1001 Ways to Market Your Books

For Authors and Publishers

Includes over 100 proven marketing tips for authors. Now you can take a more active role in marketing your books!

John Kremer

6th Edition

SELL MORE BOOKS

W9-AMA-838

Published by:

Open Horizons
P.O. Box 205
Fairfield, Iowa 52556-0205
(641) 472-6130
Fax: (641) 472-1560
Email: info@bookmarket.com
Web: http://www.bookmarket.com

Printed and bound by King Printing
www.kingprinting.com
Lowell, MA

Publishers Cataloging in Publication Data

Kremer, John, 1949-
   1001 ways to market your books: for authors and publishers.
   Sixth Edition.
   Bibliography: p.
   Includes index.
   1. Books—Marketing. 2. Publishers and publishing.
3. Authorship. 4. Self-publishing. I. Title.
II. Title: One thousand and one ways to market your books.
III. Title: One thousand and one ways to market your books.
Z278.K72 2006   070.5
ISBN 0-912411-49-X (pbk.)

1001 Ways to Market Your Books

Books by John Kremer

Celebrate Today

Do-It-Yourself Book Publicity Kit

John Kremer's Self-Publishing Hall of Fame

1001 Ways to Market Your Books — For Authors and Publishers

Tinseltowns, U.S.A. (a trivia quiz book)

Turntable Illusions: Kinetic Optical Illusions for Your Record Turntable

Newsletters

Book Marketing Update (contributing editor)

John Kremer's Book Marketing Tip of the Week (a weekly e-newsletter)

MiniGuides

Book Marketing 101: How to Create a National Bestseller

Book Marketing 102: Editorial as the First Step in Book Marketing

Book Marketing 103: Designing Your Books as Sales Aids

Book Marketing 104: 192 Marketing Ideas I've Learned from Others

Book Marketing 105: Choosing a Book Distribution Method

Book Marketing 106: Working with Bookstores to Sell More Books

Book Marketing 107: Everything You Ever Wanted to Know about Internet Marketing with a Little Help from My Friends

Book Marketing 108: How to Sell More Books via Publicity

Book Marketing 109: How to Make Money with Your Mailing List

Marketing Your Novel 101: How to Market Your Novel

Foreign Book Distributors, Wholesalers, & Sales Reps

Literary, Subsidiary, & Foreign Rights Agents

Databases

Catalogs Sales Data File (features 1,350+ catalogs that carry books)

Special Events Data File (features 18,550 special day and anniversaries)

Top 700 Independent Booksellers Data File

Public Libraries Data File (features 2,300 public libraries)

Learning Centers Data File (features 150 continuing education centers)

Table of Contents

Brief Version

Dedication

To lovers of books . . .

I hope this book helps you to get your work out to a wider audience, that it allows you to stir the hearts and minds of many, many people.

I would love nothing more than to see your book in the hands of people everywhere—readers walking down the street, browsers in the bookstores, vacationers at the beach, students in the classroom, secretaries at the office, mothers at home.

That's a great challenge, and maybe it's not possible to achieve. But it is certainly worth an attempt. Even several attempts.

Take your time. Do it right. And enjoy.

That's the best advice I can give you.

Table of Contents

Chapter 3—Establishing and Marketing Your Company, *63*

Chapter 4—The Customer Is Always Right, *81*

Chapter 10—Tips on Advertising Your Books, *237*

Chapter 11—Offbeat Advertising and Promotions, *289*

Chapter 14—Working with Bookstores, *459*

Chapter 15—Selling Through Other Retail Outlets, *511*

Chapter 19–Special Sales: Special Opportunities, *611*

Chapter 20–Authors: How to Capitalize on Your Books, *655*

Notes:

Introduction

How to Get the Most Out of This Book

Using this book has multiplied my sales.
It de-mystifies the entire process. I love it!
— Toby Rice Drews, author, *Getting Them Sober*

This book is not intended to be a textbook on how to market books. Rather, it is designed to be an organized potpourri of useful ideas, examples, tips, and suggestions to stimulate your creativity and encourage you to explore new ways to market your books. Here are a few suggestions on how to make the best use of this book:

☐ **Once you have reviewed the ideas in this book, make them your own.** Don't copy someone else's approach. Adapt each idea to your own books and your own needs, make it better, and then use it.

☐ **Remember the old 80/20 rule.** Generally speaking, 80% of your business comes from 20% of your customers. So focus your efforts on your prime markets first. Don't scatter your attention by trying to apply all 1,001 ways to market your books on each book you publish. Be selective. And maintain your focus on those markets and advertising methods which offer the best possible return for your time, talent, and money.

☐ **Again, I repeat, maintain your focus.** Take the best ideas from this book and use them. Don't go overboard and dilute your efforts by trying to do everything at once. I've seen too many marketing efforts fail because the companies had no plan, no focus, and no clear conception of what in the world they were doing in the first place (or the second place, or the third place). That's why I devote an entire chapter to planning your marketing strategy. Planning is the first and most crucial step in marketing any book, so be sure you do it justice.

☐ **Study, study, study.** That means, come back to this book after you've spent some time in marketing your books. Read this book more than once. Read other books on publishing and marketing, especially the companion reports to this book, which include *The Do-It-Yourself Book Publicity Kit, Creating a Bestseller, John Kremer's Self-Publishing Hall of Fame,* and the incredible reports included in the *Reports on CD-Rom.* Other superb titles are listed in the extended bibliography located at our web site: http://www.bookmarket.com/1001bib.html.

☐ **Review your own marketing efforts.** And do it with a critical eye. Where can you make your program better? What more can you do? What more can your friends do?

☐ **Test everything** you do before rolling it out. Don't get suckered into buying baubles when you are going for the gold. Make sure the things you commit yourself to doing are worth the cost of your time, your life, and your good name.

☐ **Every book deserves a 3-year marketing commitment.** Don't write or publish a book unless you are willing to commit at least three years to keeping that book alive. You don't have to commit to each book full-time, but do something every day for each book you really love.

Don't be afraid to mark up this book unless, of course, you've borrowed this copy from a friend or from the library—in which case, run down to your local bookseller right away and get yourself a personal copy. Or order direct from **Open Horizons** (http://www.bookmarket.com) for only $27.95 plus $6.00 shipping and handling. Or call 641-472-6130.

While you are at it, you should buy a copy for every one of your authors, your publishers, your friends, your parents, your best buds, your worst enemies, and your word-of-mouth army. Make them your promotional partners. Call 641-472-6130 to find out about our generous group discounts (50% off on each case of 12 copies).

Authors — Scattered throughout this book are boxed notes like this one. These notes provide tips and suggestions to help writers who want to take a more active role in marketing their books. Read the rest of this book to get an inside look at how book publishers go about marketing books. Read these notes to learn how you can help them. Here, then, is your first note: If you are an author, buy copies of this book for your publisher, marketing director, publicist, and editor. It will be the best investment you make in marketing your book. But, please note, that as the author, I am biased.

As you read this book, make notes to yourself. Use a marker to highlight those sections or ideas which have the greatest potential for your own marketing program. Insert plenty of sticky notes, perhaps color-coding ideas by subject (yellow for your travel books, red for your cookbooks, green for your business books). Use this book as you would a dictionary or workbook. Keep it handy. Mark it up. Scribble notes to yourself.

Above all, don't just glance through this book once and then toss it aside. If you do, you'll miss many opportunities to sell more books. Use this book every day! Open it once a day—to any page—and read the first paragraph that pops up before your eyes. You might be surprised by the ideas that one paragraph will inspire in you. You probably won't get earth-shattering ideas every day, but if you read a paragraph once a day, you will come up with at least two or three good ideas every month. And by good ideas, I mean ones that could help you to sell more books and make you thousands of dollars.

But don't forget your focus. Take the best five ideas from this book, and focus on those until you have really done them justice and they, in turn, have produced significant sales for you. Then, and only then, add more items to your book marketing to-do list. Stay focused. It's better to do five things right than a hundred things half-baked.

I have my own philosophy about publishing. I am dedicated to selling my books—not just for the money, or the prestige, or whatever—but because I don't believe in wasting my time. If I'm going to write or publish a book, then I'm going to do my best to make sure that anyone and everyone who might benefit from the book gets a chance to read the book. I believe that all writers and all publishers should be as committed to marketing their books. And that's why I've written and published this book—to make it easier for you to meet that commitment. I hope it helps.

John Kremer
April 17, 2006

P.S.— The key changes in this edition have been made to Chapter 9 (about publicity), Chapter 12 (about Internet marketing), and Chapter 17 (about selling rights). If you have read previous editions of this book, you might want to start by reading these chapters.

Two days ago I completed reading your book, *1001 Ways to Market Your Books*! As perhaps you already well know, this book is special and a must for anyone within the industry, never the less allow me to sing your praises.

This work has blown my mind. As perhaps you could imagine, my copy now is covered in highlighter ink. Perhaps I should have just pre-dipped the whole book into a vat of highlighter ink prior to beginning. The cover has dog ears, and there are numerous post-it notes adhered throughout the book. I think that gives you enough of an image, and compliments the book better than any flowery words could.

— Antonio (just antonio)

1001 Ways was my BIBLE for a full year as I took a totally unknown book published by a tiny publisher with no publicity to speak of to a sales total of over 100,000 (as of last month) and still climbing. My book, *100 Ways to Motivate Yourself*, started out at zero. I was totally unknown and had to begin by reverse shoplifting and sneaking it on to the shelves at Borders, etc. Then I got a break when I sent the audio version to Dale Dauten, the noted syndicated business columnist for King Features, who named it Audiobook of the Year for 1998. From there it just hasn't stopped selling.

If people would really use your book like a map, it would lead them out of the cave of obscurity to life, as I now have, as a full time writer. I am very grateful to you for providing such a service and making such a difference in my life. People who make a difference will never be forgotten.

— Steve Chandler, author, *17 Lies*

I recommend your book to lots of folks in the publishing industry. My copy is so laden with post-its and highlights, it looks a bit like a child's favorite blankie. Translation: I love it and use it constantly. Thanks for helping us get through this crazy business we call publishing.

— Rita Putnam, author,
As Your Parents Age: A Guide to Hassle-Free Caregiving

Chapter 1

Some Basic Fundamentals of Marketing

When life handed me a lemon, not only did I make lemonade,
I also wrote the recipe and then sold that recipe!
— JoAnna Lund, author, *Healthy Exchanges Cookbook*

The following points are basic to any marketing strategy. Read them and get to understand them before you go on to read the more practical points covered in the other chapters of this book.

1:01 Selling Is Your Responsibility

No matter how you choose to sell your books—whether through bookstores, via direct mail, via the Internet, or however else—one thing you will always have to do: You will have to sell your books. No one else can do that for you.

Even if you sell exclusively through bookstores, it is still your responsibility to see that potential readers know about your books and where to buy them. Don't expect anyone else to do your selling for you. That's your job. At best, others can only provide channels. It will always be up to you to provide the motivation for readers to buy your books.

1:02 The Two Fundamentals

There are two fundamental activities in marketing any product or service: 1) promotion and 2) distribution. In other words, you must get the word out *and* you must make sure that your product is available. One does not follow the other. Both must be done simultaneously, or neither will be as effective. Promotion will not be effective unless readers can readily buy your books, and distribution will be disappointing and full of headaches (and returns) unless your promotions help to move your books out of the stores.

1:03 Look Before You Leap

Even before you begin to promote and distribute your books, you must engage in a great number of other marketing functions. For instance, you must decide what you are going to publish (editorial). You must package your books (design). You must decide who your customers are and how you are going to position your book (market planning). You must set a workable price (financial). You must print your book (production). All of these functions are crucial to the successful marketing of a book.

1:04 Publishing as Marketing

If you haven't noticed by now, I consider every function of a publisher to be an integral part of book marketing. And, because I do, this book will cover more than just promotion and distribution. It also covers editorial, design, customer service, rights sales, and working with authors. As far as I'm concerned, no detail is too small to consider if it will make a difference in how many readers get to know about and read your book.

If you happen to be with the marketing department, I encourage you to share this book with the other departments in your company. Not only will it make your job easier, but it will also foster better cooperation among the people in your company. Indeed, if you are wise, you will buy a copy of this book for every employee (and every employer) in your company. Yes, I will benefit by this action, but so will you.

Now, with the commercial out of the way, I want to repeat the point I've been making: Marketing is a company-wide activity. It cannot be, and should not be, restricted to one department. Too many things enter into the making of a successful book (and a successful publishing company) to allow parochial interests to limit your possibilities.

Even the least recognized department of most publishing companies, the fulfillment division, has a crucial marketing impact. Many companies rise and fall based on their customer service (fast delivery, ease of ordering, cordial service representatives, customer confidence, and more). Any company which does not regard its fulfillment division as an integral part of its marketing will certainly fail.

And don't forget your authors. They are and will always be the best salespeople for their books. Read Chapter 8 to get some tips on how to make best use of authors in marketing their books.

1:05 Marketing Requires Commitment

It takes time to build a company (even longer to build a reputation). You must be prepared to spend years developing a book list, making contacts, testing various advertising methods, establishing a network of sales representatives or distributors, and doing all the other jobs that go into building a company that will be around for years to come. Don't give up. If you can make it through the first few years, you'll be well on your way to success.

Of course, this same advice applies to each book you publish. Never give up your marketing efforts as long as the book is still in print. I suggest that you do three to five things every day to market each and every book that you publish (or that you still love). It will take about ten minutes of your day (longer if you customize your contacts). If you do that, you will end up making about 1,000 contacts each year. Think of the impact that will make on your marketing efforts—provided, of course, that you spend your time making targeted contacts rather than spreading yourself thin by pursuing every little whisper in the wind.

Too many publishers have failed because they ignored this fundamental of marketing: You must be committed to what you are selling. You must believe in it. How can you sell anything if you don't believe in it—and if you're not willing to back it up with time and effort? Why publish a book if you're not going to commit your resources to marketing the book so it reaches the people who can use it and enjoy it?

> Authors: This rule applies to you, too! Don't write a book unless you are ready to back it up with your time and effort to sell the book. You are your own best salesperson. For every book you write, you should be willing to commit three years to marketing it. You don't have to market full time, but you do have to do something each day for the full three years if you really want your books to make an impact.

1:06 Marketing as an Investment

When you are just starting out, you must think of your marketing program as an investment. You cannot approach marketing as a sporadic activity. If you do, you'll just get caught up in one fad after another. That is no way to build a business or create an audience for your book.

You don't have to spend a lot of money to make an investment in your book. In fact, in my experience, the authors who simply throw money at their books are the ones who most often fail. The authors who are successful invest something else: They invest their sweat, their heart, their time, their most careful attention, and their life's blood.

1:07 For Most Effective Marketing, Be Consistent

Though consistency may be, as Emerson once noted, "the hobgoblin of fools," it is also the basis for developing a stable business. A marketing plan is essential to any success. And that marketing plan should include a clear picture of the image you want your company to present to the public. Once you've set your goals and your means to those goals, stick to them as long as they still serve your needs. Even if you are a one-book self-publisher, a consistent and persistent effort will pay off.

1:08 Velvet Hammer Marketing

Ultimately, marketing boils down to one thing: Creating relationships. That, in turn, means one thing: Making friends.

As a publisher or author, you need to develop and nurture relationships with major contacts in the media, distribution network, bookstores, book clubs, catalogs, specialty retail chains, and other key markets. Publishing and marketing are both people businesses. The more relationships you develop, the more friends you have, the more successful you will be.

The best way to develop relationships is to start by creating a list of 100 key media and marketing contacts—what I call your Kremer 100 list. Use standard off-the-shelf contact management software or a database program to create your Kremer 100 list. To kick-start your list, check out my web site at BookMarket.com to find out about the **Kremer 100 Program**.

Once you've develped your list, then mail, fax, telephone, or email those contacts at least 10 to 15 times per year. What should you send? Send a catalog. Send a press release. Send a memo about some new development— a book club sale, an article in a major magazine, an author appearance on *Oprah!* or a local television show, a list of forthcoming bookstore appearances—anything that suggests people are standing up and taking notice of your books. Send a fax responding to some current event related to your book. Phone them with the latest hot news. The key is to keep these people informed and excited about your book.

Don't expect them to find out this news on their own. They don't have time to pay attention to every book that crosses their desks. You have to take charge and keep them informed.

Joanna Lund, the bestselling book author on the QVC shopping network, calls this approach *velvet hammer marketing*. It consists of a constant soft persistent push to keep people informed and pumped up. It doesn't require a lot of money (although you can spend as much as you want), but it does require your time. Ask yourself: "How important is this book to me?" Your answer to that question will tell you how much time or money you should devote to marketing your book.

1:09 Marketing Is the Means, Not the Goal

The last four points of this chapter have, in essence, been making the same point. Effective marketing requires commitment. It requires a stable base. It requires a long-term point of view.

I have reiterated these points because I want to ensure that as you read about the wide variety of ways to market your books, you don't lose sight of your major purpose in being a publisher. Remember that marketing is the means, not the goal. If I have to tell you what your goal is, you shouldn't be publishing or writing books.

1:10 Making Friends: The Essence of Marketing

All of marketing ultimately comes down to one thing: creating relationships. If you don't understand this basic principle, you will ultimately fail as a book marketer. Indeed, you will fail in life as well.

Think of it: What is publicity? It is simply creating relationships with people in the media who, if they like your product, idea, or service, will pass on that information to their audience in the form of reviews, interviews, stories, or notices.

Think of it: What is distribution? It is simply creating relationships with bookstores, wholesalers, and sales representatives who will make your books available to retail customers.

Think of it: What are special sales? They are based on creating relationships with catalogs, premium buyers, government bureaus, specialty retailers and others who will buy your books in quantities.

Think of it: What are rights sales? They, too, are based on creating relationships with key companies and people who can exploit those rights better than you can.

Think of it: What is editorial? It is simply creating relationships with authors, literary agents, and other people who can bring you good material to polish, design, and promote.

All of book publishing ultimately comes down to creating relationships. Indeed, all of business operates the same way.

Wherever you look in business, relationships are what make things happen: networking, the old boy network, the new girl network, customer lists, sales reps visiting their customers, publicists talking with the media, luncheon meetings, conventions, trade shows, chat groups, newsletters, blogs, and more. They all have one thing in common: Their primary purpose is to enhance communication and further relationships.

Since 80% of all books are sold by word-of-mouth, your primary goal in marketing your books is to create a core group of people who will spark that word-of-mouth. I like to think of these people as the officers for your word-of-mouth army, because what you ultimately want to create is an army of people talking about your book. In that army, you'll have privates, corporals, sergeants, lieutenants, majors, colonels, and generals. The moment someone meets one of your authors, they've self-promoted themselves to at least a corporal. If they get an autograph, count them a sergeant. If they buy ten books for other people, promote them to lieutenant. You get the idea. In my *1001 Ways* army, I have at least three five-star generals: Jack Canfield, Mark Victor Hansen, and Bob Allen. They've earned every star.

Note: If you don't like the analogy of an army, then think of it as a parade, fan club, or party.

When speaking to the Women Writers of the West conference a number of years ago, I realized that when I talked about creating relationships, I was really talking about making friends. Because that is what every good marketer really does: They make friends. When you begin to think of marketing in this way, everything about marketing books becomes more fun. Suddenly there is no foreignness, no fear, no feelings of inadequacy. We can all make friends. It's a talent we've had since we were little children. Use it.

Each new edition of 1001 Ways to Market Your Books is doomed
from the minute it enters my house. For each book that we publish,
I go through John's book page by page, customizing our marketing plan
and getting new ideas on each page. When I'm done with it,
half the pages are dog-eared and marked up and the spine is cracked
in a million places. But this book has helped my books to get featured
on Oprah, and in USA Today, the Wall Street Journal, Parade,
and in 100s of other media.

— Lisa Rogak, Williams Hill Publishing

1:11 Book Sponsorships

To increase the value of the last edition of this book, I invited various book publishing service providers to sponsor this book. I've done the same for this edition. As part of their sponsorship, they were each asked to write a one-page article that provided good marketing tips to publishers and authors.

Please note that the sponsors paid to be featured in this book, but I only invited individuals who I believe provide useful services to book publishers and who would write informative articles. Because I wanted to ensure that you received good practical information, I retained final editorial approval over their contributions.

Note that I took some of my inspiration from Mark Victor Hansen and Jack Canfield who have invited many of their friends and colleagues to contribute to the *Chicken Soup for the Soul* series. While their contributors were not sponsors, they were a great help in marketing the series. I'm hoping the sponsors for this book will be at least as effective in marketing this book.

How to Double or Triple Your Income as an Author or Publisher
(Why you need to visit my site: www.PinkGoat.com)
by Fred Gleeck, The Product Guru

Less than 1% of all authors make more than $50,000 a year. Sad but true. Want to be in the 1% group? Then keep reading.

The reality of publishing is that the real money isn't made from books. It's made from all of the other products and services that you sell people *after* they buy your book. I'm the author of more than 10 books myself, so I speak from experience.

To make big bucks as a publisher you need to create a *line* of products related to your book *and* an automated system to sell them. This may sound like a daunting task but compared to writing a book it will be relatively easy.

Since people learn using different modalities, you'll need to eventually create products that can be read (books, ebooks), watched (videos and DVDs), listened to (audios of all kinds), and experienced (seminars, teleseminars, etc.). The products you create should range in price from $10 to $1000.

Don't worry. You don't have to create them all at once. But, if you don't have a skeletal line of products lined up before your book comes out, you'll be losing money right from the start. If your book is already done and printed you can always insert a postcard into the book to bounce them back to you.

Think of your book as a way to get people into your funnel to then upsell them all of the other materials that you offer. I recommend a program called WebMarketingMagic (http://www.WebMarketingMagic.com) to help you manage your online efforts.

To get people into your funnel you'll need to create bounceback offers in your book. I suggest including various kinds of offers imbedded in the text of the book itself. One of my books (page 43) says "to collect your free gift worth $47, send an email to tips@SeminarExpert.com." I also put that same bounceback offer at the bottom of each of the pages in my book. I suggest you consider doing the same.

Do *not* send people to a website. You are not certain of capturing their email address if you do it that way. Instead, ask them to email you. That way you'll be certain to get *their* email address.

When people don't buy from you directly, you don't know who they are. The only way to get them to identify themselves is to offer them a bribe, preferably a digital bribe (like an ebook or an ecourse) that has high perceived value. Offering people this bribe in your book will give them a strong incentive to get them into your funnel at *no* cost to you.

After you get peoples email addresses you'll want to send them some great content to make them comfortable buying other products and services from you. You can do this all automatically with autoresponders, another feature of WebMarketingMagic.

Each product you produce (whether audio or video) should have it's own website. Take a look at http://www.PinkGoat.com to get some ideas.

To create your audios, videos and events you'll need to learn the process before jumping in. I highly recommend that you check http://www.TheProduct-Guru.com to get a better idea of how to do those things the *right* way. I've coached many authors just like you, so feel free to give me a call and I'll make sure to help you get it done right.

To get five of Fred's books that every author or publisher should have (worth close to $90) *FREE*, go to http://www.FredGleeck.com/ebooks. You can contact **Fred Gleeck, the Product Guru** by email: fredgleeck@mac. com, or by calling 800-FGLEECK (345-3325)

Chapter 2

Planning: The Basis of Successful Marketing

> Most publishers have a front-list mentality.
> They put all their sales efforts into the first six months the book is out.
> That doesn't give you enough time for word of mouth to help.
> Make your readers your marketing team.
> Stay focused on the project for at least two to three years.
> — Dave Chilton, self-publisher, *The Wealthy Barber*

No company can be successful without some sort of marketing plan. Whether it is written on the back of a matchbook, carried in the mind of the company president, or formalized in a 200-page bound report, a marketing plan is a must. Without it, you might as well be gambling—the effect would be the same.

Before you make any plan, you should have some idea what you are getting into. To help put the business of book publishing into perspective, check out the statistics, facts, figures, and other tidbits of information at http://www.bookmarket.com/statistics.html.

2:01 Preparing Your Marketing Plan

What should a marketing plan include? At the very minimum, it should feature the following items:

- The books or lines to be offered
- The packaging, display, and pricing
- How the books will be positioned
- The audience or market for the books
- A program for reaching that market

- A list of the key people and companies you intend to contact (your Kremer 100 list).

In other words, you should have some idea of what you plan to sell, how you plan to package it, how you will create a desire for your books, who will buy the books, and how you intend to let those buyers know about the books (and where they can obtain them). Other points you should consider when preparing a marketing plan include: market research, competitive titles, budgets, schedules, and how the proposed promotion fits in with major company objectives and ongoing projects.

2:02 Positioning to Sell

No book manuscript or proposal should be given the go ahead until you have a firm idea how you will position the book. That means, that before you make any editorial decisions, you should always ask yourself the question: "Who will buy this book, and why?" The last part of that question is crucial. You should always be able to describe what needs and/or desires your new books fulfill.

David Ogilvy, author of *Confessions of an Advertising Man*, once listed thirty-two things he had learned during all his years as an advertising man. Of the items on that list, he said the most important was how you positioned your product. Results, he claimed, were based not so much on how the advertising was written as on how the product itself was positioned.

Positioning is vital when your book is not the first one published about the topic. For example, if you are publishing a new diet book, the first question a reader will ask is, "Why should I buy another diet book? The other four I've bought didn't work. Why will this one work any better?" If you expect readers to buy your diet book, you need to answer that question. And you will need to have answered that question long before you even begin to typeset the book. Because your answer to that question will not only affect how you market the book, it will also affect how you edit, design, and package the book.

> **Authors** — When conceiving and writing your books, you, too, should ask yourself the question, "Who will buy my book—and why?" And you had better have a good answer.

When Little, Brown published *Miracle on the 17th Green* by novelist James Patterson and golf writer Peter De Jonge in the fall of 1996, they positioned the book as *"The Christmas Box* for golfers." In other words, like the bestselling *Christmas Box, Miracle on the 17th Green* would make a perfect holiday gift, especially for any friends or spouses who are golfers.

This positioning clearly told women that this was a safe book for them to buy their husbands, bosses, or coworkers.

2:03 Scheduling the Publication of Your Books

The publication date for a book should not be a production decision; it must be a marketing decision. The timing of a book is a crucial part of any marketing plan. Note that the *publication date* is not the day books come off the printing press; it is the date when your book should be amply distributed to the bookstores and your major publicity should hit. For more details on how to set publication dates, see http://www.bookmarket.com/pubdate.html.

When trying to create a bestseller, timing is crucial. The *laydown* of books (the delivery of books to bookstores) must be coordinated precisely with your major advertising and publicity.

Timing is crucial to all books. No booksellers want to stock a book that has no marketing behind it, and no media want to cover a book that has no distribution. If a book gets great reviews but has no distribution, it does not sell. If it has great distribution but no critical praise or word of mouth, the book will also fail. Ideally, your new books are in bookstores a week or two before your major publicity hits.

Below are a few other examples where scheduling is important for books.

☐ College textbooks must be presented to academics before March (if not a lot sooner) for fall adoption. Summer is way too late.

☐ The *Consumer Research Study on Book Purchasing* brought out an interesting point: More art/literature/poetry books are bought in the fall than any other season. 41% are bought in the fall, while the other seasons account for about 20% sales each.

☐ To tie in with special days, you need to let retail stores know about your books at least five to six months in advance. Since the major gift industry trade shows for Christmas are held in July and August, Christmas gift books must be ready for promotion before then. Indeed, begin your promotion with BookExpo America in late May or early June.

☐ Calendars need to be promoted in May and June. August is too late, since by then most stores have already bought their supply of calendars which they then put on display in September. Note that the deadline for *Publishers Weekly*'s calendar issue is early March.

☐ Cookbooks also have seasonal trends. For example, soup and turkey cookbooks tend to sell best in the fall, as do books about entertaining at home. Books on outdoor cooking and salads sell best in the summer. Baking guides sell best in winter.

☐ Diet books do well after the winter holidays and before the summer swimsuit season.

☐ Instruction books for golf and tennis sell better in the winter when the readers are not actively playing.

☐ Smaller publishers can often gain more notice and reviews during January and February and in late summer before the major publishers announce their spring and fall lists. So consider setting your publication dates for those times.

☐ Sometimes it's wise to schedule a book's publication date at a time outside the normal expectations of the industry. For example, by being published in late fall, the bestseller *50 Simple Ways to Save the Earth* got a head start (and all the publicity) over the other ecology books which did not come out until the 20th anniversary of Earth Day in the spring.

> **Authors** — Make sure you have your finished manuscript in your publisher's hands when your contract specifies. The publisher's marketing plans often succeed or fail based on whether you meet deadlines to keep your book's production and promotion on schedule.

2:04 The Seven Seasons of Bookselling

In past years, most publishers brought out books twice a year: in the fall and the spring. Now, savvy publishers realize that there are seven seasons for selling books. The major bookselling season is still the winter holidays, which account for a large portion of bookstore sales. A second major season for bookstores is the triple threat of Mother's Day, graduation, and Father's Day. While generating about 70% of winter holiday sales, these family days have grown as a gift-giving season for books. Besides these two major gift giving seasons, there are five other major bookselling seasons during the year. Here, in calendar order, are the seven seasons of bookselling:

☐ **Valentine's Day** — This day is big for romance novels, relationship books, and sex books. Each year Greg Godek's *1001 Ways to Be Romantic* enjoys a major sales boost around Valentine's. Prima Publishing designed special Valentine's displays for their book, *How to Find the Love of Your Life* by Ben Dominitz, and made sure the book was widely available early enough to encourage sales.

☐ **Easter** — This season is especially productive for Christian books. Other books sell well around this time, especially gardening and environmental titles (to coincide with spring and Earth Day).

☐ **Mother's Day** — Publishers are now publishing gift books for this holiday. Simon & Schuster, for example, publishes a new Mary Higgins

Clark mystery for each Mother's Day. Other big sellers include novels, cookbooks, lifestyle books, garden books, and biographies.

Graduation — Every year, Dr. Seuss's *Oh, the Places You'll Go!* rockets to bestseller status as family and friends give the book to recent graduates. It has sold more than 3.5 million copies as a result. Other books that sell well include reference books and gifty advice books, such as *Life's Little Instruction Book* by H. Jackson Brown, Jr.

Father's Day — For Barnes & Noble bookstores, Father's Day is the second biggest selling season (about 20% of the winter holidays, but 50% greater than sales for Mother's Day). Golf and baseball books are the big sellers around Father's Day. But other relevant books such as Bill Cosby's *Fatherhood*, Paul Reiser's *Babyhood*, and Mariana Cook's *Fathers and Daughters* are also big sellers around this time.

☐ **Summer** — Summer is a big time for mass market paperback novels, which can be read on the beach or carried around as a person travels.

☐ **Back to School** — This season is great for children's books and the first of the fall's big books.

☐ **Halloween and autumn festivals** — According to bookseller Roberta Rubin of The Book Stall in Winnetka, Illinois, "Halloween has gotten big bookwise." Most major novels of the year are introduced during this time, which also starts the holiday gift-giving season.

☐ **Winter holidays** — This time, again, is a major selling season for booksellers and publishers. People buy gifts for many of the winter holidays, including Christmas, Hanukkah, the winter solstice, Kwanza, and New Years. Books make safe and practical gifts for the many office parties held during these days.

There are other days that can work well for selling books, including Boss's Day, Secretary's Day, April Fool's Day, Groundhog Day, and others included in *Celebrate Today* by John Kremer (http://www.celebratetoday. com). Ingram, the major bookstore wholesaler, has book codes for the following holidays: Valentine's, St. Patrick's Day, Passover, Easter, Mother's Day, Graduation, Father's Day, Fourth of July, Classroom Adoption, Back to School, Yom Kippur, Halloween, Thanksgiving, Hanukkah, Christmas, and Kwanzaa (a big holiday for selling African-American books).

2:05 Prepare a Marketing Budget

Set your marketing budget well in advance of publication. Be sure to have a clear plan of how you intend to spend your advertising dollars, reserving the major portion for your prime markets and media. Because word of mouth is still the most cost-effective way to advertise your books, set aside at least one-third of your marketing budget to be used for promotion and publicity.

2:06 Repeat, Repeat, Repeat

When planning your marketing budget, follow **the rule of seven**. This rule states that if you want your prospects to take action and buy your books, you must connect with them at least seven times within an 18-month period. That's why you should include enough money in your marketing budget so you can advertise or publicize to your major prospects at least seven times. Repetition is a key to gaining audience recognition.

2:07 Research Your Market

If you are approaching a new market, do what you can to get to know more about that market. Ask questions, conduct surveys, read the major trade and consumer magazines for that area, attend trade shows and exhibits, poll retailers, and do test markets with your potential audience. For more details on researching new or existing markets, read Chapter 5 on *How to Open New Markets*.

In preparing their Swept Away line of young adult novels, Avon joined *Seventeen* magazine's spring survey of its readers. In that survey, Avon polled thousands of readers to find out what time and place teenagers would most like to visit and what famous people in history they would most like to meet. The answers to this poll were used to plan future titles in the Swept Away line.

To keep track of new markets, check out polls and other sources of statistics (http://www.bookmarket.com/statistics.html). Also watch for these kinds of statistics in your daily newspaper and in trade magazines so you can spot new trends and markets before they become oversaturated with new book offerings from other publishers.

> **Authors** — You should research your audience as thoroughly as you would if you were the publisher and it was *your* money that was riding on the success of the book. Besides researching the audience, you should also research your competition, that is, what other related books are already in the stores.

2:08 Spotting Trends

Besides watching the changing statistics, you should also be watching for new trends in society. The first company to spot a trend has the best chance of capturing the largest share of the market.

☐ Trivial Pursuit, for example, was the first game to exploit people's fascination with trivia. As a result, it became one of the hottest selling games of the century with over a billion dollars in sales!

☐ Mabel Hoffman's *Crockery Cookery* was the first major book published describing how to use crockpots. It has sold more than three million copies since 1975.

☐ Because she was one of the first people to self-publish a book on microwave cooking, Bev Harris has sold over 1 million copies of her cookbook—all by word of mouth. Every time she goes back to reprint the book, she orders another 50,000 copies.

☐ Tom Clancy, with his *The Hunt for Red October*, captured a new trend in militaria and helped to put the Naval Institute Press on the map.

☐ Be the first or be the best. As Scott Flanders, president of Macmillan Computer Publishing once noted, "We say that there are two successful books on a subject: The first one out and the best one." My preference is to be both. That way there's no confusion in the minds of the buyers.

☐ Les and Sue Fox self-published *The Beanie Baby Handbook* in 1997. By July of 1998, they had gone back to press eight more times for an in-print total of 3 million copies while the book established itself in the #2 spot on the *New York Times* bestseller list. Here's an example where a self-publisher took a hot topic and ran with it long before any larger publishers could get a book out.

☐ The Dummies® books got there first with the best because they fulfilled the need of consumers to have fun easy-to-use computer books. As they began to dominate the bestseller lists for computer books—propelling IDG Books to the number one computer book publisher within two years—they also allowed IDG to extend the brand name to hundreds of other topics, from sex to wine, investments to taxes, dogs to chess. More than 90 million Dummies books have been sold thus far.

Authors — Be sure to protect your rights when signing any contract with a book publisher. Dan Gookin, creator of the original *Dummies* book, never got any credit for designing the look and feel of the series and the brand name because his contract with the publisher gave them all such rights. A decent publisher, of course, would have recognized his contribution and rewarded him accordingly, but you can't count on all book publishers to do the right thing.

Alpha Books, a division of Macmillan, has tried to capture the same market with their *Complete Idiot's Guides*, but their sales don't begin to compare. They, too, have extended the franchise to cover fishing, fitness, buying and selling collectibles, dealing with difficult people, decorating your home, organizing your life, marketing, gardening, dating, religion, bargain hunting, wills, starting your own business, weddings, cooking basics, raising a dog, creative writing, business presentations, project management, football, marriage, beer, golf, business letters, chess, classical music, bridge, parenting, grandparenting, 401(K) plans, skiing, mixing drinks, genealogy, baking, geography, philosophy, yoga, astrology, selling, Wall Street, car repair, first aid, and even Elvis!

> **Authors** — The sooner you can catch a trend, the more likely you are to write books that will sell—and sell well. Be alert to changes so you can ride the crest of the wave rather than the tail end.

2:09 The Benefits of Specialization

When planning your book list, you should consider how each new title fits into your current publishing program. The more you can specialize in certain areas, the greater your chances of success in those areas. Do what you do best, and do it better than anyone else. Here are just a few of the advantages of specialization:

☐ **Your company gains recognition for its expertise in your areas of specialization.** For example, Que has a good reputation for publishing practical computer books. Globe Pequot is known for its line of bicycle tour books. Nolo is recognized as the leader in law books for consumers.

☐ **You create a readership that avidly awaits your next offerings**. This creates a marketing momentum that makes each new book much easier to sell to bookstores. This becomes readily apparent in category fiction. For example, the first book in Jean Auel's Earth Children series, *The Clan of the Cave Bear*, sold 119,000 hardcover copies its first year. The next book, *The Valley of Horses*, sold 289,000 hardcover copies its first year. But the third book in the series, *The Mammoth Hunters*, really took off; it sold 1,470,000 hardcover copies within three months of publication. This same trend held true for the Harry Potter books.

☐ **You can make greater use of your house list to sell new titles** since your previous buyers will naturally be interested in new titles along the same lines as the books they previously bought. When I brought out the first edition of this book, I already had a built-in audience of book publishers who had bought my previous titles, *Book Marketing Made Easier* and *Directory of Book Printers* (both titles are now out of print).

☐ **You build name recognition**. As you publish more books in the same field, people in that field will become more and more familiar with your company name and reputation. Even if they don't buy your first or second or third book, they will buy eventually.

☐ **Specialization will strengthen your acquisitions program**. Major writers or experts in your area of specialization will begin offering you first look at their new manuscripts. Hence, the quality of your offerings will only get better as you continue to specialize.

Jeremy Tarcher publishes many new age, psychology, and self-help titles. One of their specialties within this category are books on drawing and writing. Their first book in this area, Betty Edward's *Drawing on the Right Side of the Brain*, sold more than a million copies. As a result, they attracted other writers, including Mona Brookes, author of *Drawing with Children* (with 80,000 copies in print), and Gabriele Lusser Rico, author of *Writing the Natural Way* (with more than 175,000 copies sold).

☐ **Specialization allows you to market books together as a package**, to display them together, to offer special discounts for ordering three or more different titles, to offer bouncebacks for the entire range of titles, to publish special interest catalogs, and to coordinate other cross promotions. Even better, you won't have to create a new marketing plan for each title you publish.

☐ **Specialization makes it easier to cultivate media and rights buyers**. Paul Nathan, former rights columnist for *Publishers Weekly*, once wrote that Combined Books "could almost be mistaken for a spinoff of the Military Book Club," since twenty of its military history titles had been selected for the club within three years.

Authors — When looking for publishers, first try those who specialize in the subject of your book. Not only are they more likely to be interested in publishing your book, but they are also more likely to market it more effectively than a publisher who does not specialize in the subject.

2:10 Develop Series for Continuing Sales

A variation on specialization is to develop a series of titles on the same topic. The advantages are the same as for specializing in general.

☐ Modern Publishing publishes 30 to 40 different series of children's books each year and then packages each series as a display unit. As Lawrence Steinberg, Modern's president, pointed out: One book gets lost in the midst of many other books, but six books make a display and, hence, are much more visible.

☐ Globe Pequot Press offers a series of Bed & Breakfast guide books for different parts of the country. Each book helps to sell the others, just as Fodor, Fielding, Frommer, Baedeker, Insiders' Guides, Moon Publications, Lonely Planet, St. Martin's Let's Go series, and other travel guides continue to sell year after year.

☐ Bantam sold more than 50 million copies of two series aimed at teenage girls, *Sweet Dreams* and *Sweet Valley High*. As a result of the success of these series, Bantam went on to create several other series for young adults, including *On Our Own, Varsity Coach, The Carlisle Chronicles, Time Machine, Dark Forces, Kelly Blake*, and *Sweet Valley Twins*.

☐ Since 1973, Random House sold more than 50 million copies of its Pictureback line of children's books. In two years, its follow-up Step-into-Reading series of thirty-seven titles sold over one million copies.

☐ Because of the loyalty of children, juvenile books sell well as series. Witness the following: *Berenstein Bears* series by Stan and Jan Berenstein, *Where's Waldo?* series by Martin Handford, *The Magic School Bus* series by Joanna Cole, the *BabySitters Club* by Ann M. Martin, *The Indian in the Cupboard* and its sequels by Lynne Reid Banks, *Clifford the Dog* series by Norman Bridwell, as well as series featuring *Sesame Street* characters, *Shrek*, *The Lion King*, and other TV/movie favorites.

☐ Writers often develop series when one of their books hits big. It's a natural follow-up. Once you've written one book on the subject, the second is that much easier to write (and to sell).

Spencer Johnson and Kenneth Blanchard wrote a good number of One Minute books since their first (originally self-published) *One Minute Manager* became a bestseller. Now there's *The One Minute Father, The One Minute Mother, The One Minute Salesperson, Putting the One Minute Manager to Work, Leadership and the One Minute Manager, The One Minute Manager Gets Fit*, and *One Minute for Myself*.

Similarly, Laurence Peters came out with *The Peter Plan* and *The Peter Pyramid* since hitting it big with *The Peter Principle*. The follow-ups, however, rarely do as well as the originals.

☐ The bestselling author in the world in 1995 was R.L. Stine, author of the Goosebumps and Fear Street series. With sales of more than 32 million copies, the Goosebump series grabbed 17 of the top 20 slots in the frontlist paperback bestsellers list for 1995 and the first 27 spots of the backlist paperback bestsellers list!

Even the Goosebumps parody, *Gooflumps* by R.U. Slime, nabbed several bestselling slots, as did the Spooksville series by Christopher Pike. Other knockoffs, such as Bantam's Doomsday Mall series, however, did not sell nearly as well.

The success of *Goosebumps* did not happen overnight. Scholastic first published the series in 1992, but it took awhile for kids to become more involved with the series and talk about it with their friends. Within two years, Scholastic was shipping 1.25 million copies of the series every month. By 1996, more than 90 million Goosebump books had been sold.

□ The *Chicken Soup for the Souls* series by Jack Canfield and Mark Victor Hansen has already sold more than 90 million copies. In 1996 alone, the *3rd Serving* of the series sold 1.6 million copies while *Chicken Soup for the Woman's Soul* sold 1.1 million, *Chicken Soup for the Soul at Work* sold 248,000, *A Cup of Chicken Soup of the Soul* sold 239,000, *Condensed Chicken Soup for the Soul* sold 219,000, and *Chicken Soup for the Surving Soul* sold 147,000. To follow up those sales, Health Communications also published many similar titles, including *The Sound of the Soul* by Arthur Joseph and *Gifts of the Heart* by Bettie Youngs.

□ Dover Publications publishes a collection of Ready-to-Use Alphabets and Cut & Assemble books along with many other series which they then sell by mail to regular customers.

□ When *What to Expect When You're Expecting* by Arlene Eisenberg, Heidi Eisenberg Murkoff, and Sandee Eisenberg Hathaway became a bestseller (it now has sold 11.5 million copies), the authors wrote a second book following up on where the other left off. Their *What to Eat When You're Expecting* has already sold more than a million copies. Additional books in the series have also been bestsellers, including *What to Expect the First Year* (7 million copies), *What to Expect the Toddler Years* (2.5 million copies), and *What to Expect Pregnancy Organizer* (400,000 copies). Twenty-six foreign editions have been published as well as a Spanish-language edition for the U.S. market.

□ A $100 million company was built up around a series of books which describe in fictional form the lives of young girls during different periods of American history. Pleasant Company of Madison, Wisconsin, sells 100,000 copies of most new titles in its American Girl series every year. Several years ago, Mattel paid $700 million to buy the company from its founder.

Authors — When you conceive a new book, consider the possibilities for related titles. Does the subject you are writing about lend itself to one book or a series of books? When you send a book proposal to publishers, let them know if you have any plans for additional related titles. Publishers love series because the first book in the series helps to sell the following books (and the following books, in turn, help to sell more copies of the original title in the series).

2:11 Category Books: Sales after Sales after Sales

Category or genre books can be viewed as a combination of a book series and a magazine. They tend to develop a regular following just as any magazine does. Hence, if you publish a line of romances or science fiction or westerns (such as Silhouette romances or DAW science fiction), you begin to establish an expectation in your readers. They begin to look for your new releases. This repeat readership allows you to forecast sales much more readily than for non-category fiction (which is always a gamble at best). This consistency of sales also makes it easier to convince booksellers to carry your books.

Category books, of course, need not just be fiction. Nonfiction categories such as cartoon books, automobile repair books, cookbooks, and computer books have also developed regular and predictable customer bases.

2:12 Annuals and Perennials — Directories

Another way to ensure consistent sales and income for your company is to develop an annual directory or guide. Directories can form the foundation for an entire line of related books.

☐ When Open Horizons first started out, the *Directory of Book Printers* generated the customer base for our other books on marketing. We no longer publish the directory, but we do maintain a list of book printers on our web site at http://www.bookmarket.com/101print.html.

☐ Gale Research and a good number of other publishers have established strong sales bases from their annual directories and guides. Many of their sales are to repeat customers, year after year.

☐ And, of course, annuals can become perennial bestsellers such as the J.K. Lasser and H & R Block tax books.

Directories, of course, come in at least 57 varieties, among which are yellow page listings, telephone directories, apartment guides, tourist guides, menu listings, bibliographies, field guides, consumer guides, Who's Who, buying guides, surveys, catalog collections, almanacs, databases, and more.

Authors — Writing a directory has one major advantage as well as one major disadvantage. What is the major advantage? If the directory sells well, you will have a regular source of income for years to come. The disadvantage? A directory always needs updating. Ask yourself: Are you ready to commit to the time and effort required to update a directory every year?

2:13 Develop Standing Orders

Another benefit of developing a specialty, a series, or an annual directory is that you can solicit standing orders from libraries and customers who require the latest information. When customers place *standing orders*, they are asking you to send all new books in a series without asking them for further permission. They also obligate themselves to pay for those books or return them if they don't like them.

☐ Third Sector Press established a standing order policy whereby their customers were sent each new title for a free 60-day examination. Only customers who had prepaid or paid previous invoices within five weeks were offered this review privilege. The customers benefited from this standing review policy because they get to see each new title at least three to four months before publication date. And Third Sector benefited because they thereby establish a strong continuing customer base.

☐ In 1996, sales of subscription reference books netted publishers $706.1 million (*Book Industry Trends 1997*).

2:14 Develop Continuity Series

Continuity series are a variation on the standing order mixed with the negative option of the book club. In a continuity series, customers sign up for the first title in a series and are sent all further titles until they either cancel their participation or the series is completed. In such series it is not unusual to have as many as 50% of the initial customers drop out by the fourth book in the series. Nevertheless, the series can still be a success if you start with a large enough customer base.

☐ Time-Life Books ran continuity series for years with remarkable success. Their revenues for 1985 were over $550 million. Recently, though, they've closed their continuity series publishing program. Why? The program was probably a victim of the decline of direct marketing revenues as well as the rise of Internet book selling.

☐ Knapp Press developed a 24-book continuity series titled *Cooking with Bon Appetit*. Several of the books in this series sold more than 100,000 copies.

2:15 The Value of Bestsellers

When planning your future books, always be on the lookout for any title that has the possibility of becoming a bestseller Does it cover a hot topic? Does it have an author who is willing to do a lot of promotion? Is the author a good speaker and/or TV guest? Will the book draw lots of rights interest? Has it created a buzz among booksellers or prereviewers? Does the book have a great title? Or do you believe it is the best book to come along in many years?

The above criteria are good reasons for backing a book. Once you find a great book, do everything you can to make it a bestseller. Why? Because a bestseller can put your company on the map. Here are just a few examples of what can happen when one of your books becomes a bestseller:

☐ The Naval Institute Press hit the big time when it published Tom Clancy's first novel, *The Hunt for Red October*. Not only did wholesalers, booksellers, and librarians look more carefully at the Institute's subsequent new titles, but they also began buying more backlist titles as well. In addition, book reviewers began giving more serious consideration to new titles published by the Press.

☐ It's not necessary for a title to hit the bestseller lists to have an impact on a company's growth. Ginny NiCarthy's *Getting Free: A Handbook for Women in Abusive Relationships* sold more than 80,000 copies. These sales enabled Seal Press, the publisher, to afford other projects.

☐ Getting on the bestseller lists creates a self-fulfilling prophecy. When a book gets on one of the major bestseller lists (*New York Times* and *Publishers Weekly*), it automatically gets more sales. Why? Because bookstores notice and push books that make the list. Most stores now have a special section in the front of the store which highlights bestselling books. And, even better, all the chain stores and many independent booksellers now discount the bestsellers thus giving consumers one more reason to buy those books.

☐ Another side effect of publishing a bestseller is that it makes your company more attractive to established authors. As a result, they are much more likely to submit their best work to you. And as you receive more quality submissions, your chances of discovering and publishing another bestseller increases substantially.

Acropolis Books developed a line of books from their bestseller by Carole Jackson, *Color Me Beautiful*. They published *Your Colors at Home* by Lauren Smith and Rose Bennett Gilbert, *Always in Style with Color Me Beautiful* by Doris Pooser, *Alive with Color* by Leatrice Eiseman, and *The Winner's Style* by Kenneth Karpinski.

Authors — Can you add something new to a bestselling topic? Something like what Doris Pooser and others did for *Color Me Beautiful*? If you can, you have a chance to tailgate on their success—and have a bestselling book of your own. Don't be shy about offering to write a follow-up book to a bestseller.

2:16 The Bias of Bestseller Lists

Given the power of bestseller lists to generate additional sales, you should do whatever you can to get on those lists—especially if your book is a serious contender. While a bestseller is often defined by the lists compiled by the *New York Times*, *USA Today*, and *Publishers Weekly*, these lists are not the only way to measure success. Indeed, the *NYT* and *PW* lists are more or less works of fiction.

For example, in compiling the most influential bestseller list, the *New York Times* submits a list of 36 titles (those which their editors think will be the bestselling titles for that week) to about 3,000 bookstores across the country. These stores are asked to fill in the number of copies of each title they sold during that week. In addition, there is a space at the end of the lists where stores can write in good-selling titles that didn't make the suggested list. Each week, these reports are compiled, weighted by region, and reported in the *New York Times Book Review*.

If a book is not selected for the *Time*'s suggested list of 36 titles, it has no chance to make the bestseller list that week since few bookstores bother to write in titles. As one bookstore polled by the *Times* once noted, "You can be assured that no book in that space ever makes the bestseller list."

Publishers Weekly follows a similar procedure in compiling its bestseller list. Both publications rely heavily on advance publicity from the major New York publishers to decide which books might become hot during that week. That's one reason the major publishers hype the print runs and publicity budgets for their frontlist titles.

What may surprise you is that it doesn't take a lot of sales to get on a major bestseller list. *Vox Populi* made #10 on the *PW* hardcover fiction bestseller list with 55,000 copies in print (not necessarily sold). *Mating* made that same list with only 45,000 copies in print. Robert Boswell's *The Mystery Ride* landed at #15 with an in-print total of 30,000 copies. And *Damage* stayed on the list for 14 weeks with net sales of 90,000 copies (averaging 6,500 copies sold per week over those 14 weeks).

In his column in *USA Today*, Larry King once questioned the validity of these lists: "Is Washington out of touch with what's happening or *The New York Times* best-seller list wrong? I asked five different bookstores about M. Scott Peck's all-time best-selling paperback *The Road Less Traveled*, which has been on the *Times* list for 508 weeks. None of the stores had sold even one copy, no copies in five stores. All last week. You figure it out."

The fact is that these bestseller lists only measure sales over a short period of time. In one of her *Publishers Weekly* columns, Daisy Maryles pointed out that the #2 title on *PW*'s hardcover nonfiction bestseller list had sold almost 10,000 copies that week. The #10 bestseller had sold a little over 3,200 copies, while the #15 bestseller had sold less than 1,000 copies. Now that quantity is within reach of almost any publisher, large or small.

What's wrong with these bestseller lists? Here are a few of the reasons they are fiction:

☐ Many of the reporting bookstores don't pay close enough attention to their sales to be able to report them accurately. And many don't bother to look up the numbers in their computerized systems.

☐ Booksellers who have made a heavy buy for a slow-moving title have an incentive to push that book on to the bestseller lists. Simply classifying a loser as a winner can make a difference. Wholesalers could have the same incentive to fudge a little.

☐ Some bestseller lists draw from both bookstores and wholesalers. Thus, some book sales could be duplicated. If a bookstore orders fifty copies from a wholesaler, the wholesaler reports those fifty copies as sold that week. In the meantime, if the bookstore sells twenty copies, it reports those twenty copies as sold. Later the bookstore might return the remaining thirty copies as unsold. It is quite possible, then, for a book to have sold only twenty copies while seventy copies are reported as selling in a particular week. Multiply those numbers by the number of bookstores and wholesalers reporting, and the discrepancy between real and reported sales figures could be huge.

☐ Of 88 fiction titles that made it on the *Publishers Weekly* list during 1995, 30 shipped and billed less than 100,000 copies. Of the 93 fiction books with sales over 100,000 copies in 1995, 13 never even made it onto the weekly lists. Of the top 101 nonfiction books with sales over 100,000 copies in 1995, 30 never landed on the charts! This phenomenon continues to happen year after year.

☐ *I'm OK, You're OK* had sold over a million copies before it ever made it onto a single bestseller list! Greg Godek sold more than a million copies of his self-published *1001 Ways to Be Romantic* without ever appearing on a bestseller list. Since selling the rights to Sourcebooks, he has sold another million copies, but still no appearance on a bestseller list.

☐ Bestseller lists report only sales made through a select list of bookstores and wholesalers. They ignore sales made through small independents, many specialty bookstores, other specialty retailers (such as health food stores, gourmet shops, religious stores, and do-it-yourself centers), warehouse clubs, libraries, book clubs, mail order, and institutional sales.

☐ Bestseller lists focus on too small a time frame. How many small publishers can afford to orchestrate distribution and media attention to fall within a week's time? None. The bestsellers from small publishers tend to be those lucky few that build slowly and then start to sell in significant numbers as word of mouth spreads.

☐ Big books, ones that are being promoted heavily by New York publishers and are "supposed to be bestsellers," are automatically added to the lists. Reporting bookstores are more likely to give these added attention.

☐ What are your chances of making a bestseller list if you are not one of the top ten New York publishers? Here are the facts: Only one title from a small publisher made it on the *Publishers Weekly* hardcover list in 1996. Only thirteen such titles made it on the paperback list in 1996. The numbers have been better in more recent years, but the percentage is still quite small.

☐ The two major lists are biased towards the East Coast. Ed Koch's biography *Mayor* appeared on the *New York Times* bestseller list when the only copies available were in the New York metropolitan area. The book actually made it to the top of the list before it had national distribution. Is New York really that important?

2:17 How to Make the Bestseller Lists

How, then, does a small publisher get past the New York bias of the two major bestseller lists? Simple. Copy the major publishers. Here are a few suggestions you might want to try out when you have a book you think could be a genuine bestseller:

☐ **Send letters to the major independent bookstores** and chain store outlets in major cities reminding them to think of your book when they fill out the bestseller surveys. Remind them more than once. You could also send them reading copies or samplers of your major titles. An early sampler to bookstores was one of the promotions that helped Robert Boswell's *The Mystery Ride* make it to the bestseller lists.

☐ **Send letters to major media**, especially *Publishers Weekly*, *New York Times*, and *USA Today*, to remind them that your book has bestseller potential—and to let them know what you are doing to promote the book. Remind them more than once. Note that Daisy Maryles, the editor of *PW*'s Behind the Bestsellers column, is always looking for up-and-coming titles.

Here are a few of the items that will get their attention: review copy of the book, press kit, print run, unusual sales patterns, highlights of the author's promotional schedule, current media hits, previous sales patterns for the author, and any innovative publicity plans.

☐ **Make follow-up phone calls** to both groups mentioned above.

☐ **Advertise in *Publishers Weekly*** at least three to four weeks before the book's publication date. If you can afford it, try full-page ads. Prelude Press used this technique, combined with lots of publicity, to boost *Do It* and *Life 101* onto the bestseller lists.

☐ **Advertise in the *New York Times Book Review*.** They say that editorial and advertising are separate departments, but editors do notice the ads.

☐ **Aggressively promote your books.** To propel *Life 101* to the #3 spot on the *Times* list, Prelude sent out at least one news release every week for the three weeks prior to publication date and for the five weeks after. Each news release built upon the previous ones and also announced the successes the book had thus far enjoyed.

☐ **Set up an author tour.** The major publishers almost always set up author tours for their top books. Recently, some publishers have shifted from the standard author tour to satellite tours, where an author does interviews with local TV shows around the country while sitting in a New York studio.

☐ **Get on a major TV show.** Naura Hayden's self-published book, *How to Satisfy a Woman Every Time*, jumped to the #3 position on the *PW* list after her appearances on three major talk shows (*Oprah, Joan Rivers*, and *Sonya Live*) in one week. Oprah has been known to launch many bestsellers. In fact, each selection of Oprah's Book Club, started in October 1996, immediately hit the bestseller lists. Most sold between 600,000 and 1,200,000 copies within weeks.

After author appearances on *Good Morning America* and *20/20*, Andrew Weil's *8 Weeks to Optimum Health*, shot to the top of *PW*'s bestseller list within two weeks.

Sales of Nicholas Sparks's novel, *The Notebook*, tripled in one day, right after his appearance on *CBS This Morning*.

Paul Pearsall's *The Pleasure Prescription*, published by Hunter House, made it onto *PW*'s trade paperback bestseller list after the author's first appearance on the *Montel Williams Show*. It was the first time that Hunter House ever had a book on the bestseller list.

☐ **Radio talk show campaigns can also be effective** in establishing a book. John Gray's *Men Are from Mars, Women Are from Venus* was first published in June 1992. After Gray's initial author tour, HarperCollins continued to promote the book with a nationwide radio talk show campaign. Combined with Gray's seminar appearances, the radio talk shows helped the book get on many regional bestseller lists. Finally, an appearance on *Donahue* caused the book to show up on *PW*'s bestseller list.

A number of books have also made it onto bestseller lists after being hyped by radio talk show hosts such as Howard Stern, Don Imus, or Rush Limbaugh (e.g., the *You Might Be a Redneck If...* series).

☐ **Get other major media attention.** Articles or excepts in *Newsweek, National Enquirer*, and other major magazines have propelled some books onto the bestseller lists. *The Arthritis Cure* by Dr. Jason Theodosakis jumped onto the bestseller lists immediately after Jane Brody, a syndicated columnist, reported that after eight weeks on his program, the arthritis in her knee improved enough for her to play tennis again.

☐ **Get on a regional bestseller list.** Here are just a few of the major newspapers that compile their own bestseller lists: *Chicago Tribune, Dallas Morning News, Detroit Free Press, Atlanta Journal Constitution, Hous-*

ton *Post, San Francisco Chronicle,* and *Washington Post.* The local bookstores as well as the national media pay attention to these regional lists. If you make such a list, of course, be sure to let the major national lists know about it.

When Cliff Sheat's *Lean Bodies* stayed on the *Dallas Morning News* bestseller list for 30 weeks, the Summit Group was able to generate lots of national interest in the book, including special promotions in both of the major chains.

☐ **Get on specialty bookseller lists.** For instance, the Christian Booksellers Association and Spring Arbor Distributors compile a monthly bestseller list of religious books. *Locus* magazine compiles a monthly science fiction bestseller list (based on sales in 25 science fiction bookstores). And the *Chronicle of Higher Education* compiles a list of the bestselling trade books in college bookstores (based on sales in 150 such stores).

☐ **Get on wholesaler bestseller lists.** For instance, Ingram publishes lists of its bestsellers in the following categories: children's books, computer books, science fiction, cookbooks, and more. New Leaf lists its top 50 bestselling titles in four categories: conscious living, metaphysical, wellness, and young readers. Each month, Quality Books publishes its top 40 library bestsellers.

☐ **Get on a magazine bestseller list.** *Bloomsbury Review* features a bestseller list based on sales from 30 top independent bookstores. The *Voice Literary Supplement* also features such a list. Among specialty magazines, the *Lambda Rising Book Report* features a list of bestselling gay and lesbian titles. Note that the *Wall Street Journal* and *Business Week* both have business books bestseller lists.

☐ **Be sure your books are stocked by the national bookstore chains.** When *Publishers Weekly* was analyzing the top bestsellers for 1996, they noted that "to be a contender for these top slots on the annual lists, a serious quantity of books has to move in the national chains."

☐ **Offer consumer rebates.** When Bloomsbury published Joanna Trollope's novel, *A Spanish Lover,* in England, they inserted 1.3 million copies of the first chapter in the *London Sunday Times.* They also offered an $8.00 rebate to any *Times* reader who bought the book in the first three days after publication. The book shot to the top of the *Times* bestseller list within a week.

☐ **Publish your key titles during the off seasons** when the major publishers are not bringing out their blockbusters. For instance, July and August are slow months. The Behind the Bestsellers department of *Publishers Weekly* noted that several books made the list that might not have made it at a busier time: "Since both hardcover bestseller charts are currently soft, the numbers it takes to gain a spot on the bottom of the lists are less competitive."

☐ **Relaunch a book.** When Jonathan Harr's *A Civil Action* failed to make any of the bestseller lists even though the first printing of 108,000 copies sold out, Random House decided to relaunch the book in January 1996, a less competitive time of year when books by first-time authors have a better chance of making the lists. First they offered retailers a $4.00 credit for all books sold between January 14 and February 17. In addition, they ran new national print ads and radio spots and booked the author on *CNN This Morning* and NPR's *Fresh Air*. As a result, the book finally made the bestseller lists.

In July 1997, Harmony relaunched Chris Bohjalian's novel, *Midwives*. During its first three months, the book had been chosen as Discovery of the Month by the New England Booksellers Association, hit the Maine bestseller lists for nine weeks, sold to Book-of-the-Month Club, was optioned for filming by Tri-Star Pictures, and garnered all sorts of great reviews, yet it did not make any national bestseller lists. So Harmony placed a full-page letter ad in *Publishers Weekly* announcing, "We're going to fight to get book lovers everywhere reading this book. Please help us spread the word." They offered booksellers a free reading copy of the book as well as a 53% discount on the book from July 14 to August 31. As Chip Gibson, publisher of Harmony, wrote, "We're behind *Midwives* 100% and we'd like you to be behind it, too."

When Simon & Schuster noted that M. Scott Peck's *The Road Less Traveled* had sold 176,000 copies in less than two years without making a bestseller list, they sent a letter to booksellers noting that the book was selling at legitimate bestseller levels. They then asked the booksellers to "make the extra effort to keep this title a part of your bestseller displays and if genuine, report it to the lists." This letter to bookstores along with a renewed push for publicity made the book a fixture on bestseller lists, including more than 500 weeks on *Publishers Weekly* trade paperback list (that's almost ten years!).

☐ **Treat your title as a top frontlist title.** Give it a knockout cover design. Print and mail galley copies for review at major magazines. Pre-sell the book to major book clubs prior to publication date. Get your distributor and sales reps behind the book.

Months before *Jurassic Park*, the movie, was about to be released in June 1993, Ballantine decided to relaunch the book by Michael Crichton. Probably the most important factor in its relaunch to bestseller status (it had already been a bestseller in 1990) was the fact that the reps treated the book as a bestseller launch rather than a backlist title. That meant they pushed the bookstores for larger orders, asking them to order 25 or more copies rather than the usual three or four. They also pushed the booksellers to promote the book to their customers rather than wait for readers to ask for the book. As a result, the book returned to bestseller lists in mid-January, months before the movie was released, and remained on the lists through the summer.

☐ **Go slow.** Let word of mouth build your book into a bestseller. Since most smaller publishers cannot afford to orchestrate a national laydown and PR effort that hits all in one week, those who have been successful creating a bestseller usually use the slow but sure method. Here are a few books that took that way to reach the bestseller lists:

Jeremy Tarcher published *The Artist's Way* by Julia Cameron with Mark Bryan in July 1992 with a 7,500 first printing. Word of mouth took over and orders started to increase. By February 1994, the publisher was shipping 8,000 copies per month.

When Dave Chilton self-published *The Wealthy Barber* in 1989, he took a long-term view to building the book. He did hundreds of interviews during that first year. By 1990, his book was selling ten to fifteen thousand copies a month. By 1991, his book had made the Canadian bestseller list. By 1996, it was still on the Canadian bestseller lists. With more than a million copies sold (in a country of 29 million at the time!), his book is the bestselling book in Canadian history, excluding the Bible. As Chilton points out, most publishers have a frontlist mentality and put most of their promotional efforts into the first six months. This, he says, "doesn't give you enough time for word of mouth to help." He suggests that you make your readers your marketing team while you stay focused on the project for at least two to three years.

Publishers: One word of caution: If you are serious about promoting a book so it becomes a bestseller, be sure you are prepared to deal with all the accompanying headaches: reprintings, distribution, fulfillment, returns, collections, and the cash flow crunch. More than one small company has found itself in bankruptcy because its owners and managers were not prepared to handle the demand, either materially or psychologically.

2:18 How to Launch a Bestseller (Some Case Histories)

Below are a few different strategies employed by publishers to launch their books onto the bestseller lists. Use these case histories to plan your major book launches. I have provided these case histories as checklists so you can check off those points you want to pursue.

The Big Picture by Douglas Kennedy (Hyperion)

When Hyperion launched this novel on March 26, 1997, with a one-day national laydown, here are a few of the things they did in the months prior to that day to build interest in the book:

☐ In August 1996, they bought the rights to the book when they heard about a movie deal in the works (Fox 2000 eventually bought the film rights). They offered a floor bid of $500,000 and ended up paying $1,125,000 when the book went to auction.

☐ They assigned a national marketing budget of $750,000, one-third of which went into the sell-in to bookstores.

☐ In November 1996, they sent unbound manuscripts to 200 key buyers and industry decision makers and 50 top book reviewers.

☐ Also in November, they placed a full-page ad in *Publishers Weekly* announcing their full launch campaign (which you are reading here).

☐ In December, their sales reps sent *bound galleys* [books bound from printed typeset proofs] in evidence bags, along with disposable cameras printed with the book's cover art, to 1,850 accounts. At the same time, the publicity department sent galleys to 350 additional book reviewers.

☐ In January, they sent 5,000 reader's copies to buyers and clerks at the major independents and chain stores.

☐ When *Publishers Weekly* gave the book a starred review, Hyperion sent cameras with quotes from the review to the 400 book reviewers who had received advanced galleys.

☐ They *advanced* 300,000 copies of the 400,000 first printing (that is, they took firm orders from bookstores for 300,000 copies).

☐ They designed a 12-copy floor display with a special riser.

☐ They made co-op money available to bookstores.

☐ The book was the Clyde Pick of the month at the Books-a-Million chain, which meant it was heavily displayed and promoted throughout the chain. Only one book is chosen each month for this star treatment.

☐ They sold audio rights to Simon & Schuster.

☐ They sold book club rights to Literary Guild and Doubleday Book Club.

☐ They sold foreign rights to England, France, Germany, Italy, Norway, and The Netherlands.

☐ During the week of the March 26th publication date, they ran full-page ads in the *New York Times*, *Variety*, *Los Angeles Times*, and *Hollywood Reporter*.

☐ National television spots were placed on CNN and E! Entertainment along with many local programs.

☐ At the same time, they placed transit ads in New York and Connecticut.

☐ A billboard was placed along Hollywood's Sunset Boulevard.

☐ A 30-second trailer ran in 800 Cineplex Odeon theaters.

By May, the book had made the *New York Times* bestseller list, but it did not stay on the list for more than a few weeks. Did it pay, then, to spend what they spent? Since they made some good subsidiary rights sales, they probably made a profit on the book. The sales from the book alone could not have justified the cost.

Excerpted advice from Steve Martini's *The List*

In his bestselling novel about making the bestseller list, Steve Martini reviewed some of the things his fictional publisher did to ensure a bestseller ranking for first-time author Gable Cooper.

☐ The publisher sent out 5,000 *dumps* (cardboard floor displays for books) holding 12 copies of the book.

☐ The publisher paid booksellers to place the dumps at the front of their stores. According to Martini, "Space in a single chain of stores could cost a publisher thirty thousand dollars for a single week." The publisher would spend $200,000 in the first sixty days for special display placement. "Without this, a book seldom, if ever, had a chance to become a bestseller."

☐ The publisher placed full-page ads in the *Los Angeles Times*, *New York Times*, *Washington Post*, and *Chicago Tribune* (these are the big four local newspapers, along with *USA Today* and *Wall Street Journal*, whose reviews and stories can propel a book onto the bestseller lists). Ads were also run in several high-circulation magazines.

☐ Because of his ad placement, the publisher was able to influence one of the chic tabloid magazines to name Gable Cooper one of the fifty most beautiful people in America.

☐ Ads were placed inside all New York City subway cars because New York was a "pressure point to establish buzz within the industry."

☐ Sample chapters were inserted into morning papers on publication day.

The Lion of Wall Street by Jack Dreyfus (Regnery Publishing)

Despite a one million dollar marketing campaign financed by the author, this book did not make any major bestseller lists. A previous book by Dreyfus, *A Remarkable Medicine Has Been Overlooked*, also did not make the bestseller lists, even after a $1.5 million advertising campaign financed by the author's medical foundation. Below are a few of the promotional activities promised for his *Lion of Wall Street*.

☐ Free copies were to be sent to 40,000 libraries throughout the U.S.

☐ Full-page ads were placed on publication date in ten major newspapers. A month later, more full pages ads were placed.

☐ Full-page ads were run in *Time*, *Newsweek*, and *Forbes*.

☐ Ads were placed on the TV pages of many newspapers.

☐ The author was scheduled for national radio and TV appearances.

Chances are that the book did not do well because it presented a mixed message. The book was half biography and half medical proselytizing. Note that a million dollar marketing campaign is no insurance of bestseller status. The book has to work on its own. Ultimately, for a book to get on and stay on a bestseller list, it must get good word of mouth.

2:19 Develop a Perennial Bestseller

To develop a perennial bestseller (one that sells many copies year after year), follow the same basic rules as described above except act for the long term rather than the short term. More than one small company has built its business based on one perennial bestseller.

☐ Ten Speed Press has become a well-recognized press because of Richard Bollen's *What Color Is Your Parachute?*, which has been a perennial bestseller for many years. In 1996, the book made *Publishers Weekly*'s annual bestseller list twice—once for its 1995 edition, which sold 132,000 copies in 1996, and again for its 1996 edition, which sold 183,000 copies. The book is still hitting the bestseller lists in 2006.

☐ Bernard Kamoroff built his one-person publishing company, Bell Springs Publishing, by selling 500,000 copies of one title, *Small Time Operator*.

☐ Although published with a first printing of 29,000 copies, *The Bridges of Madison County* made the *New York Times* list in August 1992 and re-mained among the top 10 bestsellers for three years running. 6.3 million copies were sold in the U.S., and another 3.7 million worldwide.

☐ Because it is used in so many classes, William Golding's *Lord of the Flies* continues to sell 300,000 copies a year in paperback.

☐ First published in 1923, Kahlil Gibran's *The Prophet* has sold almost 9,000,000 copies since Knopf began keeping computerized records. The book was on the bestseller lists for eleven months in 1992.

☐ The *American Heritage Dictionary of the English Language* sells about 200,000 copies per year.

☐ Dr. Seuss's *Oh, The Places You Will Go* continues to make the bestseller lists every year at graduation time. Many of his other books, such as *The Cat in the Hat*, *Green Eggs and Ham*, and *Hop on Pop*, continue to sell year after year. In 1995 six of the top fifteen hardcover backlist best-sellers were books by Dr. Seuss.

☐ Every year the University of Chicago Press sells 150,000 copies of its *Manual for Writers of Term Papers, Theses, and Dissertations* (known as *The Chicago Manual*). Over five million copies have been sold.

☐ Paul Samuelson's *Economics*, probably the best-known college textbook, has sold millions of copies over fifteen editions published since 1949. Besides establishing McGraw-Hill as a preeminent publisher of economics textbooks, the book defined modern economics and contributed to Samuelson being awarded the first Nobel Prize in Economics.

☐ Since 1931 when Irma Rombauer originally self-published *The Joy of Cooking*, this cookbook has sold milliss of copies. Almost seventy years later, it still sells more than 100,000 copies per year. In November 1997, Scribners published a completely revised fifth edition, the first new edition in twenty years. It, too, became a bestseller.

☐ Other perennial bestsellers include *The Elements of Style, The Catcher in the Rye, The One Minute Manager, Charlotte's Web, Where the Wild Things Are, The Little Prince, Goodnight Moon, The Little Engine That Could, The Poky Little Puppy*, and *Think and Grow Rich*.

☐ Of course, many annual guides have also become perennial bestsellers, such as the various tax and travel guides, *World Almanac, Rand McNally Road Atlas, Guinness Book of World Records, Kelley Blue Book Used Car Guide*, and *Kovel's Antiques & Collectibles Price List*.

2:22 Develop Brand Names

Even book publishers can develop brand names that help to promote their titles. Brand names can be developed not only from company names (to be discussed in greater detail in the next chapter), but also from series titles, authors, and individual books. Brand names, if they represent quality or consistency, can help to build a loyal customer base.

☐ Publishers' imprints such as Laurel, Plume, Torchbooks, Roc, Red Dress Ink, Dafina Books, Downtown Press, and Vintage Contemporaries have established strong reputations for quality. As a book reviewer in the *Philadelphia Inquirer* noted, "If I had to pick a line of paperbacks I would buy sight unseen, title unknown, it would be the Laurel series."

☐ Annual directories often develop brand names as well. How many of you would recognize *LMP*? Almost anyone who has been in the book industry for a few years would recognize this book as *Literary MarketPlace*.

☐ Simon and Schuster's 1980's series, Harold Robbins Presents, sold more because of the headline name than because of the contents of the books themselves. International rights guarantees for the series exceeded $225,000. An author's reputation can carry an entire line of books, even if he doesn't write any of them.

☐ Other brand name authors (whose new books are almost sure bestsellers) include: Danielle Steel, Kathleen Woodiwiss, Barbara Taylor Bradford, Nora Roberts, Mary Higgins Clark, Stephen King, Dick Francis, Robert Ludlum, Judy Blume, Toni Morrison, Patricia Cornwell, Elmore Leonard, Judith Krantz, Tom Peters, Stephen Covey, Dr. Seuss, Jeffrey Archer, Jeff Smith (the Frugal Gourmet), Tom Clancy, John Grisham,

Maya Angelou, Jackie Collins, Michael Crichton, James Patterson, Lawrence Block, and Ray Bradbury. This list is obviously incomplete.

☐ Even characters can become brand names. Witness Scott Adam's *The Dilbert Future*, *The Dilbert Principle*, and other Dilbert books and calendars as well as their Dogbert spinoffs, *Dogbert's Clues for the Clueless* and the bestselling *Dogbert's Top Secret Management Handbook*.

☐ Two of the bestselling series of the past 20 years, *Dummies* and *Chicken Soup for the Soul*, are trademarked. New brands include the *Don't Sweat the Small Stuff* series, *The Worst Case Scenario* handbooks, *Dr. Atkin's* diet books, the *Fix-It and Forget-It* cookbooks, *The South Beach Diet* books, *The Prayer of Jabez* series, and *What to Expect* parenting series.

☐ Price/Stern/Sloan's Wee Sing series of books and cassettes have consistently been in the top ten of B. Dalton's juvenile bestseller list.

2:21 The Importance of a Lead Title

Even if you do not develop any bestsellers or brand names, you should set priorities for your new titles. Usually this means that you will feature one or more lead titles each season. And, although these lead titles will take most of your time and money in promoting them, they do not need to detract from your other titles. Indeed, if chosen carefully and promoted well, lead titles can actually help to attract attention to your other titles.

☐ One way lead titles can help is by opening doors to reviewers and booksellers who would not otherwise look at any of your titles. A lead title for New Society Publishers in 1985 was a wall calendar featuring *Cat Lovers Against the Bomb*. The calendar appealed to many general readers, especially cat lovers, who might not otherwise have been attracted to New Society's line of social justice titles. Once readers bought the calendar, they were more likely to look into other books published by New Society (many of which were listed on the back page of the calendar).

☐ When Rutledge Hill published H. Jackson Brown's *Life's Little Instruction Book*, they found that the bestselling book help them to open many new accounts as well as pull the sales of other titles in their catalog. The book also helped pull in more customers for Brown's first two books, *A Father's Book of Wisdom* and *P.S. I Love You*, which were only modest sellers before his blockbuster hit.

Authors — Don't be jealous if your book isn't the lead title. Be happy your publisher is promoting its lead titles because these titles, if successful, often pull along the entire line, resulting in more sales for your book as well.

2:22 Build a Superb and Deep Backlist

Good list building is the only way to ensure steady income over a number of years. If you rely solely on your new titles, your company will always be in a boom or bust cycle. So when selecting new titles, be sure to look for titles that will have lasting value—books on health rather than fad diets, books with real content rather than instant non-books, books written with style and depth rather than by formula.

When you prepare your marketing plans you should be thinking ahead to how new titles will fit into and contribute to your current backlist. Think backlist. It truly forms the solid backbone of any successful book publisher.

- [ ] Bantam's backlist now includes well over 2,000 titles, of which 250 sell more than 10,000 copies per month.

- [ ] HarperCollin's backlist titles account for 70% of their paperback sales.

- [ ] According to a recent Huenefeld survey, 65% of all sales for mid-sized book publishers comes from titles more than a year old.

- [ ] College textbook publishers obtained over 80% of their sales from their backlist titles.

- [ ] Farrar, Straus & Giroux has an active backlist of 300 titles. When Flannery O'Connor's letters were published in 1979, her *Collected Stories*, which had been published eight years before, also picked up in sales.

- [ ] Cookbooks are perennial backlist sellers. At one time, six of the ten top backlist sellers for HarperCollins were cookbooks. 80% of Waldenbook's sales of cookbooks are backlist titles.

- [ ] Backlist titles will sometimes come back to the forefront due to new promotions. *Out of Africa and Shadows on the Grass* by Isak Dinesen became a bestseller as a result of the release of the movie *Out of Africa*, starring Robert Redford and Meryl Streep.

- [ ] *When I Am an Old Woman I Shall Wear Purple* put Papier-Mache on the map. Indeed, it sold better in 1991 than it did in 1987 when it was first published. Why? Because it took awhile to find its audience and generate the word-of-mouth that results in sales. In fact, booksellers chose it as one of the first runners-up for the ABBY award, which was given to books that booksellers most enjoyed hand-selling.

- [ ] A strong backlist title rarely gets returned—another good reason for developing a quality backlist.

- [ ] Independent booksellers welcome any publisher with a strong backlist. Backlist titles allow independent booksellers to compete with the discounters, chains, warehouse stores, and supermarkets which primarily feature frontlist titles.

- [ ] Publishing backlist books is just like printing money. Titles that can sell year after year are the basis of most successful publishing companies.

2:23 Plan for the Long Term

The main point of much of the above chapter has been to encourage you to develop a long-term marketing plan rather than focus only on short-term seasonal marketing plans. Your publishing company will become much stronger if you do so. Ideally, your long-term and short-term plans should mesh in such a way that each contributes to the other. If done well, your frontlist will then merge into your backlist, making it even better and better as the years go on.

All good books have one thing in common —
they are truer than if they had really happened.

— Ernest Hemingway

That's how you get a bestseller—
one interview, one book signing at a time.
— Og Mandino, author, *The Greatest Salesman in the World*

Creating a Bestselling Career

by Greg Godek, author of the
2.5-million-copy bestseller 1001 Ways To Be Romantic

"It's not about the book." [Huh?!] "It's not about the book... It's about what the book can do for you."

Books are wonderful. Marvelous. Necessary. I love books. I've written 14. Sold four million. But it's still not about the books. It's about me. My career. My image. My branding.

You want the Truth? Here it is: Creating a bestselling book is a devilishly difficult thing to do. But creating a bestselling career is eminently achievable. And one of the best strategies for creating a bestselling career is to pursue the creation of a bestselling book. [Huh? But I thought you said ...]

You see, books are the perfect focal point for any expert's career. Your book is the crystallization of who you are; the embodiment of your message; the spoken word given solid form. Books are an opportunity—and also a trap. Because it's so easy to slip into thinking that it really is about the book.

You need to step back and consider the bigger picture. If you define yourself only as an author (like Stephen King or J.K. Rowling), I wish you good luck. You'll need it. Your chances of making a living from writing books alone is approximately a hundred-kajillion-to-one. But if you're smart about it, and combine writing and speaking, then your chances are about one-in-four.

If you are overly caught up in your book's success, you're letting the tail wag the dog. Why? Well, let's take a quick look at the "publishing model" versus the "speaking model." Books sold through bookstore channels (and that's' where real bestsellers—and national images—are created) earn about a buck a book in royalties/profits. Speeches and seminars can reasonably earn anywhere from $1,000 to $10,000 per engagement. You do the math!

The secret, of course, is to create synergy between your book and your speaking career. Your book bestows credibility and opens doors to the media (which, in turn, builds your image). Your speaking career makes money—and it's easier to get booked when you have a solid image. A good combo, eh?

Why not really focus on creating a bestselling book? First, because books are rarely profitable. And second, because luck is by far the major factor in the creation of bestselling books.

When authors and publishers pursue bestsellerdom, we of course manage/manipulate all of the factors that are within our control. Things like marketing, PR, promotion, distribution, budget, title, cover, etc. Picture a pie chart: All of these factors together comprise maybe 20% of the bestseller equation. The remaining 80% is ... luck. (Luck equals things like timing, cultural trends, unconscious consumer wants and needs, generational factors, a hot movie, a war, the state of the economy, etc.)

I desperately encourage you to not build your business on luck. You might just as well list "buying lottery tickets" among your marketing strategies. If, instead, you focus on creating a bestselling career, the equation reverses itself: The controllable factors comprise 80%, and luck shrinks to 20%. Much better odds.

You need to sell about 100,000 books in one year to even approach bestseller status. A hundred friggin' thousand books! Supporting that goal is expensive and time consuming. [I know from experience: I spend $100,000 per year in marketing. (Hey, you think being a bestselling author is an easy gig? Think again.)] But you need to sell only 10,000 to 20,000 books per year to support a successful speaking/consulting career. Those are reasonable, achievable numbers—not subject to the whims of luck.

It might also help you to know that most bestselling books are a flash in the pan—good for your resume and good for your ego. But a bestselling career will sustain you, your lifestyle and your family for the rest of your life.

Greg Godek is best known for his 2.5-million-copy, self-published bestseller *1001 Ways To Be Romantic* and for his outrageous marketing techniques and creative approach to strategy and branding. He now limits his consulting to hosting monthly **BestSeller Experience Seminars** at his studio in La Jolla, California.

For more information, contact Greg Godek at 858-456-7177. Email: GregGodek@aol.com. Web: http://www.BestSellerExperience.com.

The Changing Face of Publishing

by John Harnish of Infinity Publishing

In these changing times of publishing, the days of expensive book launchings sponsored and paid for by mainstream publishers have been diluted. The rule of thumb in setting a publisher's book marketing budget is that it should be about the same amount of money as the publisher has paid the author as an advance. Authors are required by contract to contribute their efforts to promote their books in order to earn future royalties until the books go out-of-print. The window of opportunity for books to produce results in bookstore chains is limited by the bean-counters as royalties dwindle.

Evolving publishing styles, such as author-originated publishing, are attracting increasing numbers of professional authors who are marketing-smart and publicity-savvy. One of the primary attractions is that the author controls the content and retains all rights. The once-limiting windows are expanded into infinity because their books will never go out-of-print and royalties are paid monthly on all books sold. This provides authors with a promotional platform for producing long-term returns. The selective seeding of interest-rich areas is more fruitful than the scattered shotgun blast–after the bang, the flash quickly fades. The author of a digitally published book benefits from all accumulated promotional and marketing efforts. The author holds the key to opening the door to increasing book sales that will lead to media attention.

Authors have a vested interest in promoting their books to reap the harvest from all the seeds of interest they have planted along the way. The trend of media news coverage is more niche-orientated, which increases Google searches for authors of special topic books.

☐ Oprah Winfrey searched for an expert on shoplifting addictions and found Terry Shulman, Infinity author of *Something for Nothing: Shoplifting Addiction and Recovery.*

☐ The History Channel wanted to do an oral history segment about feuding in the hills of West Virginia and they found *Appalachia: Spirit Triumphant,* written by Betty Lewis and published by Infinity Publishing.

☐ Robert Pelton has published an Infinity series of cookbooks with recipes from colonial times and the Civil War era. He's a frequent speaker at historical meetings and re-enactments, where his cookbooks sell like hotcakes.

An author-originated book in print is the author's passport into an expanding world of publishing beyond the limitations of traditional mainstream houses. The editorial freedom of cost-effective publishing provides the motivated author with unprecedented benefits. If you're an author with a book that is ready to be published, you owe it to yourself to explore author-originated publishing. It has the benefits of mainstream publishing without the expensive risk of self-publishing.

Infinity Publishing is the industry-acknowledged trendsetter in author-originated publishing. Our Just-in-Time book publishing system maintains an on-shelf inventory of our 3,000+ titles. We produce our books in-house on state-of-the-art high-speed digital printers. Bookstores enjoy our liberal book return policy that helps to get more of our books into the market place. Our sister company, Spoken Book Publishing, is the only company that is setup to produce and distribute audio books for self-published authors. We take great pride in being author friendly and sponsor an annual Authors' Conference each year in Valley Forge, Pennsylvania, where authors learn latest trends in book promotion from marketing experts like John Kremer.

For more information, contact: **Infinity Publishing**, 1094 New Dehaven Street #100, West Conshohocken, PA 19428; 610-941-9999; 877-BUY-BOOK; Fax: 610-941-9959. Email: info@infinitypublishing.com. Web: http://www.infinitypublishing.com.

Chapter 3

Establishing and Marketing Your Company

Any institution worth its salt, any service worth its salt ...
ought to have a mission that's brief,
that says it all, and that everybody knows.
— Robert Coles, *The Ongoing Journey*

An integral part of marketing your books is marketing your company name and image. If booksellers, librarians, and readers do not have a strong awareness of your company, you will have a difficult time selling books. So you must, as Humpty-Dumpty pointed out to Alice, begin at the beginning.

3:01 Do the Obvious

Although it may not be necessary to point out the obvious, in the interest of being complete, I will mention that you should start your company out on the right foot. That means you should register your company, acquire all the proper permits, rent or arrange a separate workspace, get a phone, print up official stationery and business cards, and get down to business.

Try to set up financial arrangements that will help you get through the inevitable cash flow crunch. For most small publishers, printers demand payment in advance but wholesalers, distributors, and bookstores all want 90-day terms or better. The gap between the time you pay the printer and the time money comes in from the distribution network is often six months or more. While some publishers finance their business with credit cards or personal loans, there are other ways to finance your business, including pre-selling books, looking for venture capital, and forming partnerships (for more info, check out http://www.bookmarket.com/venture.html).

When Cynthia Black and Richard Cohn were building up Beyond Words, they partnered with the author of *Seeing Beyond 20/20* to finance developmental costs for the book. The author used his American Express card and they used their Visa card to get cash advances to print the cover of the book, rent a targeted mailing list, and mail 10,000 postcards. That mailing brought in 1,000 orders, which at $12.95 each, gave them enough money to print books and pay off both credit cards.

3:02 Use Your Business Cards to Network

To maximize your networking among acquaintances and business associates, learn how to use your business cards. And be sure your employees, sales people, and authors also know how to make best use of them. Here are some hints:

☐ Carry your cards with you wherever you go. Hand them out to everyone you talk to (on the street, in an airplane, at the market, wherever). More often than not, these people will be interested in your books and what you do—and will contact you again later. This technique is especially effective for authors.

☐ When visiting key contacts, give out two cards—one for them and one for their secretary (for the Rolodex).

☐ Exchange cards. Don't just give your card away. Be sure to get the other person's card as well. In fact, an easy way to make sure the other person gets your card is to ask for her card first. Once you have her card, write a note on the back reminding you of the conversation and any follow-up you want to do.

☐ When giving out your card, write your home phone number on the card before you give it to the other person. Do this only for people you really want to mark as being special.

☐ Have your office hours printed on the card, or note when you are commonly available. This will make it easier for the other person to contact you.

☐ Business cards are an absolute must at conventions, exhibits, meetings, and conferences. Don't leave home without yours.

☐ Leave your card when you tip. Enclose a card with your electric bill (one Realtor sold a house because he enclosed his card every month in his electric bill).

Business cards work a whole lot harder these days. No longer a bland black and white, business cards now come in all colors, from hot pink to fluorescent orange, with color photographs, intricate illustrations, cutouts, pop-ups, or holograms. Business cards no longer come only in plain paper, but instead come in all sorts of materials, from magnetic cards to wood, leather, fluorescent plastic, translucent cellulose, and heat sensitive materials. And, in keeping with the digital age, you can now send a virtual business card via e-mail.

Don't treat business cards as attention-getters only, they can also do a selling job for your product or service. Here are a few ways you can spice up your business card to get more attention and sales:

☐ **Offer discount referrals**. Realtor Ron McCall passes out a business card that features a list of local retailers and restaurants on the back. All of those listed on the back offer special discounts to anyone presenting Ron's card. As a book author, you could make this work for you. For example, if you have a romance novel, you could include the names of local restaurants or hotels with romantic weekend packages. If you have a book on immigration law, you could list a few lawyers who would provide discounted services to anyone presenting or mentioning your card.

☐ **Use your card as a discount coupon.** When people call you, they can get a special discount on your books if they mention the special offer or code printed on your card.

On the back of my new business cards, I offer publishers a free five-minute consulting session (worth $40.00 at my current rates). I am now making that same offer to anyone who reads this book. Call me, and I will give you five minutes of free advice. After that, you're on the clock. This offer, however, is subject to withdrawal if I get overwhelmed.

☐ **Use the back of your card for promotion.** For example, print your book cover, aphorisms supporting your book's topic, frequently used industry terms, a helpful formula or chart, or useful tips. A foreign travel guide, for example, could list the most useful phrases a traveler would need (such as, "Where is the toilet?). For his novel, *Uncommon Influence*, Terry Dodd included a useful tipping chart for average (15%) and generous (20%) tippers.

☐ **Pass on an excerpt from your book.** Robert Conklin, author of *Be Whole!*, passes out Billfold Boosters, 8-page folded business-card-size brochures which include excerpts from his book. His charts of the dynamics of positive and negative attitudes have been translated into German, French, Norwegian, Russian, Spanish, Japanese, and Braille. And his cards have been used by congressional prayer meetings, self-help groups, prison inmates, doctor's clinics, churches, hospitals, corporations, and a football team that won the Rose Bowl!

☐ **Laminate your card.** One man passes out cards with a quarter laminated to the back side so recipients would always have money for a phone call.

For color printers who can print your book cover, photo, or other four-color impact illustration on business cards, see the BookMarket.com web site at: http://www.bookmarket.com/color.html.

> **Authors** — You should have business cards printed up with your name and the title of the book or books you are currently promoting. You might even want to have the cover of your main book reproduced on the back (or front) side of the card. Once you have the cards, give them to everyone you meet who might have any interest (however remote) in your book.

3:03 Choose a Company Name

Give careful thought to what you call your company. You will have to live with it for years. Here are a few hints:

☐ Avoid names that are hard to pronounce or whose spelling is not immediately obvious. I often had cause to regret my own decision to name my previous company, Ad-Lib Publications. It's not an easy name to catch over the phone. Plus, people have come up with innumerable ways of spelling it (not quite as many ways as with my own last name—but I didn't have a choice in that matter).

☐ Peggy Glenn, in her book on *Publicity for Books and Authors*, describes how she came to change her company name from Pigi Publishing (P.G. from her initials, but often pronounced "piggy") to Aames-Allen. First, borrowing an old trick from the telephone book, she began her company name with two A's. That way her company would always be first in the various trade listings. It's a small quibble, and I certainly wouldn't recommend that anyone else follow suit because then *Literary MarketPlace* would begin to look like a big city's yellow pages. As publishers, we must remember that there are twenty-six letters in the English alphabet.

Peggy's second reason for naming her company Aames-Allen is well-conceived. It sounds very English. Plus it has the hyphenated name associated with many established publishers, such as Time-Life, Addison-Wesley, McGraw-Hill, Prentice-Hall, Amber-Allen, and others. Hence, it not only sounds like proper English, but it also sounds familiar, as if it had been around for a long time.

☐ Don't use the word *enterprises* at the end of your company name. It usually marks the amateur in the business world. Don't ask me why that is the case, but when I was working in the gift and toy industry, any such company name was always suspect. The situation may have improved in the past twenty years, but I wouldn't bet on it.

☐ Many smaller presses have wonderful names like The Lunchroom Press, The Green Hut Press, Bear Tribe Publishing, The Spirit That Moves Us, Devil Mountain Books, Milkweed Editions, Pig Out Publications, and

Peanut Butter Publishing. The disadvantage with such names is that they sound like small presses, and some booksellers still hesitate to order from small presses because of past problems getting orders or receiving credit for returns. On the other hand, these names project an alternative image that many presses want to promote—and which many readers find appealing.

☐ Bill Henderson named his publishing company Pushcart Press to honor those authors, such as George Plimpton, who had sold their books from pushcarts along Manhattan's Fifth Avenue to protest their treatment from the major publishers.

☐ In the final analysis, you must pick a name that appeals to you and projects the image you want for your company. Whatever you do, choose a company name that helps you to reach your ultimate audience. Your company name should be—and is—part of your company image. Make sure it fits.

3:04 Create a Brand Name

One of your first goals as a publisher should be to establish your company name as a brand name—one that will be immediately recognized and respected by readers. A brand name can be worth thousands, even millions of dollars, in advertising every year.

☐ One scholarly publisher with an established imprint tested a new imprint name in a direct mailing to its regular audience. The mailing under its established imprint outpulled the new imprint mailing by over 200%.

☐ In a *Publishers Weekly* article, the Bantam sales and marketing directors both asserted that they sell the Bantam name as much as any individual titles when they sell to bookstores.

☐ Kiplinger Books has established a brand name as a result of its newsletters and magazines. Now, all their books carry the Kiplinger name displayed prominently on their front covers. Kiplinger's *Make Your Money Grow* has sold over 300,000 copies.

☐ Because both the Penguin name and logo are familiar to most English-speaking readers, the company promoted Penguin boutiques (separate sections devoted solely to Penguin titles) in various bookstores. And many bookstores bought the idea.

☐ Repetition is the key to creating a brand name. If you decide to try to establish your company name as a brand name, be sure to repeat it in all your ads and to feature it on the covers of all your books.

☐ Harlequin has done such a thorough job of establishing its company name as a brand name that it comes close to being a generic term for romances.

☐ Workman has become known for a certain style of book. Most booksellers can spot a Workman book by its cover and design. Now that's a
great way to establish a brand name! While others have tried to copy
them, no one does it as well as Workman. The company specializes in
backlist titles that sell year after year—and announces that fact once or
twice a year in *Publishers Weekly* ads touting another press run for thirty
titles, listing their in-print totals to date (none less than 200,000).

☐ Klutz Press is another company well-known for its packaging and design. In fact, its book and box, book and pouch, and book with net are
all trademarked. Now that other companies are copying their format,
they've begun to mark all their books 100% Klutz Certified.

☐ In 1982, G. & C. Merriam changed its name to Merriam-Webster, which
it has trademarked. The company has gone to court many times to protect that trademark. And, to draw upon the power of its trademark, it recently changed the name of its bestselling *Webster's Collegiate Dictionary* to *Merriam-Webster's Collegiate Dictionary*. The book is the
world's leading hardcover bestseller, with almost 50 million copies sold
since 1896. The company now positions its dictionaries with the following statement: "Not just Webster, Merriam-Webster."

☐ Some companies have established their brand name so well that they can
extend the brand to almost anything. For instance, look at Virgin Records which now runs a string of music stores, an airline, a railroad, a
cola, a vodka, and a phone service.

Similarly, the Dummies brand name has carried over to many other lines
of books, starting with computer books but now covering lifestyle and
business topics as well. The name, however, doesn't translate very well.
In France, the books are for zeroes; in Poland, for the lazy; in China, for
Ding and Dong; in Croatia, for ignoramuses; and in Russia, for teapots!

☐ Berlitz, well-known for its language schools, has now extended its brand
name to travel guides. Recently, they introduced a series of travel guides
to children to extend that brand name to a younger audience.

☐ For a list of great independent book publishers that you might want to
emulate for their cover designs, editorial, or marketing, see the Book
Market.com website at http://www.bookmarket.com/101pub.html. That
page features the top 101 independent book publishers.

Authors: Use the Top 101 Publishers list to locate companies
which might do a good job publishing your book. If you'd like
your book to get special attention rather than getting lost in the
middle of hundreds of titles, these smaller publishers will suit
you well. If you'd rather go with a larger publisher, review the
list of editors also on the BookMarket.com website.

3:05 Become a Joiner

To help establish your company name, you should join one or more trade associations for the book industry. Besides giving you more visibility in the industry, membership in a trade association can help to foster working relationships with other publishers, provide you with the latest news and resources, enable members of your company to attend informative seminars, allow you to find out what's working for other publishers, and provide many other educational and marketing opportunities.

☐ The Association of American Publishers is the oldest trade association for book publishers in the United States. It functions mainly as a networking and lobbying association for the major publishers. Because of its high membership cost, many smaller publishers have chosen not to belong to this association, but join one of the other national associations listed below. **Association of American Publishers, 71 Fifth Avenue, New York, NY 10003-3004; 212-255-0200; Fax: 212-255-7007**. Web: http://www.publishers.org.

☐ PMA publishes a great newsletter, sponsors regular seminars, and exhibits member books at BookExpo America, ALA, and other conventions. It also offers an array of co-op promotional mailings, including Books for Review, Library Mailings, and Target Mailings (to buyers and reviewers of cookbooks, self-help, new age, and other topics). PMA sponsors the annual Benjamin Franklin Awards. Founded in 1983, PMA now has over 3,000 members, many of whom are smaller publishers. **PMA: The Independent Book Publishers Association, 627 Aviation Way, Manhattan Beach, CA 90266; 310-372-2732; Fax: 310-374-3342**. Email: pmaonline@aol.com. Web: http://www.pma-online.org.

Gary Blair, author of *What Are Your Goals*, wrote that the following outcomes can be tied directly to the services provided by PMA:

• International rights sold to six foreign countries, with advances totaling $15,000. Twenty-six inquiries came from the PMA display at Frankfurt Book Fair.

• Thirty-seven book reviews or feature stories.

• Three speaking engagements, which came directly from the reviews, which generated $7,500 in speaking fees.

☐ SPAN (Small Publishers Association of North America) has about 1,200 members. It also publishes a newsletter, offers co-op advertising and display opportunities, runs an annual conference, and operates a web site for members. Contact **SPAN, 1618 W. Colorado Avenue, Colorodo Springs, CO 80904; 719-475-1726; 800-331-8355; Fax: 719-471-2182**. Email: span@spannet.org. Web: http://www.spannet.org.

☐ NAIP (National Association of Independent Publishers) is a smaller organization with 300 members that offers book awards, an informative quarterly newsletter, a free 30-minute consulting session, and seminars in cooperation with the Florida Publishers Group. For more information, contact **NAIP, Betsy Lampe, P.O. Box 430, Highland City, FL 33846-0430; 813-648-4420; Fax: 941-647-5951**. Email: naip@aol.com.

☐ CLMP (Council of Literary Magazines and Presses) serves literary book publishers with a quarterly newsletter, conferences, monographs, seed grants, distribution projects, and a *Directory of Literary Magazines*. For more information, contact **CLMP, 154 Christopher Street #3C, New York, NY 10014-2839; 212-741-9110; Fax: 212-741-9112**.

☐ Join your regional book publishers association. There are now more than 40 local and regional publishing associations, including ones in Seattle, Portland, Marin County, Minnesota, Philadelphia, Florida, Texas, Houston, Tucson, Arizona, San Diego, Southern California, Northern California, Colorado, Kansas City, Illinois, Hawaii, Alaska, New England, the West, and the South. Please note that this list is not complete.

☐ Many subject areas (such as medicine and law) also have active publishing associations. For a list of regional and subject-oriented publishing associations, see http://www.bookmarket.com/pubassn.html.

☐ While you are at it, don't overlook the associations for booksellers. Membership in the American Booksellers Association helps support an association that can only strengthen independent booksellers—which, in turn, means that you are helping to strengthen one of the main outlets for your books. **American Booksellers Association, 200 White Plains Road, Tarrytown, NY 10591; 914-591-2665; 800-637-0037; Fax: 914-591-2720**. Web: http://www.bookweb.org.

Among the services that ABA offers to its member stores is the instant availability of any publisher's address, phone number, and terms just by calling ABA's toll-free phone number. You can use their web site to look up bookseller associations, independent bookstores, the latest bookstore news, and bookselling statistics. And, perhaps most important, you can become an active partner in their BookSense marketing program.

☐ There are many worthwhile regional booksellers associations as well, such as the Midwest Booksellers Association. UMBA holds an annual trade show in the fall, publishes a bimonthly newsletter, and sponsors a holiday book catalog that is mailed to 300,000 people. **Midwest Booksellers Association**, 3407 West 44th Street, Minneapolis, MN 55410; 612-926-5868; 800-784-7522; Fax: 612-926-6657. Email: info@midwest booksellers.org. Web: http://www.abookaday.com.

☐ Many of the other regional bookseller associations also hold trade shows and sponsor holiday book catalogs. Both the Mountains & Plains Booksellers Association and the New England Booksellers Association also publish membership directories which you can use to locate bookstores in those area. For a complete list of bookseller associations, see http:// www.bookmarket.com/bookassn.html.

☐ If you are a specialty publisher, you might also want to join a specialty booksellers association such as the Christian Booksellers Association or the Association of Booksellers for Children (ABC).

☐ As a publisher, you should also join any special interest writers groups that are related to the books you publish. These associations are great places to network with potential authors, reporters who cover the area, syndicated columnists, and freelance writers who write about the subject for magazines and newspapers. Most groups publish newsletters, provide membership directories, and sponsor seminars.

For example, if you publish home decorating books, you should join the National Association of Home and Workshop Writers. Other associations include writers for dogs, medicine, computers, gardens, science, poetry, children's books, travel, Christian, sports, and the outdoors. Sisters in Crime and the Romance Writers of America are active in promoting their authors and genre. Most of these groups as well as many local writers groups are listed at http://www.bookmarket.com/writers.html.

☐ If you publish books of interest to specific trade and professional associations, you should join those associations. Since you are publishing in that area, you probably already know which associations are most active. Join those. If you don't know which associations to join, go to your local library and explore a copy of the *Encyclopedia of Associations*.

Authors — You should join author associations where you can network with other writers. If you write books in specific subject areas, you should also join the trade and professional associations representing that subject as well as any consumer or hobby groups devoted to the subject.

3:06 Become a Reader

If you are serious about marketing your books, you should read everything you can to keep up to date on current events in the industry. Plus, you should never stop learning. Continue to read new books and reports on book marketing, publicity, advertising, publishing, printing, graphics, and anything else that applies to the fields in which you publish.

☐ Above all, you should subscribe to at least one trade magazine such as *Publishers Weekly, Library Journal, School Library Journal, Quill and Quire, New Age Journal*, and others (see addresses in Chapter 9).

☐ Subscribe to the *Book Marketing Update* newsletter. Edited by John Kremer, author of this book, this newsletter provides many marketing tips, resources, and key media and marketing contacts to help publishers and

authors sell more books. To order, go to *BookMarket.com*. At the same
time, read John Kremer's email tip of the week and Book Marketing
Bestsellers blog at *http://openhorizons.blogspot.com*.

☐ Subscribe to other publications such as *Subtext, BP Report, Scholarly
Publishing, Children's Books Insider*, the publishing association newsletters, and others.

☐ Subscribe to online newsletters, many of which are free for the asking.
For details on those, see *http://www.bookmarket.com/tipsconfirm.html*.

☐ Read some of the books listed in the bibliography of this book. The
complete bibliography is at *http://www.bookmarket.com/1001bib.html*.

Authors — You should also read these trade magazines and
newsletters. Not only will you get a better idea how the industry works, but you will also be able to keep up on what other
authors and publishers are doing. First choice: *Publishers
Weekly*. Second choice: *Book Marketing Update*. Then read
author publications such as *Freelance Writers Report, Writer's
Digest*, and *The Writer*. Also check out John Kremer's blog and
email newsletter as well as other online writer's ezines.

3:07 Get the Notice Out

Once you've established your company, don't hide under a bucket. Get
the word out. Let key people in the industry know that you are in business.

☐ Send notices to all the trade journals. *Publishers Weekly, Foreward*, and
Small Press Review list new ventures as a regular feature. Don't forget
the library and bookseller journals as well. And the appropriate specialized trade magazines. Finally, send me a notice for *Book Marketing Update*. Email: JohnKremer@bookmarket.com.

The addresses for the book trade journals are listed in Chapter 9. The
addresses for specialized trade magazines are listed in *Standard Periodical Directory* or *Gale's Directory of Publications*. You can also find
many of these addresses now by searching on the Internet. Start with
your favorite search engine and go from there.

☐ Send notices to key contacts in the industry: wholesalers such as Baker
& Taylor and Ingram, bookstore chains such as B. Dalton and Waldenbooks, book clubs, catalogs, and other businesses that you think might
be interested in what you are doing (and can help you to do it). Reports
and databases for these contacts are available from Open Horizons. See
our *BookMarket.com* website for details.

3:08 Get Listed Wherever Possible

As part of your publicity, be sure to have your company listed in all the appropriate industry reference books. Not only will such listings help get you orders from booksellers and librarians, but they will also add legitimacy to your company.

Certainly the most important listings for your company and its books are the Library of Congress Cataloging in Publication and Catalog Card Number offices (web site: http://lcweb2.loc.gov/pcn), Copyright Office, ISBN office, and Bowker *Books in Print*. You might also want to join the Copyright Clearance Center, which collects licensing fees for book excerpts used by schools, colleges, and corporations. Contact info for these services are listed at http://www.bookmarket.com/3.html.

Of course, you'll also want to get featured on Amazon.com and other Internet bookselling sites.

3:09 Continuing Publicity

Don't be shy about announcing other achievements as your company continues to grow. Anniversaries, new book publications, author signings, new discount and return policies, changes in employees—these are all news and should be announced to any key contacts and trade magazines which would be interested. See Chapter 9 for more ideas.

3:10 Get Involved, Become a Sponsor

When you join associations, don't fade away into the woodwork; become an active member. Get to know fellow publishers, booksellers, librarians, and others involved in the industry. Get to know their concerns, their needs, their desires—and let them know yours.

☐ As part of your active participation in the industry, sponsor awards, contests, or scholarships to give others recognition and to help them grow in their profession. Or work with your associations when they sponsor such awards and scholarships. Any such activities might not immediately show on your balance sheet, but they do help your company to gain recognition in the industry and further the image you want for your company (as long as the activities you sponsor are compatible with the image you want to project). Below, for example, are a few of the book publishers who helped to sponsor the first annual National Poetry Month in April 1996. Even more publishers have signed on since then.

Copper Canyon Press highlighted the month in advertisements, sponsored readings, and offered posters and other display materials to libraries and bookstores.

Farrar, Straus & Giroux offered a poetry audiotape sampler, a reading guide for poetry, and display materials.

Graywolf Press created poetry samplers and display materials. They also sponsored a read-a-thon, festival, and poetry bus.

☐ You could also sponsor marathons, bake-offs, and other such events. For instance, several book publishers helped to sponsor the 1984 LA Olympics. Such sponsorships have certainly helped gain recognition for Budweiser, Miller Lite, Pepsi, and Pillsbury. If your company's line of books would lend itself to such sponsorship, you should give it serious consideration. For example, why couldn't a publisher of auto books help sponsor the Indy 500 or the Daytona 500? Or a publisher of cookbooks sponsor its own bake-off? Such sponsorships take time and commitment, but they can pay off in the long run—both in increased publicity every year and additional sales.

Bridge Publications was the first book publisher to sponsor an Indy 500 racing team, the Dianetics/Penske team. They did so as part of their promotional campaign for *Dianetics*, their perennial self-help bestseller.

☐ Through its Books Building Community program, Foghorn Press donates a portion of the proceeds from every book it sells to community organizations addressing environmental, literacy, and health issues. Indeed, every book they published is done in coordination with a nonprofit association. For more details on cause-related book publishing, see the section on selling to associations in Chapter 19.

3:11 Create a Unique Selling Proposition

When you work to build up your company image, try to create a unique selling proposition that can set your company apart from others. To be honest, I'm not aware of any publishing companies that have a widely recognized unique selling proposition, such as Avis's "We Try Harder" or Nike's "Just Do It."

Wouldn't it be nice to position your company the way Perrier positioned itself? After all, it is just water, isn't it?

Can you name the companies or products associated with the following slogans? The answers, if you need help, are at the bottom of the next page.

1) Let your fingers do the walking.
2) A _____ is forever.
3) Reach out and touch someone.
4) Look, mom, no cavities!
5) Snap, crackle, pop!
6) We build excitement—_____!
7) Ring around the collar.
8) Don't leave home without it.

9) Leave the driving to us!

10) When It Absolutely, Positively Has to Be There Overnight

11) Melts in Your Mouth, Not in Your Hands

12) You Deserve a Break Today!

Of course, gaining such name recognition usually requires quite a bit of mass-market advertising. But your company name need not be recognized by everyone; it only needs to be recognized by your major prospects. So even a publisher with a limited audience can promote its unique selling proposition to that audience—and make them remember it.

☐ Kiplinger uses the following slogan in the trade ads for its consumer finance books: "Kiplinger: Brand name help for generic problems." A great slogan!

☐ Dan Poynter of Para Publishing has done that with the slogan for his *Self-Publishing Manual*—"The Book That's Launched 10,000 Books!" That number should be larger now.

☐ Amazon Books bills itself as "the world's largest online bookstore." Not to be outdone, Barnes & Nobles bills itself as "the world's largest bookseller online."

☐ Dustbooks calls itself, with some justification, "the information source for the small press world."

☐ Gateway Books calls itself "The Pioneering Publisher of Books for People over 50."

☐ Health Communications, publishers of the *Chicken Soup for the Soul* series, bills itself as "The Life Issues Publisher" while Fairview Press bills itself as "The Family Issues Publisher."

☐ Island Press bills itself as "the environmental publisher" and has clearly positioned itself to fill that market.

☐ While they don't announce their USP to the world, Steerforth Press has a definite statement of purpose: "To build a publishing house as Roger Straus did in the '40's, as Alfred Knopf did in the '20's, and to publish quality writers whose work can sell in paperback 10 to 20 years from now." That's an incredible mission!

☐ I've been considering a USP for *1001 Ways to Market Your Books*. I'm undecided between two choices right now: "The Book That Helped to Sell Over a Billion Books ... and Counting" or "The Book That Inspired More Than 100 Bestsellers." I'm not sure which to use—or to just stick with the great testimonial from Jack Canfield and Mark Victor Hansen, the one featured on the cover. If you have a favorite among these three options, email me at JohnKremer@bookmarket.com.

Answers: 1) yellow pages, 2) diamond, 3) AT&T, 4) Crest toothpaste, 5) Kellogg's Rice Krispies, 6) Pontiac, 7) Wisk, 8) American Express card, 9) Greyhound Bus, 10) Federal Express, 11) M&M's candies, and 12) McDonalds.

3:12 Persistence Pays

Follow the rules. Ignore the rules. But whatever you do, hang in there. Persist, and you will win out. One of the basic secrets of marketing is persistence. Marketing takes time. If you can persist long enough, your company will eventually get the recognition it deserves. You must give the prime book marketing tool, word of mouth, a chance to operate.

☐ For example, it took my old company Ad-Lib Publications four years and three editions of the *Directory of Book Printers* to gain the recognition it deserved. Libraries finally discovered the directory, with the third edition selling ten times faster than the second. Moreover, B. Dalton finally started carrying the book. Even then, Ad-Lib still had people calling them to ask, "Where have you been all these years?"

☐ Not only will your books sell better as you gain experience and exposure over the years, but you will also begin to receive more proposals that have greater commercial potential as writers and other contacts discover your existence. For instance, May-Murdock, a self-publisher in Marin County, quietly published books about railroading for a number of years. Finally the word got around. As a result, a leading San Francisco television personality asked them to publish his collection of commentaries.

☐ Penguin Books celebrated their 50th anniversary in 1985, and gained an incredible amount of publicity as a result. So another advantage of persistence is that someday you, too, will be able to celebrate your golden anniversary. Please invite me when you do. I love parties.

Persistence is what makes the impossible possible
the possible likely, and the likely definite.
— Robert Half

Nothing in the world can take the place of persistence.
Talent will not...genius will not...education will not....
Persistence and determination alone are omnipotent.
— Calvin Coolidge, American president

Making the Most of Media Opportunities with an Online Media Room

by Kathleen Meyer, Marketing Director for BookFlash

New technology has impacted every aspect of book publishing—even publicity. For media professionals in search of that next big story, the Internet is their first stop. A recent study shows that over 90% of journalists start researching a story by searching on the Net. That same study also shows that journalists are constantly frustrated by websites with difficult navigation, outdated or irrelevant information, a lack of PR contact, and no downloadable images and/or multimedia clips. In short, many websites and online media rooms are falling short in this age of instant information.

For the savvy book promoters out there, this presents a wonderful news-grabbing opportunity. By simply offering journalists, producers, and editors an easy-to-navigate and well-organized online media room, complete with everything they need to take a story about your book or author from start to finish, you have a great chance of scoring excellent media coverage. To help make your online media room a destination of choice for web-surfing journalists, we've put together a few guidelines:

1. Can I Call You?

Sure, it seems obvious, but you'd be surprised how many people forget the importance of providing all contact names, phone and fax numbers, email addresses, pager numbers, and mailing addresses in their online media rooms. One of the top reasons journalists use the Internet is to locate PR contact info, and according to one recent study, 45% of the time they are unable to find that vital information in online searches.

Make your PR contact info highly visible on your company website, and position it at the top of each page of your online media room. In addition, *always* provide an emergency response phone number. If a journalist is working on a deadline, their ability to contact you at a moment's notice could determine whether you receive coverage or not.

2. Playing Up Your Press Releases

Not surprisingly, journalists have indicated that press releases are the most important items in an online media room. Be sure that the press release section of your online media room is updated frequently with the latest news about your book or author. Archive all previous press releases in the press release section of your media room, and post all press releases in HTML to make them easily and instantly accessible.

3. In This Case, a Picture Really Is Worth a 1,000 Words

Downloading images for use in stories is one of the top five reasons journalists visit online media rooms. Be sure to offer high-resolution, downloadable images of your book cover, author, and any illustrations or photos from the book that would lend visual interest to a feature story or review. If available, post clips of previous radio and TV appearances. Such clips can greatly influence show producers who are searching the Net for guest experts.

4. Take It Easy on Me: Backgrounders, Story Ideas, and Fact Sheets

Help make the journalist's job a little easier and include a section in your online media room that contains additional information to help flesh out a full article or show segment about your book or author. Provide your media visitors with story ideas to tie your book into current events, backgrounders such as related trivia or topical quizzes, or fact sheets that list basic information about the book and its subject matter.

5. The Online Media Room: It's Like a Regular Press Kit, Only Better!

When creating your online media room, remember that any component of a traditional press kit can be included in your online media room. As you acquire more content such as reviews, resources, author events, and media placements, be sure to add these to your media room.

Kathleen Meyer is the Marketing Director for BookFlash, an innovative book publicity services firm offering affordable and easy-to-use online media rooms designed specifically for the unique promotional needs of authors and publishers. For information about **BookFlash Media Rooms** or BookFlash's other book publicity services, call us at 520-798-2356, visit us online at http://www.bookflash.com, or email us at bookflash@bookflash.com.

12 Ways to Sell More Books
on Radio and TV Talk Shows

by Steve Harrison, publisher, Radio-TV Interview Report (RTIR) and
Harrison's Guide to the Top National TV Talk & Interview Shows

There are many benefits of being interviewed on TV and radio talk shows. Your 800 number may ring off the hook with orders the minute you finish the interview. You can increase your name recognition and enhance your credibility. In 18 years of helping 12,000 authors get on the air, here are the strategies we've found help authors and publishers sell their books.

1. Send flyers to local bookstores before you do a show in their area. Before an interview, Mark Field, author of *The Air Courier Handbook*, sends flyers to local bookstores, urging them to buy copies of his book. If they place a large order, he'll even agree to mention their store on the air.

2. Leave flyers at stations when you do their shows. Tony Hyman, author of *I'll Buy That!*, sells more than $250,000.00 worth of books via his 800 number every year by doing radio phone interviews. At first after he did a show, listeners would call the station asking how to order, but the switchboard operator wouldn't know. Now he leaves a detailed order flyer with the producer, host, and switchboard operator so people know how to order.

3. Send an autographed copy of your book to the host. The more familiar the talk show host is with your book, the better the interview will be. And when making a point, asking the host something like, "Did you notice the chart on page 56?" will draw attention to your book.

4. Be prepared for interviews. Harvey Mackay, author of *Swim with the Sharks without Being Eaten Alive*, suggests guests know the call letters of the station, the name of the show, the producer's and host's names, the show's format, and audience demographics before getting on the air. Write out answers to questions the host is likely to ask you. Be armed with lots of specific examples, case studies, and stories to support your point of view.

5. Think of yourself as a co-host. Don't just sit back and wait for the next question to come; be an active participant. Take control of the interview when appropriate, and remember the host is depending on you to entertain and inform the audience. Address the host and callers by their first names.

6. Emphasize the severity of the problem and how your book solves it. People don't want to buy books per se. They want to buy solutions to their problems. For example, Dr. Ted Broer, a nutritionist and author of *Eat, Drink and Be Merry*, sells thousands of books and tapes on radio and TV talk shows each year. But he rarely mentions his books on the air. He spends most of the time citing study after study showing people they're quite likely to get cancer, heart disease, or some other degenerative disease unless they make some significant changes. The result? Booming book sales.

7. Tell stories that create strong feelings. Most people decide to buy on an emotional basis and then justify it with logic. One of the best ways to trigger those feelings is by telling compelling stories. Got a personal finance book? Tell a story about a couple who went through a painful divorce after years of constant financial stress and fighting over money. Then explain how their breakup could have beenavoided if they'd known the info in your book.

8. Let your passion come through. If you're an author, you've written a book because you're passionate about your topic. Make people feel you mean what you say. Be bold about your convictions. And don't worry about people disagreeing with you—that's what a talk show is all about.

9. Make it easy for people to order. Make sure you have an easy-to-remember web site address and maybe even an 800 vanity number like 1-800-JOBSNOW. Also remember people may be listening to your radio interview while driving. Say something like, "If your listeners get a pen and paper out, in a few minutes I'll give them a website and toll-free number where they can get a free credit report." Then when it's time to give the 800 number to order your book, listeners will be ready to write it down.

10. Ask the station or show to include a blurb about you on their web site along with a link to order your book.

11. Give the audience an incentive to order today. Mark Victor Hansen, co-author of *Chicken Soup for the Soul*, tells people they'll get an autographed copy of his book if they order today. Consider telling listeners that they'll receive a special bonus report or a discount if they order now.

12. Sell multiple books in a package or kit. Why sell a book for $12.95 when you can sell a book and several audiocassettes for $39.95? Or consider bundling several of your books into a set. Dr. Cass Igram, the author of several nutrition books does this and grosses over $200,000 in sales each year. For example, if you had a book called 50 Ways to Lose Weight for $12.95, you might combine it with two others books and call it the Lose Weight Fast Program available for $39.95.

Steve Harrison is publisher of *Harrison's Guide to the Top National TV Talk & Interview Shows* (info at http://www.getmajorpress.com/tvbook), the directory/database that gives you key how-to-get-on information and contacts for America's top 235 national TV shows including *Oprah, Good Morning America, Today Show*, CNN and other top programs.

Steve also publishes *Radio-TV Interview Report*, the trade magazine where you can advertise your availability for interviews to 4,000 producers nationwide. RTIR is a way to get talk show interviews without doing any work or spending a fortune on a publicist. For a FREE Info Kit call toll-free 800-553-8002, ext, 735 or go to http://www.FreeAuthorTips.com/infokit22.

Chapter 4

The Customer Is Always Right

Customers don't like it when they can't have it right away.
— Kathryn Fullmer, bookstore manager, Walton Book, Provo, Utah

To build a loyal customer base, you must begin by offering basic customer services such as the acceptance of major credit cards, toll-free phone service, and fast response. Even more important, however, you must treat your customers with respect.

Remember: Your customers are always right (almost). Make it a point to develop a loyal customer base. Treat your customers with respect. Listen to them. Serve them well, and they will continue to buy from you.

4:01 Accept Credit Cards

One way to develop a steady customer base is to accept credit cards. Why? Here are a number of good reasons:

☐ Credit card holders have better credit histories, greater household income, and more disposable income than others. Hence, they make ideal customers, especially for sales via mail or telephone.

☐ Credit card customers tend to spend more on each order. As Bob Stone wrote in his book, *Successful Direct Marketing Methods*, "The average credit card order is at least 15 percent bigger than a cash order." At Open Horizons, we found that when we started to accept credit cards, our average order jumped by 30%. Phone orders, as opposed to mail orders, took an even bigger jump.

☐ Credit card holders are more likely to buy by mail, by phone, or via the Internet. In fact, without credit cards, it's almost impossible to take an order via the web.

☐ Accepting credit cards makes it easier for your customer to order from you—and to pay you. They are also a whole lot easier for you than sending out invoices and waiting for payment. You get your payment almost instantly.

☐ If you promote your books via radio and TV talk shows, accepting credit card orders is a must since most of your orders will come by telephone within hours of an appearance.

☐ More bookstores are now placing special orders with credit cards. This allows them to get books much faster since they can place the order via phone or fax within minutes of getting the order.

How do you go about accepting credit cards? For VISA and MasterCard, start with your local bank. Ask them for an application form for credit card merchant status. You may have to check more than one bank before you find one that will allow you to process credit card orders through their system. In recent years, it has become almost impossible for smaller companies selling by mail or phone to get merchant status. But, if you have built a good relationship with your bank, they will help you get merchant status.

When I sold Ad-Lib Publications and started up Open Horizons, I had to reapply for merchant status. Well, at first I was rejected because I sell primarily via the mail, phone, and Internet. But my banker wrote a letter telling the credit card processing company that they would cover any bad charges, and my new company was instantly accepted. They were willing to write that letter for only one reason: They knew me well. I had established a good working relationship with my bank ahead of time.

If you are selling to businesses, you should also accept American Express since many businesses provide employees with this card for travel and miscellaneous expenses. If you already have an established VISA or Master-Card merchant account, it is easy to get an American Express account as well. For more information or to set up an account with American Express, call **800-528-5200**. To set up an account with Discover card, call **800-347-6673**. Accepting this card may be important for you if you sell direct to consumers. For Carte Blanche and Diners Club, call **800-432-1160**. They are looking to add more publishers to their list.

4:02 Install a Toll-Free Phone Number

If you are serious about providing customer support and service, you should install a toll-free number to make it easier for your customers to call and order from you. Toll-free numbers are so inexpensive nowadays that you really cannot afford to offer anything less. Note that with the increased demand for toll-free numbers, the FCC has added several new toll-free prefixes: 888, 877, and 866.

If you do install a toll-free number, be sure to let your key customers and contacts know that you have such a number. Have it printed on all your sales literature, catalogs, news releases, business cards, and other out-going mail. Above all, be sure it's on your order forms.

To be sure its customers have the number handy, Peachtree Publishers sends a sticky label with its toll-free number highlighted. It recently added a toll-free fax number for orders as well.

Here are a few of the advantages of having an 800 number:

☐ An 800 number makes it more convenient for your customers to order from you. In a survey conducted by CMG Telemarketing, 65% of the consumers questioned said they would not shop by telephone if they had to pay for the call.

☐ It speeds response to your direct mail offers. You can begin to receive orders as much as a week or two faster than by mail.

☐ It has been known to triple the response to such offers.

☐ It produces larger orders because it allows you to interact with your customer. If your telephone order takers are alert, they can increase sales by letting customers know about other books you publish that are similar to the ones the caller ordered.

☐ People buying by telephone have a better payment record and tend to be better credit risks.

☐ Toll-free phone numbers encourage impulse buying.

☐ Toll-free service builds good will. It demonstrates that you are responsive to the needs of your customers and open to their feedback.

☐ A toll-free number allows you to offer better customer service. It makes you more accessible to your customers so they can clear up any questions they might have about your books or service. The sooner you clear up questions, the quicker you diffuse any possible dissatisfaction—thus ensuring that the word of mouth about your company and your books remains positive.

☐ You will sell more books to bookstores since they will be able to place special orders quickly. As Penny Davis of the Earthling Bookshop in Santa Barbara, California, once noted, "It would be great if more publishers had 800 numbers. I'd be much more likely to pick up the phone and place an order."

☐ You can save money on sending out review copies. Since a review copy is only a toll-free phone call away, reviewers are more likely to respond to your news releases by calling for a review copy.

☐ If you get the voice mailbox when calling an important reviewer, editor, book buyer, or other contact, you can leave your 800 number to make it easy for them to call you back. Be sure to leave your regular number as well just in case their phone system doesn't allow them to call toll-free numbers.

☐ Reviewers and other media outlets are more likely to mention a toll-free order number where they might not mention a mailing address or ordinary phone number. They view toll-free numbers as a service to their readers while they view mailing addresses as a service (i.e., a free ad) for the publisher.

After all this promotional talk about toll-free numbers, you are probably wondering what Open Horizon's toll-free number is. We had a toll-free number for many years and will have one again, but due to problems with our provider, we had to cancel the one we had. Here are a few notes on our experience with offering an 800 number:

☐ In a three month study we conducted in 1987, we found that 28% of our orders were coming in over the phone. In 1997, about 60% of our orders came via the phone. In 2005, however, about 60% of our orders are now coming from our web site, while 30% come in over the phone and about 10% via the mail.

☐ During that three month period, 45% of our sales revenue came from phone orders.

☐ The average order size from phone calls was $57.19 as compared to an average order size of $27.04 from incoming mail—that's more than double the sales revenue! Some of that increase was due to our upsell efforts where we would tell callers about related books and our 10% discount on orders of three or more titles.

☐ It costs us about a dollar in phone charges and another dollar in labor to take an order via our toll-free number. These added costs are more than covered by the $30.00 difference in average order size between phone orders and mail orders.

☐ Nowadays, of course, our website takes most of the orders, at little or no cost. Many orders are handled automatically, especially the download data files and reports.

To use a toll-free number effectively, you must accept credit cards. You must also have someone to answer the phone during regular business hours and, if you are marketing to consumers, 24 hours a day. If you are doing a major consumer promotion, you may well need more than one toll-free line.

For those of you who are not ready to establish an in-house 800 line or for those who are expecting a huge volume of calls, you might want to sign up with a toll-free answering service. A list of such services are featured at http://www.bookmarket.com/tele.html.

For publishers just starting out, you might want to use an outside answering and fulfillment service. For a list of some fulfillment companies that are accustomed to working with book publishers, again see my website at http://www.bookmarket.com/4.html#bf. By the time you read this, we will have set up our fulfillment service with Speakers Fulfillment Services, a good Midwest fulfillment company that is also handling our online shopping cart as well as all downloads.

One aspect of 800 numbers you might want to consider is whether or not to use a vanity number such as 800-THE-BOOK (Barnes & Noble), 800-9TRU-LUV (*Bridal Solutions* catalog), 800-FLOWERS (flower delivery service with trademarked number), or 800-4BIRTHDAY (*Birthday Express* catalog). When Viking Penguin published Stephen King's *The Regulators* under his pseudonym, Richard Bachman, they established a vanity toll-free number, 1-888-4BACHMAN, so readers could get the scoop on the "lesser-known" author, as told by Stephen King. While vanity 800 numbers are hard to get (simply because there are so few numbers left), vanity numbers for the 888, 877, and 866 prefixes should be easier to obtain.

One drawback to vanity numbers is that some opportunist could piggy-back on your promotions and siphon off some of your sales by getting a similar number. In one well-known case, the hotel booking service Call Management got the vanity number 800-405-4329, which mimics the heavily promoted 800-HOLIDAY (800-465-4329). As a result, Call Management received many calls that should have gone to Holiday Inns. They booked more than $275,000 in business as a result. When Holiday Inns sued for violation of trademark, the original judge ruled in their favor. However, the Court of Appeals overturned the ruling, thus allowing Call Management to continue to use the near vanity number.

4:03 Fax for Fast Service

Twenty years ago you could still do business without a fax number, but that is no longer the case. If you are serious about business, get a fax machine and a separate phone line for it. Don't Mickey Mouse around with a single line for both your phone and fax machine. Get a separate line for each. You can also use the second line to make outgoing calls while waiting for return calls on your primary line.

Here are some of the advantages of fax machines:

☐ They are faster than letters sent by mail. Speed is often essential for press releases, price change announcements, changes in author tour schedules, and rescheduling appointments.

☐ Fax machines are easy to use. A recent Gallup survey of Fortune 500 companies found that 60% of daily fax users are faxing more than in previous years.

☐ If your fax machine is connected to a dedicated phone line, you can keep it hooked up and available for orders 24 hours a day—and with minimum labor costs.

☐ Faxes, unlike letters, still carry a sense of urgency; hence, they tend to get delivered sooner. Indeed, they sometimes get special handling, thus bypassing the normal screening of business mail.

☐ Unlike phone orders, fax orders are less susceptible to errors since all information is written or typed by the sending party.

☐ *Fax-on-demand*, where someone can call a company and get information faxed backed to them right away, is faster than phone calls, postal mail, *bingo cards* (postcards inserted in magazines that allow you to circle numbers if you'd like more information about a company) for getting information to customers when they want it. This technology, of course, has been replaced almost completely by email autoresponders and informational web sites.

☐ *Broadcast fax* technology allows you to send faxes to ten, twenty, or hundreds of people with one short phone call. Again, this technology is now rarely used when email is so much easier and cheaper.

How can you use the fax machine to sell more books? Here are just a few of the ways book publishers are now using faxes to publicize and market their books.

☐ **Process orders.** More companies are now offering to receive (and send) purchase orders via fax. Bookstores prefer to order by fax because they can order quicker (much faster than by phone) and more accurately so ISBN numbers or order numbers are correctly received.

Houghton Mifflin offers a toll-free number for fax orders (800-458-9501) and prints it on its invoices and in its catalogs.

To encourage bookstores to order by fax, Ingram (the largest wholesaler) offers an extra discount point for faxed orders.

At Open Horizons, we don't actively solicit orders by fax, but five or ten orders still come in every week. By the way, Open Horizon's fax number is 515-472-1560.

☐ **Speed up your cash flow.** Faxes can speed up the processing of credit applications and verifying credit references, thus allowing you to ship orders more quickly which, in turn, allows you to collect payment more quickly. Faxes can also speed up the resolution of credit disputes, especially when a customer questions an order or bill.

☐ **Promote specials.** If you have a hot deal to offer wholesalers or bookstores, faxes are a great way to get the word out quickly.

☐ **Announce new titles.** When you have a new book that needs an extra promotional boost, use your fax to reach the people that have to know.

☐ **Get printing quotes faster.** Many book printers now provide one-day response to quotes submitted by fax. While quotes by phone might only take a few minutes, you can never be sure the quote actually covers all that you want. If you need to be sure and want to get it in writing, then fax your request for a quote.

☐ **Publicize your books.** Fax a one-page news release to major media when you need to let them know something overnight. The news should be timely or interesting. With broadcast fax and a good media database, you can send releases to hundreds of media in a few seconds. Or you can hire one of the news services, such as Bacon's or PR Newswire, to broadcast your faxes (or emails) for you.

To promote the duct tape guys and their books, Bad Dog Press sends one-page faxes loaded with graphics, one-liners, and humor to inspire media to call them for an interview. It works for them.

☐ **Respond quickly to breaking news stories.** When *Inc.* magazine did a short side article on self-publishing, I sent them a fax correcting one point in the article that could have misled people. By sending a fax, I made it easier for *Inc.* to include a response in the next issue. That makes the magazine seem fresher to its readers.

☐ **Fax a letter to the editor.** Most magazines and newspapers now offer special fax numbers just for letters to the editor. Again, this makes it easier for people to send their reaction about a major news event before it's already old news.

☐ **Conduct surveys via fax.** When you need to survey your customers or update a directory, faxes get more responses than letters. In 1992, Gale Research found that 50 to 60% of faxed questionnaires were returned, which was a 15 to 30% increase over mailed questionnaires.

Note that many of the things faxes do well can also be handled by the web and email. For more details on selling via the web, see Chapter 12.

4:04 Use a Database Program

One of the first things you should do when you set up your company is to install a database program that will allow you to process orders, keep track of invoices and statements, maintain a mailing list, and generate the financial statements you will need to do your taxes and apply for loans.

You can use an off-the-shelf software program, as we do here at Open Horizons, and adapt it to your needs. Any database program (such as File-Maker Pro. Alpha Five, or Microsoft Access) or financial accounting program (such as QuickBooks) will do the job—but only if you know what you are doing. If you expect to grow, however, you should start off right away with a software program designed for publishers. For a list of such programs, see http://www.bookmarket.com/4.html#bp.

Besides a good order fulfillment system, you should have a database for handling all your publicity and marketing contacts. One of the secrets of effective publicity is persistence and follow-up. A database of media contacts makes it easy to do just that. Again, you can use an off-the-shelf database program or a contact management program, such as ACT or GoldMine.

4:05 Create a Customer

The first four sections of this chapter have dealt with setting up a few specific mechanisms that will enhance your service to your customers. The rest of this chapter will focus on how to create and keep customers.

Don't just make a sale; create a customer. Satisfied customers are repeat buyers. So do whatever you have to do to keep your customers happy. Make customer service part and parcel of your daily operating philosophy and way of doing business. Here are a few reasons you should provide the best customer service you can possibly offer:

☐ Customers are willing to pay more for better service.

☐ It costs five to ten times as much to acquire a new customer as it does to retain a current one. According to Tom Peters, it takes $10.00 of new business to replace $1.00 of old business.

☐ According to a study done by the American Productivity and Quality Center, 68% of customers stop doing business with a company if they receive poor service. Customers are five times more likely to leave because of poor service than because of poor product quality or high cost.

☐ Customers who receive poor service tell from 9 to 20 other people about their dissatisfaction. But they are not likely to tell you. According to a study by Audits & Surveys, only one out of 26 dissatisfied customers complains to the company offering the poor service.

☐ The average satisfied customer tells five other people.

☐ A study published in the *Harvard Business Review* showed that if you could reduce your customer drop-out rate by 5%, you could improve your profits by as much as 100%.

☐ According to American Express, best customers outspend others by 16:1 in the retail business, 13:1 in restaurants, 12:1 in the airline industry, and 5:1 in lodging.

☐ General Motors says that a loyal customer is worth $400,000 to them over a 20-year period. The average loyal customer of a supermarket is worth $3,779 in sales every year.

4:06 Fast, Friendly Service (with a Smile)

Never delay any response to your customers. Always respond to any orders, inquiries, or complaints with fast, friendly service.

☐ Process orders as fast as possible. One reason so many independent booksellers shop with Ingram and other wholesalers is because they fulfill orders the same day and ship right away. If you process your orders the same day you receive them, you'll begin to pick up orders that would otherwise go to wholesalers at a higher discount. Plus, since booksellers will be able to obtain books while the books are still hot, faster order processing will mean increased sales and less returns.

☐ Respond to inquiries the same day you receive them. The faster you respond (whether by phone, mail, or a sales representative), the greater your chances will be that the inquirer will order from you.

☐ Acknowledge immediately any back orders, out of print titles, or other books that cannot be shipped right away. Be as specific as possible about the date you will ship the order.

☐ Answer complaints right away. Better yet, resolve them. Remember, no matter how petty or ill-conceived the complaint, the customer is always right. Don't take that statement as just another platitude; make it a working philosophy that all your personnel adhere to without question.

☐ Send refunds as soon as they are requested. Stand by your guarantee, and your customers will stand by you.

☐ Ship by UPS or Priority Mail rather than book rate when the order needs to be shipped quickly or when you need to make sure it gets there at all.

The value your company puts on customer service must permeate the entire company, from top management down to the mailroom. Alan Mirken, former owner of Crown Publishing, used to spend one day a week at their warehouse—not only to check on their fulfillment services, but also to emphasize the value the top management placed on customer service.

4:07 Answer Your Phone

Keep your phone lines open for customer service and orders. According to a study done in 1984 by CMG Telemarketing, 19% of callers give up if the number they call does not answer. That's one-fifth of your potential business.

If you are a small company and have no one available to answer the phone, then install an answering machine and make sure you get back to callers right away. Again, in the CMG Telemarketing survey, 74% of callers said they were very unlikely to place an order via a recorded message. So make it clear on your out-going message that you will call back right away if callers leave their phone numbers.

If you are a larger company with a telephone operator and three tiers of secretaries, make sure they know when a call should come through to you rather than be terminated somewhere along the chain of command. As Tom Peters has noted in *The Excellence Challenge*, "The only magic of the $40 billion giant IBM is that in a $500 billion industry they happen to be the only company that answers the phone."

When you do answer, never let callers hang up until you have completely answered their questions—and have gotten their names and addresses so you can send them further information.

Finally, if you must use voice mail technology, be sure to give your callers an easy way to reach a real person. There is nothing so frustrating as being caught up in an endless loop of mechanical messages.

4:08 Don't Run Out of Stock

Always try to keep your titles in stock, readily available for any orders that might come in. Plan ahead so you don't run out right before a big promotion. Work with your various printers so that you always have good turnaround times on reprintings. And, finally, keep track of your inventory so you don't have any costly surprises.

I know that it's not always possible to follow this rule. Because of a major library review, we ran out of copies of the third edition of this book months before I finished writing the fourth edition. I know we lost some orders as a result of that delay. Exactly how many I don't know. It's hard to measure such losses.

With the publication of this edition, I was very late in getting it out. I let the fifth edition run out last August, expecting to get this edition out by October. Well, the best laid plans don't always work out. But as a result, I've had to deal with many unhappy customers. I don't recommend this. It's not fun at all. It takes the joy out of publishing.

4:09 Everyone Wins

One of the key rules of marketing is to structure your product, prices, and services so that everyone wins. Give your customers a good product (content, style, design, and promotion). Offer it at a fair price. And provide fast service. Then your customers win by getting what they want, when they want, at a price they can afford.

You win because you've gotten your books into the hands of the people who can use them—and you got paid for doing it.

While this rule makes so much sense, few companies really follow through on such a commitment. What a loss!

4:10 Go for the Additional Sale

Never fulfill an order without going for the additional sale. Include *bounceback offers* (additional offers sent with an order) in your shipping package. Send them your catalog. Or put order cards describing related titles in the books you ship out. Don't feel shy about letting your customers know of other books that might interest them. Such notices should be an integral part of your service to them.

Of course, you should also set up a program of regular mailings to your best customers. Mail to them at least two to four times a year.

4:11 Do What You Do Best

Create the best books you can, offer the friendliest and fastest service, and always let your customers know that they are important to you. Then you need not fear competition from any other source.

4:12 Offer Satisfaction Guaranteed

Offer a firm guarantee of satisfaction, and then stand by it. Sears, one of the largest retailers in the world, built its business on its unconditional guarantee of satisfaction. Why should you offer less?

- ☐ Stein & Day advertised a full refund to anyone who did not find Oliver Lange's novel, *The Devil at Home*, "one of the most moving experiences you've had in fiction in a long time." Their print ads announced the book as "the only guaranteed fiction in America." Any dissatisfied reader was invited to return the book to the publisher with comments (and the sales slip) if they wanted a refund.

- ☐ Warner Books offered an even more daring guarantee. They put a belly band around their newly published diet book, *The Pasta Diet*, announcing a money-back guarantee if the book buyer did not lose ten pounds in fourteen days. According to their reports, few refunds were requested.

- ☐ Villard Books placed a full-page advertisement in *USA Today* announcing A Great Diehl! on William Diehl's novel, *Thai Horse*:

  "We guarantee it! Villard Books is so sure you will love *Thai Horse* that we'll prove it with a MONEY-BACK GUARANTEE! Not only that, we'll let you read the entire first chapter—excerpted below—for free! Because we think that once you begin this novel, you'll have to finish it. So start reading. Experience the adventure of a lifetime—guaranteed!"

- ☐ Scribners offered a guarantee for Aljean Harmetz thriller, *Off the Face of the Earth*. But they added a catch: Customers had to send proof of purchase and a written explanation of why they didn't like the book.

- ☐ Zondervan not only featured $2.00 off coupons on the catalogs it made up for Christian booksellers to give away to their customers, but they also offered a complete money-back guarantee. Their motto for this promotion was: "Anyone can write a story. Only we guarantee you'll like it." All five novels in this special promotion were stickered with a special "Good Read Guaranteed" emblem.

- ☐ Enterprise Publishing offered a "Risk-Free, Postage-Free, 100% Money-Back Guarantee" for its *Basic Book of Business Agreements*:

(1) *The* Basic Book of Business Agreements *must save you at least $695 (10 times what you paid for it) within 6 months of purchase!*

(2) *You will recover the full cost of the book in saved legal fees the first* one *or* two *times you use it.*

(3) *Regardless of how much money it saves you, you must be completely satisfied. Look it over at our risk for 30 days. If you don't think it lives up to our claims, we'll refund your money.*

(4) *You may return the book using the postage-free return label on the reverse* [of their guarantee].

☐ Boardroom Books offers a $100,000 guarantee good for a whole year: "If the *Book of Inside Information* doesn't give you at least $100,000 worth of money-making/money-saving ideas, return it at any time up to a full year from the date you receive the book. We'll promptly refund the money you paid, no questions asked."

☐ Margaret Kent's self-published book, *How to Marry the Man of Your Choice* (which originally sold for $95.00 per copy) later appeared on the bestseller lists as a $14.95 hardcover from Warner Books. Their unique guarantee still stands: If the reader isn't married to Mr. Right within four years, she can get her money refunded. This guarantee brought the book oodles of publicity via major TV shows, radio shows, and newspapers.

☐ When Gary Fenchuk self-published his *Timeless Wisdom* quotation book, he offered a $5,000 reward to any bookseller or publisher who could find a better quotation book. He publicized this offer in various media. When no one came forward with a better quotation book, he publicized that fact as well.

Note how these publishers used dramatic guarantees to gain wide publicity for their books. Whatever money they had to pay out in refunds was certainly minimal compared to the value of the publicity and customer goodwill they received in return.

Guarantees, of course, can also be used to state your company's philosophy of doing business. Note how the following companies establish rapport with their key customers by stating their philosophy of doing business.

☐ The following guarantee is printed on the front inside cover of *Marketing Without Advertising* by Michael Phillips and Salli Rasberry:

Nolo Press, the publisher of Marketing Without Advertising, *is confident that you will find this unique small business book to be worth far more than your purchase price. If for any reason you do not agree, we will refund your full purchase price, no questions asked, no reasons requested. (We thought about asking for a copy of your financial statements before and after reading this book to make sure your business didn't in fact improve, but decided what the heck, if you trust us, we trust you.)*

The reason we make this unusual offer is that we firmly believe Marketing Without Advertising *authors Phillips and Rasberry when they write that for any small business to successfully market goods and services over the long term, they not only need a quality product, but must also go out of their way to provide excellent customer service. This is done by assuring customers in advance that if they are dissatisfied with the product they have easy to understand rights to effective recourse. One of these is to be able to ask for and promptly receive a full refund.*

So, while we look forward to not hearing from you, we will promptly and cheerfully refund your money if we do.

☐ Sierra Club offers the following guarantee on all items in its catalog:

"Lifetime Guarantee—At Sierra Club, our work spans lifetimes. So in the spirit of the Club, we offer you a lifetime guarantee on any merchandise you purchase from our catalog. If you are not unconditionally satisfied with your selection, you may return it for a prompt refund, repair or replacement."

☐ Nolo now offers a no-hassle guarantee on all their books: "If for any reason, anything you buy direct from Nolo Press does not meet your needs, we'll cheerfully refund your purchase price and we'll pay for your cost to return it to us via U.S. Priority Mail. No ifs, ands or buts."

Note that few consumers actually take a company up on its guarantee, no matter how generous it is.

4:13 Give a Little Extra

Always give your customers more than they expect. Make your books the best available. Add bonus reports or little gifts (bookmarks, cards, whatever) when you ship their orders. And, especially with your key customers, send them something special around the winter holidays, or for Valentine's, or some other appropriate occasion. But, above all, offer great service. It's great service that distinguishes the successful companies from the not so successful companies.

4:14 Keep in Touch

Keep in touch with your key customers. Let them know you appreciate their business. Send them advance announcements and pre-publication specials for your most important titles. Send them complimentary advance review copies of attractive titles. Publish a newsletter that keeps your customers up to date on your new titles. Whatever you do, don't give them a chance to forget you.

IDG, former publisher of the Dummies series, tried to stay close to its readers. As John Kilcullen, their president, asked, "How many publishers go see their customers? We do. And all of our books include reader response cards. We get thousands every week—and we read them."

4:15 Always Say Thank You

Whether you overtly say thank you with every order, or you choose to say thank you by demonstrating to your customers their importance to you (by responding to them quickly and courteously), you should always let your customers know that you appreciate their business.

Thank you!

4:16 Satisfied Customers Spread the Word

Not only are satisfied customers repeat buyers, but they are also your best advertisements. When you create satisfied customers, you are also creating walking/talking billboards for your books. So when planning your fulfillment and customer service systems, remember that word of mouth is the most productive advertising available to book publishers—and that the best word-of-mouth advertising comes from satisfied customers.

There is only one boss: the customer.
And he can fire everybody in the company,
from the chairman on down,
simply by spending his money somewhere else.
— Sam Walton, founder, Wal-Mart

Chapter 5

How to Open New Markets

You should market test every product, but books are the one product
that is almost never market tested. I've told this to several publishers,
but they still don't market test their books. I don't understand why.
That was the way we knew we had something good. If we wouldn't have
done it, we would have released a completely different book.

— Dave Chilton, self-publisher, *The Wealthy Barber*

There are a few basic steps you should take whenever you are opening a
new market for your books or other products. These basic steps apply
whether you are attempting to sell to libraries, wholesalers, bookstores,
other retail outlets, catalogs, corporations, individuals, or associations.

The following points should be considered general guidelines. As you
read the rest of this book, keep these guidelines in mind.

5:01 Ask Questions

The best way to scout a new market is to ask questions of everyone you
can locate—store owners, wholesalers, sales representatives, consumers,
magazine editors, and so on. Don't be afraid to ask stupid questions. In this
first stage of researching your market, you should not be shy or reserved. Be
open. Let them know that you are new to the market and would like to learn
more. My experience is that most people are quite willing to share their
knowledge and experience, whether in person or over the phone.

Start by questioning people you know. Use your local resources. Talk to
your local bookseller, retail outlet, library, or anyone else who might be
qualified to answer some or all of your questions.

5:02 Ask the Right Questions

Of course, it's not enough to ask questions. You have to ask the right questions. And the right people. Here are just a few of the questions you might ask:

Retail Store Owners

Where do they buy their goods? From whom? At what discount?
What trade magazines do they read?
Which magazines do they use to make their buying decisions?
What web sites do they go to when they are looking for new products?
How do they find out about new products?
Do they respond to direct mail, e-mail, or telemarketing?
Or do they require visits from sales representatives?
Which wholesalers do they use most often? Why?
Which sales representatives give them the best service?
Which wholesalers or representatives do they trust most?
Have they noticed any new trends? Any new consumer demands?
What marketing help would they like to have from their suppliers?
Also get their feedback on your books' titles, covers, and contents.

Consumers

Where do they go to buy books (or other products) similar to yours?
What factors affect their decision to buy?
How do they find out about new products?
What magazines do they read?
What web sites do they go to regularly?
Do they respond to advertisements in magazines? To direct mail?
Are there any books they'd like to see published?

Wholesalers

What discount do they require? What terms?
What is the average size of their opening order?
How do they find out about new products?
What magazines do they read?
What trade shows do they attend?
Do they use the Internet to search for new suppliers? If so, how do they use the Internet in their search?
What markets do they serve? How do they reach their markets?
Do they publish a catalog?

Sales Representatives

What territory do they reach? What markets do they serve?

What percentage do they require for their commission?

What kind of discounts do the wholesalers and retailers require?

How do they find out about new products?

What magazines do they read? What trade shows do they attend?

What new trends have they noticed?

Is there anything retailers want that other suppliers are not providing?

Are they responsive to e-mail contact?

Trade Magazine Editors

What is the size of the market?

How do products get distributed in this market?

What are the standard terms and discounts?

Who are the most reputable wholesalers and sales representatives?

Have the editors noticed any new trends in the market?

What are the critical marketing months for this market? Lead times?

What trade shows are most effective?

How do they like to be contacted with new product information?
Phone, mail, e-mail, fax, or lunch?

In all of the above cases, you should also ask for suggestions on where to go to find out more information. Get names, addresses, and phone numbers where you can. Also get feedback on the design and usefulness of your book or other product (and any displays, advertisements, or promotional material you have available).

Authors — You, too, should be asking questions. Indeed, if you have done your homework in writing your book, you will have talked to many of these people anyway. While you are gathering material for your book, also look out for any information that could be useful in marketing your book.

5:03 Read the Trade Magazines

Read the trade magazines to find out how distribution works in a particular market, what retailers are looking for, what the new trends are, how to approach advertising to this market, and other insider information. And, if the magazine is not providing the knowledge you want, write to the editor. These magazines are responsive to the needs and desires of their readers.

☐ In the gift market, you should read *Gift and Decorative Accessories* and *Giftware News*, among others.

☐ In the toy market, read *Toy and Hobby World* and *Playthings*.

☐ In the premium and incentive markets, read *Incentive Marketing, Potentials*, and *Promo*, among others.

Most of these trade magazines will send you a sample copy or even a free subscription if you request it on your letterhead. For the addresses of these magazines and others in your specialty market, check the *Standard Periodical Directory, Gale Directory of Publications, Gebbies*, or the Internet.

5:04 Read Appropriate Consumer Magazines

Besides reading the trade magazines, you should also read the consumer magazines that cover the subjects you publish. When you read these magazines, read the ads as well as the articles. Which ads appear issue after issue? (Those appearing more than once are probably successful.) What angles are the advertisers using to reach this market? What benefits do they stress? What are the buzz words for this market?

When reading articles, which topics get the most coverage? What subjects are covered in their regular columns? What are the concerns of the readers, as reflected in their letters to the editor? Remember, magazines are sold month by month. If the editors do not deliver what the readers want, the magazines will not sell. Hence, editors are sensitive to their readers' needs and tend to pick up on new trends long before book publishers do.

☐ For example, if you want to sell to camera shops and photographers, read *American Photographer, Aperture, Darkroom Photography, Lens Magazine, Modern Photography, PHOTOgraphic*, and *Popular Photography* as well as the photography department in *Popular Mechanics*.

☐ If you publish business books, read *Business Week, Forbes, Fortune, Inc., Business 2.0, Fast Cmpany*, and *Wall Street Journal*, as well as your regional business magazine and the business sections of *USA Today* and your local newspaper.

☐ If you publish books for children or on child care, read *Child Magazine, Family Circle, Parenting, Parents, Redbook, Woman's Day,* and other women's magazines, among others.

☐ If you publish new age titles, read *Body, Mind & Spirit, New Age Journal, New Frontier*, and *Yoga Journal*, among others.

☐ For gardens, read *Fine Gardening, Flower & Garden, HG, Horticulture, National Gardening*, and *Organic Gardening*, among others.

Both *Gale Directory of Publications* and *Standard Directory of Publications* list magazines by primary subject interest. You'll find that most subject interests are covered by 20 to 25 magazines. Use these directories and the Internet to find the magazines' addresses and editors. To get a sample copy of any magazine, write to its advertising department. Ask for their ad rates at the same time.

> **Authors** — You should read the trade and consumer magazines that cover the subject of your book. Read them to make sure you are covering your subject as completely as possible. Read them to get a better understanding of the audience for your book. Read them to get ideas for new books. And, finally, read them to figure out the best ways to market your books.

5:05 Join Associations

As part of your on-going research, join the trade, professional, or consumer associations in your subject areas. Most associations publish a magazine or newsletter to help members keep track of the news, people, trends, and upcoming events. Many also sponsor conventions, trade shows, seminars, or other networking meetings; publish books or reports (and market other publishers' books); keep a job bank or referral service; and offer other services that could be invaluable in researching and marketing your new books.

Here are just a few of the associations you might want to join:

☐ For crafts and hobbies, join the Hobby Industry Association, American Home Sewing Association, Association of Crafts & Creative Industries, Southwestern Craft & Hobby Association, or National Needlework Association, among others.

☐ For psychology, join the American Psychological Association, Transpersonal Psychologist Association, American Family Therapy Association, and others.

☐ To learn more about direct marketing and mail order, join the Direct Marketing Association or the National Mail Order Association.

☐ For environmental issues, join the Sierra Club, Audubon Society, Nature Conservancy, Worldwatch Institute, and others.

To locate these associations, look in the *National Associations of the U.S.* (a.k.a. *Encyclopedia of Associations*), *National Trade & Professional Associations of the U.S.*, or *Associations Yellow Book*, which are available in most libraries. Note that many national associations also have local chapters where you can network person to person.

> **Authors** — If you don't already belong, you should join appropriate associations. They provide the best opportunity to meet other people interested in the same things that fascinate you. Network with these people. It's a great way to research your books, discover background information, uncover new trends, meet opinion leaders, find out new marketing possibilities, open up speaking possibilities, solicit testimonials, and more.

5:06 Attend Trade Shows and Conventions

Each market has its own trade show (and usually more than one). Attend at least one trade show as soon as possible. There is no better place to get completely immersed in a new market. All the major players attend (media, manufacturers, other suppliers, services, distributors, and buyers). You can make more contacts and follow up more leads during a two- or three-day show than you could in a year of correspondence. When you return home from the show, of course, be sure to follow up on those contacts.

Also, if you have time, attend any appropriate seminars that might run concurrently with the trade show. These seminars can often provide a gold mine of information and contacts.

☐ If you sell to the gift market, you'll want to attend the National Stationery Show (mid-May in New York), the New York International Gift Fair (mid-January and mid-August), the Chicago Gift Show (early February and late July), the Washington Gift Show (mid-July), the Wisconsin Gift Show (late August), the Boston Gift Show (mid-September), or other regional gift shows. Attend the show nearest you.

☐ For other general merchandise markets, you might want to attend the National Back-To-School Variety Merchandise Show (mid-February in New York), Mid-Year Variety Merchandise Show (mid-June in New York), and National Merchandise Show (late September in New York).

☐ For the toy market, attend the American International Toy Fair (mid-February in New York) and the Atlanta Spring & Summer Toy Fair (late September).

☐ For the craft and hobby markets, attend the National Craft and Hobby Expo (late October), the Craft, Model and Hobby Convention (mid-January), and the National Craft Supply Market (mid-March) as well as the regional craft and hobby shows.

☐ If you want to sell your books as premiums, you should attend the Premium Incentive Show (early May in New York) or the National Premium Incentive Show (late September in Chicago).

☐ If you want to know more about direct marketing, attend the DMA Annual Conference (late October), the National Mail Order Merchandise Show (late March in New York), and Catalog Expo (June).

☐ For sporting goods, attend the World Sports Expo in mid-October, the National Sporting Goods Association Fall Market in mid-September, and the Mid America Sports Market in late February, among others.

☐ For housewares, attend the Houseworld Expo (mid-April in Chicago), the International Housewares Exposition (mid-January in Chicago), and the Mid America Hardware Show (late February).

There are many other professional meetings and seminars. For a complete list, read the appropriate trade and professional magazines. Or look into these directories, some of which should be available at your library:

☐ *Trade Shows Worldwide* — Lists 4,500 trade shows and conventions. From Gale Research, 27500 Drake Road, Farmington Hills, MI 48331-3535; 248-699-4253; 800-877-4253. Web: http://www.gale.com. Call for their catalog of other valuable directories.

☐ *TradeShows & Exhibits Schedule* — Features 11,000 exhibits and trade shows. From Bill Communications, Successful Meetings Data Bank, P.O. Box 888, Vineland, NJ 08362; 800-266-4712; Fax: 856-696-2130.

☐ **Trade Show Bureau**, 4350 E. West Highway, Bethesda, MD 20814-4410; 301-907-7626.

☐ Trade show and event guides on the Internet: http://www.tscentral.com, http://www.expoguide.com, or http://www.eventsource.com.

> **Authors** — If you ever get a chance, you should also attend appropriate trade shows, conferences, or seminars that might cover the subjects you write about. Again, they are the best way to immerse yourself totally in a new field. And a great place to make new contacts.

5:07 Check Out the Directories That Cover the Field

You can discover a lot about a new market by exploring the various listings in the directories that cover a particular field. Most markets are covered by at least one if not two or more directories that list sources, buyers, consultants, suppliers, magazines, and more.

☐ For new age topics, read these directories, among others: *Alternative America*, *Holistic Resources*, *National New Age Yellow Pages*, *New Age Directory*, *New Marketing Resource Directory*, *New Consciousness Source Book*, and *Whole Again Resource Guide*.

☐ To sell to catalogs, read the *National Directory of Catalogs, The Catalog of Catalogs, Directory of Mail Order Catalogs, Great Book of Catalogs,* and *Wholesale by Mail Catalog.*

☐ To market to libraries, check out the *American Library Directory, Directory of Special Libraries and Information Centers,* and *Directory of Federal Libraries.*

To locate more of these directories for specific fields, refer to Gale's *Directory of Directories* or check out guides on the Internet. You can also ask the directors of the related associations as well as the editors of the applicable trade journals. Both of these groups should be able to tell you which directories cover the field most thoroughly.

Authors — To research your books and the potential markets for your books, these directories can be invaluable. Go through them with a fine-tooth comb. You'll find it worth the time.

5:08 Contact the Distribution Network

Each market operates differently, with varying terms and discount structures, marketing channels, and operating procedures. To begin feeling out the territory, contact at least one or two distributors or sales representatives right away and ask them how to approach the market.

Some markets rely primarily on distributors or wholesalers, while others rely primarily on sales representatives, while still others (like the book market) use a combination of the two. Adapt your sales program to fit within the established structure of that particular market. Don't try to force some new terms or creative programs on that market until you have first become established. If your books don't fit, no one will carry them. Design your displays and programs to match the available resources within that market.

5:09 Network with Other Publishers

When approaching a new market, first talk to a few other publishers to find out what they know about the market. Somewhere along the line you will meet a publisher who has experience selling to the market or knows another publisher who does. Invite them out to lunch. Then pick their brains (while sharing your own experiences with them).

There are a number of publishing and self-publishing web sites and discussion groups on the Internet. Check them out as well. The discussion groups can be great places to interact with other people struggling with the same issues you have. Plus many publishing experts also belong to these groups. Since these come and go, search via Google or Yahoo to locate the current groups.

One of the great things about the publishing world, especially among independent publishers, is that people are willing to share information. I have never found any independent publisher who was not willing to share his or her experiences, resources, and knowledge—and I talk to about 2,000 publishers every year!

Of course, when you talk to other publishers, remember the golden rule. If you expect them to share ideas and resources with you, you should also share your ideas and resources with them. That's only fair.

> **Authors** — You should network with authors and publishers you know. You can learn a lot from others, especially if you share what you know with them. Check out the many sites on the web that are targeted at writers, or join in the chat sessions on the America Online writers section.

5:10 Use Your Local Library or the Internet

Two of the best resources you have for finding out anything—and everything—is your local library and the Internet. Especially get to know your local reference librarian. Here are just a few of the things libraries and the Internet can do for you:

☐ Help you find the directories of periodicals, associations, and other marketing possibilities.

☐ Let you know what topics and authors are hot with their patrons.

☐ Help you keep track of new books (especially competitive titles) from other publishers. Amazon.com is especially useful for tracking the sales rates of competitive titles.

☐ Provide you with books, magazines, online databases, web sites, and other resources to research new books or verify facts in manuscripts submitted by your authors.

☐ Give you feedback on your titles, covers, contents, bibliographies, and indexes of forthcoming books.

☐ Help you locate authors, experts, and celebrities who can write new books for you.

☐ Provide access to catalogs, associatons, trade shows, non-profits, and all sorts of other resources for planning your marketing steps.

> **Authors** — You should also get to know your local librarians. They can help you research your books, find out what books compete with yours, let you know which publishers are publishing books similar to the ones you are working on, and help you locate experts and opinion leaders who can help you promote your books.

5:11 Use Your Government Resources

Most government departments maintain statistics and other research that can aid you in finding out more about new markets. Your librarian or the Internet can help you locate those local, state, and national government departments which might be able to assist you.

Most of the information available from government departments is free or low cost. Not only do these government departments publish research, but they can also provide consultants or experts who can answer other questions for you. Or if they cannot provide an answer, they can direct you to someone who can. Most now also offer web sites with loads of information.

5:12 Target Mailings

In testing a new market, start by doing targeted mailings to a few prime buyers in that market. Test your offer (titles and contents of your books). Test your copy. Test your lists. Follow up with phone calls to verify your results—and your assumptions. Once you've tested your offer, you can roll out with more mailings or with advertisements and distribution via the normal channels for that market (whether via sales representatives, distributors, or wholesalers).

5:13 Test, Test, Test

Start small. Always test your marketing programs before spending a lot of money or rolling out a new marketing program. Make sure your advertisements and marketing programs are designed well—and work. One of the beauties of the Internet is the ability to get feedback, often immediately, on your titles, covers, and marketing programs. Once you've done your research and testing, then, and only then, roll out to the larger market.

One of the biggest mistakes beginning authors and publishers make is to jump into a new market without any testing. The only results of such silly behavior are disappointment, money loss, and poor sales.

5:14 Plan and Prepare

Make sure you have a good marketing plan. Then stick with it. Remember: First impressions last. Make sure the first impression you create in a new market is the one you want to live with. Then go ahead.

5:15 Be Persistent

Once you commit yourself to a new market, stick with it. Be patient. It can take time to open a new market, sometimes as long as a year or two. While you are waiting for orders, keep in touch with the major players in that market. Let them know that you are still actively interested in their market—and that you intend to be in that market for the long run.

5:16 Go Slow

Don't enter a new market until you have exploited your prime markets thoroughly. Remember the 80/20 rule. Spend most of your marketing time and money promoting to the 20% of your potential market which is most likely to produce the most buyers of your books. Only then should you explore other markets.

As a corollary to this principle, don't try to open too many new markets at the same time. You'll just spread yourself too thin and won't have the time or money to do justice to any of the new markets.

How to Use the Internet to Sell and Deliver Your Books Instantly to Your Customers — Completely on Auto-Pilot!

by Sen Ze, http://www.SenZe.com

By offering a digital version of your physical book and selling it on the Internet as a file that can be downloaded instantly from your web site, you can double, triple or quadruple the amount of money you can make with your writings.

It costs you nothing for your web site to reproduce a copy of your digital book for your online customers. In addition, your web site can sell and deliver your digital book every single day for you, automatically.

Here's what you'll need:

1. A PDF Converter — This software will convert your manuscript in Word format into the Adobe PDF Format within seconds. PDF documents can easily be locked by a password to prevent unauthorized copying.

2. A Domain Name — This is your web site address.

3. A Credit Card Processing Service — This will enable you to accept credit card orders directly on your web site. You can get this service online within minutes.

4. A Sales Web Page — This page is written in a specific way to sell your book. It's more than just a book cover and a brief description of what it's about.

5. A Thank You Web Page Containing the Download Link to Your Book — This is what your customers will automatically see after their credit card has been successfully processed.

6. A Web Hosting Account — This will store your web pages, and reproduce your digital product on demand for your Customers.

Here's a diagram to illustrate this auto-pilot selling concept:

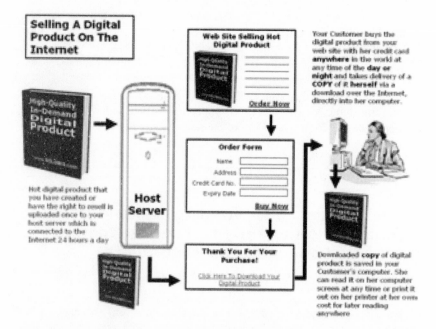

For a more detailed description on the above, other powerful concepts, and how you can get started immediately even if you've never done anything like it before, go to http://www.SenZe.com/author now.

Chapter 6

Editorial: The First Step

---

*When I started as a publisher, people used to tell me to publish
what you know and like. It all sounded naive. But I think it's true:
you have to publish books you feel passionately about.*
— Neil Ortenberg, publisher, Thunder's Mouth Press

In writing the Fifth Edition of *1001 Ways to Market Your Books*, I ran
into a problem. The book was getting too long. Since I worried how this
would affect sales of the book, I surveyed several online discussion lists
asking for feedback. Their response: About half of those who responded
said that 800 pages would be just fine, at any price, as long as I had written
it. But the other half said that I should either break the book down into two
books or edit and cut until the book was a manageable size. They said that
an 800-page book would be too heavy, too bulky, and too intimidating for
many people to use.

So I took their advice. As a result, I decided to delete most of Chapter 6
on editorial and Chapter 7 on design because they were the two least relevant chapters for people who already have a book and need advice on marketing what they already have. It was a tough decision to cut anything, but I
had to do it to keep this book manageable. By cutting those two chapters, I
saved more than seventy pages.

Now I made this decision *after* I had already written the two chapters, so
I certainly did not want to throw them out. There is some great material in
these two chapters, both for authors and publishers. That material from this
chapter is now incorporated into my mini-guide: *Book Marketing 102: Editorial as the First Step in Marketing.*

Market-Savvy Editing

by Chris Roerden and Pat Meller

A review in *The Nation* criticized the authors of *Guns in the Courtroom* for turning the "cut-and-paste function of their word processors into tools of torture." A *Milwaukee Journal* reviewer ridiculed *Southern Daughter: The Life of Margaret Mitchell* as "the worst-edited book I have read in years."

If you think editing means proofreading, you're missing the value of developmental editing from a market-savvy perspective. Here are some of our clients' many success stories.

Rewriting a Professional Book to Reach a Consumer Audience

The Battering Syndrome is a $79 hardcover edited by Chris for professionals. Its publisher, the National Crisis Prevention Institute, also had Chris redevelop this book for a lay market. She cut the length, simplified vocabulary and sentence structure, and introduced a conversational voice. Result? The popular trade paperback *He Promised He'd Stop: Helping Women Find Safe Passage from Abusive Relationships*.

Awareness of Market Needs Facilitates Mass Purchasing

When the audience for cardiac monitoring equipment ranges from high school grads to MDs, an editor must make information talk to everyone—including non-tech buyers for hospitals. Marquette Medical Electronics had Pat create its documentation, praised by the marketing reps for clarity and accuracy. They knew its value in helping them sell contracts worth millions.

Developmental Edit Turns Autobiography into Powerful Exposé

No attorney would represent the executive's wife, so Rosalyn Reeder represented herself. No newspaper would mention her lawsuit against Whirlpool and no publisher would touch *Divorcing the Corporation*, so Reeder self-published. Chris's developmental editing moved the writing from catharsis to gripping, fact-filled narrative, avoiding the pitfalls that ruin many autobiographies. The book's positive reception, even in the corporation's home territory, proved the value of market-savvy editing.

Organizing and Streamlining Gains Media Attention

Good Housekeeping reprinted a chapter from *The Safety Minute*, telling Safety Zone Press that the book's clear presentation helped them select what would most appeal to their 5 million readers. *Mademoiselle* used its safety tips as talking points for an article featuring the book. Chris's developmental editing had eliminated excess wording and reframed each warning as a direct command for action. She was asked to do the same for the second edition, which adds identity theft.

Emergency Responders Learn Complex Computer Program Quickly

Hundreds of thousands of first responders must learn to use special software for public safety. Pat created templates, styles, and flowcharts and developed training materials with the consistency and clarity required for train-the-trainer efficiency—a benefit for national security.

Clear Editing from the Start Facilitates Sub Rights Sales

The PBS series *Ancestors* selected *Genetic Connections* from Sonters Publishing for its companion guide to the TV series, the only resource picked for its program on genetics. The book, a Benjamin Franklin award winner, was easily condensed in time for the broadcast because its technical content had been made clear and user-friendly from the beginning by Chris and Pat.

Market-Savvy Thinking Uncovers Hidden Market

Chris asked successful mystery authors to review an early draft of *Don't Murder Your Mystery: 24 Fiction-Writing Techniques to Save Your Manuscript from Turning Up D.O.A.* Most said they'd like to hand something about this much-needed book to all the writers who approach them at their book signings and ask how to get published. Bingo! Chris is now marketing to experienced authors whose success attracts the book's primary market.

Chris Roerden and Pat Meller each bring more than 35 years of experience in writing, editing, teaching, and publishing to small press clients in business, academia, health, science, IT, public speaking, and more. Discover their high-quality award-winning work at their web site at http://www.MarketSavvyBookEditing.com.

Proofing Makes Perfect: Because a Book Isn't Judged Only by Its Cover

by Bobby Bershausen of Virtual Bookworm

Picture this: Fred Novelist (creative, huh?) has a great marketing strategy for his latest self-published book. He has notebooks full of ideas and potential locations for signings. Money is no object for his cover, so he contracts a top-notch artist to create a dazzling piece. Everything seems perfect, so he rushes to finish the book and send it off to the printer. Sales are good out of the gate, but suddenly stop cold. Signings are a bust and Fred just prays an AP photographer doesn't stop by. What happened?

You'd be surprised at how many Freds enter the publishing fray every day. Many authors who decide to self publish or utilize print-on-demand know most of the hurdles they will face, so they become obsessed with marketing and how the book will look. But they cut corners on proofing and publish a book that becomes a reader's exercise in *spot the errors*.

The packaging of a book can be beautiful and/or hip yet tank in sales once word gets out that it is riddled with errors. Reader reviews on Amazon and similar sites often mention errors, etc. Yet I have seen rather ugly books sell like crazy because the book is polished and reads well. Most readers (we call them that for a reason, you know) buy books they want to read, not just books that will look nice on the bookshelf.

Despite the fact that we screen every manuscript and plead for authors to send us their absolute, final product, we often receive documents riddled with grammar, punctuation and usage errors (many of which could have been easily detected using the word processor's spelling and grammar check). When we point out the mistakes, many authors seemed surprised and then complain about having to go through the whole thing again.

Sure, self-publishing and POD have some stigmas. The biggest is that technology is allowing junk into the marketplace. Unfortunately, that has happened to some extent. So if you do go the POD route, find a publisher that has a selection process so your book isn't being sold under the same imprint as a title that wouldn't even pass a tenth-grade English class.

You want to submit only the best, most polished manuscript possible. Don't rely just on the spelling and grammar check of your software (although you *should* run it as part of the editing process). And, since we often get attached to our work and can't catch even the most obvious of errors, get someone else to review it. If you can't afford a high-priced wordsmith, at the very least you should get someone who is skilled in editing (another author, a journalist, your former English teacher). And then have someone review the content. In other words, if you've written a murder mystery, have a law enforcement officer or lawyer (watch the bill) look it over. If it's poetry, have someone who appreciates verse go over it (your mechanic probably wouldn't be a good choice here, unless he recites Longfellow while changing your oil).

You've poured your heart and soul into your book, so don't short-change your baby by publishing the first or second draft. Make it shine. After all, you do want it to sell. And you don't want your former English teacher to throw eggs at you as she cries about how she failed. Once you have it polished, then worry about *how* to sell it.

Bobby Bershausen is president of Virtualbookworm.com Publishing, a self-publishing/POD publishing firm that screens every manuscript received. They also offer a returns program, book layout and design services, marketing, and website creation/hosting. For more information, contact **Virtual-Bookworm.com Publishing**, P.O. Box 9949, College Station, TX 77845; 877-376-4955. Web: http://www.virtualbookman.com.

Chapter 7

Designing Your Books as Sales Aids

---

*I know when I see a really attractive jacket that the publisher
is behind the book and, of course, I pay attention to it.*
— Leslie Hanscom, former book editor of *Newsday*

As with the previous chapter on editorial, this chapter on design has also
been cut to the bare bones. You can read more about book design, especially as it relates to marketing in my new mini-guide, *Book Marketing 103:
Designing Your Books as Sales Aids.*

"And when they open the book cartoon,
he pops out and begs them to reorder."

The cartoon on the previous page and the one below are sample cartoons that were created by Andrew Toos, who provides illustrations for books. For more information, contact **Cartoon Resource**, Andrew Grossman, P.O. Box 2921, Williamsburg, VA 23187; 757-220-3076; Fax: 757-220-3079. Email: andrew@cartoonresource.com. Web: *http://www.cartoonresource.com.*

"Man, not getting into our chain store really impacted him."

Publishing forms a minor branch of the entertainment industry,
and book design is increasingly a matter of fashion—
that is, of attention-getting. In the visual clamor of a bookstore,
the important thing is to be different; a whisper becomes a shout,
and the ugly becomes beautiful if it attracts attention.
— John Updike, novelist

How to Design Your Book Cover

by George Foster, cover designer, Foster Covers

Your book cover is your most important marketing piece. In just six seconds, people judge your book by it. Use this principle to your advantage with an attractive book cover. Here are some general tips to help you do this.

Know your audience: Look at book covers in your category. You will see common design traits you can use. If your book is about business, you'll notice that most business books appear smart and bold. Type is large and clear. Health books use vibrant color and often have a white background. Cookbooks show appetizing colors (red, yellow, and green). History covers include a picture. Fiction covers convey a mood to hook you right away, like a movie poster. Match your cover to its topic and you're off to a great start.

Think small: Does your cover look good at a small size on the Internet, a catalog page, or a book review? How about in black and white? Photocopy your cover to test this. If your background is detailed, make your title bold and a solid color. Add a drop shadow for more punch. Make your title large enough to read easily.

Type: Use fonts that match your book's category. Visit a website like myfonts.com or store.adobe.com/type, where you can type in your book title and view it in any font. Notice how the feel of your book changes dramatically when the title is displayed in different fonts. If your title is longer than four words use upper and lower case letters. A contrasting font for the subtitle is helpful, but limit your cover's fonts to two or three. Remember that type's function is to convey your message, not create clutter.

Color: Black can convey authority, romance, richness, evil, fashion, mystery, and, when combined with red, evoke danger. True crime covers are almost always black and red. Color does matter. Use it wisely to get the best response from your target audience. Red is warm and intimate and appeals to women while it is exciting, even risky, to men. Blue is reliable and intelligent, preferred by men but depressing to women. White is clinical, credible and pure. Orange is healthy, brown is rich, green is leisure, yellow is energetic, and pink is relaxing for men while therapeutic for women.

Front vs. back: Your front and back covers create a two-step selling process. The front (step 1) should show just enough to make your target audience stop and say, "this looks good" which attracts them to the back cover (step 2). The front cover's attraction is mainly emotional, not verbal. Like a salesperson who talks too much, you can chase people away. Let the back cover do the explaining. Endorsements, benefits, synopsis, special features, and claims belong here. The back cover should harmonize with the front's type and color. Include your company logo at lower left, ISBN barcode at lower right, book category (self-help/psychology) top left, and retail price ($19.95 U.S.) at top right. Keep all text at least 1/4" from the outer edge.

Refine the spine: The smallest portion of your cover has to be big at selling. In a bookstore your spine is generally the only visible part of your cover, squeezed between other books on the shelf. When designing your spine, give it strong contrast and make your title large and legible.

Smarter is better than clever: Refrain from being too clever on your cover. If you confuse, you lose. Keep inside jokes and non sequiturs inside the book where you have established context and rapport. Before publishing, test your cover by showing it, without describing your book, to bookstore owners and study their reactions. You might be surprised.

BEFORE (below left) — This cover is dynamic, but what the heck is going on? Is this about dancing? Note the subtitle says to "stop them NOW," perhaps referring to the dancers. Be careful how you position your subtitle, and resist including too many subtitles, or at least organize them so they don't create a messy cover. The title, instead of making the cover an immediate and compelling message, looks like it was added as an afterthought.

Before   After

AFTER (above right) — We're targeting teens and parents so we want to be dignified and trustworthy, yet fresh and energetic. Red and pink (and teal) score a high response from females so they are used generously. The white adds its clinical, trustworthy feel. The girls share a healthy look and attitude, reinforcing the title. The author's name is dark blue and set in a dignified serif typeface, reflecting her expert status.

George Foster is my book cover designer. He has donce a wide range of covers, can do any look, and always creates great covers. **Foster Covers**, 1401 Wonder Way, Fairfield, IA 52556; 641-472-3953; 800-472-3953; Fax: 641-472-3146. Email: info@fostercovers.com. To see some wonderful book covers, see his web site at http://www.fostercovers.com.

Design Your Book to Build Your Brand

Kathi Dunn, Dunn+Associates Design for Authors, Speakers and Experts

Did you know that your book is not just a book?

As an author and business person, you know that your book has the potential to be your strongest lead-generator, and its cover is your most important marketing tool. But did you know that your book cover should be an essential component in building your brand?

With a powerful brand, you can actively shape your clients' and your prospects' perception of you. Your talent alone will probably not take you to the top of your field. Creating and promoting your unique brand is critical to your success. If you want to be perceived as the leader in your sphere of influence, creating professional, stand-out-from-the-crowd branding is key to building the right impression and opening doors.

When developing your book cover, think about how to use your book to build your brand, as a stepping stone to imprint on your target audience.

The power of your front cover

Your choice of colors, fonts, photos or illustration style can become foundational elements of your visual brand. The message in your title and subtitle can differentiate you and drive home your promise, which is your brand.

Did you know that book distributors only carry books' front covers to sell books? Did you know that bookstore browsers spend about eight seconds looking at a front cover and 15 seconds on the back cover before making a buying decision? Now, that's the potential of a powerful brand!

Your professional publisher logo

A logo is a compact image of exactly who you are, what you do, and why you're the best at doing it. A logo is often the public's first visual contact with you or your company and therefore establishes that all-important first impression. Your logo must be timeless, unique, appropriate, and most of all, highly memorable. The best publisher logos are immediately recognizable when printed as small as a postage stamp on a book's spine or as large as a billboard, hot-stamped in one color on the case binding or splashed in many colors on your website.

Expand your brand

Once you've defined your brand, carry that into everything you do—your logo, stationery, posters, brochures, speaking materials, website, and other information products—to create that consistent and memorable image.

Branding consistency is powerful and crucial. Yet, a great brand is opportunistic, ready to evolve and expand while remaining true to its essence.

Branding doesn't just happen. It needs to be approached strategically as well as creatively. Your branding must differentiate you, it must be powerful with an original identity, it must be customer-oriented, and it must be be clever and compelling. Great brands promise consumers the very things that they value. Do your book and its marketing collateral do that?

Build your brand wisely and you will attract new clients, increase your visibility, differentiate yourself from your competition, carve out your expert status, build your income, and enjoy new opportunities.

Power-2-Be Media publisher logo, mug promoting publisher URL, their Power Selling book, and postcards promoting the book. Strategic branding and design by Dunn+Associates

---

For over two decades Kathi Dunn has helped authors, speakers and experts open doors, accelerate their careers, and develop their brands. Kathi's client list includes a host of top presenters and authors—Tony Robbins, Ken Blanchard, Mark Victor Hansen, Deepak Chopra, Sylvia Browne, John Edward, and Dottie Walters. Kathi's international award-winning design firm has created hundreds of book covers, including numerous bestsellers, and has received over 200 awards. Dunn+Associates is sought after for the powerful, distinctive, fresh, and compelling covers they deliver to their professional publishing clients like HarperCollins, Simon and Schuster, Prentice Hall, Ballantine, Hay House, Pearson Education, Random House, and Bantam.

To learn insider secrets that today's fast-track authors are using to build instantly recognizable brands, position themselves as leading industry experts, and create a profit-building empire, contact **Dunn+Associates**, P.O. Box 870, Hayward, WI 54843-0870; 715-634-4857; Fax: 715-634-5617. Web: http://www.dunn-design.com.

Interior Design: The Unsung Hero of a Successful Book

by Barry Kerrigan of Desktop Miracles

Interior design and typesetting is the unsung hero of a successful book. A great interior design combines an attractive layout that is visually pleasing, while also creating a logical structure to the layout so that comprehension and readability are enhanced for the reader.

The design of your book is vitally important to your success both with industry professionals and with your readers.

Industry professionals such as distributors, reviewers, and bookstore buyers will glance at your cover first, read the back cover and flaps, and then open the book up to inspect it. An attractive, professionally laid out book communicates that the publisher understands how to do the job correctly and that care has been taken in the development of the title.

A book that is poorly designed with layout problems, inconsistencies, and poor typesetting immediately makes these key gatekeepers more suspect of the content itself. A poor design or layout can reduce your chances of getting distribution or reviews and prevent you from getting in front of prospective customers.

The interior design is also important to the reader, even though it may be on a subconscious level. A good design is not only attractive and easy to read, but one that helps the reader understand and comprehend the information as well as the structure of the text. A satisfied reader is far more likely to recommend your book to others and to purchase your future titles.

Thanks to the technological advances of the last 15 years, attractive book design and layout is within reach of virtually every publisher.

Quality typesetting can be produced in page layout programs like Adobe InDesign and Quark XPress, and graphic eye candy like photos, illustrations, and screens are relatively easy to incorporate.

It doesn't take that much more time and effort to do it right. It just takes caring enough to do it right.

Desktop Miracles creates incredible interiors, book covers, and book jackets. As John Kremer once noted, "They do wonderful interiors, some of the best I've seen." For more information, contact Barry Kerrigan at **Desktop Miracles**, 112 S. Main Street, PMB #294, Stowe, VT 05672; 802-253-7900; Fax: 802-253-1900. Email: barry@desktopmiracles.com. Web: http://www.desktopmiracles.com.

7:01 Interior Design: A Few Guidelines

How important are looks? When *Publishers Weekly* rated the top five tax guides in 1996, *Taxes for Dummies* was rated best because of its "excellent visuals, superb writing, and friendly organization," while *J.K. Lassers Your Income Tax* was rated lowest because it tried to do too much: The "layout is not easy on the eyes." While Lassers had created the tax book category, "it has now been eclipsed in the packaging department: no small consideration for people with less time than ever to mess with their taxes."

Given the important of interiors, here are a few tips on designing the interior of your book:

☐ **Use readable type.** If the book is to be used by older people, make sure the type size is large enough. New England Press published a superb cookbook (practical content, great reviews, attractive design, and reasonable price), but the book did not sell well. Only when watching bookstore browsers pick up the book and page through it, did they discover that the typeface was too small for use in a kitchen.

☐ **Give a sense of spaciousness to your books.** Don't crowd your type. In other words, don't follow my example in this book. The text is very crowded in this book because I am too verbose. My apologies.

☐ **Make sure the typeface fits the subject** or content of the book. I used Times Roman, for example, in this book because it is a typeface that is easy to read and yet imparts a degree of seriousness to the text.

☐ **Avoid sans serif type for any long text.** Use it only when the text is short or in bite-size pieces.

☐ **Illustrations help to sell books.** Photographs, line drawings, cartoons, tables, graphs, charts, sidebars, and other illustrations all make a book more attractive and useful. Especially in this visual age where many readers have grown up watching television, graphic elements help to sell books. That's one reason the *Dummies* series has done so well.

☐ **Use high-bulk paper** to make a book look bigger when necessary. Since many readers still equate size with quality, you could use high-bulk paper to make your books look bigger and to add a feel of substance. In 1982, two titles were published on the same subject. The first, printed on machine-coated stock, measured one inch thick and sold for $17.95; the other, printed on antique finish paper, measured one and a half inches thick and sold for $24.95. The thicker book, which actually had nineteen fewer pages, sold much better in bookstores.

Remember: If your major distribution outlet is bookstores, your books should be as attractive and as inviting as possible, both inside and out. As many as two-thirds of all bookstore sales are impulse purchases. The more attractive you make your books, the more likely they are to sell. Don't pinch pennies on the inside of your book. It simply isn't worth it.

Chapter 8

How Authors Can Help Promote Their Books

All my author friends complain that their publishers don't do enough.
At least I can do it myself. You can't depend on your publisher.
You should be your own PR person.

— Henry Rogers, author, *Rogers' Rules for Businesswomen*

Many publishers are hesitant about having authors get involved in the marketing of their books. Publishers often have good reasons for such reluctance: First and foremost, many authors get a little too enthusiastic and demanding. Nevertheless, an author's help is indispensable to the active promotion of any book. If you make it clear to your authors right from the beginning where you need and expect their help (and where you don't), you will gain invaluable marketing assistance. Use it. It can make the difference between a poor seller and a bestseller.

8:01 Publishers: A Few Basic Guidelines

The best single advertisement for a book, other than giving away lots of review copies, is the author. An author is a walking, talking advertisement for his or her own book. So, don't ignore your authors. Here are a few basic guidelines on how you can make best use of your authors:

☐ **Listen to your authors.** Let them know that you are interested in using their knowledge and experience. Don't brush off their suggestions. Use their good ideas, and tell them why their other ideas are not workable for your company.

☐ **Before you sign a new author to a contract, find out what he or she will do to promote the book.** Get it down in writing. Then follow up.

☐ **Have all your authors fill out an author's questionnaire.** Make sure your authors understand the importance of completing this questionnaire as soon as possible. Let them know that you will be using the information they provide to plan a marketing campaign in which they will play a central role. For a very complete sample author questionnaire plus author contract, see my special report *Book Marketing 101: Author Contact Package* (details at http://www.bookmarket.com).

☐ **Offer your authors sizable discounts** (at least 40%) if they want to buy books to sell on their own. Better yet, offer them 50 or 60%. Remember: They can be their own best salespeople. This one change can have more impact on book sales than almost anything else you could do.

As Pat Gundry of Suitcase Books once noted, "You cannot do wrong by giving the author the most generous discount possible. He is your best marketing tool. Make it worth his time and effort to market for you constantly." Her husband, an executive at a large publishing house that recently began offering authors such generous discounts says that the program is "a great success with everyone happy all around."

☐ **Keep your authors informed of new marketing developments**—book club sales, major reviews, special sales, foreign rights, and so on. You never know when some bit of information might inspire your author to make a contact that could help you sell tons of books.

☐ **Take a personal interest in your authors.** When Random House published Glenn Doman's *How to Teach Your Baby to Read*, not only was the editor Bob Loomis an enthusiastic advocate, but also the president Bennett Cerf and his wife, Phyllis. They recommended the book to everyone they spoke to. Because Random House's commitment was wholehearted, the book got fantastic reviews, touched people deeply, and sold more than half a million copies in thirteen years.

☐ **Have your authors autograph several hundred copies of their books.** When sending review copies to major reviewers and other key contacts, send these autographed copies. Indeed, if your authors are willing, have them personalize the autographs for each key contact. These personalized copies will get more attention than ordinary copies.

☐ **Support your authors with material for doing bookstore appearances and media interviews.** For major titles and other books that lend themselves to a national tour, help to organize such a tour and pay the author's expenses. National tours are one of the best ways to establish a nationwide demand for a book—and such widespread demand can often propel a book onto the bestsellers list.

One autumn, the Minnesota Independent Publishers Association organized autograph parties featuring regional authors. The autograph parties were held over four weekends in different Twin Cities shopping centers. Why not work with your regional publishers or booksellers association to organize a similar program in your area?

In January 1989, sixteen Florida writers boarded a Romance Writers Caravan bus for a three-day, four-city promotional tour of the state. As part of the tour, they autographed books, talked to aspiring writers, and met with booksellers and distributors in Miami, Fort Lauderdale, Orlando, and Tampa-St. Petersburg. If your authors ever have a chance to participate in such a tour, sponsor them.

☐ **Send your authors to appropriate trade conventions** and other conferences. One publisher sent the author of a book on child-raising to a baby products fair. While there, the author not only sold books but also made contacts that got her TV appearances as well as invitations to speak before people who bought still more books.

Even if you cannot afford to display at an appropriate convention or trade show, you or your author should still attend. Even without a display, you and your authors can still make many good contacts. The opportunities for networking at a convention are wide open.

☐ **Encourage the formation of fan clubs** for your regular authors by providing special membership cards, posters, and other promotional material for any fans who request help in forming such a club. Also exploit existing fan clubs.

Janet Dailey, author of *The Great Alone* and *The Glory Game*, has such a fan club, and Pocket Books sends regular mailings to club members announcing new titles. It's a great way to establish a stronger bond between authors and their most ardent fans (who are also their strongest word-of-mouth supporters).

When Kathryn Leigh Scott sent out a flyer announcing her book, *My Scrapbook Memories of Dark Shadows*, to the membership of the Dark Shadows fan club, she got a 28% response to the mailing. Fans do respond—and respond well.

When Conari published Vicki Leon's *Uppity Women of Medieval Times*, they sent special mailings to its Wild Women Association, a group formed by Autumn Stephens, another Conari author. The group celebrates history's forgotten females.

When Algonquin Books published Lewis Nordan's *Lightning Song*, not only did they help establish and promote the author's fan club, but they also sponsored a National Lewis Nordan Appreciation Week from February 7 to 14, 1997.

☐ **Print your author's home address in the back of the book** so readers can write directly to him or her. If your authors don't want their home addresses public, encourage readers to write to you with the assurance that you will forward all mail to the authors the same day you receive it.

☐ **Promote tie-ins with other authors**, books, or events wherever possible. For example, be on the lookout for promotions such as the one run by the Village Green bookstore. A staff member happened to read in one of Alice Walker's books that Zorah Neil Hurston was her favorite author.

So Village Green, building on the publicity from Walker's bestselling book *The Color Purple* and the movie of the same name, ran a promotion for Hurston's book, *Their Eyes Were Watching God*. As a result, the store sold 365 copies of Hurston's book during the holiday season.

☐ **Get your authors listed** in Gale's *Contemporary Authors*, other directories of writers, and any appropriate *Who's Who* listings. These listings not only help to bring greater immediate recognition to your authors, but they also make it easier for media, librarians, and other researchers to find out more about the authors.

☐ **When you sign a contract with your authors, give them a copy of *1001 Ways to Market Your Books***. It is the most important thing you can do for your authors—and for me. Thanks. Actually, self-interest aside, it really is the most practical way to introduce your authors to the world of book marketing. Give a copy of this book to every author you sign. [Generous quantity discounts are available from Open Horizons.]

When Susan Wilson, author of *Your Intelligent Heart*, told one of the marketing people at AMACOM Books that she had read *1001 Ways to Market Your Books*, the person said (tongue in cheek), "That's a dangerous book for authors. Now they'll know enough not to need us." Then she added, "I have a copy, and I love it!"

Do not be afraid to give copies to your authors, because the fact is they still need you to get the best distribution and exposure. Indeed, informed authors are your best salespeople. The more they know about book marketing, the more help they can give you—and the more they can do on their own to generate sales for their books. That's also why generous discounts for authors can create a big impact on book sales.

☐ **Work with them on special promotions.** For more details, read the rest of this chapter—even the sections, such as the next one, which are directed towards authors.

8:02 Publishers: Use Your Authors' Connections

Although some authors are famous for their love of seclusion, most authors do have associations, connections, contacts, and friends who can be of assistance in promoting their books. Use those connections. They are a prime audience for the book.

☐ Ask your authors to compile four lists of individuals they know:

1) those who might be interested in buying the book for personal use,

2) those who might purchase the book in quantity (for businesses, associations, clubs, and other organizations),

3) those who can provide their expertise in reviewing, commenting on, or perhaps writing a promotional blurb or foreword for the book,

4) those in the media who might review the book or provide other exposure for the author and/or the book.

☐ Other lists your authors might be able to provide include:

1) the names of individuals involved in the subject area of the book, especially opinion leaders.

2) buyers of products or services described in the book,

3) companies or other organizations that might be interested in the book (either for resale to their members or for use as premiums),

4) membership directories of clubs and associations in which the author is an active member,

5) a list of media for the city in which the author lives (or has lived),

6) names of individuals who have expressed an interest in the author's previous books, articles, or other activities.

☐ Ask your authors to arrange announcements about the publication of their books in the newsletters of any associations to which they belong, in their companies' in-house magazines or newsletters, in appropriate alumni publications, and other club bulletins.

☐ If your authors work for a company or other institution, encourage them to ask the company's public relations department to issue its own news release.

☐ If the author is a regular contributor to a magazine or newspaper, that periodical might be interested in doing a review or special advertising promotion for the author's current book, especially if the book fits its editorial profile.

Because Robert Miller was a regular contributor to their magazines and because his book, *Most of My Patients Are Animals*, fit into their editorial focus, *Veterinary Medicine* and *Western Horseman* took 8,000 copies of the book to sell to their subscribers.

☐ Explore any sales opportunities with your author's college. Stetson University College of Law ordered a special alumni edition of Steve Rushing's book, *A Funny Thing Happened on the Way to Court*. 1,000 copies of the book (with the Stetson logo imprinted on the cover) were given to donors to the college.

Authors — Help your publishers ferret out these special sales and promotional opportunities. You are the one with these special connections. Make a list of them and then help your publisher follow up on these prime sales leads. Don't wait to be asked. Volunteer the information and your follow-up efforts. You are your own best salesperson.

8:03 Publishers: Provide Authors with Sales Material

Since your authors' family, friends, colleagues, and other connections are prime prospects for their books, provide your authors with any promotional material which might help stimulate sales to these special audiences.

☐ For instance, print your regular news release on legal-size paper with a tear-off order coupon at the bottom of the page. These announcements can then be sent by your authors to all their friends and acquaintances. This procedure not only allows your authors to announce the publication of their books, but also relieves them of having to let each individual acquaintance know where to obtain their books.

☐ Let your authors know that you will also supply similar announcements, advertising copy, or more formal brochures to any organization or individual acquaintance promoting the author's book in their newsletter, membership mailings, or other promotions. You could have the orders come direct to you, go to the organization or individual sponsoring the mailing, or have the recipients order through their local bookstore.

> **Authors** — If your publisher offers you the opportunity to mail out some promotional materials, take it—even if you have to share expenses (as long as you also share profits).

8:04 Publishers: Keep Your Sales Force Informed

Your authors are your best sales force for their own books. Encourage them to carry copies of their books with them wherever they go, to talk up the book with any individuals or organizations they encounter, and to always let you know what they are doing in the way of personal promotions.

The last point in the above paragraph is perhaps the most important of all: Make sure your authors keep you informed of any activities, speeches, or other events that might have an impact on the sales of their books. In turn, you should let your sales representatives and distributors know of all such activities so they, in turn, can take advantage of any such promotions.

> **Authors** — Be sure to keep your publisher informed of anything you are doing to promote your books. That way, your publisher can coordinate your activities with their own activities —and those of their distributors.

8:05 Authors, Please Note!

Although you have a right and duty to help market your books, don't get in the way of your publishers. Remember, above all, that your publishers will generally have had more experience in editing, designing, producing, promoting, and marketing books than you. Let your publishers do their job; you do yours. Here are some suggestions on how you can help your publishers do their job more effectively:

☐ **Work with your editor.** Your editor should be your main contact with your publishers. If you have any suggestions for different ways to market your book, channel those suggestions through your editor. Your editor, in turn, should pass those suggestions on to the appropriate departments within the publishing company.

☐ **Listen to your editor** when he or she makes suggestions on ways to improve the style, content, or approach of your book. That doesn't mean you shouldn't give your editor feedback based on your own knowledge and experience, but it does mean that you should listen carefully to his or her suggestions and, in most cases, follow those suggestions.

☐ **Negotiate a strong contract in your favor.** The most important clause for you should be the one stating that you can buy copies of the book at a large discount, preferably 60% or more. I know many authors who have been able to negotiate such discounts. Some even buy books on a cost plus 10% basis (authors pay the publisher only 10% more than the cost of printing the book).

Other important clauses: Keep the copyright in your name. Retain all subsidiary rights the publisher is not in a position to exploit.

☐ **Consider ways to change your book's contents** so the book becomes more marketable. For details on how you can improve the contents of your book, reread the two preceding chapters.

☐ **Answer all questionnaires and other requests for information** from the publisher promptly and completely. Use these requests as an opportunity to suggest other ways to market your books—especially those ways which draw on your own experience, associations, and expertise.

A year before Bear & Company publishes a book, they ask their authors to gather as large an endorsement list as possible. This strategy helped them to identify a network of Native American lodges, healing groups, classes, seminars, and publications. As Debora Bluestone, their publicity director, noted, "These publications aren't anything you'd find in *LMP*, but we've found our best results by working at a grassroots level."

☐ **Provide your publisher with a detailed biography** of your life, including your activities and interests. The publisher may have contacts or knowledge that can turn some of your activities or interests into promotions for your book.

☐ **Never stop thinking of ways to market your books.** Pass on those suggestions which would be most appropriate for the publisher to carry out. Also consider ways you yourself can market your books. More suggestions along this line are listed below.

> **Authors** — Read the above notes one more time. They are the most important pointers you can pick up from this book. Above all, establish a good working relationship with your editor and, secondly, fill out (in detail) the author's questionnaire your publisher sends you. If they don't send you one, create your own. Or use the Author's Questionnaire in my *Book Marketing 101: Author Contract Package*, available from Open Horizons.

8:06 Authors: Your Publisher Needs Your Help

Don't think that you can write a book and then sit back and let the publisher do the rest. While that works for a few authors, it doesn't work for most. Not if you want to reach plenty of readers. Not if you want to sell books. Not if you want to have a bestseller. Listen to your publisher. Hear what kinds of authors they like working with. Become one of those authors.

☐ "The best publicity tool we have are the authors.... The authors who network, who appear at conferences and workshops, and who maintain databases of contacts can really make a difference. We try to support and supplement their efforts whenever feasible." — Larry Hughes, publicity director, Penguin USA

☐ When booksellers were asked about Angie Fenimore's slow-selling *Beyond the Darkness*, they cited the book's not-so-sunny angle and the fact that "to sell, New Age authors must tour like troupers." — *Publishers Weekly*

☐ "We're looking for authors who will work hand-in-hand with us and find promotional opportunities for their books." — Pamela Krauss, cookbook editor, Clarkson Potter

☐ "If you really want your book to fly, you need to know that the reality of the publishing business is that publishers print and distribute. The author has to be willing to promote the book, because no one else will." — David Chilton, author, *The Wealthy Barber*

☐ "The author is what makes a book settle into the backlist. Authors can't expect their books to backlist if they're not out at cooking schools, doing local television shows, or becoming a known specialist. It's legwork, legwork, legwork." — Harriet Bell, executive editor, Broadway Books

☐ "Don't waste a single day." — Bessie Delany, 104-year-old co-author of *Having Our Say*, a bestseller and Broadway play

☐ "Nowadays, it takes so many impressions of a product before someone will buy it. So I say to my authors, 'What can you do to help create those impressions?'" — Gail Ross, literary agent

☐ "When it comes to the niche stuff, you rely on the author, and that can make a huge difference in sales." — Linda Roghaar, literary agent

☐ "You can't bring a baby into the world and expect somebody else to raise it." — Brad Hurtado, former producer, *Donahue*

☐ "Publishers concentrate on a manuscript at a time. We tell authors them they need to have a broader view. Author branding creates an understanding that the biggest asset the publisher has is the author, not the book." — Sealy Yates, literary agent for religious books

8:07 Authors: Talk, Talk, Talk

The following pages describe just a few of the ways you can use your talking ability to sell more books.

Become a Speaker

Here are a few good number of ways to use speaking engagements to sell more books:

☐ **Mention your books in any talks you give**, whether to the Lady's Auxiliary, Rotary Club, or an association meeting. Integrate the subject of your book into the subject of your talk so you can mention your books as a natural part of the talk. Then let your listeners know they can buy copies of your book in the back of the room after the talk (these sales are known in the speaking trade as *back-of-the-room sales*) or from their local bookstore. Sir Edmond Hillary used to sell at least two books for every person who attended his lectures.

At one of his Super Seminars in Los Angeles, A. L. Williams sold 7,600 copies of his book, *All You Can Do Is All You Can Do, But All You Can Do Is Enough*, in just two hours and fifteen minutes.

☐ **Here are a few other places you might want to give a talk**: bookstores, libraries (especially meetings of the Friends of the Library), clubs, churches, civic groups, chambers of commerce, schools, colleges, PTA's, writer's clubs, garden parties, businessmen luncheons, workshops, seminars, professional meetings, cruise ships, museum shows, conferences, book fairs, ski lodges, Learning Annexes, Unity Churches, and anywhere else that welcomes speakers and entertainers.

Your local Rotary group (and other service groups such as Kiwanis, the Lions, JCs, etc.) needs a new speaker every week. The people responsible for their programs are, therefore, hungry for speakers. Such local talks are a great way to build your confidence in speaking and to develop an effective book-selling talk.

Robin Newman, author of *How to Meet a Mensch in New York*, sold 10,000 copies of her book by speaking at resorts, singles mixers, libraries, museums, continuing-ed programs, synagogues, community centers, YWCAs, and department stores. As she notes, "People enjoy buying the book from the author directly. It makes the experience more personal."

The Indiana Chamber of Commerce has set up its own speakers bureau. Check to see if your local or state Chamber has a similar program.

☐ **Give them an experience.** One man makes a living with his children's books by going from school to school putting on a show and selling his books afterwards. His dog, the main character of the books, is always at his side. As he notes, "Unless an author provides people with an experience, he won't sell many books."

☐ **Give something free to everyone who attends your lectures.** Art Fettig of Growth Unlimited offers everyone a free copy of one of his verses, illustrated and ready for framing. Each verse has his name, address, and phone number. He gets many bookings and book sales through this means alone.

☐ **Give everyone a brochure and order blank.** Hand them out free during the lecture, or just afterwards. If you include some points from your talk or a list of resources that the audience can follow up on after the talk, they are more likely to take your brochure home with them.

☐ **Offer to accept credit card orders**. When Art Fettig offers his higher priced book/tape combos, he tells members of the audience to write their charge card number on the back of their business card. In this way, he often gets over $1,000 in orders per lecture.

☐ **Presell your books.** If you are giving a seminar to a corporation or a professional association, try preselling your books to the program planner so that each attendee receives a free copy of your book as part of the program. If your books will make the meeting that much more effective, the corporation will probably jump at the chance. One speaker raised his fee from $325.00 per person for each seminar he gave to $495.00 and then included his book as part of the materials for the seminar. He met no price resistance when he raised the price of his seminar.

☐ **Be available after your talk.** Ask the person introducing you to announce that you will be available after your talk to autograph books and to speak to anyone with any additional questions. Of course, those people who do not already have a copy of your book will want to buy one from you so they can get your autograph at the same time.

☐ **Inform the media.** If you are speaking at a newsworthy event, let the media know about the speech. Send them an advance copy of your talk so they quote accurately from your talk if they decide to cover the event.

☐ **Charge for speaking.** As a professional you should charge for speaking to any major seminars, conferences, clubs, and so on. These fees will help to pay your way to other speaking engagements and help to keep your promotional show on the road.

On the other hand, Bruce Sievers does not charge for his poetry readings, but he does insist on his right to sell his books after the readings. And does he sell! In one year alone he sold more than 25,000 books just as a result of his poetry readings.

☐ **Do a tour.** If the topic of your book is of interest to a specific national association with local chapters, why not set up a speaking tour with these local chapters? Linda Salzer, author of *Infertility: How Couples Can Cope*, funded her lecture tour by visiting local chapters of Resolve, the national support group for infertile couples.

☐ **As you travel, plan ahead.** Try to arrange speaking engagements wherever you travel. Beverly Nye, self-publisher of *A Family Raised on Sunshine*, bought a 30-day bus pass to tour five cities where she had previously lived. In each city she arranged with Mormon church groups and homemaking classes to give lectures, where she talked about her methods of homemaking. Not only did she make money on admission fees, but she also sold 1,500 copies in 30 days. That's 50 copies per day— which means that she made more than $250 a day just from book sales.

☐ **Invite your customers to your speaking engagements.** As you develop a list of customers, let them know when you'll be speaking in their area. Ann McLaughlin, author of *Lightning in July*, draws crowds wherever she speaks, because she sends a personalized invitation to people on her list. She speaks regularly at schools, libraries, universities, bookstores, writers' groups, book clubs, hospitals, and support groups.

☐ **When invited, go!** When Maya Angelou was invited to President Clinton's first inauguration, she did such a dramatic reading of a new poem that sales tripled for many of her books. As a result, her book *I Know Why the Caged Bird Sings*, stayed on the bestseller lists for two years.

☐ **Become a best-selling author.** It was through such speaking engagements that Wayne Dyer, Leo Buscaglia, John Gray, Deepak Chopra, James Redfield, Mark Victor Hanson, Jack Canfield, and Robert Allen all became best-selling authors. Robert Allen traveled to different cities, offered "A Free Evening with Robert Allen" seminars, got people excited about his ideas for creating wealth, and sold loads of books.

Go to Your Local Book Fairs

Over the past ten years, dozens of local book festivals or fairs have sprung up in different parts of the country. At the very least, you should attend the fairs in your area. Contact the organizers ahead of time to make yourself available for readings, talks, or other appearances. Some of the top book fairs in the country include the San Francisco Bay Area Book Festival,

New York Is Book Country, Northwest Bookfest, Rocky Mountain Book Festival, Baltimore Book Festival, Miami Book Fair International, Texas Book Festival, Southern Festival of Books (Nashville), Times Festival of Reading (St. Petersburg), Harvard Square Book Festival, LA Times Festival of Books, Printers Row Book Fair (Chicago), and Sacramento Reads!

☐ In doing her author tours, romance writer Nora Roberts often visits military bases because she is a big favorite among military wives. In addition, she visits many local book fairs such as the Kentucky Book Fair.

☐ Not only did Rabbi Kushner, author of *How Good Do We Have to Be?*, do a 12-city media tour for his book, but he also did the 15-city Jewish Book Fair circuit.

Become a Teacher

A good number of self-publishers and writers have found that lecturing at colleges and adult education classes is a superb way to market books.

☐ Melvin Powers, author of *How to Get Rich in Mail Order*, has been teaching for many years in the California college system. Not only does a description of his course get mailed to over a million potential students, but in the course description he recommends that his own book be bought and read ahead of time. He suggests that students buy the book at a local bookstore or check it out of their library. As he notes, "The result was phenomenal from a standpoint of sales."

☐ Linda Donelson, author of *Out of Isak Dinesen in Africa*, recently spent two days at Illinois College giving a convocational address and speaking to various classes. Not only did she get paid for the talks, but the college publicity department helped get her story into the local media. Many small colleges require students to attend a minimum number of convocations; hence, they are hungry for speakers. In another college appearance, she was featured in a full-page article in the local paper which, in turn, was picked up by a dozen other newspapers in central Michigan.

Become a Talker

The subhead above means just what it says. Talk to anyone and everyone you meet. As a self-promoting author, you shouldn't hesitate to talk about your book and your writing. Let people know you are an author. Naturally, they will then ask what you've written. Don't just tell them; show them the book. When your book is first published, be sure to carry a copy around with you at all times so you can show people the actual book. Also be sure to let them know where they can order the book.

☐ One author of a guidebook for handicapped travelers sat next to Abigail van Buren on an airplane flight. Of course, during their conversation the author mentioned her book. Some time later, Abigail found an opportunity to write about the book in her syndicated column, *Dear Abby*. Over two sackfuls of mail—all orders—resulted from that one little mention.

☐ When Bonnie Christensen travels, she stays at KOA campgrounds. The first thing she does when she settles in is put up a flyer at the front desk saying, "Meet the author at site #____." It draws people every time!

☐ During the 1996 campaign, Joyce Vedral, author of *Top Shape*, waited in line at a Republican party rally and, as Robert Dole passed by, she handed him a copy of her book saying, "Mr. President, you already look better than Clinton. This will make sure you stay that way!" Moments later, as Elizabeth Dole passed by, Vedral handed her another book, *Definition*, saying, "You don't need it. You look beautiful, but this will make sure you stay that way!" It got their attention. And made the news.

☐ One day at her neighborhood gas station, Pat Middleton, author of *Discover! America's Great River Road*, met a Swiss editor who was getting gas. She gave him a copy of her book and suggested a few places he might want to visit. A year later she received a copy of the Zurich daily newspaper with a major story about their interaction, her books, and the places the editor visited. Pat received a number of orders from people in Switzerland who faxed her orders with their credit card numbers.

☐ When he first published *ComputerMoney*, Alan Canton carried the book with him wherever he went. One night while standing in line for a movie, the man behind him saw the cover and began asking questions. The business editor for the *Sacramento Bee*, the man went on to write a great story about Canton's book.

☐ Do you want to meet someone? Be bold, like the people who auditioned for director Garry Marshall while he was out on the road promoting his autobiography, *Wake Me When It's Funny*. Dozens of people tried out for his next movie, *Dear God*, while seeking his autograph. Thirteen of these acting hopefuls actually got parts in the movie. What would have been their chances if they had waited for a casting call? Almost nil.

☐ Take people out to lunch. This past year, Gail Golomb of Four Geez Press took a medical librarian out to lunch to ask her to write a book review for a major special libraries newsletter. It worked.

Sell Your Books Door-to-Door

Don't laugh. Door-to-door selling can be one of the most effective ways to sell your books. People love to meet and talk with authors—and they love reading books by people they've met personally. Who wouldn't buy and cherish a personally autographed copy? Plus, you will learn so much about your readers by meeting them face to face.

☐ Gary Provost, self-publisher of *The Dorchester Gas Tank*, began his career this way. He'd take a suitcase of books to downtown Boston every day, settle down at some busy corner (around City Hall, the public library, a subway entrance, or plaza), and begin peddling his books to anyone who'd listen. He'd sell 20 to 25 books a day. That's more sales than most books make per day.

☐ Another author sold his novel, *A War Ends*, door to door. While knocking on doors one day, he met a reporter for a Los Angeles newspaper. The reporter was so taken by the author's approach to selling books that he featured him in a story. That story not only brought the author many local sales, but it also inspired a number of other feature stories nationwide, thus bringing more attention to the novel ... and more sales.

☐ Peter Gault sold 5,000 copies of his self-published novel, *Goldenrod*, by traveling across Canada setting up tables and selling books to anyone he met. At one point, he even sold books on the street in front of the offices of Canada's major newspapers. Not only did he get attention there, but he also received many reviews from major book critics. Later, while selling his books in front of Lincoln Center in New York, he met another writer, Richard Kalish, who bought his book, liked it, and introduced Gault to Martin Shepard of The Permanent Press. In the spring of 1988, he published a hardcover edition of Gault's book for the U.S. market.

☐ Dawn Hall, self-publisher of *Down Home Cookin' Without the Down Home Fat*, sold 18,000 copies within two months with the help of her family and friends. Within ten months she had sold 70,000 copies by loading her van with books and selling them to grocery stores, gift shops, health clubs, and other stores as well as through cooking demos, classes, and author appearances.

Do Radio/TV Interviews

In Chapter 9, I'll cover publicity in greater detail, but I do want to emphasize now how important it is for authors to be willing to tour, especially to do radio phone interviews and TV interviews. Don't worry if you start by doing phone interviews on small radio stations. If you do well there, you'll eventually work up to national radio and television.

☐ When Wayne Dyer first appeared on the scene with his book, *Your Erroneous Zones*, nobody knew him. So he bought up the first printing, put them in his car, and took off on a trip across the country. He went on every little radio show in every town he passed. Slowly but surely, his book began to sell. Now, of course, he is a best-selling author.

☐ To promote *Celebrate Today*, I advertised in *Radio/TV Interview Report*. From one ad, I booked 75 radio shows. My interviews, all done by phone, ranged from five-minute interviews on morning drive-time rock and country stations to hour-long in-depth interviews on news/talk radio stations. One time, when I couldn't make it back to my home in time for an interview, I had to call the station from a grocery store. The show was live, and in the background checkers were calling out for price checks. I did the half-hour interview while sitting on a grapefruit crate, but the show must go on. Remember: You can do a show from anywhere, under any conditions. So make yourself available for such interviews. They're fun!

8:08 Authors: Write, Write, Write

Write Articles

Besides selling first or second serial rights to your books (covered later in this book), you might also consider adapting chapters of your book or writing related articles for magazines. If you can sell these articles, all the better; but even if you don't, you should try to place articles in any magazine where readers might be interested in the topic of your book. Be sure to coordinate any such freelance writing with your publisher (who may already have approached the magazine about second serial rights).

Tom and Marilyn Ross did this for their *Encyclopedia of Self-Publishing*, selling short articles about self-publishing to such diverse magazines as *Southwest Airlines Magazine*, *Toastmaster Magazine*, *Pro-Comm Newsletter* and others. In each case, they insisted that the magazine include an endnote telling readers where they could order the book.

Write a Column

To gain greater visibility, write a regular column for an appropriate trade journal or newsletter.

☐ Before Lisa Shaw published *The Complete Country Business Guide*, she wrote a regular column profiling ski town entrepreneurs for *Snow Country* magazine. In return, the magazine printed a tag line naming her book and giving her 800 number. They also paid her to write the column.

☐ While networking at a trade association convention, Karen Adler met the publisher of *On the Grill* magazine. As a result, she became their regular book reviewer. Her column mentioned that she is the president of Pig Out Publications, the only company in the world specializing in distributing barbecue and grill cookbooks. It also listed her 800 number. She received calls from stores that sell outdoor grills, publishers of gift catalogs, and other retailers looking to do business with her.

Become a Letter Writer

If you want to get noticed, write letters. Write letters to the media, to bookstores, to previous customers, to anyone who might be interested in your book. For your first mailings, do it yourself. Get involved. Here is the advice of direct mail expert Gary Halbert:

> *You address those envelopes! Not your spouse, your kids, your secretary —you do it. And then, you go to your local post office and get 1,000 first-class postage stamps and you lick 'em and you stick 'em. Next, you sit down and, in one sitting, you write the best sales letter you can to those people.... And then, you sign all 1,000 letters and you fold them and you stuff them into the envelopes. Then you seal the envelopes and you take those letters to the post office.... There is something that hap-*

pens on a cellular level, something that indelibly imprints itself on your being, some kind of neural knowledge that can only be achieved by physically doing a mailing all by yourself.

Ask your publisher to provide brochures, flyers, bookmarks, or other printed material that you can mail out to prospects. Most publishers will be happy to provide such materials. One author slips a flyer or bookmark into every piece of outgoing mail, including bills. He swears it gets results.

☐ Each of the sixty-seven grandmothers featured in *From Grandma with Love* agreed to lobby their local newspapers for reviews or articles about the book. Their publisher, Alti, gave them media training, kits, and galleys to use in the promotion. As a result, dozens of reviews and articles appeared on Mother's Day in newspapers around the country.

☐ Paulette Cooper, author of *277 Secrets Your Dog Wants You to Know*, believes in sending out lots of review copies with great cover letters. She even sent a copy to Andy Rooney, who ended up doing a segment on writers who send him books he wouldn't read or mention on the air. Then, showing her book, he said, "I don't have time to read books with cute titles ... like *277 Secrets Your Dog Wants You to Know*."

Fax It

In addition to writing letters, you can fax notes to media and other key contacts. Faxes work. To solicit blurbs for her *Fast Cash for Kids*, Bonnie Drew faxed a request to a list of potential reviewers. While some responded with regrets, others were happy to do it, noting that no one had ever asked them before. From her top choices, Drew got with three great blurbs.

Email It

Nowadays email messages are even more pervasive than faxes. One plus for email is that messages go direct to the recipient, so you know that if you write a good header, your message might well get noticed.

When Nan McCarthy self-published her first romance novel *Chat* (written entirely in email format), she had a hard time getting her book into bookstores. But she noticed that another book released at the same time was stacked high in pyramids at every store. The book? *Dave Barry in Cyberspace*. So she wrote a note to the humorist in the style of Dave's newspaper column. He replied with a short note telling her not to give up. Well, she didn't. She sent her humorous note to a number of humor newsgroups where Barry's fans congregate. And they responded. Soon she had sold out of the 2,500 copies she had printed and signed on with a computer book publisher to print another 20,000 copies!

Write a Newsletter

Ask your publisher to help you develop a newsletter you can send out to your fan club, customer list, or other prospects. For example, many romance and mystery novelists have developed lists of fans to whom they send quarterly newsletters. Penguin helps Jan Karon, author of the *Mitford* novels, produce a *Mitford* newsletter that they send out to 6,000 fans.

Leave Parts of Yourself Behind

Besides carrying around a copy of your book, you should also carry extra copies of any promotional brochures, bookmarks, and news releases about your book. Give these away to people you meet. Leave some lying around the doctor's office, in the laundromat, on the bulletin board at your local grocery store, at the airport, and wherever else you go—especially places where other people have to wait and are, therefore, likely to be looking for some reading material to pass the time.

Nice looking bookmarks (printed with the title of your book, the publication date, the publisher, the retail price, your name and address, and an illustration from the book cover) have proven to be an effective way to keep an author's name before potential readers. Give these to people you meet during your daily activity. Bookmarks work especially well in casual social occasions where giving out a business card would be inappropriate.

If your books are stocked by your local retailers (and they should be!), print up some stickers or cards that point out that you are a local author. Ask the stores if they would mind if you placed these stickers on the copies of your books in stock. 90% of the stores will appreciate this bit of help.

Offer to autograph the books as well. That makes the books more valuable—and more likely to be bought. Again, provide a sticker or card that points out that these copies have been autographed. Note that bookstores cannot return books that have been autographed. Whenever I am in a different city, I always visit at least one bookstore. When I do, of course, I check to see if they have any copies of my books. If they do, I offer to autograph my books. When I did this at a large bookstore, they placed a band around the autographed copies that announced that the books were autographed—and then placed the books on a special table up front.

Give bookmarks, copies of the book's cover, or autographed copies of the book itself to the people at the cash register—or the person in the store most likely to have contact with potential buyers.

Above all, leave a good impression. Wherever you go, dress well, speak well, and act with good manners.

8:09 Authors: Work with Bookstores and Distributors

Bookstores and distributors are generally happy to work with local authors. As mentioned above, most will appreciate any copies you have time to autograph. But they also respond to visits from authors. As Pocket Books publisher Gina Centrello once noted, sending out authors to meet distributors and drivers "breeds good will, helps distribution levels, and restocks shelves. Any personal connection always helps." Indeed, some distributors actively pursue continued contact with authors.

☐ Not only was Jacqueline Susann a superb interview subject for TV shows, but she was also a tireless self-promoter, going so far as to get up at six in the morning just to meet the drivers for mass-market paperback jobbers and encourage them to place her books in the prime spots. And they responded to her personal attention. Wouldn't you?

☐ Ron Hickman, book buyer for Florida East Coast News, actively sought contact with authors. Not only did he attend the Florida Writers Conference, but he also invited authors to speak to his monthly sales meetings with the drivers. He even supplied copies of the book for the author to autograph. When Maggie Davis, author of the novel *Satin Doll*, spoke at one of these monthly meetings, sales of her book in that region were much greater than in areas where she had not spoken to the drivers.

☐ When you send promotional material to bookstores and wholesalers, send them a personal note as well. Such personal touches help to get your material to the top of the stack—and read! Indeed, Dan Berger, former book buyer for the Raleigh News Company, has said as much. He definitely pays more attention to writer's own promotional material, especially if it's newsy and interesting.

☐ As an author, you could publish a short promotional newsletter, which could be sent to major chain buyers, wholesalers, jobbers, and other buyers and opinion leaders. Keep them up to date on any new promotions, publicity, and sales that might encourage them to take a second look at your book. If you have a fan club, send your club newsletter to these buyers. That will save you from having to write two newsletters.

☐ To promote *The Love Book*, Robert Rosenheck visited eighty booksellers from North Carolina to Toronto, persuading them to "put it behind the counter or on a table. It just doesn't sell in the photo section." It worked. The book sold 50,000 copies during his tour.

☐ Millie Criswell, a romance author, is known as a sales dynamo. For her novel, *Wild Heather*, she and her husband visited 250 bookstores in the mid-Atlantic area. Partially as a result of her trips, the wholesaler Ingram sold out nationally. As her editor noted, "She'll do whatever the account wants, from sitting in the back room signing copies to meeting and greeting customers."

8:10 Authors: Do Whatever It Takes

Become an Expert

As a published author, you automatically become an expert in your book's subject. To become recognized, however, as an expert, you must also establish yourself as a reliable source of news or information. Hence, don't respond to a reporter's question if you don't know the answer. Admit the limits of your expertise if you want to become quoted as a reliable source.

As an author of a number of books about publishing, I am often called upon to consult with publishers and authors about book production and marketing. I help where I can, and when I don't know the answer I send them to people who can help them. In the same way, many editors and publishers have sent people my way because they knew I could answer the questions from their readers. I've received many book orders from these referrals.

Become a Joiner

Do anything you can to become visible. This means joining appropriate trade and social associations related to your topic (if you don't already belong). But don't just join; become active in the association's activities. If you were interested enough to write a book about the subject, you should be interested enough to become active in working with a related association.

To promote debut novelist Charlie Huston's *Six Bad Things*, Ballantine gave away sampler copies at the Edgar Awards banquet, at the Malice Domestic convention, and via mystery bookstores throughout the country. As an author, you need to let your publisher know what organizations are active in your field, especially ones where your target audience meets. This includes conventions, awards ceremonies, and bookstores.

Form Alliances with Other Authors

Besides joining organizations for writers, you should also work out arrangements with writers in other parts of the country to promote each other's work in your home areas.

- [ ] You can leave promotional material for each other wherever you go.
- [ ] When visiting bookstores and distributors, you can check to see if they stock not only your own books but also the books of the other authors with whom you are working.
- [ ] You could co-publish a newsletter that carries news and features about you and the other authors.
- [ ] And, if you go on tour, you can stay with your friends across the country (and they with you). That alone would make an author tour more cost-effective for your publisher.

Do It for Charity

While you doing promotions, do them for a charitable cause. Not only will this help you in getting publicity for your book, but at the same time you will be doing a good turn for the charitable cause by bringing publicity (and money) to it as well. Kathryn Leigh Scott sold her book, *My Scrapbook Memories of Dark Shadows*, to several PBS stations to use as a premium in their annual pledge drives. As part of the deal, she spent several days shooting generic spots for pledge drives across the country.

Set a Record

One way to get publicity for your book is to set a world record (a record that can somehow be related to your book). Note that you don't have to set a world record to gain publicity, you only have to attempt it. Actually, if you're not into setting world records, you could sponsor an attempt or announce a contest and prize for such an attempt—anything at all that associates you and your book with the world record.

Reverse Shoplift

When he travels, Greg Godek, author of *1001 Ways to Be Romantic*, places copies of his book in hotel gift shops and other retail locations. He sneaks copies on the shelves and leaves them there. If the stores sells the one copy, he knows they'll order more. Even if the store doesn't, Godek knows that every book he gets into the hands of someone will lead to more sales down the road.

Create a Web Site

Every author should have a web site for his or her books. Not only do such sites give fans an opportunity to get to know the author better, but they are also a great way to promote upcoming author appearances. We'll talk more about web sites in Chapter 12 on Internet marketing.

Change Your Name

A Canadian author named Zimmerman, author of *The Wealthy Paper Chasers*, changed his name to Cimmerman so his book would be shelved higher on the shelves (since most bookstores shelve books alphabetically by author name within each category). He also changed his name so his book would be placed near Dave Chilton's bestselling book, *The Wealthy Barber*.

Develop a Moniker

Create a sales handle that will get you noticed. It will help you get media attention, be memorable to radio listeners, and attract attention for your author appearances. Here are a few sales handles used by authors:

☐ George Roman, a psychic and book author, is known as the Beverly Hills Love Guru.

☐ Carolyn Wyman, a syndicated food columnist and author of *The Kitchen Sink Cookbook*, calls herself "the world's foremost authority on Spam."

☐ Dr. Kathy Levinson, author of *First Aid for Tantrums*, is known as the Tantrum Doctor.

Do Everything

If you have the time, you can be your own best salesperson. Sharon Scott is responsible for selling thousands of copies of two of her books, *Peer Pressure Reversal* and *How to Say No and Keep Your Friends*. Here are just a few of her activities that have helped to sell her books:

- She conducts in-service training programs for teachers, counselors, and parents.
- She speaks at many conferences, both national and international, for professionals working with youth.
- Through seminars and workshops, she has trained more than a million people in forty-one states and four foreign countries.
- She writes a *Positive Parenting* column which appears in many school newsletters.
- She is a frequent guest on local and national TV and radio shows.
- She has produced several videos based on her work.

Authors — Be careful not to overcommit yourself to the promotion of your books. Do what you can, but be sure to save time to write new books. That's what you do best.

8:11 The Value of Awards and Honors

When one of your authors or books wins an award, make sure everyone knows about it. Send out press releases. Prepare new brochures announcing the award. When reprinting the book, add the announcement to the cover of the book. Also, when publishing new books by the author, let people know that the author is an award-winning author.

Also, don't forget to submit your best designed books for consideration in many of the annual graphics or design competitions, such as the Boston Bookbuilder's and AIGA awards. These give added prestige to your company and will also result in many orders from libraries.

Some literary awards which have a major impact on sales include the following (obviously, not an all-inclusive list):

- [ ] American Book Awards
- [ ] American Booksellers Book of the Year (children's and adult trade)
- [ ] James Beard Book Awards (cookbooks)
- [ ] Benjamin Franklin Awards (small press titles, many awards)
- [ ] Caldecott Medal (illustrators of children's books)
- [ ] Golden Medallion (romance) and Golden Spur (westerns)
- [ ] Firecracker Alternative Book Awards (fiction, nonfiction, poetry, sex, politics, drugs, music, art/photo, graphic novel, kids, outstanding independent press, and my own wild idea for a category)
- [ ] Hugo and Nebula awards (science fiction and fantasy)

☐ Heartland Prizes (for a novel and a nonfiction book written from or about the midwest; sponsored by the *Chicago Tribune*)

☐ Lambda Literary Awards (gay/lesbian poetry, fiction, and anthologies)

☐ LAMMIE Awards (law books and other products)

☐ National Book Critics Circle Book Awards (biography, criticism, fiction, nonfiction, and poetry)

☐ National Book Awards

☐ Newbery Medal (authors of children's books)

☐ Nobel Prize (literature, medicine, physics, economics, chemistry, peace)

☐ Pen/Faulkner Award for Fiction

☐ Pulitzer Prize (biography, fiction, nonfiction, poetry)

☐ R. T. French Tastemaker Awards (cookbooks)

For additional book and author awards, check out *Literary Market Place* at your local library or online.

It has been estimated that the annual Hugo awards in science fiction are worth $50,000 to the winners in increased sales, higher advances and royalties, and greater subsidiary rights sales. Although the winners do not receive a cash award with the Hugo, they become instant celebrities within the genre and each subsequent book is heralded with the banner, "by the Hugo award-winning author." That banner alone sells thousands of extra books each year. Plus, the fact is that almost every Hugo novel is still in print.

William Kennedy's 1984 Pulitzer-winning book, *Ironweed*, sold more than 180,000 copies in trade paperback. If you'd like your books to be considered for the Pulitzer Prize, send four copies of each book, a photo of the author, a short bio of the author, and a $20.00 entry fee to the **Pulitzer Committee,** Graduate School of Journalism, 706 Journalism Hall, Columbia University, 116th Street and Broadway, New York, NY 10027; 212-854-3841. Even if your books don't win, a nomination can still boost sales. Only a few books are nominated for the award, and only one is selected. This weeding out process is one reason awards boost sales, because readers are then alerted to a book which has passed inspection more than once.

Awards can also help sell subsidiary rights.

Dick Lochte's *Sleeping Dog*, winner of the 1985 Nero Wolfe Award for Best Mystery Novel, was optioned for a movie and sold paperback rights. Similarly, the winner of the Jonathan Cape Young Writer's Award, Joseph Olshan, had his book *Clara's Heart* optioned by Warner Brothers for a movie, plus sold paperback rights.

Award winners often also receive money.

For example, winners of the Ernest Hemingway Award for first fiction receive $7,500, while winners of the Martha Albrand Award for first nonfiction receive $1,000. To submit books for these two awards, write to the

PEN American Center, 568 Broadway, New York, NY 10012; 212-334-1660; Fax: 212-334-2181.

Book awards sell books.

According to editor Nan Talese, "With so many books being published, prizes attest to the quality of the writing." Here are a few more examples of book sales resulting from awards:

☐ After winning the American Bookseller's Book of the Year award sales of Papier-Mâché's *When I Am an Old Woman I Shall Wear Purple* jumped from $300,000 per year to more than a million.

☐ Within three weeks after Cormac McCarthy's *All the Pretty Horses* won the National Book Award for fiction in 1992, Knopf had to go back to press twice—and the book was propelled onto the bestseller lists again for another twelve weeks. Nowadays, Barnes & Noble stores feature all the finalists for the National Book Awards and prominently display the winners once they are announced. More than 80% of all National Book Award winners since 1950 are still in print today.

☐ When Cheryl and Bill Jamison's *Smoke & Spice* won the James Beard Award, the phones at Harvard Common Press rang off the hook. Not only did bookstores and wholesalers call, but so do many major newspapers and magazines. To enter the James Beard Awards for cookbooks, contact the **James Beard Foundation**, 6 West 18th Street, 10th Floor, New York, NY 10011; 212-627-2090; Fax: 212-627-1064.

☐ When Czechoslovakian author Jaroslav Seifert won the 1983 Nobel Prize for Literature, the only English translation of his books published in the United States was a poetry book, *The Casting of Bells*, published by The Spirit That Moves Us Press. As a result, the small publisher was swamped with orders and had to return to press for another printing. Similarly, when Polish poet Wislawa Szymborska won the 1996 Nobel Prize for Literature, Harcourt Brace had to ship 17,500 more copies of his *View with a Grain of Sand*.

☐ Here are several examples where a nonliterary award had a great impact on the sales of a book. When Bishop Desmond Tutu won the 1984 Nobel Peace Prize, Eerdman's Publishing became swamped with orders for his book, *Hope and Suffering*. Again, when Bishop Carolos Felipe Ximenes Belo and Jose Ramos-Horta won the 1996 Nobel Peace Prize, Red Sea Press, publishers of Ramos-Horta's *Funu: The Unfinished Saga of East Timor*, had to rush through a second printing of 10,000 copies to meet the demand (after the first printing of 3,000 copies sold out).

Watch for other awards.

Watch for other awards that your authors might be eligible to win. Besides the Computer Press Awards, Parents' Choice Awards, Parent Council Awards, and Gavel Awards, here are a few awards they might qualify for:

☐ National Jewish Book Awards in these categories: Autobiography/Memoir, Children's Literature, Children's Picture Book, Contemporary Jewish Life, Fiction, Holocaust, Israel, Jewish History, Jewish Thought, Scholarship, Visual Arts, Yiddish Literature. For more information, write to **JWB Jewish Book Council**, 15 East 26th Street, New York, NY 10010; 212-532-4949.

☐ The Golden Rib Award for the best barbecue book is awarded each year by the Diddy-Wa-Diddy National Barbecue Sauce Contest. The 1988 award was won by Greg Johnson and Vince Staten for *Real Barbecue*.

☐ Nominations for the Firecracker Alternative Book Awards are done by readers who pick up ballots at their favorite bookstores. Ballots are also available at BookWire: http://www.bookwire.com/awards/firecracker.html. Check out this site for other awards as well.

Don't overlook other awards and honors.

Your authors or books could also win other honors not normally given to books. If such awards come your way, make sure to publicize them.

☐ *The Mathematics Calendar* by Theoni Pappas was selected as one of the "Top 100 Products of the Year" by editors of *Curriculum Product News*.

☐ The Hawaii Visitors Bureau selected M. J. Harden's *Magic Maui* as the best new guidebook in Hawaii.

☐ Joe Tanenbaum's *A Man in the Mood: Poems for Laughing, Loving and Living* won the Champion Imagination Award for its cover design.

☐ Jo Peddicord's *Look Like a Winner after 50* received a Silver Award in the National Mature Media Awards Program.

☐ The audio version of Papier-Mâché's *Grow Old Along with Me, the Best Is Yet to Be* was a Grammy nominee in the category of Spoken Word.

Authors — Help your publishers. Look for awards that might be appropriate for your book. While most book publishers are aware of the major literary awards, they are not generally aware of other awards that you or your book might be eligible to win. If you discover such awards, let your publisher know. You can search on the Internet, via your local library, or through your normal reading, especially of magazines that often give awards.

8:12 Sponsor an Award Yourself

One way to draw attention to your books is to sponsor award competitions which are in some way connected with your books. For example, if you were publishing a book on cooking with woks, you might sponsor a wok recipe contest. Using their books as prizes, a law book publisher established scholastic awards at various law schools. In another case, Addison-Wesley sponsored a national Best Teacher Award competition in connection with their book by Marty and Barbara Nemko, *How to Get Your Child a Private School Education in a Public School*. The award emphasized the value of committed teachers.

Another way to draw attention to new books while you are also soliciting new material from unpublished authors is to sponsor an award for an unpublished work of fiction or nonfiction. Viking instituted the Malcolm Cowley Prize for an unpublished work of fiction or nonfiction by an emerging American writer. The winner not only gets published by Viking, but they also receive $2,500 over and above whatever their contract specifies. Of course, when their book is published, Viking promotes the book as the winner of the Malcolm Cowley Prize.

8:13 Publishers: Encourage Interaction

Your authors can do much more than just a few media interviews and bookstore signings if you work with them and allow them to work with you. To get the most help from your authors, you should have a procedure in place by which your authors can interact not only with their editors but also with your marketing and public relations people.

This procedure should have some safeguards so your marketing people are not continuously bombarded with suggestions or wild phone calls from your authors. If you can set up such a procedure, you will find that your authors are quite willing to work more closely with you in the promotion of their books—and that this closer cooperation will lead to greater sales.

8:14 A Dramatic Example of Persistence

Here's an example of how an author, through persistence and a bit of luck, promoted her book onto major bestseller lists—a year after the book was given up as dead by her publisher! The book: *Callanetics*. The author: Callan Pinckney.

The book was launched by Morrow in September 1984 and, after a first round of publicity and 10,000 copies sold, went into a second printing of 5,000 copies. But there the book died. Because Pinckney was not a celebrity and because the book was competing against an exercise book by Victoria Principal, Morrow was not able to get more media interviews for Pinckney.

Pinckney continued to promote the book but with little effect until a fan in Chicago called her to ask if she would be coming to Chicago any time soon. Pinckney, of course, said she would be able to come if she could do a

TV show in the area. Well, the fan was determined to have Pinckney come so she arranged for the producers of *A. M. Chicago* to contact Pinckney.

Within hours of Pinckney's appearance on the show, Kroch's & Brentano's had taken 400 orders. That was in August, 1985. From there Pinckney went on to do more shows in other small cities, and each time she created another spurt of sales for her book. During this time she also personally called major book chains to let them know that Morrow still had books stored in their warehouse. She had to fight with Morrow to get them to put the books into the bookstores. After about three months of this activity, her book finally hit the bestseller lists (over a year after the book was published!) and remained on the lists for almost a year. The book went on to sell 250,000 copies and garner a $200,000 advance for paperback rights.

Weeks before the book's pub date, we sent out 3,000+ letters and postcards, at our own effort and expense. We got on the phone and called cookbook specialty stores to introduce ourselves, and asked whether they planned to carry our book. We offered to speak everywhere from bookstores to book fairs to adult education programs. We learned that autographed books sold better than non-autographed books, so once the book was published, we made it a habit to stop by bookstores during our business and pleasure travels to sign our books and chat with bookstore personnel. We sent copies of our book to our friends in the media (as well as their friends). We never let up. And, sure enough, things started to happen.

Our book's first printing of 7,500 copies sold out before its official pub date. Through our efforts, we landed an interview with Matt Lauer on The Today Show, while dozens of chefs cheered and waved whisks at the TV cameras outside NBC's Rockefeller Center studios! Within a couple of months, the book went into its fourth printing. By the end of the year, Borders cited Becoming a Chef as one of its top five bestselling cookbooks nationally for 1995. And in 1996, it was honored with the James Beard Book Award for Best Writing on Food. Even today, the book still gets its fair share of press—in publications ranging from Newsweek to Forbes!

Our publisher is not known for promoting its books via media tours, but when they saw how our efforts resulted in such unprecedented sales, they got behind us and sent us on a 20-city tour for our second book, Culinary Artistry. Published in November 1996 (and in bookstores for barely eight weeks), it was the company's bestselling book for 1996.

The moral of our story? No one is in a better position to sell a book than its author. Like it or not, your efforts as an author will largely determine your book's failure or success.

— Karen Page, co-author of *Becoming a Chef*

Making Radio Interviews Really Pay

by best-selling author Alex Carroll — www.RadioPublicity.com

I've been a guest on 1,264 radio shows over the past 10 years. I've rarely left home (most radio interviews are done by telephone), I've never spent a dime on advertising (radio interviews are free), and most importantly, I've grabbed over $1.5 Million in direct to listener book sales.

Let me share a few secrets with you...

☐ There are over 10,000 radio stations in America — most with only a handful of listeners. The 80/20 rule applies to radio like everything else. 20% of the stations reach 80% of the listeners. Wanna sell lots of books? Focus on the big shows.

☐ Many people assume that a station with lots of wattage (50,000-100,000 watts) has lots of listeners. Often wrong. Many high wattage stations are in LOW population areas with FEW listeners. Many low wattage stations are in high population areas with millions of listeners. Example: KBOI in Boise has 10 times the wattage of KABC in Los Angeles. But KABC has 10 times as many listeners.

☐ Many people assume that stations in big markets (cities) have lots of listeners. Again, often wrong. Example: WKXW in Trenton (Market #138) has 8 times as many listeners as KKLA in Los Angeles (Market #2).

☐ Bottom line, you want the shows with the most listeners. I have the only database of top radio shows based on actual listener numbers. All have at least 100,000 listeners. Wanna sell lots of books? Use my database.

☐ Some people will tell you that sending out a fax or e-mail blast is the best way to get booked on radio shows. Not anymore. Ask yourself this: Do you like reading your junk faxes and spam? Neither do radio producers ... especially the big ones. At best, this method may get you a few calls from a few little stations.

☐ The best way to get booked on big radio shows? CALL them. Why? Because they're in radio and they want to hear what you SOUND like! If somebody else is calling for you (employee, PR firm, etc.), be sure you have some interview sound clips on your website.

☐ After speaking to a big radio producer, you need to follow up by sending them a press kit that pitches your SHOW idea. Most people send them press kits and news releases that pitch a STORY. Big mistake. Stories are great for magazines and newspapers ... they're in the story business. But radio people are in show business. They want to know how you will entertain and educate their audience.

☐ There are 5 times as many radio listeners at 7:30 am as there are at 9 am. Why? People commuting to work. Tip: Pitching a morning show? Ask for an interview slot between 7:30-8:30 am. Afternoon show? 5:15-6:30 pm is the slot to get.

☐ Send thank you letters after each interview. Offer to be an emergency fill-in guest. Ask them to post favorable listings on bulletin boards like Bit-board or Radio Online. These member-only boards are read daily by thousands of radio people and have generated hundreds of extra interviews for me.

Visit **http://www.RadioPublicity.com** for a **free** list of the *Top 20 Nationally Syndicated Radio Shows*. Resources available include: Database of the top 1,364 radio shows (100,000+ listeners only); Sample press kit: "How to pitch a show instead of a story;" Audio course: "How to pitch radio producers" (listen to actual phone calls Alex made while booking 77 interviews). This is an incredibly valuable training tool for PR firms, publishers and authors.

How to Get Celebrity Endorsements and Testimonials for Your Books

by Jordan McAuley of Contact Any Celebrity

Getting a celebrity, notable VIP, or leader in your field to give your book a short testimonial or endorsement (sometimes called a *blurb*) is a great way to boost sales and garner extra publicity. Remember that this is a trade-off. You get a testimonial for your book, and the endorser gets additional exposure and/or credibility. Below is the six-step process we teach authors and writers:

1) Choose potential endorsers based on your book's subject.

If your book is about animals, for example, target celebrities and/or notable VIPs who have a vested personal interest in animals. If it's about a disease, target people who have suffered personally from it or who contribute to the disease's cause. If it's about kayaking, target people who like to kayak.

2) Ask potential endorsers to write your book's introduction or foreword.

This technique can work really well as long as you remember: flattery is key. Don't ask for an endorsement at this stage. Instead, flatter the person by saying that because of his or her expertise on the book's subject, you'd like to ask him or her to write the introduction or foreword. You may want to point out that this is a great opportunity for the endorser to get some additional exposure. When the book is published you can mention "Introduction by (Celebrity's Name)" or "Foreword by (Celebrity's Name)" on the cover.

3) Gather a list of names and contact information.

The reference area of your local public library is a good start, but you can find more accurate information online. Search Google for "celebrity contacts" or "celebrity addresses for a list of resources. If the celebrity has an official Web site, you can usually find his or her contact information there as well. Don't forget personal and professional connections. Take some time to sit down and brainstorm all the people you know who could put in a good word for you or at least pass along your request.

4) Make it as easy as possible to get a response.

Your request should include a draft of your book, a self-addressed, pre-paid FedEx or Priority Mail envelope, an easy-to-fill out testimonial form, and a personalized letter from you. If you're nervous about sending a draft of the book, you can also include a Confidentiality Letter. You may also even want to mention that the better the testimonial, the more likely it will appear in your book (and possibly on the cover) resulting added exposure for the endorser.

5) Point out the benefits of giving an endorsement.

Potential endorsers usually won't mind (and will even appreciate) the free publicity, additional exposure, and added credibility their blurb will provide when it's featured in (and maybe on) your book. Let the endorser know you'll mention his or her name and company under the testimonial as an added benefit of giving you an endorsement.

6) Follow up.

Send a follow-up letter or an email to the people you asked for an endorsement after a few weeks have gone by if you haven't heard anything after a few weeks. Know that getting a good endorsement or testimonial can take time. Celebrities and VIPs are busy, and their mail is often screened by an assistant or representative which can delay your request getting to them.

Always remember the 3 Ps for getting celebrity testimonials and endorsements for your books: be Persistent, be Polite, and be Positive.

Jordan McAuley is the President and CEO of **Contact Any Celebrity**, a research firm located in Los Angeles whose online database provides accurate contact information for over 54,000 celebrities and public figures. For more information on how to get celebrity testimonials and endorsements for your books, visit *http://www.ContactAnyCelebrity.com*.

Chapter 9

Tips on Publicizing Your Books

Ask others for advice. We interviewed more than 100 successful authors, including Barbara De Angelis, Harvey Mackay, Wayne Dyer, and Betty Eadie, and asked them what it took to be successful. The bottom line is that 90% of what it takes to succeed is publicity, marketing, and promoting.
— Jack Canfield and Mark Victor Hansen, *Chicken Soup for the Soul*

There is an old definition of publicity that still applies today as it did years ago: Publicity is doing good, and then telling the world about it. Here, then, is the essence of getting good publicity: 1) Produce a good book, and 2) Let people know about it. It really is that simple. But both steps do require patience, persistence, and attention to detail.

Publicity is not free. You must pay your dues. If you're going to invest your time and money in promotions, make sure much of it is committed to your publicity efforts. Remember: Publicity does sell books, more books than any other means of promotion.

9:01 The Three Basics of Gaining Publicity

The three basics of gaining publicity are:

1) **You must create real news about your book**, something worth publicizing. A book with solid content and style will help immensely in fulfilling this first requirement. A highly promotable author also helps.

2) **You must locate and cultivate the appropriate media contacts.** For help in locating targeted media contacts, refer to the national media directories or check out John Kremer's Book Marketing MBA Program at http://www.BookAcceleration.com.

3) **You must be persistent**; you must follow through. Ron Gold, author of *The Personal Computer Publicity Book*, asserted that the three most important PR jobs are: 1) follow-up calls, 2) follow-up letters, and 3) follow-up calls. In other words, you must be persistent. Any PR professional will say the same thing: Persistence pays. If you knock on enough doors enough times, you are bound to get through.

9:02 Dealing with the Major Book Reviewers

Of all book review media, there are about fifteen that are most important for establishing your books as critical and commercial successes right from the beginning. These include the review magazines for booksellers (*Publishers Weekly* and *Kirkus Reviews*), the major library review media (*Library Journal, School Library Journal, Booklist, Choice,* and *Horn Book*), and the book review sections of the large city newspapers (*New York Times Book Review, Washington Post Book World,* and *USA Today*). In addition, major publications such as *Time, Newsweek, U.S. News & World Report, Wall Street Journal, Entertainment Weekly,* and *People* can have a major impact.

Of course, not all would be appropriate for every book you publish since *Choice* only reviews books appropriate for college and high school libraries, *Horn Book* only reviews children's books, and *School Library Journal* only reviews books that might be acquired by school libraries.

Below are guidelines for getting your books reviewed by some of the major review media (note that the following names and addresses are subject to change and updated addresses can be located at the BookMarket web site at http://www.bookmarket.com/9.html):

☐ **Publishers Weekly**—Published weekly as a trade magazine for booksellers, librarians, and publishers, this magazine reviews about 5,000 books per year. They review almost any sort of book except reference books. Send galley copies at least three to four months before publication date to PW Forecasts, *Publishers Weekly*, 360 Park Avenue South, 13th Floor, New York, NY 10010-1710; 646-746-6400; Fax: 646-746-6631. Web: http://www.publishersweekly.com.

Here are a few of the other ways you could get into *PW*: My Say editorial, letters to the editor, news items, rights sales, spring and fall announcements, regional publishing news, and roundup articles. For details on the other ways that you can get into *Publishers Weekly*, see the BookMarket web site at http://www.bookmarket.com/pw.html.

☐ **Kirkus Reviews**—Published biweekly as a prepublication review for booksellers, libraries, agents and publishers, this newsletter reviews 80 to 100 books per issue, about 2,500 per year. They review almost any fiction or nonfiction book, except poetry, mass-market paperbacks, and picture books for toddlers. Because they are a prepublication review service and run reviews at least two months prior to publication date, they like to see galley copies at least three to four months in advance. The editors are Eric Liebetrau, adult titles and Karen Breen, children's books. Send galley copies and catalogs to *Kirkus Reviews*, VNU US Literary Group, 770 Broadway, New York, NY 10003-9595; 646-654-4602; Fax: 646-654-4706. Email: kirkusrev@kirkusreviews. com. Web: http://www.kirkusreviews.com. Submission guidelines: http://www.kirkusreviews.com/kirkusreviews/about_us/submission.jsp.

☐ **Booklist**—Published biweekly by the American Library Association, this magazine reviews about 4,000 books per year. They review almost any book of interest to the patrons of a public library, including fiction, nonfiction, children's, young adult,, and reference. Send two copies of the actual books or galley copies as soon as they are available. A review in *Booklist* constitutes a recommendation for library purchase.

Brad Hooper is the book review editor of adult books, Hazel Rochman of young adult books, Ilene Cooper of children's books, and Mary Ellen Quinn of reference books. Write to *Booklist*, American Library Association, 50 E. Huron Street, Chicago, IL 60611-2729; 312-944-6780; Fax: 312-337-6787. Web: http:// www.ala.org/booklist. For details, write for a copy of their *Procedures for Submitting Review Materials to Booklist* and *Booklist Selection Policy* (this information is also on their web site).

☐ **Library Journal**—Published monthly for public librarians, this magazine reviews about 6,000 books per year. They will review almost any book that is appropriate for a general public library, but no textbooks, children's books, or very technical or specialized books.

Send the finished book or galley copy four months before publication date to Barbara Hoffert, Book Review Editor, *Library Journal*, 360 Park Avenue South, 13th Floor, New York, NY 10010-1710; 646-746-6400; Fax: 646-746-6734. Email: ljquery@reedbusiness.com. Web: http://www.libraryjournal.com. Submission guidelines at http://www.ljdigital.com/about/submission.asp.

☐ **School Library Journal**—Published ten times a year, *SLJ* reviews 2,500 books per year. They will review any book appropriate for school library use. They do not review books after publication date. They also do not review textbooks, parenting titles, or books for teachers.

Send two galley copies or F&Gs (folded and gathered signatures) to Trevelyn Jones, Book Review Editor, *School Library Journal*, 360 Park Avenue South, 13th Floor, New York, NY 10010-1710; 646-746-6400; Fax: 646-746-6689. Email: slj@reedbusiness.com. Web: http://www.slj.com. Also send the following bibliographic information: author, title, binding(s), price(s), publication month and year, ISBN(s), and Library of Congress number or CIP info.

☐ **Horn Book Magazine**—Published bimonthly for anyone interested in children's literature, this magazine reviews about 400 children's and young adult books per year. Send two finished books or galley copies to Roger Sutton, Editor, *Horn Book Magazine*, 56 Roland Street #200, Boston, MA 02129; 617-628-0225; 800-325-1170, ext. 4; Fax: 617-628-0882. Email: magazine@hbook.com. For submissions information, go to: http://www.hbook.com/booksubmissions.html.

☐ **Choice**—Published eleven times a year by the Association of College and Research Libraries, this magazine reviews over 7,000 books per year (out of 20,000 they receive). They will review any books appropriate for college undergraduate libraries, but no books on law, pop psychology, medicine, travel, or children's topics. They review only from finished books. They have many subject editors, but send finished books to Book Review Editor, *Choice*, 100 Riverview Center, Middletown, CT 06457; 860-347-6933; Fax: 860-346-8586. Email: submissions@ala-choice.org. Web: http://www.ala.org/acrl/choice.

☐ **New York Times Book Review**—Published every week as part of the *New York Times* Sunday edition, this review does about 3,000 book reviews each year. They do not review how-to books (cookbooks, diet books, etc.) except at Christmas time. They prefer that you send galleys as soon as available and then send books when printed. The best times to send them books for review are in time for January, February, July, or August reviews. Sam Tanenhaus is editor of the *Book Review*; Eden Lipson is children's book editor. Send review copies to the *New York Times Book Review*, 229 West 43rd Street, New York, NY 10036; 212-556-7366; Fax: 212-556-3830. Web: http://www.nytimes.com/books.

☐ **Washington Post Book World**—Published weekly as part of the Sunday *Post*, this supplement reviews about 2,000 books per year. They review general fiction and nonfiction books. Send review copies to Marie Arana, Editor, *Washington Post Book World*, 1150 15th Street N.W., Washington, DC 20071; 202-334-6000; Fax: 202-334-7502. Web: http:// www.washingtonpost.com. For book review details on other major city newspapers, see http://www.bookmarket.com/newspapers.html.

☐ **USA Today**—Published five times a week, this national newspaper reviews fiction and nonfiction. They also review books in their sports, money, and life sections. Books are also featured in news stories and other regular features. Send review copies to Carol Memmott, Book Editor, *USA Today*, 7950 Jones Branch Drive, McLean, VA 22107-0020; 703-854-3400; Fax: 703-854-2053. Web: http://www.usatoday.com. For details on other ways that you can get into *USA Today*, see the BookMarket web site at http://www.bookmarket.com/usatoday.html.

☐ **Wall Street Journal**—This weekday national business newspaper reviews at least one book every day. Send review copies to Erick Eichman, Taste Editor, *Wall Street Journal*, 200 Liberty Street, New York, NY 10281; 212-416-2487. Web: http://www.wsj. com.

☐ **New York Review of Books**—Published biweekly for the general public, this tabloid reviews about 1,000 nonfiction books per year. They not only review books but also use excerpts and buy serial rights. Send review copies to Robert B. Silvers or Barbara Epstein, Editors, *New York Review of Books*, 1755 Broadway, 5th Floor, New York, NY 10019; 212-757-8070; Fax: 212-333-5374. Web: http://www.nybooks.com.

☐ **Voice Literary Supplement**—This monthly supplement of the *Village Voice* newspaper reviews all types of books but with a special focus on literary fiction. Send review copies to Joy Press, Editor, *Voice Literary Supplement*, 36 Cooper Square, New York, NY 10003-4846; 212-475-3300; Fax: 212-475-8473. Email: editor@villagevoice.com. Web: http://www.villagevoice.com.

As you may have noticed, one of the most important things to do if you want reviews from these major review media is to send books as early as possible—preferably four months in advance of the book's publication date. Send galley copies if finished books are not yet available at that time; then send the finished books when they do become available.

If you have any questions about their review policies, don't hesitate to call the magazines and ask. All the book review editors I've ever talked with have been willing to answer questions and make suggestions. When you call, also ask for their editorial calendar.

Authors — Make it a habit to read a few of these major review media every week. Not only will this reading help you to keep up on new trends in publishing and book marketing, but it will also help you to target publishers who are most likely to be interested in publishing your new titles.

9:03 Don't Overlook Special Interest Review Media

Besides the major book review media listed on the previous pages, you should also mail review copies to the book review sections of other major newspapers and magazines. Finally, you should also send review copies to any special interest review media. You can find a list of special interest book review media at http://www.bookmarket.com/9.html. Additional listings are included in the Kremer 100 program at BookAcceleration.com.

Besides sending review copies to the book sections of major newspapers and magazines, you should also be sending review copies or news releases to other general and special interest magazines. To locate those media, check out the directories at http://www.bookmarket.com/directories.html.

> **Authors** — Many of these special interest review media may not be known by your publisher, especially if your publisher does not normally publish books in that subject area. Hence, you can help your publisher by scouting out these review media as well as other special interest magazines that might be open to reviewing your books or interviewing you.

9:04 The Importance of Book Reviews

Book reviews are critically important to any book that is targeted at a general audience. No publisher can afford to advertise in all the newspapers and magazines which reach a wide audience, so the only major way to reach the most people with the least money is to obtain reviews, interviews, or other notices in newspapers and magazines. Almost any general trade publisher who relies on bookstore sales will tell you that reviews are a key factor in generating word-of-mouth and, hence, sales.

- Mexican writer Carlos Fuentes books all received critical acclaim. However, in almost every case the reviews came too late to have a great impact on book sales. When his novel *The Old Gringo* received top billing in almost every major book review supplement, the book hit the *New York Times* bestseller list within six weeks of publication.

- When the *New York Times Book Review* reviewed Michael Rogan's *Ronald Reagan, the Movie*, the University of California Press received calls from wholesalers the very next day. They took orders for 500 copies.

- Karen Friedman and Evonne Weinhaus sold 20,000 copies of their self-published book, *Stop Struggling with Your Teen*, after positive reviews in *Family Circle* and *Woman's Day*, plus author appearances on the *Today Show*, *Hour Magazine*, and *Sally Jesse Raphael*.

- Barbara Harris sold more than a million copies of her self-published book, *Let's Cook Microwave*, without paying one cent for advertising. The sales were all the result of publicity and word of mouth.

- When *Parade* magazine featured Vic Spadaccini's *The Home Owner's Journal*, he received 1,710 orders in the first week, another 1,210 orders the second week, and more than 5,400 orders over the next six months.

- Allan Bloom's *The Closing of the American Mind*, quickly rose to the top of the bestseller lists on the strength of reviews, beginning with a favorable review by the *New York Times Book Review* and followed by other favorable reviews in major newspapers across the country.

- If you can't get a review, get a notice or an article about the book. *Family Circle* featured Harold Moe's book, *How to Make Your Paycheck*

Last, in a third-page article. As a result of that one free blurb, Harsand Press sold more than 180,000 copies of the book (out of a total 400,000 copies sold). **Note:** A follow-up display advertisement in the same magazine brought in only six orders.

- Even one review can sometimes make a difference. Hugh Nissenson's book about Johnny Appleseed, *The Tree of Life*, stayed alive only because of a favorable review in *Time* magazine.

- Reviews may not always carry a book to the top of the bestseller lists, but sometimes they can make the difference in keeping a book in print. For example, Noam Chomsky's first book for South End Press, *After the Cataclysm*, sold few copies until an impassioned review appeared in the *Village Voice*. Only then did bookstores begin to feature the book.

- Enthusiastic reviews convinced Little, Brown to crank up an ad campaign for William Least Heat Moon's *Blue Highways*. Before the reviews, the only effort the publisher had made was to get an excerpt in *The Atlantic Monthly*.

- Local or regional reviews can help boost a book to the bestseller lists just as easily as national reviews. In 1990, Barry Lopez's *Crow and Weasel* made the *New York Times* bestseller list without a single review east of the Mississippi.

- Besides sales, there is one other major benefit of publicity: You can attract better authors. The reason Tama Janowitz, author of *Slaves of New York*, signed with Crown was because they offered her a real commitment to building up her public image.

9:05 How to Get Reviews: Rule #1

Send out review copies. Send out lots of them. Send out more than you think you should. Hit every major magazine which you think might be at all interested in the subject of your book. In most cases this means sending out somewhere between 200 and 500 review copies.

For other possibilities on your media list (that is, those media which are not prime prospects for reviewing your book), send a news release, brochure, and reply card offering a review copy upon request. Then send them a review copy if they request one.

Here are several examples of the impact of giving away sufficient (even abundant) review copies:

- When Epson came out with their first dot matrix printer, they sent 500 printers to the major opinion makers in the computer industry. They did not say, "Use this printer for 90 days and then send it back." No, instead they said, "It's yours. Keep it. Use it any way you want. Enjoy." As a result, by the time other dot matrix printers got their promotional campaigns underway, Epson had already established itself as the standard among the movers and shakers in the industry. So, of course, when these people wrote about computer printers, they naturally talked about Epson —simply because that was the printer they used. Note, however, that this giveaway policy would not have worked if Epson had not produced a solid, reliable printer. Similarly, sending out review copies will not help you unless your book is actually worthy of review.

- A major literary agent for some of the best-known cookbook authors says that one of the most effective ways to promote cookbooks is to send out plenty of review copies to anyone involved with food—from newspaper and magazine food editors to teachers at cooking schools and owners of gourmet cooking shops. The word-of-mouth these people create is worth any amount of regular advertising.

Budget 5% to 10% of your first printing as giveaways—for reviewers, booksellers, and key opinion makers. The majority of these review copies should be given away in the first four months or, better yet, months before your book's publication date.

9:06 How to Get Reviews: More Tips

Here are some general tips on how to go about getting reviews for your books. Use those tips which make the most sense to you within your own procedures for sending out review copies.

☐ Don't just send review copies to book review editors. In many cases, especially with cookbooks and how-to books, you'd be better off sending your books to the food or lifestyle editors. Indeed, many book review supplements at major newspapers do not review how-to books or cookbooks except around Christmas time or other special occasions. So, watch for other opportunities for reviews: newsletter editors, specialty shop owners, in-house magazines, trade magazines, freelance writers, and other authors writing books in the same subject area.

☐ Some magazines and newspapers have special sections or theme issues where they review certain types of books. For example, *Scientific American* does an annual review of science books for children in their December issue. Similarly, the *New York Times Book Review* only reviews cookbooks and how-to books at Christmas time. Other sections of the *Times*, of course, feature such books at other times of the year.

For the editorial schedules of magazines, refer to **Bacon's Media Alerts**, 332 S. Michigan Avenue #900, Chicago, IL 60604-4301; 312-922-2400; 800-972-9252; Fax: 312-922-3127. Web: *http://www.baconsinfo.com*. This directory lists the editorial calendars, profiles, and lead times of 1,100 magazines and 200 daily newspapers.

☐ Send advanced galley copies to major reviewers. *Galley copies* are copies of your book which are photocopied or printed and then bound ahead of time so you can send them out three to four months in advance of publication. These galley copies are often prepared even before you've checked all typos or done an index. Be sure to print the title, author, publication date, ISBN number, and price on the cover (which can be a plain brown or blue cover without illustrations or color print).

There are several ways you can create galley copies.

1. Go to a galley or on-demand book printer. For a short list, see *http://www.bookmarket.com/9.html#galley*. Such printers can print and bind as few as ten copies or as many as several thousand. Most jobs can be done in a week or ten days.

2. Have several hundred copies of the first print run of your books overprinted with the heading, "Advance Reading Copy — Not for Sale" on the cover. Use these copies as review copies. The disadvantage of this method is that you won't have galleys until you've printed your book.

3. Alternatively, you could print labels that provide the same information and attach them to the outside of the cover or the inside front cover of finished books. This is the cheapest alternative but, again, it means you won't have galleys to send out in advance of printing.

4. For short runs of ten or less, you can create them yourself using your laser printer or copier. Print back-to-back or print one side only and then bind the copies using comb-binding or glue binding (which many print shops or office supply stores can do for you).

☐ The basic information every reviewer needs to have at hand when reviewing a book includes the following:

1. title of book (including the subtitle)
2. author or authors of book
3. publication date
4. ISBN number
5. whether the book is available in both hardcover and softcover
6. the prices of available editions
7. the name and address of the publisher

☐ Send a cover letter with the book. This may not be read by all editors (and may well be thrown out when the receiving clerk unwraps the book), but it is indispensable for media which do have a policy of saving such enclosures. The letter should contain the following data:

1. the basic facts about the book (what does the book do?)
2. the significance of the book (what benefits does it offer?)
3. the intended audience (who will the book help?)
4. a short biography of the author (how is the author qualified?)
5. a list of the author's previous books

The first three points of the cover letter should provide a quick summary of why readers would be interested in the book. The last two points clarify the author's credentials and background.

- [ ] If the author has been published before, be sure to indicate that. Reviewers are more likely to review a book by an author who has already had several books published. Why? Because an author who has been published before has demonstrated that he or she can write books that people will be interested in reading.

- [ ] For special reviewers, write a personal letter to accompany the review copy. You might also have the author autograph the review copy. Some book reviewers will notice these little touches, and some will even appreciate the extra attention. At least one reviewer has pointed out, "You get my attention by sending letters addressed by hand. I don't open letters addressed by machine."

- [ ] Hand deliver review copies where practical.

- [ ] Clean up your list of reviewers so you are not sending multiple copies to the same reviewer. In an article in *Publishers Weekly*, on book editor castigated publishers for wasting her time by sending out duplicate copies of books. One publisher actually sent her six copies of a novel!

- [ ] Send catalogs announcing new titles as soon as possible. Pat Holt, the former book editor for the *San Francisco Chronicle*, recommends sending catalogs six months in advance.

    To promote its catalog, *Brainstorms* sent a copy along with a sticker pasted to its front cover that announced: "THIS IS MY PRESS RELEASE." The sticker encouraged radio and TV producers to call Marshall Cordell, president of *Brainstorms*, for an interview on zany gift ideas for the holidays. Stations were offered on-air samples, gift certificates, and catalogs to give to their audiences. The sticker also featured a list of the Top 10 Brainstorms Holiday Favorites, which included chocolate brain treats, alien embryo kits, toilet paper hats, and Eat Your Face gelatin molds.

- [ ] If your book is by a local author or on a hot topic, enclose a handwritten note emphasizing that. Or highlight something unique about the author. Seattle firefighter Earl Emerson got lots of off-the-book-page attention for his books because of his job. Of course, it helped that his novels feature fire chief Mac Fontana (*The Dead Horse Paint Company*) and Seattle private eye Thomas Black (*Deception Pass*).

- [ ] Do something special to draw attention to your book—to put your book at the top of the pile of review copies. Several producers at top TV shows have admitted in public that they liked little gifts and practical items in the press kits sent to them.

    To publicize his mystery novel, *First and Ten*, Douglas Anderson sent out trading cards featuring his lead character Santa Arkwright, a fictional free safety for the Buffalo Bills.

    Peter McWilliams, author of *T'aint Nobody's Biz-Ness If I Do*, sent out a music CD featuring various artists singing that song. Among those featured were Bessie Smith, Fats Waller, The Ink Spots, and Billie Holiday.

When Crown published Elizabeth Alston's *Muffins* cookbook, they accompanied review copies with a basket of homemade muffins.

Bantam packaged the review copy of Jonathan Kellerman's novel, *The Butcher's Theater*, with a letter opener piercing the cover of the book.

☐ Above all, follow up. Every review copy you send out should be followed up by a phone call or a handwritten note. When you call, simply ask if they received the review copy and whether they need any further information or would like to talk to the author?

The more I talk to those publishers who have been successful getting reviews and features, the more I'm convinced of the value of follow-up calls. According to many publishers, it is common to discover that the media did not receive the review copy, or they received it but can't find it, or any of a hundred different variations on these themes.

Most media do appreciate the follow-up call, and most do respond either by asking for a review copy, by putting the review copy they received higher up on their pile of things to do, or by passing the book on to an editor who will be able to use it in a news or feature story.

A friend of Jeff Stein's agent had been promising a review of his book, *A Murder in Wartime*, in *Time* magazine for months. Finally, as Jeff put it, "I just called up the correspondent at *Time* who covered military/national security stuff, told him about the book, and sent him a copy. He read it over the weekend and loved it. It took his own constant advocacy and pressure inside the magazine to get his review published two months later." The result? A glowing full-page review calling Stein's book, "the best military morality tale since *The Caine Mutiny*."

> **Authors** — Cooperate with your publisher. Volunteer to help by autographing copies of the book, writing personalized letters to major reviewers, hand addressing envelopes, and doing anything else that you can do to increase your chances for reviews. Above all, be sure to provide your publishers with enough information about you as a person so they can write a great author biography that will attract the attention of reviewers and other media contacts. Better yet, write a great bio yourself.

9:07 Any Review Is a Good Review

Don't worry about the kind of reviews your books receive. Any review is a good review, whether the reviewer liked the book or not. Even a bad review helps to bring attention to the book and to fix the book's title in the minds of readers. Many readers will buy a book despite a bad review—if for no other reason than to prove the reviewer wrong. Others buy out of curiosity. Still others buy because they remember reading about the book but do not remember whether the review was good, bad, or indifferent.

- *The One Minute Manager* by Spencer Johnson and Kenneth Blanchard did not receive good reviews from most critics. Nonetheless, readers loved it. So, although good reviews can help put a book on the bestseller lists, they are not absolutely necessary.

- The critics' reaction to Harvey Mackay's bestseller, *Swim with the Sharks Without Being Eaten*, was at best lukewarm. *Fortune*'s reviewer called it "a bunch of platitudes dressed up in see-through anecdotes." Another reviewer, struggling for something good to say, called the book's observations "short." Nonetheless, *Swim with the Sharks* went on to sell millions of copies.

- When quoting from a negative review, use the good parts. Most reviews have at least one or two phrases you can pull out to quote. If the review was so bad you can't find even one phrase, then simply say "as reviewed in the *Washington Post*" or, better yet, "find out why *Vogue* hated this book." Controversy always sells.

- If a reviewer clearly misunderstood or misrepresented your book, then write a letter to the editor. Point out where the reviewer went wrong. This gives you double exposure in that print media!

9:08 What to Do after the Reviews

To make your book review program really effective, you must follow up your efforts. Here are a few suggestions on how to make the most of your book's reviews:

☐ Write a thank you note to the reviewer. Moreover, if you have gotten a good response from the review, let the reviewer know what the response was. All review media are interested in what their readers respond to, and if your book received a good response and you let them know about that response, they will be more likely to review similar books in the future (if your list is specialized, those books will be yours).

☐ If your books are hardcover, print a limited number of book jackets in the beginning. Then, when the reviews start coming in, print additional dust jackets featuring the best reviews. This procedure is more costly than printing all the jackets at once, but if the reviews are good, the extra expense could well be worth it.

☐ Make copies of the best reviews and include them with news releases and review copies you send out after the first big wave of publicity. These reviews will help to convince later reviewers that the book is important, worthy of review, and of interest to their readers. When making copies of reviews, underline the most favorable and important comments.

Also, be sure to include a tag line identifying the name of the periodical and the date the review appeared.

☐ Also send copies of major reviews to your key bookselling contacts (your sales reps, distributors, chain stores, wholesalers, book clubs, foreign rights buyers, periodicals that buy second serial rights, etc.). Keep these key contacts informed of your book's publicity.

☐ Send copies of reviews to the author. Not only does this notify the author that you are promoting the book, but it also provides important feedback which the author can use in revising the book (or writing a new book which covers material left out of the current book). The reviews might also cause the author to think of other media or promotions.

☐ You can also feature copies of reviews in the bounceback offers you send to direct mail customers.

☐ Quote the best reviews in all your continuing advertisements, brochures, catalogs, and other promotional materials.

☐ When you quote reviews, give credit to the actual reviewer as well as the publication (say John Doe of the *Twin City Times* instead of quoting the *Times* alone). Reviewers remember those authors and publishers who remember them. Knopf and Dutton are two publishers who regularly credit the reviewers in their catalog copy and promotional literature.

☐ When you get a large response from a review, consider advertising in that magazine or newspaper. Obviously, if readers were interested in the book as a result of a review, other readers will probably order the book if they see another notice of the book. Be cautious, however, on your advertising outlays. Remember the results Harsand Press received with their display ad in *Family Circle*: only six copies.

After receiving a good response to a favorable review in *Entrepreneur's*, Wilshire continued to advertise *How to Get Rich in Mail Order* every month for the next year. Their ads continued to produce superb results.

☐ Advertise in a periodical after a review rather than in the same issue as the review. That way, if the review is favorable, you can quote from the review in your ad. Plus the repeated exposure of the book in the periodical will produce better results than two exposures (one ad and one review) in the same issue. These quoted reviews are especially effective when advertising in the library review magazines.

☐ If you are doing an extensive publicity campaign, subscribe to a press clipping service to keep tabs on all features that appear in print media. Note that few media will automatically send you copies of their reviews. The only way you will know about these reviews is to subscribe to a clipping service. You cannot count on reader inquiries and orders to alert you to all reviews and features that appear, and you certainly cannot expect readers to send you copies of the reviews when they order. For a list of clipping services, see http://www.bookmarket.com/9.html#cs.

☐ Keep copies of all reviews in your files, along with copies of any other promotions. Each book should have its own file.

☐ Also place a copy of the review in your media file for that particular newspaper or magazine. If you don't already have a media file, you should begin one. The file should include a record of that publication's name, address, phone number, book reviewer, other important contacts (editors, producers, etc.), subjects they review, and other notes. File a copy of every review, notice, feature, or other publicity which that publication prints about your company or your books. With new computer programs, you can keep these files on your computer for easy access.

☐ Finally, if you really want to establish rapport with the media, follow a few of the guidelines (or, at least, avoid the mistakes) that Roberta Plutzik, former Lifestyle Editor for *The Record*, once pointed out:

To prepare for a round-up of children's titles, I called a dozen publishers to request information and review copies. Most seemed not to know our paper, which has been around for 100 years, is located 10 miles from Manhattan and, on Sundays, reaches 700,000 people.

Upon publication, two copies of our section were sent to each publicist. Not one followed up, either in a gesture of appreciation or to suggest concrete ways to continue the relationship. Only one, a small press, placed us on their mailing list.

Recently, when we began planning a summer reading round-up on kid's books, we had to call every publisher all over again. In the days leading up to closing this section, publicists were conscientious about quickly sending books out. But only one, representing a small press, followed up to make sure we'd gotten the material and had the information we needed. I suggest that children's book promoters take the offense for a change by updating their contact lists and getting to know potential markets. There is life beyond the New York Times.

Publishers should begin to practice what all good salespeople must in a competitive world: outreach. We may not all have the space and time to review children's books on a regular basis, but we may respond to the well-crafted idea for thematic round-ups, profiles of engaging authors and illustrators, and trend stories.

9:09 How to Write a News Release

When sending out review copies or when soliciting requests for review copies, you should also send a news release. Often a news release is all you need to send to generate effective publicity. Indeed, Open Horizons has often had better results in sending a simple news release than in sending an entire media kit and/or review copy. Here are a few guidelines I use in writing news releases. They have worked for me, again and again.

☐ Hold the news release to one page. If you require two pages, edit more vigorously. In my experience, every news release that crosses my desk could have been edited to one page—and been more effective.

☐ If you simply cannot cut any information, try to excerpt part of the news release and put it into a separate background release or author bio. Too many news releases contain details which detract from the main news story rather than add to it.

☐ Focus on the news or benefit value of the book, not its contents. Books are not news. If you want editors to read your news release, provide answers (that is, benefits).

☐ Focus on one main benefit or idea. When writing a news release, keep it as simple as possible.

☐ Avoid making judgments about your own book, unless you are quoting someone. Such statements as, "a must reference resource," or "the new standard in the field," or "the most complete directory," are out of line.

☐ Use quotes. Memorable quotes from the author or another expert help to jazz up a news release and make it more personal. They also make a release look like a regular news story. People like to read about people. That's why reporters look for people to interview as part of any story.

☐ Quotes allow you to make strong points that would be out of place in a straight news story. Here's a quote I used in news releases for the *Directory of Book Printers*: "It doesn't matter where you are located. With this new edition you can find a quality book printer who specializes in the quantities, sizes, and bindings you want to use—at a price you can afford." The quote, from me as the author, summarized the main benefits.

Here's an even better quote that was effective in getting media attention: "Without the *Directory* I paid $12,500 for the first printing of one book—and I got plenty of production hassles. With the *Directory* I paid $4,500 for the identical job—and no problems!"

To promote *Angel Talk* by Ruth Crystal, Edin Books used *call-outs* (centered quotes) to highlight the best quotes from the author. For example, when the author described how it felt during an angelic encounter, she said, "It's like 5,000 grandmothers hugging you all at once." Now, that's vivid and memorable. I'm sure many media picked up on it right away.

☐ Top the news release off with a great headline. You want to write a headline that will grab the attention of the editor as well as the readers. Keep it short and keep it punchy.

Compare the first headline below, written by Stephanie Gallagher, author of *Money Secrets the Pros Don't Want You to Know*, with the second one sent out by her publisher. I prefer the first headline. It's stronger.

How to Spend Too Much Money on Everything
vs.
AMACOM Money Secrets Put Readers on Path to Financial Wealth

☐ The news release should read like a standard news story. It should answer the questions: Who? What? Where? When? Why?

☐ Use the inverted pyramid style of news stories. Start with the most important news or feature, then the supporting news, and end with the least important information. Note: Most newspapers, when they edit, start by cutting from the bottom of the news release.

☐ Even given the above information, place your ordering information in the last paragraph. Make it easy for the media and their audience to find how to get in touch with you. Include your 800 order line or web site. Many media still consider giving out an 800 number or web site as a service to their audience while giving out an address is advertising. Most media do not like to appear as if they are providing free advertising.

☐ Speak the language of the intended audience. If you have a book that appeals to a number of different audiences, print up special press releases focusing on the benefits of the book for each audience.

For example, for the *Directory of Book Printers*, we sent one news release to magazines for writers and publishers, another release to business magazines, and still another to association and club magazines. For media which seemed to fit no particular category but whose readers would still be interested in the *Directory*, we sent a personal letter to the editor outlining the benefits of the *Directory* for his or her readers. We did this for school journalism newsletters and genealogy magazines.

☐ Keep your news release up to date. To promote their new book, *The Entrepreneur's Road Map to Business Success*, Saxtons River Publications began a news release with a specific tie-in to another news event: "Two weeks into the new decade, the Pentagon announced it would eliminate 42,000 jobs." Such specific details are far more likely to attract the attention of an editor than a plain book announcement.

☐ For important editors, attach a personal note to the news release. Use a Post-It note or write on the news release itself.

☐ According to one newspaper editor, the glitzy press kits are the first to hit the trash. The news releases with a handwritten note tend to get read. A trade magazine editor has also noted, "I'd rather see a well-written release any day than all the fancy packaging on Madison Avenue."

☐ Start with an enticing lead that brings the editors and, ultimately, the readers into your story. For their book, *Canned Art: Clip Art for the Macintosh*, Peachpit Press wrote one of the best lead questions I've ever come across. Wouldn't you love to know the answer? Isn't it obvious?

QUESTION: What weighs 5 pounds and has 51 hands, 3 nuns, 3 hypodermic needles, 8 hourglasses, 1 Ayatollah, 12 quill pens, 3 flying squirrels, 11 skeletons, 3 Kewpie dolls, 1 recycling symbol, 180 Teddy bears, 5 windsurfers, 1 pot o' gold, 1 Pee Wee Herman, 17 butterflies, and more—all wonderfully organized and intelligently indexed?

Below is a great example of a lead sentence for a news release, this one written by Shel Horowitz for a client.

First paragraph:

"It's 10 O'clock. Do you know where your credit history is? How about your employment records? Your confidential medical information?"

Second paragraph:

"How would you feel if you found out this sensitive and should-be-private material is vacationing in computer databanks around the world—accessible to corporate interests who can afford to track down and purchase it, but not necessarily open to your own inspection?"

John's Comments: The first paragraph is great. It plays off an old line about knowing where your children are—which only makes knowing where your credit history is just that more vital.

The second paragraph is one long sentence. If I were writing it, I'd probably rewrite that sentence into two or even three sentences. But the points it makes are still important. Any media reporter would pick up this news release and know that there is something important that the author has to say.

☐ With newspapers, emphasize the local angle (if one exists).

☐ Here's an option: Instead of a standard news release, have someone write a feature article about the book or author. Send that out to your key contacts. If it's good, some publications might well print it as is.

☐ Here are a couple of other ways to spice up your news release:

Glamorize your subject—For instance, for a book on country inns, what famous people stayed at the inns featured in the book?

Stand out from the pack—Is your book the most complete? Then point it out in an unusual way: "Weighs over three pounds!"

Take the road less traveled—Take a different angle on the subject. Don't copycat other publishers' promotions.

Write an anecdote—In 25 words or less, what can you tell others about the book? Is there a story behind the book, something interesting about the author, a story in the book that can be excerpted? Tell a story. People love stories.

Localize the story—Slant the news story to a local angle. People like to read about themselves and their home towns. For my book, *Tinseltowns, U.S.A.*, we added a line at the end of each news release: "Your city, Minneapolis [or whatever], is featured on page 73!" That line got the book many local features.

Tie-in to other events or stories—See section 9:22 for many ways to tie your book into other events or stories.

☐ Be sure to top off the news release with your contact information. Print the name of the person to contact for more information. Be sure to include the contact's phone numbers (night and day) and email address. And if you provide more background material on the book or author on your web site, include the exact web site address for this information.

One note from Paul Hartunian, author of the home study course, *How to Get $1 Million Worth of Publicity...Free!*: "The one and only purpose of a press release is to get the media person to read it and contact you for more information. A press release is not supposed to be printed or broadcasted word for word. If it is, you did a bad job of writing the release."

> **Note:** For actual samples of news releases and other press kit material that have worked for other publishers and authors, see *The Do-It-Yourself Book Publicity Kit* by John Kremer. This $30.00 kit features great pitch letters, background releases, feature sidebars, and news release rewrites. The *Kit* is available exclusively from Open Horizons at BookMarket.com.

9:10 Added Touches

To improve the reception of your news release, supply the media with added material that will help them create a story their audience will heed. Here are a few examples of things that you could add to make your news release more acceptable.

☐ **Press kits**—Also known as media kits, press kits package a news release and review copy with many of the other items listed on the following pages. When you add more items to the kit, fold them so they create a staircase effect in the pocket of the kit folder. When folded properly, the top of each sheet placed in the kit should stand out and it should be easy for the editor or producer to pull out the sheets that interest them.

To publicize her *Easy Halloween Costumes for Children*, Leila Albala put together a dramatic press kit: press release, catchy cover letter, bio, photos, copies of previous articles featuring her books, and the book itself—all inside an orange folder with a color snapshot of Halloween costumes glued to the front. That media kit worked. Her book was featured in major Canadian newspapers as well as many American newspapers.

Carol DeChant, a Chicago publicist, prepares press kits with different covers to match different regions and markets. Thus, while the insides might be the same, the covers customize the press kit and make it immediately stand out in different markets.

☐ **Pitch letter**—A pitch letter (also known as a cover letter) should be personalized for the target media. It should plant a potential story idea in the editor's mind. Or a special angle on the news for that publication. Sign the letter. Make it as personal as possible. Use bulleted points to highlight the key ideas you are presenting. Don't tell everything; leave them asking for more. Keep it short. One page is best.

In her cover letter to several columnists, one author wrote, "I live with my parents in Brooklyn. We are very poor but we are honest and good and gossip-minded." That personal note got the columnists' attention.

When she realized that Houghton Mifflin, the publisher of her first novel, *Mama*, was not planning any special publicity, Terry McMillan personally sent out 3,000 letters to booksellers and reviewers.

As an alternative to a cover letter, you or your author could write a personalized note. When David Triemert sent me a review copy of *Getting Approved: Making the American Credit System Work for You*, he added a Post-It note to the book cover. It read: "John, I've yet to meet a publisher or promoter who has a plentiful supply of startup, operating, or expansion capital to work with. Here's a way you can help them through the almost inevitable cash crunch." That note got him a notice in the *Book Marketing Update* newsletter. If he hadn't written the note, I'd never have made the connection between his book and my readers.

☐ **Author biographies**—Always include a biography of your author. Spice it up with interesting tidbits about the author. Humanize the author. What incidents or experiences led the author to write the book? Again, people like to read about people.

When I sent out media kits for *Celebrate Today*, I emphasized taking the day off, so I wrote about my four gardens: vegetable, flower, herb, and berries. On the other hand, for *Turntable Illusions*, I made the assertion that I had the world's largest collection of optical illusions. No one has ever disputed that claim, including the one person I know who might well have more than I do. You, too, can make such claims—if you dare!

☐ **Photos**—As the publisher of *Time* magazine noted in one of his letters to readers, "As is often the case, eye-catching photography was crucial to the choice of subject. The strength of a picture will often make or break an item. ... We want the usual subjects doing unusual things."

Romantic Times includes a note in many issues asking authors to send their own photos: "New authors—be up-to-date and send professional publicity photos and introduce yourself."

People magazine is not interested in *things*; they are people-driven. Hence, when you pitch them, you need to pitch the author as an interesting person. And be sure to provide them with strong visual ideas. Without good photo opportunities, *People* won't do a story.

In some cases, you might want to send a photograph alone in place of the news release. Remember: A picture can be worth a 1,000 words. Just send a captioned photo. If you try this, make sure that: 1) The photo tells a story. 2) The caption is catchy. 3) The media uses photos.

> **Authors** — Have a professional publicity photograph taken of you. Make sure your publisher has a print, and keep several on hand for sending out with your personal press releases. Photographs can add that personal touch that makes the difference on whether a press release is noticed or tossed out.

☐ **Clip sheets**—In place of or in addition to a photo, you could send a clip sheet of reproducible artwork of different sizes to fit varied column widths and lengths. The artwork could consist of logos, book covers, illustrations from the book, or other camera-ready art related to the subject of the book. Clip sheets, like photos, have two distinct advantages: 1) Visuals add to the attractiveness of a news release and make it more likely that people will notice it—and editors will feature it. 2) Features that use artwork or photos tend to take up more space in the publication. The more space, the more attention.

☐ **Brochures or other promotional material**—Richard J. Oddo sent out bookmarks that featured illustrations and quoted excerpts from his book, *Within a Miraculous Realm*. I probably would not have opened the review copy except I was so taken with the bookmark that I ended up reading the entire book.

☐ **Background releases**—If the book is technical or about a relatively new subject, you might want to add a background sheet that describes the history of the subject or how the book is tied into current events. Background releases can be used effectively to flesh out a one-page news release and fill in background information that a reporter would need to write a feature article. The background release might even include information that is not in the book.

☐ **Fact sheet**—A fact sheet states the basic facts about the book (title, author, publisher, number of pages, size, ISBN number, publication date, binding, and price). To convince an editor to open the book, it might also offer some enticing tidbits from the book.

For Leonard Mogul's *Making It in the Media Professions*, Kate Bandos of Globe Pequot Press prepared a wonderful fact sheet full of intriguing tidbits from the book, such as the origin of magazines and the birth of cable television. What editor could resist such tidbits? This fact sheet makes superb use of details from the book. To find the complete details, you have to read the book!

To promote a new edition of *The Macintosh Bible*, Peachpit Press included a 25-inch long, 4-inch wide fact sheet that listed excerpts from 57 rave reviews. The back side reproduced comments from previous readers. Two people called it outstanding! Nine people said it was terrific! Twenty-nine rated it excellent! Eighty-four called it great! Five readers said it was very good! One person wrote that it was "very, very, very, very, very, very, very, very good!" One reader said the book was "almost as good as sex." Another wrote that it was "as good as sex." Another that it was "better than sex." And yet another that "perhaps it will replace sex (I said, *perhaps*)." Have you been using your reader comments as effectively as you could? As effectively as Peachpit Press?

Joe Devine of Green Stone Publications had great success with a special fact sheet, the *Human Costs of Literary Creation Finally Revealed*, which took a humorous look at the costs of writing a book. As he wrote, "The release garnered 19 reviews in magazines and newspapers, 9 radio shows (as well as on-air plugs on two other stations), 4 reprintings (including a feature in *Writer's Digest*, with pictures and all), and a 290% increase in sales. I compute that the reprints generated over 250,000 splashes and *Writer's Digest* even paid me for printing the release!"

☐ **Q&A sheet**—When soliciting interviews, include a question-and-answer sheet that features some of the best questions that might come up about the book, the author, or the subject. Make the questions provocative, intriguing, even unanswerable. Leave them wanting to know the answers, or refer them to the pages in the book where they can find the answers.

☐ **Review copy of the book**—For all major media, enclose a review copy of the book with the media kit. When Axelrod Publishing sent out review copies of *Eat to Your Heart's Content* by Dr. Kent Corral, they had the author autograph those copies. A nice touch!

☐ **Excerpts from the book**—If you do not send a copy of the book, then add a page or set of pages excerpted from the book. To enhance her news releases, Jane Hoffman sends out sample experiments from her book, *The Original Backyard Scientist*. She gives permission to reprint the experiments with any review or feature article about her book.

☐ **Blads**—As an alternative to sending a complete review copy, you could send a blad. What is a *blad*? It is an excerpt from the book printed as a booklet. It features the cover of the book with "Advanced Book Information" and the book's publication date and specifications stripped in. Inside the cover, place the flap copy, a table of contents and sample pages. Even if the book isn't completely written, you can send out excerpt blads six months or more before pub date. Blads are especially appropriate for expensive full-color books—because you can give editors and book buyers a taste of the book at a fraction of what it would cost to mail out actual copies. If they are seriously interested in reviewing the book, they will call for finished review copies.

☐ **Copies of previous articles**—If the book or author has been featured in previous reviews or articles, enclose copies of a few of the most important ones—those from major media, those that feature the book in an effective way, or those that are visually attractive.

☐ **Testimonials**—Once you've received a number of testimonials, blurbs, or reviews, include them on a separate sheet. I often do a double-sided sheet with one side featuring what reviewers have written about my book and the other side featuring what people are saying about the book. These testimonials help to add credibility to the rest of the media kit.

☐ **Catalogs**—At the beginning of each season, Running Press mails new catalogs to 300 or 400 book and feature editors at magazines, newspapers, and broadcast media. They always included a checklist of titles so the editors and producers could simply check off those new and backlist titles they would like to see. This procedure is especially effective for their children's titles. Also, many TV producers used the catalogs to find books that fit show themes they were thinking about using.

☐ **Reply card**—Many companies now include a reply card or form to allow editors to request a review copy, further information, or an interview with the author. To promote its book about Santa Barbara, Pacific Travellers Press enclosed a postpaid return postcard with their news releases. Besides offering to send a review copy of the book, they also made the following offer: "If you ever plan to do an article on Santa Barbara, we have a lot of data available on a PC floppy disk that you would be free to use in return for a mention of our book." Now, of course, you could offer access to this data on your web site.

☐ **Envelope**—Don't neglect the envelope when you send out a news release or media kit. Remember: It's the first thing anyone sees. When I sent out news releases for one of the earlier editions of *Celebrate Today*, I enclosed them in a laser-printed envelope that included the editor's name and address (no label required) and the following headline: "Name the 2006 dates for these events: Mother-in-Law Day, Birthday of the Singing Telegram, National Smile Week, and Good Nutrition Month."

☐ **Rolodex cards**—Sending a Rolodex card makes it easy for reporters and producers to file you in their Rolodex system. On the tab of the Rolodex card, include your topic, not the title of your book. For *Three Strikes and You're Out* by Mike Reynolds and Bill Jones, Quill Driver Books sent out a Rolodex card headlined Crime/Anti-Crime to make it easy for producers to locate the phone numbers of the two authors.

☐ **Other supporting material**—Enclose other items that support the news release. For example, if your book is about making home DVDs, prepare a DVD of bits from home videos and enclose it with the news release.

For Steve Hagen's *How the World Can Be the Way It Is*, Quest sent a banana squash to major reviewers. Why? Because in the book, Hagen describes seeing an odd looking vegetable in a shop. At first, when he found out it was a banana squash, his curiosity was satisfied. But later he realized that knowing its name did little to help him understand what it was. By sending the banana squash, Quest highlighted a major message of the book: seeing things as they really are (past the words we have for things). The response of the media to the banana squash and the book was overwhelmingly positive.

To promote Stephen Frey's novel of Wall Street skullduggery, *The Takeover*, Signet sent a bar of gold bullion and a roll of coins (actually a bar of chocolate wrapped in gold foil and a role of Life Savers).

For Eileen Goudge's novel *Trail of Secrets* that features a mounted policeman, Viking Penguin enclosed a police whistle, a genuine NYPD T-shirt, and an audiotape featuring interviews with real mounted police.

When ICS Press promoted *The Politics of Auto Insurance Reform* to media and major buyers, they always enclosed a bumper sticker with any news release, review copy, or brochure. The bumper sticker read: "Hit Me—I Need the Money!" An attention getter if I've ever seen one. The front of the bumper sticker also featured the title of the book, the author's name, and ICS Press's 800 number. The back of the sticker reproduced the three best paragraphs from the news release for the book.

For most small publishers, it doesn't make sense to send out a complete media kit to every media. Be very selective. Media kits are most important when approaching broadcast media. In most cases with print media, you will be better served simply sending a news release. I have had great success with one-page news releases—and nothing else! Short and sweet and to the point. Many editors prefer that.

Sometimes, however, I also enclose a testimonial sheet or background info. Other times, I'll send a selected sampler from the book (one sheet, sometimes printed on both sides). I am selective on what I send, depending on the book and the purpose of the news release.

If you are in doubt about what to include, test several packages. For instance, you can mail a simple news release to fifty media and a news release accompanied with several other items to fifty other media. Then wait and see which mailing produces the best results.

> **Authors** — Provide your publishers with any material that will help enhance their press kit: photos, copies of previous features about you, a good bio, and whatever else is suitable.

9:11 29 Ways to Break into the Media

My experience, and that of many independent publishers, is that it is far easier and more effective to get news and feature write-ups than it is to get reviews. How effective can features be? Here are a few examples:

- In 1989 *USA Today* featured Gregory Stock's *The Book of Questions* in a week-long series on the front page of the Life Section. That same week, Workman had to go back to press for another printing of 25,000 copies. The book went on to sell more than 550,000 copies in its first year.

  Peter Workman, also publisher of *The Silver Palate Cookbook* (which has sold millions of copies), believes that newspaper features are the best way to promote a cookbook. People try the recipes, then buy the book and, if the book is good, then word of mouth does the rest.

- When Abigail van Buren mentioned Jim Trelease's *The Read-Aloud Handbook* in her Dear Abby column, sales of that book were boosted to more than 200,000 copies.

So, how do you get your books featured in newspapers and magazines? Here are 29 ways you can break into print. These are not listed in any particular order of priority.

1. Work with local columnists.

Every newspaper in the country, from the largest to the smallest, has at least one reporter whose duty it is to cover local people and events. Many of these columnists feature products and services offered by local individuals and companies. These general interest columnists work hard to find interesting stories. Provide them with a good story and they will be happy to write about you. Pat Holt, former book review editor at the *San Francisco Chronicle*, once suggested that local columnist might be the best way to get your book or author noticed in major newspapers.

As I've traveled across the country, I've seen books mentioned in Herb Caen's column for the *San Francisco Chronicle* (before he passed away) and in David Cataneo's Hot Stove sports column for the *Boston Herald*.

> **Authors** — Help your publishers. You know your local newspaper and its columnists better than your publisher or, at least, you should. Write a personal, localized note to the columnist you think would be most interested in your book. Hand deliver it if you have time. Or, better yet, if you have the gumption, invite your local columnist to lunch.

2. Work with specialized columnists.

Many local newspapers also have specialized columnists such as Lee Svitak Dean's Tidbits column for the Taste Section of the *Minneapolis Star Tribune*, or Pat Gardner's Tender Years column for the same paper. In one case, Dean featured *Uncle Gene's Bread Book for Kids* in his Tidbits column and even printed the price of the book and the address of the press— Happiness Press of Montgomery, New York.

Most newspapers have columnists who cover travel, gardening, careers, business people, companies, housing, automobiles, food, restaurants, music, movies, and more. Take time for at least one week to read your local newspaper every day and make note of those columnists who you think might be interested in what you are doing. Then put them into your contact database under media. As you travel, read the local newspapers and add specialized columnists from other cities to your contact database.

If your newspaper doesn't have a columnist covering your area of interest. Volunteer to be a freelance columnist for them. For example, many large newspapers have Realtors who write regular features in their Sunday home section. When it comes time for a reader to contact someone to help them sell their house, who do you think they will call?

3. Work with syndicated columnists.

There are about 1,500 nationally syndicated columnists who write about everything from home decorating and repairs to advice about relationships, from real estate to entertainment, from business to child care. Almost all of them mention books at one time or another.

Here are the names of just a few of the many nationally syndicated columnists: Dale Dauten and Mark Nelson, *Job Talk*; Peggy Gisler and Marge Eberts, *Dear Teacher*; Ralph and Terry Kovel, *Antiques & Collecting*; Andy Pargh, *Gadget Guru*; Jan Collins Stucker, *Flying Solo* (for divorced people); and Chuck Shepherd, *News of the Wierd*.

For a copy of *Editor & Publisher*'s annual Syndicate Directory featuring 3,000 columns, call 888-612-7095. **Editor & Publisher**, 11 West 19th Street, New York, NY 10011-4234. Email: edpub@mediainfo.com. Web: http://www.mediainfo.com. The cost is only $8.50.

- *Dr. Gott*, a syndicated medical column by Peter Gott, M.D., recommended Jack Yetiv's self-published book, *Popular Nutritional Practices: A Scientific Appraisal* in answer to the following question from a reader: "I am confused about diet, weight loss, vitamin supplements, and the relation of diet to disease. Is there any up-to-date book on these subjects." Yetiv's book would not have received this superb commendation if he had not sent a copy to Dr. Gott.

- After Jane Brody featured *Kicking Your Stress Habits* in her column on personal health, Whole Person Press sold more than 100,000 copies of the book by mail order.

Authors: Why not have your family and friends from other parts of the country write into a column recommending your book as a resource that helped them out? Or ask the columnist a question that your book answers so well.

4. Self-syndicate your own column.

You can syndicate your own column to newspapers, magazines, or news-letters. Much of the column's content could be taken from your book. Or the column could form the basis for a new book!

- Jeffrey Lant, author of many books, wrote a business self-help column that he syndicated to 500 small business and opportunity publications. His column had a readership of more than two million. He also syndicated his columns via e-mail distribution to key prospects.

- To promote her series of *Backyard Scientist* books, Jane Hoffman regularly sends out articles adapted from the books to a large number of home schooling newsletters and other interested media. Many of these newsletters use her columns. Of course, each article ends with information on how the reader may order the books.

- JoAnna Lund, author of the bestselling *Healthy Exchanges* cookbooks, syndicated her food column to fifty monthly newspapers. She offered the column to the newspapers for free. Her only requirement was that the paper must send her a copy each month so she can make sure that they are including her address and toll-free number so readers can get in touch with her. She reports that "It's been working great for over three years now. We get orders every week because of it."

Authors — Don'twait for your publisher to arrange syndication. You can do it yourself. Find out which magazines or newspapers your target audience reads, write a column that would appeal to those publications, and send out a series of columns (start with three or four). Enclose a short note letting the editors know that they can use the material for free as long as they include your tag line (which provides your name, book title, address, phone number, and ordering information).

---

5. Set up your own press syndicate or information bureau.

To establish your company as a source of information related to your specialties, establish a press syndicate. Such a syndicate does not need to be complicated. It could be comprised of a simple monthly mailing of news story ideas, feature articles, and other items.

- Reebok, manufacturers of athletic shoes, sends out many of their background information releases under the auspices of their Reebok Aerobic Information Bureau. The Associated Press featured one of their releases about a study conducted by USC researchers that showed that exercising improves problem-solving abilities, concentration, and short-term memory. What a way to sell shoes! Why not books as well?

- Zondervan, a major publisher of religious books, has formed the Zondervan Press Syndicate, a free monthly feature service sent to interested newspaper and magazine editors. Each monthly mailing includes story ideas and camera-ready articles. Among the items they send regularly are feature articles, Q&A articles, word puzzles, book excerpts, cartoons, author columns, guest editorials, opinion articles, biographies, and special days of the month material.

  Zondervan also mails out a monthly newsletter, *Producer's Report*, which features interview ideas for radio and TV producers. They also formed the Zondervan Radio Network that mails out free audio cassettes to 350 radio stations. The tapes feature various lengths of recorded material, from 30-second news segments to 23-minute author interviews.

6. Volunteer to be an expert.

Let the media know that your authors are available as experts. Send them an author bio and a background news release about the author's latest book. Later, follow up with copies of other articles that feature the author (attach a For Your Information note to any follow-up copies). You might also publish a regular newsletter that you can send to all your media contacts. The key point is to keep your authors' names continually in front of the media. Don't expect an immediate response. You won't always get one. Sooner or later, though, if you have matched your author's expertise to the media's needs, some will contact you to speak to your author.

- Every week *USA Today* features a special department, Ask Money, where they invite readers to ask questions which are, in turn, answered by leading experts around the country. Do you have any authors who are qualified to answer such questions? If so, let the Money editors at *USA Today* know how to get in touch with your authors.

- *USA Today* often uses experts. In an article describing a survey on sex, they interviewed about ten authors, including Judith Sills, Maggie Scarf, Maxine Rock, Paul Pearsall, and David Viscott.

- The *Minneapolis Star Tribune* has a Fixit column, which answers readers' questions about consumer problems, from insurance to real estate. Sometimes they turn to authors to answer questions from their readers.

- *Playboy* mailed out packs of Rolodex cards to important media contacts. Each card in the pack was categorized by subject of expertise at the top and included the name of a *Playboy* editor or regular contributor as an expert. Addresses and phone numbers were also listed. Experts were provided in the areas of art, sports, music, movies, photography, books, fashion, travel, and sex. Perhaps, you could send out a pack of Rolodex file cards featuring your authors as experts.

- Many companies and associations advertise in the *Columbia Journalism Review* or *Editor & Publisher* to announce their availability as resources for interviews or background information.

- Berrett-Koehler Publishers offers a *Resource Directory of Leading Experts and Speakers*, which features seventy-eight of their authors who can speak on artistry and humor, career development, creativity, diversity, global sustainability, human resources management, leadership, organizational change, performance improvement, quality, sales & marketing, strategic change, teamwork, and visions and values. They promote the *Directory* in their catalogs as well as through press releases. It has been a major help in booking their authors as speakers and interviewees.

> **Authors** — Don't wait for your publisher to volunteer you as an expert. Do it yourself. Just keep your name before the editors of those newspapers or magazines where you would like to be featured as an authority. Send notes or other items at least once every two months.

7. Establish your company as a prime source.

State Farm Insurance prepared *A Reference Notebook of Insurance Sources* listing 200 organizations that could provide information on insurance topics (top insurance companies, trade associations, arson associations, and research groups). They then placed ads in major journalism publications (*Editor & Publisher*, *Quill*, *Columbia Journalism Review*, and *American Journalism Review*) inviting the media to send for a free copy of the report. Of course, State Farm was listed prominently as a source in the report. But, more important, the fact that they were able to compile such a report clearly suggests that they are the best source for information on insurance issues.

In another ad in major journalism publications, State Farm headlined with a question: "Need Information about Insurance?" The bottom of the ad announced, "Next time you have a question about personal insurance, call one of these numbers." They then listed five different phone numbers, one each for questions on auto, home, boat, health, and life insurance.

If you publish a series of books on the same subject, you can have a member of your staff prepare a similar *Reference Notebook* for that subject area. Or you can ask your authors to do it for their subject areas. And then send the report out to important media contacts. You don't have to push the media. Keep it low key. They'll appreciate the information without you having to convince them.

> **Authors** — As an authority, you should be able to establish yourself as a prime source. It shouldn't take a lot of work since you've undoubtedly done of a lot of the research already while writing your book.

8. Create your own speakers bureau.

One way to make your authors more available for speaking engagements with associations, groups, and businesses is to form your own speakers bureau. You can fund the bureau with your commissions from paid speaking engagements for your authors. Matthew Bender, a legal publisher, formed a speakers bureau for their authors. Not only do they book their authors for seminars and conferences, but they also book them for media interviews.

9. Sponsor a poll.

Conduct a survey related to one of your books. Then announce the results. Indeed, many books are nothing more than a summary and comment upon a survey (such as *The Hite Report*).

- Gallup did a poll for *Talk to Win*, a book by speech therapist Lillian Glass. The results of that poll were featured in many news stories.

- *USA Today* runs a short visual graphic—based on some poll or survey—on the front page every day.

10. Sponsor a contest.

One effective way to get publicity is to sponsor a contest. You can even charge a small fee for entering the contest. How about a muffin-baking contest to promote a new cookbook? Or "your most romantic moment contest" to promote a romance novel or a book on relationships. Or the best photo of the Grand Canyon for an Arizona travel book?

- The Coriolis Group, Eastman Kodak, and Borders Books & Music co-sponsored a national Digital Camera Giveaway contest to promote Coriolis's publication of *Digital Camera Companion*. The winner, chosen from all entry forms gathered at Borders stores, was given a new Kodak digital camera.

- In their quarterly *Llewellyn New Times* newsletter, Llewellyn sponsored a book review contest. They invited readers to submit a 750 to 1,000 word review of any Llewellyn title. Winners received a $20 gift certificate good towards any Llewellyn book.

- To promote the paperback edition of Terry McMillan's *How Stella Got Her Groove Back*, Signet ran a consumer contest asking readers to tell how they "got their groove back" in fifty words or less. The winner received a trip to Jamaica.

- Dawn Publications ran a Growing Up Together Contest to encourage parents to read to their children. Dawn awarded prizes up to $500.00 to parents who submitted creative reading and storytelling ideas based on any Dawn Publications picture books for children.

- Jim Miller, author of *Corporate Coach*, worked with Planned Television Arts to combine a contest with a series of interviews on morning drive time radio shows. During each show, Miller invited listeners to describe their favorite and least-liked bosses. Winners would receive a vacation in Kuwait. The contest received 4,000 entries and helped sell an additional 125,000 copies of the book. As a bonus, Miller was able to use 300 of the best entries as material for his second book, *Best Boss, Worst Boss*.

11. Solicit information or entries for an upcoming book.

USA Today often features solicitations for information in the Lifeline Section. Here are just a few such requests that have appeared:

- Mifflin Lowe, author of *The Cheapskate's Handbook*, sought the USA's biggest cheapskate. The winner received economy air fare to New York or Los Angeles. The runner-up won a $50 Kmart gift certificate.

- CCC Publications requested entries for the most humorous answering machine messages for their book, *No Hang-ups III*. They offered prizes of $1,000, $100, $50, and 50 fourth place prizes of $5. I'm sure that all entries received a promotion for the first two books in the series.

- Sandy Soule asked readers to name their favorite country inns for her book, *America's Wonderful Little Hotels & Inns*.

Other publications, of course, also publish notices of writer's needs or other requests for information. For instance, *Learning* magazine along with Fulcrum Publishing sponsored a writing contest for students to describe what it will be like in the year 2020 to go to school and learn. The best entries would be published in a book. And winning students, teachers, and schools would receive copies of the books.

12. Get listed in community news.

When your authors go on tour (or even just visit another city), arrange autograph sessions at local bookstores, libraries, or other venues. Then make sure your local contact gets the event listed in the Events section of the local newspaper. Note that some newspapers publish more than one calendar. For instance, the *Minneapolis Star Tribune* has a separate calendar for events of interest to senior citizens and families and another for art events.

13. Offer something free.

Many magazines and newspapers have special departments that feature notices about new products, free reports, free samples, informational brochures, and other things that people can write away for. While it is almost impossible to get a magazine or newspaper to do a feature or review more than once on a book, it is easy to get them to feature new free offers as often as you can come up with them. Plan to start a new promotional campaign at least four times a year for each book you publish.

How do you find something to give away free? Easy. Your books should be full of valuable information that you can excerpt in short 2-page or 4-page brochures that you can offer free to anyone who sends you an SASE or $1.00 to $3.00 for postage.

For example, a travel publisher could offer a list of the ten most exciting places in Iowa (if their book was about Iowa). Three months later, the same publisher could offer a report on holiday happenings in Iowa. Three months later, a report on how to plan your next vacation in Iowa. And three months later, a list of ten major historical sites in Iowa. And three months later....

- *USA Today* regularly features free offers in its Lifeline column on the front page of the Life Section. In October 1988, they featured a free booklet, *Acupressure for Your Beauty and Health*, from Kim's Publishing. When readers sent for the booklet, they also received promotional material on Kim's other books. The free offer was a perfect way for Kim's to develop a list of interested readers.

- *Family Circle* magazine had a Circle This column, which consisted of three pages of short items about unusual products. Publishers have sold as many as 20,000 books as a result of one mention in *Family Circle*.

- Joel Herskowitz received more than 8,000 responses from one magazine to a freebie offering for a pamphlet outlining the diet described in his book, *The Popcorn-PLUS Diet.*

- *Freebies*, a bimonthly newsletter that publishes free offers, is interested in items for kids, crafts, home, auto, garden, and teachers. Send your items or news releases to **Freebies**, 1135 Eugenia Place, P.O. Box 5025, Carpenteria, CA 93104-5025; 805-566-1225; Fax: 805-566-0305.

- Many magazines have a Things for Free department.

- *Bottom Line/Personal*, the largest circulation newsletter in the country, often features free or low-cost things to send away for. But you cannot charge their readers any postage. Send news releases to **Bottom Line/Personal**, Boardroom Inc., 281 Tresser Boulevard, P.O. Box 436, Stamford, CT 06901-0436. Web: http://www.bottomlinesecrets.com.

When you make a free offer, make it something useful. And be sure it is related to one of your books (or to an entire line of books). Then, when readers write in for your free offer, send them your report or brochure plus your catalog or advertisement for a related book.

Authors: Writing free reports to offer via press releases is one of the best ways to publicize your book after the first year. You will have to take responsibility for this. Publishers rarely think of doing publicity for books after the first few months.

---

14. Send out top ten lists.

While David Letterman has popularized top ten lists among consumers, print media (and radio shows) have always had a strong interest in top ten lists. Hence, one of the best ways to capture the media attention is to send out top ten lists and other sidebar material that fits in odd editorial places most publications have to fill.

- To publicize her *Free Vacations & Bargain Adventures*, Evelyn Kaye sent out a news release featuring the "Top Ten Free Vacations." She also gave the report away to people who listened to her radio interviews.

- Speech therapist Mort Cooper selected the "Best Funny Money Voices" to promote *Stop Committing Voice Suicide*. His list was reprinted in many places as well as mentioned on radio. Here are a few of his picks:

  Bill Clinton—"Makes hoarse voices fashionable."

  Dr. Ruth Westheimer—"Will never play a Demi Moore sex kitten."

  Donald Duck—"No wise quacks, please!"

- To promote *Cyberwriting*, Joe Vitale worked with a comedy writer for Jay Leno, to develop a humorous top ten list of reasons to read his book. Among those reasons were the facts that it's "cheaper than a night in the Lincoln bedroom and contains no ghosts of former presidents" and "rearrange the letters of each chapter title and find out what's really being stored in Area 51." Within hours of posting his top ten list to forty-nine friends, he noticed his message being spread across the Internet (confirming his theory that one thing that gets distributed via email with little or no effort is humor).

- *Autograph Collectors Magazine* sent out a press release via the Internet announcing that their annual list of the best and worst celebrity autograph signers was now available in the magazine. They hooked readers by mentioning John Travolta, Robin Williams, Brat Pitt, Alicia Silverstone, Mel Gibson, Demi Moore, Tom Hanks, and Nancy Reagan. They ended the release by teasing, "To find out who's nice and who's a stinker, contact the magazine." Within hours, reporters from *USA Today* and other media contacted them for a copy of the magazine.

15. Don't forget the wire services.

Many newspapers, which are members of one or more wire services, rely upon the services to provide their readers with national news and features. It's common for a story that goes over the AP wire to be picked up by 200 or more newspapers. That's a quick way to get your story national coverage.

What is the best way to reach these services? Start by working with a reporter at your local city newspaper. Once your local paper publishes a story, especially if it's good, encourage the reporter or the editors to put the story over the wire. It's in their interest to have their stories go over the wire. It adds prestige to their work. Besides, most newspapers are required to submit a certain number of stories to the wire services every month.

If your local newspaper doesn't do a story about your book that gets over the wires, approach the local or regional bureaus for these news services. If you can't find their names in the yellow pages, call or write to the national headquarters as follows:

☐ **Associated Press,** 450 West 33rd Street, New York, NY 10001; 212-621-1500; Fax: 212-621-7520 and 212-621-1679. Email: pr@ap.org. Web: http://www.ap.org. You can send story ideas to subject editors (sports, food, etc.). They also offer special alert wires covering medical, environmental, energy, political, high tech, automotive, financial, agriculture, and Eastern European news.

☐ **United Press International** (UPI), 1510 H Street N.W., Washington, DC 20005-2289; 202-898-8000; Fax: 202-898-8057; press release fax: 202-898-8064. Press releases: pressreleases@upi.com. News tips: newstips@upi.com. Web: http://www.upi.com.

☐ **Reuters Information Services,** 3 Times Square, New York, NY 10036; 646-223-6100. Web: http://www.reuters.com.

There are other general news services such as the Gannett News Service, Copley News Service, Knight-Ridder, Scripps Howard, and Newhouse as well as many specialized news services such as Bloomberg Business News, College News Service, National Catholic News Service, and Alternet (for alternative newspapers). When Diane Pfeifer was promoting her *Angel Cookbook*, she sent out a vegetarian Lenten press release which was picked up by the Catholic newswire service. It went into many diocesan newspapers across the country and resulted in a major sell-through at retail.

16. Submit your story to your local news bureau.

Major media often have bureaus in other cities. According to Allan Hall, technology editor at *Business Week*, when submitting news stories to the major magazines, submit the story twice—one copy to the main editorial office and the other to the nearest bureau of the magazine. The chances are far greater that your local bureau will respond to your news release. Why? Because it is their job to find local newsworthy events, people, and products.

17. Track down the right reporters.

Sometimes you might have to contact four or five different editors at a newspaper before you find the one who would be most appropriate for your book. It's worth the effort to track down the right editor or reporter.

• One publisher had to send three review copies and make calls to five different editors at *USA Today* before he located a freelance writer from California who was interested in writing about his book. His persistence paid off with a front page feature in the Life Section of *USA Today*.

• Alan and Denise Fields, self-publishers of *Bridal Bargains: Secrets of Throwing a Fantastic Wedding on a Realistic Budget*, got a feature story about their book in the *Wall Street Journal* by contacting the magazine reporter. Why that reporter? Because the Fields had discovered that the bridal magazines were refusing advertisements from mail order discount bridal companies. Of course, this policy created a controversy in the magazine industry—something the magazine reporter would be interested in probing. As a result of that article, Alan Fields received a call from *People* magazine which, in turn, resulted in a two-page spread with their toll-free number!

18. Track down freelance writers.

To get into some newspapers, it often pays to track down a freelance writer who does a lot of work for those newspapers *and* who specializes in writing about subjects related to your book. Here's how one publisher located a freelance writer: "I called and asked who the family editor was. I wrote her but I received no response. So I called again and this time asked for the assistant family editor. I wrote her as well. As a result of these two letters, one of them contacted a freelance writer living nearby. She wrote a superb article featuring our book."

Be on the lookout for any freelance writers who are working on books or articles dealing with subjects covered by any of your books. Send them review copies of appropriate books. For example, in one issue of *Publishers Weekly*, Marilyn Stasia requested review copies of mystery paperbacks for a feature article she was doing for the *New York Times*.

Authors — You can help your publisher by tracking down freelance writers, reporters, local news bureaus, and other media contacts that your publisher's publicity department has not yet discovered. As you travel, make note of the newspaper reporters writing about your topic. You can be your publisher's minor league scout.

---

19. Submit to a different department.

Sometimes one section of a newspaper or magazine will reject your news release where another will eagerly embrace it. It isn't always easy to tell which will like it. So, even though your news release was rejected by one department, you can always resubmit the news to another department.

- If the Parade Picks department of *Parade* magazine (which features forecasts of movies, records, and books) does not pay attention to your book, submit it to the Bright Ideas to Make Life Better department (which features new ideas on gardening, nutrition, health, parenting, and other how-to subjects).

- Besides its feature stories and interviews (sometimes of authors), the inflight magazine of American Airlines, *American Way*, also features short snippets on interesting travel trends and unusual sights in its Sojourns section—a perfect opening for travel books.

- To promote David Pryce-Jones's book on improbable deaths, *You Can't Be Too Careful*, Workman sent copies of the book to the obituary writers at major newspapers. Along with the copy, they sent a note suggesting that the writers review the book for their paper's review pages.

- Besides the regular departments, watch for seasonal features such as the perennial holiday gift section in many major magazines. Here's the story of the publicist of Down East Books who happened to notice a listing about holiday gift features in the *Book Marketing Update* newsletter:

    I noticed a blurb that Playboy might be looking for unusual gift ideas for their Christmas issue. We are currently publishing a very unusual book in a signed, limited edition called Penobscot River Renaissance. The possible marriage was just quirky enough that I thought it might work —it did! Playboy will review the book for their Christmas issue (with direct response information, no less).

20. Write a letter to the editor.

Submit a guest editorial to the newspaper. Write about something that really moves you. Write about the subject of your book.

- Don't think that op-ed pages are worthless for publicity. They can be very effective. When Anthony Lewis praised *Under a Cruel Star: A Life in Prague 1941-1968* in the op-ed pages of *New York Times*, the publisher had to go back to press for a second printing of 3,000 copies.

- The buzz for Gary Aldrich's *Unlimited Access* book about the Clinton White House picked up a notch immediately after his op-ed piece in the *Wall Street Journal*. In response to the demand, Regnery Publishing had to move up the publication date for the book by three weeks.

- Jacques Werth, author of *High Probability Selling*, wrote a letter to the editor in response to an article on "Love the Ones You're With" that appeared in *Sales & Marketing Management*. He offered a few points from his book in response to a sidebar in that article on "Five Ways to Sell More to Current Customers."

- USA Today offers a special editorial fax number for letters to the editor (703-854-2053) as well as an email address: editor@usatoday.com. "Letters most likely to be published are timely, brief and direct. Include your name, address, day and evening phone numbers for verification."

Besides the letters to the editor page, many newspapers and magazines offer other opportunities for their readers to give them feedback.

- To encourage its readers to send news of successful direct marketing campaigns, industry news, and other items, *Direct* magazine lists its Direct Hotline number prominently as well as its fax number. It now also encourages submissions direct via email.

- Readers of *Popular Mechanics* are invited to call any of eleven departmental editors via special hotline numbers between 3:00 p.m. and 5:00 p.m. every Wednesday. Readers are encouraged to express opinions, ask questions, and offer story ideas.

- *Nation's Business*, the monthly magazine of the United States Chamber of Commerce, features the Entrepreneur's Notebook, a full-page column written by a reader on any subject of interest to business owners.

> **Authors** — This tip is primarily for you. Who better to write an editorial or op-ed piece about your subject than you? As the author of a book, you have the credentials. Use them. Look for current events that relate to your book. Then give your opinion about those events in the light of your book. Don't, however, go overboard. Keep the commercial subtle.

21. Join a press association.

Freelance writers and journalists often join associations to mingle and network with other journalists. There are press associations for many interest groups, including a Catholic Press Association and a Computer Press Association. There are also writers associations for garden writers, children's book writers, travel writers, and so on. For a list of such associations, see http://www.bookmarket.com/writers.html. Why should you seek out and join these associations. Here are a few reasons:

☐ You can find professional writers for new titles.

☐ You can make connections with magazine and newspaper editors, radio and TV journalists, and freelance writers.

☐ You can be the first to learn about editorial changes. Most press associations notify members of such changes long before others know.

> **Authors** — If you write regularly in one subject area, you should look into joining the press association that covers your subject. Membership will give you an opportunity to meet and network with other writers and editors. Then, when you submit articles or news releases to these editors, you should get a far better reception.

22. Use co-op publicity programs.

To supplement your other promotional efforts, you might participate in a co-op publicity program or pay for a listing in one of the PR programs that are sent to editors and producers. Below are a few of them.

☐ **KSB Links**—This newsletter is sent to the media three times a year by KSB Promotions to highlight books and authors. For more information, contact KSB Promotions, 55 Honey Creek N.E., Ada, MI 49301-9768;

616-676-0758; 800-304-3269; Fax: 616-676-0759. Email: pr@ksbpro-motions.com. Web: http://www.ksbpromotions.com.

For *The Well-Fed Writer*, Peter Bowerman got close to 80 review copy requests between the initial insertion and ongoing KSB web listings.

Lisa Roberts, author of *How to Raise a Family and a Career Under One Roof*, also had success with *KSB Links*: "Just this week, over 50 requests for review copies have come in, in addition to the 25+ that came in last week. These requests are ranging from big wigs like the *L.A. Times* and Lifetime Television to radio stations and periodicals. The range is astounding as well, from the Christian Family Book Club (who picked up the title) to *Playboy* magazine to senior citizen magazines."

☐ **Leading Edge Review**—This publication, which features paid reviews of new age books and cassettes, is sent to 2,500 new age bookstores, 1,000 print and broadcast media, and is also distributed to 45,000 consumers via bookstores and wholesalers. For more info, contact *Leading Edge Review*, Sheila Grams, P.O. Box 308, Viroqua, WI 54665; 608-637-7206; Fax: 608-637-3719.. Web: http://www.leadingedgereview.com.

☐ **PMA's Books for Review newsletter**—PMA does a co-op mailing to 3,700 book reviewers four times a year. The mailing consists of a 4-page brochure listing about 40 books (with cover photo, short description, subject, and pricing). For details, write to PMA, 627 Aviation Way, Manhattan Beach, CA 90266; 310-372-2732; Fax: 310-374-3342. Email: pmaonline@aol.com. Web: http://www.pma-online.org. Those publishers who have used this service average between 10 and 20 requests for review copies, with about half that number resulting in reviews.

23. Distribute news releases via a PR service.

If you want to get your news out fast nationwide, you could work with one of the publicity services that distribute news releases electronically to news rooms around the country. Here are two such services:

☐ **PR Newswire**, 1515 Broadway, New York, NY 10155; 212-832-9400; 800-832-5522; Fax: 212-832-9406. Web: http://www.prnewswire.com. They distribute news releases electronically to 1,000 newsrooms across the country (both newspapers and broadcast). They also distribute news releases via email and the Internet.

☐ **North American Precis Syndicate**, 201 East 42nd Street, New York, NY 10017-5793; 212-867-9000; Fax: 212-983-0970. Besides news release distribution, this company can also handle multimedia releases and camera-ready releases.

Jo Peddicord used NAPS to distribute a news release about her book, *Look Like a Winner After 50*. The release generated 1,260 newspaper articles in thirty-seven different states with a total readership of sixty-one million. Most of those placements were with smaller newspapers. Note: Not all releases get that much response.

24. Distribute camera-ready news or feature stories.

Dr. Tony Hyman regularly sells over $100,000 in books every year by placing only three ads. How does he do it? He writes a short news story about his book, *Cash for Undiscovered Treasures*, and then distributes the story to 7,000 newspapers in camera-ready format designed for standard newspaper layouts. His stories are formatted and distributed by Metro Creative Graphics for about $1,200 per article.

Tony writes his own stories, but he makes sure they follow standard journalistic style so they read like a real news or feature story. His experience is that about 200 newspapers pick up a story. And from that exposure, he sells some 1,600 copies of his $22.95 book. He grosses anywhere from $35,000 to $40,000 per story. To keep his book alive, Tony places three stories each year, with each story having a different slant. As a result, some newspapers have carried more than one story about his book.

You could try to distribute your own camera-ready news stories, or you could use one of the services, such as Metro Creative Graphics, that regularly distribute such stories for a small fee. Both PR Newswire and North American Precis Syndicate, listed above, also distribute such stories. Here are a few other companies that offer this service:

☐ **Metro Editorial Services**, 519 Eighth Avenue, New York, NY 10018; 212-947-5100; 800-223-1600; Fax: 212-714-9139. Email: mes@metro-email.com. Web: http://www.metroeditorialservices.com. Besides sending out monthly mailings of camera-ready releases, this company also offers thematic sections such as Health and Fitness, Garden Time, Spring Home Improvement, and so on. Metro also offers a free clipping service for first-time participants of their services.

☐ **News USA**, 250 East 54th Street, New York, NY 10022; 888-563-5200. Web: http://www.newsusa.com. News USA will write, edit, typeset, print, and distribute a 100-word feature in their monthly tabloid of camera-ready articles which is sent to over 10,000 newspapers.

☐ **Family Features Editorial Services**, 8309 Melrose Drive, Shawnee Mission, KS 66214-3628; 913-888-3800; 800-443-2512. Web: http://www.culinary.net. This company specializes in full-color thematic sections for the food and lifestyle pages of newspapers.

25. Fax it.

Most media are equipped to receive news releases via fax. If you have a machine and access to media fax numbers, try sending some releases via fax. Don't, however, use faxes unless your story has a real news value or immediacy. If there is one thing media people resent, it is having their fax machines (and their own time) tied up receiving puff stories.

Many fax machines and computer fax cards can be set up to send the same fax to several hundred recipients whenever you want them sent. If you send them late at night, you can avoid the daytime fax rush, have your story on the editor's desk in the morning, and save money using the lowest late night phone rates. Most media databases include fax numbers and email addresses as well as phone numbers.

26. Email it.

More and more media people have email addresses and are receptive to receiving letters and product promotions via email. Indeed, according to a recent survey sponsored by the Columbia School of Journalism, a third of all editors go online daily (to do research, verify references, find sources, and check email). Most media contacts I've talked to prefer email news releases because they are easy to skim, edit, and respond to.

To be safe (so they know it's a news release) and at the same time grab their interest, you should add a subject header with a good headline such as "Celebrate New Year's Every Month of the Year"—a headline I used right before New Year's Eve when promoting my book of holidays and anniversaries called *Celebrate Today*.

One morning while driving around doing errands, I heard a story on NPR's *Morning Edition* talking about the Stop the Holiday Movement in India. To accommodate its many religions, India has over 40 public holidays plus many other special holidays whenever someone important dies. Since many businesses frown on employees taking the day off all the time, the Stop the Holiday Movement wants to cut down on holidays to attract more international businesses. When I got back to my office, I immediately emailed a note to *Morning Edition*. Here's the note that I sent that day:

I enjoyed your little story about the Stop the Holiday Movement in India on this morning's Morning Edition. But it did shock me. Because I'm actually working on the exact opposite cause in this country. I'd like to make every day a holiday. That's why I wrote my book, Celebrate Today. I'll send you a copy of the book. Meanwhile, here are a few reasons to take tomorrow off:

Midsummer Eve (aka St. John's Eve)
1st round-the-world flight in a single-engine airplane
Birthday of the Saxophone (1846)
Birthday of the Typewriter (1868)
Bobbit entered the English language (1993)

P.S.—I've actually set up a National Special Events Registry so people could get official recognition of their own holidays.

Morning Edition did not use my email message on their show, but it was a good attempt to respond immediately to something heard on radio or TV. And next time, who knows?, it might work. Someday, that show will feature my book. It's just a matter of time, and I have lots of it.

27. Put your information on the Internet.

If you have a web site, make sure you make your news releases and other promotions available on your site. Thousands of people will visit your site every year, especially if you are listed with all the major search engines. More details on computer publicity will be featured in the next chapter.

28. Teleconference.

If you are holding a press conference or major media event, you might want to arrange a teleconference hook up with distant media. Several years ago, Dow Jones-Irwin conducted a workshop based on its new book, *Service America*, that was beamed via satellite to 150 universities and corporate sites across the country. As a result of that initial push in publicity, the book sold 55,000 copies in the first year.

One of the easiest and yet most effectives ways to speak before a large audience without having to travel is to speak on teleconferences organized by newsletters, web sites, consultants, and other marketers to the audience you are trying to reach. I've spoken at teleconferences organized by the National Speakers Association, Jay Conrad Levinson's Guerrilla Marketing group, Robert Allen's protege group, *Book Marketing Update*, and many writers groups. You can reach a lot of people without leaving home.

29. Go for the top!

Always aim for the highest first. Target those media which you want to reach, and don't give up until they surrender. If your book or author is right for a particular magazine or TV show, don't ever give up until they say yes. Remember: They need you more than you need them. You actually do them a disservice if you give up too soon. Aim for the top. In time, you'll get it.

Some of the top print possibilities include *Time, Newsweek, USA Today, People, Vanity Fair, Entertainment Weekly, O Magazine, Family Circle,* and major newspapers.

Several years ago Greg Godek, author of *1001 Ways to Be Romantic,* called me and said, "I have $25,000 to spend on promoting my book during the next three months. How should I spend it?"

My answer: Don't spend it. Put it in the bank. Instead, mount a letter-writing campaign to Ann Landers. My idea was to send Ann Landers something every day for a month—a letter responding to one of her columns, a note excerpted from the book, a personal postcard, a handwritten Post-It note attached to a news release, and so on. If done with humor and just the right personal touch (and, of course, if the book is right for Ann Landers), I was sure it would work. Greg, however, decided not to go with my advice. Next time, I know what I will advise him: "Give me the $25,000, and I will guarantee you placement in *O Magazine.*"

In my experience, you will always get more effective publicity if you target the top media and really work with them to get a story about you or your book. That means developing a list of the top media (your Kremer 100 list). And that also means personally contacting members of your Kremer 100 list at least once a month—by mail, by phone, by email, or in person.

9:12   The Importance of Author Interviews

Author interviews are useful in propelling a book to bestseller status. Few radio and television shows actually review books, but many of them do interview authors. And despite what you might think, radio and television shows are not incompatible with either selling or reading books. Research shows that book sales are helped by television exposure (via talk shows and interviews), and that people who watch a lot of TV also read a lot of books. Indeed, key television shows sell more books than reviews in such major print media as the *New York Times Book Review*.

Interviews, of course, can appear in print as well. Both print and audio or video interviews have certain advantages over book reviews. Here are a few of those advantages:

☐ They tend to be more personal and intimate. They give the reader a better feeling for the author's intent in writing the book as well as the author's qualifications.

☐ More people watch talk shows and read newspaper/magazine features than read book review sections.

☐ The author has greater control over what will be covered in the interview; hence, the author can be sure to include more promotional comments about the book.

☐ Most interviews are longer than reviews and, in general, the greater the length, the greater the impact.

☐ Interviews are usually more involving, lively, and interesting than book reviews.

9:13   Tips on Obtaining Interviews

The basic guideline for obtaining interviews is the same as that for obtaining any publicity. You must be persistent, and you must follow through. Of course, you'll have an easier time arranging interviews if your authors are interesting and entertaining speakers and if your books appeal to the personal interests of a wide audience. Here are a few tips on how to arrange interviews in the various media:

☐ Know your media. Don't try to get interviews on a show or in a newspaper section where your book doesn't fit.

☐ Pitch trends. If you can't offer the media any type of scoop, then offer them a story about trends. If possible, give them more than one example of such a trend.

☐ Write a good pitch letter. Paulette Cooper sent a letter to Lucy Howard at *Newsweek* pitching buzzwords used by people in a profession related to one of her books. Within two weeks, she had her plug.

☐ Demonstrate to editors or producers that your author will do a good interview and that the book will interest and benefit their audience.

☐ Prepare a professional media kit which includes a copy of the book, a biography of the author, a news release or brochure describing the book, a list of questions that will produce a good interview, and a list of previous author interviews (where and when), including copies of any print interviews.

☐ The list of questions is crucial. Make sure the questions are interesting, concise, entertaining and, above all, cover the important points you want to make during an interview. Many interviewers will not have time to read the book, so the only thing they have to go by is the information you provide. One question almost all interviewers ask is: "How did you come to write this book?"

When I promoted my movie trivia book, *Tinseltowns, U.S.A.*, I included a list of questions. Invariably, interviewers chose to ask many of them as part of any interview. Here are a couple of the questions I sent them:

What Iowa town is the future birthplace of Captain James T. Kirk?

Who built the first movie studio? And where was it built?

What is the name of the first town to star in a beer commercial?

What building was used for the exterior shots of the *Daily Planet* building in the *Superman* TV series?

☐ Telephone the stations or newspapers and make contact with someone who can make decisions on interview subjects. Then mail your press kit to them. A week or two later, follow up with another phone call to your contact. At this time, ask if he or she is interested in setting up an interview or requires any further information about the author. Note: The best times to call editors and reporters is usually in the morning.

☐ Sing for your supper. When Mel Parker of Warner Books was pitching *Publishers Weekly* for Bob Rosner's *Working Wounded*, he sang one of Rosner's entries on the pros and cons of entrepreneurship to the tune of "Both Sides Now." It worked.

☐ Don't give up. If the first person you contact isn't interested in an interview, try someone else at the same media. While arranging interviews for Peter McWilliams, author of the *Personal Computer in Business Book*, Ron Gold was rudely turned down by the business editor of a major Southern newspaper. But he didn't give up. His next call was to the computer editor at the same paper. As it happened, that editor had been wondering how to get in touch with McWilliams; hence, he was only too glad to set up an interview.

☐ When you send out review copies, indicate those parts of the book which would be most appropriate for the interviewer to read. You might want to attach Post-It notes to the relevant sections of the book and highlight the liveliest passages.

☐ Don't assume because a media has never featured a book that they won't feature one. Rudra's *Mastery: Insights and Wisdom from 33 Remarkable People* was the first book *Continental Magazine* had ever serialized. That serialization would not have happened if Rudra had given up without sending a book.

☐ Seminars can help you gain media attention. Whenever you are giving a bookstore talk or a seminar at a learning center, be sure that the local newspapers and other media know that you will be in town. That's the perfect time for them to interview you—either prior to you coming or at the time you are in town.

When Lisa Shaw, author of *Moving to the Country Once and For All*, did a weekend seminar for Vermont Off Beat, a reporter for *USA Today* saw her seminar in the catalog and called her for an interview. Lisa ended up on the front page of *USA Today*'s Life Section.

The Rules by Ellen Fein and Sherrie Schneider was slowly selling by word of mouth until they started to do seminars around the country. Warner decided to piggyback those seminars for some extra promotion by inviting the media to attend for free. Within months, the book got articles in *New York* magazine, *LA Times, Time*, and *USA Today*. In addition, the authors appeared on *Sally Jessy Raphael, Leeza, Imus in the Morning*, and *Oprah*.

☐ For some easy-to-use forms to help you research the media, write great news releases, set up interviews, and book author tours, see the workbook that was designed to accompany this book: *The Do-It-Yourself Book Publicity Kit* (available at BookMarket.com).

Authors — Prepare a list of interview questions and give these to your editor (who should hand them on to the publicity department). Also, you should highlight those sections of your book which would be of most interest to interviewers. Work with your publisher to refine the questions and the sections of the book to be highlighted.

9:14 The Value of Print Interviews

Don't neglect newspaper and magazine interviews when you are arranging author tours and interviews. Press interviews have several advantages over radio and TV interviews:

☐ They are more concrete.

☐ They tend to linger longer in the minds of readers.

☐ Readers can read them at their leisure.

☐ You can collect and copy press clippings more easily and send them to key contacts.

☐ Print interviews are more likely to be syndicated, which can result in features being published in as many as 200 other newspapers.

☐ Print interviews are more likely to inspire other feature stories.

William Zimmerman, self-publisher of *How to Tape Instant Biographies*, is a firm believer in the power of the press. He's had feature spreads in *Business Week*, *Washington Post*, and *New York Times*. The *Times* feature story brought in over 2,000 inquiries for his book.

9:15 Radio Interviews Via Telephone

Radio interviews are an easy and effective way to promote your authors and books. In many cases, radio stations will handle interviews with the author over the phone. It is possible to organize a national author tour without your author ever leaving his or her home. Radio stations like the idea because it means that any author, no matter how famous or how busy, can be accessible to them even if they broadcast from Missoula, Montana. Besides, authors usually make superb guests; they are articulate, intelligent, know a lot about their special areas of interest, and are usually better prepared than many celebrities to answer impromptu questions.

Authors, of course, love the idea because they do not have to bear the long hours of travel. Publishers love the idea even more because such interviews are much less expensive than full author tours. Plus they are easier to arrange because of fewer time conflicts or tight schedules. For publishers with limited funds, here are a few ways to get the name of your books and authors in front of the people who schedule such interviews.

☐ Pay for a listing or display advertisement in one of the expert listings services or directories.

Yearbook of Experts, Authorities, & Spokespersons—This directory lists authors, individuals, and organizations willing to speak on any topic. The yearbook is distributed free to 7,600 media, including thousands of radio producers, as well as over the Internet. Write for an information kit from **Broadcast Interview Source**, 2233 Wisconsin Avenue N.W., Washington, DC 20007-4104; 202-333-4904; Fax: 202-342-5411. Email: editor@Yearbook.com. Web: *http://www.yearbook.com*.

Directory of News Sources—Published by the National Press Club as part of its membership directory, it is circulated to all club members. A listing in the directory includes a web site listing and a hyperlink to your web site. For more information, contact **National Press Club**, 529 14th Street N.W., Washington, DC 20045; 202-662-7525; Fax: 202-662-7512. Email: membership@npcpress.org. Web: *http://www.npcpress.org*.

☐ Pay to be listed in one of the following periodic interview newsletters that feature authors and other experts.

Radio-TV Interview Report—This newsletter is sent to 4,700 radio and TV producers. *RTIR* suggests that an appropriate response to a half-page ad will be fifteen or more calls from producers. For more information, contact Bradley Communications, P.O. Box 1206, Lansdowne, PA 19050; 610-259-1070; 800-553-8002; Fax: 610-284-3704. Email: marketingcoord@rtir.com. Web: http://www.freepublicity.com.

When I used this service for *Celebrate Today*, I booked seventy-five interviews from my first full-page ad. Gary Blair, author of *What Are Your Goals?*, attributes the following success to advertising regularly in *RTIR*: 366 radio appearances, 7,413 copies of his book sold at full retail via an 800 number, $110,824 in total revenued, and $92,291 in profit.

☐ Book your own radio interviews using one of the following directories or booking systems.

The Radio Talk Show System—This system features a book, audiotape, and a database of 915 radio shows. Contact Pacesetter Publications, P.O. Box 101330, Denver, CO 80250; 303-722-7200; Fax: 303-733-2626. Email: jsabah@aol.com. Web: http://www.sabahradioshows.com.

RadioPublicity.com—This report plus database features the addresses and contacts for the 900 largest morning talk radio shows. Contact: AceCo Publishers, 924 Chapala Street #D, Santa Barbara, CA 93101; 805-564-6868; 800-322-6946; Fax: 805-963-1644. Email: alex@radiopublicity.com. Web: http://www.radiopublicity.com.

Talkers Directory of Talk Radio, Talkers Magazine, 650 Belmont Avenue, Springfield, MA 01108; 413-739-8255; Fax: 413-746-6786. Email: info@talkers.com. Web: http://www.talkers.com. Features the names, addresses, phone, fax, email, and web site info on hundreds of talk stations and individual hosts.

Gordon's Radio List, North Ridge Books, P.O. Box 1463, Lake Forest, CA 92609; 949-855-0640; Fax: 949-855-4860. Email: info@nrbooks.com. Web: http://www.nrbooks.com. A list of 1,100 locally produced and nationally syndicated radio shows, with show descriptions, URLs, and email address for both hosts and producers.

☐ Pay to have a news service send your story out by satellite feed. Here is one service that feeds radio stations:

News/Broadcast Network, 149 Madison Avenue #804, New York, NY 10016; 212-889-0888; Fax: 212-696-4611.

☐ Send a review copy and author information to a radio news service, such as the following:

ABC Radio Networks—Send news releases to this newswire service that is sent to 3,000 subscribers. Contact ABC Radio Newswire, 125 West End Avenue, New York, NY 10023; 212-456-5193.

Wireless Flash News—They send a twice-weekly show prep service called *Wireless Flash* to many radio stations. This service offers lifestyle news, trivia, and entertainment features. Contact Wireless Flash, P.O. Box 639111, San Diego, CA 92163; 619-220-7191; Fax: 619-220-8590. Email: newsdesk@flashnews.com. Web: http://www.flashnews.com.

☐ Pay to have your news release send out via email by one of the Internet news services. Details on these services will be presented in Chapter 12.

☐ Form your own radio network. To promote its Christian authors, Zondervan formed the Zondervan Radio Network, consisting of 250 stations that asked to receive monthly cassettes featuring news, stories, interviews, and commentaries based on their books. Segments ranged from 60-second sound bites to 27-minute interviews. Zondervan also sends out a monthly newsletter of interview ideas featuring their authors. Besides religious topics, their authors speak on health, sex, parenting, business, politics, investments, children, abortion, and other current topics.

☐ Launch your own national radio show. Fodor's recently launched a weekly, two-hour radio talk show called *Fodor's on the Road*. The show, heard on 67 stations around the country, is simulcast on Fodor's web site at http://www.fodors.com.

Random House donated its recordings of "Breakfast at Random House" discussions to public radio stations around the country. More than 50 stations signed up for the syndicated series. The first airing of the series proved so popular that the series ran for a second time.

☐ Join someone else's network or arrange to produce and/or host your own local radio show. Donna Montgomery, a semi-regular guest on one of the major radio shows in Minneapolis, Minnesota, was able to arrange her own 2-minute segment named after her book, *Surviving Motherhood*.

☐ Work to get an interview or other feature on National Public Radio. Many of their shows, especially *All Things Considered*, feature interviews with authors. An interview on *Fresh Air* helped to push Robert Boswell's novel, *The Mystery Ride*, onto the bestseller lists.

When one of their authors appeared on NPR's *Science Friday* to discuss a book on making calculus easy, Prometheus sold more than 100 books in the fifteen minutes after the show ended. Orders continued to come in for a week after the show. Two other authors who had also appeared on the show did not do as well. Why? Because their publishers did not ask the host before the show to mention their 800 numbers. If you want orders, mention your 800 number some time during the interview.

After Daniel Pinkwater, NPR's book commentator, enthusiastically praised the children's books published by Northland Publishing, the publisher's phone rang off the hook. Retailers asked to set up accounts, wholesalers increased their stock, and sales went up at the various chains. Plus they sold $5,000 worth of books at retail. How did they get

Pinkwater to mention their books. Simple. They sent him a package of books, and the quality of their books sold themselves.

☐ Try to book interviews on other major national shows or networks. For instance, Bloomberg Radio interviews are heard on at least 30 affiliate stations. The nationally syndicated radio show, *Pet Talk America*, is heard on 38 stations as well as on the Internet at http://www.pettalk.com.

The publicists for Lee Covington, author of *How to Dump Your Wife*, were able to book him on Howard Stern's radio show by using off-the-wall faxed press releases and endless follow-up phone calls. That one interview resulted in more than 1,000 orders for the book.

When Paula Langguth, author of *Bounce Back from Bankruptcy*, did an interview on *Smart Money with the Dolans*, by the time her office manager got off the phone with the first order, nineteen messages had come in from other callers. They were still getting orders months later.

☐ Work to get interviews on major local shows. When Tony Hyman, author of *Trash or Treasure*, appeared on Roy Leonard's show on WGN radio in Chicago, he sold $25,000 worth of books.

Some 30,000 callers simultaneously tried to call a New Orleans radio station when they heard that Stefan Paulus, author of *Nostradamus 1999*, would be answering questions on a call-in talk show. The calls overloaded a circuit that disabled telephone service in a 30-block radius.

After a seven-minute appearance by Ruth Crystal, author of *Angel Talk*, on WWYZ-AM in Hartford, Connecticut, the station received more than 4,000 phone calls the following week. Even with local stations, be sure the receptionists have your phone number because many listeners will call the station for more information.

By working only with 10,000 watts and up radio stations, Diane Irons, author of *The Real Secrets of Beauty*, has sold as many as 400 books after a good interview.

☐ Make sure the radio prep services know about your author. Keep them informed of your author's radio interview appearances. Give them quirky or controversial tidbits about your authors or their books. Here are a few radio prep services:

Interprep, Steve Holstein, Editor-in-Chief. Email: holstein@interprep. com. Web: http://www.interprep.com. Launched in 1994 as the first web site dedicated to radio show prep.

Radio Prep Web Center, American Comedy Network, 91 River Street, Milford, CT 06460; 203-877-8210. Web: http://www.americancomedy-network.com. If you can pitch your book in a funny way, this prep web site would be interest. The same for the one below.

The Comedy Wire, Michael King, Michael King Productions, Dallas TX; 214-905-9299; Fax: 214-845-8016. Email: mikek120@mindspring. com. Web: http://www.comedy-wire.com.

For a list of other prep services, surf to http://www.radiodirectory.com.

☐ Get listed in GuestFinder. This world wide web service features paid listings of authors and others who are open to doing interviews. For more information, surf over to http://www.guestfinder.com. This service is operated by a self-published author.

☐ Get your book listed in *R&R* (Radio & Records). This weekly newspaper for the radio and record industry often features offbeat books that would interest disc jockeys (especially for the morning drive-time shows). Send review copies or news releases to **R&R (Radio & Records)**, 10100 Santa Monica Boulevard, 5th Floor, Los Angeles, CA 90067-4004; 310-553-4330; Fax: 310-203-9763. Web: http://www.rronline.com.

When my book on kinetic optical illusions, *Turntable Illusions*, was featured in this newspaper, I received many requests from producers in all parts of the country. Plus the producer for *Friday Night Videos* called to arrange a segment on the book.

☐ Also send information on your book and author to *Talkers,* the monthly newspaper for the news/talk radio industry. Send to **Talkers,** 650 Belmont Avenue, Springfield, MA 01108; 413-739-8255; Fax: 413-746-6786. Email: info@talkers.com. Web: http://www.talkers.com.

☐ Note that most radio hosts and producers also read *USA Today*. Again and again, as I travel around the country, I hear radio shows using stories from *USA Today* in their news segments and as filler material during the morning drive-time shows.

☐ Send an audiotape interview of the author or someone reading the book to radio stations. When William Morrow published John Irving's novel, *A Prayer for Owen Meany*, they sent a boxed cassette reading by the author to the book trade and major media.

B&B Audio offered oldies station WJMK in Chicago fifty copies of its *Love Tactics* audiotape to give away to listeners of its Club JMK program for singles. Each time the station gave away a copy, they said, "If you didn't win, you can get *Love Tactics* by calling B&B Audio at 1-800-3-LISTEN."

Richard Paul Evans, author of *The Christmas Box*, put together a two-hour program, *The Magic of the Christmas Box*, that featured an interview and *Christmas Box* music. The show was syndicated nationally.

☐ Offer free copies of your books to radio and TV shows. When I promoted *Tinseltowns, U.S.A.*, I offered ten free copies of the book to any radio show that would interview me. These copies were to be given away as promotion for my interview or during the actual interview. As a result of this one promotion, I was interviewed on over fifty shows, some lasting as long as an hour and a half.

To promote *The Wealthy Barber*, Dave Chilton sent twenty free copies to major radio and TV shows. In the letter that accompanied the books, he told the stations to give the copies to their camera people, reception-ists, hosts, and other employees. As he wrote in the letter, "I guarantee that once they read the book, you'll want me on your show." And he was right. As a result of those media appearances, his book became one of the top bestsellers in Canada for two years running.

☐ Fax information to the radio stations. Make sure the faxes are graphic and interesting. Humor publisher Bad Dog Press is already famous for its humorous and always interesting media faxes for their *Duct Tape* books. They get lots of response—and bookings—as a result of those faxed releases.

☐ Instead of using a publicity service to book interviews, Quill Driver Books hired a woman part-time to make phone calls and send faxes to broadcast media. During the first six weeks, working three days a week, she booked many media in California as well as the national weekend *Today* show.

9:16 How to Do Radio Phone Interviews

Here are a few tips, based on advice from authors who have done many phone interviews, on how to do a successful phone interview.

Tips from bestselling author Joanna Lund:

☐ Set up your room so there will be no interruptions.

☐ Prepare flash cards highlighting the major points you want to make.

☐ Have a page in front of you with the call letters of the station, the names of the producer and host, the city and state of the station, their phone number (in case you get disconnected), the time of the interview, and space to write down the names of callers so you can address them by name.

☐ Keep a glass of water handy.

☐ Send a thank you note.

Here are a few additional points from Jack Canfield and Mark Victor Hansen, bestselling authors of *Chicken Soup for the Soul*:

☐ Average one media interview every day. Do as many as you can.

☐ Be willing to do interviews any time of the day.

☐ Set up an 800 fulfillment number. They use a vanity number: 800-Soup-Book.

☐ Give listeners an incentive to order. They promise listeners an auto-graphed copy if they order right away.

☐ Be prepared for interviews. Write down your key points as easy to re-member sound bites.

☐ Mention your book title frequently during the interview.

☐ Use stories to communicate. People are more easily motivated by the stories you tell than any points you make.

☐ Continually visualize your success. Both Mark Victor Hansen and Jack Canfield cut out the *New York Times* bestseller list, wrote their book in as number one, and framed it in their offices.

Dr. Cass Igram sells $250,000 worth of books via radio shows every year. His best show was a 45-minute interview on WWDB in Philadelphia where he sold $45,000 worth of books. One of the ways he ups his take from any shows is to bundle several books together. Here are some of his tips for doing successful interviews:

☐ Keep a prop in front of you. Igram keeps a dollar bill in front of him to help him focus on his purpose.

☐ Don't get caught up in trying to give too much information. Instead, repeat your key points over and over again.

☐ Keep your answers short and to the point.

☐ People want to be entertained first, then educated.

☐ Before the show, ask the host if he has a personal interest in your topic. If you can get the host to talk about your topic, it will make for a stronger show.

☐ Change the pitch of your voice so you don't come across monotone.

☐ Be sincere.

☐ Stress the uniqueness of your book.

Here are a few more tips from other authors who have successfully sold books via radio phone interviews:

☐ **Tell your listeners to take time to get a pencil and paper** because in a few minutes you will give them three tips. When Joe Sabah was doing interviews for his get-a-job book, he offered three tips "I guarantee will get anyone a job." The reason you give them time to get their pencils is so they have it ready when you give out your phone number.

☐ **Give away some useful information with each interview.** This demonstrates to listeners that you have even more information to offer them. Paula Langguth, author of *Bounce Back from Bankruptcy*, always gives out lots of detailed information during her interviews and, as a result, gets at least twenty calls from every interview.

☐ **Work with local bookstores.** For some books, radio talk shows won't have much impact on sales unless you also contact bookstores ahead of time. For her book, *277 Secrets Your Dog Wants You to Know*, Paulette Cooper did 120 radio shows with little impact on sales. When she started contacting bookstores two weeks ahead of an interview in their local area, she started seeing an impact on sales. With every bookstore who agreed to order books, she told them that she would mention their name during her interview.

☐ **Offer free shipping if they order right away.** One publisher waives shipping costs if listeners, when ordering the book, mention the name of the radio show where they heard the author being interviewed. That way the publisher can track which shows produce the best results.

9:17 The Impact of TV Talk Shows

One appearance on a major network or syndicated TV talk show such as *Good Morning America* or *Oprah!* can sell thousands of books. As a Waldenbooks manager once noted, "Give me a *Phil Donahue Show*, and I'll sell you a million books." Nowadays, booksellers would say the same thing about *Oprah!* or *The Today Show*.

Even local TV talk shows can produce dramatic sales. Don't ignore TV just because you think viewers do not read. That is not the case. TV viewers do read, and they do respond to reviews and interviews they see on TV.

☐ **The daytime talk shows can sell books!** Louise Hay's appearances on *Oprah!* and *Donahue* catapulted her book, *You Can Heal Your Life*, onto the bestseller lists. Even before the book hit the bestseller lists, it had sold over half a million copies.

After Paula Begoun appeared on *Oprah!*, her *Blue Eyeshadow Should Be Illegal*, sold 40,000 copies. Since she was such an informed and entertaining guest, she has been invited back on *Oprah!* at least once a year.

When Marianne Williamson, author of *A Return to Love*, appeared on *Oprah!*, HarperCollins took back orders for 35,000 copies of her book by the end of that day. By the end of the next day, back orders had risen to 120,000 copies! The book became a bestseller within days.

Montel Williams, another TV talk show host, has also been known to propel books onto the bestseller lists. In late 1996, Paul Pearsall, author of *The Pleasure Prescription*, appeared on *The Montel Williams Show*. Within four weeks, the book had sold 75,000 copies and reprints had been ordered for another 100,000 copies.

Nora Hayden's appearances on *Oprah!, Joan Rivers*, and *Sonya Live* in one week pushed her self-published book, *How to Satisfy a Woman Every Time*, near the top of the bestseller lists.

A plug on Oprah still produces magic. A November, 2004 appearance on *Oprah* by Dr. Nicholas Perricone led to *The Perricone Promise* being ranked No. 1 on Amazon.com the next day, followed by the paperback edition of *The Perricone Prescription* at No. 2., the hardcover of *The Perricone Prescription* at No. 6 and *The Wrinkle Cure* at No. 7. *The Perricone Prescription Personal Journal* rose to No. 18. Perricone also had the No. 1 and No. 2 books the next day on Barnes&Noble.com.

☐ **The late night shows can also help sell books.** Bill Sand's book about his life in prison, *My Shadow Ran Fast*, did not sell well when first published. However, during an appearance on the *Tonight Show*, he so captivated the audience that he was invited back for a second show. Those two appearances alone were enough to put the book on the *New York Times* bestseller list. Also, within two weeks of his appearance on *The Tonight Show*, James Randi's *Flim-Flam* sold 7,000 copies.

☐ **The early-morning talk shows also sell books.** When Becky Barker appeared on *Good Morning, America* to promote her self-published book, *Answers*, ABC got more than 800 written requests for more information plus hundreds of phone calls. It was one of the largest responses they'd ever had to a segment on the show.

When H. Jackson Brown, author of *Life's Little Instruction Book*, appeared on the *Today* show, Waldenbooks sold 10,000 copies that day.

After Dr. Jason Theodasakis, author of *The Arthritis Cure*, appeared on the *Today* show, NBC received so many calls from viewers that they booked him again a month later. The publishers had to go back to press immediately for another 110,000 copies.

☐ **The evening news shows also sell books.** The day after Andrew Weil, author of *Spontaneous Healing*, appeared on *Prime-Time Live* during the May sweeps period, both Knopf, his publisher, and ABC were flooded with phone calls. Sales jumped almost 1000% during the next 24 hours.

☐ **Cable shows can also sell books.** After Vincent Bugliosi, author of *Outrage: The Five Reasons Why O.J. Simpson Got Away with Murder*, appeared on CNBC's *Rivera Live*, the publisher sold 20,000 books the next day. The next night, when Bugliosi appeared on CNN's *Larry King Live* to debate Alan Dershowitz, 40,000 more books were sold immediately. Within two weeks, the book had 400,000 copies in print.

When Warner Books published Stephen Davis's story of the rock group Led Zeppelin, *Hammer of the Gods*, not only did *Rolling Stone* magazine serialize the book, but MTV got wind and began plugging the book free of charge. As a result, this hardcover book sold over 70,000 copies.

9:18 How to Arrange TV Talk Show Appearances

Here are a few more tips on how to arrange TV appearances for your authors. These tips supplement the general suggestions for obtaining interviews outlined in previous sections.

☐ Allow four to eight weeks lead time for TV talk shows. That means you must begin contacting the show producers at least four weeks ahead of the date your author will be available.

☐ To locate the producers and hosts of national TV news and talk shows, get a copy of *The Top National TV Talk Shows* published by Bradley

Communications. To order, call 800-989-1400 or go to http://www.free-publicity.com.

☐ When you call, first talk to the receptionist at the station to confirm the name of your contact. In this business people change jobs often so even if you use the most up-to-date directory, chances are that some of your major contacts will have moved on.

☐ Once you've confirmed the name of the booking agent (producer, talent coordinator, or whatever their title might be), have the receptionist transfer your call to that person. Give him or her a good pitch for your author. Tell exactly how your author can enliven the show. This pre-call can save you time and money because often the person will either tell you that the show doesn't do such interviews or will refer you to someone else at the station who would be more likely to be interested in your particular author or subject.

☐ Once you've alerted the person that you will be sending him or her something, send your press kit that same day.

☐ When pitching the afternoon talk shows, pitch a show idea. Wrap up your author in a great show. For example, describe how your author can take someone out of the audience and change their life, their relationships, their finances, their love life. If you know of regular people who have used the author's diet, financial program, ideas, or whatever, let the producers know that you can put them in touch with real people who have had success using the book.

☐ Within five days of the day you expect the person to receive your press kit, follow up with a phone call. Don't wait for anyone to call you. They're not about to. In this follow-up call, you must make your best pitch. The pitch should be well-rehearsed and short (no more than 30 seconds). If you cannot get your pitch down to three or four sentences, then you are not likely to get anyone's attention.

☐ Remember that the attention span of a person while watching TV is very short, so your description of why anyone would be interested in what your author has to say must be equally short. Don't become pushy; such tactics rarely work. If someone says no, go on to call the next person on your list. If the person indicates they will think about it, suggest that you'll call them back again in a few days. Then do so.

☐ Don't make the same pitch to every show. Remember that most TV shows have different needs. Late night shows want humor or celebrity gossip. Early morning shows want practical advice. The daytime talk shows want drama and conflict—or good advice on how to avoid drama and conflict. The evening news shows want scandal or controversy—or good commentary on such events.

☐ Wade West, a media trainer with MediaPower, points out that print media talk to the head while broadcast media talk to the gut. He suggests that you pitch a strong selling point. Focus on a problem and then offer the solution (your author and his or her book). Other possible pitches: controversy, current news stories, predictions, trends. Look for ways to explain a complicated news story in a single sound bite. Feed them stories that will capture their imaginations.

☐ When you do receive a booking, send a letter out to the person right away thanking him or her for the booking and confirming the exact time and place. This confirmation letter will prevent any later misunderstandings or mishaps. You can find a sample confirmation letter, with all the details that should be in such a letter, in the *Do-It-Yourself Book Publicity Kit* by John Kremer (available only through Open Horizons).

☐ The real secret, of course, in obtaining interviews is to keep on calling. If the first person rejects your pitch, call the second; if the second also rejects your pitch, call the third. Continue calling until you get a booking. If your author or the subject of the book is at all interesting, you should have no trouble obtaining a good number of interviews.

☐ Be persistent with the major shows that you feel really should feature your authors. Send those shows new information at least once every two months, if not more frequently. Make sure your news releases and other info target the show's needs. Relate the book to a current crisis, problem, or news event. But, above all, keep in touch. One self-published author took over a year to get on *Oprah!*, but she kept her name in front of them until they finally called her.

☐ Send TV shows a photo of you or, better yet, a video. As one *Dateline* producer noted, "On television, we want to know what you look like."

☐ Include a phone number where the author can be reached day or night. It's common for a news producer call at midnight on Sunday.

☐ It's best to start your new authors out with appearances on local shows so they can get more experience dealing with the hectic environment of a TV studio during the taping of a show.

☐ You might find it easier to book the national network shows by working through your local network affiliate. If your author makes a good impression on their talk show, then the local affiliate might be willing to help you book the author on a national show.

☐ When sending your press kit to local and national shows, include a videotape of your author in action. This videotape could be taken from a previous interview where the author performed well, or it could be a demo tape of the author during a simulated interview taped especially for the press kit. In either case, the tape should give program directors a great opportunity to see how well your author comes over on TV. Major TV shows want to see a tape at some point, so have one ready to send.

☐ Bribe your children. Trish Gallagher, author of *Raising Happy Kids on a Budget*, offered a $50 prize to whichever of her children got her on

Oprah! Her five-year-old won by writing a letter that essentially said, "My Mommy wrote a book. Please have her on your show." It worked.

☐ Call 800-421-9600. That's the advice that publicist Arielle Ford gives to authors who want to be on *Oprah!* That's the Science of Mind prayer line. Some authors swear it works.

☐ Stay on top of the news. CNN has a 24-hour phone line which you can call if your book relates to a breaking news story. They always need experts to shed lights on current events.

☐ Keep getting publicity. Eric Marcus, author of *Breaking the Surface*, got on *Oprah!* because the show's researchers had run across an article where he had been interviewed the year before.

☐ Get to know the shows. Find out what they like, what kind of programs they do, how they like to appeal to their audience.

☐ Buy something expensive and in the spotlight. Okay, not every author can do this, but it did work for novelist Sandra Brown. Just around the time her novel, *Exclusive*, was published, she went to Christie's and became the proud owner of the tiara that Audrey Hepburn wore while filming *Breakfast at Tiffanys*. CBS, ABC, and Fox all interviewed her about her purchase, filming her as she held a copy of her book.

☐ You can do a national TV tour without leaving your home city. How? By doing a show on your local public-access cable television channel and then marketing the tape to public access cable outlets across the country. Your cost: duplicating fees for the tape and mailing costs.

☐ Along with a copy of your book, here are two other items you should bring to all TV interviews:

1. Bring along any visual aids or props that will help to make the interview more interesting. For example, bring fire extinguishers or alarms for a book on fire safety. Or cakes and cookies for a dessert cookbook. Or regional craft items for a book on travel. When Dr. Aubrey Hampton, author of *What's in Your Cosmetics?*, appears on shows, he shows viewers how to create safe hair and skin care products by using ingredients found in most kitchens (such as yogurt, green tea, or citrus fruits).

2. Also, bring an index card with the author's name typed in all caps on one line and the title of the book on another. Bring this card to make it easy for the show's production crew to flash the information on the screen while the author is talking.

☐ Always send a thank-you note. In 1997, a CNBC host remembered a 1985 show where Harvey Mackay, author of *Swim with the Sharks*, was the guest. Why did he remember the show? Because Mackay was "one of the few authors who sent me a thank you note." He told Mackay that the note had really made a difference. What did Mackay do? He called his office that day and had a specific thank you note sent to the host via Federal Express for delivery the next day.

9:19 More Ways to Obtain TV Coverage

Author interviews are not the only way to get coverage on television. Here are a few more options:

☐ Send information on your books (or information *from* the books) to various television syndicates, such as Med*News, which each week syndicates three 2-minute segments on health and medicine.

☐ Send out video news releases (VNR). If you choose this option, have it produced by professionals. Make sure it is identified as a PR release, is one to four minutes in length, and features more than a standup news reporter or two talking heads. See the next page for the names of some companies that can help you produce a VNR.

To support a national tour by Dr. Bernard Lown for the book *Peace: A Dream Unfolding*, Simon & Schuster sent out four-minute *Peace* videos to stations across the country.

DWJ Television went to the top of the Brooklyn Bridge to interview Nick Telch for a VNR about his book, *America Then & Now*, which features photos taken years ago with recent photos taken at the same spot (the Brooklyn Bridge was one of the spots featured in the book). HarperCollins used the VNR to support a satellite media tour of the author.

Warner produced a special VNR to promote Madonna's book, *Sex.* Over 47,000,000 people got a sneak peek of the book when the VNR aired on network, local, and cable TV stations worldwide.

☐ Set up an author tour via satellite. By producing an interview locally and feeding it to stations across the country via satellite, your author can do a 20-city television tour in less than four hours. Here are two companies that specializes in producing satellite author tours:

On the Scene Productions, 5900 Wilshire Boulevard #1400, Los Angeles, CA 90036; 213-930-1030; Fax: 213-930-1840. Web: http://www.onthescene.com. They also produce and distribute VNRs. On the Scene went inside Attica Prison to interview Donald Frankos, a Mafia hitman and author of *Contract Killer*, for a satellite broadcast to promote the book published by Thunder's Mouth Press.

Planned Television Arts, 1110 Second Avenue, 3rd Floor, New York NY 10022; 212-593-5820; Fax: 212-715-1664. Web: http://www.plannedtvarts.com. Their Sunrise Satellite Tour offers their clients the opportunity to reach dozens of morning television shows in a few short hours. PTA also produces B-roll newsfeeds, video news releases, electronic press kits (EPK), Morning Drive Radio Tours, and TelePrint Conferences. PTA's 20/20/20 publicity campaign, which consists of a 20-city Morning Drive Radio Tour, a 20-city Sunrise Satellite Tour, and a 20-city TelePrint Conference (to major newspapers) can be done for about $10,000 to $15,000.

When the Ebola virus killed fifty people in Zaire, Random House and PTA worked together to carry out a crisis response publicity campaign for Richard Preston, author of *The Hot Zone*. The campaign included a 22-city satellite TV tour as well as a 20-city TelePrint conference.

☐ Send out video news releases via satellite. In a survey conducted by News/Broadcast Network, news directors preferred the following subjects for VNR topics: 39% health/medical topics, 27% hard news, 15% consumer news, 6% unusual features, and 4% business news. There are many companies which can provide VNR production and distribution. Here are a few of them:

Medialink, 708 Third Avenue, 9th Floor, New York, NY 10017; 212-682-8300; 800-843-0677. Web: http://www.medialinkworldwide.com. Distributes but does not produce VNRs.

National Satellite, 8075 W. Third Street #504, Los Angeles, CA 90048; 213-857-0777; Fax: 213-939-9475. Email: natsat@aol.com.

News/Broadcast Network, 149 Madison Avenue #804, New York, NY 10016; 212-889-0888; Fax: 212-696-4611.

Worldwide Television News, 1995 Broadway, 8th Floor, New York, NY 10023; 212-362-4440; 800-526-1161; Fax: 212-496-1269.

The cost of having one of the above companies produce, distribute, and monitor a video news release ranges from $8,000 to $25,000. Distribution costs from $3,000 to $8,000, depending on coverage.

Authors — Visit your local TV stations. Call ahead of time to get the name of the person you want to meet. Since you are a celebrity, they should be happy to interview you, if even for a short two-minute interview. Get experience doing local shows before attempting to hit the national shows.

9:20 Organizing Effective Author Tours

Author tours can be expensive, a hassle to put together, and very wearing on the author, but for some books they can make a great difference for sales. In general, author tours are not productive unless the author is a celebrity and/or the subject of the book has a wide appeal or is connected to a current issue of interest to many people.

Author tours are not easy to arrange. Not only do you have the additional expense of long-distance phone calls, but you must also fit interviews into a tighter schedule since you cannot afford to pay for the author to stay more than a day or two in any one city. Nevertheless, for certain authors and books you will want to arrange such tours. Note that if you hire an out-side publicity service, it will cost you about $3,000 per city to book and co-ordinate an author tour.

The *Do-It-Yourself Book Publicity Kit* by John Kremer includes work-sheets and procedures to help you organize author tours with a minimum ef-fort. Here are a few suggestions to make the tour more effective:

☐ **Consider doing several short tours rather than one long one.** Not only would this be easier on your author, but it could also save you money (especially if you can organize the mini-tours around your author's normal business or vacation travel).

☐ **Here are the major cities** that publishers regularly schedule for author tours: Atlanta, Boston, Chicago, Dallas, Houston, Los Angeles, Miami, New York, Philadelphia, San Diego, San Francisco, Seattle, and Wash-ington, D.C. Second tier cities include: Cleveland, Denver, Kansas City, Milwaukee, Minneapolis, New Orleans, Palm Beach, Pittsburgh, Port-land, San Antonio/Austin, and Saint Louis.

☐ **Arrange for a local contact** in each city, someone who can pick the author up at the airport and take care of any other driving during the author's stay in the city. This local contact could be one of your sales representatives, a friend or relative (yours or the author's), or a profes-sional media escort.

☐ **When booking interviews, don't forget other possible appearances** that could boost sales for the author's book. Check to see if any book-stores would be willing to host an autograph session. Try to schedule a speaking engagement for the author with a local club, association, or business. Have the author visit any key wholesalers, distributors, or other sales outlets. Look into any local celebrations or other events.

Warner Book books its authors into other venues to support their book-store signings and media interviews. Richard Simmons worked out on center stage in many malls. Alice Medrich whipped up chocolate truffles in local gourmet shops. Robert Ballard recreated the last night of the *Ti-tanic* for students. Kirk Douglas signed his latest novel in the lobbies of movie theaters.

☐ **Call the regional bureaus** of Associated Press and United Press Inter-national and ask that your author's appearances be listed in their Day Book. The Day Book is a calendar of events which is checked every day by media sources which subscribe to the AP or UPI services. This could, again, result in additional interviews or other coverage.

☐ **Be sure the local newspaper calendars** list any author appearances.

☐ **Do a road show.** To promote their books (including *Pirate Utopias* and *Chaosophy*), Autonomedia/Semiotexte sent the six-member Bindlestiff Family Circus on a cross country tour where they performed sideshow acts and comedy at colleges, rock clubs, and theaters. The fire-eaters and blockheads took turns pitching the publisher's 100+ titles. The performers toured the country in a bookmobile.

☐ **Hold a launch party.** To kick off the publication of *Final Curtain* by Margaret Burk and Gary Hudson, Seven Locks Press hosted a luncheon on the *Wild Goose* yacht, formerly owned by John Wayne. Pfeifer-Hamilton, another small publisher, has launched books in museums, art stores, and sports bars.

☐ **Do something unusual.** To promote his book, *Bad As I Wanna Be*, NBA star Dennis Rodman showed up at a Barnes & Noble signing in New York City wearing a complete wedding ensemble, including dress, veil, gloves, and bouquet. Not only did this appearance gain him plenty of notice in the press, but it also resulted in a 35% increase in sales of the book throughout the Barnes & Noble chain.

☐ **Do a virtual tour.** In 1996, W.W. Norton and Pacific Bell used video-conferencing to promote Walter Mosley's mystery, *A Little Yellow Dog*. While Mosley read selections from the book and answered questions from the audience at the Pasadena Public Library, his presentation was videocasted live to three other libraries in California. Attendees at the other sites were able to participate in the question-and-answer session.

> **Authors** — If your publisher wants to arrange a tour for you, cooperate. Note, however, that a tour is wearing and time consuming. If your publisher declines to book a tour, you can book your own. That's what Harvey Mackay did for his first book (with the help of a PR company). Indeed, he spent about $3,000 per city for his 26-city tour. But, in his case, it was worth it. That tour helped to put his book on the bestseller lists.

9:21 Distribution Is Everything

Make sure you have distribution before arranging an extensive author tour or major media interviews. If there are not enough books in the stores to cover the anticipated demand, the entire effort can be wasted. This means, at the very minimum, that you should give advance notice to the booksellers in each city the author will be touring. Even better, you should have your sales representatives or distributors make sales calls just prior to your author's appearances. Here are a few other things you can do:

☐ Pay for a listing of your author tour in the weekly *Bookselling This Week* email newsletter. For ad rates, contact the **American Booksellers Association**, 828 S. Broadway, Tarrytown, NY 10591; 914-591-2665; 800-637-0037; Fax: 914-591-2720. Web: http://www.bookweb.org.

☐ Arrange for distribution yourself. When Beverly Nye organized her own author tour, she checked the yellow pages of each city for retail bookstores. She called each store to let them know that she would be doing interviews and to confirm how many copies of her book they had in stock. She then drove around to each store peddling her books and confirming that each store would have sufficient stock to cover the demand.

☐ Work with a major book chain to ensure that your books are carried in each city your authors will be visiting. Then have your authors mention that the books are available at that chain if the viewer cannot find them elsewhere. For example, Waldenbooks worked with Fairfield Press to ensure that *The TM Book* was in stock when TV shows promoting the Transcendental Meditation program were aired in different cities.

☐ If all else fails (and you don't have a toll-free order line), have your author give out your web site or the phone number for a fulfillment service. Listings of some book fulfillment services can be found at http://www.bookmarket.com/4.html.

9:22 How to Make Waves by Making News

Besides being featured in reviews and interviews, your authors and books can also be publicized via regular news or feature stories. Indeed, some of the best publicity for books and authors comes outside the normal review or interview channels. Don't overlook any chance for publicity. Make news. Find a news hook. Connect your books or authors with news that's already happening or about to happen. Below is just a short list of ways you can hitchhike publicity for your books with other news.

Anniversaries

Schedule the publication of your book to coincide with an appropriate anniversary. Here are just a few anniversaries that have been used as promotional tie-ins by publishers:

☐ **College**—Globe Pequot Press published *The Illustrated Harvard* to coincide with that university's 350th anniversary.

☐ **Current events**—Congdon & Weed's published the book *One American Must Die* to commemorate the anniversary of the terrorist hijacking of a TWA jetliner.

☐ **Deaths**—Grove Press published Warren Beath's *The Death of James Dean* on the anniversary of Dean's death.

☐ **Sports**—Donald I. Fine set the publication date of Maury Allen's *Roger Maris: A Man for All Seasons* to coincide with Maris's 25th anniversary of breaking Babe Ruth's homer record.

☐ **State**—Putnam's *Make Way for Sam Houston* tied in with the Texas Sesquicentennial celebration.

☐ **TV show**—the CBS/Library of Congress "Read More About It" book promotion project featured a number of books about soap operas on the 30th anniversary broadcast of *As the World Turns*.

To locate such anniversaries, see John Kremer's *Celebrate Today Special Events Database* (http://www.celebratetoday.com).

Book Anniversaries

Celebrate the anniversaries of book classics by republishing the classics or by publishing new related titles.

* To celebrate the 50th anniversary of the publication of Margaret Mitchell's *Gone with the Wind*, Macmillan published a golden anniversary facsimile of the original edition. Meanwhile, Outlet Books excerpted part of Ronald Haver's *David O. Selznick's Hollywood* for release as *David O. Selznick's Gone with the Wind*. Several other book publishers also brought out related titles.

* Dutton celebrated the 60th anniversary of the publication of A.A. Milne's *Winnie-the-Pooh* by publishing *The Winnie-the-Pooh Journal*.

Authors' Birthdays

You can celebrate authors' birthdays by publishing or re-releasing their books. For example, July offers the following author birthdays: George Sand (1st), Hermann Hesse (2nd), Franz Kafka (3rd), Nathaniel Hawthorne (4th), Beatrix Potter (6th), Robert Heinlein (7th), Jean Kerr and Marcel Proust (10th), E. B. White (11th), Henry David Thoreau and Pablo Neruda (12th), Isaac Bashevis Singer and Irving Stone (14th), Erle Stanley Gardner (17th), William Thackeray and Yevgeny Yevtushenko (18th), Ernest Hemingway and John Gardner (21st), Stephen Vincent Benet and Amy Vanderbilt (22nd), Raymond Chandler (23rd), Alexandre Dumas, pere and John D. MacDonald (24th), Paul Gallico and Carl Jung (26th), Alexandre Dumas, fils (27th), Gerard Manley Hopkins (28th), Alexis de Tocqueville (29th), and Emily Bronte (30th), among many others.

By the way, if you'd like to celebrate my birthday, it's January 16th.

TV Series

Publicize books that are tied in to continuing TV series such as the various soap operas or to miniseries such as *Roots* or *Shogun*. Genealogy books, for example, have always sold better after showings of *Roots*.

* The miniseries, *Dreams West*, was part of the CBS/Library of Congress "Read More About It" project. The project, in connection with this miniseries, promoted books about America's westward expansion.

* After the six-part PBS series, *Joseph Campbell and the Power of Myth*, appeared, Princeton University Press saw its 39-year-old Campbell title, *Hero with a Thousand Faces*, hit the bestseller lists. Doubleday sold over 250,000 copies of the companion book to the series.

- When Shirley MacLaine's *Out on a Limb* miniseries aired, the book once again hit the bestseller lists. Indeed, all four of MacLaine's previous books went right back onto the bestseller lists. One of the books featured in this miniseries (the book fell on MacLaine's head, thereby starting her on her quest) was *A Dweller on Two Planets*; within a week Harper & Row received 2,000 orders for the book. Meanwhile, sales of all new age and metaphysical books jumped 95% at B. Dalton stores.

- After the airing of *World without Walls* (a documentary about aviatrix Beryl Markham) on a local PBS station, North Point Press sold 20,000 copies of Markham's book, *West with the Night*, within two weeks—in the Bay area alone! Once the show aired nationally, the book hit all the major bestseller lists and sold more than 375,000 copies.

Movies

You can also tie-in the publication dates of books with the release dates of movies. The obvious beneficiary of such tie-ins are the directly related books about the movie or the books which formed the basis for the script. But other books can work as well. I'm sure, for example, that fly-fishing books sold better after the movie, *A River Runs Through It*, hit the screens.

- In 1947, Lippincott and Universal Studios promoted Betty MacDonald's bestselling book and soon-to-be-released movie, *The Egg and I*, by setting up a stunt. They hired Jim Moran, a professional screwball, to hatch an ostrich egg while reading a copy of the book.

- Ecco's *Rope Burns*, a collection of short stories from a corner man, sold fewer than 9,000 copies in its first four years. But it got a new cover and title (*Million Dollar Baby*) when the Clint Eastwood movie was nominated for Best Picture in 2005.

Broadway Shows

While Broadway shows don't have the national impact of television series or movies, they can still be used as promotional tie-ins. Marion Boyars set the publication date of Charles Marowitz's *Potboilers: Three Black Comedies* to coincide with the October opening of the Broadway show, *Sherlock's Last Case*, starring Frank Langella.

Local Interests

Make special note of any local angles when sending out press releases or review copies. For example, if the author has lived or still lives in the region, note that fact (perhaps by placing a label on the cover of the book announcing that the author is a local resident). As an alternative, you can take a local event and make it of national interest.

- When I sent out review copies of *Tinseltowns, U.S.A.*, I localized each release to that city. Since more than 400 towns and cities were featured in the book, it wasn't hard to find a local angle for all major newspapers.

- When a Peanut Advisory Board survey uncovered that most Americans identify peanut butter as a fun food, they decided to capitalize on that perception. How? They convinced the town of Peanut, Pennsylvania (population 140), to stage a Peanut Butter Lovers' Festival to raise money for a local library and food bank. To publicize the event, they erected signs at the city limits saying, "Welcome to Peanut, Pennsylvania. We're Nuts About You!" They also invited national media to attend and sample the world's largest peanut butter and jelly sandwich. While only 950 people attended the event, one of them was the governor of Pennsylvania. Stories about the event were featured in Associated Press, UPI, CNN, CNBC, *Washington Post*, *Wall Street Journal*, and local TV affiliates in New York, Baltimore, Philadelphia, and St. Louis.

Retailing Promotional Tie-ins

Whenever you can associate your book with a retail promotion, whether local or national, do so. Frederick Warne published several Beatrix Potter books to tie in with "The World of Beatrix Potter" department store display which toured eleven major cities.

Holidays

Many books are published to coincide with major holidays, such as Christmas, Hanukkah, Easter, Halloween, Valentines, Mother's Day, and others. Many retailers try to coordinate promotions with these holidays.

- Dolphin scheduled the publication date of Bill Cosby's book *Fatherhood* for Father's Day, 1986.

- The publication date for the book, *How to Make Love All the Time*, by sex therapist Barbara De Angelis was set for Valentine's Day. The book became a bestseller.

- Sierra Club Books launched *Peace: A Dream Unfolding* by Patrick Crean and Penney Kome on November 11th, Veterans Day.

- To promote their *Duct Tape* books, Pfeifer-Hamilton sent out a news release featuring the top ten uses for duct tape around the holidays. This list got reprinted in many newspapers.

- To tie in with Mother's Day, Impact Publishers conducted an Almost Perfect Mother-in-Law contest to promote *The Other Mother* by Yvette Strauss. The winning 200-word essay on "why your mother-in-law is almost perfect" received a gift certificate for two tickets to Hawaii for the mother-in-law and her son-in-law or daughter-in-law. All entries had to be validated by a participating bookstore.

Special Months

Time your book's publication date with a month that suits your book's subject. September is Back to School Month; June is Dairy Month; May is Barbecue Month; April is School Media Month.

- Learning Publications found out the hard way. They sent out press releases in June for their book called *Joyful Learning—Learning Games for Children Ages 4 to 12*, but they did not receive any notices for the book until September because that is the time when people's interest again returns to educational issues.

- For the celebration of National Poetry Month in April, several publishers became participating sponsors. Alice James Books, Arte Público Press, Beacon Press, Calyx Books, Boyds Mills Press, Harry Abrams, and Bantam Doubleday Dell were among the sponsoring publishers who highlighted poetry titles during that month. Many media also committed themselves to greater coverage of poetry. These media included *Vanity Fair, Mirabella, Elle, Metropolitan Home, New York Times, The Nation, New Yorker, Harper's Bazaar*, and NPR's *Fresh Air*. This annual month has become an effective promotion for poetry books.

> **Authors** — To locate all the special months, weeks, and days, refer to the *Celebrate Today Special Events Database*. It includes more than 18,500 possible media tie-ins, from National Eye Health Care Month to French Fry Friday. This database costs $30.00. Web: http://www.celebratetoday.com.

Special Weeks

Arrange your book's publication date or big promotions to fall within weeks that tie in with the book's subject. April has Library Week and Secretary's Week; October has Children's Book Week and Fire Safety Week; June has Gay Pride Week; July has Special Recreation Week for the Disabled; and August has Psychic Week, National Smile Week, and National Scuba Diving Week. For any subject, there's at least one week that fits.

- Peggy Glenn arranged for major publicity during Secretary's Week for her book on *How to Start and Run a Successful Home Typing Business*. As a result, the book received feature stories in a number of major newspapers and magazines.

- You can sponsor your own week. Simply send in the information to the **National Special Events Registry**, P.O. Box 205, Fairfield, IA 52556-0205; 641-472-6130; Fax: 641-472-1560. Email: JohnKremer@book-market.com. Web: http://www.celebratetoday.com. The following information is required: name of the event; dates of event (day, week or month); if dates are changeable, an explanation of how they change from year to year; sponsor's name, address, phone numbers, email address, and web URL; and an explanation of what the event is. You can also send nominations to *Chase's Annual Events* by calling 312-540-4536.

- Azriela Jaffe, author of *Honey, I Want to Start My Own Business*, created two holidays. The first week of May is Acknowledge Your Supportive Spouse Week and the Friday after Labor Day is Honey, I Want to Start My Own Business Day (notice how well it ties in with her title). For the week in May, she sponsored a national award for the best supportive spouses (who would receive awards donated by sponsoring companies). Teleflora, one of the sponsors, promoted the event throughout their network of 20,000 florists.

- *Random Acts of Kindness*, published by Conari Press, has inspired the creation of a special week (the week of Valentine's Day) called Random Acts of Kindness Week. As of 1997, 480 communities and 75 cities were sponsoring activities for that week. Articles in *Family Circle* and *Teaching Tolerance* brought a flood of calls into the offices of Conari from people wanting to get involved. Conari prepared posters, buttons, and T-shirts to celebrate the week and then advertised to booksellers via *Bookselling This Week*.

- Beverly Naidus, author/illustrator of *One Size Does Not Fit All*, designed the poster for 1997's Eating Disorder Awareness Week in February.

Special Days or Celebrations

As there are weeks and months for almost everything, there are also special days and/or celebrations as well. For example, besides Mother's Day, May also has Biographers Day, Native American Day, Tax Freedom Day, No Socks Day, National Hoagie Day, and Armed Forces Day.

- Look in *Chase's Annual Events* (available at your local library) to discover special days, weeks, and months that might fit in well with your books. This book is especially useful for local celebrations. *Celebrate Today*, mentioned previously, has more listings for national events.

- Grove Press scheduled the beginning of a nationwide author's tour to coincide with World Hunger Day, October 16th, for *World Hunger: Twelve Myths*, by Frances Moore Lappe and Joseph Collins.

- For *Tall Ships of the World*, Globe Pequot Press planned a promotional tie-in with the Fourth of July Tall Ships Parade in New York City.

Current Events

Scan the daily newspapers for any current news that you might use to further publicize your books. Be on the lookout for offbeat as well as headline news.

- The author of a book on how to stop snoring noticed a short item about a wife filing for a divorce because she could no longer stand her husband's loud snoring. The author quickly sent off a copy of his book to the judge hearing the case. The judge, in turn, announced in court that he felt the book could save the couple's marriage. Of course, that statement made the local news and was later picked up by the wire services.

Soon feature articles all over the country were spreading the word about the book. As a result, the book went into four printings.

- When the Green Bay Packers won the Super Bowl in 1997, Barry Sears sent out news releases noting that the Packers had been modifying their diet over the past year to eat more protein and less carbohydrates to keep them in the zone, as described in *The Zone* by Barry Sears. Several key Packer players used Joe Masiello, an advocate of the Zone Diet, as their trainer. Two days before the game, Masiello was quoted as saying, "The team that's in the Zone will be able to sustain a level of energy over the other team, and this will be a hard-fought game."

- In 1996, several publishers made use of the presidential primaries and race as a way of drawing attention to their books. Random House, for example, set up shop in the lobby of the Sheraton Wayfarer in Manchester, New Hampshire, to give out copies of *Primary Colors* to the press covering the Republican primary debate.

- Velvet hammer marketing specialist Joanna Lund organized a Presidential Pie Primary during the final months of the race between Clinton and Dole in 1996. She started by calling both candidates to get their favorite flavors. It took three calls to each campaign office to get their favorites —Clinton liked pineapple, apricots, and pecans; Dole liked anything with chocolate. Lund developed cheesecake recipes for each candidate and then sent out news releases headlined: "Vote for the Pie Worthy of Being Served in the White House." She encourage people to make both pies at home, and let each family member vote on which flavor they liked best. She ended her release by saying, "May the best pie win!" Many radio stations and 100 newspapers announced her primary and, as a result, she got three things: 1) the names of all the people who entered, 2) results that closely mirrored the actual results of the '96 election, and 3) follow-up publicity. She'll be at it again in 2000 with a news release that announces, "Ignore all the other polls. Use the pie primary to predict the winner!" The total cost of her campaign? $350.00.

Authors — Here is a good reason for you to read your daily newspaper or weekly news magazine. Your publisher cannot possibly notice or follow up on all the potential tie-ins to current events. You are in a far better position to do so. Hence, when you notice a potential tie-in, either let your publisher know or follow up on the item yourself.

Natural Events

Associate your book with a natural event, anything from eruptions like Mount St. Helens to regular events such as the coming of Halley's Comet.

The predictable events obviously work best because you can plan your publishing calendar around the events.

- A number of publishers brought out books to coincide with the return of Halley's Comet, including Hunter House's *Tales of the Comet* and Polestar-Nexus's *Mr. Halley and His Comet* (which was also the premier book in a series of children's books about men and women of science).

- One author from a small town in Missouri is always called upon by major media when any major earthquake occurs. Why? Not only is he an expert on earthquakes, but he has written several major books about earthquakes.

Conferences and Conventions

Set your publication date to coincide with an important conference or convention. Look especially for any conference, trade show, or convention that relates to the subject of your book.

- Princeton University Press scheduled their main publicity campaign for the book, *Makers of Modern Strategy from Machiavelli to the Nuclear Age*, to coincide with a major conference on "War in History and War Today."

- The University of North Carolina Press publicized the book, *North Carolina Quilts*, to tie in with a quilt exhibit at the North Carolina Museum of History.

Charity Events

Contribute your books as prizes for a charity event, anything from the semiannual public television fund-raisers to special campaigns such as the Statue of Liberty renovation.

- For an auction to benefit the Mercantile Library in New York City, science fiction author Isaac Asimov offered to include the name and occupation of the highest bidder in his next short story.

- Barron's donated a small portion of its profits from the children's book, *Pickles*, to the North American Riding for the Handicapped Association.

- To commemorate its 25th year in business, Jossey-Bass adopted the San Francisco Public Library by making a commitment to give them a copy of every new book they publish during the coming 25 years. Of course, they made sure other people knew what they did and, as a result, they received national as well as local publicity for their efforts.

- In cooperation with the American Lung Association, Scholastic launched a Proud to Be Smoke Free awareness campaign. As part of the campaign, Scholastic released *The Berenstain Bear Scouts and the Sinister Smoke Ring* by Stan and Jan Berenstain. The Bears were also featured on promotional material with the American Lung Association logo. The publisher and association also planned an extensive community outreach program (schools, libraries, bookstores, and media) to emphasize the importance of healthy lungs and to stop the formation of smoking habits.

- When Mickey Mantle died in 1995, Peachtree Publishers sent out a press release announcing that one of Mantle's last written statements was his contribution to *Home for the Holidays*, a gift book benefiting Habitat for Humanity. As Mantle noted in his contribution, "It's really nice to be able to use the name of Mickey Mantle to give something back." At the bottom of the news release Peachtree noted that "Sales of 10,000 copies of this book will provide the funds to build one house for a family on the Habitat waiting list."

- In 1997, Berrett-Koehler joined with several other business book publishers to form the Consortium for Business Literacy. One of the major purposes of the consortium was to encourage the formation of business reading groups where people would come together and discuss the ideas presented in the latest business books. To facilitate the groups, Berrett-Koehler published a free *Guide to Starting a Reading Group* and offered quantity discounts on books used by the reading groups. They also published study guides for some of their books.

Local Book Fairs and Other Festivals

Tie-in the publication of your book with a local book fair, ethnic festival, or other celebration. If nothing else, this should get you a feature in the local newspaper or, at the very least, a notice of some kind.

- For example, if your book is aimed at an Hispanic audience, one of your best promotions would be to give away sample chapters of your book to people attending Cinco de Mayo festivals.

- Redbird Productions promoted *Cream and Bread*, their book on growing up in a Scandinavian community, at any festival or event where people of Scandinavian descent might attend. As a result, in less than two years they sold over 27,000 copies of their self-published book.

Authors — Look out for any of the above promotional tie-ins for your book. Indeed, if you know of any such promotional tie-ins when you are submitting your manuscript or book proposal to publishers, tell them about the tie-in right away. Such tie-ins make the book more attractive. As a result, you are more likely to interest publishers in publishing your book.

Top 10 Lists

One of the great tools of publicity is the creation and annual announcement of a Top 10 list. Blackwell's lists of the best dressed and worst dressed celebrities make news every year. Blackwell doesn't create these lists just for fun; he's got something to sell to the fashion industry.

David Letterman's lists of 10 every night make news almost every morning on many radio stations around the country. Why? Because they are funny. Do they help to promote his TV show? You bet they do.

If you have a book on surviving cancer, why not create a list honoring the top 10 famous people who are helping to create awareness for cancer checkups and/or raise funds for on-going cancer research? If you publish travel books, create a list of the top 10 new things to see or do in the state, country, or area your books cover. If you publish business management books, honor the top 10 business managers of the year.

Look at the famous lists that make news every year: the *Fortune* 500, the *Forbes* 400, the *Sports Illustrated* swimsuit issue, *Time*'s person of the year, *People*'s 50 sexiest people, *Newsweek*'s list of the top colleges, etc. Why do magazines create such lists? Because they help to sell magazines. These issues are always among the top-selling issues of the year for these magazines. Media love lists because their readers and listeners love lists.

If you can create a real list that's worthy of news, you can reap major publicity year after year after year. All-star games are just lists. Pro bowls are just lists. The top 25 college basketball teams are just lists. But these make news week after week, year after year, both before the major event as well as during and after such events. The Oscars, Emmys, Tonys, and other such awards are just lists—lists that make major news for the movie, TV, and stage industries every year.

Some lists make news every day. What do you think the Dow Jones Average is? It is based on a list of 25 stocks, yet investors watch this number for signs of a strong or weak economy. There are also the S&P 500, the Nasdaq 100, as well as other indexes—all aimed at providing some insight into the economy while also publicizing the companies or organizations who develop these lists.

When you create a list, you can choose to develop it yourself (like Blackwell does), involve a prestigious panel, allow a specific group of people to vote (such as the Oscars), or encourage the public to vote (such as the baseball All-Star game).

Halls of Fame

To get on-going publicity for a subject area that you specialize in, why not form a hall of fame recognizing the people who have contributed most to that area. Halls of fame are not just for sports. Sure, there are halls of fame for baseball, football, basketball, golf, tennis, wrestling, swimming, the Olympics, etc., but there are also ones devoted to teachers, agriculture, accounting, advertising, jazz, bluegrass, blues, cable TV, African-Americans, women, police, radio, entrepreneurs, bird dogs, aviation, car collectors, conservation, ecology, lingerie, cowboy artists, and self-publishers.

I began the self-publishers hall of fame about ten years ago. It now has honored more than 300 self-publishers who have gone on to fame, fortune, or some other significant contribution to society. I maintain the hall of fame on my web site (http://www.bookmarket.com/selfpublish.html). In addition, I've compiled a 200-page book featuring the honoree's stories. Not only does this book inspire those who might want to self-publish, but it also includes many insights on how to market books more effectively, drawn from the real-life success stories of great self-publishers. The Self-Publishing Hall of Fame on my *BookMarket.com* web site enables my web site to score high when people search on the phrase "self-publishing" via Google and other major search engines.

For travel, there is the HHonors Frequent Traveler Hall of Fame sponsored by Hilton Hotels, which honors King Tusk (an elephant with the Ringling Brothers Circus), the Energizer Bunny, Ashrita Furman (a Guinness Book of World Records holder), Superman, and David Letterman.

Anyone can create a hall of fame. And there's plenty of room for new ones. For example, in my database of 500 halls of fame, there are no halls devoted to explorers, fat people, thin people, novelists, psychologists, book cover designers, publicists, or politicians (other than Louisiana politicians).

A hall of fame allows you to create on-going publicity as you call for new submissions, announce new inductees, hold induction ceremonies, and open a museum to honor the members of the hall of fame. Make your publishing company a tourist destination by establishing a small hall of fame devoted to your subject. Sell books there. Your books.

9:23 43 Other Publicity Ideas

Here is a checklist of 43 additional ways to obtain more promotional exposure for your books and authors:

☐ **Send out announcements of any major author appearances** (at local bookstores, national conferences, or other events).

☐ **Announce any major author signings**, subsidiary rights sales, premium sales, reprintings, new editions, or other newsworthy sales news. Send this information to the major book trade publications and any other key media contacts.

☐ **Send out unusual news releases.** Ballantine, as part of its promotion for Robert Shea's *All Things Are Lights*, sent out postcard releases featuring the cover of the book. They also sent out custom-made candles, which tied into the book's title.

☐ **Write a skit.** Janet Martin and Allen Todnem of Redbird Productions developed a funny skit to help promote their book, *Cream and Bread*, on local radio shows. They also developed a slide show based on the book to present at meetings of Scandinavian-related organizations.

☐ **Send out audio tapes, Cds, or mp3s.** Simon & Schuster produced a cassette of one-minute tax tips to help promote its perennial bestseller *J. K. Lasser's Your Income Tax*. They sent this tape to radio stations in thirty major cities with a request that one tip be featured each day for three months. As an added incentive, they also sent each station 90 copies of the book to be given away as prizes over the three-month period.

☐ **Send out videotapes or DVDs.** To promote their *The Book of Inventions*, World Almanac produced a one-minute videotape, *History of Inventions in 60 Seconds*, which they sent to television stations nationwide. World Almanac also sponsored a contest for the best invention by a reader of the book. As a prize, the winner of the contest was featured in a later edition of the book.

☐ **Don't forget your local newspapers.** They are sure to be interested in any local company which is expanding or offering new products. Let them know of your company's new books, big sales, new personnel, expansion plans, and other items that might interest their readers. Open Horizons has had a number of such stories in our local press—and we've always gotten orders for our books as a result. In a town of 10,000 people you'd think everyone would already know about us, but that isn't the case. Think of the possibilities if you're located in a city of 200,000.

☐ **Send releases to appropriate college newspapers**, in-house publications, association newsletters, alumni newsletters, club newsletters, and other off-the-beaten-track publications. The readers of these publications are generally more responsive than magazine readers or radio audiences.

☐ **Try alternate news hooks.** Learning Publications originally publicized their book *Joyful Learning* as a fun way to learn. Nothing new there. But when they began publicizing the book as a way to help underachievers, the media jumped on the story. Now the book filled a definite need.

☐ **Create a splash with your publication parties.** Try something unusual. Hold the press party at a unique place—on a ferryboat, in a penthouse, at a haunted house, in the middle of Yankee Stadium, in front of city hall, at an art gallery.

When Crown published George Lang's *Cafe des Artistes Cookbook*, they invited the press to a black-tie dinner at a major restaurant. Of course, the press came. They rarely turn down a free lunch, much less an extravagant dinner.

For *Eating Rich: Recipes from America's Wealthiest Families*, Peter Pauper Press held a publication party at Lyndhurst, the former palatial home of financier Jay Gould.

For the book, *The Best Companies for Women*, Simon & Schuster held a party at Time, Inc. headquarters (Time was one of 52 companies named in the book). They then invited representatives from all 52 companies to attend the party.

In 1997, Workman launched Sheila Lukin's *U.S.A. Cookbook* at a star-spangled celebration, complete with 75-piece marching band and a fire-works display over New York's East River.

To promote his book, *The Fine Art of Jumping Off Cliffs!*, Mike Dixon jumped 80 feet from a bridge into the icy waters of the Pacific Ocean in Alaska. After jumping, he tried to read from his book, but lost the book in the icy churning waters. Good try, though.

☐ **Hold your author signings at unusual locations.** Yankee Books fea-tured a special author signing at the Mondavi Winery in California for *Italian Provincial Cookery* by Bea Lazzaro and Lotte Mendelsohn. Other places authors and publishers have done signings include bars, donut shops, libraries, funeral homes, candy stores, garden clubs, cruises, sporting goods stores, airport shops, Jewish community centers, art gal-leries, trains, planes, museums, music theaters, and parking lots.

☐ **Write a letter to the editor** responding to something having to do with one of your books. I've seen such letters in local and national newspa-pers, trade magazines, and other consumer magazines. They can create a great impact on book sales.

☐ **Reply to television commentaries and editorials.** When you hear the announcement that "this station welcomes opposing views from respon-sible spokespersons," why not respond—especially if the subject is re-lated to your book and you can contribute a new insight regarding the situation.

☐ **Call in to radio talk shows.** When Captain Bob, author of *Fire Up Your Communication Skills*, heard John Gray being interviewed on KFRC, the biggest morning drive-time station in San Francisco, he called in and plugged his own book as he made a comment on romance.

☐ **Keep columnists aware of your book.** Write to Mary Ellen with a help-ful hint. Write to John Dvorak about some computer question. Write to any major columnist if you can somehow tie your question or comment in with your book.

☐ **Have your say in the pages of *Publishers Weekly*.** More than one author (and publisher) have written columns for the My Say section—a perfect way to gain exposure before the most important people in the book trade, all of whom read *Publishers Weekly* every week. Send your 850-word essay to **Publishers Weekly**, Attn: My Say, 360 Park Avenue South, 13th Floor, New York, NY 10010-1710; 646-746-6400; Fax: 646-746-6631. Web: http://www.publishersweekly.com.

☐ **Send subsidiary rights sales information** to *Publishers Weekly*. When I sold book club and U.K. rights to *Mail Order Selling Made Easier*, that information was in the Rights column. Also, when I sold rights for the *Directory of Book Printers* to the Writer's Digest Book Club, that was highlighted in the Rights column. If I can get in, so can you.

☐ **Make the news.** Mayhaven Publishing, a small Midwestern publishing company, received two-thirds of a column in *Publishers Weekly*'s news section when they instituted a no-returns policy in August of 1996. They were quoted as saying, "We realize this is a risky decision, but we have decided to opt for certain sales and far fewer headaches."

☐ **Work with regional reporters.** When *Publishers Weekly* declined to review *Rudyard Kipling in Vermont*, Tordis Isselhardt spoke once again with Steve Sherman, the freelance writer who covered New England for *PW*. Steve proposed a BookNews piece to the appropriate editor, and the book got coverage.

☐ **Get on the cover.** When writing or editing a book, look for ways to mention the name of the major trade journal or consumer magazine covering the subject of the book. Mention the periodical either as a resource or in some other complimentary way. Notice how many times I've mentioned *Publishers Weekly* in this book. It was not all by accident. Not, of course, that I think *PW* would review this book just because I've mentioned them fifty times in this book, but when they do review the book they might look more favorably on it. Who knows? Look what happened to the group who recorded the song, "On the Cover of *Rolling Stone*." They made it, didn't they? So what if it was the back cover?

☐ **Give something away free.** When promoting our *Directory of Book Printers*, we offered a free report on how to save money in producing your books. Many periodicals published this free offer where they might not have published the news release about the *Directory* itself.

To promote the 4th edition of *1001 Ways to Market Your Books*, I sent out news releases offering a copy of a special report, *29 Ways to Get Publicity for Your Books*, for only $5.00. That report was essentially just an excerpt of section 9:12 of this chapter. Of course, when people ordered that report, they also received a promotional brochure about the book. Once they read the sample, how could they refuse the rest?

Offering such reports is one of the best ways to keep your book alive even years after it was first published. The new reports are news! The best thing about free reports is the fact that you can create more of them, offering new reports every three months or so.

☐ **Make a prediction.** Forecast a trend. Predict anything related to your book that is likely to happen. Predictions can make news, especially if an expert makes the prediction—and authors are considered experts.

☐ **Give a copy of your book to a major news figure.** Jeffrey Lant sent a copy of his *Unabashed Self-Promoter's Guide* to Rosalyn Carter when her first book came off the press. As a result, he received mention in several news articles.

Proctor Jones, who self-published a collection of photographs as *Classic Russian Idylls*, sent a copy to President Reagan. A few weeks later he received a call from Reagan thanking him for the book. Of course, he let the news media know about the President's reaction to his book.

When President George Bush announced in a discussion about education that he personally had vowed to learn how to use a computer, Simple Software sent him a copy of their *Easy Instruction for Using Your Computer* to help him get up and running quickly.

President Clinton is famous for carrying around books—and reading them. Just after Super Tuesday in 1992, he was photographed carrying Sara Paretsky's mystery, *Guardian Angel.* Delacorte's publicity director Roger Bilheimer noted that he was "pleased when a candidate shows such exceptional taste in books. It certainly helps to sway my vote."

☐ **Run for president or some other high office.** That always makes news. Back in the late 60's Pat Paulsen ran an off-the-wall campaign for the presidency. Meanwhile, he received lots of press coverage which helped boost his career as a comedian. Later he wrote a book about the campaign. Of course, if you win the election, all the better. By this time I think almost every major political figure has published at least one book—and many of their books are novels (which sold not so much for their literary value but because of the people who wrote them).

☐ **Write a song.** Carol Bayer Sager wrote a song to celebrate the publication of her first novel, *Extravagant Gestures.* Johnny Cash also wrote a song to accompany his book *Man in White*, the story of the apostle Paul's conversion.

☐ **Use celebrity spokespeople.** Michael York and Dudley Moore talked about the Capra Press book, *Voices of Survival in the Nuclear Age*, during their appearances on major TV talk shows.

When publicist Lynn Goldberg was booking TV coverage of a new novel that was billed as "the first literate crack novel," she said, "I could try to get the 31-year-old first time author on *Oprah*, but I think it would be more important if I got people like maybe New York Mayor David Dinkins or writer Jimmy Breslin talking about the book."

When Ken Osmond, who played Eddie Haskell on *Leave It to Beaver*, did one radio interview for *Brainstorms* catalog, they received 450 catalog requests in one hour.

☐ **Promote your mistakes.** When Cliffhanger Press found out that they made fifteen typographical errors in the first edition of Arlene Shovald's mystery, *Kill the Competition*, they promoted a Find-the-Typo Contest. Anyone who could locate 15 or more errors in the book were given their choice of an error-free second edition or copies of three other titles from the company's list. This contest got a lot of ink—indeed, probably more than if the book had been error-free.

☐ **Give an award.** SouthWestern Publishing Company gives a Gold Book Award to any of their authors who have sold more than one million copies of a book. Thus far, they've given out sixty-four such awards. Each time, of course, they've received press coverage for both the company and for the book and author receiving the award.

☐ **Set up a hotline number** to promote your books or services. How about a hotline for tax help? Or gardening tips? Or recipes? Or travel tips? With 900 numbers, such a hotline could actually be a moneymaking proposition in itself. The cost to you is minimal. You will need a dedicated phone line, an answering machine with a long continuous-loop tape, and someone to write and record the tips. Of course, if you do a 900 number, you will probably use a service bureau.

To promote his copywriting services, Robert Bly set up the Advertising Hotline. When you dialed his hotline, you heard one of several 3-minute taped marketing seminars, such as *10 Ways to Stretch Your Advertising Budget* or *12 Questions to Ask Before You Create Your Next Ad Campaign*. The messages were changed about once a week.

To promote his piano books, Duane Shinn offered a 3-minute Dial-a-Piano lesson by calling (503) 664-6751. This lesson provided a free sample of the teaching style he uses in his books.

Alan and Denise Fields set up a toll-free phone number that brides-to-be could call to get updated information not contained in their book, *Bridal Bargains*. When *People Weekly* featured them in a three-page article, they reprinted the Field's toll-free number.

☐ **Get interviewed on religious radio stations.** Many authors report incredible success with interviews on the hundreds of religious radio stations around the country. You have to have the right book, something that will appeal to middle, conservative America, but if you do, you will sell books. For a directory of religious media (1,500 radio stations, 330 television stations, 375 radio producers, 235 television producers, 490 periodicals, 310 book publishers, and more), get the *Directory of Religious Media* from **National Religious Broadcasters**, 9510 Technology Drive, Manassas, VA 20110; 703-330-7000; Fax: 703-330-7100. Email: info@ nrb.org. Web: http://www.nrb.com.

☐ **Watch the bestseller lists.** While few media that publish bestseller lists will tell you what stores are polled, you can still use the polling to promote your book. Bill Chleboun, compiler of the local bestseller list for the *San Francisco Chronicle*, made the following offer to local publishers: After he polled bookstores every Tuesday, he'd tell you which books were on the list. Also, if you called and said that you were interested in finding out how one of your books was doing in the local stores, he would check on this as he made his round of calls. What a great way to create awareness of an important title with major booksellers!

☐ **Send out news releases on CD** or make them available on your web site. Dialogic Corporation sent out a disk with the news release provided in nineteen different IBM word processing formats. Not only do you make the editor's job easier, but you also attract their attention. If you do decide to try this, however, make sure you include a printed hard copy of the news release as well.

☐ **Make your news release visual.** For instance, for a Campbell genealogy, you could include a photo of the author in kilts or print a plaid border around the news release.

☐ **Mount a campaign.** Josh McDowell, author of *Why Wait? What You Need to Know about the Teen Sexuality Crisis*, worked closely with the national Why Wait? campaign. In the first five months the book sold over 90,000 copies.

☐ **Name a street after one of your authors.** City Lights celebrated its thirty-five years in publishing by encouraging the city of San Francisco to rename twelve streets after local authors and artists. Now when you visit San Francisco, you can walk down streets named after Ambrose Bierce, Richard Henry Dana, Dashiell Hammett, Jack Kerouac, Jack London, Frank Norris, William Saroyan, and Mark Twain.

☐ **Send copies to opinion makers.** When Warner Books published John Naisbitt's *Megatrends*, they sent copies of the book to the chief executives at the 500 largest corporations in the country. As a result, they generated very effective word of mouth for the book. And the book went on to become a bestseller.

☐ **Form a fan club for your authors.** There are more than 1,000 fan clubs in the United States. While most of these fan clubs are for movie stars and musicians, some authors also have fan clubs—Lewis Grizzard, for instance. Also many romance novelists. One of the great advantages of a fan club is that you have a built-in instant word-of-mouth generator for every new book the author writes.

☐ **Stay alert to media opportunities.** Watch for news items that you can use to promote your books. Also watch for news items about other books that you could tie into your books.

In a column, *Publishers Weekly* asserted that *How to Profit by Setting Up Your Own Corporation* "holds the record for being in print longer than any other book in its class." *PW* also noted that the book had sold 300,000 copies in thirteen years. Well, I knew a book on the same subject that had sold more and been in print longer: Ted Nicholas's *How to Form Your Own Corporation Without a Lawyer for Under $75.00*, which was self-published in 1972 and sold 900,000 copies. So I called the author and the new publisher Dearborn Trade and alerted them to the error. They followed up and, as a result, got more publicity for their book. Now, if I had been alert, I would have called the *PW* and told them, thus reaffirming my reputation as an expert in book publishing.

☐ **Encourage your authors to read their books for the blind.** Blind people are not likely to buy a book anyway, but they will talk to their friends about books they've heard.

☐ **Talk, talk, talk.** When promoting his book, *Swim with the Sharks Without Being Eaten Alive,* Harvey Mackay talked to anyone who would listen. On one airplane flight, he noticed a passenger reading his book. Well, that got him started. He introduced himself and then launched into a 20-minute speech. He talked loudly enough that people could hear in the back row. To explain the commotion, one of the flight attendants announced who Mackay was and also gave out the name of his book over the loudspeaker.

☐ **Piggyback on other's publicity.** When Michael Bolton began promoting his children's book, *Secret of the Lost Kingdom,* Lifetime, publisher of a Bolton biography, made sure their book was in the stores in plenty of time to take advantage of all the publicity.

☐ **Take part in a controversy.** Choose sides. Issue a commendation. Issue a protest. Get involved. Challenge the other side to a debate. Media like nothing more than a good fight.

☐ **Get noticed by the major media**—especially those read by other media. According to a survey of 1,700 opinion leaders taken by Erdos & Morgan, the *Wall Street Journal* is the nation's most influential print media. Besides the *Journal,* most media people read at least one of the following major papers: *USA Today, New York Times, Washington Post,* or *Los Angeles Times.* They also pay attention to the three major weekly news magazines: *Time, Newsweek,* and *U.S. News & World Report.*

When Alan and Denise Fields got their self-published book, *Bridal Bargains,* featured in a *Wall Street Journal* article, they didn't receive a lot of orders but they did get a call from an editor of *People.* That call resulted in a three-page article which, in turn, generated 200 to 300 calls a day. Besides many calls from people wanting to order the book, they also received calls from other media, several literary agents, and a number of major publishers who wanted to buy the rights to the book.

9:24 Five Promotions a Day

When I wrote the previous editions of this book, people kept coming up to me to thank me for writing a wonderful book—and then they'd start making excuses for why they hadn't followed up on any of my suggestions. Well, you don't have an excuse any more. In this edition, I'm giving you the basic rule—a rule that forbids excuses. I call it the **rule of five**.

All it takes is five promotions a day. Really, that's all it takes. Mail a letter. Send out a news release. Phone someone. Take an editor to lunch. Do a phone interview. Give a speech. Jot down a postcard. It need not require much time—15 to 20 minutes is enough—but it can make a world of difference on how well your book sells.

I don't want any more excuses. If your book hasn't sold, there is only one reason (provided the book has any merit at all). And that reason is this: You're just plain lazy. If you spend just ten minutes a day *every day* on every book you love, you will generate an incredible momentum for your books.

There is no reason why any of your books should die after six weeks in the marketplace. Books, like diamonds, are forever—provided you are willing to put a little elbow grease behind their promotion and you use those ten minutes a day wisely.

Now get off your rear end and start doing your ten minutes a day right now. Don't wait. I mean it. Don't wait. This book will still be here when you're done with your ten minutes.

Authors — If you really want to help your publisher promote your book, take the last point to heart. Just make five contacts each day. It need not require much time or money to gain public exposure for your books. Just make five promotional contacts every day, and your book will get noticed.

9:25 Publicity Generates More Publicity

When you are pursuing media exposure, remember these four essential points:

☐ **75 to 80% of all news is planted**. That means, that most of the news you read in newspapers and magazines or hear on radio and TV has come out of news releases sent to the media by businesses, associations, government offices, and other organizations or individuals with something interesting to say.

☐ **If you can provide real news for the media, they will be glad to feature your authors and books**. That's why you should keep refining your news hooks until you find one that really meets a need. Don't send out a press release announcing any book until you can show that the book provides at least one benefit for potential readers—whether that benefit be entertainment, information, instruction, or enlightenment.

☐ **Publicity begets more publicity.** Once you get the ball rolling, it will often go on by itself. Local news features are often picked up by the wire services and spread across the country. Local radio and TV shows can lead to bookings on network shows. One or two features in major review media, and soon every newspaper in the country is calling to ask for a review copy (or simply reprinting the review from a major source).

4. **If at first you don't succeed, try, try again.** Persistence, above all, is the key to success in generating favorable publicity for your books and authors. Believe in your books and authors, keep on plugging away, and the reviews and features will come.

How I Got in the *Chicago Tribune*

I called the book editor at the Chicago Tribune and excitedly told him about my book. He was nice enough to say he'd look at it. I followed up a week later, and he said he gave it to a woman in another section, Lifestyles, I think. I left tons of messages on her machine, but she never called me back. Finally I got her at her desk, and she said she'd passed it on to the Womanews editor. I then left tons of messages on the Womanews editor's machine, but never heard from her either. Just when I was about to give up, a writer called me. She was assigned to write about me by this last editor, who I never even spoke with. That one brief article boosted sales astoundingly! The lesson: Be persistent! It may take an embarrassing amount of calling, but once you get the piece in print, you will not only get sales, you will have a valuable piece for your press kit, which is crucial.

— Jill Spiegel, author of *Flirting for Success*

Book Promotion Time Line

by Kate Siegel Bandos of KSB Promotions

The Recommended Book Promotion Time Line on the next page is reproduced by permission of Kate Bandos, president of KSB Promotions. Use this promotion time line as a guide to planning your publicity activities. If you plan carefully, you will be able to time your activities so you can fit in all the promotions you'd like to carry out.

Kate Bandos, a veteran of more than 30 years in book promotion, was formerly publicity director for Globe Pequot Press, Pelican Publishing, Acropolis Books, and M. Evans & Company. Now she acts as an independent publicist for many small publishers. For more information, contact Kate Bandos at **KSB Promotions, 55 Honey Creek N.E., Ada, MI 49301-9768; 616-676-0758; Fax: 616-676-0759.** Email: pr@ksbpromotions.com. Web: http://www.ksbpromotions.com. Ask her about her *KSB Links* publication.

Recommended Book Promotion Time Line

provided by KSB Promotions — telephone: 616-676-0758, fax: 616-676-0759, e-mail: pr@ksbpromotions.com, web site: www.ksbpromotions.com

Task	Time In Weeks
1 Create overall plan	
2 Interview author/prepare bio	
3 Write book description	
4 Create information sheet for sales reps	
5 Select media to get galleys/releases/books	
6 Solicit expert endorsements	
7 Present to book clubs	
8 Present to magazines for excerpts	
9 Write promotional copy to be sent with galleys	
10 Send galleys to book clubs & magazines	
11 Follow-up with book clubs/magazines	
12 Make additional galley follow-ups	
13 Submit trade announcement info	
14 Submit info for special trade features	
15 Write media releases	
16 Prepare other media kit materials	
17 Contact major TV shows if appropriate	
18 Review media selection	
19 Review overall plan	
20 Finalize & print releases, etc.	
21 Mail electronic & newspaper releases	
22 Send out review copies	
23 Begin scheduling interviews/media training	
24 Stage publication day event if appropriate	
25 Begin book & release follow-ups	
26 Continue scheduling interviews	
27 Review plans & evaluate responses to date	
28 Implement second efforts	
29 Compile promo sheet of review quotes	
30 Send promo schedule & update sheet to reps	
31 Create & implement new campaign	
32 Plan campaign for the new edition	

Time In Weeks: 28 24 20 16 12 8 4 0 4 8 12 16 20 24 28 32 36 40 44 48 52 60 Done

(Publication Date)

Spreading the Word about Your Book:
How a Book Publicity Firm Works

by Celia Rocks, Principal, Rocks-DeHart Public Relations

Authors come to us because they want their very important message—one that may have taken an entire lifetime to develop and articulate—to be visible to their market. Many have no idea what to expect from the process but they do know that publicity is the most economical, credibility-building way to get their message to as many people as possible.

Here is what a great publicity firm should do for you:

1) Help you craft the brilliance of your book—your expertise, your intellectual property, the "thing" you can articulate, communicate, and speak on better than anyone else—into a message that's meaningful to readers, potential clients, and the media.

2) Package your message in such an innovative way (via press releases and press kits) that it can be successfully pitched to local, regional, and national radio, television, newspapers, magazines, and Internet publications to obtain third-party news media credibility.

3) Let your distributor reps know about upcoming media hits so they can sell more books through the bookstore systems.

4) Continue the process with another outstanding press release and targeted pitch. Plug away at media exposure so that competing books never have a chance to take over the top position. Success breeds success ... media breeds more media.

5) Help you integrate your book's message into other materials. That might include a website, a keynote speech and speaker flier, a brochure, a new set of business cards—even another book as you become a leader in your genre.

6) Create a platform that will help you sell more books. This may involve hosting seminars, speaking at conferences, sending out VIP packages to the movers and shakers in your industry ... and so forth.

Hopefully, you now have a feel for the process. Now, a few tips for finding the perfect publicist for you and your book:

☐ **Commit to going to the next level.** Make sure you have done your homework and your book's message is breakthrough. Please give your publicist the best possible book to work with—even if this means delaying the publication date until you have a great product.

☐ **Look for a publicist who can see the big picture.** He or she must be proficient in everything from spotting and/or creating unusual book promotional opportunities to working with publishers to coordinating media appearances. Most importantly, a good publicist will guide you in leveraging the coverage you get into being a sought after expert (which means more publicity!).

☐ **Find a publicist who fits your values and culture.** For instance, if you are very detail oriented, make sure his or her reporting system meshes with your level of accountability.

☐ **Make sure your publicist can help with every aspect of your image.** No matter how brilliant your book might be, it's all for naught if you don't dress properly, speak clearly, or use confident body language.

☐ **Manage expectations.** We've worked with high school dropouts who became self-made multi-millionaires to Nobel Prize winners to international singing sensations to *Wall Street Journal* and *BusinessWeek* bestselling authors. These clients all have a common story: They plugged away one day at a time with a clear direction for success. There are no overnight sensations.

In closing, the job of a public relations firm is to create enough buzz so that when your name or the name of your book pops up, someone will say, "I've heard of that book" or "I saw an article on her in *Fast Company*" or "Isn't that the author I saw on Oprah?" Those casual words belie the sweat, tears, and midnight oil that went into orchestrating the events that led to them. But you will know the truth ... and so will your publicist.

Celia Rocks is president of Rocks-DeHart Public Relations, a full-service book and author publicity firm that has been serving clients, big and small, since 1992. RDPR's mission is to help professionals use their books as powerful tools for growing their businesses.

RDPR has a national reputation for excellence and a strong client following. Celia has worked on the *For Dummies* series of books, a publishing phenomenon, since its inception, boasting 120 million books sold. Celia and her business partner, Dottie DeHart, recently published *101 Publishing Tips for Speakers and Consultants*.

For more information, contact **Rocks-DeHart Public Relations**, 306 Marberry Drive, Pittsburgh, PA 15215; 412-784-8811; Fax: 412-784-8610. Email: Celia@rdpr.com. Web: http://www.rdpr.com.

Here's a note John recently received from a consulting client: "Thanks again for recommending Celia Rocks to handle public relations for my book. Celia has done an outstanding job in a very short time period, in a very cluttered category, on a small budget. Here are some of the press highlights Celia has arranged for me in these short six weeks: CNBC, CNN, *Los Angeles Times, Christian Science Monitor, Wall Street Journal*, and Business News Network. Please pass the word. Celia is great at PR!"

The 14 Most Common Publicity Mistakes Authors Make

by Pam Lontos of PR/PR

Many authors make crucial mistakes in their publicity campaigns. While some of the mistakes are more detrimental than others, the costs can be staggering. For example, saying the wrong thing to a reporter may cost you a quote in a national magazine. And you never really know who would have read the interview. Maybe a reporter for *USA Today*, or maybe Oprah's producer (or maybe even Oprah herself).

Everyone makes mistakes; but being aware of the more common ones, allows you to take action to avoid them. Here are some of the ones to avoid:

1. Thinking their book will become a best seller from one book review or TV appearance. Fame and name recognition take time and repetition to build. In fact, a person will need to see your name around six or seven times before they actually remember it. So regardless of what you've heard, there's no such thing as an overnight success.

2. Not being unique in their approach. No one wants to hear the same old message over and over again. So develop a hook, or unique angle that sets your book apart from others. For example, if your book is about relationships, you can focus your message to "relationships after retirement."

3. Thinking they can't get into a large publication. Many new authors feel intimidated by the big name publications. They envision high-powered magazine editors schmoozing only with celebrities. In reality, editors scramble daily to find people to interview who have knowledge on the latest trends. Realize, too, that editors must find new and exciting people to interview, so the more knowledgeable people they can add to their database, the better.

4. Thinking small publications don't matter. Every opportunity can lead to unexpected successes. One client made time to do an interview for a small, new travel publication. When the article came out, an editor with *Time* read it and called to do an interview. She got one sentence in *Time*. This sentence was read by a national TV news producer and she ended up with a camera crew at her home from the *NBC Nightly News* with Tom Brokaw.

5. Thinking their ideas are wonderful. Touting your experience and explaining all the reasons why your book is wonderful to an editor is not an effective way to pitch your ideas. In fact, this is an immediate turn-off. Realize that an editor or reporter only cares about one thing: their readers.

6. Pitching themselves, instead of a story for the audience. Always pitch the media by highlighting the benefits you and your book can offer their particular audience. Consider what uniqueness you can offer and why their readers or viewers will be interested in what you have to say. They only care about your credentials after they like the story you are proposing.

7. Pitching the wrong person. Pitching your ideas to the wrong media contact will likely frustrate them. If you want to score an interview, you need a reporter. Be sure to have the proper contact's name.

8. Not finding out what reporters really want. As you present your ideas to a reporter, ask questions about what they and their audience are looking for. Then make changes to your idea based on their responses. Don't try to sell your idea if it isn't a good fit; instead, promote alternate ideas and emphasize your ability to address a variety of issues that fit their audience.

9. Not answering the reporter's questions. Always let the interviewer lead the conversation, because she most likely has an agenda for the story's development already in mind. Don't attempt to take over the conversation or talk about points the reporter doesn't want to cover.

10. Not getting to the point. Audiences love to hear firsthand accounts of experiences relating to the topic because it helps them know you on a more personal level. But don't overload the reporter with unnecessary information that isn't directly related to the story. If you can't convey your message in a short amount of time, then your answer won't be used.

11. Not respecting the reporter's time. Reporters work on time-sensitive deadlines, and nothing will irritate them more than you being inconsiderate. So before you start pitching your ideas, always ask if they are on deadline. If yes, ask for a more convenient call back time.

12. Not gearing their pitch to the specific media. If you get a "no" from an editor, always ask, "What do you need?" Then adapt your presentation on the spot. The more you learn about their needs and customize your message for their audience, the more likely you'll be featured in their publication.

13. Making it an advertisement for their book. Interviews and articles are not the right place to go on and on about your knowledge. You must let your information speak for itself. By giving solid, useable information, audiences will automatically know how great your book is and want to buy it.

14. Not understanding the importance of frequency of publicity. While it takes a long time to build your name recognition in the marketplace, it takes no time at all for people to forget you. So you must maintain the frequency of your publicity throughout your career. Otherwise, you become old news. Ask yourself, why does Coca-Cola still spend millions on advertising?

Pam Lontos is president of PR/PR, a publicity firm for authors. Former VP of Sales for Disney's Shamrock Broadcasting, she is the author of *Don't Tell Me It's Impossible Until After I've Already Done It*. PR/PR gets its clients interviews, articles, and reviews in national newspapers and magazines. Clients have been featured in *The Wall Street Journal, Cosmopolitan, Reader's Digest, Fast Company, USA Today*, etc. **Call 407-299-6128** or see http://www.prpr.net. "PR/PR has gotten my name into so many magazines that I've had to get a new filing cabinet to hold them all." — Brian Tracy

Building the Best Network

by Rick Frishman of Planned Television Arts and Jill Lublin

Helping

The ideal time to build your network is when you are in a position to help others and you don't need their help. Or as President John F. Kennedy advised, "The time to repair the roof is when the sun is shining." Stephen Burgay, Senior Vice President of Corporate Communications for John Hancock Financial Services, calls this *implicit networking* because you have no agenda. In contrast, "explicit networking is when you have an agenda such as needing a job, wanting to change jobs, or being on the move."

Implicit networking builds goodwill and can position you for tomorrow. Help others whenever you can because it might motivate them to assist you when you need help. Usually, you need networking most when you are no longer in a position of power. So give early to build relationships that transcend changes in your circumstances.

Give generously and gladly. Don't just fill expectations - exceed them - exceed them beyond your contact's hopes. Don't brag or broadcast your generosity to others or repeatedly remind those you helped of your largesse. Create an example of generosity that others will admire.

To build your network, give your product or perform your service for free to the right people. Write it off to goodwill; consider it an investment. Usually, people are more willing to try things that are free and will remember when they receive something of value, especially when it comes at no cost. The object is to get your product or service out there, to let its quality speak for itself and to impress those who are in a position to help. If it's really good, your contacts will spread the word and endorse you, your product, or service.

Getting Organized

Create a detailed network database on your Rolodex, Palm Pilot, or address book or simply start a separate card or computer file. Also, investigate the numerous computer programs that provide contact-organizing services. They include ACT!, TeleMagic, Goldmine, and tons more.

Collect as many names as possible because you never know when a contact could lead you to the perfect fit. Successful networkers collect business cards and contact information as if it were money. A contact whom you have barely met may have heard about you, been impressed by you, or think that you or your product/service are fabulous and want to hook you up with his or her network.

Divide your contact database into three groups.

A Group — Top, most important network members. The people whom you feel could help the most.

B Group — Other, less important contacts whom you actually met.

C Group — People you do not know but have heard of, seen, read articles by, and would like to meet.

Get into the habit of collecting business cards and making notes. Carry a small notebook or a personal digital assistant, such as a Palm Pilot, at all times to record names and pertinent information. Keep notebooks and writing implements in your car, briefcase, purse, office, boat, and near all computers and phones.

Review and update your network database on a regular basis. Update all changes as soon as they occur. At the least, scan your database once a month and go over it from top to bottom every three months. The more familiar you are with you list, the more easily and quickly you will be able to link network contacts when the need arises.

With 195,000 new books published in just the past 12 months, how can an author rise above the sea of titles fighting for consumer and media attention? With PTA's intensive online marketing campaign. One of the first companies to launch a book onto the best-seller list, PTA has been arming authors with the competitive edge they need to sell books, raise their brand awareness, and get their message heard for over two years.

How does it work? Through the technologies of online ordering, ezines, blogs and mailing lists, we have successfully set up promotions that compel thousands of readers to buy your book in a short period of time. The resulting boost to sales acts as a catalyst to attract more attention from reviewers, booksellers, and the book buying public. As many as one million online consumers, will receive information about the book.

Our best-seller campaign usually works best for business books, how-to books, health books, and news-making books. If your title does not fit into these categories, do not despair. Call and tell us what your book is about and we'll tell you if it can work.

For more information, please contact: Brian Feinblum at feinblumb@ plannedtvarts.com. Web: http://www.plannedtvarts.com.

Three Ways to Choose the Right PR Agency

by Willy Spizman and Jenny Corsey, The Spizman Agency

Everyone knows that PR is essential to success in the publishing field. But how can a smart author find the perfect PR pros to get the job done right? Here are three strategies to consider when selecting an agency.

Choose an agency that knows how to transform authors into authorities. Media outlets depend on expert commentary to make their stories substantial, well rounded and credible. Marketing guru Al Ries is the branding expert who transformed an industry by pioneering the concept of Positioning. Our agency positioned the marketing expertise of Al and Laura Ries, co-authors of *The 22 Immutable Laws of Branding* in the media and earned coverage in top trade publications such as *Ad Age* and *PR Week*, but also business outlets such as *The Wall Street Journal, Forbes, Business Week*, and *Bloomberg News*.

Choose an agency that thinks like the media. Think like a reporter, a producer, or a blogger. For example, when we launched a PR campaign for stress management expert Dr. Kathleen Hall's book *Alter Your Life: Overbooked? Overworked? Overwhelmed?*, we pitched her commuter stress solutions to media in cities where rush hour traffic ranked the worst. Not surprisingly, New York and Detroit were among the first to bite. Her expertise was most useful to these cities. *Fortune* ran a column on commuter stress with Dr. Hall's stress techniques. CNN International shot a segment with the author on commuter stress in London. Her book received millions of media impressions with outlets such as Associated Press, ABC News, *Parents, Cosmopolitan, USA Weekend*, and *Chicago Tribune*.

Choose an agency that specializes in award-winning results. Measurable results determine the success of your publicity. In 2002, The Spizman Agency earned the Gold Bulldog Award for Excellence in National Media Relations for solid and consistent PR results for Bruce Blythe, CEO of Crisis Management International and author of *Blindsided: A Manager's Guide to Catastrophic Incidents in the Workplace*. We mobilized a national campaign that offered Bruce's expertise to top media and secured coverage from NBC's *Today Show*, NPR, CNN, *20/20, The Wall Street Journal, Newsweek, Business Week, USA Today, Smart Money, Fast Company, 48 Hours,* CNBC, and MSNBC.

PR provides a powerful voice for authors to tell their stories, establish themselves as experts, and make a vast impact on book sales. The proof lies in measurable results. At the Spizman Agency, we are committed to tangible, results oriented service. We believe that our longevity, record of repeat business and documented local and national coverage for clients is testimony to a philosophy that works.

The Spizman Agency is a full service public relations firm that specializes in marketing, promoting and publicizing books, products, and leading edge authors. Experts at transforming authors into authorities and people into personalities, they have worked with many best-selling authors and publishers as well as first-time authors launching books and literary careers.

The agency's public relations and marketing campaigns have resulted in millions of book sales worldwide and thousands of appearances on top media outlets including *Oprah, Good Morning America, Today, NPR, Time, Early Today, CNN, The Wall Street Journal, ABC Evening News, CNBC, MSNBC, Nightline, Larry King Live, People, USA Today, Fast Company, Fortune, Money, Business Week, Entrepreneur, Newsweek, Cosmopolitan, Southern Living, Parents, Woman's Day*, and *ForeWord*.

Contact: **The Spizman Agency**, Willy Spizman, 5280 Cross Roads Manor, Atlanta, GA 30327; 770-953-2040; Fax: 770-953-2172. Email: willy@spizmanagency.com. Web: http://www.spizmanagency.com.

Chapter 10

Tips on Advertising Your Books

There are two rules and two rules only in direct marketing:
Rule #1: Test everything.
Rule #2: See Rule #1.
— Malcolm Decker's Ultimate Rule

The most effective way to promote your books is to combine advertising with your publicity efforts. Although publicity and word of mouth may be sufficient by themselves to put some books on the bestseller lists, most books will benefit from some well-planned and well-placed advertising.

As one librarian noted in *Publishers Weekly*, "I confess I tend to buy books that are advertised. I have learned that, in most cases, books that are advertised have a real commitment from publishers."

When advertising to consumers, you have six options: direct mail, telemarketing, magazine advertising, newspaper advertising, radio/TV commercials, and Internet ads. Of course, you can apply these six basic options in a variety of ways. Moreover, there are many other lesser known advertising approaches which have been used successfully by book publishers.

When planning your advertising campaign for each book (or for your entire line of books), you must decide which approach or method will produce the best results for that particular book (or series of books). In making your decision, you must consider the subject of the book, its audience, its price, its format, your advertising budget for the book, its method of distribution, and its competition. In addition, you must consider how the advertising will fit into the promotions for your other books and with the company image you want to project.

10:01 Some General Guidelines

No matter what approach you decide to take with your advertising, there are certain basic principles that apply to almost any kind of advertising. The following pages feature a short checklist of such principles:

☐ **Test, test, test.** Whenever you place any ad or do any direct mailing, be sure to test before committing your entire budget to that specific approach. Test everything that is important. Test the advertising copy. Test the lists or media. Test the price. Test the offer. Don't, however, waste your time testing little details such as the color of the envelope or small changes in copy.

☐ **Select your audience carefully.** Choose magazines or other media with a reader profile similar to your book buyer profile. Select lists made up of recent book buyers rather than a compiled list.

☐ **Track the results of your advertising** so you know which media are producing the best return on your investment. Use these results to guide you in placing further advertising, not only for the current book but also for future related titles. The basic principle here is to continue using the advertising media and approaches which are producing results before trying other media or approaches.

☐ **Focus your advertising efforts on a few select approaches.** Don't scatter your attention by trying to advertise everywhere in every way. It won't work. Only when your prime approaches no longer produce a good return should you test other approaches.

☐ **Make sure you have distribution.** For example, if you are going to advertise on national television, make sure you have mass distribution—that your book is available in all local bookstores. Of course, if you are going for a direct sale on television, then you don't need mass distribution. In that case, however, you will need to make it easy for people to order by offering a toll-free number, charge card privileges, and a clear and firm guarantee of satisfaction.

☐ **Have enough books in stock** to handle the anticipated demand created by your advertising. Don't roll out a big advertising campaign if you don't have enough stock on hand and a smoothly functioning fulfillment department.

☐ **A toll-free 800 line and acceptance of credit cards** will almost always increase response to any advertising regardless of the media, whether print advertising or TV advertising.

☐ **Focus your advertising on a prime objective**: more sales for a particular book, more sales for your entire line of books, creating an image for your company, creating a brand name, or whatever. The clearer you are in your own mind about what your objective is, the more effective you will be in creating and carrying out an advertising campaign.

☐ **Set a marketing budget**, and stick to it. Most general trade book publishers spend about one dollar per book for advertising, or about 6% of the retail price of the book. About half that amount is spent on *push advertising* (ads directed to bookstores, wholesalers, libraries and other institutional buyers) and half on *pull advertising* (ads directed to the consumer). Decide for your own company how much you will spend for each book and where you will spend it.

☐ **Advertise to sell.** Remember Claude Hopkins basic rule: "The only rule of advertising is to make sales."

☐ **Repeat what works.** If an ad works once, continue to use it until it no longer pays off.

10:02 The Advantages of Direct Mail

I must admit that of all advertising methods I prefer direct mail. In 1996, U.S. mail order sales hit $290 billion ($151.3 billion in consumer sales, $78.4 billion in business-to-business sales, and $60.3 billion in nonprofit donations). According to Robert Coen of McCann-Erickson, expenditures for all forms of advertising in 1997 topped $109 billion, with direct mail leading the pack with almost $36.6 billion in expenditures (compared to $31 billion for television ads).

Why do companies spend so much on direct mail? Below are just a few of the advantages of direct mail. Note: These same advantages apply to most Internet marketing as well since Internet sales are essentially just a form of direct marketing.

☐ **It is quicker to produce.** You can prepare and mail a small promotion within days or weeks rather than months. Hence, it is perfect for testing prices, titles, offers, and potential audiences. More elaborate and carefully targeted promotions do take longer to prepare, but even then they usually require a shorter lead time than most other media.

☐ **Response is quicker.** Not only is a direct mailing quicker to prepare, but response time to direct mail is usually quicker as well. Thus you can project the final results of a mailing more quickly and accurately than you can with most other advertising.

☐ **It can be cheaper, especially for smaller tests**. Using a computer to generate the sales letters, I have done personalized first-class mailings to lists as large as 500 for only the cost of paper, envelopes, and postage (about 40¢ per piece).

☐ **It does not require as much design time**. A standardized direct mail format (letter, response card, folder or brochure, and return envelope) is much easier to design and produce than a magazine advertisement or television commercial.

☐ **It can be highly targeted.** If you choose lists carefully, you can target your mailings more selectively than you can with most other media. You can reach almost any market segment, buyer profile, or area of the country you feel is most appropriate for each book.

☐ **It allows you to target hard-to-reach consumers.** Direct mail allows you to reach audiences you could reach through any other method.

Rodale Press has sold over a million copies of their book *Stocking Up* since its 1977 publication. Only 10% of those sales were made through bookstores. Indeed, of Rodale's $250 million in 1996 book sales, $212 million were the result of their direct marketing efforts.

☐ **It is more flexible.** After testing a promotion, you can change almost anything right away without waiting. You have complete control over the media, the audience, and your offer.

☐ **It can offer more details**. You can pack a lot of information into one envelope, far more than you can on a full-page magazine or newspaper ad, or in two minutes or even a half hour on radio or TV.

☐ **There is less competition.** Your advertising message does not have to compete with other advertising messages or editorial matter. At least, it doesn't have to compete once the envelope is opened.

☐ **Direct mail can be more personal**. Not only can letters be personalized via mail-merging techniques, but you can use more informal language in writing your letter and can direct your letter to the specific interests of the reader.

☐ **It is easier to respond to.** The inclusion of an order card and return envelope makes it easier for the consumer to respond to direct mail as compared to magazine ads (unless you include a bind-in card opposite the advertisement or include a toll-free order number).

☐ **It is easier to keep.** A direct mail piece is more likely to be retained for future reference than a magazine ad since many readers find it inconvenient to tear an advertisement out of a magazine or will be reluctant to do so. Other forms of advertising (radio, TV, and telemarketing) offer nothing to retain.

☐ **It can be used to test.** You can build an advertising campaign with more confidence by testing small lists, then building to larger lists, and then rolling out to a full list or lists.

Strawberry Hill Press turned to direct mail after selling only 3,000 copies of Stephen Chang's *The Book of Internal Exercises*. They started small with a four-page direct mail letter to a list of 10,000 proven buyers of health books. When that mailing pulled a 9% response for a net profit of $9,000, they tested a variety of other lists which, in turn, produced a net profit of $40,000. When they finally rolled out to larger lists, they sold almost 100,000 copies of the book within a year (for a net profit of $150,000).

☐ **It can build a list of loyal customers.** Direct mail allows you to build and maintain an in-house list of prime prospects for your future books (and backlist books). Furthermore, you can make money renting the list. Strawberry Hill Press, in the example noted above, also had over $20,000 worth of list rental income in that same year.

☐ **Direct mail helps bookstore sales.** When Rudolf Flesch's *The Art of Plain Talk* was first published, it sold 1,800 copies through bookstores in two years. Not happy with these results, Flesch persuaded his publisher to test a direct mail campaign. Within seven months, the publisher sold 40,000 copies via direct mail. But the really good news was that they also sold 45,000 copies through bookstores (with no other marketing efforts of any kind!).

Disadvantage

Just to be fair, there is one major disadvantage of direct mail if you market your books primarily through bookstores. Bookstores do not appreciate it when publishers advertise books for direct sale to consumers; they would much prefer that you send those consumers to them.

Several years ago one bookseller in Manhattan returned 20 copies of *The Great Getty* to Crown Publishing after he noticed a coupon soliciting direct orders in a *New York Times Book Review* advertisement. Indeed, there have been other cases when several booksellers boycotted publishers who were soliciting direct mail orders for titles normally sold through the trade.

If you are going to use direct mail to sell books that you are also selling through bookstores, be sure to tell your bookstore accounts how your direct mail will help their sales not hinder them. Tell them about Rudolf Flesch's experience noted above. Or remind them of how well Reader's Digest books sell through bookstores whenever they do a sweepstakes promotion direct to consumers.

10:03 14 Ways to Use Direct Mail

Direct mail can be used for other reasons besides making a direct sale. Here are just a few other ways you can use direct mail to increase the sales of all your books:

☐ **Obtain inquiries**—You can use an inexpensive direct mail package to obtain inquiries about your books which you then follow up with a more expensive and elaborate informational package to obtain a sale.

☐ **Obtain leads**—Use direct mail to obtain leads for direct sales representatives or telemarketing staff. This method would be useful for high priced series or collections (encyclopedias, continuity series, or multi-volume reference works). It is also useful for sales to independent retail stores, libraries, schools, and colleges.

☐ **Offer free trials**—One of the most effective ways to sell expensive books is to offer a 15-day (or 30-day) free trial period. When a customer sends in a request, send the book with an invoice. Upon receipt of the book, the customer has 15 days to return the book if not satisfied or pay the accompanying invoice.

☐ **Supplement retail sales**—Harlequin uses direct mail to make sales they would not reach through retail stores. According to their president, Harlequin's direct sales do not cut into retail sales. This additive effect of direct mail sales has also been noticed in many other industries, such as the toy and gift industries.

☐ **Boost retail sales**—The publishers of Reader's Digest Books have found that many of the people they mail to actually buy the book at a retail bookstore rather than order direct by mail. Inevitably when they make a mailing on a backlist title, bookstore sales also increase.

☐ **Increase sales to libraries**—By increasing consumer demand via the mails, you also increase the number of people who go to libraries to request the book. Whenever there is a demand for a book, libraries will order the book. You can also stimulate college library sales by mailing to college instructors rather than direct to librarians.

☐ **Make special sales**—To reach potential volume buyers (for premium or catalog sales), direct mail followed up by telephone calls is the most cost-effective way to advertise.

☐ **Sell subsidiary rights**—One of the most cost-effective ways to sell licensing or other subsidiary rights is to reach potential buyers via direct mail and then follow up with telephone calls.

☐ **Publicize your books**—Most publicity is generated via direct mail, again followed up by telephone calls.

☐ **Maintain contact with key customers**—Direct mail can be used to send newsletters, updates, and other customer communications to help you maintain contact with your key customers. Such continuing contact can lead to better customer relations and, hence, to more sales. My recommendation: Contact key customers at least once every two months.

☐ **Build your customer list**—One of the great advantages of direct marketing is that you can build up a list of buyers who are interested in the areas related to your specialty. Many direct marketers will even lose money on their first mailings just so they can build up their list—not only for their own future use but also to rent to others.

☐ **Conduct research**—Use direct mail to do market research and surveys. Many published surveys, opinion polls, and other research is already conducted via this method.

☐ **Prepare new editorial material**—You can use direct mail to help you prepare your editorial content. For example, direct mail is the most cost-effective way to update directory listings.

☐ **Sell advertising**—If you publish directories or other reference books where advertising is accepted, you can sell advertising space by mail.

10:04 The 3 Fundamentals of Direct Mail

The following three elements are vital to the success of any direct mail promotions. If one of these is missing or inadequate, the chances of success are slim.

1. **The offer**—Your books must be worth the cost. Make an irresistible offer, and your chances of success are much greater than if the book is inadequate or the price is too high (or too low).

2. **The advertising copy**—The format of your direct mail is not nearly as important as its message. The copy must speak to the interests of the reader. The letter must stimulate the reader to act.

3. **The list**—You can have the best offer and the most irresistible copy in the world but, if you mail to the wrong list, none of that will have any effect. Hence, of the three fundamentals, many direct marketing professionals would insist that the list is the most important.

According to Ed Mayer, direct mail success is dependent on the following ratios: 40% lists, 40% offer, and 20% everything else. Bob Hacker, another direct marketer, asserts that success is based 30% on the offer, 30% on the lists, 20% creative, and 20% costs (if you pay too much, you'll never recover). While direct marketers might quarrel about the percentages, most are quite clear on the priorities: list, offer, and advertising copy.

10:05 How to Improve Your Offer

The most important element of your offer is the book. If the book answers a definite need, your offer may need little else to be effective. Nonetheless, here are a few other suggestions on how you can improve your offer to make it more enticing to the mail order buyer.

☐ **Offer a premium for buying the book**. As a publisher, an ideal premium would be another printed product (brochure, booklet, or book) related to the main book offer. When I first offered the *Directory of Book Printers* for direct sale, I gave buyers a choice of four reports for ordering early: 1) *20 Ways to Save on the Printing of Your Books*, 2) *16 Points to Consider When Selecting a Book Printer*, 3) *70 Full-Color Catalog and Brochure Printers,* or 4) *68 Books about Publishing and Self-Publishing*. The response to these premiums was so great that I included the first two reports in the third edition of the *Directory*. Whatever premium you do offer, be sure it has a high perceived value regardless of its actual cost.

☐ **Set a time limit**. If you limit the availability of the book or a special offer (such as the premium offer described above), you can increase the response. At the very least, most people will respond more quickly (which can be important if you require a faster inflow of cash).

☐ **Offer a discount** if they order within a certain time limit or if they order more than one book. For years, AdLib Publications offered a 10% discount to anyone ordering three or more books at the same time. And because of this offer, they seldom got orders for two books. When customers ordered more than one book, they invariably ordered three or more. Indeed, they received many comments from customers saying that they couldn't resist the discount.

☐ **Offer payment options**. Allow payment by credit card, check, billing, or whatever. The billing option is almost an absolute necessity if you are selling to companies. Indeed, a credit or bill-me offer has been known to improve results by 50% or more. Installment payments, for items costing more than $25.00, can also improve results.

☐ **Make it easy for them to order**. Allow customers to order by phone, to call collect, or to call via a toll-free number. Or, if you'd prefer mail-in orders, provide a *BRE* (business reply envelope) to make it easier for customers to send in the order.

☐ **Offer a free trial period**. The free trial period works particularly well for advertising in card decks where your advertising message is so limited by the available space that you almost have to offer people a chance to see the book itself if you expect them to buy it. Nowadays, of course, you could offer the free trial via sample chapters on your web site.

☐ **Offer a demo.** Computer software companies have discovered that one of the best ways to attract the interest of potential buyers is to offer a free limited download of their program. Perfume manufacturers have discovered that scent strips are a superb way to give consumers an experience of their product. Warner Books actually inserted a short sample chapter of Gallatin Warfield's *State V. Justice* novel into an issue of *Publishers Weekly*. Some mass-market publishers are now offering previews of forthcoming books in other related books.

☐ **Guarantee satisfaction**. Offer a 30-day money-back guarantee, a lifetime replacement warranty, or some other form of guarantee that assures them you will stand by your product. Then stand by it.

☐ **Offer several versions of the product**. One version could be standard and the other a higher-priced and more exclusive version. You could, for instance, offer a limited edition of a book, an autographed copy, or a hardcover/softcover option. Generally speaking, you can never sell two items through one mailing package (unless your mailing package is a catalog), but you can sell two different versions of the same item—and make it work for you. In a mailing for the Third Edition of the *Directory of Book Printers*, I offered a book (for $13.00 postpaid) or a Deluxe

MailMerge Computer Edition (for $30.00 postpaid). About 15% of the resulting orders were for the higher priced edition.

☐ **Make a special offer**. For example, send discount coupons to all your customers in celebration of your company's anniversary saying, "It's our birthday, but you get the present!" The coupon could offer $5.00 off for any order regardless of size. Note: The more believable your special offer is to your target audience, the more likely it is that it will succeed.

☐ **Offer special benefits to repeat buyers.** Give them an added discount. Or send an exclusive mailing only to your best customers.

☐ **Run a sweepstakes**. Sweepstakes can increase orders by 50%. For more on sweepstakes, see Section 11:29.

☐ **Offer free shipping.** In one of their recent catalogs, Turtle Press offered free shipping to customers who returned a completed and signed survey. While they lost some money on shipping for small orders, they made money on the larger orders and, at the same time, got many great testimonials to use in ads. The new ads boosted their sales even more.

☐ **Offer rush service**. People appreciate fast service. If you offer special shipping, people will respond. Quick service is especially important when you are offering seasonal books such as holiday gifts, gardening books, or summer travel guides. Turtle Press is currently getting the best response to their catalogs by offering 2nd day shipping on all orders over $50.00 at no extra charge. This shipping upgrade created a big jump in the number of orders they received over $50.00.

☐ **Offer free books to every 100th customer.** Or make some other special offer that draws people in.

☐ **The possibilities are endless.** In his *Profitable Direct Marketing*, Jim Kobs listed ninety-nine proven direct response offers. Here are a few of them: Mystery gift offer, cash discount, early bird discount, seasonal sale, enrollment period, charter membership, prepublication offer, write-your-own-ticket offer, negative or positive option, lifetime membership fee, short-term introductory offer, and executive preview charge.

10:06 How to Design Effective Direct Mail Letters

Although the format of your direct mail package is not nearly as important as the advertising copy itself, variations in format can have measurable effects on the response. Hence, in this section I will be describing not only how to write more effective advertising copy but also how to design your direct mail programs to produce greater response.

First, to help you set your priorities, note that Murray Raphel asserts that the letter accounts for 65 to 75% of the orders from any direct mail package while the brochure accounts for 15 to 25% and the order form accounts for 5 to 10%. So be sure to spend time writing your letter. Here are a few hints:

☐ **Sell the benefits.** Above all, write copy that sells the benefits that can be derived from reading the book. Don't leave any doubt about what the benefits are. And don't expect the readers to guess what the benefits are from a listing of the book's contents. Tell them. Spell it out in clear language that any bozo could understand. As Zig Ziglar once pointed out, "No one buys anything until they can picture themselves utilizing or enjoying the benefits of your product or service."

☐ **Offer a benefit right away.** The first paragraph, indeed the first line should pique the interest of the reader. It should inspire the reader to read on. You must capture the reader's interest right away, or the entire letter will fail simply because the reader stops too soon.

☐ **Use "you" copy.** Write in a personal, comfortable style. Don't use overly long sentences or paragraphs. Underline words to make a point. Vary the length of paragraphs. And begin sentences with "and" or "or" or "but." In short, write in a conversational tone as if you were writing to a good friend rather than being graded by the queen's grammarian.

☐ **Remember the classic formula** for writing direct mail copy that sells: AIDA—Attention, Interest, Desire, Action.

First, get the reader's attention.

Second, once you have their attention, keep them interested by asking questions, answering questions, giving examples, and stating benefits.

Third, stir their desire by demonstrating to them all the advantages of owning the book you are offering.

And, finally, inspire them to act. Ask for the order. Make it easy to order. And don't let them delay.

☐ **Above all, ask for the order.** Make your offer clear to potential customers in simple, direct English. Repeat the offer again on your response card or order form.

☐ **Include a second order form** in your mailing package. This second order form could be printed in your brochure. Not only does a second form reduce the chance of a person losing the ordering information (price, address, etc.), but it also encourages pass-along orders.

☐ **Don't be afraid to be redundant.** Repeat if necessary. Say the same thing several times just to be sure that the reader has gotten the point. You don't have to repeat everything in the same paragraph, but you should repeat your main offer and the major benefits of the book several times in your mailing package—at least three times. Repetition helps to make your point clear and avoids any possible misunderstandings. You can even repeat the exact same sentence again later on in your letter. If it's a good sentence, it can bear repeating.

☐ **Use key words that people respond to.** Here are a few of those words: *you, your, free, new, bonus, satisfaction guaranteed, order now, success.* According to research done at Yale University, the following twelve words are the most persuasive: *discovery, easy, guarantee, health, love, money, new, proven, results, safety, save, you*. Of course, there are other effective words. Use the ones that suit you best.

☐ **Use testimonials in your letter.** When I mailed out a letter offering the *Directory of Book Printers*, I included the following testimonial both as teaser copy on the front of the envelope and as the lead to my letter: "Without Kremer's *Directory* I paid $12,500 for the first printing of one book—and got plenty of production hassles. With the *Directory* I paid $4,500 for the identical job—and no problems!" That testimonial not only summed up the two main benefits of the *Directory*, but it did it in an objective, yet dramatic way.

☐ **Direct your offer to the people reading the letter.** If you switch lists and the customer profile is different, you should rewrite your letter if necessary to appeal to the new audience.

☐ **End each page of a letter with an incomplete sentence** so the reader will turn the page. End the page by offering a special benefit or asking a question. Answer the question on the next page.

☐ **Write as much copy as you need to tell your story.** No more, no less. But note: A two-page letter tends to pull better than a one-page letter, and a four-page letter tends to pull better than a two-page letter.

☐ **Add a P.S. at the end of your letter.** Time and time again, a postscript has proven effective in increasing orders. Use it to restate the key benefit of your book, to offer an added inducement to order, or to offer a guarantee. The P.S. is one of the most read parts of any direct mail letter. Many people read the postscript before they read the letter.

☐ **Letters should look like letters.** Use typewriter type in your direct mail letters. It still works better than fancy laser typefaces—perhaps because it seems more personal and less high-tech.

☐ **Use ragged right text**, instead of justified text. It's more personal.

☐ **Highlight important points.** Besides underlining words, you might also circle certain words or write something in the margin (using legible handwriting). Don't overdo this, but use whatever seems appropriate to emphasize a point or make the letter more personal.

☐ **Personalize your letter.** Don't use computers just to merge the recipient's name into the greeting and body of the letter. Have a reason for using the person's name. Better yet, use some other details that demonstrate you know the reader's background.

Merrill Lynch sent a personalized letter to some of its key Investment Retirement Account clients detailing what their present holdings were and how their retirement value would change if they switched to a new program Merrill Lynch was offering. To personalize the letter even more, each letter was signed by the client's financial consultant. Sales for the program doubled as a result of this single mailing.

☐ **Develop more personal salutations.** Rather than writing "Dear Customer" or "Dear Reader," start your letter with "Dear Plant Lover" or "Dear Fellow Publisher." Address the audience directly.

☐ **Get their attention.** Use the recipient's name. Use color, Use boxes. Draw their interest.

☐ **Use a great headline.** How important is a headline? Judge for yourself. When *Sports Illustrated* began promoting its new *Sports Illustrated for Kids* via insert cards, it changed the headline on the card after it received some complaints. The original headline read: "Hey Dad, kids love sports too!" The changed headline dropped the first two words. When they made the change, response to the card dropped by half. The lesson learned? The personalization of the "Hey, Dad!" was vital to appealing to the mostly male audience of *Sports Illustrated*. If you test any part of your news releases or direct mail letters, test your headlines. They are far more important than you might think.

☐ **Be honest.** Keep your words and style believable. Don't exaggerate, and don't use hype. I have always found it to be more effective to be completely open and honest in my letters.

☐ **Offer free information.** Give the reader some free information in your letter: predictions that affect his or her well-being or business, news, trends, unusual facts, advice, or how-to instructions. Make sure the information offers the reader a reason to continue reading your letter.

☐ **Use involvement devices**, such as stickers, tabs, stamps, rub-offs, tokens, coins—anything to get the reader involved. Also known as action devices or hot potatoes, these involvement devices almost always improve results. Walter Weintz, who mailed more than 100 million pennies while circulation director for *Reader's Digest*, once noted, "I wouldn't even put out a mail-order mailing without some form of hot potato in it." And, as direct mail expert Axel Andersson observed, "I am surprised that coins have not been used more frequently. I don't know of any mailing with one that has failed."

Graphics Arts Monthly enclosed a quarter with a request for reader feedback. They wrote, "There's no way we can pay for your time ... perhaps the coin will help brighten the day of a child you know."

☐ **Print your name and address in many places** (at least once on each enclosure in the mailing package). First, this prevents the loss of an order when the customer misplaces the order form. Second, it adds a greater measure of credibility to your offer. If you were not proud of your product, you would try to hide your name.

☐ **Print some teaser copy on your envelope.** One of the first barriers any direct mail letter faces is at the mailbox. Many letters are thrown away without being opened because the outside envelope did not inspire the recipient to open the letter. To avoid this, print some teaser copy on the envelope that suggests a benefit that would interest the recipient.

Along with a window showing a connect-the-dots puzzle, the envelope of a *Games* mailing included the following teaser: "Connect the dots and discover a surprise from *Games* magazine! Gift pencil enclosed." Anyone interested in *Games* magazine would open such an envelope. The dots, when connected, spelled out the last name of the recipient.

☐ **Make the envelope look important.** Design it to look like a telegram, a bill, a check enclosure, a priority letter, an important business letter, or a personal letter.

☐ **Use an unusual envelope.** For instance, use an extra-large envelope, an envelope with multiple windows, a flaming red envelope, a brown paper bag, or a mailing tube. Or use some special effects on the outside of the envelope—stickers, seals, commemorative stamps, tokens, cartoons, rub-offs, or embossing.

☐ **Use actual stamps.** Use precanceled bulk mail or first class stamps rather than a bulk mail indicia. If you're making a large mailing, use metered bulk mail rather than a printed indicia (bulk metered mail is not easily distinguished from first class metered mail; hence, it actually looks very businesslike). Or, finally, you could have a bulk mail indicia printed in red ink so it looks like metered mail (check with your post office to make sure you do this exactly according to specifications).

☐ **Include a reply envelope** in your mailing, with or without return postage guaranteed. A pre-addressed reply envelope makes it easier for the person to respond. It's also more secure than a reply card by itself. Any time you ask for a check or credit card payment, you are better off including a reply envelope. Note that American Express, as a security measure, requires any orders charged to one of its cards to be inserted in an envelope.

☐ **Break any of the above rules** if it makes sense to do so. However, if you do break a rule, make sure you thoroughly test your mailing promotion before you roll out to a large audience.

☐ **Keep a swipe file.** Save every direct mail package, catalog, flyer, ad, letter, or whatever that you find effective (whether because of its copy, its layout, its color, its graphics, or whatever).

Authors — Write a direct mail letter solicitation for your book. Make it benefit oriented. Write at least six to twelve pages. Sell, sell, sell. Writing such a letter will give you a new perspective on your book.

At the very least, it should help you discover what benefits might be missing from your book. That's one good reason for you to try writing such direct mail letter *before* you finish writing the book.

10:07 How to Get the Best Lists

Of the three fundamentals of direct marketing, perhaps the most important is the list. Put simply, if you mail to the wrong list, neither your offer nor your message will have any impact whatsoever. Here, then, are a few tips on how to generate, maintain, and select mailing lists that will produce the greatest results for your direct mail program.

☐ Clean your list regularly. Since 20 to 30% of all addresses change every year, clean your house list at least every six months. To clean a list, simply print "Address Correction Requested" on the envelopes of any mailing to your list. The post office will charge for each address correction they return. Not only do individual consumers move with such regularity, but so do businesses and personnel. Job titles change, people get promoted or switch jobs (or companies), businesses expand, businesses move, companies go out of business—these are all responsible for the deterioration of business mailing lists.

☐ Your own house list will usually offer the best return on any mailing, even when some of the buyers may have originally bought books unrelated to the book you are currently offering. Of course, buyers of previous titles in the same subject area are your best prospects of all.

☐ The next best list is buyers of similar books from another publisher. If your book is not directly competitive with the other publisher's books, you should be able to rent the list. Most book publishers who do direct marketing rent out their list.

☐ Or, perhaps better yet, you might be able to arrange an exchange of lists with such a publisher. If you do exchange lists, make sure that the lists are as nearly equivalent as possible (in terms of average unit of sale, recency of list, number of buyers in relation to inquirers, number of names on the list, etc.). Open Horizons, for example, has exchanged lists with Para Publishing, publisher of *The Self-Publishing Manual*, and McHugh Publishing Reports.

☐ When you have exhausted all lists of buyers of related titles, test lists of buyers of items which are related to the title you are offering. For example, if you have an organic gardening book, you could rent a list of buyers of organic pesticides. No matter what your subject, there is a list out there somewhere that targets the audience for your book. Here are just a few of the lists that are available for publishers of gardening books:

   ☐ 259,000 last 12-month buyers from *Gardener's Supply Co.* catalog
   ☐ 250,000 members of the National Arbor Day Foundation
     (89% have flower or vegetable gardens)
   ☐ 189,000 buyers of products from the *Smith & Hawken* catalog
   ☐ 212,470 gardening book buyers from Sunset House
   ☐ 274,100 12-month garden book buyers from Rodale Press

- ☐ 155,000 subscribers to Jerry Baker's newsletter (as well as 324,000 book buyers)
- ☐ 763,000 subscribers to *Organic Gardening* magazine
- ☐ 70,000 active members of the Organic Gardening Book Club
- ☐ 28,100 active members of the Successful Organic Gardening Continuity Program (Rodale Press)
- ☐ 4,098,000 subscribers to *Better Homes & Gardens*
- ☐ 72,000 gardening enthusiasts who bought software from Parsons Technology
- ☐ 99,000 subscribers to *Fine Gardening* magazine
- ☐ 1,600,000 buyers from the *Spring Hill Nurseries, Breck's Dutch Bulbs*, and *New Holland Bulbs* catalogs
- ☐ 245,000 subscribers to *Horticulture* magazine
- ☐ 108,000 buyers of items from the *White Flower Farm* catalog
- ☐ 892 garden supply dealers (compiled)
- ☐ 72,000 garden stores and nurseries (compiled)
- ☐ 2,195 garden clubs or 72,715 garden club members (compiled)
- ☐ 1,085 seed, nursery, and gardening supply catalogs (compiled)

☐ In almost every case, a list of mail order buyers will outperform a list of inquirers or a compiled list. Nevertheless, if no other buyers lists are available, your next best choice is a targeted compiled list. Open Horizons, for example, regularly rented the R.R. Bowker list of U.S. book publishers, a list that always performed well even though compiled (and full of duplicates).

☐ You can, of course, compile your own business mailing lists by going through the yellow pages of city telephone books. Many libraries have collections of the yellow page directories from most major cities. In fact, compiled lists from phone books are available now to anyone who owns a computer with a CD-ROM drive or Internet access.

☐ Membership lists of related organizations can also be superb sources of book buyers. Open Horizons uses the PMA membership list which, next to its house list, is its best performer. Indeed, our list now includes close to 90% of the PMA membership.

☐ Subscriber lists are also effective. Why? Because most newsletters and magazines are sold by direct mail. Also, of course, periodical subscribers are proven readers; hence, they are more likely to buy other reading material by mail.

☐ Other list sources: attendees at a convention or trade show, members of clubs, book club members, Internet interest groups.

☐ When selecting lists, get recommendations from three or four different list brokers. In such cases, you will undoubtedly receive duplicate recommendations from these brokers. These duplicate recommendations are likely to be the best lists to test first. List brokers won't cost you any money because they get paid by the list owner. For a list of list brokers and managers, see http://www.bookmarket.com/lists.html.

☐ Use the Internet to search for lists. The best source I've found is at the web site of American List Counsel (http://www.amlist.com).

☐ Get hotline names whenever possible. Hotline names are names of people who have bought within the past 30 to 90 days. Recent buyers are the most likely candidates to buy again.

☐ *Merge/purge names* (names that appear on two or more targeted lists) are the best potential customers. Such lists outpull any other list.

☐ When you are considering a list, get samples of promotions which have worked with the list. Ask the list owner to provide samples or give you the names of some previous renters. The best samples to review are those from repeat renters of the list (no sane direct marketer would ever rent a list twice if it had not performed well the first time). When you get samples, look for any similarities in appeals, copy, or format. These should give you insight into how to approach the list with your offer.

☐ As part of your long range list research, try to get your own name on the lists which you might potentially use. Code your name so you will know when that list is used. You can, for example, code your name by using different initials for each list (J. L. Kremer for one list, J. A. Kremer for another, John F. Kremer for still another, etc.).

How do you get on other lists? Buy something, make an inquiry, ask for their catalog, join an association, or simply ask to be put on their mailing lists for their latest offers. Two of the main advantages of being on a list you might rent is that you will get a good idea of 1) how often the list is rented, and 2) what sort of mailers rent the list.

For example, I've been on some lists that are rented out four or five times a week—that's too often to be effective for many promotions, especially ones for higher-priced items. I've also been on lists which, it turns out, were rented primarily to chain letter opportunists—again, not a list you'd ever want to use.

☐ To expand your own in-house list, offer a low-priced book or report that appeals to the same audience as the rest of your books.

Peachpit Press binds in a postcard offering something free in almost all of its new books. For instance, in their *Windows 3.1 Bible*, the bound-in postcard offered a free *Windows Game Book* and *Windows Goodies Disk*. This is an excellent way to build a list, no matter where the customer bought your book, whether direct or in a store.

To add names to our list, Open Horizons has offered inexpensive reports including *How to Create a Bestseller* for $3.00, *29 Ways to Get Publicity for Your Books* for $5.00, *How to Sell Books via the Internet* for $5.00, *50 Creative Book Marketing Ideas* for $5.00, *Wholesalers and Li-*

brary Jobbers: A Select List for $5.00, and *Choosing a Distribution System* for $5.00. We offered these through press releases, small classified ads, and as giveaways. Although in most cases we made little money on these offers, we did add a good number of regular customers to our house list. These low-priced reports, then, function the same as loss leaders: They bring in the customers, and once these customers discover all the other books a publisher has to offer, they order more—enough, in the final analysis, to make the entire proposition pay off.

☐ Offer freebies to attract potential customers. Just be sure to offer a freebie that is related to your main line of books. Such offers can bring in as many as 20,000 inquiries when offered in a magazine with national circulation (such as *Family Circle* or the *Bottomline Personal* newsletter).

☐ Add a section to your catalog order forms which gives your current customers an opportunity to "Do a friend a favor." Ask them to give you the names of any friends who they think would like to receive your book catalog. This friend-get-a-friend technique has worked well for a good number of mail order companies.

☐ According to Donnelley Marketing's *Survey of Promotional Practices*, manufacturers use the following means to build their customer databases (the average company uses three to four different means):

84%	Premium Offers / Rebates
74%	Consumer Information Inquiries
68%	Contests / Sweepstakes
53%	Trackable Coupons
42%	800/900 Phone Number Promos
26%	External Mailing Lists
16%	National Consumer Surveys
5%	Warranties / Registrations
5%	Retailer Frequent Shopper / Reward Programs

> **Authors** — If you know of targeted lists (associations, magazine subs, catalog buyers, or other possibilities) that would be appropriate for your book, let your publisher know. They might not use the list, but it doesn't hurt to let them know it exists —and it may lead them to other lists that work even better.

10:08 How to Make Best Use of Card Packs

Card packs, those ubiquitous collections of loose postcards advertising from thirty to two hundred offers, are still a major form of alternative direct marketing. You can choose from some 750 card packs, at least one for almost any audience you want to target (from engineers and doctors to sales managers and craft store owners). Before you decide to use one, though, you should be aware of the disadvantages as well as the advantages of advertising in such response decks.

Disadvantages of Card Packs

☐ Since they are cooperative advertising vehicles, it is quite possible to have several of your competitors also advertising in the same pack. Actually, this could be an advantage or a disadvantage depending on how your book measures up to the other books in price and offer.

☐ Because of the small card size it is often difficult to sell books which require detailed explanation or extensive copy.

☐ Again because of the size limitation, it is often impossible to offer multiple order or payment options.

☐ You can't offer a business reply envelope (though you can offer a business reply card).

☐ Returns and bad debts tend to be higher among card pack buyers as compared to magazine advertising or regular direct mail.

☐ Since many packs are mailed only two or three times a year, they may not allow the best timing for your book promotions.

☐ Since card pack advertising may be more widely distributed than your own direct mail package, such advertising can tip off your competitors to your new offers.

☐ Response rates are low, anywhere from .1% to 1%, generally to the low side.

Advantages of Card Packs

☐ Card packs offer one of the lowest costs for direct mail advertising ($17.00 to $20.00 per thousand as compared to $300.00 to $500.00 per thousand for your own packages).

☐ They are easy to use.

☐ Per inquiry or per order insertions are quite easy to arrange in many of the packs (especially with the recent oversaturation of the market).

☐ Card packs are superb lead generators.

☐ Card packs offer fast response. You can expect to receive half the response from your ad within 12 days of receiving the first response.

Questions to Ask Before Using Packs

☐ Is the list made up of buyers? (Mail responsive lists are better than compiled lists.)

☐ If it is a list of buyers, how much did they spend on the product? (The price should be at least as high as the price of your book offer.)

☐ What is the source of the list? (Make sure it's a reputable source.)

☐ How often is the list cleaned? (The more often it is cleaned, the better the list.)

☐ How often is the pack mailed? (The better packs are mailed four to six times a year, thus allowing you more opportunities to follow up on the success of a card placement.)

☐ Is it mailed to the same people each time, or to different lists? (Different lists are often better since they allow your offer to reach new prospects each mailing.)

☐ Does the pack offer an A/B split for testing? (A/B splits allow you to mail one offer to half the list and another offer or format to the other half. Such splits enable you to test which offers or formats produce the best results.)

Tips on Using Packs

☐ Use packs that are sent to mail responsive names rather than to compiled lists. However, avoid hotline names which often represent current respondents only rather than paid buyers.

☐ Position is important. Some studies have shown that cards in the first half of the pack produce twice the results of cards in the second half of the pack. Hence, if you have to pay a premium for position, it may well be worth the extra payment.

☐ Free trial offers work better than credit card sales. McGraw-Hill has consistently found that 10-day free trial offers work the best for their books.

☐ If you do use such free trial offers, expect some debt collection problems and some returns (up to 30% of all orders). Factor these considerations into your calculations when figuring whether participation in the pack will pay off for your book.

☐ Note that offers for higher priced books are more likely to pay off for you as compared to lower priced books. Again, card packs are best for generating inquiries or leads that can be followed up with sales letters, telemarketing, or direct sales visits.

☐ One option that worked well for Caddylak Systems was to offer three or four books on the same card. Although each book in itself was low priced ($9.95 to $14.95), multiple-copy orders usually made participation in the pack pay off. Since Caddylak published a line of some forty related books, any orders generated through the card pack usually resulted in additional sales. Caddylak later offered higher priced books (usually $49.95 or higher) through card packs. Hence, while the lower priced offers may have helped them build up a good list of buyers, they were probably not making a profit for Caddylak.

☐ Always state the price of your book in the ad.

☐ Lay out your offer horizontally. Customers read the pack this way.

☐ Use graphics or a photo of your book in the ad. Multiple colors also work better than a single color. Note that many card pack publishers will throw in a second color free to encourage you to test their pack.

☐ Use headlines that will compel the casual browser to read on:
FREE CATALOG! or FREE SAMPLE! or 50% OFF! or SAVE $10.00!

☐ Ask for a business card rather than having buyers fill out an order blank. Buyers with business cards are more qualified buyers. Also you can learn more about a buyer from a business card than you can from any information they fill out in an order blank. To encourage the sending of business cards, many card pack participants now print a light line saying, "Tape Business Card Here," over the coupon area.

☐ Give them plenty of room to fill out their return address, just in case they don't attach a business card.

☐ Cards are one-second billboards. Most cards receive no more than a one-second glance from pack recipients as they flip through the deck. That one second is all you have to gain the attention of the recipient and earn a second chance to make a sale. Design your card with this one-second rule in mind. Don't overcrowd your card. Keep it simple.

☐ Call for action right away. Card packs are designed for immediate response. If the recipient puts your card away for later referral, chances are they will never respond. So ask them to call your 800 number right away for a free sample copy. Or ask them to fill in the card now for a one-month, no-obligation trial.

☐ Many card packs accept per inquiry or per order advertising. Indeed, in many packs up to 30% of the cards are p.i. or p.o. ads. With per inquiry or per order ads, you only pay the card pack publisher for actual inquiries or orders you receive. For example, if you received 100 orders for a $19.95 book, you would have to pay the card pack publisher about $1000.00, or about 50% of your total income from orders you received. Similarly, you might have to pay $2.00 to $5.00 for each inquiry you received. When requesting a p.i. deal, make it clear to the pack publisher that if the results are good, you will be placing more ads.

☐ Some pack publishers will sell on a space available basis which could save you up to 50% of the pack cost. If you choose this option, you run the risk that the pack will fill up and your ad won't run.

☐ Other packs offer a 15% discount for advertising agencies and card brokers. Many also offer such a discount for direct placement or for your first placement in their deck.

☐ Many card pack publishers will typeset, design, and write the copy for your card. Many offer this service free to first time users (in the hopes, of course, that you will become a regular participant in their pack).

☐ Some book publishers who use card packs regularly report no fall off of orders with larger packs (when packs go from 40 to 60 cards).

Card Pack Inquiry Services

If you'd like to test card packs without spending a lot of money, you might try one of these card pack inquiry services. These companies will advertise a short listing describing your book (your book will be listed with 25 to 50 other products). They charge for each inquiry they generate (but they require an upfront deposit of $150 to $500).

☐ **Cata-List**, Venture Communications, 60 Madison Avenue, 3rd Floor, New York, NY 10010-1681; 212-684-4800; Fax: 212-576-1129. Web: http://www.adventure.com.

☐ **One-Stop Catalog Shop**, Visual Horizons, 180 Metro Park, Rochester, NY 14623-2666; 716-424-5300; Fax: 716-424-5313. Web: http://www.visualhorizons.com.

Ad-Lib Publications advertised the *PR-ProfitCenter* database through one of these services. We received about 300 inquiries, but the sell-through was very poor. But, again, the cost to test is quite inexpensive. If you have the right book or books for card pack audiences (primarily small businesses), such programs might work well for you.

10:09 Other Direct Mail Options

When using direct mail, you have a number of different format options which have proven successful for other companies. If any seem appropriate for your company, test that format against your current format. If it proves successful for your books, you might switch all or a large portion of your mailings to that format.

Classic letter package

Perhaps the most common direct mail promotion is the classic letter package consisting of a letter (anywhere from two to twelve pages in length), outer envelope, BRE (business reply envelope), order form, and a lift letter, brochure, or both. Why is the classic letter package so common? Because it works, time and time again.

If you include a *brochure* in your classic direct mail package, here are a couple of hints for making it better:

- A two-color brochure almost always outpulls a one-color brochure.

- Put your selling message, the prime benefit, on the front cover. Most people never read past the front cover if it does not pull them in.

- Make sure your brochure describes the complete offer. That way, even if the brochure gets separated from the rest of the mailing package, the customer can still place the order.

Lift letters are short letters usually printed on half-sheets of paper to supplement the sales story laid out in the longer full-size letter. When original, lift letters can be effective in increasing results. That's why they are called lift letters: They generate a lift or increase in response.

Card decks or card packs

Rather than mailing one or two cards in another company's card deck, you could offer your entire line of books in card deck format, with one or two books offered per card. Publishers like John Wiley and McGraw-Hill, who service a professional audience, are among the most extensive users of card decks. Among the card decks John Wiley has published are the following: *Human Resources Card Deck, Educators Card Deck, Art Educators Card Deck, Woman-at-Work Card Deck, Elementary Educators Card Deck*, and *Career & Personal Advancement Card Deck*. Not only do they offer their own books in these card decks, but they accept advertising inserts from other companies as well.

☐ Academic Press offers a separate deck aimed only at buyers of microbiology books.

☐ St. Anthony Messenger Press replaced its Christmas gift catalog with a card deck to offer its line of religious books to over half a million customers. Results were "beyond anything else we've ever done."

☐ Garden Way produces an ads-only periodical of direct response cards, called *Gardener's Marketplace*, to sell its line of gardening books and cookbooks. The *Marketplace* is mailed twice a year, in the spring and fall, to almost one million gardeners. This format has been effective for them, with one card alone bringing in over $40,000 in orders.

Catalogs

Almost every book publisher uses this format once they've developed a list of books long enough to justify the cost. Many publishers, however, only send the catalogs to bookstores, wholesalers, and libraries. A growing list of book publishers are beginning to use catalogs to reach book buyers directly. Catalogs can produce excellent results if your own in-house list is large enough or your book list is specialized enough to allow you to target your catalog mailings to specific lists.

Why do people buy from catalogs? According to a recent Gallup survey, 36% of the respondents buy from catalogs primarily because they are more convenient than shopping in retail stores, while 19% like the variety that is available in a catalog, 17% the lower prices, and 6% the higher quality. Remember these percentages when planning and designing your catalog.

☐ The Pleasant Company of Middleton, Wisconsin, does more than $100 million in business per year primarily through its catalogs, which feature the American Girls Collection books as well as the accompanying dolls, toys, clothing (doll clothes as well as life-size clothes for girls), cooking kits, furniture, fashion accessories, trading cards, postcards, calendars, bookmarks, stationery sets, scene settings, magazine, and other items.

☐ When Loyola University Press published three separate catalogs (one for the bookstore trade, one for libraries, and one for consumers), they had a seven times increase in sales. Don't try to make one catalog fill all needs. It might be better for you to produce two or more catalogs, each targeted to specific audiences.

☐ O'Reilly publishes a catalog that is sent direct to software programmers. This catalog is designed for consumer orders only.

☐ To promote its frontlist titles for fall 1993, Henry Holt sent out a catalog in a postcard billfold format that unfolded to feature ten book covers on one side and short excerpts or testimonials on the other side.

☐ Note that printing and computer technology is getting to the point that you can publish one-to-one full-color catalogs personalized for each customer. To make use of this technology, you will have to develop and maintain an extensive database of information on your customers or else develop a system that captures that information when they call. One company in Europe, Toets 9220, already publishes 48-page catalogs personalized for each person who calls to get information on specific subjects. They use a voice-response system to capture the information necessary to prepare and publish the personal catalogs.

Dover format

Besides mailing special interest catalogs, Dover Publications also mails up to eight 11" x 17" flyers folded to fit inside a #10 business envelope. Each flyer features a separate line of about forty books (for example, paper dolls, crafts, graphic arts, or science). Although most books sell for under $5.00, Dover does well with these mailings because the average order is much higher, with most customers ordering three or more books.

Tabloid catalogs

New Society Publishers printed seasonal catalogs on tabloid-size newspaper stock which allows them plenty of room for describing and illustrating their new and backlist titles while being inexpensive to print.

Magalog (catalog in magazine format)

You can also send out a catalog in magazine format (also known as a *magalog*). A magalog includes useful editorial matter as well as sales information and ads for your products. One advantage of this format is that it is more likely to be saved during the first sorting of mail—and it also has a better chance of being read. And a mailing that can produce those effects has a much better chance of making the sale than a mailing that gets tossed out without being opened at all.

☐ Rodale sent out a magalog, *Prevention for Pets*, promoting *The Doctor's Book of Home Remedies for Dogs & Cats*. That publication won an Echo award from Direct Marketing Association and sold many books.

☐ John Wiley issued a catalog in magazine format, even giving it a fancy title, *Excel*, and volume and issue numbers. Their first issue was in the summer of 1985. I haven't seen any further issues, so the format may not have produced the results they had hoped it would.

☐ A number of larger companies, including IBM, AT&T, and FedEx, have been publishing magalogs for years.

☐ Doubleday published *D Magazine* to promote new titles, usually by featuring excerpts from the books but sometimes also featuring interviews with the authors.

Books or booklets

You can actually use books as a direct mail promotion to sell other books. Aspen Publishers uses short mass-market paperbacks to sell subscriptions to its newsletters.

☐ To promote its hardcover book, *New Choices in Natural Healing*, Rodale Press sent out a 50-page booklet bulk rate. *The Doctor's Vest-Pocket Sampler of Natural Remedies* actually provided remedies for many common ailments, from sore throats and hot flashes to asthma and leg cramps. It also described how to prevent gum disease, beat PMS, cure ulcers, and more. Plus it offered teasers for curing hemorrhoids, cold sores, diarrhea, chronic fatigue, constipation, and more. Anyone who read the booklet and tried out a few of its natural remedies would be sure to buy the complete book. To make the offer irresistible, Rodale offered a free 21-day trial and a free gift, *5-Minute Cures*, just for looking. It was a dynamite package that sold lots of books.

☐ Time-Life first tested a booklet mailing against its control large envelope mailing for its *Mysteries of the Unknown* series. Although the booklet beat the control package, the management of Time-Life considered it a fluke and didn't roll it out. Later, though, they would use booklets to sell other series successfully, including its *World at War* series.

Self-mailers

Self-mailers are mailing formats which do not require an envelope. They come in different sizes and formats—from simple folded leaflets to large folded brochures printed on card stock. Self-mailers offer many advantages:

☐ They are generally easy and quick to design and produce.

☐ Since they require no outside envelope, they are cheaper to produce (but, note, they rarely outpull envelope-enclosed mailings).

☐ Because they are in one piece with no outside envelope, they require no collating and stuffing; hence, labor costs for preparing them for mailing are much lower.

☐ They get immediate attention for recipients. Hence, they are often used for mailings to bookstores and libraries.

Postcards

Publishers have used postcards to announce single titles. Postcards have a sense of urgency and informality which might be right for some titles. Plus, they are inexpensive to produce and mail. Single postcards have been used to build retail traffic, generate leads, announce one-shot sales, send customer service messages, and keep retailers informed of on-going publicity. Double-postcards have been used effectively by magazines for years.

☐ Christine Adamec, author of *There are Babies to Adopt*, mailed out a simple postcard to some 400 radio stations to announce her availability as an expert for interview. As a result, she was interviewed by more than 15 radio shows. Cost? About $125.00.

☐ To promote the new edition of *Creative Cash*, the author Barbara Brabec mailed out 5,000 postcards to her own customer list that hadn't been cleaned in 18 months. Her cost for the mailing was $180.00 for printing plus $950.00 for postage. Besides getting 964 address corrections (at no extra cost), she also received 153 orders, which amounted to over $2,500.00 in sales.

☐ As part of the prepublication promotion for its coffee-table book on the Broadway play, *Rent*, William Morrow sent out a targeted postcard mailing to ticket buyers for the play.

Broadsides or posters

These formats can be effective for single titles with appealing graphics. Any use of broadsides or posters, whether for single titles or multiple titles, requires careful planning and graphic design. Posters are often sent to bookstores in the hope that the booksellers will display them in their stores.

Book jackets as brochures

Book jackets or covers, printed on the inside with further details about the book, make excellent promotional brochures. They are especially effective when sent with press releases, with mailings to booksellers (who can get a better picture of how the book will look on their shelves), and with prepublication announcements. When you get your book printed, order overruns of the cover. When printed along with the book, the additional cost is minimal since setup and plates have already been paid for.

☐ Every distributor and sales rep insists upon having printed covers to help them present the book to their customers. Often the book cover is the only thing any retailer sees before placing an order for your book.

☐ Mayfield Publishing, a college textbook publisher, prints the inside of cover overruns with promotional information about the book. They send these covers to professors about two weeks before they send out complimentary desk copies. That way, when the professors get the desk copy of the book, they will already recognize the book and be more open to putting it at the top of their pile of things to look at more closely.

Statement stuffers

You can print small 8½" x 3½" flyers announcing new or backlist titles to send out with your invoices and statements. These statement stuffers are cheap to produce and can be effective in selling related titles. You could also insert your announcement in statements sent out by banks, catalogs, credit card companies, and magazines. The cost to participate in a statement stuffing program is much less than mailing out first class yourself. Plus, your announcement is guaranteed to be sent to proven creditworthy buyers.

To promote their Boston guidebook, *In and Out of Boston (with or without) Children*, Globe Pequot Press inserted statement stuffers in with the billing statements of the *Boston Globe*. As a result of this promotion and many others, they have thus far sold over 300,000 copies of the guide.

Stamp sheets

Stamp sheets have been used for years to sell magazine subscriptions via sweepstakes mailings. Most of these sweepstakes promoters have begun selling books as well as magazines. Plus, some book publishers are now also using the format on their own.

☐ In early 1993, Time Warner rolled out a national test featuring 99 books (75% of the titles were from other publishers). The stamp-sheet mailing, which included a sweepstakes, reached 1,000,000 prospects. Bantam also tested a sweepstakes stamp-sheet mailing to sell their titles.

☐ To sell professional medical titles, Little, Brown uses a sheet of full-color stamps bearing cover illustrations for their medical books. Recipients can select the stamps for the books they'd like to receive, stick them on the order form, and send it in. Such offers work well if your covers are designed to sell your books and if you offer billing privileges.

☐ Rodale Press, which promotes many of their titles through direct mail and television advertising, also sells some of their health titles through Publishers Clearing House sweepstakes mailings. Rodale reports that PCH's sales do not cut into Rodale's direct sales to consumers.

Videos and DVDs

If you sell a high-priced book or series, you might try sending videocassette or DVD versions of your catalog to your top prospects. Not only will they attract people's attention, but they are also far less likely to be thrown out without being viewed. Royal Silk, a catalog of high-priced clothes for women, now offers a version of its catalog on videocassette. They charge $5 or $10 for it. They have found that people who order via the videocassette catalog spend an average of $20 more per order.

Newspaper clippings

Sales & Marketing Digest encloses only one item in its direct mail letters: an ad that appears to have been torn out of the financial section of a newspaper. They've been using this format for several years, so it's apparently working for them. A number of book publishers have also used newspaper clippings to sell books.

CD-Roms

Many major companies are now using CD-Roms as a dramatic and often effective way to grab and hold people's attention. Here are just a few of the advantages of this new medium:

☐ They are still novel enough to attract attention.

☐ CD-Roms are great involvement devices. If designed well, they encourage interaction by involving recipients in answering questions, filling in the blanks, or making choices on what parts of the program to see.

☐ They can pack an incredible amount of information, with many options to choose from.

☐ Computer owners have attractive demographics: high income, college educated, home owners.

☐ You can create animated displays with great graphics.

Here are just a few of the companies using CDs to market their products: General Motors received 300,000 requests for an interactive disk that demonstrated one of its new Buicks. Ford Motor distributed 25,000 disks for its upscale sports sedan, the Merkur XR4Ti, with the following selling message: "Take a test drive on your disk drive." Chase Manhattan Bank sent out a disk to demonstrate its Electronic Funds Transfer service.

Newsletters

Because newsletters combine useful information with an advertising message, they can be one of the most effective ways to market books. Above all, they tend to be read—and that is always the first step towards selling anything by mail!

☐ The *Book Marketing Update* newsletter was begun in 1986 as an advertising vehicle for Open Horizon's books. The first two issues were sent to 20,000 publishers for a total cost of about $10,000. From those two issues we grossed about $35,000 in sales (with about a 4% response rate). From our experience, I would suggest these pointers:

1. Keep the newsletter short.
2. Publish monthly or bimonthly (repetition is important for creating the greatest impact).
3. Start small. Keep testing until you find the right format and audience.

☐ Many other publishers are currently using newsletters to promote their books, including AMACOM Books, Backboard Press, Bantam (*Word of Mouth*, their consumer cookbook newsletter), Children's Book Press, Harper & Row (*Harper's Web*, their junior books group newsletter), Nolo Press, Para Publishing (*Publishing Poynters*), Ransom Hill Press,

Simon & Schuster (*Inner Sanctum*, for crime fiction and mystery books), and John Wiley (*Wiley Ideas*).

Questionnaires

Questionnaires and surveys can be used as a direct marketing vehicle. For instance, Omniartists/Sirius found that when they sent out questionnaires for their *Acquisitions and Development Directory* for motion pictures, they also pre-sold the directory to many of those people and companies listed in the directory. Their mailing package, which included a flyer, questionnaire, and sample page, drew a 5 to 10% response for the $159.00 directory.

10:10 Marketing via Your Telephone

Most publishers now offer toll-free service for incoming orders and customer service. The cost of a toll-free number is so low and the returns so great that few companies can afford not to offer the service. For details on the advantages of offering toll-free service, see Section 4:02 in this book.

While the installation of a toll-free number can have a great impact on your sales, you should not limit your telemarketing to passive order taking. As long as you have the customer on the phone, take the opportunity to make additional sales or to ask questions of the book buyers (to discover, for instance, how they found out about your books and why they decided to order your books). If you prepare a standard script for your order takers, they can easily increase your book sales without any additional cost.

After you have organized an effective system for handling incoming orders, you should consider establishing an outgoing telemarketing effort as well. While some consumers resent the invasion of telemarketing sales calls into their homes (and rightly so), outbound telemarketing can still be an effective sales tool for your company. Here are a few ways to use outbound telemarketing to your advantage:

☐ **Test a list fast**. You can test a list of a thousand names within a few days by using the telephone. If the results are good, you have reason to expect a follow-up mailing to a larger portion of the same list to produce comparable results. Such a test is clearly not as reliable as a test mailing, but it can provide you with quick feedback on which of two or more possible lists is likely to produce the best results. According to one telemarketing expert, calls to 100 people will give a response equivalent to a direct mailing to 1,000 people.

☐ **Test an offer fast**. Use telephone calls to test alternate offers (for example, to test which of two premium offers will produce the most sales).

☐ **Follow up inquiries and leads**. For example, you could call instructors who have been sent examination copies of textbooks to check whether they will be using your book in their classes and, if not, why not.

☐ **Research your market**. For example, make phone calls to a sampling of doctors to see if they'd be interested in a book on gall bladder operations. Or perhaps, you could use the same phone calls to ask open ended questions that encourage the doctors to tell you what kind of information they do need. Then you can produce books that would fill that need.

☐ **Increase sales**. Telemarketing can increase the response to an offer by as much as five or ten times. For example, if a list would normally yield a 5% response to direct mail, telemarketing might increase the response to 20 or 25%. Such increases may be attributed to the more personal nature of phone calls, to the greater opportunity for give and take in a phone conversation, and/or to the greater immediacy of phone calls.

☐ **Upsell**. When customers call to order one item, you can take that opportunity to sell them additional items, or sell them a higher-priced book on the same subject.

☐ **Sell new editions**. Buyers of previous editions of reference books and manuals are the best prospects for new editions. You can make calls to your own in-house list of buyers offering a prepublication special.

☐ **Sell new titles to your in-house list**. Your in-house list is your best prospect for any new titles, especially related titles. With a proper computer order entry and tracking system, you should be able to sort out those previous customers who are most likely to buy certain titles. You could then use telemarketing to produce enough prepublication orders to pay for the cost of producing the new title.

☐ **Open new accounts**, especially among booksellers. This application offers the greatest potential for producing profitable orders via telemarketing. You can use the phone not only to open new accounts but also to alert previous customers of new titles or offers.

☐ **Cut sales costs**. Telemarketing can be an inexpensive substitute for direct sales visits. Indeed, with bookstores which are located out in the boondocks, phone calls may be the only practical way to keep in touch with them. For smaller publishers who are not able to set up sales representatives, telemarketing offers a viable alternative, especially if it is used to supplement direct mail offers.

☐ **Collect delinquent accounts**. Probably more publishers use outbound phone calls for this reason than for any other.

☐ **Create publicity**. Outbound phone calls, of course, are also an essential element in any aggressive publicity campaign. Phone calls are often the only practical way to follow up previous contacts. Also, since phone calls allow a certain give and take, negotiations for author interviews and appearances are much easier to conduct over the phone rather than through email or snail mail.

☐ **Save customer time**. Not only can customers order faster over the phone, but they can also check on the availability of your books (especially backlist) and discuss any problems that might have come up in regard to any of their orders.

☐ **Build good will.** A toll-free phone number demonstrates that you are responsive to the needs of your customers and open to their feedback. Answer your phone. Be open to calls from your customers.

☐ **Answer questions**. You can answer questions over the phone that you could never answer in a print advertisement or catalog.

☐ **Conduct a teleclass.** People dial a special phone number and are connected to a group call, complete with interaction. In March 1997, author Judy Sabah conducted a teleclass on *How to Be Totally Debt Free, Including Your Home Mortgage, in 5-7 Years, on Your Present Income.*

10:11 Tips for More Effective Telemarketing

Telemarketing sales have grown from sales of $161 billion in 1987 to sales of $385 billion in 1996. Business-to-business marketers spend more money on telemarketing ($35.9 billion in 1995 out of a total of $71.8 billion in advertising expenditures) than any other means of advertising. Because telemarketing costs run high (anywhere from $1,200 to $2,000 per thousand names), response rates must be high. While response rates for consumer telemarketing can range as high as 15% to 25%, you cannot expect such response rates unless your telemarketing campaign is carefully designed.

Telemarketing, to be effective, must be highly organized. You cannot play it by ear. You must plan every step of the process if you hope to make efficient use of what is one of the most expensive and effective media for making sales. Here are a few tips:

☐ **Use highly targeted lists.** Don't waste your phone time on general lists or random canvassing of phone books. Your own in-house list of buyers and inquirers or outside lists of buyers are your best prospects. Of all factors in any telephone marketing campaign, the list is the most important. Again, the offer and the audience must match.

☐ **Make a clear, specific offer**—one that can be easily stated in a few sentences. Make it easy for the listener to either say yes or no.

☐ **Have a definite script which your callers must follow.** Be sure to spend time training your callers to handle any customer questions or other responses. You should anticipate most questions in your script and have clear answers already prepared for the most prevalent ones.

☐ **Hire only phone callers who can handle rejection**, who can terminate a phone call politely and proceed right away with the next call. The best callers are those who can be casual in their tone and presentation while sticking to the script.

☐ **Accept purchase orders, C.O.D., or credit card sales**. Don't expect people to send checks in response to telephone sales calls.

☐ **Prepare a simple but complete order form** that allows your caller to record the order easily while continuing to talk with the customer.

☐ **Record responses.** Each phone conversation, whether resulting in an order or some other response, should be recorded in writing and filed with your records. With outside lists, ask operators to check off a simple form recording the number of responses for each general category (orders, requests for more information, simple rejection, vehement rejection, hang-ups, no answers) rather than writing a complete memorandum.

☐ **Outbound sales calls can be more effective as follow-ups to previous mailings than as cold calls.** Such a one-two punch can be more effective than phone calls or mailings made independent of each other. For example, Enterprise Publishing used outbound telemarketing to solicit feedback from customers. These outbound calls often resulted in further sales—about 10% of their sales came via outbound telemarketing.

☐ **Don't call too often.** For its encyclopedias, book clubs, and continuity programs, Grolier has a policy of not telemarketing anyone who has been called within the past three months. They also make an effort never to call anyone twice about the same product.

☐ **Make it as easy as possible for potential customers to reach you.** While continuing your outbound telemarketing, also work to make it easy for people to call you. Advertise your inbound numbers (both regular and toll-free numbers).

☐ **Whenever anyone calls you, try upselling**—that is, let them know what else you have to offer them. This upselling doesn't have to be aggressive, but certainly it makes sense to let incoming callers know what else you have to offer. Whenever anyone calls Open Horizons to order a book, we let them know that we publish an entire line of books, reports, and newsletters on publishing and marketing.

☐ **Offer a special service.** To increase incoming phone traffic, offer a special service for those customers who are not ready to order anything. Then, when they call, offer them a limited-time special or tie-in merchandise. Banana Republic offers their catalog customers a Climate Desk phone service. Customers can call this toll-free number to find weather information for their travel destinations, including high and low temperatures for various seasons, average rainfall, political situations that might affect travel, medical requirements, health precautions, State Department regulations, and clothing needs. Where appropriate, Banana Republic also suggests clothing or travel books that might be useful. Of course, any clothing or travel books that they recommend, they also sell.

☐ **Use call processing.** If you receive many incoming calls, you might want to use voice mail, which functions like an automated receptionist. Here are just a few of the benefits this technology can offer you:

1. Automatically routes calls to the right department.

2. Answers all calls without your intervention, thus saving on the number of people you need to hire to answer your phones. All calls are answered by human voices (which can be taped by you).

3. Can take orders right over the phone, with the callers leaving all required information by voice message or by punching the appropriate touch-tone numbers on their telephone pads.

4. Allows callers to leave messages for various people (so those people can get their messages by just checking their telephone mail box).

5. You can program sales messages that callers access by pressing the right touch-tone numbers. You could have separate sales messages for each title on your list. Or you could have separate messages for your sales reps, for booksellers, and for individual customers.

At one time, Book-of-the-Month Club installed a voice mail system, but later they abandoned it. I'm not sure why, although I suspect it might be because many consumers resent the impersonal nature of such systems. I much prefer a real person answering the phone and, I suspect, most other people do, too. If you use such a system, make sure you give callers a quick way to talk to a real person.

☐ **Market with a 900 number**. While 900 numbers were originally dominated by sexploitation schemes, many newspapers, TV networks, and Fortune 500 companies are using such numbers to poll their markets, provide information, and sell products. The great thing about 900 numbers is that the caller pays for the call.

Windsor Peak Press promoted a 900 number in the back of their *Bridal Bargains* book. Readers could dial the 900 number to get updates on bargains listed in the book. The cost to readers was 75¢ per minute. After paying the phone company and service bureau, Windsor Peak netted $300 to $400 per month from the 900 number.

Authors — Your telephone can be one of your most potent marketing tools. If you do decide to help your publisher by calling major buyers or by conducting an outbound marketing test, be sure to coordinate your efforts with your publisher.

10:12 Advertising in Newspapers

While newspaper advertising outside of the book review sections is not used by many publishers, it has produced fantastic results for publishers who have the money to commit to an extensive national campaign. Here are a few ways publishers have used newspapers to advertise their books:

☐ **Encourage bookstore sales.** Robert Ringer used newspaper advertising to market several bestsellers, including *Winning Through Intimidation*, *Looking Out for #1*, and *Crisis Investing*. His technique was quite simple: He wrote superb mail order copy, took out large ads in major newspapers, and then directed orders to bookstores rather than to his own publishing company. His aggressive advertising campaign combined with the cooperation of the major book chains pushed his books onto the bestseller lists and enabled him to sell mass-market rights for close to a million dollars. Such techniques obviously won't work for everyone (if they did, you'd see many more publishers trying the same thing). His technique worked because his books were general enough to appeal to a wide audience and because he was a superb promoter, making good use of publicity to enhance the effect of his ads.

☐ **Sell books direct to consumers.** Some self-publishers, such as Ted Nicholas, Benjamin Suarez, and Joe Karbo, are all famous for their mail order promotion of books via national advertising in newspapers and magazines. In these cases, they usually went for the direct sale, with all orders coming to them.

☐ **Supplement book reviews** and other promotional activities. Most book publishers use advertisements to supplement book reviews. Hence, they tend to focus most of their advertising in the book review sections of major national newspapers.

☐ **Target specific audiences.** Other publishers advertise in sections targeted to a specific audience (for example, advertising a cookbook in the food section of a newspaper).

☐ **Offer coupons.** As part of a $250,000 promotional campaign for Mark Sullivan's *The Purification Ceremony*, Avon placed ads in *Sports Afield* and newspapers featuring a $5.00 consumer rebate coupon.

☐ **Insert an excerpt.** Several publishers have placed full-page ads in *USA Today* and other newspapers featuring the first 500 words of a major new novel. Publishers also have bound in short book excerpts into national magazines. As part of the $800,000 marketing budget for Philip Shelby's *Days of Drums*, Simon & Schuster inserted an excerpt into *Entertainment Weekly*. Similarly, St. Martin's inserted a 32-page excerpt booklet of *Beyond Midnight* into *Romantic Times* magazine.

☐ **Offer free copies.** To generate word-of-mouth around publication date, advertise in newspapers and magazines to offer free review copies to the first 250 or 1,000 respondents. For instance, Dutton placed an ad in the *Wall Street Journal* offering the first 250 respondents a free autographed copy of Stephen Frey's financial thriller *The Inner Sanctum*.

For Jonathan Kellerman's novel, *When the Bough Breaks*, New American Library placed direct response ads in seven newspapers (*Los Angeles Times, New York Times, Washington Post, Chicago Tribune, Boston Globe, San Francisco Chronicle,* and *Toronto Star*). In the ads they offered free copies of the book to the first 500 people to respond in each city. When NAL sent the free copy to each respondent, they also included a 30% discount offer for Kellerman's second novel, *Blood Test*. While NAL did not make any money on this special promotion, they did stimulate word of mouth for Kellerman's novels.

As part of the initial promo for the novel *Beaches,* Bantam placed ads in the *Los Angeles Times* offering two free copies to the first 2,000 people who wrote in (one copy for themselves and one for their best friend).

☐ **Advertise in the classified sections** of newspapers. Such advertising is only effective in newspapers where books are regularly advertised, such as the *Wall Street Journal* or the *San Francisco Chronicle* with its special book mart section. Some classified ads are made up only of words; others are small display ads in the classified section. Hacker Art Books has advertised their sale catalog in the *Wall Street Journal* every year since 1952. They would not continue to do so if it did not pay off.

☐ **Advertise in specialized newspapers**. If you have the appropriate book, look into advertising in specialized newspapers such as those for army and navy bases, colleges, specific religions, ethnic languages, minorities, and so forth. Ace Books, for example, advertised *The Specialist* by Gayle Rivers in armed forces newspapers.

☐ **Advertise in alternative weeklies.** For a directory or info on advertising in 125 weeklies, contact the **Association of Alternative News- weeklies**, 1020 16th Street N.W., 4th Floor, Washington, DC 20036-5702; 202-822-1955; Fax: 202-822-0929. Web: http://www.aan.org.

☐ **Co-op ads with local booksellers**. Advertise through co-op ads with local booksellers. In such cases the publisher pays all or part of the costs of the ad if the bookseller buys a certain number of books. (See Chapter 12 for more details on offering co-op ads.)

10:13 Tips on Advertising in Periodicals

Many of the tips given in Sections 10:05 and 10:06 for direct marketing also apply to any print advertising, but here are a few additional suggestions for improving the response to your ads:

☐ **Use a strong headline.** The most important element of most newspaper and magazine advertisements is the headline. The headline must offer a strong benefit, one dramatic enough to get the attention of the reader.

☐ **Use a second color.** A number of tests conducted over a period of twenty years in the *Long Beach Press-Telegram* showed that two-color ads (one color plus black) outsold non-color ads by 64%.

☐ **Use illustrations or other graphic elements.** According to some studies conducted by McGraw-Hill, illustrations increase readership of ads. And increased readership will usually result in increased sales.

- [ ] **Cite testimonials.** Testimonials in the advertising copy usually increase response. They are more believable than straight ad copy.

- [ ] **Create a sense of urgenc**y by putting a time limit on the offer.

- [ ] **Use a strong border.** With smaller ads, the border becomes more important. It should clearly set the ad off from surrounding editorial matter or other advertisements and yet not distract the reader's attention from the advertisement's message.

- [ ] **Design your ad to look like editorial.** Advertisements which look like editorial copy have been effective in producing sales.

- [ ] **Put a coupon in the ad.** Make it easy for the reader to order your book. Even Robert Ringer put coupons in his national advertising; in his case, though, the coupons directed the readers to the nearest chain bookstore. In general, ads with coupons pull better readership than ads without coupons. If you use coupons, place them on the lower outside corner where readers can cut out the coupon without having to ruin the entire page.

- [ ] **Repeat your address.** Make sure your address and phone number are printed several times in the ad, once outside the coupon and once in the coupon itself. Thus, if someone has already clipped the order coupon, other readers can still find out where to send the order. For that same reason, your basic offer (the name of the book, the cost, and any special conditions) should also be repeated outside the coupon.

- [ ] **If you are using classified ads, make every word count.** Don't be penny wise and pound foolish. If you need more words to describe your book adequately, then use more words. At the same time, don't waste words. You need to strike a balance between minimum word count (and, hence, minimum cost) and an adequate description of the benefits your book offers (and, hence, maximum sales results).

- [ ] **Start small.** Use smaller display ads before you place larger display ads. Indeed, many publishers have found that a series of smal display ads will often outpull a large ad. Not only do smaller ads cost less, but a series of smaller ads can create multiple impressions that one larger ad cannot do.

- [ ] **Maintain a swipe file.** Whenever you see an advertisement with a good headline, attractive layout, well-written copy, or something else that attracts your attention, save that ad. Put it in a separate file, called your swipe file. Then, when you write and design your ads, borrow the best ideas from the ads in your swipe file.

Authors — You, too, should maintain a swipe file of your favorite ads. Refer to it whenever you need some examples of good copy to stimulate your ideas when writing promotional copy for your books.

10:14 Advertising in Magazines

Magazines offer something most newspapers cannot offer: targeted readership. If you publish books on specific subjects, you might want to test direct ads to the readers of magazines covering the same subjects. For example, NTC Business Books advertises its direct marketing books in *Direct* magazine. There are magazines aimed at almost any audience you'd ever want to reach. Here's a checklist of a few samples:

[ ] animals (*Cats, Cat Fancy, Horseman, Birding, Ranger Rick*)

[ ] art (*Art and Auction, North Light, Graphic Arts Journal*)

[ ] business (*BusinessWeek, Forbes, Business 2.0, Inc., Entrepreneur*)

[ ] children (*Highlights for Children, Humpty Dumpty, Parents*)

[ ] clubs (*American Legion, Rotarian, Kiwanis, National 4-H News*)

[ ] computers (*PC World, Laptop Computing, Eweek, MacAddict*)

[ ] crafts (*Crafts, Workbasket, Fiberarts, Woodworkers Journal*)

[ ] ethnic/minorities (*Ebony, Jet, Colors NW, Scandinavian Times*)

[ ] entertainment (*Entertainment Weekly, Premiere, Variety*)

[ ] farm (*Successful Farming, Farm Journal, Ohio Farmer*)

[ ] food (*Bon Appetit, Gourmet, Saveur, Food & Wine, Fine Cooking*)

[ ] genre (*Fantasy & Science Fiction, Romantic Times, Analog*)

[ ] health (*Prevention, American Health, Family Doctor, Men's Health*)

[ ] history (*American Heritage, Civil War Times, History Channel*)

[ ] home (*Better Homes & Gardens, Inspired House, House Beautiful*)

[ ] homemaking (*Good Housekeeping, Family Circle, Woman's Day*)

[ ] lifestyle (*Interview, Playboy, Cosmopolitan, Seventeen*)

[ ] literary (*New Yorker, Grand Street, Paris Review, Pig Iron*)

[ ] men (*Maxim, FHM, Details, Esquire, Men's Journal, Stuff, Genre*)

[ ] music (*Blender, Country Weekly, Dance Spirit, Juice, Opera News*)

[ ] new age (*Balance, Dragonfly Review of Books, Parabola, Shift*)

[ ] news (*Newsweek, Time, U.S. News and World Report*)

[ ] people (*People, Us, National Enquirer, Globe, In Touch, Star*)

[ ] political (*American Prospect, Nation, Clamor, Dissent, Earth First*)

[ ] regional (*Mpls, New York Magazine, Houston Living*)

[ ] religion (*Church Herald, Columbia, Guideposts, Jewish Journal*)

[ ] science (*Scientific American, Transpersonal Psychology*)

[ ] sports (*Golf, Running, Sports Afield, Sports Illustrated*)

[ ] trade (*Gift & Decorative Accessories, Playthings, Publishers Weekly*)

[ ] travel (*Budget Travel, Travel + Leisure, Where to Retire, Rail*)

[ ] women (*First for Women, Self, O, Lucky, Working Woman*)

And many more, including alumni magazines, company publications, in-flight magazines, scholarly journals, entertainment guides, Sunday magazine sections of local newspapers, gossip tabloids, and professional journals. For a complete list of such magazines, see the *Standard Periodical Directory*, *Ulrich's International Periodicals Directory*, or *SRDS Business Publication Rates and Data*. You should be able to find one or more of these directories at your local library. The top magazines in each of these areas is featured in the Kremer 100 program.

The same basic rules apply to magazine advertising as apply to newspaper advertising. The one exception is that since you can target your audience more selectively with magazines, you can and should write more specific ad copy appealing to the special interests of the readers of each magazine. Here are a few tips on getting the most for your money through magazine ads:

☐ **Go for publicity first.** Don't advertise in a magazine until you've gotten some publicity in that magazine to test its pulling power. In one study conducted by The Wirthlin Group in 1994, when people had to choose which source of information would impact their buying decisions most, 17% selected newspaper articles, 15% selected magazine articles, and only 4% selected magazine ads. Those with higher incomes placed even more reliance on feature articles.

☐ **Ad space is negotiable.** According to *Publishing News*, one out of four magazines negotiate ad rates. So, if you don't like the rates on their ad cards, negotiate.

☐ **Advertise in regional editions of national magazines**. You can buy space in regional editions for much less than the cost of the entire national edition. One company ran a single ad in a regional edition of *Time* magazine and then used reprints of that ad for its window displays and direct mailings for the next five years. Hence, by advertising in the regional edition of such a well-known and respected magazine, the company was able to gain a level of credibility with its customers it could not have gained in any other way.

☐ **Arrange per order ads**. Many magazines will accept a per inquiry or per order arrangement for books which they feel will interest their readers. Similarly, some magazines will run an advertisement for free if you will dropship the orders for them. In this case, orders are sent direct to the magazine; then the magazine processes the order, takes its cut, and sends the order on to you (with their check) for dropshipping. In such cases you will be expected to give a discount of anywhere from 40% to 60% to the magazine. Globe Pequot provides ad slicks to special interest magazines that the magazines can use when they have unsold ad space. These ads (either full-page or two-page spreads) offer Globe's books for sale through the magazine publisher on a per order basis. Not only does Globe get free advertising, but they are also able to go to bookstores and tell them that full-page ads appear regularly in major magazines.

☐ **Offer free excerpts from your books** to magazines in exchange for a tagline at the end of the article telling readers how they can order the book (your company name and address, the price of the book, and other ordering information). When an in-flight magazine contacted one publisher for permission to serialize a book on business management, rather than charge a fee for the serial rights, the publisher offered to let them run the excerpt for free as long as ordering information was listed at the end of the article. As a result, the publisher received over 1,000 orders.

☐ **Buy remnant space.** Ask the magazine to let you know when they have unsold space, which can be bought at a fraction of the usual cost. Of course, when you rely only on remnant space, you have no way of controlling when and if your ads will appear. Hence, remnant ads are best used for titles which are not time sensitive.

☐ **Use classified ads.** You can test some magazines by using classified ads. Not only are classified ads an inexpensive way to advertise, but they can often pull better than normal display ads. Classified ads are a superb way to compare the pulling power of different magazines. The main disadvantage of using classified ads is that it is tough to sell books costing more than $5.00 through the classifieds. Why? There are two basic reasons: 1) the space limitation of classifieds may not allow a complete description of the benefits of your book, and 2) classifieds do not attract as affluent an audience as normal display ads.

There are, however, apparent exceptions to the rule. Jay Levinson used classified ads for many years to sell his self-published book *Secrets of Successful Free-Lancing* for $10.00. Why did his ad work where others didn't? Because he avoided the two main limitations of classified ads 1) by writing a long ad that described the benefits of his book in a clear and appealing way, and 2) by placing his ads in upscale periodicals such as the *Wall Street Journal* and professional artist and writer magazines.

☐ **Use Selectronic printing to target readers.** Some magazines (including *American Baby*, *Farm Journal*, and *Medicine*) offer Selectronic printing that allows advertisers to target individual readers with personalized ads or messages. This personalization, of course, costs money, so this technology should only be used for specialized, relatively high-priced books.

☐ **Ask for their media kit.** When you write to magazines to request their advertising rates, ask for a sample issue, rates for display and classified ads, the names of their editors and book reviewer, their editorial schedule for the coming year, and copies of any reader surveys they have recently conducted. For instance, a survey of *Crafts 'n Things* subscribers showed that 70% of their readers had purchased craft books in the past year. Moreover, 75% of their readers own more than 10 cookbooks and 50% had purchased books by mail. What a prime audience for books!

☐ **Use the magazine's support services.** Some magazines will prepare and typeset your advertisement for you—in the hopes, of course, that the advertisement will pay off for you so you will continue to advertise in the magazine. Also, when you advertise in some trade journals, they will provide you with a variety of other marketing programs. Here, for example, were a few of the marketing support services provided by *Target Marketing* to their advertisers:

List rental—You could mail to their entire list of 42,000 direct marketers (free one-time use of their list).

Market research—They would prepare a survey of 1000 of their readers for your company. They would print, mail, and tabulate the survey for you free.

Research studies—All half-page or larger ads in certain issues were analyzed and studied for their effectiveness and recall by an independent research company.

Purchasing reports—They sent confidential reports on their readers' projected buying plans.

Reader service—They forwarded leads to advertisers when readers requested more information about ads by using the enclosed reader service cards in each issue.

Ad display mounts—They mounted up to five of your ads for greater visibility at trade shows and exhibits.

Forbes ad—You could share space in *Target Marketing*'s full page ad in *Forbes* magazine at no extra cost.

Bonus distribution—Besides its regular subscriber mailings, *Target Marketing* is also distributed free at nearly 40 trade shows each year, giving you additional exposure to new buyers.

Special catalog ad rates—If you wanted to insert a 4-page or 8-page catalog, you can do so for half what it would normally cost you.

Editorial support—When space was available, *Target Marketing*'s editors make every effort to support advertising with free publicity.

Other services that magazines might provide (either at cost or for free) include the following: article reprints, product sampling to prospective buyers, convention or trade show promotions, advertising design and layout, and directory listings.

Authors — Write to magazines that cover the subject areas you write about. Ask for sample issues, ad rates, editorial schedules, and the names of appropriate editors. Not only will this information help you in planning promotions for your books, but it could also come in handy when researching and writing the book. Get to know these magazines well. They could be the key to your success.

10:15 How to Advertise on Radio

Radio is not a common advertising vehicle for books. About the only books I've heard advertised on daily radio are mass-market paperbacks. For example, Dell conducted a national radio campaign of 60-second spots on late night and drive time network shows and major market radio stations for *Shattered Moon* by Kate Green.

Nonetheless, you might consider using radio even if you don't have mass distribution. For instance, you might advertise a regional title such as the *Boston Ice Cream Lover's Guide* on local stations. Or you might advertise a rock biography during a syndicated top 40 show or on several local rock stations. Or how about a religious title on a religious station?

Or, perhaps best of all, market a Spanish-language book to an Hispanic audience via a local ethnic radio station or a national network. According to one source, 90% of all U.S. Hispanics listen to Spanish-language radio stations as compared to only 75% viewing Spanish-language television and only a little over 50% reading Spanish-language newspapers.

In each of these instances, you could advertise a specific title to a highly targeted audience. In such cases you would not need to have mass distribution as long as you had local distribution or offered to accept credit card orders via a toll-free number.

You do not need to limit your advertising to national radio network or syndicated shows. You can also advertise on local AM or FM radio stations which have different audience profiles, from rock to country, from all news to easy listening, from sports to religious. Just select the audience profile that fits your books. Here, then, are a few guidelines to follow if you decide to test advertising your books on radio:

☐ **Match your books with the format** and audience profile of any radio stations you intend to use for advertising.

☐ **Advertise on a syndicated radio show** for the lowest cost for the widest possible reach. For instance, a 30-second spot on *Live from Gilley's* use to cost only $250.00. This show, which aired on 256 stations, had an estimated audience of 335,000 listeners.

☐ **Advertise on the radio networks.** Note that the major radio networks actually offer several possible divisions that enable you to target your audience more specifically. For instance, ABC radio used to offer the following networks. Call them to verify their current lineup is.

ABC Contemporary—262 affiliates (CHR and AC formats)
ABC Direction—362 affiliates (AC and Country formats)
ABC Entertainment—555 affiliates (Country and AC formats)
ABC Information—622 affiliates (News, Sports, and Talk)
ABC Rock—80 affiliates (AOR, Rock, CHR)
ABC Talk—116 affiliates (Talk and Call-in formats)

As part of its $250,000 marketing campaign for novelists Glenn Meade's *Brandenburg*, St. Martin's ran 30-second radio spots on the CBS Spectrum Network.

☐ **Buy time through a media rep network**. Besides the major networks, you can also buy spot time on local radio stations across the country by working with a media rep network. For more information on some of the fifty media rep groups in the country, see SRDS's *Spot Radio Rates & Data* directory.

☐ **Try per inquiry ads.** Per inquiry ads are still available in some radio markets, but they are not that easy to find. If you'd like to try offering books direct to consumers via per inquiry radio advertising, work with a media rep group. For instance, about 90% of Katz's direct response advertising placements are done on a P.I. Basis.

☐ **Both radio and TV rate cards are negotiable.** Remember, if they don't sell the time, it is gone forever. Hence, if they have open time, they will be willing to negotiate a lower rate than the one on their rate cards.

☐ **Prepare spots for local radio.** Take the following hint from Thomas Rider, owner of Goerings' Book Center of Gainesville, Florida: "Why don't trade publishers manufacture 45-second spots and make them available to booksellers the way glossies are available for newspaper ads? Then all that booksellers and local radio stations would have to produce would be the *donuts* [short announcements at the beginning and end of commercials], which most radio stations wouldn't charge for anyway. Production costs would be very low for publishers, and practically nonexistent for booksellers."

☐ **The best time for running ads on radio are during its prime time hours**, the morning and afternoon drive times. Afternoon drive time has one advantage over the morning drive time: As a rule, people are more relaxed and happier as they head home for the evening. Hence, they may be in a better mood for buying.

☐ **Radio requires frequent repetition for maximum effect.** You are better off concentrating your ads during a short period of time rather than stretching them out over a longer period. In order words, focus all your ads during one week rather than spreading them out over several weeks.

☐ **Repeat your main message at least three times** (in different ways). And repeat your book title and company name at least twice.

☐ **30-second spots can sometimes work as well as 60-second spots** and are less expensive. Indeed, some studies indicate that people listen more attentively when an announcer speaks more quickly. Thus, you may find it more effective as well as cheaper to squeeze your message into 30-second spots.

☐ **Take time to make your lead-in effective.** With radio, you have about three seconds to attract the attention of the listener.

☐ **Use professional announcers and studio equipment** to make your commercials. Don't skimp on production.

☐ **If you are asking for a direct order, you will also need to repeat the ordering information at least twice.** Don't try for a direct order unless you use a 60-second or two-minute spot. You simply would not have time to repeat your basic message and the essential ordering information in less than 60 seconds.

☐ **Listen to the tape of your radio commercial** on your car audio system. The closer you can get to simulating how it will actually sound on ordinary car radio speakers, the more accurately you will be able to judge its effectiveness.

☐ **Since radio is an audio medium, consider using appropriate music** to heighten the impact of your commercial. Or use other audio effects to enliven the presentation.

☐ **Here are a few of the advantages that radio offers over television:**

1. Commercial time is significantly less expensive.

2. Changes to the content of any radio commercial can be made more easily, more quickly, and less expensively than with almost any other media. In a pinch, even you can make the commercial.

3. Radio audiences can be pinpointed more specifically.

4. Radio is a more pervasive medium. It can be heard in the home, in the office, on the beach, and while driving to and from work.

5. Radio is not as seasonal as television.

10:16 13 Major Ways to Advertise on Television

Television has one great advantage over radio: Not only can it be heard, it can be seen. Studies have shown that people's memories improve as much as 68% when they have a visual element to help them remember something. Hence, if your book lends itself to a visual presentation, you might find that television commercials will produce greater sales than radio commercials or print advertisements.

On the down side, of course, television costs more. To make it worth your while, your TV commercials must be effective. Publishers have developed a number of ways to increase the effectiveness of their TV promotions.

General TV Commercials

Some major publishers have begun to run TV commercials to promote bookstore sales and reader recognition. While a television campaign for a major author would formerly cost as much as $750,000, with computerization, it can now cost as little $150,000. Several advertising agencies, including Franklin Spier, The Mesa Group, and Ziccardi & Partners, specialize in preparing TV ads for book publishers.

☐ In the past year, for example, Ziccardi prepared TV spots for Stephen King's *The Green Mile*, Caleb Carr's *Angel of Darkness*, Stephen Cannell's *King Con*, and Sidney Sheldon's *Best Laid Plans*.

☐ Similarly, during the past year, Franklin Spier's output of broadcast ads has increased from 43 in 1995 to 60 in 1996 as book publishers have begun using TV commercials more and more.

☐ William Morrow placed national TV ads during *The X Files* and *The Late Show with David Letterman* for Brad Meltzer's thriller, *The Tenth Justice*.

☐ The Mesa Group has prepared television commercials for major authors from Putnam, Viking, and Ballantine and placed ads on *Good Morning America*, *Oprah*, and CNN.

☐ McGraw-Hill has placed a series of MTV-like TV spots portraying the company as a forward-thinking purveyor of information. The ad included this line: "No one really knows where the next big thing will come from, but if you're looking, we can give you a pretty good place to start—the McGraw-Hill Companies. Keeping the world up to speed."

☐ Bridge Publications, the publishing arm of Scientology, has used TV commercials for years to drive bookstore sales. In the summer of 1997, they placed 30-second TV ads on MTV, CNN, The Learning Channel, VH1, Discovery, BET, Lifetime, USA, ESPN, and other cable channels for their latest title, *Scientology: The Fundamentals of Thought*.

☐ New American Library promoted the *Weight Watcher's Quick Start Program Cookbook* through 30-second spots during two-week periods in each major city. The bookstore chains found that sales of the book increased by 40% during those two weeks, and that sales remained high for at least another week after the commercial stopped airing.

Direct Response TV Commercials

According to a recent study, direct response television is one of the fastest growing areas of direct marketing. DRTV sales totaled $72.7 billion in 1995 and rose to $122 billion by 2000.

☐ Time-Life Books has used direct response commercials to sell various series of books on topics such as World War II, cooking, and home repair. The advantage of selling such continuity series is that the overall sale (if the buyer continues with the entire series) is high enough to cover the cost of expensive TV time.

☐ Bantam advertised the Loveswept romance series via TV ads and a toll-free order line. They offered four romance novels (plus four additional free novels) for only $9.95 plus postage and handling. After people paid for their first set, they'd be shipped four new novels each month for their approval. Anytime they wanted to stop receiving monthly shipments, all they had to do was send in a written request to Bantam.

☐ Hal Lindsey's *Countdown to Armageddon* was advertised via two-minute commercials asking viewers to order through a toll-free phone number. Within 90 days, they sold 370,000 copies of the book via television ads.

☐ Mikhail Gorbachev's book *A Time for Peace* was also sold via two-minute commercials in smaller cities where the book would not otherwise be generally available. In this case, the TV commercials were used to supplement bookstore sales in major cities.

☐ In 1997, Rodale ran a DRTV campaign for a number of its individual titles, from *New Choices in Natural Healing* to *The Doctor's Book of Home Remedies for Dogs and Cats*. Their goal was to sell books—and they did—but a side benefit was the promotion of the Rodale brand name across several book titles.

Commercials Related to TV Shows

☐ Dolphin got free 30-second spots on the syndicated show *Lifestyles of the Rich and Famous* to promote their book named after the show. The show, which is syndicated to some 200 stations across the country, ran the commercial each week for three months. If you have a book which is somehow tied into a TV series, try to arrange a similar promotion.

☐ Berkeley advertised the book *Return to Treasure Island* after each episode of the miniseries of the same name. The miniseries ran for ten weeks on the Disney Cable Channel. Berkeley paid for the advertising.

☐ Every time Jeff Smith's cable show *The Frugal Gourmet* moved into another market, sales for his book of the same name picked up dramatically. Morrow supported bookstore sales in these new cities by offering co-op advertising to local booksellers. Eventually as the show moved into more and more markets, the book became a national bestseller.

☐ Another TV tie-in, Knapp Press's *New York's Master Chefs*, sold more than 110,000 copies through telephone sales generated by the show of the same name. Another 40,000 copies were sold through bookstores.

☐ Collins promoted their *Day in the Life* Series by televising documentaries based on the books as well as by organizing traveling exhibits of the photos included in the books. Carl Sagan's *Cosmos* and Kenneth Clarke's *Civilizations* both gained wide publicity and bestselling status as a result of their associated television documentaries.

Cable Channels

The multiplication of cable channels has opened up many possibilities for advertising and other promotion of books, especially with the special-interest channels such as the Travel Channel, Food Channel, Inspirational Network, and HGTV. Besides contributing programming for these channels, you might also want to look into advertising selected titles.

☐ Lonely Planet prepared a series of video tapes, *Destination Fitness*, that ran as a series on the Travel Channel.

☐ Thomas Nelson Publishers, in cooperation with the Inspirational Network (ISPN), has run spots ads, direct response ads, as well as special programming sponsorships on this religious network.

CNN Airport Network

You can also advertise your books on the CNN Airport Network. In early 1998, O'Reilly advertised an entire line of computer books on the network. Earlier, Ballentine supported the publication of Lorenzo Carcaterra's first novel, *Apaches*, by running commercials on the *Today Show, Good Morning America, CNN Headline News, Larry King Live*, and the CNN Airport Network. As a result, the book jumped onto the bestseller lists.

Local Cable TV

Don't overlook local cable TV shows when planning your TV promotions. Local cable TV is still quite inexpensive as compared to local network TV. If your book can be linked in any way with a popular cable feature, you have a chance of making the commercial pay for itself.

Home Shopping Networks

Submit your books for sale via the home shopping shows and networks. These networks sell books—lots of books! Especially QVC. While some of the networks will buy product on a nonreturnable discount, many are now buying product on a consignment basis (they pay only after the sale and return anything that doesn't sell). What do they look for in a product? It should be new, easily demonstrated, preferably exclusive, high quality, and the right price point (more than $15.00). Below are the four major home shopping networks.

☐ **QVC Network**, Vendor Relations Department, 1200 Wilson Drive, West Chester, PA 19380-4262; 484-701-1000; Fax: 484-701-1356. Email: vendor_relations@qvc.com. Web: http://www.qvc.com. To become a QVC vendor, visit http://www.vendor.studiopark.com or call 888-NEWITEM.

Founded in 1986, QVC reaches 65 million households, introduces 250 new products each week, and has sales of more than $2.5 billion per year. With an audience primarily of females, its bestselling product categories are jewelry, apparel, cosmetics, and cookware.

Their big book subjects are cookbooks and romance novels. QVC calls itself "the bookstore that's in 65 million homes." In 1995, QVC sold more than 2.2 million books. Since then, book sales have become an even larger part of their sales.

The first time that the QVC Network featured a full hour of books, they took in $360,000 in sales. Later, a single pass across the screen sold 400 copies of a book about Harley Davidsons. The book, a $39.95 retail value, was discounted to $29.95 for the few minutes it was featured.

Judy Mazel, author of *The New Beverly Hills Diet*, sold more than 2,500 copies in three minutes during her debut appearance on QVC. *Mr. Food* by Art Ginsburg sold a million copies over a number of appearances. *The Alternative Medicine Reference Guide* sold 40,000 copies in four and a half hours.

One author star of QVC is JoAnna Lund, who originally self-published her *Healthy Exchanges Cookbook*. It took her more than six months of persistence to get on QVC. During that first appearance, she sold 3,500 books in twelve minutes on a Thursday afternoon. During her second appearance on a Friday evening, she sold 6,300 books in six minutes. Since then, she has gone on to become QVC's bestselling author, selling more than a million cookbooks. During a seventy-minute appearance, she sold more than 200,000 cookbooks.

☐ **Home Shopping Network**, Purchasing Department, 1 HSN Drive, St. Petersburg, FL 33729; 727-572-8585; 800-436-1010; Fax: 727-573-3702. Web: http://www.hsn.com. Founded in 1983, HSN reaches 709 million homes and receives about 175,000 calls per day. Write for their Vendor Information kit. They ask that you send them a filled out Partner Information Sheet, Invoicing Information Sheet, and Product Presentation Sheet along with a photo of your product (not a sample). If it's something they want, they act quickly.

☐ **Shop at Home Network**, 5388 Hickory Hollow Parkway, Antioch, TN 37013; 615-263-8000; 800-359-1515; Fax: 615-263-89496. Web: http://www.ishopathome.com. Founded in 1986, this fourth largest home shopping network reaches over 30 million TV households. 50% of their customers are men (a larger percentage than the other three shopping networks). They had $40 million in revenues in 1996. Specialties: sports memorabilia. You can pay them to test your product on their network.

☐ **ShopNBC**, 6740 Shady Oak Road, Eden Prairie, MN 55344; 612-947-5200; 800-676-5523(customer service); Fax: 612-947-0188. Web: http:// www.shopnbc.com. Founded in 1991, this is the third largest home shopping television network. It reaches 48 million households and had sales of $106 million in 1997. Formerly known as ValueVision, this network is not a big market for books.

Not all authors appear on QVC to sell books. Wolfgang Puck has appeared on QVC selling cookware, while Paul Prudhomme appeared selling his line of spices. Kenneth Wilson, author of *American Glass*, appeared on QVC to sell glass objects. Nonetheless, his book was displayed prominently on the set and his appearance on QVC, according to his distributor, "generated many sales through the bookstores."

Infomercials

Infomercials are the long-form television commercials that blend information and entertainment with direct sales. Most infomercials run late at night or during the day on weekends. According to one study, 40% of those who have ever watched an infomercial have bought a product off of a TV ad at some point. While books alone rarely sell via an infomercial, books do sell as part of a tape/book package. Indeed, some of the all-time bestselling infomercial products were based on books.

☐ In the late 1980's, The Beckley Group marketed its *Millionaire Maker Course* through one-hour TV shows. They purchased an entire hour during which time they presented an informational seminar on how to get rich in real estate. Interspersed throughout the hour were commercials which presented the hard sell for the course. The advantage of this format is that the hour-long shows, packed with information of interest to the potential buyers, presented the soft sell while the commercials closed the sale. Their courses sold for $295.00, and orders were taken via credit card, C.O.D., or check. They sold as many as 20,000 courses in one week. That sounds like lots of sales, and it is, but note that this is a high-risk way to sell anything. The Beckley Group had C.O.D. refusal rates as high as 30%. And, when they offered a later (and weaker) course on credit cards, they were also hit with a blizzard of returns which, in due course, led to their bankruptcy.

☐ The *Making Love Work* infomercial by author Barbara De Angelis not only won the 1994 NIMA Award for best infomercial, but it also grossed more than $70 million in sales. In 1996, it pulled in another $48 million in sales. With personal development and relationship products, "the person is the product."

☐ The *Personal Power* series by Tony Robbins grossed more than $250 million in product sales. In addition, it helped Robbins to land on the *New York Times* bestseller list with several titles.

☐ Before John Gray's *Men Are from Mars, Women Are from Venus* hit the airways as an audiotaped infomercial product, the book had been selling 70,000 copies per month. Once the infomercial aired, bookstore sales increased to 200,000 copies per month. The book became Harper-Collins's best-selling hardcover in its history.

☐ You don't have to create your own show. Instead, be on the lookout for potential partnerships or tie-ins. For example, Ron Krannich's *Discover the Best Jobs for You* was featured in a 1993 infomercial for *The Edge: Rx for Success*, a book/tape package selling for $149.95.

☐ In 1989, sales of juice extractors totaled about $10 million. After 2 years of juice extractor infomercials, retail sales of juicers totaled $380 million in 1992. Avery Publishing sold hundreds of thousands of juicing books as a result of those infomercials.

☐ Be sure to follow-up on infomercial sales or home shopping network sales. *As Seen On TV* products are big sellers in catalogs and stores. Here is one company that can help you sell your *As Seen on TV* book to catalogs and mass merchandisers: **TeleBrands Corp.**, 81 Two Bridges

Road, Fairfield, NJ 07004; 201-244-0300; Fax: 201-244-0233. Web: http://www.telebrands.com.

☐ For other infomercial resources, search here: Web: http://www.dtrtv.com.

According to Greg Renker of Guthy-Renker, infomercials have a 1 in 800 chance of success, with only 1 in 100 ideas making it to the testing stage and only 1 in 8 becoming a success at roll-out. Note that a typical infomercial costs anywhere from $100,000 to $450,000 to produce. Plus you have air time to buy. As a result, infomercials are not within the practical marketing budgets of most publishers. You should look for opportunities to work with experienced infomercial producers such as Guthy-Renker, Inphomation, or Hawthorne Direct.

Videotape Advertising

Advertise on videotapes. If your book is tied in with a movie or other popular videotape title, you might arrange to advertise your book at the end of the videotape. Since many readers, after seeing a miniseries such as *Shogun* or a movie such as *Out of Africa*, buy the book to read, you may find a similar immediate response to popular videotape titles.

Advertise in the TV Magazines

One other way to reach television viewers is by advertising in TV listings magazines. For instance, you could advertise in *TV Guide*. Although *TV Guide* is a print medium, it is so closely connected with TV viewing that you can reach much the same audience for a fraction of what it might cost to advertise on TV itself. Of course, the impact of a print ad is not as great as the impact of a TV commercial.

If you want to cut the cost even more, advertise in the cable TV guides. Book-of-the-Month Club, Grolier, and Franklin Mint have all advertised in the *The Cable Guide* network of magazines serving 600 cable systems (with a total circulation of more than 5.5 million). Similarly, Doubleday, Grolier, and Encyclopedia Brittanica have all inserted direct response ads in *On Cable*, a network of magazines with a circulation of almost 1.5 million.

Get Your Book Featured in Someone Else's Commercial

While it may be difficult to get your product featured in someone else's commercial, it sure beats paying for the commercial yourself. Be alert to the possibilities. A summer 1986 commercial for Bartles & Jaymes wine coolers featured David Ogilvy's book, *Ogilvy on Advertising*. The Books on Tape logo was highlighted in a promotion for the Isuzu Rodeo.

Game Show Giveaways

Get your product given away on game shows as *The Price Is Right* or *Wheel of Fortune*. While not all books are appropriate for game show giveaways, many can be packaged with another product. For example, you could give away travel guides with a Mediterranean cruise, a diet or exercise book with home exercise equipment, a microwave cookbook with a microwave oven, a dress for success book to accompany a new wardrobe, or a racy novel to accompany a fancy waterbed.

Here is a company that can help you get placed on game shows: **Game Show Placements**, 7011 Willoughby Avenue, Hollywood, CA 90038; 213-874-7818; Fax: 213-874-0643. Email: gsp@ix.netcom.com. Web: http:// www.gspltd.com.

Cinebooks had good success promoting their movie guides as giveaways on various TV game shows, such as *Jeopardy, Wheel of Fortune*, and *The Price Is Right*. To get their books featured, they worked with one of the placement firms listed below. It cost them $100 plus copies of their books for every mention on a show. They were able to select which shows they wanted their books to be featured on and how often.

Product Placements in TV Shows and Movies

Besides offering giveaways in game shows, you can work to get your book featured as a prop or character in TV shows and movies. This effort is known as product placement. Below are two companies that have helped book publishers make connections with TV and movie producers.

☐ **Creative Entertainment Services**, 1015 N. Hollywood Way #101, Burbank, CA 91505; 818-842-9119; Fax: 818-842-9568. Web: http:// www.acreativegroup.com/ces. They helped West Publishing, a major legal publisher, get product placement on *Law & Order* and *Feds*.

☐ **UPP Entertainment Marketing**, 3401 Winona Avenue, Burbank, CA 91504-2549; 818-526-0111; Fax: 818-526-1466. Email: info@upp.net. Web: http://www.upp.net. "Since our goal is to get their products seen, we don't simply want to have piles of books as set dressing, we want them to figure into the story or be used by a character." For one scene in *Notting Hill*, they got an entire row of *Frommer's* guides placed directly behind star Hugh Grant. They were also able to place a *Frommer's* guide in a character's carry-on bag in *American Pie II*. The *Dummies* series has been featured in *Master of Disguise* and *Kingdom Come*.

10:17 Tips on Producing Television Spots

Although major TV commercials cost $70,000 or more per 30 seconds to produce, you can create an effective commercial for less. While you balance budgetary constraints against the need for a quality production, don't try to do it all yourself. Use your in-house staff where your expertise is strong (for example, possibly in copywriting), but hire professionals where your expertise is weak (for example, in video production). TV audiences are accustomed to high quality production values and will notice any commercials which are not carefully produced and edited (and will not respond to such ads). Below are guidelines for designing and producing TV commercials.

☐ The key to success, according to regular TV advertisers, is media buying skills. If you do not have knowledgeable media buyers, don't do the buying yourself. Use a professional agency. Since TV rate cards are highly negotiable, make sure your buyers are skilled negotiators. The money you save could make the difference between profit and loss. The Beckley Group had as many as twenty buyers negotiating for media time whenever they rolled out national TV campaigns.

☐ If you are working with a local TV station, let them provide all the technical production assistance (equipment, camera operators, lighting technicians, directors). Often they will provide such assistance for a minimum cost as long as you are buying time on their station. In most cases, don't let them write your commercial unless you want it to sound exactly like every other local commercial on the station.

☐ Television is a mass medium. Don't use it if you don't have mass distribution (either through bookstores and mass market outlets or through a toll-free telephone order-taking system).

☐ While ad agencies often use storyboards to lay out the story line of a commercial, you may not need one especially if your commercial is well-written, with all the action clearly described in the script. Storyboards can add from $300 to $700 to the cost of a commercial.

☐ The best way to save money is to do most of the work at the preproduction stage rather than during the taping when costs can skyrocket, especially if you have to stop to work out a problem. Hold preproduction meetings to make sure everyone understands the script and knows what to do. Check the scripting details, the lighting, the timing. Hold a dress rehearsal. Never go before an expensive camera crew until you are sure that the production will go smoothly.

☐ Tape more than one commercial at a time. Since you will generally have to pay for a minimum amount of production time regardless of how much time you actually use (as well as travel and set up time), make the best use of the production time by taping two or more commercials or variations at the same time.

☐ When you plan the taping of your commercial, arrange the segments so that editing costs are kept to a minimum. Editing can cost anywhere from $250.00 per hour on up.

☐ TV is a visual medium. So create a strong visual message in your commercial. If the commercial can make its point even with the sound turned off, then you have a sure winner. Use music, sound effects, and words to enhance the visual impact not to replace it. If possible, show your book in use. If it is a cookbook, show someone using it to create a scrumptious meal. If it's a mystery, tease the viewers with a look at the unsolved crime.

☐ As with radio, commercials on TV must gain the attention of the viewer within the first few seconds. Make sure your commercials have a captivating lead-in.

☐ And, again, as in radio, don't be afraid to repeat.

Touch them with tenderness, and you will give them love.
Touch them with love, and you will give them the world.
Touch their todays, and you will touch their tomorrows.
— Johnson & Johnson TV commercial

To build word of mouth for your book,
you need to touch people's hearts, or minds, or inner souls.
— John Kremer

Kilroy Was Here – Making Your Mark Online

by Cathy Stucker, the Idea Lady

A strategy that has been successful for my clients is one I call, *Kilroy was here*. Named after the ubiquitous graffiti left around the world by the military, it is a simple way to leave your mark online and send book buyers to you.

This strategy will help you sell more books by increasing your name recognition in your target market, building your reputation as an expert in your field, attracting the attention of customers and the media, and getting links to your Web site to generate targeted traffic and higher search engine rankings. Each of the techniques takes very little time, and no money, to implement.

☐ **Put press releases online.** When you send a release to the media, be sure to include online distribution services, such as PRWeb.com. Add the release to the media room of your Web site.

☐ **Post articles online.** Add original content to your Web site, and encourage others to link to it. Publish a reprint policy to let them know how they can use your articles on their sites or in their newsletters. Offer your articles to non-competing sites in your niche. Post them to online article banks, such as EzineArticles.com.

☐ **Participate in online forums and discussions.** Answer a question raised by another member, post a link to a resource on your site, or offer a list of tips. Add helpful comments to blogs. Always include a brief signature with a link to your Web site.

☐ **Create your profile on Amazon.com** (even if your book isn't published yet). Post reviews and other content, and identify yourself as, "author of . . ." To do this, from the Amazon.com home page click on (Your) Store, then Your Profile.

☐ **Offer testimonials.** When you find a product or service you love, send a testimonial. Ask that your name, Web site and/or book title be used with the testimonial.

Do not be overwhelmed by all of the opportunities available for online visibility. Start today and do a little each day. The results will amaze you!

As the Idea Lady, Cathy Stucker helps authors, entrepreneurs, and professionals attract customers and make themselves famous. Cathy is the author of *The Mystery Shopper's Manual, Market with Articles, Selling eBooks Online, Free Publicity 101*, and many other titles. She has achieved top search engine rankings and national publicity, and shows her clients how they can do it, too. Get a free subscription to her marketing tips newsletter, **Bright Ideas**, at http://www.IdeaLady.com. For details on implementing the strategies in this article and many more ways to sell your books, visit http://www.SellingBooks.com.

Chapter 11

Offbeat Advertising and Other Promotions

Money will come when you are doing the right thing.
— Michael Phillips

While most books are advertised through direct mail, newspapers, magazines, radio, and TV, a good number of other creative methods have been used both by publishers and other companies to advertise and promote their products. This chapter presents a collection of some of those methods. When you consider using these offbeat advertising methods, don't think of them as gimmicks. Rather, think of them as sales tools which should be integrated into your other advertising and promotional activities. Few of these methods will work alone; they must be part of a well-planned and well-executed advertising strategy.

11:01 Inserts in Shopping Bags

Some paper bag companies are now offering to insert advertising messages inside shopping bags at a relatively low cost per thousand. If you have a line of cookbooks, beauty and diet books, or romance novels, you might test this new method.

11:02 Printed Bags, Cartons, and Matchbooks

You might also test having your advertising message printed on the outside of grocery bags and other shopping bags where people besides the recipient will see your ad. Some producers of milk cartons are also offering to print appropriate advertising messages on the outside of their cartons. And, of course, there are always matchbooks, a longtime advertising vehicle for correspondence courses which might also work well for do-it-yourself books and business opportunity or career books.

11:03 Ad Specialties and Premiums

When you advertise your books, you might offer a premium with the book—for example, a slide chart with baseball schedule for a book on baseball, a calorie counter slide chart for a diet book, or a coupon clipper for a book of moneysaving ideas.

You could also send ad specialties with your news releases and review copies to draw attention to your books. Or send them to key bookselling contacts to remind them to push your books. How about an imprinted coffee cup with a cookbook? Or matchbooks with a fire safety book?

Try to match the premium or advertising specialty to the contents or style of your book. Please don't send any more pens. But how about stickers, decals, buttons, balloons, memo cubes, note pads, rubber stamps, golf balls, calculators, paper clips, rulers, playing cards, yo-yos, thermometers, magnetic message holders, wine glasses, pot holders, key tags, ice scrapers, or any number of other items?

For more information about ad specialties, send for a free booklet, *Specialty Advertising: The Medium That Remains to Be Seen*. Write to the **Promotional Products Association International**, 3125 Skyway Circle North, Irving, TX 75038-3526; 214-252-0404; 888-IAM-PPAI; Fax: 214-594-7224. Web: http://www.ppa.org.

Authors — If your publisher offers a premium or advertising specialty with one of your books, ask the marketing department to provide you with a supply so you can hand them out to your contacts.

11:04 Calendars

Calendars are a superb way to advertise your books. Of course, they are also a superb way to advertise your calendars. Send copies to all your main bookstore accounts and other key contacts.

Whenever you send promotional calendars, do not send generic calendars simply imprinted with your company name. Use photos or illustrations from one or more of your own books to enliven the calendar. One approach you might use is to print an illustration from a different book for each month—ideally from a book whose publication date is printed in large red numerals on that month's calendar. To do this, of course, you will have to schedule at least one new book for each month of the coming year and will have to commission artwork for that book ahead of time.

A calendar that would have great appeal for booksellers would be one with different promotional ideas outlined for each day or week or month of the year—a calendar similar to the promotional calendars that used to be featured in *American Bookseller*.

At the 1991 BookExpo America, Open Horizons published an edition of *Celebrate Today* which we called the *1991 Book Promotion Calendar*. Besides featuring special days, weeks, and months for the last six months of 1991, the calendar featured advertising and cover art from many of our books. We handed out 1,000 copies of this calendar to people who came by our booth. As a result, we received many follow-up book orders, prepublication orders for the 1992 calendar, and a write-up in the *Washington Post*.

11:05 T-Shirts and Other Apparel

T-shirts are walking billboards. If you can convince people to wear your T-shirts (especially bookstore personnel), then you'll have a much better chance of getting your books noticed. How about baseball caps for a book on baseball, sun visors for a book on golf, muscle T-shirts for an exercise book, or bikinis for a diet book?

One way to distribute such imprinted apparel is to offer a free T-shirt with every order of ten or more books. Or give them away to a sampling of people at a public event (for example, imprinted baseball caps at a baseball game). Or give them to people who will wear them on crowded streets at lunch time (when many office workers do their shopping for reading material). Or do as many publishers do: Give them to booksellers and other attendees at the annual BookExpo America Convention. Or, at the very least, have your convention booth workers wearing the T-shirts.

Remember that the main value of any imprinted item is to draw attention to your books and to act as reminder advertising. To accomplish these goals, the imprinted items must be seen (that's one reason imprinted lingerie isn't all that effective). If you are using imprinted apparel, be sure to get them into the hands of people who will wear them. I like wearing book T-shirts when I fly. I always get lots of comments in the terminals and airplanes.

Dell offered T-shirts imprinted with "It's Heaven ... and Heller" to promote Joseph Heller's book, *God Knows*. New American Library offered T-shirts to promote Stephen King's *Skeleton Crew*.

For *Celebrate Today*, I gave T-shirts featuring the book cover to sales representatives for my bookstore distributor. This kept our new book in the front of their minds when they went out to sell books to bookstores.

> **Authors** — If your publisher doesn't supply imprinted apparel to promote your book, that shouldn't stop you from making your own—and wearing it wherever you go. With a computer and color printer, you can now print your own T-shirt print-on transfers which you can then iron on a plain T-shirt. So you can create your own T-shirt quickly and with little cost.

11:06 Party Kits

Bantam Books offered a *Sweet Dreams* pajama party kit free to anyone who requests one. The kit includes one of the latest novels in the *Sweet Dreams* romance series for young adults, menu ideas for the party, game ideas, and other items to enliven a pajama party.

How about a similar kit for a wine and cheese party to promote a cookbook or book on wines? Or a trivia party kit to accompany a book of lists, records, or ratings? Or a dance party kit to accompany the biography of a rock star? Or a going away kit to promote a travel book? Or a birthday party kit for a children's book?

11:07 Fan Clubs

Many authors already have fan clubs. If so, work with those fan clubs to promote new books or reissues from your authors. And, if there are no fan clubs, why not organize some by putting query coupons in new editions of your authors' books, especially those authors who have three or more books published by you? Fan clubs can be an effective way of starting the word-of-mouth bandwagon for a new book.

In addition to author fan clubs, you could also organize a fan club for your company or a special imprint. For instance, Scholastic offered a free *Babysitter's Club* starter kit in the back of their young adult novel, *Kristy's Great Idea*, a book in the *Babysitter's Club* series.

Algonquin used the Lewis Nordan Fan Club to build the promotional buzz for his novel *Lightning Song*. As part of that promotion, they mailed letters to members of the fan club asking them to recruit new members. "When you fax us or send a postcard with the name and address of a new fan," Alqonquin wrote, "We'll send you and the person an advance copy of *Lightning Song*." A nice incentive for signing up new members!

If you'd like to join the John Kremer Fan Club, go to the BookMarket. com web site and sign up for my free *Book Marketing Tip of the Week* ezine. I'll be sure to include you in my Fan Club. It will be fun!

> **Authors** — If you have a fan club, be sure to let your book publisher know about it. If you don't have one, why not start one? If you're too modest to start one yourself, ask a friend or your publisher to start one for you. You deserve one.

11:08 Local Distribution of Flyers

If you have a local guide (for example, the *Boston Ice Cream Lover's Guide*), why not print up some flyers and have them distributed in the local area by neighborhood kids or by a professional distribution service? Start by testing a small area and see if you get any sales. If you do and the sales are enough to cover your expenses, distribute some more over a wider area.

Your book, however, doesn't have to have a local angle. You could easily target other books for such distribution. For example, how about distributing flyers about your new auto care book under the windshield wipers of targeted cars at shopping centers, in downtown parking lots, or at the beach?

11:09 Public Posters

Why not poster the town? Whenever I visit New York, I always see thousands of posters decorating construction sites announcing new plays or movies. Why couldn't a book be publicized in the same way? Especially in New York. I think such postering could be especially effective for celebrity biographies and entertainment titles (rock music, movies, sports, or artists).

11:10 Samples

Another ubiquitous phenomenon I've noticed on New York streets are the people giving away samples (cigarettes, candy, whatever). Again, why not give away samples of a new book? Holt, Rinehart and Winston printed sample chapter brochures of Marek Halter's new novel *The Book of Abraham*. I don't know how these were distributed, but certainly some could have been distributed quite effectively on the streets of New York. What a marvelous way to get word of mouth going.

You could also distribute samples through participating bookstores, exhibits, conferences, book fairs, meetings, author speaking events, and other group events or public areas. Distribute samples anywhere there are plenty of people who might be interested in the book being sampled. When you distribute samples, make sure your book is widely available in local bookstores so people can buy the book once their interest is sparked.

- Daytimers, through 1,500 trained counselors, has distributed more than 750,000 samples in one year. They have found sampling to be the best method to introduce their time schedulers to new audiences.

- Bantam distributed sample copies of *McDonald's: Behind the Arches* by John F. Love to employees (and former employees) of McDonald's.

- Bantam also sent samplers of their Bantam Travel Guides to travel agents and airlines.

- When Globe Pequot Press discovered that they had the only *Guide to Eastern Canada*, they convinced the Canadian tourist information centers to stuff a brochure about the book in with their infopacks sent to travel inquirers. The tourist bureaus were happy to do it because the book promoted tourism in eastern Canada.

- Perigord Press sent advance reading copies (with a special wrapper and seal) of Joseph Wambaugh's novel, *The Blooding*, to the book trade, media, and top law enforcement professionals.

- When Warner Books published John Naisbitt's *Megatrends*, they sent sample copies to the chief executives of the 500 largest corporations in the country. As a result, they "created a groundswell of acknowledgment" for the book.

- Atheneum sent five postcard teasers (one each day for a week) to key book reviewers and booksellers for David Lindsey's novel, *In the Lake of the Moon*. The postcards featured excerpts from the book.

- If your book has a targeted audience, send samples to opinion leaders. On the other hand, if your book is a mass-market book, get copies into the hands of as many people as possible.

- At the ABA Convention, John Wiley gave away booklets excerpted from Jeff Slutsky's book on *Streetsmart Marketing*. These *Bookseller's Street Smart Marketing Tips* described many clever bookstore promotions. The booksellers loved the handouts.

Authors — You can help by giving away samples to key opinion leaders in your field (or by providing the names of these people to your publisher). And, if you are ever feeling adventurous, you can give away sample chapters of your books on the streets of New York; or Sleepy Eye, Minnesota (for a book on better sleeping); or Santa Claus, Indiana (for a children's book); or Valentine, Nebraska (for a romance title); or Rome, Iowa (for an Italian travel guide), or wherever appropriate for your book. Again, be sure to get your publisher involved in such a promotion. And be sure the media hears about it.

11:11   Stadium Advertising

Berkeley used multimedia advertising in Yankee Stadium to promote Mickey Mantle's autobiography *The Mick*. Jove also used stadium ads for Jerry Kramer's football book, *Distant Replay*. Certainly, you could do the same with any book that would appeal to a sports audience or other public audience. You don't have to limit such advertising to baseball or football stadiums. You could also use basketball fieldhouses, boxing gyms, dance halls, or convention centers—wherever, again, an audience interested in the topic of your book might gather.

11:12   Blimps, Balloons, and Skywriting

Goodyear is probably better known for its blimp than for any other advertising it does. Currently a number of other companies are now flying blimps as well as hot air balloons to publicize their name at public events. Although such extravagant advertising may not be appropriate for a single book, it might be appropriate for your company as a whole or for a series of books (for example, a series of adventure novels).

Skywriting or banners flown from an airplane could also work well for a single title. Since such advertising can be expensive (up to $500 per tow), your book should have mass-market distribution and appeal or strong regional interest. For example, how about flying a banner over the beaches of Cape Cod announcing the *Boston Ice Cream Lover's Guide*?

- Random House had a plane fly over the beaches of Long Island on the Labor Day weekend carrying the following banner: "Get the new best-seller—*Through A Glass Darkly*."

- To promote Stephen Frey's *The Takeover*, Signet paid for aerial banners to fly over the beaches of Long Island, Cape Cod, New Jersey, and Laguna Beach.

- As part of the half million dollar campaign for Steve Alten's suspense novel *Meg*, Doubleday flew aerial banners over the beaches of Cape May, Cape Cod, and Los Angeles.

- As long as we're talking about high-flying promotions, how about trying to place one of your book characters as a balloon in the annual Macy's Thanksgiving parade? What are your chances? Not very good, but the exposure is so great that it could be worth the attempt. Your character could join Snoopy, Mickey Mouse, SpongeBob SquarePants, Spiderman, and other stars of the parade. If Macy's does select one of your characters, they build the balloon (you share the construction costs with them). If interested, contact Macy's vice president of special productions in care of the main New York City store. Web: http://www.macysparade.com.

11:13 Next Exit: Billboards

Billboards can be effective as reminder advertising to reinforce other forms of advertising or promotion. Dell, for example, has used billboards combined with national advertising and an author tour to promote Joseph Heller's novel, *God Knows*. Dell also used a billboard on Sunset Boulevard to advertise Kate Green's first novel, *Shattered Moon* (the setting for the novel was Hollywood and its environs).

Billboards work best for book publishers in areas where there is a high density of book buyers. You might try billboards in Silicon Valley, for example, to promote a series of books about computers. Or, if you publish a travel guide or atlas that is well distributed in gas stations, restaurants, or tourist spots, you might try billboards announcing that your guide is available at the next exit.

One of the elements that went into the successful promotional campaign for the self-published *The Messengers* were billboards scattered throughout Portland and Seattle. Those billboards helped the book get lots of attention.

A few pointers: Use no more than six to twelve words in the ad. Motorists usually have the billboard in view for only a few seconds, so the message has to be simple and clear (hence, the book's message probably also has to be simple and clear). Try placing billboards where there is high foot traffic as well (for example, on Sunset Boulevard). Again, billboards are most effective when used as reminder advertising combined with effective publicity and other promotions.

Here are a few more books which have been promoted on Sunset Boulevard billboards: *The Blooding*, by Joseph Wambaugh (Perigord Press), *Max Headroom: The Picture Book of the Film*, by Steve Roberts (Vintage), *Nice Guys Sleep Alone: A Survival Guide to Dating in the '80s*, by Bruce Feirstein (Dell), *One More Time*, by Carol Burnett (Random House), and *Secrets*, by Danielle Steele (Dell).

11:14 Display Billboards in Malls

Many shopping malls and airport terminals now offer space on their walls for billboard advertising. Why not test one of your major books (a general book that would appeal to an affluent audience) in a mall billboard, especially one near a chain bookstore?

• Day-Timers has found that its billboard advertising in airport terminals has yielded thousands of inquiries and orders every week.

• Avon advertised the mass-market edition of Spencer Johnson's *The One Minute Sales Person* in nine top-market airport terminals. To complement these billboards, they placed a full-page advertisement in the Business Travel supplement of *USA Today*.

- To supplement its national radio and TV ad campaign for Michael Crichton's *Airframe*, Knopf placed billboard ads near airports and lightbox ads in airport terminals.

11:15 Transit Advertising

While they are not yet standard media for book advertisements, buses, subways, and taxis have been used to advertise books. If you do advertise any of your titles via such transit ads, try to include a "Take One" order pad attached to the ad so that interested commuters can easily remember the title of the book and where to buy it.

- A few years back one author, who was able to buy transit ads quite cheaply because of a family connection, filled the buses of New York with ads for his new novel. As a result, he received publicity in *Publishers Weekly*, the *New York Times*, and other major newspapers in the city. He also sold a lot of books to people who saw the ads in the buses. If I recall, he even got on a local bestseller list.

- New American Library used transit advertising to promote the paperback edition of *Smart Women, Foolish Choices* by Connell Cowen and Melvyn Kinder.

- In addition to a billboard on Sunset Boulevard for Brad Meltzer's thriller *The Tenth Justice*, Rob Weisbach Books also placed transit advertising in the Metro North commuter railway in New York and Metropass in Washington.

- One novel, Gael Greene's sexy *Blue Skies, No Candy*, had its advertising posters removed from 3,000 New York City subway cars. Why? Because its cover depicted a woman's hand on the zipper of a man's pants. According to Warner Books, when the ads came down, the sales for the book shot up. Controversy sells!

Transit ads can appear on the outside as well as the inside. Use outside ads on buses and taxis in the same way as a billboard ad. One advantage of transit ads over billboards is that the transit ad travels all over the city. To promote Richard North Patterson's legal thriller, *Silent Witness*, Ballantine placed ads on the sides of buses in the author's hometown of San Francisco.

Several services (such as Wheeler, Inc. of Long Island City, New York and Advan of San Francisco, California) offer moving ads on delivery trucks. How much does it cost to place such an ad? About $9,000 per month. Advan claims to deliver 33,000 impressions a day—impressions which reportedly are effective in building a company's image. Again, if you are trying to make an impact on a local level (either for a mass-market novel or a regional title), such advertising might well be worth the expense. Mike Cutino, publisher of *New York Sports Scene* magazine, claimed that 75% of his 125,000 circulation came from billboards on trucks.

A relatively new variation on the standard transit ad is known as moped advertising. In this case, a company pays a person on a moped to drive around (at a beach, in certain areas of the city, or at some public event) carrying a small billboard advertisement. Moped advertising has the advantage of allowing you to specifically target the areas and audiences you want to reach. You can also test more cheaply than with other transit ads which usually require a minimum number of ads (the cost, while cheap per advertisement, can quickly add up to become expensive).

11:16 Other Billboard Ads

A few other billboard-type ads which have been used include bench ads (at bus stops or park benches), sandwich boards carried around in heavy pedestrian traffic, picket advertising, parking meter ads, shopping carts, ski lifts, bumper stickers, food court place mats, airline sick bags, the nasal strips on athlete's noses, and Johnny Ads (yup, you guessed it, these are ads in public toilet facilities). For links to more opportunites for outdoor displays, see http://www.outdoorsystems.com.

One way you might use such billboard advertising is to hire pickets to carry signs advertising one of your books in front of a major bookstore in a high traffic area. Before you do this, be sure you obtain the permission of the bookstore owner. Also, this type of advertising would probably be more effective if the advertising message were humorous or warmly appealing in some way. Alfred Knopf first introduced literary sandwich boards in 1921 when he sent sandwich board pickets to New York's financial and theater districts to promote *Zell, Moon-Calf*, and other novels. He made sure that the bookstores in the area had window displays of the books as well.

- The *Denver Quarterly* placed advertisements on bus benches in Denver which read, "Keep Denver literate. Read." The ads, which also featured their name and number, proved effective in obtaining new subscribers.

- The sides of New York City bus shelters are now adorned with large full-color advertising posters which are protected by glass and illuminated at night. If you want to create an impression with the major media located in New York, you might place ads in midtown Manhattan.

- During the mad cow scare in England, one enterprising farmer near Birmingham, England, decided to increase his revenue by selling advertising space on the sides of his cows. He charged $450 per week for the cow placards. As he noted, "The cows are losing money while they are feeding [since they cannot be sold], so they might as well start paying for their upkeep." He sold eight such ads.

- One advertising agency in England hired London cabbies to talk up Siemens phones during March 1997. The cabbies were even trained to weave the important features of Siemens phones into normal conversation. Wouldn't books be a natural for this? Hire some New York cabbies to cruise near the *New York Times*, CBS, NBC, and a few other midtown media locations and talk up some of your books.

- In October 1997, the Russian Space Agency announced that it was going to step up efforts to sell advertising space on its Mir space station. If you have the right book, you can play to the entire world and beyond!

If you'd like to explore other out-of-home advertising opportunities, check out Standard Rate & Data's *SRDS Out-of-Home Advertising Source*, which features 2,000 such programs, from billboards and bus shelters to event marketing and transit ads, from movie theaters and sports stadiums to in-room hotel ads and in-store ads. For details, contact **SRDS**, 1700 Higgins Road, Des Plaines, IL 60018-5605; 947-375-5000; 800-851-7737; Fax: 847-375-5001. Web: http://www.srds.com.

11:17 Business Cards

The use of business cards has already been discussed in Section 4:01. The only reason I mention them here is that you should think of your business cards as wallet-sized billboards and use them accordingly. Business cards can be one of your most effective promotional tools. Be sure to remind your authors, editors, and marketing representatives to carry a few of their cards with them at all times. Business cards are great facilitators of networking opportunities. To promote their new fall books at the ABA Convention, Sourcebooks printed business cards which featured the cover of each of their books on one side and a short summary of the book plus the company's address on the back.

11:18 The Yellow Pages

People rarely look at the *Yellow Pages* unless they are interested in buying something. Advertising in the *Yellow Pages* may be a great opportunity for you to sell books, especially if you publish a regional title that would be of interest to people who use the *Yellow Pages* to do their walking for them. For example, if you published a local restaurant guide, why not advertise the guide under the Restaurants section of the *Yellow Pages*? Whatever you do, don't list your company under books; list it under your subject specialty.

There are 6,400 Yellow Pages directories published in the United States. Many of these directories offer per inquiry advertising deals or split runs to encourage national advertisers to run an ad. Indeed, you need not limit your advertising to local directories. It is possible to buy space through a national network of *Yellow Pages* if you have a book that would interest a specific national audience. One food company, for example, advertises cents-off coupons for their frozen pizzas under the Pizza listing in local phone books.

How about a foreign travel guide listed under Travel Agencies? Or how about an ad for a book about dog or cat care under the Veterinarian listing? If you have been thinking about advertising in any telephone directories, here are some resources to contact:

☐ **Yellow Pages Publishers Association**, 820 Kirts Boulevard #100, Troy, MI 48084; 248-244-6200; Fax: 248-244-0700. Web: http://www.yppa. org. Send for their 20-page booklet, *National Yellow Pages Advertising Fact Book*. 76.7% of all adults refer to the *Yellow Pages* in a typical month. The *Yellow Pages* are referred to 49 million times a day. 50.0% of *Yellow Pages* references result in a purchase of a product or service.

☐ **The Berry Company**, 3170 Kettering Boulevard, Dayton, OH 45439-1924; 937-296-2121; 800-366-2379; Fax: 937-296-2037. Email: berryco @lmberry.com. Web: http://www.lmberry.com. This major yellow pages publisher sells ads for most areas of the country.

☐ **National Yellow Pages Marketing Programs**, 2625 Cumberland Parkway N.W. #295, Atlanta, GA 30339; 770-432-9325; 800-755-9325; Fax: 770-432-9331. Web: http://www.natlyellowpages.com. Sells ads for any yellow pages directory in the country.

☐ The following two books will help you buy and design *Yellow Pages* ads that work: *Advertising in the Yellow Pages* by W. F. Wagner and *Getting the Most from Your Yellow Pages Advertising* by Barry Maher.

11:19 Other Directory Listings

Don't forget to get your books and company listed in appropriate bibliographies and other directories. Also, consider advertising in the annual directory issues of magazines that are most applicable to your line of books.

• If you publish craft books, you should certainly be listed in the periodic directory issues of *Creative Product News*—and you should also consider advertising in such issues. Dover Publications, Chilton Book Company, and Horizon Publishers all advertise in this trade magazine.

• I make sure that Open Horizon's books, including this one, are listed every year in *Literary Market Place*, the *Directory of Directories*, *Books in Print*, and other business and writing directories.

Authors — Look for directories (and trade periodicals which feature directory listings) appropriate for your books. Since you probably do more reading in your field than your publisher does, you are more likely to spot such directories. When you do find some, ask your publisher to contact them for listing information and, if the budget permits, advertising rates.

11:20 In-Store Advertisements

Some grocery stores and shopping malls now provide their own in-store background music programming. Often they also sell advertising on these broadcasts. Campbell Soups has used such in-store ads to build consumer interest in their LeMenu frozen dinners. Why couldn't a publisher of a series of romance novels use similar in-store ads to build consumer interest in their books? Two major advantages of such advertising are that it reaches buyers *when* they are in a buying mood and *where* the product is readily available for purchase.

Just in time for the holiday season, Warner Books joined forces with MediaOne, the nation's second largest in-store advertising network, in a $100,000 advertising campaign in 70 grocery chains with 7,000 outlets nationwide. The campaign featured high-impact ads at the checkout counters for two of 1992's hottest bestsellers: Sidney Sheldon's *The Doomsday Conspiracy* and Alexandra Ripley's *Scarlett*.

11:21 In-Flight Catalogs and Product Samples

A relatively new development is InflitePaks, which feature direct marketing solicitations distributed inside airline snack packages. America Online, one of the companies that has used this service, has reported that the conversion rate for AOL's diskette giveaways was faster and higher than with other promotions. Other companies that have used this service include *Newsweek*, Book-of-the-Month Club, and Toshiba.

☐ Sky Marketing provides product samples to 75 million airline passengers, 16 million car rental customers, 6 million cruise line passengers, and 12 million hotel guests each year. Contact **Sky Marketing**, Hanger 5, LaGuardia Airport, Flushing, NY 11371; 718-899-0424; Fax: 718-899-0551. Web: http://www.skymarketingltd.com.

☐ SkyMall drops five million catalogs via major airlines, the LodgeNet hotel interactive system, and their web site. Oone million airline passengers are exposed to the catalog each day. SkyMall's average order is $100.00. Executive Book Summaries, Nightingale Conant, Successories, and *Entrepreneur Start-Up Guides* have advertised via SkyMall. For more information, contact **SkyMall**, 1520 E. Pima Street, Phoenix, AZ 85034; 602-254-9777; Fax: 602-254-6075. Web: http://www.skymall.com.

11:22 Movie Theater Commercials

Theaters often intersperse commercials with movie previews before the main shows. I've seen ads for Wrangler jeans, GE radios, and O'Dell's butter (besides, of course, the popcorn and candy commercials produced by Coke,

Pepsi, or Seven-Up). If you are publishing a book that ties into a movie, you might test an advertisement in movie theaters during the run of the movie. You will probably find it effective to promote the book for several weeks before and after the movie as well as during the run of the movie.

How effective are such pre-movie commercials? While the same number of people will see a commercial in movie theaters during one month (if the commercial has national coverage) as will see an average commercial on television (about 30 million), one study reports that over four times as many people will remember the movie commercial the day after as will remember a TV commercial.

☐ While such movie ads are effective, they can be expensive—as much as $500,000 per minute for a national run. Perhaps a better way to expose your books to a movie audience is to participate in *The Popcorn Report*, a pre-movie newsreel featuring video news releases from sponsoring companies. For a fee of about $20,000, your video news release is featured in 500+ theaters across the country. For details, contact **The Popcorn Report**, West Glen Communications, 1430 Broadway, New York, NY 10018-3396; 212-921-2800; 800-325-8677; Fax: 212-944-9055.

☐ National Cinema Network offers commercials on 9,000 movie screens as well as the *Movie Times* bimonthly digest, movie ticket couponing, concession promotions, lobby displays, sweepstakes, and other promotions in movie theaters. For details, contact **National Cinema Network**, 4900 Seminary Road #110, Alexandria, VA 22311; 703-931-6011; 866-NCN-BIGP; Fax: 703-998-9121. Web: http://www.ncninc.com.

☐ To promote a new Mexican cookbook, *Food from the Heart*, by famed restauranteur Zarela Martinez, Macmillan placed specially produced commercials before the airings of movies in two Upper East Side movie theaters near the author's restaurant, Zarelas. With five shows a day on five screens per theater, the book received 350 promotional spots each week for a total audience of 30,000 to 40,000. Macmillan ran these spots for two months.

☐ In July 1997, the Franklin Spier ad agency created a 30-second movie trailer for John Gray's *Mars and Venus on a Date*. This trailer appeared in Cineplex Odeon theaters in fourteen major markets.

11:23 Ads in Mail Order Catalogs

Some mail order operations have accepted outside advertising in their catalogs. For example, *The Sharper Image* catalog carried four ads in each monthly issue. *Bloomingdale's* carried as many as twelve ads in their catalog. While advertising in these high-ticket catalogs is expensive, it might be appropriate for promoting an expensive limited edition title. You should also watch for other catalogs which might offer more affordable advertising rates and better demographics for your particular titles.

11:24 Coupons and Special Offers

Coupons and other special offers have worked well for many book publishers. Certainly any cookbook publisher should be able to arrange cross-promotions for ingredients, cooking tools, aprons, or other kitchen utensils. How about offering free gambling tickets with a mystery novel set in Las Vegas? How about convincing tourist attractions to offer two-for-one specials to accompany a travel guide? To accompany an investment guide, why not work with a reputable stock brokerage house to offer 10% discount coupons for brokerage services?

- Addison-Wesley arranged for special offers to be included with several of their books. In cooperation with the National Gardening Association, they offered a free subscription to the *National Gardening* magazine with any purchase of *Gardening: The Complete Guide to Growing America's Favorite Fruits and Vegetables*.

- For an updated edition of *The New Joy of Photography*, Addison-Wesley tucked in coupons worth $10.00 in film processing charges from Kodak.

- Rand McNally included $700 of travel coupons in the *2005 Road Atlas*.

- Bantam worked with Clairol to cross-merchandise their Loveswept romances and Clairol's Pazazz Sheer Color Wash. Each heroine in the *Delaneys of Killaroo* trilogy was described as having hair the color of one of the new shades being introduced by Clairol. To support sales of the novels, Clairol inserted 750,000 book samplers of the trilogy (provided by Bantam) in Pazazz displays placed in 10,000 food and drug stores. In addition, 50¢-off coupons for Pazazz were bound into every novel.

- To promote *Sprouse's Income Tax Handbook, 1989*, by Mary Sprouse, Penguin printed a coupon redeemable for a free copy of her $7.95 trade paperback, *How to Survive a Tax Audit*.

- As incentive for purchasing *The Birds Around Us*, illustrated by Robert Dawson, Ortho offered four reproductions from the book as frameable prints for only $6.95 plus the order form in the book.

- In 1992, Penguin featured The Great Summer Getaway promotion, in which they offered discounts worth up to $100 off TWA airline tickets when readers bought two paperbacks and sent in a coupon. The promotion featured two to three different books each month.

11:25 Rebates

Rebates are offers to return part of the purchase price to the buy if they fulfill certain requirements. Why offer rebates? Here are eight good reasons:

- ☐ Booksellers are more likely to stock and feature your books if you offer some sort of consumer promotion.

☐ Consumers are more likely to buy your books if you give them an incentive. According to one study, 65% of all consumers report that rebate offers do affect their decision to buy one product over another. In 1986, 50 billion dollars were offered in consumer rebate programs, yet less than 10% of that money was actually redeemed.

☐ If you require customers to send in a receipt (or a coupon from the book) in order to get a rebate, you get a chance to sell them additional titles on your list. When you send them their rebate check, also enclose information on related titles.

☐ Of course, you should also add them to your mailing list so you can let them know about new titles you publish.

☐ Rebates give you an opportunity to track book sales in different parts of the country (and in different markets). You can also conduct some market research at the same time—by asking the consumer to answer a few questions when they send in their request for a rebate.

☐ With rebates you can offer a discount on your books without hurting the bookseller's profit margin or causing other unnecessary administrative hassles (which would result if you offered direct cents-off coupons).

☐ Rebates can be used to encourage readers to sample a series of books.

☐ Rebates have also been used by other manufacturers to move surplus inventories. Perhaps publishers could use rebates to sell stagnant backlist titles or to remainder titles direct to consumers. Such rebates could replace the current attempts to remainder books in place.

Here are a few examples of how book publishers have used refunds and rebates to encourage sales of their titles:

• For a new series of gardening books, Houghton Mifflin offered a rebate to any reader who bought a second book in the series. All the consumer had to do was fill in a coupon and send it direct to Houghton Mifflin for a rebate.

• To promote its line of fourteen cookbooks from the California Culinary Academy, Ortho Information Services combined rebates along with cents-off coupons. Whenever a customer bought a book in the series, they received a $3.00 rebate coupon packed inside the book. When the customer mailed the coupon into Ortho, they were sent back a $3.00 rebate check as well as two bounceback coupons each worth $1.50 towards the purchase of other cookbooks in the series.

• Prentice Hall also offered an in-pack rebate as well as special coupons to promote *The 1989 Mobil Road Atlas and Trip Planning Guide to the United States, Canada, and Mexico.*

• To build up interest in *La Mattanza: The Sicilian Madness* by Charles Carmello, Paperjacks ran a large advertisement in *USA Today* offering a $1.00 refund to anyone who mailed in the ad coupon, a cash register receipt, and the ISBN/UPC number from the book's cover.

- In the fall of 1986, Reader's Digest Books offered a $1.00 rebate to anyone who sent them a bookstore receipt proving that they had bought a Reader's Digest book. At the same time, they also invited bookstore customers to participate in one of the $6,000,000 sweepstakes offered by their mail order division.

- A **coufund** (a cross between a coupon and a refund) is a new form of refund that has yet to be tried by publishers. It's a standard coupon that is only valid after the customer glues three or four proofs of purchase on it. Like any other coupon, the coufund is redeemed at the cash register. Why not try offering a coufund for your books?

11:26 Sweepstakes

In a poll done by *Premium/Incentive Business*, 96% of companies which ran sweepstakes accomplished their goals. For these companies, sweepstakes helped to increase sales, public awareness, brand recognition, and/or store traffic. Here are a few of the many ways different publishers have used sweepstakes to promote their lead titles:

- For Pat Booth's novel, *Palm Beach*, Crown offered a free vacation at the Breakers, a luxury resort in Palm Beach. An entry form, printed on the inside flap of the hardcover book, could either be clipped out or copied and then sent to the sweepstakes office. To encourage bookstore promotion of this sweepstakes, Crown also offered to give the same vacation to the owner of the bookstore where the winner had obtained the sweepstakes information.

- Abingdon Press ran a Win a Trip to the Holy Land consumer contest to help promote William Gentz's *The Dictionary of Bible and Religion*.

- To promote the tie-in novel for *The Jewel of the Nile*, Avon ran a consumer sweepstakes with a grand prize trip to Morocco where the movie had been filmed. To draw attention to the sweepstakes, Avon provided bookstores and travel agencies with floor displays, brochures, and movie posters.

- Villard offered a $10,000 scholarship and ten personal computers in a "Dollars for Scholars" sweepstakes to promote *The Princeton Review: Cracking the System: the SAT*. Sweepstakes coupons were available at stores which displayed the "Dollars for Scholars" poster and shelf talker.

- Harlequin offered consumers a chance to have their dreams come true by winning a Rolls-Royce or a trip to Paris in their First Class Sweepstakes. The sweepstakes was announced on the covers and in four-color inserts of all fall releases in Harlequin's romance novel series. Harlequin also provided stores with posters and shelf talkers to draw attention to the sweepstakes. Entry forms were available in each book as well as on point-of-purchase coupon entry pads.

- Bantam sponsored a sweepstakes to promote its series of books featuring Disney characters. The prize? A free trip to Disneyland.

- New American Library received 250,000 responses when they gave away the car used in the movie, *Christine*, in a sweepstakes promotion for the mass-market paperback reprint of the Stephen King novel.

- NAL sponsors twenty promotions for the 450 books they publish each year. In one case they calculated that they sold 21% more books than they would have without a promotion. In another case, they received eight times more floor displays in stores because of a sweepstakes.

- For Clark Howard's novel, *Quick Silver*, NAL/Signet offered an instant win sweepstakes with a grand prize of $1,000.00 and 100 second prizes of $25.00. Each copy of the novel contained a bound-in Quick Silver scratch-off card. To help promote the sweepstakes, NAL provided stores with an eye-catching 36-copy floor display.

Sweepstakes are an excellent way to spur interest in one of your books, especially one which you are backing with a major advertising budget (because sweepstakes work best with highly visible titles). Sweepstakes can also boost response to direct mail promotions by as much as 50%.

If you decide to offer a sweepstakes, you should hire a company which specializes in managing sweepstakes and other contests. The legal requirements for sweepstakes are so exacting that you shouldn't try to offer one without advice from an experienced consultant. Besides helping you to meet the legal requirements, such companies can provide creative development, prize selection and acquisition, judges, and fulfillment. They are well worth any additional cost. For more information, contact one of the following companies which specialize in sweepstakes, contests, and other promotions:

☐ **Don Jagoda Associates**, 100 Marcus Drive, Melville, NY 11747; 631-454-1800; Fax: 631-454-1834. Email: info@dja.com. Web: http://www.dja.com.

☐ **FAC Services Group**, 111 E. Wacker Drive, Chicago, IL 60601-4884; 312-552-4510; Fax: 312-552-4555. Web: http://www.frankel.com.

☐ **Gage Marketing Group**, 10000 West Highway 55, Minneapolis, MN 55441; 612-595-3851; Fax: 612-595-3856. Web: http://www.gage.com.

☐ **Marden-Kane Inc,** 36 Maple Place, Manhasset, NY 11030-1962; 516-365-3999; Fax: 516-365-5250. Web: http://www.mardenkane.com.

☐ **The Sweepstakes Center**, 2290 East Avenue, Rochester, NY 14610; 716-256-0080; Fax: 716-244-0628. Email: sweepnet@ice-net.com. They prepare custom or shared sweepstakes from concept through fulfillment. Call for their free *Sweepstakes Guide* and sample kit.

☐ **Ventura Associates**, 1040 Avenue of the Americas, New York, NY 10018; 212-302-8277; 888-463-9249; Fax: 212-302-2587. Email: sweepspros@aol.com. Web: http://www.sweepspros.com.

11:27 Other Contests

Another way to generate interest in your books is to sponsor contests which are in some way connected with the contents of your book or series of books. Unlike sweepstakes, these contests could be tests of knowledge, skill, or some other capability.

- Bantam sponsored a cover-girl contest to help promote its *Sweet Dreams* series of novels. Bantam also sponsored a Choose Your Own Adventure writing contest to help promote its series by that name. The winning manuscript, in this case, was published by Bantam as part of the series.

- In the back of #12 in their *Sweet Valley High* series, Bantam printed two dozen contest questions based on the first twelve books of the series. Bantam received over 20,000 entries. Winners were randomly chosen from those who answered all the questions correctly. The prizes included a trip to New York City to meet Francine Pascal, creator of the series, as well as tickets to a Broadway show and a visit to the set of *All My Children*. The contest had its desired effect. Sales of backlist titles increased. As an added benefit, Bantam was able to develop a list of teenage romance readers. Bantam has sent these readers newsletters and announcements of new series that might interest them.

- Perhaps more than any other publisher, Bantam uses contests to promote its series. To promote Marcia Leonard's *Eating*, one of four titles in their What I Like series, Bantam sponsored a baby photo contest targeted at parents. The winner received $1,000 towards their child's education.

- John Magel, author/illustrator of *Dr. Moggle's Alphabet Challenge* published by Rand McNally, offered a set of alphabet blocks enclosed in a handmade cherry case as a prize to the reader who correctly identified two hidden words which he had designed into the book's illustrations. Besides identifying the two words, the winning reader also had to explain in 40 words or less the significance of those two words.

- Morrow, publisher of *Who Killed the Robins Family?* by Thomas Chastain and Bill Adler, offered a $10,000 prize to the reader who submitted the best answer to the title question.

- To promote its line of *Ramona Quimby* young adult novels by Beverly Cleary, Morrow sponsored a Ramona Quimby Look-Alike Contest in 1984. Contestants had to go to bookstores to fill out the entry blank and submit a photo. Winners were chosen by a random drawing.

- Putnam ran two contests to promote Eric Hill's *Spot's First Easter*, one of nine books in their Spot Lift-the-Flap book series. First, they ran a Draw Spot Contest for children, ages 3-10. Then, they ran a window display contest for bookstores displaying the drawings. In this way, they were able to promote both consumer and retailer awareness of the entire book series.

- Houghton Mifflin and five Twin Cities bookstores ran a Curious George Word-Search Contest for children through a full-page ad in *Minnesota Monthly*. Houghton Mifflin provided 75% of the $1,200 ad cost through co-op moneys due the five bookstores; the bookstores each paid $60.00 as well. All the participating bookstores reported increased sales of *Curious George* titles plus a large mail order response to the contest. The prizes for the contest were children's dictionaries.

- Avon Books sponsored a Howard Cosell sound-alike contest for Cosell's *I Never Played the Game*. They backed up the contest with full-size color posters of Cosell, in-store displays, co-op advertising, radio contest promotions, and national broadcast and print publicity.

- During the summer of 1990, Llewellyn sponsored a book review contest in which previous customers were invited to write a 500-word review of a Llewellyn title. Those who wrote the best reviews of any title received a $20.00 gift certificate good for other Llewellyn titles. Llewellyn still encourages such reviews.

11:28 Brandstanding and Sponsorships

Brandstanding is the linking of special events with specific brands or products. For instance, Budweiser and Pepsi sponsor a number of different sports events each year. Millers sponsors golf games. Virginia Slims sponsors tennis tournaments. If you publish books about sports, recreation, or even travel, you might consider sponsoring a sports event as a means to gain more recognition for your books. Why couldn't a publisher of an exercise book help to sponsor a run-for-fun event? According to the *IEG Sponsorship Report*, worldwide spending on special events marketing now runs $15 billion. Each year in North America, companies spend $3.85 billion on sports sponsorships and $2.1 billion on arts and social sponsorships.

If you decide to sponsor an event, ask for product exclusivity, arrange to hand out samples, prepare signage for the event, confirm how many tickets you will get for guests, ask for permission to use their mailing list, and ask about other ways you can work with them to promote the event. Below are a few events recently sponsored by book publishers.

- When Bantam launched its Sweet Dreams line of young adult novels, it tied into a series of nationwide fashion shows sponsored by *Seventeen* magazine.

- As an official sponsor of the 1996 Mrs. America Pageant, Topaz had the right to use the winner in personal appearances. Topaz even considered asking the winner to appear on the cover of one of their romance novels.

- Bridge Publications sponsors an Indianapolis 500 race car (driven by 4-time winner, Al Unser, Sr.) to promote *Dianetics*, a self-help title. They promoted this sponsorship with a front cover ad in *Publishers Weekly*.

- How about sponsoring an attempt to break a world record? If the record were broken, the chances are that your company name or book title would be mentioned in *Guinness*, which currently sells over one million copies every year. That's a lot of free advertising.

11:29 Book Fairs

Participating in local book fairs is an excellent way to introduce your books to new readers at a relatively low cost (from $75 to $300). Most of the people who come to such book fairs are avid readers who, if they like one of your books, will order others as well. Make sure everyone who passes your booth gets a brochure or catalog.

Some of the best-known book fairs include New York Is Book Country, Miami Book Fair International, Northwest Bookfest, Texas Book Festival, Rocky Mountain Book Festival, San Antonio Inter-American Book Fair, San Francisco Bay Area Book Fair, Times Festival of Reading in St. Petersburg, Small Press Book Fair in New York, Southern Festival of Books in Nashville, Sacramento Reads!, and other fairs in Chicago, Boston, and Seattle.

- Miami Book Fair International attracts over 150,000 readers every year and many major authors. Publishers have reported sales of $5,000 to $10,000 during the book fair.

- The Philadelphia Publishers Group donated $3,000 worth of books to a city-sponsored literary celebration called Philadelphia Ink. The celebration included a book fair, seminars, and book readings, plus drawings for seven free collections of books.

- At the Great Midwestern Book Show in 1985, AdLib Publications sold $600 in books. Other small presses did so well that they had to close early because they had run out of stock on most of their titles.

- Open Horizons exhibited at the 1992 San Francisco Bay Area Book Festival. Not only did we sell $500 worth of books to individuals who came by the booth, but we also sold 20 copies of our *Turntable Illusions* book to the Exploratorium museum store. We coordinated our exhibit at the book fair with a seminar presentation at the Multicultural Publishers Exchange national conference and with several media interviews.

- Peter Gail of Goosefoot Acres Press sold about 100 books at the local Buckeye Book Fair in Ohio. At some festivals he attends, he gives out food samples from his book, *The Dandelion Celebration*.

11:30 Other Festivals and Fairs

Besides participating in book fairs, seek out other fairs, festivals, or conferences which might offer a market for your books. For example, if you publish books on crafts, why not exhibit at some local craft shows? Or, how about exhibiting your books on automobiles at a car show? Or books on sailing or fishing at a boat show?

- When Signe Carlson exhibited her book *North of Skarv Island* at Scan-Fair in Portland, Oregon, she sold 52 copies of the book in one day.

- Redbird Productions sold more than 27,000 copies of their self-published book, *Cream and Bread*, by exhibiting at any festival which might be attended by people of Scandinavian heritage.

- Mystery writer Connie Shelton met the mystery reviewer for *Publishers Weekly* at a mystery conference in Arizona. While the reviewer had missed reviewing her first title, Connie reports that "since that meeting she has reviewed every other title we've submitted."

- When Patricia Fry published *The Mainland Luau*, she found a list of 75 barbecue events in the *National Barbecue News* and wrote each organizer. Almost everyone responded. She received four types of responses:

  1. Some decided to display her book at their events.
  2. Some sold the book.
  3. Some handed out order forms and flyers.
  4. Some asked for copies to hand out as door prizes.

11:31 Multilevel Marketing

Multilevel marketing (sometimes known as *network marketing*) has successfully launched many products, including Amway, Shaklee, blue-green algae, vitamins, beauty products, and more. It's useful for promoting products that need to be explained to be appreciated. If you are interested in this means of advertising and distribution, check it out carefully beforehand. Many network marketing plans are little more than pyramid schemes, which draw governmental scrutiny. Also, multilevel marketing is still associated in many minds with fly-by-night operators and zealous proselytizers. Perhaps someday someone will come up with a way to draw upon the strengths of multilevel marketing without incorporating its weaknesses.

- Several years ago, Medallion Books, which made a concerted effort to promote general trade books via a multilevel marketing scheme, lost $4,500,000 during its year of operation. Among its titles were *The Chocolate Lover's Cookbook* by Billie Little, *Personal Power Program* by Bret Lyon, *Immune for Life*, an illustrated Bible, and several novels. The company eventually went bankrupt.

- In late 1992, The Book Network promoted mass-market paperbacks from a variety of publishers through a multilevel marketing program that offered members 25% off all orders. The program, however, did not offer enough incentive to get a real multilevel bandwagon movement going.

- Melvin Powers of Wilshire Book Company has been successful selling some of his motivational titles to multilevel marketers. In one month alone, Wilshire sold 15,000 copies each of *Think and Grow Rich, The Magic of Thinking Success, Think Like a Winner*, and *Psychocybernetics*.

- Diane Pfeifer of Strawberry Patch produced a teaser sampler booklet for a cookbook she was doing that involved a multilevel product. Using a free voice-mail recording, she sold thousands of these booklets to major distributors to give to their downline.

- John Cummata of Financial Independence Network made the 1996 Inc. 500 by selling his book *Debt-FREE and Prosperous Living* (plus newsletters and tapes) via a multilevel marketing network. Over five years, he built his network to a core group of 55,000 financial-independence consultants as well as 1,260 certified financial-independence consultants who offered his material via investment seminars around the country. While he was first building his company via direct mail solicitations, he found that his marketing costs were about 60% of his overall income. In network marketing, he points out, that "60% goes to the people who put together the sales organization."

11:32 Waiting Room Copies

To promote your books, especially series, you could provide free waiting room copies to doctors, dentists, and other offices where people have to wait. Most doctors would be happy to display such books if they appeared to be of interest to their patients. If you do provide waiting room copies, make sure you have a clear sales promotion in the back of the book or, better yet, in the front of the book.

The Children's Reading Institute sent waiting room copies of one of their titles, *Germs Make Me Sick*, to doctors around the country. The book's cover even had a special imprint saying, "Waiting Room Copy. Please Do Not Remove." The Institute bound into each copy 20 tear-out postcards that promoted their Let's Read and Find Out series of science books.

11:33 Cross Promotions

When editing and marketing your books, look for ways to cross-promote your book with another product. If you can piggyback your book advertising with a major consumer product, you'll be able to get far greater exposure than you could ever get on your own—at little or no cost to you!

- When Beth Ann Herman wrote her first novel, *Power City*, she deliberately embellished the descriptions of the Maserati owned by the novel's main character. Why? In the back of her mind, she was hoping to convince Maserati to cross-promote her book with their cars. And, indeed, she was able to do just that. When her book was published, the book-signing party was held at the Maserati dealership in Beverly Hills. As a result, Maserati spent a lot of money to promote the party and her book.

- Janet Dailey's novel, *Tangled Vines*, featured a story of true love set in the Napa Valley grape-growing area. When Dailey went on tour to promote the book, Vichon Vineyards came along to introduce a new wine at the bookstores she visited.

- Princess Cruises sponsored a travel sweepstakes to promote James Michener's novel, *Mexico*. Michener, who had lectured on previous Princess cruises, agreed to do so again. In addition, he gave press interviews while on board the ship.

- In addition to buying 100,000 copies of the photographic essay, *The Meaning of Life*, to give to anyone who test-drove their new model, Mazda also placed 10-page excerpt advertisements in thirteen Time Warner magazines (*Life, Sports Illustrated, Time*, etc.), sponsored a CBS television show based on the book, and sponsored a related photographic exhibit that was displayed in a dozen upscale shopping malls. Since this costly promotion resulted in many more test-drives and actual car sales, Mazda was happy with the results. Little, Brown, of course was also happy. Besides selling the 100,000 premium copies, the book went on to become a bestseller.

- In an unsolicited cross-promotion, Calvin Klein featured a model holding a copy of *Postcards* by E. Annie Proulx in an underwear ad that appeared in *GQ* magazine.

- A few years ago, novelist Fay Weldon created a lot of controversy when she was paid a large sum by Bulgari to feature one of their watches in *The Bulgari Connection*.

- To promote Carole Matthews's *A Minor Indiscretion*, Hodder/Headline joined with Nescafe Cappuccino and handed out 85,000 copies of two of the author's backlist titles to coffee-buyers. The book went on to become both a Sunday *Times* and *Bookseller* bestseller.

- Warner paired with Crystal Light to push James Patterson's *Suzanne's Diary for Nicholas*. Warner got book placement on Crystal Light displays in supermarkets, while the beverage got play in newspaper ads for the book. The two joined together on a sweepstakes. Each side paid for its own advertising, just agreeing to give the other placement. As Warner noted, "We're reinforcing his name and hitting the women's audience that his other books don't tend to get."

- Lauren Chattman, author of *Mom's Big Book of Baking*, did a one-day national satellite TV tour for Jif peanut butter. Lauren appeared with her 7-year-old daughter and, although she was primarily plugging Jif in a paid sponsorship, she was introduced as author of the book. Many stations flashed the cover of the book on the air. And Harvard Common Press, the publisher, reported significant sales as a result.

- In *No Boundaries*, a book of nature photography from Creative Publishing, Ford Motor Company paid for a number of plugs, from a long-distance shot of an SUV climbing a mountain to a slogan as the book's title. As part of its sponsorship, Ford shouldered a share of both production and marketing costs and donated a vehicle for a contest.

- For Artisan's *The Ford Century*, a history of the company and its effect on culture and business with a foreword by actor Paul Newman, Ford paid $150,000 in marketing costs and joined in developing the content and paying for some production costs. As the book packager Tehabi noted, "Ford was really supportive of the fact that we didn't want to dance around controversial issues. We don't hide the issues that might have been hidden in a promotional book."

Authors: When writing your books, consider the promotional possibilities. Are there any ways to cross-promote your book with a major sponsor or consumer product? If so, let your publisher know. But, please, don't be crass or blatant. Don't let the promotional possibilities determine or color the content of your book. Your book—and your reputation—are far too important to be distorted by any commercial message.

11:34 Co-Op Ads

Cooperative promotions allow publishers to share mailing and labor costs while promoting their titles to specific markets. Because co-op mailings are so much less expensive and time-consuming than doing your own promotions, they allow you to promote to marginal markets that you might not otherwise approach. Here are a few established co-op marketing programs that you might want to use:

☐ **PMA Co-op Mailings**—PMA sponsors many co-op programs (to libraries, bookstores, reviewers, and target markets). For more information, write to the PMA: The Independent Book Publishers Association, 627 Aviation Way, Manhattan Beach, CA 90266; 310-372-2732; Fax: 310-374-3342. Email: pmaonline@aol.com. Web: http://www.pma-online.org.

☐ **Perspectives Press**—This publisher does an annual co-op mailing to adoption and infertility agencies, professionals, and families. Contact Perspectives Press, P.O. Box 90318, Indianapolis, IN 46290-0318, 317-872-3055. Web: http://www.perspectivespress.com.

☐ **Evolutionary Products**—This company organizes co-op mailings for new age titles to bookstores, reviewers, and distributors. Contact Evolutionary Products, 1653 N. Magnolia Avenue, Tucson, AZ 85712-4103; 520-323-1190; 800-777-4751; Fax: 520-320-9338. Email: info@newagemarket.com. Web: http://www.newagemarket.com.

☐ **Publishers Support Services**—This publisher offers co-op mailing programs to doctors, lawyers, hospitals, and Jewish markets (gift shops, bookstores, social services, etc.). For more information, contact Publishers Support Services, Five Star Publications, 4696 W. Tyson Street, Chandler, AZ 85224; 480-940-8182; 800-545-7827; Fax: 480-940-8787. Email: info@fivestarsupport.com. Web: http://www.fivestarsupport.com.

☐ For other co-op marketing opportunities, check out John Kremer's blog at http://openhorizons.blogspot.com. The blog features updates on such marketing opportunities as well as other book-related news items and answers to questions from readers.

11:35 Use Alternative Media

Besides the card packs mentioned in Chapter Ten, there are now a good number of other alternative media (ride-alongs or piggybacks) that might be effective for marketing books. With the high cost of postage, these alternative media are making more sense, especially if you want to reach a mass audience. What are some of the advantages of piggybacking your advertising message with someone else's?

☐ Your offer receives an implied endorsement from the company sponsoring the alternative media.

☐ The cost is 75 to 80% less than a solo mailing.

☐ With over 2,000 such programs available, it's possible to target almost any mass audience.

For details about these alternative media, send for a free copy of *Everything You Ever Wanted to Know about Package Inserts and Co-op Mailings* from **Leon Henry Inc.**, 200 N. Central Avenue #200, Hartsdale, NY 10530-1940; 914-285-3456; Fax: 914-285-3450. Email: lh@leonhenryinc.com. Web: http://www.leonhenryinc. com. Leon Henry is a leading source of alternative media programs.

The following pages describe a few of the alternative media you could use to promote your books:

☐ **Package insert programs**—Advertising inserts are sent along with merchandise shipments from catalogs and direct marketers such as Book-of-the-Month Club, Great Christian Books, Hanover House, Field Publications, and Lillian Vernon. Besides the strong implied endorsement, package insert programs allow you to reach hotline buyers. Barnes & Noble Books by Mail offers a package insert program through Direct Media.

☐ **Statement stuffers**—These advertising inserts ride along with customer invoices, statements, and renewal efforts from banks, credit card issuers, cable services, phone companies, utilities, and other monthly billers. These allow you to reach creditworthy customers at a low cost, but one disadvantage is that statements are a negative buying environment (the recipients are being reminded of a debt).

☐ **Ride-along programs**—Your advertising message is inserted into other direct marketer's prospecting programs. Besides package inserts in their merchandise shipments, Columbia House, Doubleday Book Clubs, and Waldenbooks also include other companies's advertising messages in their promotional or follow-up mailings. Many magazines polybag catalogs and other direct offers from other companies along with their magazines. Seminar companies prospect for attendees in this fashion.

☐ **National co-op mailings**—These co-op programs, which reach large audiences, feature a mix of coupons and direct response inserts. Such programs are usually packaged in 6"x9" full-color envelopes.

Cox Direct, 8605 Largo Lakes Drive, Largo, FL 33773; 800-678-2743; Fax: 813-399-3061. Their Carol Wright programs are mailed regularly to 30 million families, 14 million older adults, and 2.8 million Hispanics. Their Golf Direct program is delivered to one million golfers. And their Val-Pak coupons program distributes coupons to 53 million households and one million small businesses.

Madison Direct Marketing, 10 Glenville Street, Greenwich, CT 06831; 203-532-9000; Fax: 203-532-9272. Web: http://www.madisondm.com. Their direct mail programs that go to expectant families, new parents, young families, teens, Hispanics, *Playboy* subscribers, and active adults.

Supermarket of Savings, 188 Broadway, P.O. Box 8527, Woodcliff Lake, NJ 07675; 201-307-8888; Fax: 201-307-1200. Sends co-op mailings to 7.5 million young families (with 15 million children).

☐ **Sampling programs**—Samples are handed out at various locations (such as hospitals, pharmacies, schools, or malls) or through key professionals (such as nurses, childbirth educators, or teachers).

EventNet USA, 9812 S.W. 92nd Terrace, Miami, FL 33176; 800-764-5325; Fax: 305-595-2441. Web: http://www.eventnetusa.com. This mall sampling company hands out samples at events at 1,100 malls around the country. Reader's Digest Books used this company to distribute sample books from its Healthy Living Book Series as well as surveys to senior citizens who participated in mall walking programs.

First Moments, 55 Northern Boulevard, Greenvale, NY 11548; 516-484-5740; Fax: 516-484-2950. They present samples, coupons, and advertising inserts to new parents. Their new parents package is hand delivered by nurses to 3.8 million mothers in 3,800 hospitals. Their expectant parents package is delivered to two million parents through 10,000 childbirth educators. They also deliver packages to Hispanic parents.

RMI Direct Marketing, 42 Old Ridgebury Road, Danbury, CT 06810-5100; 203-798-0448; Fax: 203-778-6130. Web: http://www.rmidirect. com. Distributes sample packs to two million seniors through 7,500 senior citizen centers and children's birthday bags through Circus Pizza.

☐ **Welcome packs**—Besides Welcome Wagon and the sampling programs described above, also watch for welcome packs given out at trade shows, conventions, and conferences. For example, 100,000 welcome packs are given out to attendees at the Organic Gardening Flower Show.

Many magazines and associations pass out welcome packs to new members or subscribers. For example, *Vegetarian Times* sends 120,000 welcome packages every year to new and renewal subscribers.

☐ **Take-one displays**—Your inserts or brochures are placed on racks in high visibility locations. Programs reach families (Good Neighbor), college students (College Take-Ones), travelers (Tourist Take Ones), golfers (MarketSource), and other easily targeted markets.

☐ **Catalog request services**—Feature your catalog in request services provided by Nationwide Shopper Systems or Publisher Inquiry Services. These mailings allow consumers to request catalogs that interest them. These services charge a small fee per catalog ($1.00 to $3.00) to consumers who want to receive them. Your cost, then, is simply to mail out the catalog to requesters.

Publisher Inquiry Services, 951 Broken Sound Parkway, Building 108, P O Box 5057, Boca Raton, FL 33431-0857; 561-998-7929; 800-555-4053; Fax: 561-998-7940. Publishes *World Famous Catalogs*. Patty Sachs of *Celebration Creations* reports that "The P.I. Services program got me into a profit situation." Cedco, a publisher of books and calendars, advertises in this publication on a regular basis.

☐ **Catalog blow-ins or bind-ins**—Advertising postcards or other material are inserted into catalogs that are mailed out from such companies as PC Mall, Swanson Health Products, Gardener's Choice, Performance Bicycle, Gurney Seed, Gander Mountain, and American Entertainment.

☐ **Coupon booklets**—You could offer a cents off coupon for any book published by you. Home Coupon Direct, for instance, mails 40 million coupon books five times a year to consumers across the country.

☐ **Newspaper FSI's**—These full-color *free-standing inserts* feature display ads, coupons, and direct response offers in Sunday newspapers. Remnant space in FSI's is less expensive. Costs include printing and distribution.

Latin-Pak Direct Marketing, 29500-22 Heathercliff Road, Malibu, CA 90265-4189; 310-457-5846; Fax: 310-457-8449. Their FSI programs are delivered eight times per year to 3.2 million Latino households.

Valassis Inserts, 19975 Victor Parkway, Livonia, MI 48152; 313-591-3000; 800-437-0479; Fax: 313-591-7358. They distribute to 56 million households every Sunday.

Want Publicity for Your Book?
Use These Formulas for Creating
Compelling Media Hooks

by Steve Harrison, publisher, Book Marketing Update

Want to get lots of publicity for your book? The first thing you need to do is to forget about your book.

That may sound strange but the fact is the media doesn't really care about your book because they can't interview your book. What they want is a compelling show or article which will immediately capture the attention of their audience. Your hook (also known as an *angle*) instantly tells the producer or journalist why they should interview you. It should be featured prominently in any press releases or pitch letters you send to the media.

Here are some examples of hook formulas you can use to create press materials to promote your own books:

Local angle: Anytown Author Offers Tips to Parents of Kids with ADD
(you should definitely pitch the media where you live)

News tie-in: Presentations Expert Grades President Bush a C+ for the State-of-the-Union Address
(send to media the day after the State of Union)

News tie-in: Business Author Calls General Motors Strategy Flawed
(at this writing General Motors was in news for its problems)

Celebrity Tie-in: Why Celebrities Like Dennis Quaid and Meg Ryan Can't Stay Married
(send to media the day after a celebrity divorce announcement)

Annual Event Tie-in: How to Throw a Killer Super Bowl Party
(send to media a few weeks before the Super Bowl)

Controversial Question: Is Spanking Child Abuse?

On-Air Quiz: Can Your Audience Identify These Famous Failures?

Pop Culture Tie-in: How Realistic Is The TV Show "24"?

Holiday tie-in: Tips for Surviving Your Spouse's Office Holiday Party

What They Don't Tell You: Buying or Selling a House? Here Are Five Things Your Realtor Won't Tell You

Steve Harrison is co-owner of Bradley Communications, which offers many publicity resources for authors and publishers including *Radio-TV Interview Report* (RTIR), *Book Marketing Update, Harrison's Guide to the Top National TV Talk & Interview Shows*, and the National Publicity Summit. Get free info on them at www.BookMarketingUpdate.com/Resources

These angles were excerpted from Steve's article of "25 Formulas for Compelling Media Hooks" which you can get free at http://www.Free AuthorTips.com/HookFormulas.

Chapter 12

How to Sell More Books Via the Internet

*Word of mouth is how we build careers in the romance business,
and our focus in 1998 is to generate word of mouth.
The Internet is an integral part of this strategy.*

Carrie Feron, executive editor, Avon

When I first included an entire chapter on selling books via computer, I still had to make a case for publishers having web sites and selling via the Internet. That is no longer the case. Most publishers now count on 10 to 50% of their income coming from Internet sales. The Internet has had a major effect on smaller publishers because, for once, the playing field between large and small book publishers has been leveled. We can play with the big boys on this field.

A real revolution has happened in the past fifteen years, one that offers publishers much greater reach and impact than any other marketing innovation of the past century. That revolution is the Internet. It is still in its infancy, but the opportunities it offers are limited only by your imagination.

While the Internet continues to be over-hyped, it truly does offer publishers and writers an economical way to reach readers and book buyers around the world with offers that can change by the minute. Never before has there been such a low-cost, flexible, wide-reaching means for testing and carrying out all sorts of promotions.

In 1994, I had to give publishers copies of the ubiquitous AOL disks just to get them to go online and explore the web. I don't have to do that anymore. Most authors and publishers understand the need for a good web site for publicity, book sales, word-of-mouth, and rights sales as well as the ability to sell internationally. The world of the Internet is here to stay.

- More email messages are being sent out today than *snail mail* (letters sent via the post office). The number of emails sent today outnumbers letters by at least one hundred times.

- According to a 1997 ActivMedia survey:

  20% of web sites weren't trying to sell anything
  20% were trying to sell but were doing so unsuccessfully
  30% earned less than $1,000 per month
  20% generated income of $1,000 to $9,000 per month
  10% generated $10,000 or more per month

  Obviously, these numbers are now irrelevant since most web sites are either trying to sell or promote something or are relying on ad income to keep running. Of course, there still are millions of web sites that exist simply because they feature the hobby or passion of the web site owner.

- According to a survey conducted by Netsmart Research, eight out of ten Internet users routinely use the web to research products and services (and report that the web helps them make better buying decisions).

- Where do people go to buy books? Of those people who participated in the Michigan Business School's *HERMES Project*, 14% bought books online, while 25% bought via direct mail or catalogs, and 87% bought at retail bookstores (percentages don't add up because some people used more than one channel).

- The Book Industry Study Group has noted that "Most book buyers already know what book they're going to buy when they enter a bookstore, whereas online book buyers are greater impulse buyers."

- For current statistics on Internet usage, check out the following sites: Forrester Research (http://www.forrester.com), Nielsen Media Research (http://www.nielsenmedia.com), and ClickZ Network (http://www.clickz.com/stats).

12:01 Why You Need to Set Up Your Own Web Site

The following pages will introduce words and concepts that are exclusive to the web. We'll try to define them as we go along, but you will not really understand them until you actually spend a little time web surfing (using *web browser* software such as Firefox, Opera, Safari, or Internet Explorer to search the Internet for information).

If you intend to market your products or services via the Net, you need to learn the basics by using the web regularly. Many of the jobs of creating, maintaining, and marketing a web site can be farmed out, but if you don't understand the way the web works, you won't be able to communicate your needs very well to those who will do the designing and marketing of your web site.

The one fundamental thing you have to do if you want to sell via the Internet is to set up a *web site* (a collection of web pages that fit together as a unit). Such a site gives you a worldwide 24-hour sales and marketing presence. In the beginning of the commercialization of the web, the most successful sites were selling advertising space. In the near future, however, most sites will be built on a direct marketing model where the focus is on selling products or services, generating sales leads, finding partners, cutting distribution costs, and providing customer service.

On the following pages are a few of the ways you can market your books via the Internet. Use this list to help you develop a focus for your site. Be selective. That means, take time to select and prioritize those things you want your web site to do for your books and your company. Then work to design and market your site to accomplish those goals.

Sell your books direct to the consumer.

One of the primary reasons most small publishers should set up a web site is to sell more books. The web offers you (as an author or publisher) direct access to your readers. Use that access to sell books.

- Rodale has set up many web sites to promote its various books and magazines. It discovered that it costs them about $20,000 to launch a web site that duplicates a direct mail package that costs $75,000 to design and test. Their web sites at one point were selling 4,000 books a month. One of their sites, http://www.sexamansguide.com, did well selling a 500-page book for $40.00. Of course, the anonymity of ordering a sex guide online makes this book a perfect book to sell online.

- At a cost of $25,000, Prentice-Hall Direct set up a web site (http://www.phdirect.com) where it sold 400 business and motivational titles. The company also had a presence on its sister division's web site, the Macmillan SuperLibrary, which was receiving 1.2 million hits per day in 1997. 33% of people who used the SuperLibrary site said that the online bookstore was their favorite part of the site.

- In 1998 Simon & Schuster announced that it planned to bring in $100 million in annual online revenues from its SuperSite (http://www.simon-says.com) and its ancillary web sites.

- Troll Communications created the Planet Troll site (http://www.troll.com) which featured a virtual playground as well as an online bookstore. Their web site features animated children's trivia games, creativity programs for writing and drawing, other fun activities, teaching tips, and other interactive applications for children, parents, and teachers. In their online bookstore, users can search a database by age or category of interest and make purchases via a secure online transaction.

- With Open Horizons I've seen telephone sales drop dramatically as most customers now order via our BookMarket.com web site. The cost for serving our customers has thus dropped considerably.

Sell book-related information.

Using appropriate software provided by your web site provider or designer, you can arrange to sell information from your books and deliver it via email or the Net. Your customers can pay directly by entering credit card information or digital cash data into forms on your web site. Once your web site receives the appropriate payment, it releases the information direct to the customer via email, download, or access to additional pages on your site. You could make money twenty-four hours a day without any intervention on your part once the software and web site are set up. Check with your web site provider and/or designer to discuss what options you have in setting up such a system.

- In fall 1997, Atlantis Publishing launched PinkMonkey.com to sell study notes and guides to high school and college students. All sales and distribution of these study guides was handled via the Internet, thus making the notes available to students twenty-four hours a day, seven days a week, at a price much lower than printed study guides.

- BookMarket.com offers data files (such as the *Catalog Sales Data Files* and *Top 700 Independent Bookstores*), miniguides (such as the *Foreign Book Distribution* report, and web courses (such as John Kremer's new Book Marketing MBA programs) to supplement the material found in this book. Anyone seriously interested in selling their books will want this additional information.

- Springhouse charged nurses to access continuing education tests and articles from their web site.

Send customers to distributors or to retail outlets to buy your books.

If you sell books through bookstores, you might want to make it easy for visitors to your site to find local bookstores where they can get your titles. Some publishers choose to feature any bookstore that has placed direct orders with them. Others choose to link their site with a generic site of bookstores, sites such as AllBooks.com, BookZone, or the American Booksellers Association bookstore search site.

- The McGraw-Hill site (http://www.books.mcgraw-hill.com) featured a keyword searchable database of the American Booksellers Association directory of bookstores. In addition, the site made it easy for readers to test drive the complete text versions of select computer books three months *before* publication date. McGraw-Hill expected these advance previews to work like bound galleys in creating advance interest in a book.

- Travel publisher Rough Guides was the first to place an entire book online with complete and free access. Their 1100-page *Rough Guide USA* book still draws lots of page views. More important, however, is the fact that the next edition of the book had a threefold increase in sales compared to the previous edition.

- Not only does the web site of Moon Publications feature book lists and reviews as well as articles from their *Travel Matters* newsletter, but it also features the addresses of hundreds of travel bookstores which carry Moon travel handbooks.

- The web site of religious publisher Baker Book House (http://www. bakerbooks.com) provides a title search engine, new titles, author guidelines, company history, special sales information, a calendar of author speaking events, newsletters, bestseller info as well as links to the search engines at the American Booksellers Association and the Christian Booksellers Association.

- The web site of Chronicle Books (http://www.chronbooks.com) also features new titles, author guidelines, and a link to the ABA search engine.

Expose your books and authors to millions worldwide.

The Internet allows you to promote your books to millions of potential customers around the world. Or, if you like, you can target a local audience by participating in one of the many city-specific sites now forming on the Net (most sponsored by local newspapers).

- Soon after the Online Bookstore published Bernice Chesler's *Bed & Breakfast in New England* online, the book made the *Boston Globe*'s bestseller list. The online version gave the book added visibility that helped the book over the sales hump.

- Frederick Warne set up a site devoted to Peter Rabbit (http://www.peter-rabbit.com) that features books and licensed merchandise for sale, listings of exhibitions and performances, biographical info on the author, newsletters, faqs, and interactive games.

- Even in a slow month, the home page of Insider's Guides gets at least a million hits.

Many companies and authors are now creating sites for individual titles. Here are a few books and authors who have received this special treatment:

- *Nimitz Class* by Patrick Robinson, published by HarperCollins—http://www.nimitzclass.com. The publisher had a *Sink the Nimitz* game designed for the web site, which began getting thousands of hits in the first week. The book quickly hit the bestseller lists. The major publishers, however, eventually abandon many of these great sites, including this one.

- Random House set up the Seussville site (http://www.seussville.com) to highlight Dr. Seuss and his books. Even as early as 1996, the site was getting half a million hits each month.

- Author Nancy Friday had her own web site (http://www.nancyfriday.com) where she invited discussion of the relationships between gender, power, beauty, and sexuality. Her site also offered forums, polls, and links to online bookstores that sell her books.

- John Wiley set up separate web sites to support Neil Salkind's *The On-line Epicure* as well as Wayne Gisslen's *Professional Cooking*. Among other things, each site featured recipes, a Q&A forum, and reviews.

Serialize your book.

One of the ways to expose your book to people on the net is piece by piece. Keep them coming back for more. If your book is highly interesting, widely anticipated, or just plain good, it should grab the attention of many visitors who will come back week after week to read more. Some of those people will, of course, become impatient waiting for the entire book to be serialized. Their only option, then, is to buy your book. Be sure to make it easy for them to do that.

- Times Books partnered with the Microsoft Network to serialize Fred Goodman's *The Mansion on the Hill* on MSN's Music Central. Anyone on the Internet could read a synopsis of the book, artist biographies, song clips, and interview sound bites. Subscribers to MSN received the full serialization as well as additional enhanced content.

- Peterson Guides serialized Kenn Kaufman's *Kingbird Highway* on its site (http://www.petersononline.com), posting additional chapters every other Friday.

- Jonathan Guttenberg, director of new media at Bantam Doubleday Dell, once pointed out that "one of the things people like most about our web site is the ability to sample the book."

- One key group of people that will always benefit from serialization are unknown poets and novelists. By allowing readers to sample your work for free, you give them a risk-free way to decide if they want to buy your book. I would never publish a novel by an unknown author without giving readers a complete opportunity to sample the book as fully as they need to. For poetry books, give Internet visitors the opportunity to hear poets reading their poems.

Set up a chat area.

To build greater rapport between your authors and your customers, spon-sor online discussion groups, chat areas, or support groups for your books and authors. Also explore the new software programs that allow you to pro-vide voice support as well via the Net. Note that some of these programs al-low your customer service reps to interact with customers via text chat, Internet telephony, or two-line interaction.

- For Kenn Kaufman's *Kingbird Highway*, Peterson Online allowed read-ers to chat directly with Kaufman on its Ask the Experts feature.

- At their free consumer sites devoted to *Animorphs, Magic School Bus*, and other series, Scholastic allows visitors to join online fan clubs where visitors can swap ideas, download pictures, and hear the latest news.

- Simon & Schuster's web site included bulletin boards for Betty Eadie, *Star Trek* and others. It also featured monthly moderated reading groups.

- Broadway Books set up a site for *The Fourth Turning* by Neil Howe and William Strauss (http://www.fourthturning.com). The book describes a series of historic cycles, or turnings, that characterize and predict socio-cultural patterns among U.S. generational age groups. The web site, with its discussion forums and monthly author columns, became, according to the publisher, "a virtual town hall meeting on our nation's future." 300,000 page views were logged during the first three weeks. After ten years, the site is still active.

- You can host a live interactive event using Live Meeting. You can register for a 14-dfay free trial at http://www.livemeeting.com.

- If you aren't ready to set up your own chat areas, you can have your authors participate in discussions via various online chat groups or via email using Yahoo Groups or similar sites.

Sell advertising on your pages to other companies.

Currently about 1,000 sites (out of billions) carry significant amounts of advertising (other than Google AdSense). One percent of the sites get ninety percent of the advertising dollars being spent on the Internet. According to Jupiter Communications, most of that advertising revenue will continue to remain with a few large sites. What this means for most publishers is that if you plan to make money on your web site via advertising sales, you will have to draw a crowd to your site. While 10,000 hits per month will get you started, you won't get much income from ad sales until your hits per month are in the millions.

- In 1997, Random House invited bookstores to advertise on the Books@ Random site. Ad packages could be paid with Random House co-op dollars. Whether a store advertised or not, the site continued to list booksellers for free in its store locator directory. HarperCollins, Simon & Schuster, and TimeWarner also sell advertising on their sites.

- *Arthur Frommer's Outspoken Encyclopedia of Travel* web site earned 75% of its revenues from advertisers such as United Airlines and Hilton.

- Some authors who have set up blogs report earning several hundred dollars a month from Google AdSense clickthroughs.

Create a subscription site.

You can create exclusive content on your site that people can access only if they subscribe to the additional service.

- *Money* magazine had two sites. The first site, Money.com, offered plenty of information and advice for free. Money.com Plus, on the other hand, was a subscription-based personal finance web site. It offered expanded use of the latest interactive technology to help users manage their finances and make investments online. Services included email alerts, portfolio tracking, stock finders, historical graphs of stocks, fund indices, a Q&A forum, financial calculators, and a searchable library of *Money* back issues.

- Hoover's Inc., publishers of proprietary information on 11,000 U.S. companies, generated 60% of its online revenues from advertising and 40% from subscriptions. "We're big believers of offering free, high-quality information supported by advertising, with deeper, more robust information available on a subscription basis," said CEO Patrick Spain. "Neither revenue model," he added, "would be enough by itself, but together, we're profitable." Hoover's charged $10 per month for unlimited access and had several thousand subscribers.

- Houghton Mifflin partnered with the PoliticsNow web site to create a subscription-based site devoted to transforming the way political science was taught. Students who owned Houghton Mifflin textbooks could access the PoliticsNow Classroom site for $15.00 per semester; those students without had to pay $25.00 per semester. The PoliticsNow site has since been dismantled by its partners.

- Besides their free consumer sites devoted to *Goosebumps* and other series, Scholastic set up the first subscription-based web site for teachers and students, the Scholastic Network.

Set up a pay-per-view section.

Set up a section of you site where people have to pay per use to view or download the information you have to sell. Such a service offers an alternative to those people who are not ready to commit to a subscription or for those who only want one piece of information from your site.

Provide customer support via your web site.

You can cut your customer support expenses by providing some support functions via your web site. According to *Executive Insights*, companies that are connected to their customers via their web sites are finding cost savings of 50% to 90% in sales, customer support, distribution, and other areas.

Federal Express, for example, allows customers to track their shipments directly. Customers get their information more quickly than via a phone call, and FedEx saves $3.00 that would have been spent if they had to answer the phone. Similarly, when Hewlett-Packard made their printer driver library available on their web site, 1.2 million people downloaded drivers in the first two months. Previously, customers called HP two million times a month for new print drivers. Since those calls cost HP $14.00 each, HP saved $8 million per month by providing easy access to their printer drivers.

- In 1997, HarperCollins launched a web-based order tracking system that allowed wholesale and retail customers with passwords to get timely information about the shipping status of their book orders.

- Houghton Mifflin set up the Education Place web site (http://www.edu place.com) to offer a wide variety of resource material for teachers and students. The site is linked to Houghton Mifflin's School Direct online bookstore (http://www.schooldirect.com).

Create contests and customer loyalty programs.

Create loyalty programs, contests, or other reasons to keep customers or browsers coming back to you. Several years ago Bad Dog Press offered free stuff to their 50,000th visitor. Certainly some people, in hopes of winning, came back to visit the site on a regular basis. Bad Dog also ran a *Wacky Uses of WD-40* contest.

Carry out publicity campaigns via the Internet.

There are many ways you can use the Internet to carry out publicity programs and create word-of-mouth for your books. Just having a web site is enough to draw the attention of media, since many reporters and producers use the web to locate authors or experts who can comment on breaking news stories. Indeed, the producers of many radio and television shows (including *Oprah*) already cruise the web to find potential guests.

Here are a few other things you can do via the Internet to publicize your authors and books: distribute news releases electronically, respond via email to media inquiries, track news and issues via computer news sources, research media, and provide background information.

- To promote Tom Clancy's eighth Jack Ryan novel, *Executive Orders*, Putnam set up a web site that featured the opportunity to vote for Clinton, Dole, or Ryan for president in 1996. While Clinton won the real election, Ryan ran away with the Putnam election.

- Planetary Publications had excellent responses from journalists who browsed their site. A writer from *Cosmopolitan* asked to feature some of the stress-related information from one of their books. ABC's *Prime Time Live*, which contacted them via their web pages, planned to do a segment using their information.

- Most author and publisher web sites now include full media kits on their web sites, with author bios, photos, background releases, and so on.

Build your customer lists.

Build email lists of customers that you can come back to with new products or services. There are a number of ways that you can capture the names, addresses, phone numbers, and/or email addresses of people who visit your site. Among other techniques, you can use guest books and email newsletters. These will be discussed in more detail later in this chapter.

- Open Horizons encourages visitors to its BookMarket.com web site to sign up for John Kremer's free *Book Marketing Tip of the Week* email newsletter. While we do not gather any names or addresses, we are able to send promotional messages to these subscribers along with the regular editorial content of the newsletter. The weekly ezine has become a great way to introduce new products and seminars to our key customers.

- Prentice Hall Direct worked to add email addresses and fax numbers to its 3.5 million-name customer database.

Offer your free catalog on site.

Put your catalog on your web site with complete information on how consumers can order any book. Or allow people to request your catalog.

- Soda Creek Press, publishers of the *Mysteries by Mail* and *Manderley* catalogs, experienced a 4% sales conversion rate on catalogs requested via their web site versus a less than 2% sales conversion rate from their direct mail campaigns. Sadly, this company has now closed.

- HarperCollins has a 10,000 title searchable database, audio clips, games, excerpts, listservs, and more to provide browsers with enough information about their titles to enable customers to make a buying decision.

- Bantam Doubleday Dell provides a downloadable version of their browsable catalog. The downloadable version allows online booksellers to import title listings and book cover images to their sites to make it easier to sell BDD books.

Survey your customers.

Use your web site to ask your customers questions. You can set up a survey page on your site or make it easy for customers to reply by email. As an alternative you can use a service such as Beach Tech (http://www.beachtech.com), which provides email and web form-based surveys and tabulation for other companies.

- As part of its SimonSays site, Simon & Schuster includes reader ratings and reviews for all its titles.

- In a survey of visitors to its site, Random House discovered that users like finding out more about authors; in fact, the more they find out about a book and its author, the more likely they are to buy the book. "Readers want to feel closer to their favorite authors," they noted. "We can provide a depth of information about a writer you could never get from a book jacket or an ad or even a television interview,"

- At his New Entrepreneur web site, Roger Parker features a *What's Your Blog Marketing IQ?* quiz. The quiz quickly establishes a need for the information Roger has to offer on his web site, including his *Relationship Marketing* book.

Collect information from visitors.

You can use your site to gather information from visitors that you can use in marketing your books or in creating new books.

- Grace Housholder uses the web site for her humor book, *The Funny Things Kids Say Will Brighten Any Day* (http://www.funnykids.com), to sell books, provide information about organ donation, and collect funny kid stories for future books.

- Jay Conrad Levinson, author of the *Guerrilla Marketing* series, partnered with Microsoft to publish his *America at Work* in monthly installments in their small business site (http://www.microsoft.com/smallbiz). As part of these installments, Levinson fielded questions and then used the feedback to improve the final version of the book.

Set up a registry service.

If you have books appropriate for gift giving, you might want to set up a registry service for weddings, birthdays, or holiday giving. As an alternative, you could offer gift certificates.

Offer coupons.

Most companies have been reluctant to offer coupons via the Internet because web coupons can be changed (either made for a higher price or a later expiration date) and printed out at will. To keep this from happening, Interactive Coupon Network launched an online couponing service (http://www.coolsavings.com) where images can't be manipulated before printing.

Provide information.

Provide related background information that draws potential customers to your site. Establish your site as the place to come to for information in your area of expertise. As Kathleen Hammond, president of Hammond, once noted, "Unless you have the capability for online delivery, you're in trouble. Consumers want and need customized products."

- Open Horizon's Bookmarket site is designed to provide plenty of information for any author or publisher looking to sell more books. Among other services, we provide lists of book printers, POD services, publicity services, cover designers, catalog/magazine printers, bookstore lists on the web, mailing list providers, telemarketers, newspaper book reviewers, fulfillment companies, book clubs, and much more. In addition, we feature hundreds of book editors of interest to writers. We update 20 to 30 pages on the site every week.

- Para Publishing, publishers of *The Self-Publishing Manual*, features more than 400 pages of information, resources, and help for authors and publishers. Check out http://www.parapublishing.com.

- Attorney Gregory Siskind offered a thousand pages of government forms and other details on immigration law. Since setting up his web site, his practice expanded to six states. Two-thirds of his business came from his web site and monthly email newsletter.

- Updated daily, Zondervan's web site features a calendar of events, links to religion news sites, audio highlights, weekly and monthly columns by a number of its authors, the monthly Zondervan Press Syndicate, author interviews, ad slicks for retailers, and more. As part of their site, they posted a model letter for people to discuss doctor-assisted suicide.

- Simon & Schuster's web site for Frommers Outspoken Encyclopedia of Travel features 6,000 pages of bargain travel information and a daily on-line newsletter with information on more than 200 cities.

- Fielding's has placed two of its books, *Fielding's Guide to the World's Most Dangerous Places* and *Fielding's Guide to Worldwide Cruises*, on-line in a searchable database format. Their *Dangerous Places* book has become their most successful book.

- National Academy Press, the publishing arm of the National Academy of Sciences, is the only major publisher to offer full-text versions of its entire line of books. They currently have 5,000 titles online. Check out their site at http://www.nap.edu.

- Bantam Doubleday launched the Bold Type site (http://www.boldtype.com) to feature fiction and narrative nonfiction from noted authors. They encouraged visitors to forward, print out, or freely distribute copies of material from the site. The site is now an independent book review site.

- Random House set up a separate Teachers Resource Center (http://www.randomehouse.com/teachers) to provide teachers with free information on their books and authors. The site provides author bios, interviews with authors, dozens of teacher's guides, and an index of books by theme, discipline, author, and grade level.

Custom print books sold off the web.

With the advent of on-demand printing, it is now possible for someone to order a book online and to receive a customized print copy within days of placing their order. Each book in the future could be created by your customers as they select which chapters they want in their individualized books.

In addition to offering the full text of 5,000 titles online, National Academy Press allows Internet users to order a book or an excerpt online and receive a customized print version in a few days. Within a year of posting the first 1,700 titles, their sales increased by 17%.

Create downloadable e-books.

With standard e-book formats and shopping cart systems, it's now possible to allow visitors to your web site to download your books for instant gratification. Downloads can feature entire books, shorter reports such as the *50 Creative Ways to Market Your Books*, databases such as the *Top 700 Independent Books*, audiobooks, seminars, audio seminars, custom courses, correspondence courses, and much more.

Provide updates.

Updates are especially useful if you sell books, software, or other information. Many software companies allow buyers to download updates and fixes for free for the first year and for a small fee afterwards.

- Open Horizons has set up special update pages on our BookMarket.com web site to allow readers of this book to have the most current address for any company whose address is mentioned in this edition. To check on current addresses, go to http://www.bookmarket.com/1001add.html. Never assume that any address given in any book is up-to-date. The moment a book is published, some addresses will already have changed.

- International Media Communications, publishers of *The Business Travel Adviser for the European Union*, provided a password to everyone who bought the book. The password allowed the purchaser to access the book's web site which provided updated information as well as supplemental data such as train schedules, weather, restaurant reviews, and entrée prices.

- Penguin's Time Out series of travel books, based on the *TimeOut* magazines, is supplemented with an online guide (http://www.timeout.co.uk) to weekly events taking place in each city highlighted in the series.

Publish a newsletter or blog.

Publish an online newsletter or other update service to keep customers, media, and retailers up to date on your authors, books, and company. Open Horizons publishes the weekly email newsletter, *John Kremer's Marketing Tip of the Week*, which is reposted to BookMarket.com to make it available to anyone on the web. I also write several blogs which are hosted at other web sites (Publishers Marketplace and OpenHorizons.blogspot.com). I doubt there's an active web site now that doesn't offer at least one free newsletter.

As an alternative, you can provide space on your web site for your customers to set up their own blogs. For example, Rough Guides offers their readers space on their web site to post their travel thoughts and experiences in a journal. They make it very easy for any individual to set up a travel blog at http://travel.roughguides.com/planning/journalhome.html.

Join associate sales programs.

Join associate sales or referral programs to generate income for your site. Many retail sites offer associate programs where they pay you for any referrals you make to their site (or pay you a percentage of any sales that come as a result of your referral). The natural fit for publishing sites are those associate sales programs offered by Amazon.com, Powells.com, and BookSense.

Also check out referral programs offered by other retailers, for example, music retailers, sports retailers, travel sites (Frommer's, for example, gets a commission for each booking it refers to Travelocity), or gourmet shops. Some of these sites are listed on the 101 Referrals page of the BookMarket site at http:// www.bookmarket.com/top101.html.

Some of the best associate programs to get involved with are those that offer major dollars for any referral or sale. That usually requires a high-priced service or product such as a seminar, tape set, software program, or similar item. Such associate sales have contributed many thousands of dollars in sales each month to Open Horizons.

Sell access to your material.

You can sell, license, or provide access to your copyrighted material to other sites. This licensing of content could, ultimately, become the most productive ways for book publishers and authors to profit from the Internet.

- Time Inc. offers financial service companies the opportunity to purchase bulk access licenses to Money.com Plus which the companies can then give as an added value premium to their clients.

- The University of Illinois Press sold excerpt rights and an author profile for Susan Cayleff's *Life and Legend of Babe Didrikson Zaharias* to Golfweb, the world's leading web site on golf.

- Foghorn Press licensed material from its recreation titles to Pacific Bell Interactive Media for its At Hand web site. Among Foghorn's guidebooks, the following were featured at the At Hand site: *California Golf, California Camping, California Beaches*, and others. The At Hand site also featured how-to tips from Foghorn authors.

- Besides its own web site, Rough Guides also had a site at HotWired. Their partnership with HotWired earned them $100,000 in shared advertising revenues and made their name better known.

- Time Inc. bought the web rights to Dr. Andrew Weil's Ask Dr. Weil web site which had been part of HotWired's site. Weil's site averages more than a million hits every month. Here is a case of an author who has created a brand name web site that draws visitors and publishers alike.

- Joan Price, author of *Joan Price Says: Yes, You Can Get in Shape*, partnered with FitnessLink. In return for FitnessLink hosting and maintaining her web site, she wrote a monthly column for them. Her columns, for the most part, were adapted from her book.

- Fodor's licensed the content of its Mobil Travel Guides to MapQuest, an interactive mapping web site.

- The *New York Times* Women's Health site (http://www.nytimes.com/women) included licensed material from *The New Our Bodies Ourselves* and *The Harvard Guide to Women's Health*.

- Richard Nelson Bolles, author of *What Color Is Your Parachute?*, signed a contract with the *Washington Post* to provide his job-hunting expertise to the their online site (http://www.washingtonpost.com/para-chute). His Job Hunting Online section provided information on how to use the Internet to find a job, columns by Bolles, discussion areas, as well as Bolles's picks of the most useful career-related sites on the web.

- Hoover's licensed its *Hoover's Company Profiles* of major public and private companies to dozens of online services, including America Online, Reuters, and OneSource. In addition, all the information is on their web site as well. Electronic publishing revenues became the key source of income for Hoover's starting in 1997 (in contrast to a 50/50 split with print in 1996).

Upload your annual report.

IBM featured its annual report on its web site for many years. Among other things, their web site annual report allowed investors to compare five years of IBM's performance on more than a dozen financials including net earnings and total revenue. Book publishers who are incorporated could profit from doing the same with their annual reports.

12:02 How to Set Up Your Own Web Site

In setting up your web site, be sure to create one that has its own distinct identity. That means that you should get your own domain name rather than put your service solely on a shopping mall or online service. A domain name makes it easy for people to find you. Open Horizon's domain name, for example, is *bookmarket.com*. Here are a few more reasons why you should have your own domain name:

☐ It protects your trademark or company name. Otherwise, another company or similar product could take a domain name that others would think of as yours. For example, in the beginning days of the web, a free-lance writer registered the domain name mcdonalds.com. It cost McDonalds a lot of time and money to get that domain name back for their own use. Simon & Schuster was luckier. When they wanted to register Simonsays.com, they found that someone had already claimed the name just ten days earlier. He, however, sold them the name for a nominal fee and some free books.

☐ Most people, when searching for a company or product, first try to search for the company by typing in www.yourcompany.com or www.yourproduct.com.

☐ Having your own domain name says that you are big enough to merit your own domain. It allows you to stand out much more than you would in a combined web site or mall.

☐ You can switch service providers easily since you take your domain name with you regardless of who is providing the actual server where your site is hosted. For small businesses, it doesn't pay to host your own site on an in-house computer (since the cost of hardware, software, and support is high). Instead, select a host service that can provide you with a secure and fast connection to the web as well as other services you might require to make your site operational. Don't try to save money by using a low-powered Web host.

☐ Your own domain name allows you to create a short memorable name that people will remember, that is easy for you to repeat over the phone, and that will fit on your business card.

☐ Domain names can be worth a lot of money. Early in 1997, Mecklermedia paid The Internet Company more than $100,000 for the Internet. com domain name. Several months later, a Texas company bought the domain name business.com for $150,000, the highest price yet paid for an Internet domain name.

☐ When creating a web site, reserve multiple names. Indeed, register separate web names (and perhaps design separate web sites) for your company, your major book titles, your major authors, and your key subject areas (or key terms in those areas). Ideally, for example, I should have OpenHorizons.com and 1001Ways.com as well as BookMarket.com. I haven't gotten those names, but I do have JohnKremer.com as well as JohnKremer.org and JohnKremer.net to protect my name. There's nothing worse than having someone else own your name.

To reserve a domain name, go to GoDaddy.com, OOOdomains.com, or 1and1.net. The cost is under $10.00. Try to get the .com URL address for your web site, since that's the defacto default in the world of the Internet. Other domain name extensions, such as .net, .org, .info, etc. can be useful when the .com is not available and is not part of a brand you are building.

For hosting your site, contact the company that provides your current Internet service. Most such companies also provide hosting services. For example, EarthLink, one of the largest Internet service providers, also provides web hosting with your unique domain name. You can also set up sites at Yahoo, Google, and other major sites.

For a low-cost hosting service, try 1and1.com. I've been using them for thirty of my sites, including HotTimesCoolPlaces.com, NovelBestsellers.com, PromotingYourBooks.com, JohnKremerSentMe.com, AllBooksFree.com, Book Acceleration.com, BestsellerGhostwriter.com, SelfPublishingHallofFame.com, BookMarketingBestsellers.com, and CelebrateToday.com.

12:03 How to Design Your Web Site

Once you have a domain name registered and have arranged for a hosting service, you then need to start designing your web site. You have three basic options on how your web site can be designed. They are::

1. Basic Information Site — Such a site features information about your books (a catalog), a way to order (a shopping cart), and a means for visitors to get updated information on new books or promotions (a newsletter). Such a site might also include biographies of authors, sample pages from books, and a few other pages. The site might also include separate information sections for bookstores, media, teachers, or other targeted audiences. Many book publisher and author sites fit into this category. The main disadvantage of such a site is finding ways to entice web users to come back.

2. One-Page Direct Sales Site — Such sites are essentially a long sales letter with few or no other links other than the option to buy. These sites can be very effective for higher priced books or packages (book, tapes, and other items). To be effective, you need lots of links to your site, active affiliates who sent customers to your site, and other offline promotions to keep people coming to visit. The drawback to such a site is that there is little reason for a person to revisit the page if they decided not to buy the first time.

3. Interactive Content-Rich Site — These sites serve web users by providing reasons for the users to come back again and again to interact with other visitors, read articles, join in discussions, comment on a blog, play games, do puzzles, answer surveys, do research, and give feedback. As users come back more often, they exposed to more opportunities to make a decision to buy your books, both backlist and frontlist. The BookMarket.com web site, with its updated pages on printers, PR services, editors, POD services, etc., is an example of such a site. Many web sites designed to reach kids include many interactive games and other activities. News and blog sites with their constantly updated pages are another example.

The main disadvantage of such sites is that they take time and money to design and keep up-to-date. Plus, they can distract users from buying books (if not designed properly). But they will rank high in most search engines, almost always higher than the basic sites or one-page sales sites.

Here are some tips on how to go about designing an effective site, regardless of which of the above formats you choose to use:

☐ **Take a look at other web sites**. Check out which ones you like the best. What features make the site easy for you to use? What content appeals to you? What designs do you like best. Select the best elements of your favorite sites and incorporate those features into your site.

☐ **You can create the site yourself using software** such as *Microsoft Frontpage* or you can hire someone who has experience designing and creating such sites. Before you hire someone, check out the sites they've already created. Make sure they can handle the kinds of features you want to incorporate into your site (shopping cart, database searches, easy and frequent updates, or whatever else you want).

☐ **Start slowly.** Keep it simple in the beginning. You can take time to build and revise your site. There is no rush to have everything perfect from the start. Start with the basics. You can add shopping carts and database wizards later.

☐ **Place an emphasis on content.** Provide good, usable content that is updated on a regular basis. Your books should provide you with plenty of content.

☐ **Give away some freebies.** You can provide any level of content for free, from simple pages of information to downloadable files packed with data or graphics. Jelly Belly Online (http://www.jellybelly.com), for instance, offered a free sample of Jelly Belly jelly beans to the first 500 visitors each day who filled out a survey form. Of course, the only way people could get the samples in this case was to provide their names and addresses. According to one reporter, the 500 free samples were already given out by 9:00 a.m. on they day he visited the site!

☐ **Make it easy for people to get around your site.** Especially make it easy for them to get to your home page and site map (if you have one). That's easy to do: Just provide links to your home page and site map on every page in your site.

☐ **Maintain your image.** Don't try to create an image that is different from your regular real world image. Use the web as an adjunct to your other marketing and promotion.

☐ **Avoid using too many graphical elements**, animation, sound, or other whiz-bang elements that slow down the appearance of your web site. Remember that many users still have slow connections as well as little patience. *Microsoft Frontpage* tells you how long a page will take to load on a 28.8 modem. Keep that time under a minute if possible.

☐ **People want to be entertained.** What causes people to come back for return visits? According to IntelliQuest, 56% return to entertaining sites, 54% like attention grabbing sites, 53% extremely useful content, 45% information tailored to their needs, 39% thought-provoking content, 39% visually appealing sites, 38% imaginative sites, and 36% highly interactive sites.

☐ **Make your site graphically pleasing.** What do web site designers recommend? Among other page design elements, they suggest: Make everything as big as possible. Don't use a lot of text. Use lots of white space and margins. Don't make people scroll (whenever possible).

☐ **Make it Web TV friendly.** Since it is possible that many people in the future will be surfing the Internet via TV sets, PDAs, or cell phones, where scrolling won't be as easy, think about designing your site to match the size and shape of a television screen or, at least, keep the page sizes small. In this case, use more graphics than text. Use larger fonts. Use fewer links, thus allowing for a more linear presentation.

☐ **Provide people with a way to register with your site** to receive updates or further information from your company. You can set up an email newsletter for this purpose. Most site providers can set up and maintain an automatic sign-up system for the newsletter that allows users to sign up without your intervention and allows you to send out a newsletter or sales message to all people on the list with one email message.

☐ **Make your web site friendlier for sight-impaired readers.** As a start, offer a text-only version. For more info on making your web site more accessible to the sight-impaired, check out the Trace R&D Center at http://www.trace.wisc.edu/world/web/index.html.

☐ **If you have a large potential market overseas, design your site with certain pages that are written in the language** or languages of your target audience. At the minimum, make your offer, information page, and order form available in other languages. There are some web resources that make it easier for you to translate certain pages into other languages. If you do set up foreign language pages, be sure to register your site with foreign-language search engines.

☐ **You can set up your web site so people can enter your site from any of a number of pages on your site.** For instance, you could have a home page where most people would enter your site. But you might also have a bookstore, library, events listing, directory, chat area, or detailed article that would attract many first-time viewers who would go on to view other parts of your site. In fact, if you have a site that could attract a number of different special interest groups, you might set up entrance pages for each group. For instance, Open Horizon's BookMarket web site attracts writers to its book editor pages (the site ranks #1 in Google for sports book editors, first novel editors, etc.). Once visitors land at one of these pages, they have access to the entire web site. If someone is interested in book editors, they will soon be interest in book marketing.

☐ **Add pages to your site.** The more pages you have in your site, the more likely it is that your site—or at least some part of it—will be picked up by the Internet search engines (described later). Since most people find out about a site by doing searches on these engines, the more pages you have, the more visitors you are likely to attract.

☐ **Be sure to title your home page** with a headline that will attract the most viewers to your web site. Many search engines use the title as one of their main ways of selecting sites to show to requesters. The first paragraph of text after your title is also often used by search engines to rank listings, so be sure your first paragraph contains key words about the contents of your site. As a matter of practice, each page on your web site should follow similar principles.

☐ **Use metatags.** To increase your rankings in some search engines, you can also add metatags at the top of your HTML page (*html* is the code language for designing web pages). An example of a metatag would be the following: <meta tags="key words" Content="book, books, publisher, publishers, publishing, marketing, sales, advertising, publicity, promotion, writing, authors, directory">. This is one of the metatags on Open Horizon's home page. It tells search engines some of the key words that a person might use to search for the information on Open Horizon's bookmarket.com site. These metatags do not show up on any home page viewed by a web browser, but can be looked at if you open the source code in your web browser. Ask a friend to help you with this if you are not familiar with using your web browser to view source code.

☐ **Somewhere on your site, include a link page** to other relevant sites. Also add links to relevant sites wherever appropriate on your site. Web surfers love sites with lots of links and might return to your site often just to make use of your links. Also some of the search engines rank web sites by the number of links they have to other sites (and the number of other sites that have links to it).

☐ **Accept credit cards.** If you plan to take orders via your web site, be sure to list that you accept credit cards since these are the main way people are currently paying for things bought on the web. Plus it makes your product more accessible to people overseas.

☐ **Give other payment options.** For example, provide a certifiably secure site so people feel safe leaving their credit card information. Also accept mini-payments via PayPal or other such digital payment services.

☐ **Make it easy for people to order.** Don't just provide your email address or an order form on your site. Also include your toll-free number, street address, and fax number. One site started with only a web order form. When it added other ordering options, its sales volume doubled.

☐ **Provide a shopping cart** such as those provided by Amazon.com and other retail sites. Shopping carts are especially valuable if you have multiple items for sale. Your Internet service provider or site designer should be able to help you put together a shopping cart.

☐ **Bookmark it.** On your home page, include the words, "Make this page a bookmark." This tells people to make your site one that they will come back to again. Don't assume that they will bookmark your site on their own. Make it clear why they should bookmark your site (to get updates, discover the latest ideas, to enter on-going contests or surveys, etc.).

☐ **Avoid frame-based sites.** Many surfers hate web sites that feature frames, but a more important reason to avoid frames is that they negatively affect your site's rating on many search engines (since some search engines ignore anything in frames).

☐ **Provide useful information on your site.** When Pfizer wanted to promote Zyrtec, a new allergy medication, on their web site, they designed an interactive house on the web where allergy sufferers could find out all the latest information on how to allergy-proof each room of their houses, including how to clean drapes, bathe pets, and use air filters. In addition, they worked with the National Allergy Bureau to include updates on pollen counts for various parts of the country. Pfizer even created a separate domain name for this part of their site. Now allergy doctors are giving out http://www.allergyinfo.com to all their patients!

☐ **Add games to your site.** Games are proven tools that are known to increase web site traffic and repeat visits. As Michael Simon, president of E-Pub Inc. recently observed, "Gaming is shaping up to possibly become the killer app that the web has been seeking." If you cannot afford fancy arcade-style games, you can set up simpler contests, trivia games, puzzles, crosswords, or other activities that encourage people to come back again and again.

☐ **Add chat areas to your site.** According to a recent *Business Week* article, adding a chat area can increase web site traffic by 50%.

12:04 30 Ways to Market Your Web Site and Books

With several billion web sites, it takes something to stand out. Given that most users visit about twenty web pages per day, it would take one person several lifetimes to visit just the home page of every site and many, many lifetimes to visit every page. Currently, 1,000 sites account for half the traffic on the web. How, then, can you make your site one of those top 1,000?

The old rule, "If you build a better mousetrap, people will beat a path to your door," simply does not apply to web sites. Once you build your web site, you must market it. Now that might seem rather silly since I have been recommending that you build a web site as a way of marketing your books —and now I'm telling you that you will have to market your new marketing tool. So why go through all the trouble of setting up a web site?

Here are four good reasons: 1) To keep up with the Joneses (you need to keep up with your competition or lose business to them). 2) A web site will allow you to reach an audience you are not currently reaching via any other means, especially a worldwide audience. 3) Much of the marketing for your web site must occur at the beginning. Once you have done the basics, your ongoing web marketing doesn't have to require a lot of extra time. 4) Every little action you take to market your web site will also be working to market your book. Here, then, are thirty ways you can market your web site:

1. Add your email address and URL.

First, add your email address and web site URL to your business card, letterhead, catalogs, brochures, advertisements, packaging, and other marketing materials. Your URL (universal resource locator) is your web site address. Besides adding your email and URL to your marketing materials, include them in your book and every letter you send out.

2. Add a signature to your email messages and newsgroup postings.

One of the best ways to get people to visit your site is to feature your site in the your email signature. Keep your signature less than six lines. Be sure to include your name, email address, web site URL, and the names or features of one or two of your products or services. Here is a great email signature, which I'm sure attracts a lot of people to her web site. I checked out her web site and found the report and ezine useful:

Marisa D'Vari Author / Writer / Speaker
Free 78 page special report: How to Attract Celebrity Status with the Free Media when you subscribe to free, twice-monthly publicity tip ezine.
See sample at http://www.deg.com/ESS/ezine.htm

Janet Hardy, publisher of Greenery Press, sends frequent informative posts to relevant newsgroups and mailing lists. With every post, she adds her .sig file (signature) at the end. As a result she gets a dozen inquiries each day and sells many books.

Jacques Werth, author of *High Probability Selling*, generated about $400 in orders per month from posting notes and his signature on a few lists.

3. Submit your web site to the major search engines.

Search engines are large databases where most web surfers go to when they want to research a new topic. They are the major way that most people will find out about your site. Here are the five major search engines where you should list your site: Google (42% of searches), Yahoo (28%), MSN Search (14%), AskJeeves (6%), and AOL (8%). Amazon recently launched a search engine (A9.com) that might grow into a major search engine. And Microsoft will launch a new search engine at Live.com. Of the seven major search engines I featured in 1998, only Yahoo still exists as a major site.

Web search engines take anywhere from a few minutes to four weeks to list your site's home page and up to six additional weeks to list the rest of the pages on your web site (if they go beyond the first page). In the above section on designing your web site, we listed some design elements you can use to increase your rank in these search engine listings (such as titles, metatags, links, key words at the beginning of your site, and the frequency of changes at your site). Since search engines can list hundreds of thousands of pages in response to one query, it is important that you do everything possible to increase your ranking (few people will look at pages beyond the first ten to thirty listed in any web search). For more information on designing your web page for search engines, check out the Search Engine Watch web site at http://searchenginewatch.com.

A month after you make your submissions to these search engines, you might want to review how your site ranks by the key words people might use to search for your site. To do this, go to Rank This! (http://www.rank this.com). This site allows you to check search engines to see how you rank. Plus the site has useful information on how to increaase your rank.

Also go to each major search engine on your own and see how your site ranks for the top five or ten keywords you think people would use to find your web site. If you can't find your web site in the first fifty listings, you have work to do. But now you'll have the data to help you do that work because, in searching for your site's rank, you will have gathered a list of sites which are getting better rankings. Check out those sites and try to figure out why they are getting higher rankings. Then change your pages accordingly.

4. Submit your web site to the subject-specific search engines.

To discover industry-specific search engines and directories, check out Internet Sleuth (http://www.isleuth.com), which is a search engine of search engines. It will provide you with a list of specific search engines where you can submit your site. Also search on "search engine sites" in the major search engines.

While 80% of web visitors use the five major search engines, people who have a specific interest often visit specialized search engines that better suit their needs. Here are two sites devoted to scientific literature: http://citeseer.ist.psu.edu and http://www.scirus.com. For scholarly papers, use http://scholar.google.com. For students: GradeWinner.com for preteens, Teenja.com for teenagers, and 24HourScholar.com for college students. In addition, LookSmart has two sites for parents: ParentSurf.com for parenting resources and GoBelle.com for active mothers. Congoo is a search engine that promises free access to premium content, with an emphasis on subscription trade magazines. Accoona.com is a news business news search service.

5. Submit your web site to the major web directories.

Besides the search engines, people also go to web directories when they want to find out more information. The major such directory, Yahoo, is as actively searched as any of the search engines. Below are two of the major directories where your site should be listed. Select your category carefully. Check out the directory site before selecting the category for your site. It can make a lot of difference in how many people will discover your site.

- [ ] **BizWeb** (http://www.bizweb.com) — A business search site.
- [ ] **Yahoo!** (http://www.yahoo.com) — The major directory on the web, Yahoo! gets as many hits as any search engine. It is #2 behind Google for people searching for sites on the web.

6. Pay for top billing.

You can pay to have your site featured on Google or Yahoo. All major search engines have programs where you can pay for positioning as a sponsored listing (you pay every time someone clicks on your link). You can limit how much you'll pay and you can quit at any time, so your risk is limited. You should test this option to see if it brings your web site more traffic. The highest paid listings (positions 1, 2, and 3) get most of the clicks.

To get a higher placement, you have two options. First, you can bid more for positioning (in other words, you can pay more per click). Or you can wait for your site to naturally rise to the top because it gets more clicks than the sponsored sites listed above you. For this second strategy to be successful, you have to write a great short ad that pulls people into your site.

7. Submit your web site to the What's New web pages.

These What's New pages only feature new sites or new pages. Here are a few of those pages:

- ☐ **Librarians Index to the Internet** (http://lii.org/search/ntw) — The best source of new web sites and new things on old web sites.

- ☐ **New Web Listings** (http://www.newweblistings.com) — Only lists new web sites. Drops sites after a few months.

- ☐ **URL Wire** (http://www.urlwire.com) — Eric Ward's news of top web launches and events since 1994.

8. Submit your web site to news services on the web.

Many search engines as well as other sites offer news about the web. C|NET News (http://news.com.com), one of those sites, is a division of the cable computer news show. This site features new sites and other web news. It's also a good place to get the latest news and info on online marketing. Two other great sites are ClickZ (http://www.clickz.com) and WebProNews (http://www.webpronews.com/submit.html). You can submit articles as well as news about your new site at all three of these news services.

9. Submit your web site or company to specialized database sites.

Here, for instance, are a few special database sites where you might want your company, books, or authors to be listed:

- ☐ **American List Counsel** (http://www.amlist.com) — Features 10,000 mailing lists. If you offer mailing lists for rent, be sure you're listed here. If you are looking for lists to rent, look here also.

- ☐ **Edith Roman Associates** (http://www.edithroman.com) — Offers a database of 30,000 direct mail lists. Be sure yours is listed if you have one. Other web sites devoted to mailing lists include SRDS on the Web (http://www.srds.com) and Marketing Information Network (http://www.dmnetwork.com).

- ☐ **GuestFinder** (http://www.guestfinder.com) — Another paid listing service for book authors and others who want to be featured guests on radio and TV shows. Listings cost about $150 per year.

- ☐ **Newsletter Access** (http://www.newsletteraccess.com) — Features 5,000 subscription newsletters. If you publish one, be sure it's listed here.

- ☐ **Speakers Platform** (http://www.speaking.com) — Features many of the best speakers. Basic listings are free.

☐ **ProfNet's Expert Database** (http://www.profnet.org) — You can search here for the bios of 4,000 leading experts from colleges and universities. Again, be sure you are listed if you qualify.

10. Submit your web site via submission services.

URL submission services submit to many sites (search engines, directories, malls, and what's new pages) at the same time. **Please note:** I wouldn't use these services. They really don't help. They list you in a lot of junk web sites so you get lots of spam and not much else. These junk web sites don't help your link ratings; indeed, they often hurt your Google PageRank rating.

11. Announce your site to the email newsletters that feature new sites.

With most email newsletters, you must be a member of the list before you can post to it. Most offer a free subscription. Here are a few of the email newsletters (sometimes also known as *mailing list discussion groups* or *listservs*) that feature new sites:

☐ **Net Surfer Digest** (http://www.netsurf.com/nsd/index.html) — You can subscribe to this email newsletter at their web site.

☐ **The Scout Report** (http://scout.wisc.edu/Reports/ScoutReport/Current) — Submit site suggestions to scout@scout.wisc.edu.

☐ **Ken Leebow's Incredible Blogs** (http://incredibleglogs.com). You can email him suggestions at Leebow@gmail.com. Ken is also the author of the *300 Incredible Things to Do on the Internet* series.

12. Announce your site to books that list web sites.

Try to get listed in the new editions of any books about the Internet or world wide web. Note that most of these books are updated regularly. You can search for such books on Amazon.com. Be sure to contact Ken Leebow listed above. His series includes many bestsellers.

13. Publicize your web site with computer magazines.

Many computer magazines devote a section to web site listings. In fact, there are now a number of magazines, such as *Internet World, Internet Shopper, The Web, the net,* and *Yahoo! Internet Life,* that are devoted solely to the Net. Be sure to let these computer magazines know about your new web site. In fact, this opportunity to get notices in computer magazines is one of the main reasons why you should have a web site, since these magazines can introduce your books and authors to an entirely new audience.

Greg Godek, author of *1001 Ways to Be Romantic,* had his World of Romance site (http://www.godek.com) featured in *The Web*'s Bookmark. In that same issue, the Lonely Planet site (http://www. lonelyplanet.com) was featured as an essential web site for travel info.

Many magazines list their web sites and editorial email addresses in their publications. Why? Because they want to be contacted via their email addresses. They are looking for the latest information, and email is the quickest way to keep media up to date.

14. Publicize your web site with other special-interest magazines.

Many special-interest magazines still feature new web sites or updates of interesting sites. Hence, your new web site will be another way to make the news in special-interest magazines for your product or service area. According to Cahners Publishing, trade magazine readers learned about new business web sites through the following ways (most reported more than one):

> 74% via trade magazine articles
> 65% via trade magazine advertisements
> 59% via links from trade magazine web sites
> 58% via word of mouth
> 35% via trade magazine promotions
> 18% via direct mail

15. Publicize your web site with general-interest magazines.

The major news magazines as well as many other general-interest magazines still have sections that feature unusual online tidbits and news. *People* magazine, for instance, has a BYTES section that features online tidbits and *Newsweek* has a Cyberscope section about web sites, software, CD-ROMs, and computers.

16. Publicize your web site with newspapers.

USA Today and many local newspapers feature new web sites. Peterson Online has been called a site which, according to the *Atlanta Journal-Constitution*, "lets your browser take wing." The *Baltimore Sun*, via its *SunSpot Books* web site, invites authors to be included in their web page directory of local writers. Check to see if your local paper has a similar directory or would be interested in doing a news story about your web site.

17. Advertise in magazines and newspapers.

If you advertise in magazines or newspapers, include your URL and email address. Advertising URLs works to draw visitors. According to a study conducted by Fifth Interactive Media, two-thirds of those surveyed reported visiting a company web site because of a magazine or newspaper ad. 54% of the ads in the first twenty pages of the March 1997 issue of *Good Housekeeping* featured URLs. Now almost 100% of magazine ads feature web site URLs.

18. Publicize your web site online.

Use one of the following email news release services to let computer and online journalists know about your site. When you send out an email news release, be sure to include your web site URL and lead with a headline that features some benefit of your site. Most of these services not only send out the press release to registered journalists but they also post the news release on their web site. Such posts get picked up by Google, Yahoo, and other search engines and RSS syndicators.

☐ **BookCatcher** (http://www.bookcatcher.com). Provides a free press release service.

☐ **EReleases** (http://www.ereleases.com)

☐ **EzineTrendz Article Submission** (http://www.ezinetrendz.com)

☐ **Internet News Bureau** (http://www.internetnewsbureau.com)

☐ **News Release Wire** (http://www.expertclick.com/NewsReleaseWire)

☐ **The Open Press** (http://www.theopenpress.com). Provides a free press release service.

☐ **PR Web** (http://www.prweb.com/about.php)

☐ **PR Leap** (http://www.prleap.com)

☐ **PR.com** (http://www.pr.com/press-releases)

☐ **Press Release Net** (http://www.PressReleaseNet.com)

☐ **Send2Press Newswire** (http://www.Send2Press.com)

☐ **24-7 Press Release** (http://www.24-7pressrelease.com)

☐ **Xpress Press** (http://www.xpresspress.com)

19. Get listed in other online directories.

For instance, your college alumni association probably has an online email and/or web site directory. Check out John Kremer's listing at his alma mater (http://www.macalester.edu/~alumni). Many other associations will have similar searchable listings. Open Horizons is featured in the membership directory of PMA (http://www.pma-online.org).

20. Post messages regularly to online groups.

Usenet newsgroups are old news. Few people visit them anymore since their purposes are now served by online chat groups and discussion services. Do join some of the online chat groups and discussion services to meet other people interested in what you are writing about and to allow you to display your expertise to a potentially key market.

When Nan McCarthy self-published her romance novel *Chat*, she had a hard time getting it into bookstores. But she noticed that another book released at the same time was stacked high at every store. The book? *Dave Barry in Cyberspace*. So she wrote a note to the humorist in the style of his newspaper column. He replied with a short note telling her not to give up. Well, she didn't. She sent her humorous note to a number of humor newsgroups where Barry's fans congregate. And they responded. Soon she had sold out of the 2,500 copies she had printed and signed on with a book publisher to print another 20,000 copies! In October 1998, Pocket Books heavily promoted her series of three novels, *Chat, Connect*, and *Crash*.

21. Post messages to discussion lists.

Unlike newsgroups which are available for anyone to read and to search past messages, discussion groups are available by subscription only. Most subscriptions are free, but you must be a member in order to post to the group. To discover discussion groups that are devoted to a subject covered by your site, search the following directories:

☐ **CataList** (http://www.lsoft.com/lists/listref.html) — This site lists more than 12,000 lists and includes the number of subscribers in each list.

☐ **Topica Lists** (http://lists.topica.com) — You can set up a free discussion list covering your favorite topic or use their services to handle your ezine email.

☐ **Yahoo Chat** (http://chat.yahoo.com) — Yahoo's chat groups.

☐ **Yahoo Groups** (http://groups.yahoo.com) — Search for discussion groups based on Yahoo. Or create your own group.

Connie Evers, author of *How to Teach Nutrition to Kids*, is actively involved in several listservs, all related to her niche: school nutrition professionals, coop extension specialists, and dietitians. She always attempts to "contribute valuable, free information when I feel I have expertise in the area." Her involvement has generated many inquiries and is responsible for most of her online orders, which amount to about fifty books per month.

22. Write a FAQ.

A FAQ is a *frequently asked questions* text that is posted to newsgroups, listservs, or web sites. Written by a knowledgeable person, the FAQ answers the basic questions that a new person might have when first encountering a newsgroup or listserv. If you encounter a discussion group and discover that there are a lot of questions about some specific problem—and you are qualified to answer them—then you might want to submit a FAQ to the group. Before web sites became prevalent, most informative articles were posted as FAQs to newsgroups and discussion lists.

To increase interest in her book, *Freelance Writing*, Marcia Yudkin wrote a FAQ file on freelance writing and then announced its availability on various online services as well as the Internet. In response, a perfect stranger offered to archive the FAQ on his web site and post it automatically every week to a newsgroup on writing. As a result, her FAQ was highly recommended in *Internet World* and sold many books.

As an alternative to an informative FAQ, you could post a humorous story tied into your book. Nothing travels faster than humor on the Net.

23. Send entries to email newsletters and blogs.

Many email newsletters and blogs welcome submissions from outside individuals and will allow you to post a little signature ad at the end of your message. Many blogs also encourage comments from readers on the posted articles. This is another chance for you to expose your knowledge and book to interested readers. Use Google, Yahoo, or Bloglines.com to locate blogs. For email newsletters or ezines, check out the following online directories:

- ☐ **Freezine Web** (http://www.freezineweb.com)

- ☐ **ZineBook** (http://www.zinebook.com)

- ☐ **Ezine Universe** (http://www.ezine-universe.com)

- ☐ **Zinos** — (http://www.zinos.com)

- ☐ **Ezine Directory** — (http://www.ezine-dir.com)

24. Develop a response template.

Design and save an email message that you can send back to unsolicited email or to anyone requesting information. This response template should be headlined by a key benefit of your product, describe your product, offer one or two testimonials, make an offer they can't refuse, and make it easy for them to respond back. Also include your email address and web site URL. Now instead of trashing unsolicited email, send them your marketing message. Most email programs allow you to automate responses. You can also use autobots to send responses to specific requests.

25. Submit your site for an award.

Many sites and publications offer awards for the top web sites, including Lycos's Top 5% of all web sites, Magellan's 3-Star Site, *USA TODAY*'s Hot Site, IPPA Award for Design Excellence, and MSN's Pick of the Week. Once your web site is established (and can be considered really hot or real cool), submit your site for an award. Below are a few sites where you can nominate your site for an award (some awards, such as Netscape's What's Cool section or Lycos' Top 5%, don't accept nominations):

- ☐ **Cool Site of the Day** (http://www.coolsiteoftheday.com) — This oldest cool site selects a new site every day.

- ☐ **Komputer Klinic**, Kim Komando, Columnist. Email: komando@ komando.com. Web: http://www.komando.com. She features web sites in her radio show, newspaper column, and weekly email newsletter.

- ☐ **Web Digest for Marketers** (http://www.wdfm.com) — Features short reviews of marketing-oriented web sites. Great newsletter.

Peterson Online was selected by *USA Today* as a Hot Site. Bad Dog Press's web site earned over 60 design and content awards, including the Web Crawler Select, *USA Today* Hot Site, and Starting Point Hot Site. Open Horizon's BookMarket site was honored with the first PE/URL award from *Publishing Entrepreneur* magazine.

26. Advertise direct.

Advertise via direct mail to key accounts letting them know where they can find you on the web. For example, Barry Sears, author of *The Zone*, sent out postcards to anyone who had registered at his site. The postcards offered a discount on his latest book.

27. Advertise on billboards.

Joe Boxer displayed its web site URL on a 6,000-square-foot billboard in New York City's Time Square. Besides its URL, the billboard also displayed Joe Boxer's email address and email greetings from many of its customers (displayed on a 100-foot electronic zipper).

28. Advertise on TV.

Besides using billboards, Coldwell Banker, a national real estate firm, broadcast direct response TV ads to promote its web site and generate sales leads for its brokers. Its web site, which features home-buying information and a database of listed properties, gets a major jump in traffic on Sundays when the spots air as well as on Mondays when people access the site from their workplace computers. Their web site logs 70,000 to 80,000 visitors every week and generates 700 to 1,000 leads for its brokers.

30. Link TV to the Internet.

Intel's Intercast technology allows users to receive TV broadcasts and web pages simultaneously via cable, dish, or antenna. When the home shopping network QVC mentioned its iQVC web site simulcasts during its TV broadcast, there was a fourfold increase in hits at the web site.

31. Put your URL on premiums.

PlanetOut, a large gay-themed site, promoted its URL with imprinted pens, mouse pads, buttons, and packages of condoms (which they gave out at conferences). Star Telecom Network offered a series of prepaid phone cards that feature collectible site graphics from nonprofit web sites.

12:05 27 Ways to Use Your Web Site to Market Itself

Besides getting listed in all the right places and actively publicizing and advertising your web site, you can also do things on your site to attract more people. The design of your web site, as discussed previously, contributes heavily to getting people to your site, but here are a few other things you can do on an ongoing basis to attract more people:

1. Establish links with others.

Besides getting listed in the major search engines, getting links from other sites is probably the most effective action you can take to promote your site via the web. The best way to get these links is to search for like-minded sites, ones that you would be proud to link to. Then place a link to those sites on your site. Once you've done that, contact the sites and ask if they'd like to exchange links. Tell them that you've already linked to them but would appreciate a return link. When sending this email, provide the HTML text to link to your site. For example: <A HREF="http://www.book-market.com">BookMarket.com</A> — Sell more books! Get a free subscription to the Book Marketing Tip of the Week.

- When Kiplinger's *Personal Finance* magazine recommended Russell Brown's *Strategies for Successfully Buying or Selling a Business*, Brown traded links with Kiplinger's web site. As a result of the recommendation and link, he was able to sell several hundred copies of his book.

- At *New Age Journal*'s web site, they invite visitors to post their favorite links and comment on them in the New Age Link Forum.

- Rand McNally has linked its web site to a select list of the best tourist sites. By providing visitors with only the best tourist sites, Rand McNally is establishing itself as a reliable source of travel information.

2. Provide other sites with a button link to your site.

When you offer to link with a site, provide them with details on how to download a graphic image representing your site. Check to see which sites currently link to you. Some search engines allow you to monitor how successful your linking program is by listing which sites are linked to your site.

☐ **Alta Vista** (http://www.altavista.com) — Enter your web site URL into their search form as follows: link:http://www.yoursite.com. The form will return the names of the sites where links to your site were found. In mid April 2005, this site showed 1,770 links to BookMarket.com. In April 2006, Alta Vista showed 2,800 links to BookMarket.com.

☐ **Ask Jeeves** (http://web.ask.com) — Enter links to yoursite.com into their search form. In April 2005, this site showed 1,430 links to BookMarket.com. In April 2006, Ask Jeeves showed 3,010 links, more than double what it showed one year earlier.

☐ **Google** (http://www.google.com) — Enter link:yoursite.com into their standard search box. In April 2005, Google showed 161 links to Book Market.com. In April 2006, Google showed 188 links.

☐ **MSN Search** (http://search.msn.com) — Enter link:yoursite.com into their search box. In April 2005, MSN Search showed 2,070 links to BookMarket.com. In April 2006, it showed 4,821 links.

☐ **Yahoo** (http://search.yahoo.com) — Enter link:http://www.yoursite.com into their search box. In April 2005, Yahoo showed 1,780 links to Book Market.com. In April 2006, it showed 2,790 links.

As you can see, the results vary considerably. But one thing I noticed between searching in mid-April 2005 and mid-April 2006 was that links to the BookMarket.com web site nearly doubled on almost every search site in one year's time. That's incredible. I didn't do anything systematic to generate that many new links. My guess is that the links came as the result of the reputation I had already set for the web site. Plus, my on-going link exchange program with other web sites.

I'm not sure why Google shows such a small number of links when all the other sites show a good number more. I would guess that they are only showing the links from web sites rated highly for PageRank as well as content. When I searched in Google to locate web pages that include the term BookMarket.com, I found 15,800 pages in mid-April 2006. So it's obvious that Google is very selective when listing sites that link to a web site.

3. Exchange banners.

To increase your presence on another site, ask them to exchange banners (rectangular graphics) with you. The banners, when clicked on, send people to your site via your link.

4. Join a banner exchange program.

A banner exchange program acts as a central clearinghouse for web sites that want to have their banners displayed on other sites. In return, each site in the exchange inserts HTML code to allow the banner exchange clearinghouse to rotate banners on their site. Here's one such site: BannerSwap (http://www.bannerswap.com).

5. Sell banner ads on your site.

Besides exchanging banner links for free, you can sell banner ads. If you want to sell ads on your site, be sure to evaluate the following points:

☐ What pages on your site have enough traffic or are targeted enough to be of interest to advertisers?

☐ Evaluate your site traffic. Check your server logs to discover how many people are coming to your site, where are they coming from, how much time do they spend on your site, and which pages attract and/or hold their attention. To attract advertisers, you will need to know these numbers and be able to verify them.

☐ Commission an independent site audit which should reaffirm your analysis of your site and will also add credibility with potential advertisers.

☐ Determine how and/or who will sell your site ad space. You can do it yourself, hire someone else to do it, or contract with an advertising agency.

☐ Develop a rate card, with cost per thousand, sponsorship opportunities, and other sales information.

☐ Evaluate how you will process and position the ads, what reports you can offer advertisers, how many times you'll show specific ads, and how you will track the response to ads. In short, you will have to develop or select software to help you carry out these important functions.

6. Hire a web advertising network.

If you want to make money selling banner ads without going through a lot of work, hire a web advertising network. Also check out these networks if you want to buy space on other sites. Online ads, according to research conducted by Find/SVP, shows that 39% of users clicked on an ad before making an online purchase. DoubleClick (http://www.doubleclick.net) sells for some of the largest web sites, from USA Today Online to Travelocity.

7. Design an effective banner ad.

Most banner ads have a click-through rate of 1 to 2%. That means 1 to 2% of the people who see the ad go on to visit a site. What kind of banner ad is most effective? Here are some tips on designing effective banner ads:

☐ **Animated ads pull better than static ads**, usually by 30 to 40% but up to as much as 400% more. In addition, animated banners increase click-through rate by 25%.

☐ **Put the words "Click Here" somewhere in the banner.** According to one study, these words can increase click-through rates by 44%. Toshiba America found this tip increased their response rate to 5.7% on three search engine sites.

☐ **Add color.** Bright colors such as green, blue, and yellow outpull black and white ads.

☐ **Larger banners pull a higher response.**

☐ **Banner ads should be changed frequently.** Response rates drop by half once browsers have seen the banner several times. Banner ads wear out after 200,000 to 400,000 impressions.

☐ **Contests don't work.** According to an analysis of 2,000 banners and half a billion impressions, one study found no significant improvement in click-through for banners that featured contests.

☐ **Simpler ads load faster** and have more time to create an impression. So keep your ads simple.

☐ **The word "free" boosts click-through** by 10 to 35%.

☐ **If possible, get your banner placed at the lower right hand corner of a page rather than at the top.** According to a University of Michigan graduate student study, banners placed next to the scroll bar generated a 228% higher click-through rate than ads at the top of the page. This is an older study; it might no longer be true to current practice.

8. Pay for banners on appropriate sites.

When you cannot exchange banners or you want to guarantee exposure on specific sites, you will need to buy exposure. Use the above points to design an effective banner ad. Then search out those sites which will get you the best exposure for the people you want to reach. Finally, negotiate a good price for placement of your banner ads. If possible, pay for actual hits or orders on your site coming from the banner on their site; this is known as pay per inquiry or pay per sale advertising.

The average charge for a targeted banner ad is about $30 per thousand impressions. With an average 2% clickthrough rate, you can expect about 20 visitors to your site for your $30 payment. Hence, expect to pay about $1.50 per visitor. Think now: Can you afford to pay $1.50 per visitor? Do visitors turn into customers at a high enough rate to justify the cost?

As an alternative, you can pay for keyword banners on hit sites. For example, some of the major search engines sell keywords linked to your banner ad. If the keyword you purchase is entered by someone using the search engine, your banner will come up. Such banner ads, while more expensive, are more likely to reach your target audience.

* When HarperCollins relaunched its site (http://www.harper-collins.com) with a 10,000 title searchable database, they bought banner ads all over the web, including CBS Sportsline, ESPN, Salon, Slate, and Yahoo!

* When Preview Travel bought keyword banners on Yahoo! and other search engine sites, their clickthrough rate went from the standard 2 to 4% up to 25%.

* Through testing CyberGold discovered that paying consumers to click on a banner increased clickthrough by thirteen times (more people clicked on the banner that paid them $5.00 than the banner that offered no pay).

9. Run interstitial ads.

When I wrote this chapter in 1998, the hottest new thing was interstitial ads—commercial messages that appear during the download delay between one web page and another. Experts predicted that 20% of web advertising dollars would go into interstitials during the next few years. Well, they were wrong. Interstitials currently play a very small role in web advertising. Funnily enough, plain old text ads (Google AdSense) make up the bulk of successful web advertising.

Berkeley Systems made heavy use of interstitials in its online quiz show *You Don't Know Jack!*. Interstitial ads popped up between every four questions in the 15-question quiz. Because of the intrusive nature of interstitials, general brand advertisers, such as 7-Up and Plymouth, are drawn to it. A study commissioned by Berkeley Systems showed that consumers exposed to a single interstitial were 64% more likely to recall seeing advertising for a specific brand, compared to a 30% increase in traditional banner ads.

10. Develop a chat ad-bot.

Black & Decker has collaborated with Planet Direct to develop an advertising robot in the shape of a Dustbuster vacuum that pops up and volunteers cleaning tips and product information whenever someone in a Planet Direct chat group mentions dust or housekeeping.

Another option is to place a banner in a chat area. The great advantage of such banners is that they stay visible for a much longer time while the individual is participating in a chat. But, while chat is still hot, chat advertising hasn't made much news lately.

11. Run a contest.

If you want to attract people to your site and keep them coming back, run an ongoing contest that requires them to come back to your site more than once.

- Foghorn Press, publisher of outdoor recreation books, ran a favorite snapshot contest featuring people in the outdoors. The grand prize winner, judged by the staff at Foghorn Press, won a weekend getaway at Sorensen's Resort Cabins in the High Sierras.

- Hotel Discounts's Trip from Hell contest drew tens of thousands of new visitors to their site. As a bonus, they received hundreds of riotous tales of vacations gone bad—tales that were added to their site to give it additional content that would attract even more visitors.

12. Donate a prize for another site's contest.

Search out relevant web sites that are hosting contests and offer your book as a prize. Many contest sites would welcome additional prizes to give away since they add more excitement and value to the contest.

13. Set up a gift registry.

To capture the names, addresses, and email addresses of visitors to your site, ask them to sign up in your guest book. Give them a reason to sign up. Offer them ongoing information whenever your site is updated. Send them a monthly email newsletter. Or offer them a discount on orders. For example, Fisher Scientific offers a free 20% off discount certificate on Fisher purchases if people sign up in its site's guest book. Or make them give you their name and email address before they can get a free valuable report that you offer. Before you can get a free list of 400 literary agents, for example, you have to sign up for Authors Team's twice-monthly email newsletter.

14. Set up a guest book.

In order to capture the names, addresses, and email addresses of visitors to your site, encourage them to sign up in your guest book. Give them a reason to sign up. Offer them ongoing information whenever your site is updated. Send them a monthly email newsletter. Or offer them a discount on orders. For example, Fisher Scientific offers a free 20% off discount certificate on Fisher purchases if people sign up in its site's guest book. Your site host provider should be able to help you set up a form that will allow people to easily sign up for your guest book.

15. License content that will attract people to your site.

If you find some great content that would go well on your site, ask the webmaster or creator of the content if you could post it to your site as well, along with a link back to their site. In some cases you might have to pay for the rights to use the content. In most cases, though, you'll be able to use it freely in trade for a link, credit line, or article they can use on their site.

- Open Horizon's bookmarket web site features short articles that we requested permission to add to our site after seeing a post in a discussion list or ezine. We always give full attribution as well as a link to the site of the contributor. Check out the free reports on the bookmarket site at http://www.bookmarket.com/reportmain.html.

- Our PromotingYourBooks web site also features many items reprinted from other people's ezines and web sites.

- Want to add some current content to your site? Then add an RSS news feed to your site. Most news sites offer the possibility of adding a news feed for specific content to your web site. In other words, if you run a crafts site, you could host a news feed about crafts news and features. If you don't know how to do this, ask your web designer or one of the news sites for help in doing so.

16. Create content for other sites.

Another way to attract visitors to your site is to give content (an article, graphic, or piece of software) to other sites. For example, Jim Clemmer allows anyone to copy and distribute the columns and book excerpts featured on his web site (http://www.clemmer-group.com). In return, any reprinting must include the byline and author description as included in the originals. In addition, the user must send a message to Jim describing how he or she plans to use the article.

WilsonWeb has a 13-point copyright and reprint policy statement which allows single copies of articles to be printed for individual use or forwarded as a single email but does not allow reproduction on another web site. They do sell reprint rights in print form only. See their entire policy statement at http://www.wilsonweb.com/copyright/reprints.htm.

Below are a number of web sites that encourage contributions of articles to their sites, with full attribution to the contributor. These articles are then syndicated to other web sites and ezines. Note that these article collection sites are among the most trafficked independent sites on the web. If you want to attract more traffic to your web site, model it after one of these.

☐ **Article City** (http://www.articlecity.com)

☐ **Article Dashboard** (http://www.articledashboard.com)

☐ **Article Garden** (http://www.articlegarden.com)

☐ **Article Marketer** (http://www.articlemarketer.com)

☐ **Article Teller** (http://www.articleteller.com)

☐ **Articles Submit** (http://www.articles-submit.com)

☐ **Associated Content** (http://www.associatedcontent.com)

☐ **Buzzle** (http://www.buzzle.com)

☐ **Ezine Articles** (http:// www.ezinearticles.com)

☐ **Go Articles** (http://www.goarticles.com)

☐ **Idea Marketers** (http://www.ideamarketers.com)

☐ **The World Wide Information Outlet** (http://certificate.net/wwio)

17. Create content to attract the right visitors to your site.

Mark Welch, a probate attorney in California, developed a directory of probate attorneys for the entire United States, listed state by state. Guess who was at the top of the California list? Yes, Mark.

Two years ago I began compiling the names of editors in two categories: cookbooks and first novels. Since that time, I've added editors for business, children, health, religion, sports, and light reference/humor. I feature 1,250 editors. If you do a Google search for book editors in any of these categories, Bookmarket.com is #1 in four categories, #5 in two others, and #6 in another. That brings BookMarket.com lots of traffic for a key target audience: new authors of books. What started as a hobby sideline has become a major source of traffic. You can do the same for potential audiences. Find out what they search for on the web and provide it for them.

18. Create a search engine, directory, or index.

Make your index so good people will want to come to your site first to look for other links in your subject area. You can go two ways with an index: Offer a comprehensive index for your subject area or offer a select list (top 20, top 100, or such). I took the selective approach in my BookMarket site. The site features a select group of the Top 101 sites in seven areas: publishing, book marketing, general marketing, Internet marketing, experts (focus on book authors and publishers), referral programs, and celebrations.

19. Give out an award.

Create a Top 100 list of sites devoted to your subject area or create some other sort of award. Then notify the sites that they've won the award and tell them how they can post the award logo to their site. You could send the HTML code with your message, so all they have to do is cut and paste the code into their site. Or you can tell them where to go on your site to grab the graphic and HTML code. Be sure to include a link to your site in the HTML code.

Gebbie Press, publisher of media directories, set up an award program to honor the Radio Station of the Month. To begin, they sent an email message to a hundred radio stations. In two days, two dozen stations said they'd like to participate. Gebbie sent these stations an award graphic which they could use on their sites. All stations also provided a link back to Gebbie's site.

20. Create a hall of fame.

I had two reasons for creating the Self-Publishing Hall of Fame: First, to honor authors who self-published successfully, and secondarily, to increase my web site rating for self-publishing. Now, when you search Google for the term self-publishing, my BookMarket web site comes in at #8. Once potential self-publishers visit the hall of fame, they can then see all the other valuable resources available to them on the BookMarket web site.

In March 2005, I opened an additional web site for more detailed listings of those honored in the hall of fame (http://www.SelfPublishingHallOfFame. com). While that web site is still a work in progress as I write, it will soon become a destination web site of its own, plus provide me with additional income from Amazon sales of books featured on the site as well as a small percentage from any clicks on the Google ads featured on the side.

Any publisher can create a hall of fame. Nothing limits you from honoring those in your field who have done great things. If you publish books on baseball and you don't want to compete with the Baseball Hall of Fame in Cooperstown, you could create a specialized Baseball Hall of Fame honoring amateur players, first basemen, relief pitchers, middle relief pitchers, first base coaches, baseball fans, or whatever.

There are currently some 500 halls of fame in the United States, most with buildings or rooms devoted to the honorees, but more halls of fame are now being created on the Internet. Perhaps, someday, your hall of fame will become so recognized that someone comes along to ask you to create a destination tourist site for that hall of fame.

You don't have to be an expert to create a hall of fame; you just have to be passionate and informed about the subject—or get qualified people involved to help you make selections and create stories about the honorees. If you don't want to create a hall of fame, think of something else that would attract visitors to your web site.

21. Sell sponsorships.

While 70% of online ad spending is on banners, 24% is spent on sponsorships of appropriate sites. Look for companies or sites which might be interested in sponsoring your site or parts of your site. Then contact them with a specific proposal. Give them a good reason to sponsor your site.

When Knopf published Nicholas Negroponte's *Being Digital* on the Internet, they charged sponsors for any hits they received from those who read the book online. For instance, Knopf hyperlinked a phrase such as "public relations" in the book. Then, when people clicked on that link, they were taken to a PR agency's web site. The agency, then, paid Knopf a small fee for each such connection.

22. Create partnerships.

Look for ways you can work with other site owners to add value to their sites while also adding value and traffic to your site.

In 1998 InfoSeek made a minority equity investment in Hoover's Inc., a publisher of reference materials about major companies. As part of the deal, InfoSeek added an icon link on its home page to Hoover's site in order to give web searchers quicker access to financial statements, public offerings, and stock quotes about the companies in Hoover's database.

23. Syndicate your content.

There are any number of ways to syndicate your contact via the Internet, and more ways will be developed before you read this. You can use RSS to syndicate content or you can use other methods. On my travel blog at http://traveltriviatime.blogspot.com, I feature two syndicated items: quotations from QuotationsPage.com and a Daily Factoid from SurfnetKids.com. Check out their web sites to see how they syndicate material using just a bit of JavaScript code. I will be syndicating some quotes myself using a very simple graphic that I will change every day. Those who accept the syndicated content will have to do nothing to enjoy the change of quotes each day. All they'll have to do is include the following code on their web site: <a href="http://www.waybackwords.com" border="1" src="sports.gif" width="198" height="250"></a>.

24. Join affiliate programs.

Use affiliate programs (also known as *associate programs*) to add content, value, and income streams to your site. Probably the best known referral program is the one operated by Amazon.com. Once you have officially signed up as an associate, Amazon pays a commission for any book sales resulting from your referral. Amazon has thousands and thousands of web sites in their associates program. Check out Associate Programs (http://www.associateprograms.com) for more details on how to make money with affiliate programs. Also check out ClickBank.com for its referral program.

During the past year, I've made about $20,000 from affiliate programs where I recommended a site, book, or program to visitors of my BookMarket web site. I know a number of authors and publishers who make a living simply through such affiliate programs. Indeed, I know people who have made more than $30,000 in a few days via associate programs.

25. Set up your own affiliate program.

To drive traffic to your site, you might want to offer a referral program for other sites. To make a referral program work, your site has to sell something that other sites believe will attract others and generate response. Almost every major retailer on the web offers a referral programs. If you use one of the standard web shopping cart programs to handle sales on your site, you probably already have the mechanism for setting up an affiliate program of your own.

Most of the web sites that rely on a one-page sales letter are successful because they have many affiliates sending traffic to their web sites. Without that traffic, a one-page letter won't produce enough income to pay off.

26. Make a free offer.

Then advertise it via news releases, email, your ezine, newsgroup postings, and links. Keep your link partners and other relevant web sites informed about your free offerings. Be sure to let any get-things-for-free web sites know about your free offer. Here are some top sites:

☐ **All Books Free** (http://www.allbooksfree.com)

☐ **All Free Things** (http://www.allfreethings.com)

☐ **Free Books for All** (http://www.freebooksforall.com)

☐ **Free Cool Offers** (http://www.freecooloffers.com)

☐ **The Free Site** (http://www.thefreesite.com)

☐ **Free.com** (http://www.free.com)

☐ **Tons for Free** (http://tonsforfree.com)

27. Encourage visitors to tell a friend.

Include a Tell-a-Friend button on your web site that sends information on your web site directly to friends of your site visitors. All they have to do is click on the button and enter the email addresses of their friends. For more information and a free trial button, check out http://www.tell-a-friend-wizard.com.

eMarketer ezine once reported on how people find websites. Note that friends and relatives have a major impact.

> 78% — Search engines
> 62% — Other web pages
> 53% — Friends and relatives
> 44% — Print media
> 6% — Usenet
> 6% — Email
> 2% — Television

12:06 Marketing Via Email

In 1992, only 2% of the U.S. population had email access. Today, probably 95% of the population has such access. It's no surprise, then, that many companies use email as a way to market their products to target audiences. In this section we will look at some of the ways businesses are already using email to market their sites and products.

Send out mass mailings.

Just as in direct mail, you can send out email to thousands of addresses in a very short time. Indiscriminate mass emailings are known as *spam* and are not welcome. But, if you develop a targeted list via the guestbook on your web site or via postings on newsgroups and if you keep your message short, your mass emailing could produce returns as high as 9%. You can do such a mailing on your own, but most companies wisely choose to use an outside provider who will charge from 10¢ to 20¢ per address for mass emailings. Here are a few of the best-known mass email list providers:

☐ **Direct Effect Media Services** (http://www.directeffectmedia.com) — They consult on all online marketing efforts.

☐ **DirectQlick.com** (http://www.directqlick.com) — Offers more than 8.4 million opt-in email addresses.

☐ **E-PostDirect** (http://www.epostdirect.com, 800-409-4443) — Offers many business email lists.

☐ **L.I.S.T. Inc.** (http://www.l-i-s-t.com) — Opt-in business lists.

☐ **PostMaster Direct** (http://www.postmasterdirect.com; 212-625-1370) — Their lists are 100% opt-in. That means that people have chosen to be on the lists. They offer many lists, with interests running from scuba diving to Java scripting. Using a PostMaster list, Ichat rang up sales of $50,000 in five hours. In another mailing to 30,000 members of the web design and promotion list, Ichat saw its sales quadruple within four weeks. Pride Vitamins got $3,000 in orders from a $600 mailing. Their message was three lines long, because they sent prospects to their web site to close the order.

☐ **SilverPOP** (http://www.silverpop.com) — Email marketing specialist.

When the Hayes Conference Center of San Jose, California, sent postcard invitations to meeting planners at Sun Microsystems, the response was dismal. When they sent a second invitation via email with a link to their web site, they received responses from 150 planners and got an additional 800 hits on their web site.

Houghton Mifflin discovered the power of email when it offered to donate one book to a children's hospital for every 25 emailed holiday wishes sent to its web site before December 31st. By early December, their web site had received 67,000 replies. By December 11, they had to call off the promotion because they couldn't handle the volume. Houghton Mifflin ended up shipping 2,500 books to children's hospitals across the country.

Send out news releases.

Use email to send out news releases to media contacts. More and more media people are open to receiving email letters and news releases. As editor of the *Book Marketing Update* newsletter, I prefer email news releases to faxed news releases. Why? Very simple. With email releases I can edit the text on my computer and insert it into the newsletter with little effort. With faxed or print news releases, all the information has to be re-keyed.

To send out news releases, you can use services such as PRWeb or Press Release Net. A list of such services was listed earlier in this chapter. A more up-to-date list can be found at http://www.bookmarket.com/12.html.

Send out promotions to bookstores.

Since many bookstores now have web sites and email addresses, you can email regular promotions to them or send them a monthly newsletter via email. That's what McGraw-Hill does with its Virtual Card Deck. Each month they email to bookstores twelve virtual postcards that feature upcoming titles as well as select backlist. Each full-color postcard features a brief synopsis of the book as well as a photo of the book's cover. Zondervan also offers free email newsletters for bookstores and media.

Rent out your email list.

Once you have developed a significant email list (5,000 or more names), you can rent it out to others to use. One of the best ways to do this is to work with one of the list companies featured earlier. All of them can build, manage, and broker your list. Many can also provide you with forms and list infrastructure via their sites. In return, they split list rental income 50/50 with you.

Note: Don't rent out your list unless you give people a chance to opt out of the list. It's very bad Internet etiquette to rent out a list where people have not had a chance to opt out. In general, you'd be better off not selling or renting out your list unless you absolutely need the income.

Answer your mail.

If you have a web site and you place an email address there for people to contact your company, be sure you answer that email—and answer it fast. People expect a fast response to email. Xerox, for instance, generated global good will because Bill McLain, their "Voice of the Web," answered any question submitted to him, even if the question had nothing to do with Xerox or copiers. He answered about 350 questions per day. As for handling complaints, Bill said, "My style for complaint email is simple. I assume that Xerox is at fault and try to help in any way I can." As part of his work, he developed about 80 boilerplate responses, but he still responded personally to each question.

Always provide an opt-out option.

When sending mass emailings, always offer recipients an option to get off your list and stay off it. In a test conducted by American List Counsel and Xoom Software, positive response increased by 51% when a company offers an opt-out option and an explanation as to why the email offer was being sent.

Use an autoresponder.

To answer simple routine questions, you might set up an autoresponder (an email address which can automatically send a form message to anyone who sends email to that address). Your site provider or shopping cart program should be able to set you up with autoresponder options.

Other uses for an autoresponder.

Here are a few other ways you can use an autoresponder:

☐ **Background news release information**—When sending out news releases, especially to online media or media email lists, you can provide them with additional background information via an autoresponder (as well as on your web site).

☐ **Catalog requests**—Set up an autoresponder that people can use to request a printed or email version of your catalog. Make this autoresponder available on your web site as well.

☐ **Book samples**—Provide book excerpts or sample pages from your book catalog.

☐ **Updates**—You could provide daily, weekly, or monthly updates of your products or other information to your customers, sales force, representatives, or other contacts.

☐ **FAQs**—Set up frequently asked question files on autoresponders so anyone can access crucial information at any time.

☐ **Sales letters**—You can send sales letters to inquirers. When someone requests your sales letter via the autoresponder, you can also arrange to send them a follow-up letter automatically (using a system such as Databack's SlowPoke autoresponder).

☐ **Short online email courses**—You can offer a week-long course via autoresponder where the recipient gets a new lesson each day for a week, or every week for so many months.

12:07 Marketing via Email Newsletters

Email newsletters are one of the most important marketing tools available via the Internet. An email newsletter is a periodic email message sent out to a list of people who have chosen to subscribe. Most email newsletters are currently free, but some do charge a subscription fee. Since you would be using an email newsletter to promote your product and web site, your newsletter would probably be offered for free.

Some newsletters, such as *This Is True*, offer two versions, a limited one for free and a more detailed or more frequent one for a subscription fee. For $24, you can get a year's subscription to the full version of *This Is True* which is sent out every week and does not include any third-party advertising. Or you can opt for the free version which is sent out every week, arrives later than the paid version, does not include all listings of the paid version, and includes third-party ads. *This Is True* currently has 150,000 subscribers from 121 countries! And every issue, paid or free, includes promos for the books which have been compiled from previous issues.

How many web sites do you know that get 150,000 hits every week? An email newsletter can be the best Internet promotion you can carry out for a book. Just listen to what Hal Croasmun, former publisher of the *Build Your Business Daily Tips* email newsletter, has to say about newsletter promotions: "We have had good response from search engines, banner ads, exchanging links, and posting to discussion lists. But the best response we have had comes from the community we are building with our online newsletter. It takes a lot of time and work, but by providing value to other people on the net, you can establish the kind of relationships that cause people to want to refer others to you." Croasmun now operates the Script for Sale web site (http://www.scriptforsale.com).

If you'd like to create your own email newsletter, first consider what kind of newsletter or mailing list you want to create. Here are some options:

☐ **A periodic newsletter**—You can generate the content or solicit submissions from your readers or other experts. My *Book Marketing Tip of the Week* is such a newsletter.

☐ **An alert service**—You send out notices of web site updates or other news from your company. Zondervan allows customers and media to subscribe to their Email Alert Service, which provides information on its new and upcoming books in thirty categories. One alert, *Pastor's File*, is designed to help pastors. Other alerts include a *Daily Bible Verse, Marriage Builder*, and *Family Matters*.

☐ **A public relations list**—You send out a periodic email press release to media or customers. This is the kind of email publication most web sites offer when they have you sign up to their guest book. They send you periodic updates on new products, changes in products, or service updates. One of Zondervan's alert services is *Zondervan News Service*, which describes Zondervan books that bring perspective to current events.

☐ **An unmoderated discussion list**—Most mailing list discussion groups take this format. An example is the Publish-L discussion list (http://www.Publish-l.com).

☐ **A moderated discussion list**—In such a list, the list owner takes responsibility to edit all submission to the discussion and sends out a daily or weekly digest.

For most promotional purposes, you will want to have subscriptions to your online newsletter be open rather than closed. *Open* means that anyone can join the list. *Closed* means that only qualified people can join the list. Open lists are far easier to administer since they can be done with list management software (such as majordomo or listserv).

To set up an email list or discussion group, ask your site host service if they can manage your list. If not, there are list service providers such as PatronMail and SparkList that can handle larger lists. When you establish your email newsletter or discussion list, be sure to get it listed in appropriate directories of ezines). You can Google for such directories.

Below, now, are a few of the ways you can use an email newsletter to make money and promote your business or service.

Build credibility with potential or current customers.

Larry Chase, president of Chase Online Marketing Strategies and publisher of *Web Digest for Marketers*, gets 60% of his consulting and seminar business as a result of his monthly newsletter, which reaches 75,000 readers online and in print (reproduced in *Advertising Age* magazine). He charges $500 for two hours of phone consulting. Below is the closing text for his monthly online newsletter (note his subtle sales messages):

> See the newest marketing categories and reviews added to Larry Chase's Search Engine For Marketers.
>
> Click here to see Larry Chase's Speaker Topics.
>
> Get Larry Chase's top picks in 40 marketing categories. Go to Larry Chase's Search Engine For Marketers now.
>
> Advertising in WDFM: This newsletter reaches over 40,000 decision-making marketers. Started in April 1995, WDFM was the first email newsletter about marketing on the Internet.
>
> See my new "Need-to-Know Marketing Sites" guide at:
>
> http://www.wdfm.com/n2k/FYINeedtoKnow5.htm
>
> Cordially, Larry Chase: Publisher, Web Digest For Marketers http://wdfm.com
>
> Author: "Essential Business Tactics f/t Net"
>
> Sample chapter at http://LarryChase.com. Ph: (212) 619-4780 Contact Larry.

John Wiley offers a number of free email *Dummies Daily* newsletters to anyone interested in the the various topics covered by *Dummies* books.

Azriella Jaffee, author of *Honey, I Want to Start My Own Business*, published by HarperBusiness, set up a free email newsletter, *Entrepreneurial Couples Success*, to attract potential readers for her book.

Offer a two-tier system.

Offer two versions of your online newsletter, one that is free, the other for pay—just as *This Is True* does. Or use the online newsletter to provide samples of a paid printed newsletter. Open Horizon's *Book Marketing Tip of the Week* is used not only to promote our BookMarket.com site, but also to provide samplers of our printed *Book Marketing Update* newsletter. Our hope, of course, is that people who sample our weekly tip will want to subscribe to the biweekly printed newsletter.

Sell ads in the newsletter.

Since most email newsletters are focused on a special interest or audience, they offer advertisers highly targeted audiences. Rates vary from about $10 per thousand subscribers for general lists to about $20 per thousand for focused lists. Note that such ads can produce dramatic results. For instance, a travel sponsor to the Internet Sales mailing list received close to 3,000 additional hits on its web site, over 250 emails, and $34,000 in sales. You can sell the ads yourself by contacting appropriate web sites or other potential advertisers, or you can work with one of the email newsletters featured at Email Results (http://www.emailresults.com).

Open Horizons sells 5-line classified ads in our *Book Marketing Tip of the Week* at a cost of only $5 per thousand. We don't actively solicit ads but began including them in the ezine when too many people began sending us promotions for seminars, teleseminars, and other items that the newsletter was beginning to look like an advertising sheet rather than an informational tool. By charging for such listings, we cut out a lot of these messages.

Offer a bannerlink option.

Besides offering advertisers sponsorship of your newsletter, you could also offer them a banner ad on your web site, especially on the page or pages where back issues of the newsletter are archived.

Advertise in email lists.

If you want to get more visitors to your site or more subscribers to your online newsletter, try advertising in related or non-competing online newsletters. The key to building a list is to advertise on other ezines or trade articles with related ezines.

Contribute to other online newsletters.

Most email newsletters and some blogs are continually looking for additional good content. If you have a great short article to offer, send it on to the editor of the newsletter. These newsletters generally welcome submissions from outside individuals and will allow you to post a little signature ad at the end of your message that sells your service or newsletter.

12:08 Selling Books Via Amazon.com & Online Booksellers

Besides the book sales and promotion you can do via your web site and email, you can also work with online bookseller such as Amazon.com, BN.com, BookSense.com, and others. Amazon.com, with billions in annual sales and millions of customers from around the world, is the best known bookstore on the Internet. Indeed, it is the best known book-related site on the Internet. For that reason, make sure your books and authors are featured as completely as possible on Amazon.com.

For more details on the ways that you as an author or publisher can help Amazon.com sell more of your books, check out their **Publisher & Vendor Guides** by visiting their Help department (link at bottom of most pages). In their guides, you'll find most of the things you can do to help them sell more of your books.

Below are a few of the things you can do. Note that you can carry out similar promotional activities on the other online bookselling web sites as well, but focus your attentions first on Amazon.com.

☐ Send them advance notice of your upcoming books. Use their online submission form.

☐ As an author or publisher, you are invited to add comments to your book listings at Amazon.com. They also encourage you to provide them with a description of the book, the table of contents, index, book cover graphic, sample pages, review excerpts, and other items to enhance your book's listing. Be sure to do that. As they say, "We rely on publishers for most of the descriptive material we post on a book's detail page."

☐ You can also encourage your customers to post reviews or testimonials of your books. Check out all the 5-star ratings for *1001 Ways to Market Your Books* for examples of great testimonials.

☐ Authors are invited to participate in online, self-guided interviews, which are featured with their titles at Amazon.com.

☐ Send them your cover art as a .gif or .jpeg file. Cover art really helps to sell books online. As in bookstore browsing, Amazon.com users like to be able to see the book. A cover image helps with that.

☐ To work more closely with Amazon.com, subscribe to their monthly mailing list that provides updated info about their policies.

☐ Amazon.com encourages you to update your book listings and to send them any corrections.

Below are some of Amazon.com's programs that can help you get more visibility for your books on Amazon.com as well as make more money from sales of your book there.

☐ **Online Book Content Form** — Amazon.com now features reviews from many magazines on its web site. If you get a good review somewhere, make sure they include it with your book listing. You can submit reviews via this form accessible via their publisher's FAQ. You can also submit other book-related information using this form.

☐ **Look Inside!** — If you provide Amazon.com with content pages from the inside of your book, they will feature a Look Inside! highlight on the book cover for your listing. People can then sample the content of your book. This content will also help your book show up for keyword searches that include a word used in the sample chapters of your book. This is just another way to help potential readers discover your book.

To join Amazon.com's **Search Inside the Book Program**, fill out their form (accessible after you complete the Online Book Content Form). Once accepted into the program, you'll also have to send Amazon.com a physical copy of each book you want included in the program.

Here's the main benefit according to Amazon.com: "When customers search for books on Amazon.com, we use the actual words from *inside* participating books—not just the author, title, and keywords supplied by the publisher—to return the best possible selection of books. With this powerful new search feature, customers can discover books that may never have surfaced in previous search results!"

☐ **Associates Program** — You can link to Amazon.com from your web site to have them fulfill your orders. Even better, you can set up as an Associate referral site and gain a percentage of every sale resulting from your link. Their main page includes a link on the bottom of the left side to various ways to make money with Amazon.com. The Associates Program is one of those ways. Every book featured on BookMarket.com that I know the ISBN of has an Amazon associates link.

☐ **So You'd Like to Guide** — You can write a guide on how to do anything, whether you're an expert on that subject or not. Obviously it makes most sense to write guides on your expertise. The guides are currently limited to a 100-word minimum and a 1,500 word maximum. To access this opportunity, go to any book page at Amazon and click on the Create your guide link under So You'd Like to...

For example, I wrote a guide, *Self-Publish and Create a Bestseller*, which is now featured on the book page of every book I listed in the guide (in rotation, of course, with other guides). So now my name is in front of anyone buying one of the major books on self-publishing. People read these guides and are also encourage to rate them.

Chris Epting wrote a guide, *Plan a Road Trip*, that featured only his own travel trivia books. Thus far, it's been read 230 times. That means 230 people were exposed to his entire list of related titles.

☐ **Listmania** — Amazon.com allows users to create all sorts of book lists on whatever hits their fancy. Any list you create will be featured on the pages of the books you feature (in a rotation with lists created by other readers and authors). It's a great way to tie into related books and get your name and book noticed by people already looking to buy competitive titles. If someone lists your book in a Listmania list, be thankful! It means that you'll get exposure on many related title pages.

☐ **Tagging** — Amazon.com now allows readers to tag any book with key words. Be sure to tag your book for key words that you think people would use to find your book on Amazon when they don't know the title or when they're simply searching for books in a specific subject area.

Here are the tags I've added so far to my *1001 Ways to Market Your Books* listing: marketing online, book marketing, books, self-publishing, writing books, book author, authors, book publicity, publicity, book-selling, promoting books, self-promotion, book promotion, promoting online, and Internet marketing.

☐ **Customer Reviews** — Amazon.com encourages customers to write reviews of all books. You can write reviews of other related titles and include your book title as part of your signature on the review. This is one way to piggyback on the popularity of related titles. If you have time, write a review for every book related to your book's subject. But only write reviews for books that you have actually read and enjoyed. Don't be critical, glib, or superficial.

Dan Poynter, author of *The Self-Publishing Manual*, has written 198 book reviews on Amazon.com as of April 2006. 1,739 people have said that his reviews were helpful to them.

☐ **Customer Images** — You can now add more images to your book's page besides the book cover. There's a link under the book cover on Amazon.com where you can share your customer images. Apparently it would be possible to share a customer image that include your book's cover on the page featuring a competitive title. I haven't tested this out, but it seems within the parameters currently set up for this feature.

If you note the current listing for *1001 Ways*, I've added a photo of myself speaking at BookExpo America, a copy of the new cover for the 6th edition, and a photo of one reader's copy packed with sticky notes and tabs. These images can only help sell the book.

☐ **Customer Discussions** — This is a new beta program where users can share their questions, insights, and views about books and other products. Amazon is encouraging people to give reviews, ask questions, compare products, and join in the group discussions.

I used this section to alert browsers on the page featuring the 5th edition of *1001 Ways to Market Your Books* that a new edition is coming out by May 15th. I encouraged readers to wait to buy the new edition rather than buy one of the used copies currently offered for sale.

☐ **Citations** — When you send in the table of contents, biography, index, and other key sections of your book to Amazon.com to enhance your book's listing, be sure to include a bibliography, even if there isn't one in the physical book. Each citation you make will be noted on the pages of the books you cite (in the Citations section). If your book is included in the Search Inside! feature, then any chapter that mentions a book will also be included in this Citations section.

This is just one of a number of ways to get your book featured on the pages of related titles, including the bestselling titles! For example, according to Amazon.com, 30 other books cite *1001 Ways* in the bibliography or in other text.

☐ **AmazonConnect** — This powerful new program allows readers to receive messages directly from their favorite authors. It opens what could be an incredibly intimate channel of communication between you as an author and your readers. Participating authors can post messages on their book detail pages and to the home page of readers who have bought their books on Amazon.com. Essentially, this program allows you to write a blog on Amazon.com!

Amazon.com shoppers can subscribe to receive every new posting from their favorite authors. These new postings will appear in the user's *plog*. That's Amazon.com's new name for a personalized web log of their activity on Amazon.com, including author postings, changes in their orders, new products that have just been released, and much more.

Lee Goldberg, author of many mystery books based on TV series such as *Diagnosis Murder*, writes a blog on Amazon.com where he simply reposts some of the posts he creates for his *A Writer's Life* blog. Here is what he has written about why he blogs on Amazon:

I have an Amazon blog. It doesn't take much effort to maintain, since it mainly consists of repurposed material originally posted here. The blog can be read as a stand-alone Lee Goldberg blog, or my posts can show up, along with those of other authors, in a reader's plog on your Amazon home page. I get a couple dozen positive votes from readers on each new post, but still I wondered if enough people were reading my Amazon blog to make it worthwhile and if it made any difference in the way people viewed me or my books. Now I know. I got this comment from Karen Oberst, a librarian in Oregon:

> We get a lot of plogs, since as a library we order a great deal from Amazon However, the only ones I look forward to are the ones by Lee Goldberg. I so appreciate the backstage look at both the television industry, and how the writing is done. Thanks, Lee for your informative posts, and for taking the time to update them so often.

The comment made my day. I never knew that libraries bought books on Amazon. The comment also told me that people are reading the posts and that maintaining the *Readers Digest* version of this blog over there is doing me some good.

In one of his posts, he noted that he had rearranged his books when visiting bookstores and supermarkets. He also reposted comments from several other authors who had done the same thing.

Well, Amazon.com allows you to comment on other author's blogs (and even encourages you to do so), so I did. Here is what I wrote about that:

Oh, I love this. For years I've recommended that authors take a proactive role in getting good placement for their books in bookstores and other retail outlets. Hooray for all bodacious authors! — John Kremer, author, *1001 Ways to Market Your Books* (a new 6th edition coming in May).

☐ **Amazon Shorts** — These are new short works from well-known authors that are available only on Amazon.com (you have to give them an exclusive for a minimum of six months). These short stories and essays are delivered electronically and sell for only 49 cents. Amazon.com notes the following benefits to authors for participating in this new program: it can promote the author's backlist titles, maintain author visibility between published books, introduce readers to unfamiliar authors, provide a new outlet to sell short fiction, and create an author profile page.

For publishers, the main benefit is the ability to feature excerpts from forthcoming books to boost pre-orders or to sustain on-going sales. Amazon wants pieces that are between 2,000 and 10,000 in length. They are encouraging participants to contribute new items on a regular basis. If you'd like to participate, email them at amazon-shorts@amazon.com. Tell them why you would be a good addition to their program.

I plan to submit an Amazon Short consisting of the pages from this chapter devoted to selling books on Amazon.com. I'll give it a nice title such as *How to Sell More Books on Amazon.com*. That should get some attention and, I hope, sales.

☐ **Reading Group Guides** — Amazon.com encourages publishers to provide guides for reading groups. At this time, you can only submit the information for such guides via FTP. If you don't know what that means, ask your web site provider to help you submit the information. For a reading group guide, Amazon.com needs the ISBN, title, author's name, discussion questions, author bio, author comments, and the RGG source (name of the publisher). Here's an example of a Reading Group Guide (this is the example that Amazon.com uses):

About the Book: "The questions, discussion topics, and author biography that follow are intended to enhance your group's reading of Deborah Simingtown's *Moose Crossing*. In this enchanting tale, Nora leaves New York and moves to a small Vermont logging town.

"The novel is populated with a quirky cast of characters to whom Nora finds herself drawn. We witness her struggle to come to terms with her past while living in a town where secrets are public property."

Discussion Questions: "What understanding does Nora have of small-town life and love? How do her ideas come to change during the course of the novel?"

"Why do you think Simingtown chose to make her romantic hero a forest ranger? Why do the woods, of all places, play a healing role in Nora's inner battle? What is the significance of the covered bridge that Roger builds?"

"After Herb fires Nora, she decides to return to New York. What does she fear in Vermont? What makes her reluctant to leave?"

Author Bio: "Deborah Simingtown was born and raised in Vermont. She is firmly established in the New York literary scene, and won the coveted Bartleby award for her first novel."

☐ **Amazon Fishbowl** — This new weekly podcast is hosted by Bill Maher where he interviews book authors. Thus far, he is leaning heavily toward interviewing famous authors from bigger publishers. We can hope that policy will change soon, or that Amazon.com will add other programs favoring lesser known authors and books. If you'd like to host such a podcast, you can always propose such a program to Amazon.com. They are always looking for ways to feature and sell more books.

☐ **Amazon Wire** — This is a free original podcast about books, movies, music, and those who create them. Any Amazon.com visitor can listen to the podcast online or download it for playing on their iPod.

The April 2006 podcast featured interviews with *Oceans 11* movie director Steven Soderbergh, Chris Stein of Blondie, and Steven Drozd of The Flaming Lips. It also included an exclusive audio essay from *Freakonomics* author Stephen Dubner on teaching monkeys to use money.

☐ **Amazon Marketplace** — You can also sell your book directly to people on Amazon.com by clicking on the Sell Yours Here link on your book's page at Amazon.com. You can set your own price. Be sure to indicate that your book is new and signed (that makes it more valuable as a collectible). When someone orders from you via this link, Amazon.com collects the money and sends you the order to fulfill. Then once a month they send you a check for 85% of your sale price minus 99 cents. They even give you a postage credit for sending the book via media mail. It's real easy to set this up.

When I checked Amazon.com's listing for *1001 Ways to Market Your Books* on April 15, 2005, there were 37 listings for new and used copies of my book for resale by others. Most were new copies probably obtained from Ingram, so I'm making money on most of those sales just as if Amazon.com had made the sale directly. And such sales still count towards their bestseller rankings!

If you are worried about people selling used or review copies of your book on Amazon, stop worrying. It's not worth the worry. Remember: Every book that gets into the hands of a reader somewhere will result in the sale of another copy (if your book is any good).

If you are still worried about used copies, there's a simple solution: Sell your own new copies at a price lower than the used copies listed by other sellers at Amazon. You'll still make money on the sale as long as the used copy price isn't too low.

☐ **Auctions and zShops** — As an alternative, especially if your book isn't listed on Amazon.com, you can set up an auction or a zShop. An auction is similar to what you would offer on eBay.com, while a zShop is essentialy a retail shop set up within Amazon.com that makes use of Amazon.com's shopping cart services. Both alternatives are explained on the Amazon.com web site.

☐ **Amazon's Honor System** — This system allows you to sell books on your web site, have Amazon.com collect the credit card payment, and send the order and money to you (less their fee). If you don't qualify yet for online credit card services and are not using PayPal or a similar service, then Amazon's Honor System certainly is a viable option.

- **Amazon.pl XML Associate Engine** — Among Amazon.com's suggested web services is this software program, which allows associates to quickly and easily add thousands of Amazon.com products to their web sites. To use this service, you do not have to know any programming languages but you do need to know how to create an HTML web page and insert links. It costs $100 to set up and $30 per year to license.

- **Amazon Product Feed** — A similar program using a free perl script to provide real-time listings of books on your web site. Details about this option are at http://www.mrrat.com/aws/index.html.

- **Associates Shop** — This free service allows you to set up in a store at Amazon.com to feature all your recommended books (for example, all the books you recommend in your bibliography) and then link to it. As the developers note: "Every time someone clicks one of your referral links and does not buy the product he clicked for but another one, you earn only 5% referral fees. With our shop he puts the article to his shopping-cart directly, so you will earn much more than without the shop!" Find out more at http://www.associatesshop.com.

- **Other Shopping Programs** — Which of the options (listed above and below) you choose to use will depend on which works best with the way you think along with which works best with your web site design. Having looked them all over, I'm currently leaning toward using AWS Content Management System (listed below). Within a few months all my web sites will include a book shop linked intimately to Amazon.com. Your information web sites should have something similar to help you monetize the value of your web site beyond your own book sales.

AMZ Lists (http://www.amzlists.com)

AWS Content Management System (http://www.awscms.com)

Mall Socket (http://www.mallsocket.com)

OK Mall (http://www.okscripts.com/okmall/index.php)

- **Buy X, Get Y Paid Placement** — Amazon.com provides one key advertising option: the Buy X, Get Y paid placement, which links two books together with a suggestion to buy both. You can pay to have your book title linked with a better known or better selling title. Your title is linked on the page of the better-selling book, bolded, and given an additional 5% discount to encourage sales.

Nominations for the BXGY program must be submitted one month before the desired start date but not more than three months in advance. You can only link with one other title at a time. BXGY promotions are displayed on the first or the 16th of the month following receipt of payment (by check only at this time). It currently costs $1,000 for a one-month link to a top 250 title; only $750 for a title ranked over 250.

Some self-published authors who have paid for this placement program have report significant up-ticks in sales. It is certainly worth testing.

☐ **Customer Discussions** — Amazon.com is testing a new beta feature that provides a forum for customer discussions. As they write, "Customer Discussions allow you to share your questions, insights, and views about products available on Amazon.com with other customers and sellers. Read what others are saying about hot products, get knowledgeable answers, read product comparisons, and join in the fun of easy-to-use group discussions."

You can always start a new discussion at any time by simply entering a discussion topic. When you click on the blank discussion topic form, it pops up a larger form to post the topic and your discussion. Then you simply click *post* to include the discussion on that product page. Here is another opportunity for you to be featured on the Amazon.com page for a related title. Use it wisely.

In April 2006, I posted the following notice in the product forum for the 5th edition of *1001 Ways*: "I want everyone who visits this page to know that my new 6th edition of this book will be off the press in mid-May 2006. Amazon.com should have copies within a week after that. Please be patient. I will have the new edition out soon. Thanks." It was just one more way that I alerted Amazon.com customers to the new edition before it was available on Amazon.com.

☐ **Amazon Rankings** — If you want to know how well your book ranks against other books on Amazon.com, here are several estimates on what the Amazon.com rankings mean in terms of actual book sales:

Amazon.com Rank	Average Sales Per Week
75 to 100	265 copies
100 to 200	235 copies
200 to 300	175 copies
450 to 750	90 copies
750 to 3,000	40 copies
3,000 to 9,000	5 copies
10,000 on up	5 or less copies

Here's another estimate of what the Amazon.com sales ranks mean, based on sales at Foner Books:

Amazon.com Rank	Average Sales Per Day
100	30 book sales per day
1,000	10 book sales per day
10,000	2 book sales per day
100,000+	1 book sale per week

☐ **Product Wiki** — Amazon.com allows customers to create encyclopedic entries (aka *wikis*) that contain customer-editable product information. Not all book pages will include a link to do this, but for the title listing for *1001 Ways to Market Your Books*, I created a Product Wiki featuring my short discussion of of marketing as building relationships.

☐ **Amazon Audiobooks** — Amazon.com is developing a new store to offer downloadable audiobooks to its customers. If you are a publisher of audiobooks or other spoken audio content and would like your products to be included in their store, email them at digital-audio@amazon.com. That's all it takes to find out more. Do it today if you already have MP3s of books, seminars, talks, chapters, ebooks, teleseminars, etc.

☐ **Miscellaneous Promotions** — Amazon.com continues to explore new ways to promote and sell more books. Stay alert to what they are doing differently, and latch on to those that make sense for you.

In one promotional effort, Amazon.com recruited John Updike to write the first and last paragraphs of a detective story called "Murder Makes the Magazine" and asked its visitors to write the remaining paragraphs. Within weeks it had received more than 100,000 paragraph entries. Each day, Amazon.com selected one more paragraph entry to add to the story.

Check out other online bookseller sites as well as other retail sites to see what programs they offer to help you sell more books. Amazon.com, being the most visible retailer on the Internet (rated #12 in traffic), is the one you should give most of your attention to, but don't ignore the others. By the way, BN.com is ranked #509 in traffic by Alexa.com as of April 15, 2006 while Powells.com is ranked #4,749; Booksamillion.com at #11,390, Borders.com at #369,588, and BookSense.com at #68,675.

If you want to support independent booksellers, join BookSense.com's affiliate program as well as Amazon.com's. That way you can give your web site visitors two ways to buy books: via the Internet big box retailer or via independent bookstores.

Other retail sites such as Walmart.com (ranked #217), Target.com (#180) and Costco.com (#470) are also ranked quite high. By comparison, Book Market.com is generally ranked around #80,000.

12:09 Creating an Amazon.com Bestseller Campaign

One of the biggest trends in book marketing is the on-going campaigns to create Amazon.com bestsellers. Because sales at Amazon.com can be tracked so easily and affected by direct Internet promotions, many authors have seen Amazon.com bestseller campaigns as a major way to draw attention to their books. And they are right.

I think such campaigns have been overdone, but I do know their power in getting attention for your book online. So I still encourage authors to do an Amazon.com bestseller campaign at least once in the life of their book, no matter how new or old the book is.

Have you done your Amazon.com promotion yet? When do you plan to do it? It is still one of the most effective online sales tools ever created for books. Its power to draw attention and create sales is still unparalleled, especially for having a fast and measurable impact on the sales of a book.

- If you ever thought of doing your own Amazon.com bestseller campaign, then you might want to check into the campaign that was done for Diane Lu's *Daughter of the Yellow River*. Why? Because she had so many participants, including people mailing to their lists as well as dozens and dozens giving away free reports, audios, etc. to buyers of her book. Her list of movers and givers could be contacted to help you as well, especially if your book is on relationships, health, self-help, business, motivation, or related topics. To check out Diana Lu's offer, see http://www.bookbonuses.com/lu.

Diana's book went from an Amazon.com ranking of 304,648 on Tuesday, April 4, 2006, to a rank of 8,366 on Wednesday afternoon, a rank of 4,516 on Thursday morning, a rank of 992 by Thursday afternoon, and 271 by late Thursday evening. Her sales campaign began on Tuesday and went through Thursday.

Now that rise is nice, but it doesn't signify enough sales to justify what it might have cost her to mount the campaign—at least not by the numbers alone. But think of how many people were exposed to her book. Think of how many will end up buying the book weeks or months later. Think of how many people will be inspired to talk more about her book after seeing the promotion.

- Here's what Jason Oman reported about *Conversations with Millionaires* when he used an Amazon.com campaign: "In 76 days from my book's release with no money spent on promotion, no PR, no public speaking, and self-publishing, we went to #1 on Amazon.com for 29 hours."

- If you want to see how an Amazon.com bestseller campaign can feature a wonderfully designed web page to make the sales pitch, see: http://www.trainone.com/special/april4. It includes great graphics, a short video from the author, some fresh bonuses, and an attractive web page design.

Except for one thing, it would be a perfect page. What is the one caveat? It takes too long to load with a slow Internet connection. So if you model this page in your Amazon.com promotions, have an alternative for people who still have slow connections to the Internet.

The page promotes Jeff Gitomer's *The Little Red Book of Sales Answers*. Gitomer is a succinct author who provides practical information that anyone can follow. His ezine *Sales Caffeine* has 80,000 subscribers!

How did I find out about this promotion? Not through a newsletter. Not through an email campaign. Instead, I found out via an RSS feed to a blog I regularly follow. What does this mean to you? It means that when you do your Amazon.com promotion, be sure to include all avenues: website updates, ezine promotions, and lots of notices on blogs.

Gitomer's book ranked #623 at Amazon.com on Wednesday, April 5th, and #3 by Thursday morning (according to a friend, the book did hit #1 some time on Wednesday or Thursday).

- After being rejected by New York publishers, cellular biologist Bruce Lipton signed on with an independent press that relies heavily on Amazon.com sales. More than 42,000 copies of his *Biology of Belief* have sold in six months.

- Mary Shomon's *The Thyroid Diet* "spent the month before publication in the Amazon top 100, and publication week in the top ten, with two days at #5, generating three printings in the first week of publication, and landing me a space on the *NY Times* bestseller list!" How did she accomplish all this before her publisher's marketing campaign had begun?

  She made sure Amazon.com had all the information it needed to feature her book prominently (she didn't wait for her publisher, HarperCollins, to do this). She made sure her web site (http://www.thyroid-info.com) had high search engine rankings. She had massive distribution to key buyers via her thyroid and diet newsletters. And she carried out an Amazon.com bestseller campaign on the book's publiciation date.

- John Du Cane, publisher of Dragon Door Publications, supported a bestseller campaign for Pavel Tsatsouline's *The Naked Warrior*. As a result of the campaign, the book reached #2 on Amazon.com's bestseller list and #1 on Amazon.com's Health, Mind, & Body list. In less than a week, they sold 2,000 copies of the $40 paperback. Several years later, the book is still ranked at #7,957 when I checked in April, 2006.

- When Randy Gilbert began his first campaign for his self-published book, *Success Bound*, it was ranked at #67,131. By 10:31 a.m. on the day he pressed the GO button, his book jumped to #81. By 8:36 p.m. that same day, it hit #10. Hours later it hit #5.

  The next morning, agents and publishers called wanting to buy rights and asking to have first look at his next books. For days afterwords, he received calls and emails from dozens of literary agents and foreign rights buyers. His book is currently published in Chinese, Finnish, Korean, Greek, Spanish, Japanese, and Hebrew.

Create and carry out an Amazon.com bestseller campaign.

Below are the basic steps you need to take to create and carry out an Amazon.com bestseller campaign:

- ☐ **Locate your campaign partners.** Your partners should include all the authors, publishers, ezine editors, bloggers, and web site owners you know who have something to sell to a similar audience to the one you want to reach. If these people aren't already in your network, you need to do more research using Google or another search engine to target the web sites with the highest rankings for your key words.

☐ **Send out emails or make phone calls** to all your potential partners. Ask them to join your bestseller campaign. Why would they want to participate in such a campaign? Easy. They will get promotional exposure to everyone who receives the sales promotion since their bonus offering will be featured in the sales copy. In addition, they will get to add each buyer's name to their list when those buyers come to their web site to download their bonus.

☐ **Compile great bonuses.** You must get a list of 20 to 30 bonuses to be included in your promotion. Help your partners identify the bonus they can offer that will be most attractive to the lists you will be mailing to. Remember: The bonuses often determine whether or not someone acts right away to buy your book. They might buy your book anyway, but to get them to act right away, you must offer must-have bonuses.

Here are a few items your partners could offer: reports created from book excerpts, an audio interview, a recorded speech, a discount coupon for consulting, a report created by consolidating several articles, a teleseminar. Don't include any hard copy bonuses. All bonuses should be delivered via online downloads (cheaper and a lot easier to fulfill).

☐ **Write the sales letter.** Once you've compiled the list of bonuses, you need to write a compelling sale letter, making an offer that knocks the socks off your readers. If you're not good at writing sales copy, research some of the others sales letters previously used in bestseller campaigns. Copy their structure and language, but adapt it to your book's benefits (and reasons to buy) and the bonuses included in your offer.

☐ **Send the sales letter to your partners**. Let them know which day to drop the mailing. They should send out the sales letter on the day of your promotion (or not sooner than the night before). Remember: Anyone offering a bonus should also mail the promotional sales letter to their customer list, include a notice in their ezine, post a notice on their web site, and/or include a post in their blog.

☐ **Drop the letter.** Again, the letter should be sent out the day of the promotion. You need to have the letter go out to at least 300,000 peope to have any impact on sales. Better yet, it should go out to a million or more. Your goal is to sell at least 250 books online in one day. In general, .05% of those on a cold email list will become buyers. 3% is in the high range of returns for a really strong list.

☐ **Send buyers to Amazon.com**. Be sure that your letter sends people to Amazon.com to buy your book—and that they buy during certain hours. That's the only way your book stands a chance of breaking out from the huddled book masses. Provide the readers with a direct link to your book page on Amazon.com.

☐ **Tell them how to get their bonuses**. In the sales letter, be sure to tell them to email you their receipt from Amazon.com. Once you receive their emailed receipt, send them a return email with a link to the page where they can get the download links for all the bonuses included in your campaign. Note: Only 50 to 65% of buyers will actually go get the bonuses.

☐ **Send a thank-you note** to your partners. And provide them with the details on the success of the program: How many people bought your book. What rank did your book achieve. Samples of any thank-you emails you receive from buyers.

☐ **Now do something more**. Any bestseller campaign only works if it is part of an integrated marketing plan. Doing an Amazon.com campaign is really worthless if you are not doing some other things to help keep your book high on the list. For most of the past 5 to 10 years, my *1001 Ways to Market Your Books* has hovered between 4,000 and 10,000 in the Amazon bestseller list.

☐ **Partner with other campaigns.** If you want to be successful in doing additional Amazon.com bestseller campaigns, be sure to participate in other author's campaigns as well when you are asked. Remember that you are creating relationships that could last for years and profit you in many ways beyond the one-time campaign.

The above points cover the basic steps you need to carry out in doing an Amazon.com bestseller campaign. Don't ignore any step in the process. Don't fudge it. Don't think you can run such a campaign without any partners. Don't settle for poor partners. Go for the best partners, with the largest email lists, most visited web sites, most active blogs. Again, use this campaign as the first step in creating a relationship that you can build on.

Biggest note: Don't roll out such a campaign without at least 300,000 people receiving the promotion. Do the math. Make sure that you gather together enogu partners to do a credible campaign. Don't cheat here.

Do a BN.com bestseller campaign.

As an alternative to doing an Amazon.com campaign, you could do one where you send buyers to BN.com. It's less competitive, so you could hit a higher rank with few sales. In addition, sales at BN.com count towards the bestseller lists compiled by Barnes & Noble. Plus, high rankings in the online store will get the attention of the buyers for the Barnes & Noble retail stores. Note BN.com updates bestseller listings every hour.

Rick Frishman and Jill Lublin promoted *Networking Magic* via a BN.com bestseller campaign. Within days, they hit #1 on BN.com and remained #2 for several days afterwards. Their book also hit the Barnes & Noble bookstores bestseller list. For four months afterwards, their book remained in the upper 1,000 bestselling titles on BN.com. In addition, their book also hit #38 on Amazon.com.

Do a BookSense.com bestseller campaign.

If you are really adventurous, you could try a *BookSense.com* bestseller campaign. In such a campaign, you'd end up sending people to buy from the web sites of independent booksellers via a *BookSense.com* link. Such sales would then help you to attract the attention of independent booksellers and also contribute to any bestseller campaign you are doing in the outside world (thus counting toward the major bestseller lists, such as the *New York Times* and *USA Today* lists.

12:10 Sell Books Via Google and Other Search Engines

As I've written before, most people find out about web sites through the major search engines. Google is the big dog on the block, but the others are also important. In this section, I'll be describing many of the programs that Google makes available that can help you to achieve a high search engine ranking for your key words, help you sell more books, and help you promote your books around the world. The strategies described here and the basic programs offered by Google will be matched in some way by the other search engines. Once you've mastered Google, work on some of the other search engines as well.

Search Engine Optimization

The the most important thing you can do to help yourself with search engine rankings is to optimize your site for the search engines. The key to this is to model the web sites that already rank high for your key words in those search engines. Review the top 30 sites. Study them thoroughly. Then try to model them, continuing to test various changes until you hit on the changes that are actually resulting in higher rankings for your web site. Most changes you make should be reflected in higher rankings within a few days if your web site is spidered regularly. If you are already in the top 50 sites for your key words, your web site is probably being spidered daily.

Because my main *BookMarket.com* web site has a relatively high Google page rank of 6, most changes I make on the web site can result in dramatic rises for any key words I target. I've been able to make a few key changes on a web page and have it come out of nowhere to rank #10 or higher within a few days. I doubt I could do that with a lower page rank site.

In research conducted using eye movements while viewing search result pages, it was discoverd that 100% of the people see the first three organic results, 85% see the 4th position, 60% see the 5th, 50% the 6th and 7th, 30% the 8th and 9th, and 20% the 10th. Few pages go beyond the first page or two of search results, so you clearly want to rank in the top 10 results if at all possible.

More important than eye movements, however, are actual click-throughs where someone actually clicks to visit the web site listed. 27.4% of all organic clicks are for the #1 listing. This click-through rate drops to 12% by the #3 position. It doesn't get better after that.

For *BookMarket.com*, I've done a lot of SEO work to make sure the site ranks high for many keywords. Here are the results as of April 15, 2006:

> book marketing — #1 and #2
> book editors — #6 and #7
> book publishers — #7
> business book publishers — #6
> business book editors — #1 and #2
> children's book publishers — #20
> children's book editors — #3 and #4
> cookbook editors — #5
> cookbook publishers — #63 (very competitive because
>   of all the fund-raising cookbook publishers)
> sports book editors — #1 and #2
> sports book publishers — #3
> health book editors — #1 and #2
> health book publishers — #3 and #4
> fiction editors — #3
> fiction book publishers — #2
> novel editors — #1
> novel publishers — #2
> first novel editors — #1 and #2
> first novel publishers — #1

The above keyword phrase was where my web site jumped from out of nowhere to #1 in ten days by modeling the site of the previous #1 site. It worked wonders. And all it took was a few word changes in this case.

I used to be #7 and #13 for self-publishing, but in the past few months my site has dropped out of sight. That won't be for long. Tonight I implemented a new strategy for keeping it rated higher.

Of course, no steps would be sufficient or even make a dent unless the page actually deserves to be at highly rated. That's where content comes into play. Over time, Google does an incredible job of sorting through web sites to find the best content. They are not easily fooled.

Google AdWords

With Google Adwords, you can pay to be linked to any number of key words. If you want to be seen whenever anyone searches for "organic gardening," you can pay to be featured in the paid listings section. Now, if you're already in the top 10 listings for that search term, you don't have to pay to be featured, but some SEO (search engine optimization) experts say you get the most clickthroughs to your web site when you combine organic listings (the listings that pop up naturally when someone searches for a term) and paid AdWords listings.

With paid listings, you can attach your book web site to any key words or search terms you can afford to pay for. And with Google AdWords, there is little risk, because you can limit how much money you want to spend at any one time and you can also drop out whenever you want. If you want a lot of traffic quickly, Google AdWords is a key tool for getting that traffic. Here are a few more points about the AdWords opportunity:

☐ **Go for the top 3 paid listings.** It doesn't really pay to be #5 or #6 unless that is all you can afford. In the study of eye movements cited on the previous page, 50% of people saw the first paid listing, 40% the 2nd listing, 30% the 3rd, 20% the 4th, and 10% the 6th through 8th. As for click-throughs, 51% of paid click-throughs are for the #1 position. It drops dramatically after that. Note that the click-throughs for paid listings are significantly less than those for the organic listings.

☐ **Bid for misspellings.** To get the most bang for your buck, bid for keyword misspellings and plurals. There's less competition for these versions. For example, if your keyword is *horse riding*, you could bid for *horses riding, hors riding, horse ridin, riding horses, riding hors*, etc. Note that when people are typing into search engine forms, they often are typing fast and misspell words simply by leaving certain letters out.

☐ **Bid for keyword modifiers** such as *free* or *speedy* or *cheap* or *easy* or *blog* (e.g., free beading crafts, cheap knitting kits, easy crafts, do-it-yourself knitting blog). These combinations are less competitive and, thus, less expensive, but can still draw very targeted traffic.

☐ **Use the Keyword Tool** (https://adwords.google.com/select/KeywordTool External) to help you decide on what keywords to bid on. Type in any word or phrase, and it will return a list of suggested words to include in your AdWord bid. This tool will also search any website page and recommend keywords to generate traffic to that page. You can then view those words by advertiser competition, search volume, and cost. It's an incredible tool to use in deciding what to bid on.

☐ **Get featured on Amazon.com.** Google AdWords can also get you listed on the Amazon.com pages of other books—if the key words you have paid for pop up on that page. For example, on my *1001 Ways* page at Amazon.com on April 15, 2006, BookSurge offer print-on-demand services, Infinity Publishing offer POD publishing services, and Toseeka.com offered helpful links for book publishers.

Interestingly, Toseeka.com's page featured five AdWords ads (that's all!), so they were paying to have people click over to their site to click on additional ads where they would earn income on every click. I wonder if this circular sales logic actually works.

☐ **Target demographics.** Google AdWords is now offering advertisers an opportunity to target ads by choosing up to three demographic categories. That could allow you to really target the audience for your book at a reasonable cost. Check it out at http://adwords.google.com.

☐ **Target other author's names.** To promote his novel Tropic/of/Cubicle, Roderick Maclean set up an AdWords campaign consisting of the names of popular contemporary authors who write like he does: John Irving, Michael Chabon, Dave Eggers, Hruki Murakami, Arundhati Roy, Bret Easton Ellis, David Foster Wallace, and Jonathan Safran Foer. Because no one was buying these names, he paid the minimum 5 cents per click. His ad read as follows: Some novels are destined for greatness. Other novels are named Tropic/of/Cubicle. www.tropicofcubicle.com.

His main competitors for AdWords for these authors were bookselling sites like Amazon that include many authors' names in their Adwords campaigns. He limited his AdWords exposure to only searches by disabling Google's content network, where ads appear on other sites besides search sites. He also limited his campaign to U.S. searches (because his publisher couldn't handle a lot of foreign orders).

During the three days he ran his campaign, 1,298 people searched for Michael Chabon, 835 for John Irving, 714 for Dave Eggers, etc. During the one day David Sedaris was included in his campaign, he got 500 searches but only one click-through to Maclean's site, so Google cut off his name because it wasn't producing enough click-throughs. (Google has little patience for non-paying ads.)

While his campaign sidn't sell a lot of books, another author or publisher who can target author's names or book titles could possibly make a lot of money if they write a good short ad. If you decided you wanted to try this, test a few different ads until you find one that gets clickthroughs and, more importantly, book sales. You don't want to pay for a lot of clickthroughs that don't result in sales. If your ads only cost 5 cents like his did, you could afford to have about 100 clickthroughs for every one book sale. But if your ad costs more, you'll have to determine exactly how many sales you need per clickthrough to break even on book sales.

If the author or book title that you are targeting costs too much per clickthrough (because there are many other companies bidding for those terms), why not try misspellings? Instead of Neal Pollack, bid for Neil Pollack or Niel Pollack or Neil Polluck.

You do have to be careful when bidding on other people's names, because a Google search for my name, even spelled the way I spell it (John Kremer), turns up a German scientist, a teenage football hero, an American school teacher, a doctor, a sports attorney, a psychologist, a snowboarder, as well as a good number of John Kremers who were born and died in Minnesota (my home state). Plus a John Kremer 1987 Supra Turbo car. As well as, of course, dozens and dozens of references to me.

Google AdSense

Google AdSense allows you to place Google AdWords ads on your web site and get paid for any click-throughs that your website visitors make to those featured links. Many websites are now being created simply to take advantage of this new revenue source. I know of websites that are making $30,000 up to $200,000 per year from the click-throughs on their active websites. I also know of other websites making a few hundred dollars every few months from Google AdSense. It will only be a big money-maker for you if your web site gets lots of visitors.

I believe that every web site should have a Google AdSense ad block featured on every page. Most of my sites now have them. My BookMarket. com web site will also have them once I redesign the site later this year. Not only can AdSense provide you with additional income but it also provides a service to visitors of your web site. If you do not want to offer a paid service, then add the Google Related Links service described below.

Google Related Links

Webmasters can place Related Links units on their site to provide visitors with links to useful information, including related searches, web pages, and news. Anyone can host a unit on their each web page and start serving links to content that is targeted to that page's topic. This service allows you automatically to add fresh dynamic content to your website without doing additional work once the Google link is in place. Unlike AdSense, you don't get paid for any searches that takes place via this Related Links service.

Google Groups

Google Groups is a free online community and discussion group service that offers the Web's most comprehensive archive of Usenet postings (more than a billion messages). You can create your own group or join in the discussions of any existing group. There are groups covering any subject interest discussions you could possibly want to join in on.

Google News

Google News offers updated news covering the world, the U.S., sports, entertainment, business, science, technology, health, etc. On your Google News home page, you can create personalized news listings that allow you to track web news for any key words you want to track. On my home page, I track my name, book marketing, and self-publishing. You can also get Google news via RSS feeds (more on these later).

Google Alerts

On the Google news page, you can also sign up to receive news alert emails for any key words you want to track. I get Google news alerts for my name, my company name, bestselling books, and self-publishing. I get daily updates on any activity in the news or new entries on the web. You can use these to monitor developing news stories, keep up-to-date on your industry or competitor, get the latest gossip about a celebrity, etc. You can have the alerts track web site changes, news alerts, and group posts.

Using Google News and Google News Alerts can help you to keep informed about your hobbies, interests, book topics, favorite authors, etc. It can also help you to track media coverage, potential news story tie-ins, and media personal changes. Make the Alerts an active part of your book promotion research and follow-up. With Alerts, you can respond to news stories as they happen. Wow, what a service!

Froogle

This is Google's shopping search site. Be sure you're featured on this search engine if you have a retail web site. Their book listings are linked to *booksamillion.com* and some of the other online booksellers. You can list your products for free on Froogle. Google encourages you to keep your product listings up-to-date by uploading new product feeds any time you have new changes to make. You can access the Froogle Merchant Center at any time using your Google Account, which also lets you access Gmail, Google Groups, Google Answers, etc.

Google encourages other web sites to use its various services and incorporate them into their own sites. You can create links to the Froogle search engine to display results on your web site.

Google Local

Any retailer or other business can sign up to be listed in the Google Local search engine for free. It's like having a free Yellow Pages listing on the Internet.

Google Earth

Google Earth is a new service that allows you to see real photos of almost any location on earth. In larger cities, the photos can be very detailed. Again, Google is encourage other web sites to link to this service via special software tools. Some web sites are using these tools to create Google Earth *mashups*, which feature the Google Earth photos combined with interesting, weird, or unusual factoids. If you create a great Google Earth mashup (or have an experienced programmer create one for you), you could feature that mashup on your web site and generate a lot of traffic. Media are covering interesting Google Earth mashups as one of the hot topics of the Internet right now. Travel editors are especially interested in these combinations.

Google Labs

Google Labs (*http://labs.google.com*) are the pages where Google introduces its latest services or potential services. By checking these pages regularly, you can latch on to the latest Google fads before the media catch on to them and then hitch your website media promotion to Google's roll-out of the new services.

Here are a few of the services currently in their labs: Google Extensions for Firefox, Google Page Creator, Google Video, Google Reader (to read

RSS feeds), Google Dashboard Widgets for Mac, Google Transit (public tranportation information currently available only for Portland, Oregon), and many more. Graduates of Google Labs include personalized search, Google Maps, Google Scholar, Google Desktop, Google Deskbar, Web Alerts, and Google Glossary.

Google Answers

You used to be able to access this service from the Google home page, but the link doesn't seem to be there anymore, so link at *http://answers. google.com*. This service offers answers from 500 carefully screened researchers at a price you choose. It's tough now to get featured as one of these researchers, but you can always answer any question yourself as well —and point people to your web site for further answers. It's a good way to get additional notice and display your expertise.

You can also use this service to get answers to questions at a price you can afford, since you can set the price you will pay for the answer. I've seen people offer as little as $2.50 all the way up to several hundred dollars.

You can search by key words to locate questions and discussion on any subject you want to follow. This can be a great place to begin building relationships with like-minded people.

Google Search

You can add the Google Search box to your web site and get paid for doing so. Check out the Google Search box on the home page of our *Book Market.com* web site to see it in action. If you use our search box, we get paid for any click-throughs you follow on any paid listings resulting from those searches.

Google Sitemaps

By joing in this program, you can submit all your web pages to the Google index and get detailed reports about the visibility of your pages on Google. With Sitemaps you can also automatically keep Google informed of all changes to your web pages. This service will keep your search results in Google fresher (and likely higher as well).

You can use their Sitemap Generator to create an XML Sitemap. To find out more about Google Sitemaps, go to *http://www.google.com/services* and click on Sitemaps. This page also describes many of their other services for website creators, including the Video Upload Program, Google Analytics, and Books Partner Program.

Google Video

The Google Video service at *http://video.google.com* allows you to upload videos of any length for exposure via this Google service. You could make money with your videos. Here's Google's description of this service:

We're accepting digital video files of any length and size. Simply sign up for an account and upload your videos using our Video Uploader (please be sure you own the rights to the works you upload), and, pending our approval process and the launch of this new service, we'll include your video in Google Video, where users will be able to search, preview, purchase and play it.

Google Book Search

Google Book Search is the controversial attempt by Google to make all books searchable on the web in their entirety. Many publishers think that this service violates their copyright, and they may be right. But I believe you can control your copyright and still participate in this incredible new tool to expose your book to thousands, potentially millions of new readers. And get paid for it!

By matching the content in your books with user searches, Google Book Search connects your books with the users who are most interested in buying them. Once they land on one of your book pages, they are able to preview a limited number of pages. If they like what they see, Google provides links to most of the major bookselling sites on the web so people can buy your books online. People are also able to search for any book reviews online as well. The page also links to the publishers website as well.

Any clicks on Google AdWords listings on your book pages will also generate income for you. Whenever those clicks generate more than $100, you get a check. If your books are popular, this could mean big money.

To participate, you simply apply online telling Google which books you want to include in the program, what prices you want to set for complete online access, where to link to, and so on. Then send them a copy of the book or upload the book on their servers as a PDF file.

☐ Here's what Osprey Publishing had to say about their experience with this program: "The great thing about Google Book Search is that you get there through a general search. If you put in the name of a particular battle, for instance... we're pretty much always right there in the results, in the top half of the first page... We have a large range of titles and every single one was accessed within weeks of being indexed." When users decided to buy the books, 30% went directly to their site while 40% went to Amazon.com.

☐ When Penn State University Press was required to cut their backlist inventory, they switched the bottom portion of their list to print on demand and feature those titles in the Google Book Search program. With each book searched, the PSU Press website is the first link on the Buy This Book links list. Since their titles have been listed on Google Print, visits to their website have increased 124% and they tripled sales of their POD backlist titles.

☐ Crossways, a religious publisher, had been using Google AdWords as their main source of new website visitors. With their participation in

Google Book Search, their website visits have increased and their authors are clamoring to have their titles featured in this program.

☐ Google Book Search now also allows you to sell online access to your books directly through this service. You choose which books you want to offer under this program. And you get to experiment with the price you want to charge for people to access your books.

Google Base

Google Base (http://base.google.com) is Google's attempt to create a combination auction site and classified ad site. You can, however, add just about any content to this site and then assign *attributes* (that's Google's term for tagging). You can share information, recipes, ideas, and more. Remember, they say, "our goal is to organize the world's information and make it universally useful and accessible, and the world's information certainly includes almost anything you might wish to contribute. We encourage you to submit your item, whether it's your store inventory, collection of original poetry, or research paper on cancer receptors."

Google Calendar

Google Calendar is a new beta program that allows you to maintain your personal, business, hobby, and volunteer calendars all in one place. The one key feature in this Calendar that can be used for marketing books is the ability to mark an event on your calendar as *public*. By making it public, anyone else using Google Calendar can search for events related to their interests and thus find yours. It's a way to market all your appearances to people intersted in what you have to offer.

Google Smackdown

This is a service provided by Paul Bausch, the author of *Google Hacks*. If you want to find out which keywords you should be optimizing for, use Google Smackdown at http://www.onfocus.com/googlesmack/down.asp. This tool allows you to test any two keywords against each other to see which ones appear on the most web sites. This is a good indication of what web users are seeking. Below are a few of the numbers I generated using Smackdown to search for book publishing and marketing terms:

    bestsellers — 241,000,000
    book sales — 16,200,000
    book publishing — 12,900,000
    selling books — 9,160,000
    self-publishing — 7,980,000
    print-on-demand — 7,190,000
    best-selling books — 3,910,000
    book marketing — 1,130,000
    book printing — 963,000
    book promotion — 896,000
    book selling — 603,000

When I first used used this tool to do similar searches about six months ago, the results were magnitudes less. That suggests an incredible growth of web pages surveyed by Google compared to just a year ago.

Now go to Yahoo!

After optimizing your site and making use of all the great wonders at Google, take time to visit Yahoo! and make use of all its extra services such as My Yahoo, Yahoo Alerts, Yahoo 360! blogging service, Yahoo Search Marketing (formerly Overture), Keyword Selector Tool, View Bids Tool, Yahoo Mail, Flikr, and Yahoo Web Services.

☐ **Sponsored Search** is Yahoo's pay-per-click placement, where your chosen keyword paid listing appears next to search results in Yahoo!, MSN. com, CNN.com, and AltaVista. **Content Match** is where your pay-per-click listings appear alongside articles, product reviews, and other information on partner sites.

The value of Yahoo's Sponsored Search and Google's AdWords is that they allow you to get exposure to people searching for key words where you don't naturally rank high. This becomes incredibly valuable if you are unable to optimize your web site so it ranks within the top 10 web sites for key search terms. If your web site doesn't rank high for a keyword like "Florida travel," you can pay for a Sponsored Search listing that ranks you #1. Indeed, using Yahoo's View Bids Tool, you can find out exactly how much you'll have to pay to rank #1 or #2 or #3.

☐ Using their **View Bids Tool**, I discovered that ArborBooks.com paid $4.95 to show up #1 on Yahoo when someone searched on the keyword self-publishing. Xlibris paid $4.81, iUniverse $4.80, About Books $4.80, BookSurge $4.02, Infinity Publishing $4.01, and Instant Publisher $2.60. EBay and Amazon.com both paid 10¢ for the self-publishing keyword. The cheapest bidder was Watchmaker Publishing at 5¢. This is a great tool to help you find the keyword phrases you can afford! For example, I found that I cound have self-publishing bestsellers for only 10¢ since no one else was bidding for that term. Now that I could afford.

To access the View Bids Tool, go to Yahoo.com and click on the Ad Programs link to the right of the search box. This page gives more information on Yahoo's paid advertising programs. Now click on the Find out more link. On the resulting page, click on the Pricing tab. On the Pricing page, click on the View Bids Tool link. This will pop up another window where you can do your search.

Let's look, for another example, at "Florida travel." Type those words into the search box and click search. When I did this just now, I discovered that OrlandoFreeVacation.com bid $1.17 to be the top Sponsored Search link for "Florida travel." DiscountHotels.cc bid $1.10, Universal Studios.com bid $1.06, and so on. Now that's too much to pay for a click-through to a web site only selling a book.

But, if you search for "Florida travel book," the costs goes down considerably. The top bid was 28¢ by hotels-and-discounts.com. Then 27¢ for the #2 position for SkyAuction.com. And only 11¢ for the #3 position taken by alibris.com. Now, if I had a Florida travel book, I might bid for that #3 position for 12¢. That might be worth it if the click-throughs converted to book sales at a good rate—for instance, for every twenty click-throughs to my website, I sell one book. The cost of that sale then becomes $2.40. If I have the margin, that makes perfect sense.

The neat thing about pay-for-click advertising is that you can test different keyword combinations until you find the ones that really do pay off in additional website visits and book sales. Now with this tool, you don't have to go in blind on the bidding. You can find out exactly how much the top listings are paying, and then decide if you can outbid one of them to become a top site yourself. This is well worth it if your site is top rated in the *organic results* (the non-paid listings that show up).

☐ **Yahoo Publisher Network** is their program equivalent to Google's Ad Sense, where any website can earn money from displaying Yahoo Sponsored Search ads on their website.

☐ **Yahoo Alerts** offers a service very similar to Google Alerts. Make use of both services, because they seem to pick up on different stories and/or different perspectives, so you sure not to miss any developing stories or news angles you could use in promoting your books and authors.

Watch out for the world!

China is hot. In another few years, you will have to pay attention to other search engines besides Google and Yahoo. Why? Because the Chinese will have their own search engines like Baidu (already the fourth most visited web site on earth) and Soguo.com. Similarly, Alibaba (the Chinese auction site) could become bigger than eBay.

12:11 Blogging Your Way to Success

Blogs are web sites that are continuously updated and indexed by date, with the most recent entries at the top of the page or at the front of the web site. That's a simple definition of what a blog is, but most people think of blogs as being web sites where people share their opinions or experiences.

Blogs have become ever more popular as a marketing tool. Why? For one major reason. Search engines like Google and Yahoo spider the blogs more often than other web sites (*spidering* means that the search engines follow all the links on the web site to find any changes or new pages on the site). Blogs have two attributes that attract this increased spidering: 1) a continuous stream of new content provided by the main blogger as well as by those who comment on the blog, and 2) lots of links, both inbound and outbound, suggesting a more popular web site.

A key action that feeds into both of these attributes is the tradition of bloggers to interact with each other, to read and comment on each other's posts, and to encourage controversy. Bloggers have broken many news stories, especially in the fields of politics and the media. They are hot, hotter right now than any other media.

Here are a few ways you can use blogs to promote your books, authors, company, brand name, and ideas.

Create your own blog.

To create your own blog, you can work with Blogger.com, Live Journal, Typepad, or any of the other sites or software that enable you to set up a blog. I've created three blogs using Blogger. They each took me just a few minutes to set up. Here are my three blogs: http://openhorizons.blogspot. com (about marketing books), http://teleseminars-free-reports.blogspot. com, and http://traveltrivia time.blogspot.com. Blogs at Blogspot (which you access via Blogger) are free to set up and continue using. You can host the blogs at blogspot.com or on your web site.

Once you've set up your blog, begin posting ideas, content, photos, etc. Add your personal opinion or insight to your posts. In your posts, begin commenting on posts from other blogs. Such comments help you to trade links with other blogs. Bloggers have their own community and often comment on each other's blog posts. Here is why you should blog:

☐ A blog establishes your expertise much in the same way as writing books, but in this case, a blog establishes your expertise on the web.

☐ A blog helps to get you more attention on the web, thus exposing you, your ideas, and your book to more people.

☐ A popular blog with lots of links to your web site (or as an integral part of your web site) helps to increase the rating for your web site.

☐ Blogs are immediate. You can respond to what's happening in the news, make announcements, and send out timely information.

☐ Blogs are the hot news of the day. All media are enchanted by blogs. Bloggers are getting big book contracts.

☐ Search engines love blogs.

☐ Blogs are interactive. People can make comments on each post and you can respond to those comments as well.

Syndicate your blog.

One of the neat things about blogs is that blogging sites and software providers make it easy to syndicate your content by using RSS. *RSS* (really simple syndication) uses XML feeds to syndicate content to anyone who chooses to subscribe. XML is a variation of HTML, a language for creating web pages. As a user, you can use feed aggregators such as bloglines, My Yahoo, or other services to keep track of blogs you 'd like to read.

One of the reasons why blogs are so much better than email newsletters is that you don't have to fight the spam filters. Anyone who subscribes to your blog will be notified of any additions to your blog and can then go directly to that new post and read it without any filtering. If you publish an email newsletter, consider duplicating the content on your blog for those who would rather access your information that way.

How to blog effectively.

To create an effective blog, one that will get noticed and linked to, you have to think and act like a blogger. Here are a few basic actions that should help your blog get noticed:

☐ **Post every day,** even multiple times each day, if you want people to revisit your blog on a regular basis.

☐ **Interview interesting people.** One popular blog activity is to interview people and post the interview to the blog. One good interview can provide you with enough blog material for an entire week. Especially with your comments added. Good interviews add to your credibility.

☐ **Use a layout that makes it easy to read your blog.** And to locate previous posts. And to comment on your current posts. Most blogging sites and software make this part of creating blogs a snap.

☐ **Stir the pot.** Say something controversial. Or poke fun at something. This gets the interaction going better than anything else.

I read in a newsletter that George Washington would beat George Bush if he were to run today. I responded on my blog that Washington would have beaten any modern-day president—if he didn't have to run a campaign. The moment Washington campaigned, he'd be in big trouble. "His wooden teeth wouldn't help him on TV. And his speech patterns would get him kicked off *American Idol* in three seconds flat. I don't think he could win a campaign in this media age, no matter how noble his intentions. Plus, once he ran, he'd run into trouble with his background. He'd be caught in too many lies about cutting down cherry trees and tossing coins across the Potomac. Then, of course, there's the problem of him owning slaves. It would all come out in a gory campaign, and he would not know how to defend himself. He'd have trouble making it through the primaries, much less the general campaign." That post drew many comments and posts from other blogs.

☐ **Recycle content.** As you post, you can always post some of the content from your book. The one strength you have over many bloggers is the content you've already created, content you can recycle into your blog to establish your credibility and to link your book to current events.

☐ **Post a blog roll.** A *blog roll* is a list of other blogs you find interesting, especially blogs that cover the same subject as you cover. Blog rolls create linking opportunities. Once you link to another blog, you can ask them if they'd consider linking to yours.

☐ **Comment on the content of other blogs.** To become an integral part of the blogging community, you must comment on other blogs, link to them, and encourage them to link to your content. Be sure that top bloggers learn about your blog. This community is very much a community built on relationships. If you create relationships with other bloggers, your blog will begin to stand out, get noticed, and get read.

☐ **Link to your web site.** Be sure to link to your web site on your main blog page as well as in some of your posts.

☐ **Do Q&A.** My *Book Marketing Bestsellers* blog gets content from the questions I get every day that I answer via email. I recycle that content on my blog. If I'm going to answer a question for free, I can at least get content out of it. These Q&A posts are often the most popular posts.

☐ **Be truthful.** Always tell the truth. When possible, speak the sweet truth.

Search for blogs.

To search for blogs that might be interested in covering your book, author, subject, or company, google your keyword + "blog." Or use the blog-specific search engines such as Technorati.com, Pubsub.com, or Blog lines.com. Besides your keywords, you can also search on your title, author, company name, brand, or a competitor's title, author, company, or brand.

Link with blogs.

There are a number of ways to get links from blogs. Try these:

☐ Ask for links from the bloggers. Offer to trade links.

☐ Arrange to be interviewed by the blogger.

☐ Provide some inside information to the blogger.

☐ Offer free content to the blogger.

☐ Ask the blogger to review your book.

☐ Comment on a post from the blogger and link to your website in the comment.

Use blogs to sell books.

Powells.com increased daily visitors from 55,000 to 70,000 as a result of its blogs and bookcasts (podcasts of authors). Powells has the largest and most active book sales site of all independent bookstores. Their web site and stores accounted for $57.6 million in sales during 2005.

Use blogs to create books.

A good number of bloggers have gotten generous book contracts to write books based on their blogs. Some have even gone on to sell lots of books. I think blogs are a great place to work out ideas for new books.

☐ Maddox, a blogger at The Best Page in the Universe, presold over 7,000 copies of *The Alphabet of Manliness*, through the Amazon link on his site. His book soared to #1 at Amazon.com after an email he sent out to the 143,000 people on his list (gathered from the million or so monthly visitors to his site at http://www.Maddox.Xmission.com).

☐ Robert Hamburger, a pseudonymous blogger at Real Ultimate Power, sold 35,000 copies of his book soon after it was published.

☐ Blogger Mr. Max, author of *I Hope They Serve Beer in Hell*, sold more than 30,000 copies of his book and became a celebrity on college campuses, thus earning some great speaking fees. He gets about 400 email messages every day from his fans.

Use a blog to piggyback on current trends.

Warren Whitlock created a blog called Potter Marketing to tie into consumer interest in the latest Harry Potter book. Since that book was all the news when it first came out, selling millions of copies on one day, his blog about the book's marketing, created quite a stir as well. He picked up hundreds of links to his web site as a result of his simple and time-limited blog.

Potter was really big. What's the next big thing? Think about it. Then blog about it. It's so simple to do. Just think: What upcoming event that will get a lot of interest can you blog about? The new TV season? The hot new TV drama or comedy? The latest reality TV show? The Oscars. The NFL football season. A new celebrity romance.

Do a blog tour.

Tom Dolby did a virtual book tour where content about him and his books reached more than 50,000 reacers via blogs. According to him, his Amazon.com numbers shot way up, and "booksellers that I visited in Manhattan over the following several days appeared to be constantly in the process of restocking their copies, so I know it had a positive impact."

The Girlfriends Cyber Circuit (http://gcc.blog-city.com) tours two authors a month on 25 like-minded blogs by female writers. It's an dynamic exchange network that can produce great awareness.

You can create your own blog tour by contacting specific blogs that talk about your subject. At each such blog, note their *blogroll* (the list of blogs they recommend) and contact those blogs as well. Soon you'll have a full-fledged tour in place where all the blogs review your book or interview you on the same day. What a way to go!

12:12 Podcasting Your Way to Success

Podcasting is just a fancy word for putting audio content on your web site or other web sites on a regular basis. Think of it as a radio show that is broadcast over the Internet or can be downloaded to an iPod. With more people accessing the Internet via broadband connections, audio and video are going to be the hot new ways of attracting attention to your web site and distributing your content. Here are a number of ways to incorporate audio into your Internet book sales plans:

☐ **Sell content as audio MP3 or podcasts.** Apple Computer has become the best friend of content creators as its iTunes and iVideo stores are getting consumers accustomed to paying for content. iTunes is already featuring podcasts and audio talks, both free and paid. Be sure to market your audio products here as well as other new audio marketplaces.

☐ **Broadcast your own radio show.** You can feature your podcast on your web site and also upload it to a number of podcast sites. Many radio shows are now available as podcasts as well as one-time broadcasts.

☐ **Syndicate the audio version** of your book.

☐ **Get reviewed.** There are many podcasts which do reviews of books.

☐ **Podcast your book.** EarthCore was the world's first podcast-only novel. You couldn't find it in stores. You couldn't download the full audio. The only way to keep up with the novel was to subscribe to the podcast.

☐ **Producer audio samplers.** Give people a taste of your book via audio. Offer the first chapter of a good novel. Or a meaty chapter from a how-to book. Holtzbrinck was the first major publisher to podcast. They started with weekly 30-minuted podcasts which presented excerpts of 10 minutes each from three titles (including author readings, interviews, and supplementary materials. They did podcasts in fiction, science fiction, non- fiction, and self-help. 40,000 people visited their podcast website in the first month and 10,000 downloaded podcasts.

☐ **Podcast you thoughts** rather than write a blog. Or do both. Bestselling Christian author Max Lucado offers commentary via his UpWords podcast. Some current literary podcasts include The Literate Loser, Book Snark, The Poet Guru, Book Buffet, and Book Voyages.

☐ **Get interviewed.** There are many podcasts that do interviews. You can seek out the reviewers and interviewers via some of the podcast directories featured below.

☐ **Interview others.** You can create a lot of valuable content by simply interviewing interesting people in your field. First, you can offer the interview as a free or paid teleseminar, then podcast it (again free or for a charge), sell it as an MP3 download, sell it as an audio CD, or incorporate it into a much larger product selling for hundreds of dollars.

☐ **Podcast to cellphones.** With software from Pod2Mobile, you can adapt your podcasts so they work with cellphones. And you can incorporate ads into your podcasts. Random House recently bought a minority stake in cell phone publisher VOCEL and then teamed up with HIT Entertainment to bring *Thomas & Friends* stories to cell phones. VOCEL also provides cell phones with the *Princeton Review, Living Language* study guides, Prima Games strategy guides, eHarlequin daily excerpts, and *Cliff Notes* cheat sheets.

☐ **Work with Audible.** It has 90,000 hours of books, newspapers, magazines, interviews, and speeches as well as 237,000 subscribers. It sold $63 million of audio product in 2005. During the fall of 2005, Audible's download of Thomas Friedman's *The World Is Flat* was the number one album on iTunes, outselling music by all the top stars. AudibleAir allows people to download books directly into their Treo smartphones.

☐ **Interview with Audio Showcase.** This service from Allan Hunkin will create a podcast interview for $1,250 and then market it to more than 60 podcast directories for only another $350. For more information, go to http://www.podcast.biz.

☐ **Sell online.** Websites like BurnLounge, Weedshare, and Peer Impact let anyone sell songs and albums online, including audiobooks.

Warning: Don't start a regularly scheduled podcast until you know that you are ready to handle it. Until then, create and promote your podcasts one at a time. Once you do decide to podcast regularly, I suggest sticking with once a week or once a month.

Podcasts are easy to create, inexpensive, and convenient for your audience, since they can listen to it at any time via their iPod. Podcasts also allow you to showcase your personality. To create a podcast, all you really need is a computer, a quality microphone, and an audio recording software. Keep the podcasts short. Three to five minutes of great stuff is better than 20 minutes of boring chatter. Create a show, something interesting and entertaining so people will want to come back for more.

If you decide to create a podcast, you don't have to categorize it under books. For example, you'd be better off categorizing a travel or recreation guide under sports or entertainment rather than books. Many podcast directories allow you to categorize your podcast under more than one category.

Once you create a podcast, you need to get the word out so people can find what you have to offer. Below are some of the major web sites that aggregate podcasts and offer accessible directories for people interested in various topics. Be sure to list your podcasts with these directories.

☐ **Podcast.net** — Lists 27,000 podcasts not counting duplicates, including book and poetry podcasts such as: *The Literate Loser, The Secrets of Harry Potter, Audio Library in Persian, The Poet Guru, Barlett Reads, PotterCast: HBP, Voices in Wartime, Cruncy Thoughts, Commuter Reviews, BookBuffet.com, Mind & Media Radio, Authors WithOut Limits, Nextbook, Fiction Fan, The Bookcast, A Way with Words, KCRW's Bookworm, Book Voyages, Page Turners, Podictionary,* and more.

☐ **Podcastalley.com** — Features 18,800 podcasts (total episodes: 530,000). The directory features many book-related podcasts, including *Really Scary, Teachings for the New Age, Page Turners, The Comic Geeks, The*

Da Vinci Notebooks, Scribe, First Voice Books, Rip Books Radio, Leadership Talk with Jerry Bowyer, ThoughtAudio.com Backstage, Christian Daily News, UpWords with Max Lucado, Podreading, Story Spieler Podcast, Book Look, Eye on Books Bookcast, Ghostly Talk, Writers Voice, Popped Culture, and others. This site is also the best place to go to find out how to go about making and distributing a podcast.

☐ **Odeo.com** — Offers three services: A directory of podcasts, the Odeo Syncr software that allows anyone to download podcasts to MP3 players, and creation tools. They categorize podcasts in many categories.

☐ **Apple iTunes Store** — Apple's store currently allows free access to thousands of podcasts. One podcast they offer is *Last Minute Book Reports* from Disney Online. Note: You have to download the iTunes software if you want to access their podcast directory.

☐ **Podcastdirectory.com** — You can search podcasts by popularity, tags, region, genre, language, buzz, and on a Google map.

☐ **iPodder.org** — Features about thousands of podcasts, including many book-related podcasts: *Pinky's Paperhaus, Scribe, Comic Geekos, Jack Fish: A Spy from Atlantis, Pipeline Comic Book Podcast*, and *Bound Cast*. Their iPodder software allows anyone to subscribe to podcasts and have them easily downloaded to your iPod or audio player.

12:13 Videocasting Your Way to Success

According to *DM News*, broadband's increased penetration into homes will change Internet advertising as many TV broadcasters begin to adapt to Internet media. What this means to you, as an author or publisher, is that you need to update your marketing to include video as well as podcasts.

Video, of course, is far more expensive than audio podcasts, but the payback could be very rich. You can start your videocasting career using an inexpensive video camera and later move towards better video, better sound, and better scripts. While you can't compete with the TV networks and other multimedia companies, you can begin small with short videos broadcast via the Internet on iFilm, Google Video, and YouTube.

• Many of the cable networks now feature online broadcasts, including Food Network, MTV, PBS, and CNN. Comedy Central offers its Mother Load clip service where users can watch clips from the previous night's *Daily Show* alongside a giant ad. Some of these clips get viewed, shared via email, or blogged about hundreds of thousands of times in just a few days. The average visitor now shows up at the Comedy Central website three times a week compared to the previous twice a month.

• ABC News now has an afternoon webcast done by the anchors of *World News Tonight*, and NBC runs *Meet the Press* online several hours after it has run on TV. During the NCAA basketball playoffs, CBS SportsLine served up 14 million video streams of the action. Episodes of major TV dramas are now being downloaded at iTunes for $1.99 each for viewing on video iPods. It won't be long before people are buying episodes of your speeches, seminars, workshops, and classes.

- *Microchunking* is the name of the game. That's where longer TV shows are now being cut into pieces and sold individually, just as songs are now being downloaded song by song rather than CD by CD.

- AOL's video search function (http://television.aol.com/in2tv) allows Internet users to watch more than 14,000 classic TV shows.

- Even print media like *Forbes* and *New York Times* are now running video content featuring audio and/or video reports from their reporters. *DM News* has recently launched a turnkey package that will let companies create and promote lead-generating video webcasts or on-demand video commercials. Advertisers will be able to choose between flat-rate charges or cost-per-lead pricing.

- When AOL put the 2006 Super Bowl TV commercials up for a vote, more than 22 million video streams were recorded in the first 24 hours and 42 million streams within days. 895,000 votes were cast for the favorite Super Bowl commercial.

- For George Shuman's debut novel *18 Seconds*, Simon & Schuster created a promotional web site that involves the visitor in solving the crime via videos of several crime scenes, a flashback of the dead person's last 18 seconds of life, and other involvement devices. To promote the web site (http://www.18secondsthebook.com), they advertised in the *Publishers Lunch* ezine (http://www.publishersmarketplace.com). The promotional game was involving but could have used better music. My bet, though, is that people who visit the web site will want to read the book. Check it out as an example of what can be done to promote a novel.

- The summer 2006 hot movie was a grade-C thriller called *Snakes on the Plane*. How did it become hot? It became a cult classic five months before the movie hit the theaters. Fans made their own movie trailers to promote the movie. One Georgetown law student hosted an all-SoaP, all the time blog in hopes of being invited to the premiere. And he got invited by New Line because of all the buzz he created.

Below are two major ways you can use video on the Internet to market your books.

Promote your book via YouTube.com.

If you haven't seen the *Brokeback to the Future* movie preview yet, you have got to watch it. Just wonderful. Really funny—especially if you've seen one or both movies. It is well done, creative, and has money-making or attention-grabbing potential. Watch it and open your mind to new possibilities: http://www.hot timescoolplaces.com/utube1.htm.

If you created something like this, you'd have the Internet viral hit of the week. This movie preview has been viewed millions of times. What if your book were simply mentioned at the end in the credits? Think of the audience you could reach. YouTube now attracts nine times more viewers than iFilm, the other major do-it-yourself movie site. YouTube visitors view 30 million videos every day! And, more important, upload 35,000 new ones!

Create book trailers.

Book trailers are mini-movies created with Macromedia Flash to act like movie trailers to entice readers to take a chance on a new novel. These trailers could evolve into an incredible marketing tool and, eventually, into an incredible new medium for publishing. This is your chance to get in on the ground floor of a new book promotion and publishing format.

There are a number of companies that are working in this area creating some very interesting promotions. Check out Circle of Seven Productions (http://www.cosproductions.com), VidLit.com (which does trailers and Naked Author interviews for nonfiction books), TrailerMill.com, and KidVidLit.com (for children's books).

KidVidLit.com created a trailer featuring a day in the life Meg Cabot, author of the *Princess Diaries*. They also created ones for *Bone* by Jeff Smith, *The Gift of Nothing* by Patrick McDonnell, and *Nicky Deuce: Welcome to the Family* by Steven Schirripa and Charles Fleming.

Mine Falls Press created several book trailers for Michael Alan's two novels. His trailers are great. They are entertaining and fun to watch. They made me want to read his books. Check out his trailers at http://www.minefallspress.com/wheelVid/wheelwright/play.asp.

Circle of Seven Productions was the first company to put book trailers in movie theaters. The first one to play was for Christine Feehan's *Dark Secret*.

12:14 Profit from User-Created Content Sites

Book publisher Tim O'Reilly has been one of the prime promoters of *Web 2.0*. Web 2.0 is user-created content. The central idea is simple. It is, according to O'Reilly, "harnessing collective intelligence." That's what is driving Google search, blogging, wikis, tagging, social sites, and more. If you want to profit from this new trend, create a web site that invites user interaction or, better yet, user creative input. You can use your book as the core of the website, but you need to find a way to get users involved.

Let's look at a few of the tools that allow for user-created content and an expanded living web. Here are a few of them:

☐ **Ajax** — It's a fancy acronym for *asynchronous JavaScript and XML*. Ajax is a web development technique for creating interactive web applications, that is, programs on the web that actually do things. It's used to create many interactive web sites.

☐ **Wikis** — Wikis are web sites that allow users to create, edit, delete, and maintain the content on that web site. The most famous example is Wikipedia, the user-generated web encyclopedia. It is also one of the most fascinating web sites in existence because it has so much cooler content than a normal encyclopedia. Why? Because the people who create it are the same people who use it passionately.

At some point in your career as an expert, you should contribute entries to Wikipedia and also comment on or edit other entries covering your field of expertise. Also you could use a free wiki program to create your own user-generated content site.

☐ **RSS** — This syndication protocol allows people to subscribe to updated information from any web site. It's the protocol that has driven the success of blogs and keep people coming back to read a blog day after day. You can use RSS to let people know when your website changes so they can return to see the new content. RSS isn't just for blogs. It's for any regularly updated content on the web.

☐ **APIs** — These are the openings that some websites offer to allow other websites to make use of their content in creative ways. It's what allows any website to set up an Amazon.com storefront that is more than just an associate link to Amazon.com. It allows other websites to grab content from another website's database and use it in a different way.

☐ **Mashups** — These are websites that take information streams from two or more web sites and blend them together to create something entirely new. One famous example is the one that displays on a local Google map the location of apartments for rent listed on Craigslist (which itself is a user-generated collection of classified ads and the world's seventh largest website, one that is run by only 19 people!).

You can profit from user-generated content in two ways. First, you can create websites that depend on user-generated content. Unless you are a programmer, you probably would need to partner with talented people to create such sites. The second way you can profit is by working with user-generated websites to promote and sell your books, authors, brand, or company.

The following websites are not listed in any special order. Please note that the list is not complete. It's just a sampling that crossed my awareness in the past few months which I think you might be able to use to promote your books. For every web site listed here, there are a dozen imitators or originals which may or may not have more visitors or more impact. The following listing is simply a guide to get you started. If you find something that works, use Google to identify other web sites where you could do the same thing (whatever it is that works in promoting your books).

Del.icio.us (http://www.del.icio.us)

This site was founded as a way for people to store and share their favorite web bookmarks. The smart thing the founders did with this site was to allow user to create their own tags instead of funneling them into a small selection of standard tags. Del.icio.us is essentially a user tagged search site that allows users to discover websites in a completely different way.

To make use of this site to market your book, begin sharing and tagging your own bookmarks (even if they are all pointing to your websites) and encourage others to do the same. That way your websites could rise in awareness on this hot site which was recently bought by Yahoo, which hopes to incorporate the tagging concept into all its search products.

User-created tags is an incredible concept. I have a web site I plan to create that draws upon one of the databases I've been selling. That database of specialty retailers is too hard to keep up-to-date, is too restricted by the tags I've created, and is very incomplete. By creating a readily accessible website where everyone is invited to add their own favorite independent shops and tag them as they see fit, I hope to expand the now almost useless database into a product driven by advertising.

From a database of 2,000 shops selling toys, cookbooks, travel books, craft items, new age gifts, etc., I hope this site will generate a listing of a million such shops, all user-tagged and commented upon.

Most retail yellow pages listings currently on the Internet don't do a good job of easily identifying stores by category. Even more important to someone who wants to sell to these stores is the fact that none of these sites currently list the name of the buyer. My site, which will go by the name of HotStuffCoolPlaces.com, will encourage people to include the name of the buyer or manager in the listing. That way book authors and publishers will still be able to use the database that is created to target independent shops that might be interested in selling special-interest books. That was the reason I created the database in the first place. The neat thing about this new website is that it will be user-created, user-maintained, and user-promoted!

Gather.com (http://www.gather.com)

What is Gather.com? Here is their mission statement: "There's finally a place where you can express your unique perspectives. Share your voice via the articles, images, reviews, or audio you publish about the things you know and love. Then start to Gather. Start by connecting with friends, family, and colleagues. Then share your content by publishing. As the content of other members interests you, subscribe to what they publish, be it short stories, photographs, songs, or podcasts."

Gather.com is now hosting a new *Ask the Author* program. Their first guest was Deborah Tannen, author of *You're Wearing That? Understanding Mothers and Daughters in Conversation*. Gather.com members were able to talk to her for several hours via the website.

In May 2006, the program will feature Terri Jentz, author of A *Strange Piece of Paradise*, and in June, Jonathan Safron Foer, author of *Everything is Illuminated*. So far they are picking big-name authors or those supported by major publishers. But I think that with enough demand from Gather.com members or a subgroup of them, Gather.com might expand this program to include many more authors, more than just once a month. It's your job as a member of Gather.com to ask for more. Perhaps with a program hosted by you. Gather your forces and see what happens.

MySpace (http://www.myspace.com)

News Corp. paid $580 million for this social networking site when it was still just a small piece of the Internet. Now it's a Goliath! It's signed up as many as 270,000 new members in one day! Someday soon it could pass Yahoo as the most trafficked website in the world.

MySpace allows users to create their own little online space where they can add photos, videos, music, blogs, and other notes—and then share them with their friends. The idea is to build a network of friends online who share your music favorites, hobbies, etc. It's become a hot meeting spot for more than 70 million teenagers and other young people (and some of us older folks). And it's become the perfect place to build and promote a career as a musician or comedian.

In December 2003, Dane Cook began building his MySpace page to showcase his comedy routines. In building his network, he approved every *Be My Friend* request and soon had a million MySpace friends. On his page he relentlessly plugged his CDs and appearances around the country. Soon he was invited to host *Saturday Night Life*, made a deal with HBO, and had a hit comedy album. Now every comedian is hoping to duplicate his feat.

Why not an author doing the same thing? If you have a book that would interest a younger audience, why not flog it on a MySpace page and create a network to help you flog it? I'd be happy to add you to my network of friends on MySpace. Let's build a network of authors and publishers.

Some publishers with MySpace pages include New Concepts Publishing, Blindside Publishing, Scapegoat Publishing, and featherproof books. Also, of course, see my space at http://www.myspace.com/johnkremer.

Other social networking websites include FaceBook (popular with college students, with 7 million users on 2,000 campuses), Digg (a techie news site where users contribute links to news stories and blog opinion pieces and then vote on which should be featured), and iMeem.

Flickr (http://www.flickr.com)

Flickr, now owned by Yahoo, is one of the most popular websites for sharing photos. It's become a worldwide virtual scrapbook with lots of viral features to encourage networking. For example, you can click on a button to automatically add a photo to your blog. Flickr photos are also a popular feature in web mashups. Visa used Flickr photos in a recent TV commercial, and it's common now when news happerns around the world for the first photographs to be posted to Flickr before they hit the newswires.

The site also encourages tagging as a way of sharing photos. A group of 3,500 members formed around the "squared circle" tag and now share more than 26,000 pictures. You could start a group by inviting people who share a particular tag (e.g., crocheting, muffin baking, or bungee-jumping).

Yahoo bought Flickr for $35 million because it had an active user base of millions generating content, millions categorizing that content, and many thousands sharing that content around the Internet. Yahoo's hoping to have its half-billion users expand that content manyfold.

Plum (http://www.plum.com)

Using this new web site's *plummer* tool, users can grab information from any computer source (web pages, blogs, photos, podcasts, photos, RSS feeds, etc.), remix it, annotate it, and save it to a collection which can be shared with others. Plus, users can connect with other collections and mash them together. I see this web site as being a good place to collect research and notes for a new book or to collaborate with others on a new book. Plus it can be a great way to share your expertise with others, again especially when you are working on a new book. When I checked in April 2006, the site was still in pre-Beta mode, but it does seem interesting.

Mercora (http://www.mercora.com)

This site allows anyone to download its Mercora player and use it to program up to five radio stations with your favorite music. You can also use it, of course, to listen to the stations created by other people. In the short time this site has been up and running, more than 60,000 stations have been programmed. I plan to use this site personally to program a radio station to go along with a music-related book I want to write. Using this program, I can allow people to listen to the music as I comment on it. Of course, there's nothing in this site that would prohibit you from starting up a talk station instead of a music station. I can see, for example, quite a demand for a John Kremer 24-7 talk station (of course, my wife would never listen).

eBay (http://www.ebay.com)

The largest sales site on the Internet, eBay accounts for more sales than Amazon.com or Walmart.com. If you learn the rules for doing eBay auctions and feel comfortable setting up such auctions, it is possible to sell books via eBay auctions. I know some pubishers who have been making goog money selling books on eBay. The auction site is certainly a good place to auction off hurts, remainders, and overstock. Since you can auction just about anything on eBay, you can also use eBay to test market potential titles and covers.

Since I don't use eBay, I can't tell you a much more about how to work with eBay to sell books. If you are interested in selling on eBay, buy one of the many books on the subject or check out some of the more expensive but also sometimes more detailed reports that are for sell on eBay or ClickBank.

ClickBank (http://www.clickbank.com)

If you want to get started inexpensively in selling information products via the Internet, ClickBank is the place to go. Not only can you upload your ebook, audio MP3, PDF report, or other electronic item onto ClickBank, but you can also use the ClickBank shopping system to list and sell the product, process credit card payments, enable the downloads, and bank the profits. And you can do all this without setting up a website, knowing a bit about HTML, or trying to figure out the intracacies of a shopping cart system.

ClickBank offers two other key benefits for selling ebooks:

☐ You can set up an affiliate program so that other websites and ezines can make money selling your ebooks. The only way to be successful selling products on the Internet is to develop partners who can also make money helping you to sell your products. An affiliate program makes it easy to convince other websites to partner wit you.

☐ You can also join the affiliate programs of many other information producers, thus expanding the items you sell and the money you can make. There is a wonderful array of products for sale on ClickBank, so no matter what your subject interest, there will be dozens of products that you can feel comfortable selling as good values to your customers.

Even after you grow your business to the point that you have your own website, shopping cart system, and affiliate program, you can still offer your products via ClickBank as well.

Fundable.org (http://www.fundable.org)

This for-profit website lets anyone raise money for any purpose, from making a movie to publishing a book, from organizing a concert to planning a class reunion. People needing funds simply create a page explaining how much they need, why they need it, and when they will need it. Then they can start collecting pledges from other members of Fundable.org. If the desired amount is raised by the deadline, then Fundable collects the money from the pledgers and forwards the money to the fundraiser.

Most Fundable money drives ask for pledges between $500 and $5,000. The average pledge is $30. If you need money to publish a book and think you can make a convincing case, the Fundable might be a tool you can use. Pledgers are not repaid but usually get a gift in return—such as a copy of the book, a ticket to the event, a credit in the film, or something similar.

Squidoo (http://www.squidoo.com)

Squidoo, started up by viral marketing master Seth Godin, is designed as a user-generated how-to reference encyclopedia. Anyone who is an expert or think they have something to say about something can create a lens. There are lens about every subject you want to know something about. And you can create your own lens as well. When the site gets up and running in a big way, lens masters will get paid a royalty for every ad that is placed on their lens which generates any income. But, for now, you should look on building a lens as a way of gaining greater visibility on the Internet and getting some quality links to your web site (from your lens, if not from any others).

12:15 Create a Dynamic Press Room to Attract the Media

If you are carrying out an active publicity campaign, then you need to create a press room on your web site, a place where reporters, editors, and broadcasters can go to find out more about your company, your books, and your authors. Here are some things you should include in your press room:

☐ Copies of your past year's news releases.

☐ Latest news on your company's sales, marketing efforts, etc.

☐ Downloadable, high-resolution photographs of your authors, brand images, book covers, and other relevant images.

☐ Author bios, complete with what they've written, their expertise or platform, and something about each of them as a person.

☐ Audio and video clips featuring short interviews with your authors. Include printed transcripts for use by reporters.

☐ Q&A pages featuring suggested questions for each author — related to the new titles you are promoting.

☐ A calendar that features a day-by-day schedule of any author tours or interviews. Make it easy for potential interviewers to locate when and where you might be available.

☐ Backgrounders — Provide background information on your latest books, information that you could not fit in your news releases — and should not try to fit into your news releases.

☐ FAQs — These might include more detailed information on subjects that you specialize in.

☐ Review copy request forms — Include a way for media to request review copies, author interviews, or other items.

☐ Awards and honors — List any awards and honors for your company, authors, or books.

☐ Copies of reviews and print interviews.

☐ Each book and/or author should have its own featured virtual media kit.

12:16 Marketing Books Via the Internet: A Publisher

Here's how one publisher is using the web and email to market its books. Zondervan, a division of HarperCollins that publishes Bibles and religious books, have adopted the Internet and email as major ways of marketing their books. Here are a few of the things they've done.

☐ **Zondervan Bible Store** (http://www.amazon.com/zondervan) — In cooperation with Amazon.com, this store makes it easy for readers to find the right Bible for their needs. It features more than 400 Bibles, segmented into six types: study, devotional, youth/children, reference, specialty, and Spanish-language. To help customers select the best Bible for themselves, the store features the top-selling Bibles in each category.

☐ **Church Leader Internet Portal** (http://www.zondervanchurchsource. com/clip) — Offers a central web meeting place for pastors and church leaders. This site offers links to other sites dealing with counseling, worship, news, religion news, humor, academic information, colleges, libraries, sermon illustrations, travel, leadership, writing resources, government, weather, sports, and more. CLIP also provides pastors with a weekly news report, *Church Leader Briefing*, as well as a Bible Verse-A-Day, Daily Church Word Vocabulary Builder, Today in Church History, Ministry Quote of the Week, and a Calendar of Church Dates.

☐ **Email Alert Service** — Keeps interested individuals informed of new books and other events sponsored by Zondervan. They offer email alerts for about 50 specific topics, from ministry and worship to family to counseling to travel. They encourage their readers to recommend their Email Alert Service in online discussion groups, chat rooms, and so on.

☐ **BodyBuilder Newsletter for Pastors** — This newsletter offers periodic news, recommendations, articles, interviews, statistics, letters, and other information to help pastors achieve a more effective ministry.

☐ **Daily Thought** — A free inspirational newsletter that anyone can sign up to receive each day.

☐ **Zondervan News Service** — This service is available on the website or via periodic email alerts. It offers a summary of current issues and points out the Zondervan resources that bring perspective to those issues.

☐ **Order Tracking for Retailers** — At their main web site (http://www. zondervan.com), retailers can sign up to track all their book orders. All they need is their Zondervan customer number and a purchase order number (or invoice number or specific ISBN). What a convenience for retailers! And what a labor-saver for Zondervan.

☐ **Website for Academics** (http://www.zondervan.com/academic) — At this site, college instructors can locate all the material they need to conduct classes in the wide range of topics that Zondervan books cover.

☐ **Zondervan's Speakers Directory** — This section of their main web site features all their authors who are willing and able to speak to groups and the media on various subjects. Users can search for speakers by topic.

☐ **They feature their partners.** — On one page, they feature links, graphics, and a long description of the key magazines, groups, and centers that they work with to develop and sell books. Among the groups are Focus on the Family, Youth with a Mission, Center for Relationship

Development, Congress of National Black Churches, and National Association of Evangelicals.

☐ **Retailer Email Alert Service** — Lets retailers know of new titles and promotions. It is an interesting and effective way to remind stores of merchandising possibilities for Zondervan books.

12:17 Marketing Books Via the Internet: An Author

Here's an example of an incredible website built up by *New York Times* bestselling author David Bach, author of the *Finish Rich* books. Check out his web site at *http://www.finishrich.com*. Look at all the opportunities he offers for consumers and businesses to get involved with him:

☐ **Learn Tab** — This tab offers a free newsletter archive, David's blog, an audio seminar, worksheets, calculators (rent vs. buy, time value, and latte factor), advice on hiring a financial advisor, success stories, and lots of free reports.

☐ **Books Tab** — An order page for all his books and audios.

Come See David

☐ **Live Events Tab** — Features all his seminars and talks, FinishRich meet-ups, how to become a FinishRich instructor (he's franchising himself!), how to book him for a speech, the Great American Homeowner Challenge Tour (a 14-city tour via a fancy bus), and author bio.

☐ **Shop Tab** — Features opportunities to buy his books, coaching programs, home study courses, and other merchandise.

☐ **Media Tab** — Features highlights of his print clippings, TV appearances, and online publicity, including links to his regular column in the *finance.yahoo.com* section.

☐ **Partners Tab** — Bach has partnerships with Wells Fargo Home Mortgage, Yahoo! Finance, Scotiabank, Bank of America, and Van Kampen Investments. All of these partners undoubtedly pay him a good amount of money for his stamp of approval. Wells Fargo, for example, is sponsoring a 3-year initiative to help more Americans become homeowners.

☐ **Contact Us Tab** — You can contact them with general questions, media inquiries, partnership opportunities, licensing, consulting, speaking, and to share your success story. They also have a frequently asked questions section. And a section devoted to financial advisors who would like to license his top seminars in their area.

12:18 Other Web Sites That Can Help You Sell Books

There are many other web sites, of course, that can help you sell books. Here are just a few of them. This is clearly not an exhaustive list. Take it as a sampler of what can be done via the Internet.

America Online (http://www.aol.com)

America Online, with millions of customers, is the leading online service. Its many forums, departments, and stores can help you sell many books.

☐ **AOL's book maven** is Bethane Patrick, who writes about books, authors, and the publishing world in her blog.

☐ Their **Book Clubs** section offers chat rooms where you can talk with other like-minded readers, information on the media book clubs, and reading group guides (from http://www.readinggroupguides.com). You can pay up to $900 to have your reading group guide featured by this website. For details, contact Carol Fitzgerald at carol@bookreporter.com. They also do Ask the Author features. They offer 1,800 reading guides to a monthly audience of 200,000 visitors. If you offer special discounts to book clubs, RGG spotlights such offers.

☐ **AOL Journals** provide you with space for a blog. If you already have a blog, you could run the same content here as well.

☐ **Black Voices** features a member center, forums, interviews, and reviews featuring black authors.

Microsoft Network (http://www.msn.com)

After AOL, Microsoft Network is the second largest online service. It offers a number of programs of interest to book authors and publishers.

☐ **MSN City Guides** feature local news, calendars, and articles for selected cities. These guides can be great places to work with if you have a local or regional title. Check out the local site for your area. Then contact the webmaster for more information.

☐ **MSNBC.com** features excerpts from books by authors who appear on NBC's *Today Show* and *Dateline*.

☐ **Slate** (http://www.slate.com), a literary and entertainment magazine developed by MSN, features book reviews, author interviews, and articles (many written by book authors). *Slate* culture editor Meghan O'Rourke reported that the serialization of Walter Kim's novel *The Unbinding* drew 3,000 to 9,000 people a day. "If you're going to write a novel, the deal we're offering is very good. It's not an insignificant amount of money for just working on the novel."

Salon Magazine (http://www.salon.com)

Salon Magazine, an interactive magazine of books, arts, literature, and ideas, has recently formed distribution alliances with many web sites. Salon's Table Talk reader forum is one of the most popular forums on the Internet. Salon encourages submissions of books, authors, and excerpts from independent publishers. Submit to. **Salon Media Group**, 101 Spear Street #203, San Francisco, CA 94105; 415-645-9200; Fax 415 645-9204.

BookWire (http://www.bookwire.com)

BookWire, an online book site owned by the publishers of *Publishers Weekly*, features news items, article reprints, and bestseller lists from *PW*. The following services are just a few that BookWire offers authors and publishers as tools to help sell more books. Most charge a few, but a couple of the services are free.

☐ **EventCaster** — An events calendar service where you can list bookstore and other literary events. The service is free if you enter each event by hand into their online form. You pay a fee if ou want to submit many events in spreadsheet format. Each week, NetRead forwards the event information to event editors at newspapers, magazines, and online calendars at Yahoo and Digital City.

☐ **Meet the Author** — Features paid interviews with authors.

☐ **BookWired Forum** (http://bookwiredforum.ipbhost.com) — A forum for sharing information, chat, and ask questions. You must be a member of BookWire to participate.

☐ **BookWire Reviews** — You can pay to be featured in these reviews as well as in Books in Print.

☐ **Bookwrap Central** (http://www.bookwrapcentral.com) — Bookwraps are author interview video clips.

☐ **Publishers Pages** — You can host your book and publisher pages with BookWire.

☐ **Bowker Market Links** (http://www.bowkermarketlinks.com) — Offers a way to sell books online.

☐ **PubEasy** (http://www.pubeasy.com) — Over 11,000 booksellers in 110 countries use PubEasy to place orders, check availability, and find information from more than 3,300 ppublishers and imprints.

☐ **Pubnet** (http://www.pubnet.org) — An EDI provider to 3,000 booksellers and 150 publishers, wholesalers, and distributors.

Other web sites that feature books and authors

Here are a few other web sites that feature authors, books, and book-related information.

☐ **Head Butler** (http://www.headbutler.com) — Features news and reviews about books, music, movies, and new products. Jesse Kornbluth, formerly the head book man at AOL, is the editor. He also writes a book blog for AARP. You can email him at headbutlernyc@aol.com. You can submit your own reviews of favorite books as well.

☐ **Latino Writers** (http://groups.yahoo.com/group/marcelalandres) — This group led by Marcela Landres features paying markets for Latino writers. She also publishes the *Latinidad* newsletter.

☐ **Cafe Press** (http://www.cafepress.com) — With this website, you can create more than 80 products (T-shirts, bumper stickers, buttons, hats, bags, coffee cups, tiles, journals, etc.) that feature your book cover, author's photo, or brand image. And then send people to your new online store which they host to buy your products. You have no up-front cost. Each product is created one at a time as the demand requires.

☐ **Writer's Weekly** (http://www.writersweekly.com) — Features a weekly newsletter by Angela Hoy for freelance writers. Includes writer's guidelines, classes, forums, and more.

☐ **RawSistaz Literary Group** (http://www.rawsistaz.com) — Reads, writes, and discusses book by African-American authors.

☐ **eReader.com** (http://www.ereader.com) — If you publish ebooks, you should have your ebooks featured in the world's largest ebook store. For more ebook stores, see http://www.bookmarket.com/ondemand.html.

☐ **AbsoluteWrite.com** (http://www.absolutewrite.com) — Publishes a great free ezine for writers called *Absolute Write*.

☐ **Armchair Interviews** (http://www.armchairinterviews.com) — Features audio interviews with authors.

☐ **BookCrossing** (http://www.bookcrossing.com) — The home of catch and release books. Register a book you've read (or your own book), put a label on the cover, and then leave it out in public somewhere to be picked up (a park bench, airport terminal, etc.). Then check back at this site to see where your book has traveled.

☐ **Romance Divas** (http://www.romancedivas.com) — A web site featuring romance novelists. Includes reviews, features, blog, forum, and more.

☐ **Romance Junkies** (http://www.romancejunkies.com) — Features book reviews, author interviews, and more.

☐ **Duotrope's Digest of Fiction Fields** (http://www.duotrope.com/digest) — Features a database of 800 markets for short fiction and poetry. A good place to research possible book review sources, especially for genre and literary novels.

☐ **Deviant Art** (http://www.deviantart.com) — This site is helping little-known artists to promote their original art as well as sell prints of many of the entries. A wonderful site for up-and-coming artists.

☐ **Pure Volume** (http://www.purevolume.com) — This site allows you to sample the work of many new musicians and groups. You can even download many songs for free. You also have the option to pay to download some songs after you listen to them. It's another great web site for singers and musicians who have produced their own music.

☐ **CdBaby** (http://www.cdbaby.com) — Founded by a musician, this site helps garage bands and other unknown musicians to sell their self-produced music CDs. The site has sold more than a million CDs already!

☐ **IndieDocs** (http://www.indiedocs.com) — This more commercial site features all sorts of movies including experimental, self-distributed, IMAX, and more. Plus books about movies, producers, directors, and reference.

☐ **URL Trends** (http://www.urltrends.com) — For a quick check of your website rankings, this site provides the incoming links according to Google, Yahoo, MSN, and Alexa as well as your Google PageRank and Alexa Rank. Use URL Trends to check on your competitors' web sites, other related sites, and especially those web sites where you'll be trading links or creating other joint ventures or relationships.

☐ **Book Marketing Bestsellers Blog** (http://openhorizons.blogspot.com) — My blog on book marketing. Update 10 to 15 times a month.

☐ **Teleseminars & Free Reports Blog** (http://teleseminars-free-reports. blogspot.com) — My blog on teleseminars and free reports. I'd be happy to announce your teleseminars and free reports here. Just send me an email. Be patient. When I'm really busy, I won't be able to get to everyone's posting. Sorry.

☐ **Promoting Your Books** (http://www.promotingyourbooks.com) — My website featuring lots of great advice, especially for novelists.

☐ **John Kremer Sent Me** (http://www.JohnKremerSentMe.com) — Features resources that I recommend for which I get paid a referral fee. Lots of good information included on this site, so check it out at least once.

For a more complete and updated list of great websites, check out John Kremer's *Marketing Top 101* list (http://www.bookmarket.com/top101.html). It includes the top booksellers, publishers, book marketing websites, book cover designers, type designers, book publicists, book printers, and more. Even more resource web pages are featured at http://www.bookmarket.com/files.html.

Also, since website addresses can change so readily, some of the sites mentioned in this chapter might have changed since we gathered the information for this book. If you run across any wrong email addresses or URLs, please let us know so we can provide updates. Email us at JohnKremer@ bookmarket.com. We will post any updates in the exclusive area for updates to this book on Open Horizons BookMarket.com website at: http://www. bookmarket.com/1001add.html.

12:19 Last Minute Findings and Suggestions

This is the last chapter I worked on before sending this edition off to the printer, but even then I couldn't incorporate all the new things I've learned recently without doing a major repagination of the entire chapter. So, here are a few bonus updates of last minute tips I couldn't let you miss out on.

Email Updates

☐ **How do most people now get opt-in email** such as your ezines? 26% of such opt-in emails now go to Yahoo addresses; 21% go to Hotmail addresses; and 13% to AOL addresses. That means 60% of your email newsletters are probably going to only three email domains! That's incredible. Less than 10% of opt-in commercial emails now go to users at their business address [Lyris Technologies].

☐ **Email users now have multiple email accounts.** That means that you are not only competing for attention with other emails going to their main account, but you are also competing for their attention with the other email accounts users access. 30% of email users have one account; 37% have two accounts; 19% have three accounts; and 13% have four or more accounts!

☐ **What's the hot day for email?** Nowadays, it's Friday. According to an ExactTarget study, Friday gets the highest open rate for emails—and the second highest click-through rate (6.5%). Sunday has the highest click-through rate of 6.9%. Most other days, though, also have a click-through rate around 6%.

☐ **Authenticate your email.** Your commercial email and ezines may not be delivered soon unless you authenticate your email. The formats for doing so are still being worked out, but do check out this technology as soon as you can so your email gets through.

Using the Internet

☐ **How are people going online in the U.S. today?** 42% access the Internet via broadband at home; 22% via dial-up at home; and 13% from email access outside the home. 23% of Americans still do not have regular email access [Parks Associates and Cnet].

☐ **What are people doing online?** According to a study done in November 2005 by the Pew Internet and American Life Project, here are the percent of Internet users who performed the following computer tasks each day. This information should give you a good idea of the best ways to reach Internet users.

    77% — Read and wrote email.
    63% — Used a search engine.
    46% — Read news.
    29% — Did job-related research.
    18% — Sent instant messages.
    18% — Banked (That's a lot more than I would have guessed!)
     8% — Participated in a chat room.
     5% — Booked travel.

3% — Read blogs.

3% — Participated in an auction.

What the above tells us is that the two best ways to reach people on the Internet are through email (ezines, viral messages, etc.) and search engines (via search engine optimization and pay-per-click). What is most interesting, especially given the media hype, is how few people read blogs. What is even more interesting is that it is the same percentage as the number who participate in Ebay and similar auction sites—and some people are making a lot of money on Ebay!

☐ **Online holiday spending hits $30 billion.** According to Nielson/Net Ratings, 2005 non-travel holiday spending between October 29th and December 23rd totaled $30.1 billion in 2005. Consumers spent $5.35 billion on apparel, $4.82 billion on computer hardware, $4.79 billion on consumer electronics, $2.95 billion on books, and $2.3 billion on toys and video games.

68% of holiday shopping in 2005 was done at brick-and-mortar stores (down from 78% in 2002). On the other hand, e-commerce accounted for 27% of holiday sales (up from 16% in 2002). Research shows that online marketing benefits from convenience, lower prices, and product selection, along with the ease of searching via Google and Yahoo!

The most shopped sites during holiday 2005 were eBay, Amazon.com, and Walmart.com, in that order. Customers ordered 108 million products from Amazon.com during this holiday season. Amazon.com also sold 600,000 gift certificates during that time.

Web Site Promotions

☐ **Be interviewed online.** Every Tuesday *Budget Travel* answers questions online. In April, Andrew Doughty, author of *Maui Revealed*, was the answer man of the month.

☐ **Make changes.** Yahoo.com made one change on its web site, something that produced enough extra clickthroughs to generate an estimated $20 million in additional annual revenue. What was the one thing? They moved the search box from the side of the page to the center.

☐ **Create a timely online poll.** Then publicize it. That's what Mary Foley, author of *Bodacious! Woman: Outrageously in Charge of Your Life and Lovin' It!*, did in early April. She did an online poll: Is Katie Couric's decision to leave her well-established position on NBC's *Today Show* to become the first solo female anchor on *CBS Evening News* a brainless decision or bodacious behavior? She announced her poll via an email news release on the eMediaWire Newswire. The poll was taken on her Bodacious Woman Awards web site at http://www.bodaciouswoman awards.com/katiecouric.

On another of her web sites (http://www.gobodacious.com), she gave away 500 physical copies of her book. In addition to those two web sites, she has a serious of other web sites that are tied together, each serving a different purpose: BodaciousBlog.com, BodaciousWomensClub. com, bodacious-motivational-speaker-mary-foley.com (aka speakermary foley.com), and YourBoMo2Go.com.

☐ **Publish for the Sony Reader.** This new Sony ebook reader might be the first to be successful. I doubt it personally. It will take a dedicated book reader to pay $300 to $400 for the reader, plus more for the books. The problem for publishers is that Sony decided to incorporate a new proprietary ebook format (BBeB). That was stupid.

The Reader does fit nicely into your hand and doesn't weight more than most hardcover books, so it doesn't have that usability issue. Plus, it's supposed to be highly readable with no backlit screen. And has a long battery life. But I still don't think that it's the breakthrough product. That will come, but this is not it. Sorry.

Sony already signed up most of the major publishers to produce ebooks in its format (Random House, HarperCollins, TimeWarner, Penguin, and Simon & Schuster)

Internet Trends

Here are a few Internet trends for the coming year, according to *DM News*, a trade newspaper for the direct marketing industry:

☐ **Buzz marketing or word of mouth will be big.** For publishers, that means you need to make better use of the viral nature of the Internet. I believe Internet marketing will become (and should become) a much bigger part of every publisher's marketing plans.

☐ **E-commerce will be more about interactions** rather than transactions. The key to successful web sites is creating relationships with your visitors, not just a one-time sale.

☐ **The Internet will be used more for branding.** Authors and publishers should be incorporating the Internet into any branding plans. I believe that all authors should be thinking about branding whenever they are writing or promoting a new book.

☐ **Online publishers will place more content behind walls.** In other words, more web sites will begin charging for more of the content they present on their web sites. If you have a big content web site, you might also consider this as a possible revenue source.

☐ **Blogs and other consumer-generated media will proliferate.** Indeed, for many media companies, this is the biggest challenge—harnessing this content and making it available to more people. Publishers are already doing this by offering book deals to many well-known bloggers.

☐ **Walmart.com might overtake Amazon.com** as the largest online retailer. Any growth in Internet retail markets will only give us more opportunities to make sales. That should be a good thing for us.

Using AdSense to Make Money from Your Old or Out-of-Print Material

by Eric Giguere, author of *Make Easy Money with Google*

Most non-fiction books eventually stop selling because they're outdated in some way. This is especially true of technology books—often outdated the day they're published—but it applies to almost any book. The obvious solution is to publish a new edition of the book with revised material, but that's not always possible. The publisher may not want to revise the book. Or you may not be interested enough in the topic anymore to do the revision. Either way, you don't normally see more money from that book once it's stopped selling. But, now with Google AdSense, you can make more money from your old material by putting it on a website and displaying targeted advertisements next to the content.

How you do this is very simple. First, obtain the rights to the material if they're not already yours. This may require some negotiation: if your book's not formally out-of-print yet, ask the publisher to revert the rights back to you. If they're unwilling, ask them if you can at least have the rights to place some of the book content (like the most important chapters) on your own website. They may be more amenable to that.

Once you have the rights, convert the material into a set of HTML pages. How easy this is depends on whether or not you have electronic versions of the original text. If you have to retype everything, it's probably not worth the effort. Note that you can also extract the text from the PDF files that the publisher might have sent you at some point during the proofing process.

Converting the content to HTML will probably take several hours to do a good job of it, so don't underestimate the time this step will take. Here are a few rules to keep in mind:

☐ **Put each section or subsection on its own page.** Don't do one chapter per page. This will expose the reader to more advertisements, which means more chances for you to make money, and it also ensures that the advertisements that are shown are better-targeted.

☐ **Keep simple search engine optimization (SEO) principles in mind** when you create the page. SEO is important because a lot of your traffic will be from the search engines, so you need to make sure that the search engines can find your content appropriately. For example, the title of the HTML page should be the title of the section, not something like Section 12. Even the name of the HTML file itself should be based either on the section name or else the keywords that best describe what the section's about. Place the section title in an <h1> headline tag. Highlight the occasional important keyword in bold. Rewrite a few sentences here and there if necessary. There's lot of material about SEO available for free on the Internet to guide you.

☐ **Organize the web pages intelligently.** Make sure that each section links to the next and previous sections in the book, that there's a table of contents page listing all the sections, that each section also links back to the table of contents. Make it easy to jump around the book.

☐ **Put the pages up on a site.** If you don't have your own site, get one. It's cheap and easy. Get your own domain name. Never use someone else's free domain name.

☐ **Join AdSense.** Once your site is up, apply to join Google's AdSense program. AdSense is a program that allows you rent space on your web pages to Google, who then uses it to display advertising. You get a cut of the money they make from the advertising – whenever a visitor clicks an ad. For a quick summary of how AdSense works, see http://twowords. ericgiguere.com/adsense.html or read my book, *Make Easy Money with Google*. There are other advertising programs out there as well, but AdSense is the best to start with unless the content of your book doesn't fit within AdSense's content guidelines.

☐ **Place the AdSense code** (you literally cut and paste it) on your pages. You'll start seeing contextually-selected advertising. Whatever you do, though, don't click any of the ads yourself – you'll get yourself kicked out of the program.

☐ **Start getting traffic to your site.** Submit it to the various search engines. Place a link to it in your email signature. Tell your mailing lists about it. Encourge other web sites to link to your new site.

If you're into blogging, you can also republish the content in a blog, either in addition to the website or as a replacement to the website. Blogs can be real traffic generators, so they're good to have.

You probably won't make a lot of money with this, but it's definitely possible to make some money this way. And doing this simple program might make you see your content in a whole new light. You might find yourself wanting to use the content as the basis for further articles or even books.

Eric Giguere wrote *Make Easy Money with Google: Using the AdSense Advertising Program* as a gentle introduction for non-technical people to making money using Google's AdSense program. You can learn more about the book at http://www.memwg.com or by mailing Eric at ericgiguere@ ericgiguere.com.

Simple Strategies to Sell More Books on Amazon.com

by Randy Gilbert, an Amazon.com bestselling author

Tip #1 — Review Other Books and Let People Know You're the Expert

If you're like me, you have just about every other book in your subject area and have read them all. Use your expertise to review other books in such a way as to give yourself credibility.

In addition to becoming known as the person people can trust, people will find out what books you've written because you are going to close each review with *Your Name, author of Your Book*. This is a legitimate credential that Amazon wants you to use (because they like it when you sell lots of your books and wish everybody did).

Tip #2 — Review Your Competitor's Book and Sell Your Book, Too

In addition to reviewing all of the other books in your subject area, you should post a review of the books that might be considered your competition. For those of you who are unfamiliar with writing book proposals, these are the books you identify as being available to people who are looking for information in your subject or specialty area.

Since you're going to put your name and book title at the bottom of a very well-written review that makes you look like the true expert in your field, many people will take the time to search for your book and buy it too.

The thing I like most about doing this is, whenever your competitor is receiving a boost in sales, perhaps due to some good PR they've received, your name and book will be seen more often as well and your own book sales will inevitably rise.

Tip #3 — Use Listmania and Become the Expert in Your Subject Area

On every sales page and on Your Profile page, there's an opportunity to create a list of books for whatever reason you choose. It's called **Listmania**. This is one of the easiest and most effective things you can do on Amazon to brand your name and become known everywhere as *the expert* in your subject area.

Some people create really corny lists, but not you. Create lists of books in your subject area and write short (200 character) reviews that'll position you as the top expert in your field.

When you create a title for your Listmania List, think of it as a Headline or a Hook and use it to grab the attention of the person browsing for a good book. You'll be the one to catch their attention.

I love Listmania, because your lists show up on every sales page of the books (or products) that you've listed, which allows you to put your branded contact information on every sales page for the books in your subject area (or any other area you choose).

Tip #4 — Become the Answer-Man on Amazon

If you're an authority in a field (which you are as an author), there is a wonderful feature on Amazon that has your name written all over it (or it should have your name all over it). It's called **So You'd Like To...** guides, which are the places where you can post your how-to articles. Use this to show the world you can help them find the answers to difficult questions and solve their pressing problems.

In your articles you will list all of the books that are appropriate to the topic, which then does a magical job of posting your articles everywhere in your subject area. So, when your perfect customer is out looking for an answer, they will quickly be introduced to you. This is the ultimate article publishing phenomenon and Amazon has brought it to you free of charge.

A word to the wise: Don't pitch your book. Just write interesting articles and people will want more of what you write. They will eventually want to buy your book because you are the one answering their questions and meeting their needs.

Randy Gilbert is the author of the Amazon.com bestseller *Success Bound* who now helps other authors sells more books via Amazon and other online retailers. The above tips were excerpted from *Eight Strategies Any Author Can Use to Sell More Books on Amazon.com*. For a free copy of the complete article, go to http://www.BookMarketingUpdate.com/Amazon.

Chapter 13

Getting Distribution

Distribution is the name of the game. It is everything.
The better your distribution network, the more books you're going to sell.
— Avery Cardoza, *The Complete Guide to Successful Publishing*

The key to bookstore sales is two-pronged: 1. You have to get your books into the stores (distribution). 2. You have to get them out of the stores (advertising and publicity).

You won't make any bookstore sales if you do not have your books in the stores when your advertising and publicity hits the public; hence, you need to get distribution. But once you get distribution, you must be sure to promote your books so that they move off the booksellers' shelves into the hands of readers rather than back into your warehouse as returns.

No sane booksellers will carry your books for long if you do not provide advertising and promotional support that will help them sell your books. The average turn at retail for bookstores is somewhere between three and four times a year—that means that booksellers, in effect, replace their entire inventory of books about every three or four months. Booksellers can't afford to stock books on their shelves which do not have sufficient demand to turn at retail within six months at the latest. For the sake of completeness, some larger bookstores might carry a few titles just to fill out a special section but, even then, they will not tolerate slow moving books for long.

How do bookstores get the books they stock? In a survey of independent bookstores, 51% of the booksellers said that they used publishers as their primary source of supply, while 12% bought primarily from one wholesaler, 23% bought from more than one wholesaler, and 14% gave no response. Of course, many of the booksellers who used publishers as their primary source also bought from wholesalers as their secondary source.

13:01 Why Bookstores Buy from Wholesalers

Bookstores have many good reasons for buying from wholesalers or distributors rather than direct from a publisher. Here are just a few of them:

☐ By combining a number of smaller orders, bookstores can usually get a higher discount from distributors.

☐ They can eliminate the paperwork necessary to deal with many smaller orders by consolidating those orders with one distributor or wholesaler. Not only do they save time in ordering, but they also save time when unpacking books and paying bills. It's far easier for them to keep track of one bill than many bills.

☐ If a book doesn't sell, they can use their credit on returns to buy other books from the distributor. In the case of a one or two-book publisher, they could be stuck with no options for using the credit.

☐ Distributors and wholesalers tend to be more reliable. They usually ship books faster than publishers. Even major publishers are two to three times slower than wholesalers in shipping books.

13:02 Distributors and Wholesalers

Because there is such a wide variety of wholesalers and distributors in the book trade, the distinction between the two is not always clear. In this book, however, we will make a distinction between the two functions.

A **distributor** stocks books, sells them to its accounts, handles all fulfillment, and pays for the books on consignment (i.e., usually 90 to 120 days after the books are actually sold). All good distributors require exclusivity. The main advantage of using a distributor is that they have sales reps which sell your books to the major chains as well as many independent bookstores.

A **wholesaler**, on the other hand, functions as an order taker for its accounts. Wholesalers generally do little promotion outside of a catalog, order books as the need arises or in small stock quantities, and pay for the books usually in net 30 or net 90 (although most trade wholesalers are now demanding consignment terms). Wholesalers do not require exclusivity; they'll buy from any publishers who have books their customers want.

One way to look at the difference is as follows: Distributors work for publishers while wholesalers work for bookstores.

13:03 Distributing through Distributors

Why, then, use a distributor to represent your books when you could simply sign up a number of wholesalers to carry your books or do it yourself? Here are a few reasons why publishers use distributors:

☐ Distributors have sales representatives, seasonal catalogs, and other active means of promoting your books.

☐ Since they have established marketing channels, they can often move more books than you could move on your own.

☐ Because they tend to represent fewer books than wholesalers and often specialize in certain kinds of books, they are more likely to promote the titles they carry.

☐ The major chain stores no longer buy directly from smaller publishers; hence, you need a distributor or established wholesaler to fulfill any chain store orders.

☐ Distributors will work with their client publishers to design effective book covers, plan marketing campaigns, and provide other feedback to make the books more salable.

☐ They handle all the order taking, warehousing, shipping, collection, and returns. What a relief!

The two main disadvantages of using distributors are that, one, they stock books on consignment (usually paying 90 to 120 days after they've sold the books) and, two, they usually ask for a hefty discount (effectively, as much as 60 to 70%).

Distributors vary widely in their ability to cover the book trade or other outlets. Hence, avoid signing an exclusive deal with a distributor unless they can demonstrate that they offer full coverage of the market you want to reach. At the minimum, they must have sales representation in major areas of the country, must make regular visits to key chains and wholesalers, and should offer other means of promotion (such as catalogs and mailings).

You can find the names and addresses of the major book distributors at http://www.bookmarket.com/distributors.html. Below are the names of a few distributors who work with indie publishers:

☐ **General distributors**: Consortium Book Sales, Greenleaf Book Group, Independent Publishers Group, Midpoint Trade Books, National Book Network, Publishers Group West, SCB Distributors.

☐ **Library distributors**: Quality Books and Unique Books.

☐ **Religious distributor**: Faithworks.

☐ **Specialty distributors**: AK Press Distribution (radical social and political books), Angler's Book Supply (fishing titles), Business Books Network, Royal Publications (health, new age).

13:04 Selecting a Distributor

Distributors differ widely in their specialties and capabilities. If you choose the right one, both you and the distributor will prosper. On the other hand, if you choose an inappropriate distributor, you'll have locked your-self into an exclusive relationship that could take months or years to re-cover from.

You should put time and effort into talking to different distributors and finding out which one is right for you. Treat your search as seriously as you would treat the quest for a spouse. This is a long-term relationship. The distributor should consist of a group of people who you wouldn't mind working with *and* being identified with for years. Do not sign up with any distributor where there is any question of ethics, reach, capabil-ity, or effective sales.

Can you make money under their contract? Do they have the capacity to sell your genre of books? When selecting a distributor for your books, be sure to ask each of them for the following information. The more hard questions you ask at the start of this relationship, the fewer tough surprises you will discover later on.

☐ **The discount they require from you**—Be sure to verify how they figure the discount. Get a firm idea what the resulting average discount will be (since many require a discount on net sales, the actual figure you pay them can vary depending on the net sale price). Most distribu-tors ask for a discount of 15% to 30% of the net sale (which may, in turn, be discounted 40% to 55% from the retail price).

Before deciding on a distributor, calculate detailed projections of what their payment terms will mean for your cash flow and income. If the numbers don't work out, negotiate with the distributor before you sign a contract. If they want you, they will bend.

☐ **Their terms**—How often will they pay? How often will they report sales? How soon after sales are made will they pay? Generally speak-ing, most pay monthly 90 to 120 days after the sale, but some pay only after they have collected from the accounts who bought from them. Most also report sales monthly.

☐ **Their territory**—Are they asking for exclusivity? If so, what territory do they cover? What markets do they serve? Is the exclusivity only for a certain territory or market, or for the entire book trade? Do they have complete market penetration? In what territories are they strong? Make sure their strengths match your market needs. If you publish books of special interest to people in the West but the distributor is strongest in the East, they would not be a good match for you.

☐ **Insurance**—Do they insure your books while on consignment in their warehouse? If so, for how much?

☐ **Stability**—How long has the distributor been in business? How suc-cessful have they been? Do they make payments to publishers on time?

☐ **Size**—How large is the distributor? Do you want to be with a large distributor who has more clout with the chains? Or do you want to be with a smaller distributor who may be able to give you more personal attention? Publishers Group West (PGW), with over $170 million in annual sales, is the largest distributor. National Book Network, with $80 million in annual sales, is the second largest. The third largest is Independent Publishers Gorup.

☐ **Number of publishers**—How many publishers do they represent? Do they have a large turnover in publishers (not a good sign)? Are the books published by their current publishers in competition with yours? Are they compatible? Would your titles fit? Check out their catalog to see what subjects they are strong in. If they have lots of titles in your area of specialization, chances are greater that they will sell your titles effectively (provided they don't represent established competing publishers). Where will you fit in their hierarchy of publishers? You want to be important enough to them that they listen to you.

☐ **Number of sales representatives**—How many sales reps do they employ? Do they have reps covering all areas of the country? Are their reps good? Ask some bookstores that last question. When you sign up with a distributor, you are essentially hiring their sales force, so you should make sure that sales force is adequate and qualified.

Are their representatives *house reps* (paid by the distributor) or *commission reps* (who carry other publishers' books as well)? Since commission reps often represent anywhere from 10 to 30 other publishers and/or distributors, they sometimes won't do as good a job as a house rep in showing your books. Your distributor's catalog could well end up at the bottom of their bag—under 25 other catalogs.

Publicist Karen Misuraca found that the regional sales reps of APG were very helpful when she needed to know the best stores for author events and media contacts for major cities. APG's Toronto rep faxed her "a fantastic list of media with hot prospects starred" In addition, he explained which stores were the best independents and even offered to set up the events for her. Now, that's a good sales rep!

☐ **Other contract provisions**—Ask to see a sample contract. Check to see what the duration of the contract will be. If need be, how can the contract be terminated? Is there a clear termination clause?

What are your responsibilities? What are the responsibilities of the distributor? Be sure you and the distributor share risks. Be wary of any contracts with a low percentage sales fee and high charges for storage, shipping, collection, catalog listings, or other marketing fees.

For an extensive article comparing distribution agreements, see "Apples and Oranges: An Analysis and Comparison of Distribution Agreements" on Ivan Hoffman's web site at http://www.ivanhoffman.com.

☐ **References**—Ask for the names, addresses, and phone numbers of other publishers they distribute. Phone these references, and check to see how well the distributor has served them. How many books did the distributor sell? Did they pay on time? Any problems? Any dramatic successes? Is the distributor responsive to publishers' questions and needs? Ask detailed probing questions.

☐ **Customer references**—As long as you are checking references, you should also ask for the names of some of their bookstore accounts. How well do they service their accounts? What kind of reputation do they have? Do they turn orders around quickly? Do they provide good customer service? Obviously you would not want a distributor who has a dishonest, sloppy, disorganized, or otherwise unhealthy reputation.

☐ **Key accounts**—Do they sell to the major accounts, such as Barnes & Noble, Borders, Books-A-Million, Amazon.com, Ingram, and Baker & Taylor, directly through house reps? Or do they use commissioned reps? Ideally, they should be handling the key accounts in house.

☐ **Reports**—Ask to see copies of any reports that the distributor provides to their client publishers. Be sure that they provide an accurate accounting of sales by title. In addition, they should identify which stores have purchased each of your titles. Without reliable and consistent reports, you can't do your job in tracking how your books are doing.

☐ **Return rates**—What are their return rates for the company as a whole? If the returns are too low (less than 10%), the distributor probably does not do a good job of placing books into the bookstores in the first place. If the returns are too high (more than 30 or 40%), they may be pushing books too hard and taking unnecessary risks. You definitely don't want to be stuck with too many returns, especially if you go back to press to print more to handle the initial demand.

☐ **Bad debts**—Will they cover bad debts? Or pass them on to you? Do they require a reserve fund against returns and/or bad debts? How much of a reserve? How is it determined?

☐ **Financial statements**—If you have any questions about the viability of a distributor, ask to see their financial statements to verify that they are sufficiently well-financed. You don't want to tie up your stock with a distributor who is teetering on the edge of bankruptcy. Note that several distributors have gone belly up in recent years because they did not have strong financial backing.

☐ **Catalog**—Look at their catalog. Is it professionally designed? Would you like to see your books in their catalog? Do they offer any other promotional activities?

☐ **Their sales expectations**—Ask them how many of each title they expect to sell. Are they enthusiastic about your titles or only lukewarm?

☐ **Accessibility**—Are the key staff members easy to talk to? Do they answer your questions promptly? Do they return your phone calls? Is the distributor located nearby so you can visit them regularly? When you visited their facilities, did you feel welcome? Taken care of?

☐ **General reputation**—Who owns the distributor? Are the owners deeply involved with the company? How often does the staff turn over? Rapid turnover might indicate deeper problems.

The larger distributors are very selective in taking on new publishers. Once you've decided which distributor you'd like to handle your books, you're going to have to sell them on taking you on as a client. The best way to do that is to present them with a solid, detailed, doable marketing plan. Make sure your books look like a topnotch retail book. And include any prepublication testimonials, especially from celebrities, booksellers, or media. Then follow up with phone calls.

When a self-publisher was told by a major distributor that they would likely pass on her book, she phoned every bookstore in her area and, as a result, developed a list of fifteen stores who said they would carry her book if the distributor took it. She faxed these names to the person making the decision at the distributor. When she called back a few days later, that person was excited to take on her book. The moral of this story? **If you want distributors to pay attention to you, get bookstores to speak for you.**

When another self-publisher wanted to get the attention of a potential distributor, he sent a portable tape recorder and a personalized tape-recorded message. That got their attention—and their approval.

As with any potential market for your book, you have to convince them that you have created a good product, that it has an audience (one that is served by that market), that others think you have a great product, and that you are going to do additional promotions that will help them sell your book. Distributors are human. If you do some of their work for them, they are far more likely to say yes to you.

Since many distributors don't want to take on one-book publishers, PMA set up a trade distribution program. This program encourages PMA members to submit their titles to a committee which judges how appropriate the books are for retail trade distribution. About 30% of the books submitted are selected for distribution through The Small Press Selection program of Independent Publishers Group. While many of the publishers have gone with the IPG program, some use their selection to convince other distributors to carry their books. For details on this program, contact **PMA**, 627 Aviation Way, Manhattan Beach, CA 90266; 310-372-2732; Fax: 310-374-3342. Email: pmaonline@aol.com. Web: http://www.pma-online.org.

13:05 How to Work with Distributors to Sell More Books

Once you have signed up with a distributor, keep in touch with them. Let them know about your upcoming titles. Send them review copies as soon as they are off the press. Get their feedback on the cover designs, titles, and contents of your books before you go to press. Also, get their feedback on your promotional plans. Let them help you help them. The more you communicate with them, the more they can sell. Below are some more tips on how to work with distributors:

Stay in touch.

Nourish personal contacts. Go to your distributor's sales conferences, if they will let you. Visit their premises at least once a season. Talk to the sales manager frequently. Also talk to your sales reps personally as often as you can. Make sure these people understand your whole line of books and your frontlist books in particular.

If a particular title isn't selling well, it may simply be that no one besides the author has figured out what it's all about and how to present it. So make a nuisance of yourself. Your sales will improve as a result. Publishers who don't have contact with their sales force get forgotten.

Go to BookExpo America.

Use BookExpo America as an excuse to talk to all the sales reps, wholesalers, staff members of your distributor, and other publishers you can lay your hands on. This once-a-year mardi gras of the publishing industry is an invaluable time to cement relationships. Get to know people. Personal contact means a great deal in the publishing business.

Get projections.

Get projections from your distributor of how many copies of a frontlist title they think they can sell. While a projection may only be a rough estimate, it is a guide by which you can set your print run. Once the book is at the blueline stage, call your distributor again and check how many frontlist orders they have received thus far. At that point you might want to adjust your print run up or down.

Monitor your sales.

Read your sales reports as soon as they come in. If there's an obvious problem with prepublication sales targets for a frontlist title, call your distributor immediately. It may not be too late to remedy the situation before the end of the current season. In 1990, Dawson Church of Aslan Publishing was stunned to get a copy of his September sales report showing only 192 sales for his lead frontlist title, *Your Body Believes Every Word You Say* by Barbara Levine. He called his distributor right away. Working together, they came up with a plan of action to get sales rolling. As a result, the book sold 6,000 copies that season and even more copies later.

Most distributors work with two seasons: spring and fall. The spring season runs from February to June or July, with catalog copy due by early September so catalogs will be available at the sales conference in December. The fall season runs from July or August through January, with catalog copy due by March so catalogs will be available for the sales conferences in May and BookExpo America in late May or early June.

Identify your lead titles.

Identify a lead frontlist title each season and put the bulk of your marketing efforts behind it. Tell your distributor which title is your lead title, and ask them if they can give it special attention.

In spring 1992, Aslan's publicist Eileen Duhn made calls to many magazines and other media outlets. She had three Aslan titles to promote, each of them fairly commercial: *Magnificent Addiction, Voices from the Womb,* and *More Than Just Sex.* But she got her foot in the door with *More Than Just Sex* and used the interest that book generated to coax reviewers to consider the other titles as well. That's the job of a lead title.

Market your books properly.

Ask your distributor for the names of publishers who have the best and most cost-effective marketing campaigns. Get copies of their marketing plans and follow their example where it fits in with your books.

Give your marketing plan to your distributor well in advance. Most distributors want your marketing plan along with a New Title Information Sheet, usually about four months prior to the start of a new season. A good marketing plan makes a difference in the degree of attention a distributor pays to a book.

Even if your marketing budget for a new title is less than $5,000, mention it. $5,000 might sound like a lot for a small publisher, but if you total *all* the costs of your marketing campaign for a new title you may be surprised. Your marketing budget includes the cost of the book's cover, announcements, ads, direct mail pieces, staff time to carry out your marketing plan (you should pay yourself a decent professional wage for your time), publicist's salary, special promotions, a portion of your catalog, and anything else you are doing to promote a new title.

Other noteworthy items to tell your distributor include national print or electronic media appearances, significant ads (*Library Journal, Publishers Weekly, New York Times*, etc.), and the size of the first printing, if it's large.

Write good marketing copy.

If you spend 1,000 hours publishing a book and devote half an hour to dashing off a few clumsy paragraphs to describe the book, you have just made a poor allocation of time. In the first eight months at one new distributor, they saw close to a hundred frontlist books with copy so poor that even a well-intentioned and persistent sleuth would have had a hard time figuring out what the books were about. The purpose of the promotional copy is to reveal, not obscure.

This promotional copy is vital. If you are not adept at writing copy that sings, hire someone who is. Even if it costs you $250 for two hours of writing, it is worth it. Why? Because you can use this copy on the book jacket, in your ads, in your new title information sheets, in your catalog, in your distributor's catalog, for ABA, for Bowker—in short, for selling lots more books than you would have sold had you not produced professional writing.

Get feedback on your covers and titles.

Treat your distributor as a free cover and title consultant. The people who are going to have to sell a product should obviously have a say in what it looks like, since they are the ones who have to present it to the buyers. Books are no different. Most distributors have weekly sales meetings. If you have several different cover designs or titles that you are considering for a new book, send them along to your distributor and ask for their feedback. Don't feel like you're imposing on your distributor. Any good distributor *insists* on being involved in such decisions.

Observe deadlines.

According to several distributors, the single dumbest thing a publisher can do is to not publish on time. If you miss your book's publication date, you have not only disappointed the distributor but you have also jeopardized your relationship with the sales reps, bookstores, and readers.

Besides getting your book out on time, you also need to observe your distributors deadlines for catalog copy, cover graphics, and other information they need to sell your books to their customers. If you withhold or delay this information, it hurts you and your distributor. It hurts the distributor in the form of catalogs late to the printer, overtime charges, extra staff hours, missing information to sales reps, and general aggravation. It hurts you in the pocketbook by jeopardizing sales of your books.

You might think that with one or two hundred client publishers, distributors wouldn't really notice publishers who send their information in on time and correct. But they do. And so do their reps. Distributors, like everyone else in business, naturally gravitate to people who are reliable. It is with such people that they form their strongest relationships. When the chance for a special promotion comes along, or a special push to the sales reps, or a free ad, distributors will call on the publishers they know are on the ball.

Send graphics and other information about frontlist titles.

Cover graphics are particularly important. For a publisher not to provide cover graphics in time for catalog production is a terrible disservice to the book. One year, one distributor's catalog was filled with many white boxes with only the title of a book inside. What happened? Publishers didn't provide cover graphics on time.

A book gets to be frontlist just once. If during this critical period, the sales reps are walking into the stores and showing the buyers blank boxes, the number of orders inevitably falls. The cover is your single most important marketing tool for a new title.

Also provide your distributor with extra jackets or covers, tipsheets or title information sheets, and, if your book contains photos or color illustrations, a 16- or 32-page sample signature (a *blad*). These items are essential ingredients for a good sales kit.

Do co-op advertising with your distributor.

Many distributors offer co-op ads in *Publishers Weekly, Library Journal*, and other trade publications. Such ads can be more cost-effective than doing your own ad. Also, you might advertise in your distributor's catalog or newsletters if the rates and the coverage are reasonable. Bookstores will notice, and the staff at the distribution company will certainly notice.

Besides requiring that all new titles be listed in the fall and spring announcement issues of *Publishers Weekly* and *American Bookseller*, National Book Network requires that "All books *must* be advertised in Bradley's *Radio-TV Interview Report*!!" NBN knows that without this minimal promotion, few books will sell via bookstores.

Don't ignore your backlist.

And don't let your distributor ignore your backlist either. Since backlist sales are the core of a publisher's income, this is a critical question to ask when you are considering a new distributor. To get attention, you could offer a 50% special discount on your backlist for the first three months after you join a new distributor. Or see if they could have their reps sell directly from your catalog for the first season, in addition to their own catalog.

Monitor backlist sales monthly, and notice which books are slipping. To keep your books fresh, send current reviews for those titles to the reps. Note that you should have direct access to your reps, including their names, addresses, and phone numbers. Most distributors print the addresses and phone numbers of their sales reps in their catalogs.

Make sure your reps know your backlist. During one of Atrium's spring sales conferences, Gerry Clow of Bear and Company held a backlist quiz for the sales reps, giving them clues so they could guess the correct title or author of each book. And the reps got most of the answers right—a tribute to the clear line identity of Bear titles.

13:06 Distributing Through Wholesalers

Instead of distributing your books exclusively through distributors, you might want to set up your own accounts with major wholesalers. In this case you would make your own sales presentations to the wholesalers (either by mail, over the phone, or through direct visits), take their orders, and handle all fulfillment and collection on your own.

Wholesalers can often provide you with as much distribution to the book trade as can a distributor. For instance, more bookstores order through Ingram and Baker & Taylor, the two largest bookstore wholesalers, than through any other distributor or wholesaler.

The advantages of using wholesalers rather than distributors are:

☐ Wholesalers usually require a smaller discount (typically 40% to 55%). Most are now requiring 55% if you want them to stock your titles.

☐ They pay by invoice usually within 60 to 90 days, rather than stock books on consignment. While this statement was true when I wrote the first edition of this book, it is now inaccurate when talking about bookstore wholesalers. Most such wholesalers are now asking smaller publishers to ship them books on consignment, with payments due 90 days after the sale.

☐ They do not require exclusive contracts. Instead, they will stock any books for which there is customer demand.

The disadvantages of using wholesalers rather than distributors are:

☐ Wholesalers tend to be passive order takers. Although they often publish catalogs of titles they stock and do some telephone marketing, none of them have sales representatives who regularly call on bookstores to promote new titles.

☐ Since they carry many more titles, they cannot promote your individual titles as aggressively as can a distributor who has fewer titles to offer.

☐ Wholesalers do not offer complete fulfillment or collection services for publishers. Since many wholesalers try to stretch payment terms, it might be said that they create collection problems rather than solve them.

Since wholesalers do not require exclusivity, you should try to set up accounts with as many as you can comfortably service. Ingram and Baker & Taylor, of course, are essential for any general books, but if you publish highly specialized titles, you should also seek out wholesalers who specialize in your subject area.

When approaching wholesalers, you will need to show them your catalog of books, your upcoming list, your promotional plans, your terms and discount schedule, and your returns policy. If you can demonstrate to them that you are producing quality books with general appeal, offer standard terms, and are well enough capitalized or committed (so that you will still be in business when—and if—it becomes necessary to return books to you), you should have no trouble selling your books to them.

To help you understand the best way to approach wholesalers, I have reproduced on the following page the results of a survey I conducted for the *Book Marketing Update* newsletter.

How Do Wholesalers Find Out About New Books?

Here are the ways that 200 major wholesalers report that they find out about new books (note that they gave multiple answers to the question):

142   Direct mail from publishers
127   Reviews in trade magazines

124   Advertisements in trade magazines
119   Sales calls from representatives and/or word of mouth
82   Telephone calls from publishers
65   Reviews in newspapers
36   Advertisements in consumer magazines and newspapers
14   Other (bibliographies, conventions, authors)

From this survey, it is obvious that wholesalers do pay attention to their direct mail—and respond by buying. Reviews and advertisements in trade magazines are also effective in getting their attention. Direct contact through sales reps or phone calls are also effective.

What Influences Wholesaler's Decision to Stock a Title?

Once you get a wholesaler's attention, you must still convince them to stock your book. How can you influence their decision? Here are a few criteria they use to judge a book's appropriateness for their market:

72   The book fits their subject interest and/or market
27   Sales potential of the book
21   Customer requests
18   Author's reputation and/or sales history
15   Price
14   Promotional plans and publisher support
12   Terms and discounts
11   Past sales of similar titles
10   Cover design

In our survey, this question was open-ended (fill in the blank). The above numbers summarize the wholesaler's answers to this question.

From this survey, obviously the most important criterion to most wholesalers is whether the book fits their subject interest or market. Hence, above all, you must match your promotions to the interests of the wholesalers. When you send them your catalog or a new title for consideration, be sure to point out how your book or books are appropriate for their markets.

Other factors enter in, but they play a more important role for certain types of wholesalers. For instance, mass-market jobbers are influenced by the author's reputation, the cover design, and publisher's promotional plans, while library wholesalers are more influenced by customer requests.

Personally, I have found that wholesalers are far more influenced by the cover design and packaging of a book than they are ready to admit. Don't ignore the cover simply because it seems unimportant in this survey.

13:07 Working with Ingram Book Company

Ingram, the 24th largest privately owned company in the United States, is the largest wholesaler to independent bookstores. They stock more than

450,000 titles. They currently distribute several billion dollars worth of books each year at wholesale. They also distribute an additional $5 billion worth of magazines, software, videos, and audios.

Because Ingram offers a large selection of books, toll-free ordering, fast shipping, and easy returns, many booksellers prefer to order through them rather than go direct to the publisher. Almost all reorders for books, whether from major publishers or smaller publishers, now go through wholesalers such as Ingram. As a result, if you want to penetrate the independent bookstore market, you need to get your books into Ingram's system.

Submit requests and information to **Ingram Book Company**, Publisher Relations Manager, One Ingram Boulevard, LaVergne TN 37086-3629; 615-213-6803; 800-937-8222, ext. 35350; Fax: 615-213-5565. Email: pubrel@ ingrambook.com. Web: http://www.ingrambookgroup.com. For new publishers, go to http://www.ingrambookgroup.com/new/publishers.asp.

Ingram is now working directly only with publishers of 10 or more titles. If you are a self-publisher or a small publisher with fewer titles, Ingram now asks that you sell to them via a distributor. You might try Partners, Biblio, Midpoint Trade, or some of the other distributors listed on my Bookmarket. com web site: http://www.bookmarket.com/distributors.html.

If they choose to stock your titles, Ingram will ask for a 55% discount with net 90 day terms on consignment (that means that they'll pay you 90 days after they make a sale, not 90 days after you ship books). And you pay the freight. If you want your books stocked by them, you'll probably have to live with these terms. But it doesn't hurt to try to negotiate better terms. If Ingram asks you to pay freight both ways (both in sending books to them and in accepting returns from them), don't accept those terms if at all possible. When you have to pay shipping both ways, it makes it too easy for Ingram to return books they should keep in stock.

Don't give up if Ingram says no the first time or even the second time around. When Ingram rejected their *Stop and Smell the Rosemary* cookbook three times (after receiving a galley copy, a finished printed book, and a fancy press kit), the Junior League of Houston called their Barnes & Noble regional buyer and explained their situation. The B&N buyer gave them the name of her representative at Ingram and suggested they call him. They did and, after talking with him for 30 minutes, he went to work to get them accepted. Within five days, their contract with Ingram arrived by fax.

Ingram takes an active role in promoting the books they carry. Here are just a few of the services they offer to bookstores:

☐ **Monthly magazines**—In their monthly magazines *Advance* and *Paperback Advance*, which are mailed to about 9,000 bookstores, Ingram lists the major new titles they have begun to offer. As a publisher, you may buy advertising in these magazines to help promote your books.

☐ **Microfiche**—ReadyStock is a weekly microfiche service listing all titles currently in stock in Ingram's warehouses. By using this service, booksellers can special order any title in stock for their customers and expect shipment within days (rather than weeks or months which seems to be the standard when they order direct from many publishers).

☐ **Telephone promotions**—Ingram offers telephone promotions of titles with wide appeal. When bookstore customers call in, they are asked if they would like to hear about some interesting new titles. If yes, then the telephone operators describe the new titles being promoted that week. Some publishers have reported sales increasing by 600% during the week they paid Ingram to promote one of their titles.

☐ **Bestseller lists**—Ingram publishes its own bestseller lists, both for general hardcover and softcover books and for specific areas like computer books, inspirational titles, cookbooks, how-to books, and so on. Booksellers use these lists as guides for ordering titles.

☐ **Ingram Books in Print Plus**—Ingram, in conjunction with the R.R. Bowker Company, has developed a database of over 800,000 titles on a CD-ROM laser disc. This database allows booksellers and librarians to identify and acquire almost any book still in print.

☐ **Bookshelf**—Ingram issues a monthly full-color consumer buying guide which they provide to bookstores at their cost ($5.00 per 100). The guide lists bestselling books as well as potential bestsellers.

☐ **Special catalogs**—Ingram produces special interest catalogs, some aimed at consumers (such as their gift and computer book catalogs) and some aimed at booksellers for title selection (such as their guide to business and economics books or their *Independent Press Review* mini-catalog). In every case, you may buy advertising space in the catalog to promote your titles in that category.

☐ **A.I.D.**—Ingram provides an Automatic Inventory Distribution program which allows booksellers to automatically receive a certain number of copies of any new title selections made by Ingram's own buying staff.

☐ **ROSI**—Ingram also provides a Recommended Opening Store Inventory selection service for new or expanding bookstores. ROSI is a computerized printout of bestselling titles by subject categories based on the popularity of those titles in a particular region. The bookseller can then edit the printout to their own needs and return it as an order.

☐ **Statement stuffers**—Ingram will insert your advertising flyer into their microfiche and statement mailings. The cost? About $1,000.00.

☐ **Other services**—Ingram offers inventory control systems, co-op advertising summaries, audio/video and software stock, and other services that aid booksellers.

☐ **Book signing program**—Through this program, you donate 100 books for Ingram staff. You spend one hour signing books for the staff at their bookstore where employees can buy at a discount. In return, they will pitch your book to the 30,000 bookstore orders that come in that week.

Because Ingram offers so many services to booksellers and because many of these services rely on their in-house selection of book titles, you should make a special effort to get your books stocked by them.

If you get a chance, visit the main offices of Ingram and meet with the buyers in person. Be prepared to give them an engaging presentation of your forthcoming titles. When Harvey Mackay was promoting his *How to Swim with the Sharks without Being Eaten*, he met with Ingram CEO Philip Pfeffer. Afterwards he visited Ingram's telemarketing center where he met with each of Ingram's 75+ telemarketers. During his talks, he passed out shark-shaped lapel pins and signed copies of his book. As a result, he and his book became more than just a few words on a computer printout.

Ingram provides publishers with access to an automated stock and sales system so they can check out Ingram's sales on any title (even competitive titles). Call 615-213-6803 and punch in the ISBN number of the title you are interested in. Or call 800-937-0995 for stock levels.

13:08 Working with Baker & Taylor

Baker & Taylor is the other major wholesaler to booksellers (and an even larger wholesaler to libraries). To get your books listed with them, contact **Baker & Taylor, New Presses**, 1120 U.S. Highway 22 (08807-2944), P.O. Box 6885, Bridgewater NJ 08807-0885; 908-541-7460; Fax: 908-541-7863. Web: http://www.baker-taylor.com. Check out their supplier information page at: http://www.btol.com/supplier.cfm.

When you complete your Advance Book Information forms for listings in the *Books In Print* database, send a copy to Baker & Taylor as well. Also send any other information about the book (brochures, copy of the cover, etc.) that will aid them in their title selection.

When your books come off the press, send a review copy to Baker & Taylor right away. These review copies will be evaluated by their staff of librarians for selection in their Final Approval Program. If your books are selected, the opening order would be for zero to 100 copies. Three factors affect their selection of a book:

1. sustained demand for your books,
2. the viability of your company (how long has it been in business, how actively does it promote its books, etc.), and
3. whether you offer normal terms of doing business.

Currently, Baker & Taylor, like most of the other major wholesalers, is requiring a 55% discount, 90 day terms, freight paid by the publisher, and books fully returnable for 100% credit without prior authorization, shipping labels, or invoice numbers. They are also requiring new vendors to pay a one-time service fee of $100 to defray their costs in setting up a new vendor account (this fee is waived for members of the Publishers Marketing Association). But they also state that "you may set your own policies in line with your marketing strategy." If your books sell primarily to libraries, you should take this last advice to heart and offer Baker & Taylor a shorter discount and net 30 day terms.

Baker & Taylor is especially strong with libraries. If you are a new or small publisher, you can expect that as many as 75% of your library orders will be placed through Baker & Taylor. Here are just a few of the services that Baker & Taylor offers its bookstore and library customers (and where you might have advertising or promotional possibilities):

☐ **Final Approval Program**—Some libraries order every title that is selected by Baker & Taylor for inclusion in this program.

☐ **Cataloging**—Baker & Taylor catalogs all new titles they stock. The cataloging of these titles encourages library and school orders because it makes the books more accessible and easier to process. In fact, one of the major reasons libraries order from Baker & Taylor is to get the accompanying cataloging card sets.

☐ **Special orders**—Baker & Taylor offers one-stop buying to its customers. Hence, even if your books are not stocked by any of its four centers, they will still order books from you when a customer requests your books. Such orders trickle in (one or two copies at a time) until such time that the demand warrants a larger order.

☐ **Bookfinder Microfiche**—B&T offers a weekly microfiche listing of the books in their inventory as well as their *Tradeweek* magazine on microfiche (which provides current information on new books, major buys, publicity campaigns, author tours, and a cross-check of bestseller lists).

☐ **B&T Link**—Their CD-ROM database gives their customers access to more than 1.4 million books, audios, and videos. Through this database, bookstores and libraries can place orders electronically. 50% of their customers currently use this feature.

☐ **Journals**—Baker & Taylor publishes two bibliographic journals which they send to libraries to encourage orders. *Forecast* goes to 18,500 public libraries in the United States and Canada. *Directions* goes to about 7,800 academic and special libraries. Your books will be listed in the appropriate journal or journals if selected for the Final Approval Program. Plus, you can also advertise in either journal.

☐ **Book Alert**—Baker & Taylor also publishes a catalog of new titles which it sends to more than 4,500 booksellers and 4,000 libraries. Advertising is also accepted in this catalog.

☐ **Independent Press Quarterly**—For smaller publishers B&T offers this advertising opportunity, a quarterly magazine which is sent to 12,000 bookstores and public libraries. They also publish a *Multicultural Catalog, Hot Picks in Mass Market and Trade Paper*, and catalogs for travel, academia, videos, computers, religious books, and children's books.

☐ **Library bestseller list**—Each month *Library Journal* lists those fiction and nonfiction titles which are most in demand by libraries from Baker & Taylor nationwide. Baker & Taylor also advertises that all new titles reviewed in *Library Journal* may be ordered through them.

☐ **Exhibits**—Baker & Taylor exhibits selected titles at overseas book fairs, including the Moscow and Frankfurt book fairs.

☐ **Overseas representation**—Their Baker & Taylor International division is one of the major reps of American books in European markets.

☐ **Telemarketing**—After placing an order, a customer can hear a 50-word promotion for a book. Titles promoted under this program must be in stock in all four warehouses.

☐ **Warehouse shipment stuffers**—B&T will insert publishers' flyers into each shipment of books to their customers. The cost to participate is $775.00 per market (public library, trade bookstores, schools, academic, or continuations). Or you can pay only $375.00 per market for a regional mailing (to customers of only one of the four regions).

☐ **Other services**—As with Ingram, Baker & Taylor offers statement stuffers, approval programs, and other special services.

As with Ingram, all these services mean that Baker & Taylor has developed a loyal following of booksellers and librarians who will not order a book which is not available through their programs. Hence, it would be worth your while to spend some time to get your books selected for Baker & Taylor's Final Approval Program.

13:09 Working with Other Wholesalers

According to one major independent distributor, 30% of their sales are to the top three chains, 25% to the major wholesalers, 25% to the regional wholesalers, chains, and major independent bookstores, and the final 20% to the other 4,500 independent bookstores.

While courting the two largest wholesalers and the major chains, don't overlook the many regional and specialty wholesalers who service booksellers and librarians. To attract these regional and special wholesalers, you must woo them the same way you woo Ingram and Baker & Taylor: Produce great books. Offer standard terms. Let them know about forthcoming books early enough so they can have them in stock before publication date. And support your books with sufficient advertising and promotion.

Here are the names of a few of the best known wholesalers (for more details, please see John Kremer's special *Book Distribution MiniGuide):*

☐ **General and regional wholesalers**—American West Books, Bookazine, the distributors, Koen-Levy Book Distributors, Partners, Southern Book Service, and Sunbelt Publications.

☐ **General library wholesalers**—Blackwell North America, Brodart, Eastern Book Company, Emery-Pratt, Midwest Library Service, and Yankee Book Peddler (a division of B&T).

☐ **Academic and special library wholesalers**—Academic Book Center, Scholarly Book Center, and others.

☐ **Medical wholesalers**—Login Brothers Books, J. A. Majors Medical Book Company, Matthews Book Company, Rittenhouse, and others.

☐ **New age wholesalers**—Abyss Distribution, DeVorss Book Distributors, New Concepts, New Leaf Distributing, and others.

☐ **Miscellaneous wholesalers**—Book Tech Distributing (computer books), Cromland (computer books), Music Book Service, NACSCORP (college bookstores), and Small Press Distribution (60% of their sales are of poetry titles; 72% of their sales are to independent bookstores).

Many of these wholesalers offer services similar to the ones offered by Ingram and Baker & Taylor. For instance, the distributors will distribute 500 of your flyers free if they stock your title. They also offer telemarketing (a 10-second mention of your title) on all incoming and outgoing sales calls (cost: $200 for about 2,000 calls per week). You can advertise in their catalogs and checklists for as little as $28.00. They publish special catalogs and checklists in the following categories: women's studies, regional titles, children's books, life enhancement, gay and lesbian studies, fall announcements, health and nutrition, cookbooks, holiday giving, and African-American.

In dealing with wholesalers, remember the following key points:

☐ **Make them earn their discounts.** Don't offer them higher discounts unless they buy in quantity. For instance, don't offer more than 20% discount for orders of 1 or 2 books. Offer 50% discount only if they order at least 25 or 100 copies. Or you can base the discounts you offer them on their total orders during the past twelve months.

Since I originally wrote the above paragraph, wholesalers have become more selective and more aggressive. As they began offering higher discounts to bookstores, they began demanding higher discounts from publishers. Many of the general wholesalers will not stock your titles anymore unless you accept their terms, which currently ask for 50 to 57% discount, net 90, free freight, on consignment. If you must accept these terms from the general wholesalers, at least don't offer them to wholesalers who order only one or two copies at a time.

☐ **Offer net 30 terms.** Don't let any wholesaler ever go beyond 90 days in paying their invoices or statements. When ProMotion Publishing was contacted by a major book wholesaler who wanted to order a quantity of books, they rejected giving the wholesaler any terms, pointing out that they do "business the old-fashioned way, we pay cash for what we get and get paid cash for what we sell." A few weeks later the wholesaler came back with an order—under ProMotion's terms.

☐ **Check credit.** When receiving orders from new wholesalers, check their credit carefully. Ask them to prepay until their credit is established.

☐ **Keep your wholesalers informed** of new developments with your books and authors.

☐ **List those wholesalers who stock your books** in your catalog and new product announcements.

☐ **Offer the same terms and discounts to all wholesalers.** If you want to offer different terms or discounts, you can make a distinction between stocking and non-stocking wholesalers. Or you can make a distinction by the number of books they order.

☐ **Try to set up accounts with at least three to five wholesalers** to make it easy for booksellers to order from their favorite wholesalers. For instance, successful Latin American publishers have found that they need to use at least a dozen different Spanish-language wholesalers to cover the U.S. market for their books.

13:10 ID's—Independent Distributors

Independent distributors (otherwise known as *IDs* or *paperback jobbers*) are responsible for the distribution of most mass-market paperbacks and magazines. These jobbers are local agencies which distribute to booksellers, schools, drug stores, food stores, airport news outlets, newsstands, and other paperback outlets. Most of them get their stock from national distributors such as Kable News Company, Select Distributors, Warner, and Simon & Schuster Mass Merchandise Company rather than direct from book publishers. In recent years, many of these local agencies have consolidated. Where there used to be 182 wholesale jobbers in 1994, there are now less than 40. The two largest national jobbers are:

☐ **Anderson News,** National Offices, 6016 Brookvale Lane #151, Knoxville, TN 37919; 865-584-9765; 800-390-1543; Fax: 865-450-3159. Web: http://www.andersonnews.com. Serves 40,000 outlets in 45 states. Owned by the same people who own BooksAMillion.

☐ **The News Group,** New Vendor Review, 300 Lackawana Avenue #7, West Paterson, NJ 07424-2900; 973-237-9600. Web: http://www.the-newsgroup.com. New book publishers information: http://www.thenews-group.com/main/vendor/NGBooks.htm.

Although most of their business involves magazines and mass-market paperbacks, some of these local jobbers also carrying hardcovers and trade paperbacks, especially bestsellers and regional titles. If you publish regional titles which might interest these jobbers, you should check to see if your local jobber handles anything other than magazines and mass-market paperbacks. You might find a willing helper for your local distribution. To find a local jobber, ask a local grocery store or drugstore (magazine department).

In May, 1997, United Magazine Company bussed a baker's dozen of romance authors across the Midwest on a five-day tour. The authors would jump out at grocery stores and other book outlets and sign autographs. Similarly, on Valentine's Day, Portland's Bay News Company coordinated romance author signings at a Fred Meyer grocery store and a Target.

Tom and Marilyn Ross met with the truck drivers of their local jobber, San Diego Periodical Distributors, to promote their book on *Creative Loafing*. This meeting helped them to get greater local distribution for the book than they could have accomplished on their own time. Also, as mentioned previously, Jacqueline Susann was famous for her breakfasts with such truck drivers, working to convince them to give her books the best positions in the paperback racks. If you want good distribution of your books through the IDs, get to know the drivers or find a way to motivate them (through a contest, display incentive, or other means).

13:11 Distributing Through Other Publishers

Some publishers distribute other publishers. If you have developed a line of books and are looking for trade distribution, you could contact another publisher whose publishing philosophy and marketing prowess you admire. You might find them amenable to taking on distribution of your line.

Most publishers who distribute other publishers' books require a discount of as much as 25 to 30% of the net price of the book. In turn, they take care of all sales visits, distribution, fulfillment, and collection. The publisher is still responsible for editing the book, plus all advertising and promotion.

What are the advantages of distributing through another publisher? Besides the benefits of sales representation, fulfillment, and collection, distribution via a larger publisher provides your line of books with more credibility and clout. It also provides your company with instant access to the major trade accounts.

What are the disadvantages? First, a larger publisher will always give first priority to their own line and only then focus on the other publishers they represent. Second, few larger publishers will distribute smaller book publishers unless they are producing at least three or four new titles each season (spring and fall).

Here are a few publishers who distribute other publishers' books. Most of the smaller publishers listed here have been distributed by major publishers for at least three years, so it must be working for them.

☐ **Amherst Media**, an independent publisher of how-to photography books, distributes similar books from other publishers to camera shops and the photography market.

☐ **Penguin Putnam** distributes books for The Monacelli Press, Overlook Press, Rough Guides, Reader's Digest Trade Books, and others.

☐ **Random House** has a separate division, Random House Distribution Services, which handles trade distribution for Rizzoli, Candlewick Press, and Rugged Land. As Random House president Phil Pfeffer noted in early 1997, "We have identified client distribution as an area with significant growth potential."

☐ **St. Martin's Press** distributes Universe, Vendome Press, Rodale, etc.

☐ **W.W. Norton** distributes Texere, Newmarket Press, Bloomberg Press, The New Press, Rio Nuevo Press, and Foul Play Press, among others.

☐ **Watson-Guptil** distributes books for Allworth Press and Parent's Guide Press.

☐ **Simon & Schuster** distributes for AAA Publishing, ibooks, Meadowbrook Press, Baen Books, and others.

For an extensive list of publishers who distribute books—with contact names, addresses, and phone numbers—order John Kremer miniguide on book distribution available at BookMarket.com.

An alternative to being distributed by a larger publisher is to join with a group of other publishers to form your own distribution. That's what the Independent Literary Publishers Association and Wisconsin Authors and Publishers Alliance did. Both of these efforts, however, are no longer operating. To succeed, such a group effort must be set up as a real business.

Other regional book publisher associations have experimented with temporary distribution arrangements. For Expo 86 in Vancouver, The Mountaineers Books and Sasquatch Books organized a group of 25 small presses in the Pacific Northwest and put together a catalog of the best travel books for the region. This *Expose Yourself to the Pacific Northwest* catalog was distributed at the Expo and to bookstores in the region. Pacific Pipeline, a regional wholesaler, handled fulfillment. Not only did the presses receive many orders as a result, but they also received lots of publicity.

13:12 Selling to Bookstore Chain Stores

Rather than go with a distributor, you could handle your own distribution through wholesalers, chain stores, and direct sales to independent booksellers. In that case, you would have to make your own sales to the major chain stores. The three major chain stores, Barnes & Noble, Borders Group, and Books-A-Million, account for almost 50% of retail bookstore sales. So you cannot afford to ignore them if your books are of general interest. Here are the addresses of the chains.

☐ **Barnes & Noble**, 122 Fifth Avenue, New York, NY 10011; 212-633-3300; Fax: 212-675-0413. Web: http://www.bn.com. They operate 650 Barnes & Noble superstores as well as 500 B. Dalton mall stores. To located addresses for Barnes & Noble stores, see: http://www.barnesand noble.com/frames/storeLocator/storeLocator_findstore_home.asp.

☐ **Borders Group**, New Vendor Acquisitions, 100 Phoenix Drive, Ann Arbor, MI 48108; 734-995-7262. Web: http://www.bordersgroupinc.com. They operate Borders and Waldenbooks stores. To submit your titles as a new publisher, see: http://www.bordersgroupinc.com/artists/publishers. htm. To locate local Borders stores, see: http://www.bordersstores. com/locator/locator.jsp?tt=gn.

☐ **Books-A-Million**, Director of Merchandising, 402 Industrial Lane (35211-4465), P.O. Box 19728, Birmingham, AL 35219; 205-942-3737. Email: marketing@booksamillion.com. Web: http://www.booksamillion. com. To locate stores, see: http://www.booksamillion.com/ncom/books?id= 2975376204251&stores=1.

Working with these major chains is no picnic. Among other problems with the chains, small publishers report the following: excessive returns, returns without prior notice, damaged returns (with credit deducted automatically), multiple shipping addresses, deductions for statistical shortages, delayed payments, and collection problems. It is common practice for the chains to return books for credit so they don't have to pay as much on their overdue invoices—and then turn around and reorder those same books!

Even given these problems, most publishers who want to reach a general audience through bookstores will have to work with these major chains. To make it easier, here are a few guidelines and suggestions on how to sell your books to chain stores:

☐ The major chain bookstores have all cut back on the number of vendors they will buy from. Hence, in the beginning, you will not be able to sell to them direct. If they like your book or books, they will order through one of the major wholesalers or distributors. Later, if they begin to sell $100,000 of your books every year, they may take you on as a vendor. There are exceptions to this rule, but not very many.

☐ In most cases, the chains are looking for publishers who can offer a steady flow of new books of broad general interest each season.

☐ They are more likely to take on a book from a small publisher if the book fills a need, especially a mass market need.

☐ The books from smaller publishers that are finally chosen for the major chains' backlists often start off as good sellers in some of their local stores. So one way for a small publisher to make it into the chains is through selling well in the local stores of that chain.

☐ Most chains have central offices that buy for all stores in the chain. In some cases, individual stores may also buy regional titles or other books of special interest to their customers. In addition, both Barnes & Noble and Waldenbooks have regional buyers in larger cities around the country. These buyers can place orders for all stores in their region. Any store manager can also order books for his or her store. Often a regional buy will become a national order if the book takes off at the local level.

When Aaron Silverman and Molly Maguire self-published the *Raymond Chandler Mystery Map of Los Angeles*, they sold the map to the local B. Dalton and Crown stores. The Hollywood B. Dalton store sold 20 copies in five days, while ten Crown stores each sold ten copies each in ten days. Of course, they all reordered.

☐ The best way to begin contact with the major chains is to call and ask for the name of their buyer who would be the most appropriate person to send your materials to. Since some of the chains buy by subject area, ask for the name of that buyer first. Then, on a regular basis, send that person information about your forthcoming books.

☐ Sometimes it can pay to start at the top. That's what Joseph Turton did for his self-published book, *My Freshman Manual*. He was so persistent in keeping the Borders president informed of his book's sales at the local Borders shop that the buyers requested, "Now please stop sending all those letters!" when they notified him that they would be stocking his book nationally. Of course, it didn't hurt that his book sold 345 copies in four-and-a-half months at his local Borders in Westlake, Ohio.

☐ Once you have books in hand, send the chain buyers a copy of the bound book before you call to ask for an order. Especially with new or unknown publishers, they would prefer seeing a finished copy of the book so they can verify for themselves that the book is of high quality in both production and contents.

☐ Keep your key contacts informed. Let them know about any major rights sales, publicity, new promotions, and author appearances. Especially inform them of any strong local promotions you'll be doing so they can order books for their local outlets.

After Waldens and B. Dalton placed large preliminary orders for his first book, *Swim with the Sharks without Being Eaten*, Harvey Mackay called up the president of Crown Books to let him know what the other chains had ordered. Although Crown had originally passed on the book, they subsequently placed an initial order for 5,000 copies.

☐ Check out their merchandising programs, such as front of store placement, end-cap display, counter display, etc. While these programs will cost you some money, they ensure that the chains will have your book in stock during the promotional period.

For example, as part of their promotion of the new edition of *The TM Book*, Fairfield Press worked with Waldenbooks to do a special co-op advertising test in a number of major cities.

☐ Send each chain a new title buy sheet (several chains provide you with a standard form to fill out) for each new title you publish. Be sure to fill it out completely and provide the chains with as much information about the new title and your marketing plans as possible.

☐ Be persistent in collecting from the chains. That keeps them honest.

☐ Be cautious about selling too many books to the chains. For one thing, returns from chain stores average about 15% above those from independent bookstores.

☐ A recent study indicated that 38% of the chain store buyers found out about new titles by reading direct mail promotions sent by the publishers themselves. In another study of smaller chain stores conducted by the *Huenefeld Report*, over 90% of the respondents reported that catalogs and flyers were the most effective way (other than personal visits) for publishers to keep them informed. Hence, don't be hesitant to mail information about your new books to these buyers.

☐ Work with the editors of chain newsletters such as Walden's *Xignals* (sent bimonthly to 250,000 science fiction book buyers), *Crime Times* (for mystery fans), *WaldenCooks* (for cookbooks), *Fiction Finds* (first novels and midlist titles), and *Walden Journal* (for business titles). For example, when books are promoted in *WaldenCooks*, sales have sometimes increased by as much as ten times.

A B. Dalton newsletter with a rave review almost single-handedly put Knopf's cookbook, *The Vegetarian Epicure*, on the bestseller lists.

☐ Finally, don't put all your eggs in the same basket. While the major chain stores may have a significant impact on retail sales, don't overlook the smaller regional chains and the great number of independent and specialty stores. For the names and addresses of many small regional chains as well as the top 700 independent bookstores, order the *Top 700 Bookstores* data files at http://www.bookmarket.com.

13:13 Distributing through Independent Sales Reps

If you decide to handle your distribution, you could use sales reps to cover certain regions of the country or certain markets. Or you could have commission representatives handle all your sales calls, from visits to the major chains and wholesalers to regular trips to see independent booksellers.

Note that most sales reps will not take on a new publisher. They want established publishers who are doing at least 6 to 12 new titles every season and who produce a catalog at least twice a year.

To set up your own network of sales reps groups, contact the **National Association of Independent Publishers Representatives**, PMB 157, 111 East 14th Street, New York, NY 10003-4103; 888-624-7779 Fax: 800-416-2586. Email: greatblue2@rcn.com. Web: http://www.naipr.org. They can send you a list of their membership.

Look for reps who don't have too many lines already because you could get lost in their sales bags. If you cannot get a major rep because of conflicts in the lines they carry, look for one of the smaller reps or a new one who is still hungry.

Write or call those sales representatives who look like they could fill your needs. To cover the entire country, you will probably have to contact four to eight groups since few of them cover more than ten states. For the book trade in general, reps are divided into six areas: New England, Mid-Atlantic states, Southeast, Midwest, Southwest, and West Coast. When you write to the sales rep groups, send them the same information you would send to a wholesaler or chain store. After a week or so, call up the rep groups. While they might not be in when you call and might not return your call, a phone call will get you noticed more readily than mail.

When contacting reps, call on them early, well before the selling season. For the fall season, contact them in February or March. For the spring season, contact them by August or September. Again, the earlier, the better. Your phone calls should be brief and to the point. Let them know how many titles you publish (and plan to publish), what your lead titles are, and what marketing you are currently doing.

Most sales rep groups ask for a commission of 10% on all retail sales and 5% on all wholesale and chain sales in their area, irrespective of whether they made the sale or not. Their commissions are paid on net sales made after returns and collections have been taken into account.

Generally, sales representatives will visit most larger bookstores in their area twice a year (spring and fall). The main advantage of having sales reps is that many booksellers still respond better to sales visits than to direct mail. The main disadvantage of having sales reps is that they only sell; they do not handle warehousing, fulfillment, and collection as distributors do. Plus, if you have sales reps, you have to do more accounting since you will have to calculate their commissions as well as the other calculations you make in your monthly accounting.

One caution on setting up independent sales reps: Check their references as thoroughly as you would for distributors. When I was consulting in the gift industry, one of the companies I worked with hired a new rep without carefully checking his references. At first, everything seemed fine. He sold many new accounts and, hence, seemed to be doing a good job. Unfortunately, he sold most of those accounts by telling them that they didn't have to pay for 90 to 120 days and if they hadn't sold the product by that time, they could return it for full credit (not standard practice in the gift industry). Meanwhile, he collected his commissions. Only when we began having problems collecting these accounts did we discover what he had done. The company ended up with a loss on his accounts.

If you decide to hire a commission rep group, get a signed contract with them. You should also provide them with the sales materials they need to sell your book, including seasonal catalogs, extra covers of your books, tip sheets, and 3-part NCR order forms.

Here are a few other things that publishers have done to support and inspire their independent sales force:

☐ To promote their April, 1993 title, *How to Fly*, Corkscrew Press sent each of their reps a ticket for the $21 million California lottery. The tickets played off the ISBN number for the book:09-4-40-42-25-2. In their letter to the reps they wrote, "Now there are two ways to make a fortune with us: the long shot and the sure shot." The long shot was the lottery. The sure shot was for the reps to earn their standard commission by selling large quantities of *How to Fly*.

Authors: Help your publisher promote your book to the sales reps. When Jim Miller, author of *Corporate Coach*, discovered that his publisher was unable to spend much money promoting his book, he convinced his publisher to allow him to fund a contest for the sales reps. He offered all-expenses-paid trips to Kuwait (where he owned a timeshare condo) for the two salespeople who sold the most copies of his book. As a result, the book sold 25,000 copies rather than the 8,000 the publisher had expected to sell.

☐ Offer your sales reps *push money* (some monetary incentive to push a new book, line of books, or display). For example, if you want your reps to push a new line of books, offer them an extra $5.00 or $10.00 when they sell a specific amount of books into one retail account. While push money is not common among book sales reps, it is common in other retail fields. If you do offer such an incentive, arrange to send the check directly to the individual reps. Make sure the reps know that the money is coming from you because they sold the line.

☐ Attend the seasonal sales conferences. Prepare brief but effective sales presentations for each book. If you can carry it off, do what Harvey Mackay did when he attended Morrow's national sales meeting to promote *Swim with the Sharks without Being Eaten*. Instead of talking about his book, he told the reps how they could serve bookstores better—based on the answers he had received from actual booksellers he had interviewed. Then, to top off his speech, he told them many details about his editor's life, thus graphically demonstrating a major thesis of his book: get to know the people you deal with. As a result of his talk, Mackay got what he wanted: the reps remembered him and, because they did, they recommended his book to retailers.

☐ Listen to your reps. They can provide you with valuable feedback on your covers, book content, sales plans, and promotions.

☐ Keep your sales reps informed of all publicity and promotional attention that you receive. Email them whenever something new happens, a book club sale, a media hit, another rights sale, and so on.

13:14 Hire Your Own Sales Reps

Most major publishers hire their own network of sales reps to cover the entire country. Having your own reps is, perhaps, the best of all distribution alternatives. The only difficulty with hiring your own reps is that you need to have at least $350,000 in net annual sales to the book trade before you can justify the cost of hiring even one rep. With salary, travel expenses, and other costs, each sales rep will cost you from $40,000 to $70,000 per year.

If you decide to hire a rep or two, start small by hiring one or two to cover your own region first. In that way you can keep their travel expenses down while you test the effectiveness of having reps for your line of books.

13:15 Handle Your Own Distribution

As an alternative, you can test the effectiveness of hiring reps by first asking some of your regular personnel (sales manager, editors, or yourself) to handle the local sales calls. In this way you can get experience on what works best for your company before you commit your time and money to organizing a separate department for sales representatives.

Another advantage of handling your local sales in this way is that you give your sales manager and editors experience in the field. Prentice-Hall use to require that all new employees begin by going on the road for three years before they are allowed to edit or market books. A number of other companies also encourage this policy. Only by going out into the stores can you see what kind of books are actually selling, what kind of merchandising actually works, and what sort of people buy your books. Moreover, being out in the field is one of the best ways to get ideas for new books.

If you do decide to use your employees part time as sales reps, train them well before you send them out. Make sure they know your list of new titles, not only the names of the books but also why the store should carry them—why, for instance, these new titles will interest the bookstore's customers. Be sure they are familiar with your backlist—which titles are selling best, what other titles might interest a particular group of people, any titles you are offering at a special discount, and so on. Finally, have them memorize your company's payment terms, discounts, returns policy, co-op advertising terms, and any promotional programs you offer. Don't send out anyone you do not feel will represent your company in a professional manner and in keeping with the image you want to project. And don't force anyone to go out who really does not want to go.

To supplement your own direct sales, you could also use direct mailings and telemarketing to cover the bookstores, wholesalers, and other buyers. The next chapter on Working with Bookstores goes into more detail on how to handle your own distribution through bookstores.

When Papier-Mâché decided to leave their distributor and do its own distribution, they used a marketing firm to represent them to national accounts (wholesalers and chain stores). To reach independent bookstores, they used direct mail and telemarketing, plus they phoned the top 1,200 bookstores four times a year.

13:16 What Distribution System Should You Use?

As a publisher, you have five basic choices for distributing your books to bookstores. They are as follows:

1. Work with a distributor and let them handle all sales and fulfillment to bookstores and wholesalers.

2. Work with another publisher who will act as your distributor to bookstores and wholesalers.

3. Work with wholesalers to service the independent bookstore accounts while you service the chains (though the chains might want to order through wholesalers as well).

4. Hire sales representatives (commissioned or in-house) to represent your line of books while you handle all order entry, shipping, and collections.

5. Do it yourself by relying on some individual sales calls to the major buyers as well as direct mail, catalogs, and telemarketing.

Which alternative is right for you? Here are some pros and cons of each alternative:

1. Distributor

Pros—1) You'll have sales reps going into stores to present your titles. Such live presentations still work. 2) You won't have to handle order taking, shipping, returns, collections, sales commissions, and other details of day-to-day selling to the trade. 3) You could save money on combined trade ads, exhibits, catalogs, and other promotions.

Cons—1) You give away a large percentage (from 60 to 70% of the retail price). Of course, you also get lots of services for that percentage. 2) You don't have as much control over the sales reps as you would if you hired your own. 3) You could get lost in a catalog that might feature as many as 200 other publishers. 4) You receive no payments until 90 days after the sale—or even later. 5) If you put all your eggs in one basket, you expose your company to greater risks should the distributor go belly up. Many publishers have lost money when distributors got into trouble.

2. Publisher who distributes

Pros—1) Besides the same pros as listed for distributors, you also can take advantage of the publisher's reputation and contacts to advance more of your books into the trade—especially if the publisher is one of the top twenty. 2) Since most publishers who distribute do not take on lots of additional lines, you won't be as lost as with some distributors.

Cons—1) The publisher's sales reps are more likely to favor the publisher's titles over any distributed lines. 2) Discounts and other costs may be too high. 3) Again, you can get lost in their catalog.

3. Wholesalers

Pros—1) Your discount will be less (generally 50 to 55%) than with a distributor. 2) You might get paid sooner, though that is becoming less likely as more wholesalers go to consignment terms. 3) You can get quick entry into the market without waiting for catalogs or sales visits.

Cons—1) No sales reps visit stores for you. Essentially, wholesalers are passive order takers. 2) Since most wholesalers are now also asking for consignment terms, you could have lots of copies sitting in warehouses. The more wholesalers you sign up with, the more extra copies you have to print to supply consignment copies with all wholesalers. 3) You have to do more paperwork than with distributors. You have to track payments from many accounts rather than just one. 4) Your distribution to the retail trade will generally be less effective than through distributors or sales reps. To make up for lack of sales visits, you'll have to do more advertising to the trade or make more phone calls. That can cost money.

4. Sales representatives

Pros—1) You'll have greater control over your sales force. 2) You won't get as lost in a catalog with other publishers. 3) You should get more effective representation.

Cons—1) You have to manage and service your reps, including keeping track of commissions. 2) You have to handle all order taking, shipping, returns, collections, and other fulfillment functions. 3) You have to warehouse titles. 4) You have to hire more people to handle fulfillment.

5. Do it yourself

Pros—1) You can put the money you would otherwise put into discounts and commissions to sweeten your deal to bookstores or, perhaps better yet, to promote your books direct to the consumers. 2) You have greater control over your fate. It's you or nothing. 3) You don't have to deal with the long lead times you have to consider when preparing catalogs or working with advance sales through reps.

Cons—1) You have to handle all sales and all fulfillment. 2) Generally speaking, smaller publishers who do it all themselves do not have effective retail distribution (although many do well selling direct to consumers). 3) It will be difficult to sell into the chains. Most chains and many independent bookstores don't want to open a new vendor account just to buy one or two titles. 4) Most bookstores don't want to buy direct from a small publisher because they wonder if they'll be able to get credit for returns. Will the publisher still be in existence? Will the publisher have other titles they can order to take advantage of the credit due them?

In some cases you might find it to your advantage to combine one or more of the five alternatives described above. You could use wholesalers to handle the chains and reorders while you obtain direct sales from other bookstores by direct mail, catalogs, and telemarketing.

To provide you with another perspective on the alternatives available to you, here are the results of a survey that Publishers Marketing Association conducted among its membership of small and midsize publishers:

Of the following sales techniques (commissioned reps, direct marketing, foreign sales, house reps, and telemarketing), most publishers rated direct marketing as the most successful for them (3.78 on a scale of 1 to 5, 5 being highest). Commissioned reps rated 2.53 while house reps rated 2.66. Tele-marketing rated 2.21 and foreign sales 2.19.

Of the following sales channels (catalogs, consumer ads, direct mail, co-op ads, sales force, and telemarketing), those same publishers rated direct mail as providing the best return on their time and money (3.60 on a scale of 5). Catalogs rated 3.34, sales force 3.15, telemarketing 2.60, co-op ads 2.23, and consumer ads 2.08.

13:17 Why Exhibit Your Books

One of the most effective ways to get your books known to booksellers is to exhibit your books at their conventions. Not only can you show your books to as many as 5,000 booksellers, but you can also attract new distributors, corporate buyers, and subsidiary rights buyers.

The major book show in the United States is BookExpo America, which is held around Memorial Day. In 2005, attendees included 7,700 book buyers, 2,200 librarians, and 17,400 publishers, media, and other visitors. For details on exhibiting, contact **BookExpo America**, Reed Expositions, 383 Main Avenue, Norwalk, CT 06851; 203-840-5814; 800-840-5614; Fax: 203-840-9814. Email: info@bookexpoamericacom. Web: http://www.book expoamerica.com.

Many of the regional booksellers associations hold book shows in early autumn. These shows can often be a more cost-effective arena for showcasing your books and authors.

Other major shows include the Frankfurt Book Fair (held in October at Frankfurt, West Germany), the Bologna Children's Book Fair (held in the spring in Bologna, Italy), the Christian Booksellers Association Convention (July), the American Library Association Convention (June/July), the Canadian Booksellers Association Convention (July), and National Association of College Stores (April).

When planning your exhibits, don't forget other trade shows. For example, if you publish children's books, you might exhibit at the toy show in February. Or, if you publish craft books, exhibit at the annual craft shows (Dover Publications exhibited at Quilt Market). Or, for travel books, you could exhibit at the International Travel Industry Expo in mid-April.

If you publish academic books, you should consider exhibiting at professional conferences such as those sponsored by the American Institute of Biological Sciences, the American Sociological Association, or the American Political Science Association, to mention a few.

Besides selling books, here are a few other reasons why you should attend at least one of these shows or conferences every year:

☐ **Sell books.** That means you should be prepared to take orders at the show, to offer special discounts for orders placed at the show, to staff your booth with sales oriented people, and to have catalogs and brochures ready to give out to all who attend.

At one BEA, Crossing Press took orders for 5,000 books. They lured booksellers to their booth by offering food samples from their new cookbook, *Street Food* by Rose Grant.

At the 1986 BEA in New Orleans, Basil Blackwell wrote almost $12,000 in business while the University of Chicago Press sold $60,000 worth of books. Many publishers, however, especially smaller ones, are quite pleased if they sell $200 to $3,000 worth of books.

At the National Association of College Stores convention, Berkeley wrote orders for more than 40,000 units.

In 1985, 17% of all bookstore orders from Christian publishers were placed at the CBA Convention in Dallas.

☐ **Display new books** to the trade and to any media in attendance at the show. Book shows are superb times to give away samples of your books to opinion makers—especially booksellers. But note that giving away books won't guarantee attention, so be conservative.

At the 1988 BEA, Algonquin Books gave away 1,600 sample copies of Clyde Edgerton's *The Floatplane Notebooks*. At the same convention, Open Horizons gave away 1,500 reading copies of *Tinseltowns, USA* (it had no impact on sales, not one iota).

For BEA in Anaheim, California, Avery gave away a bound sample chapter from their *Guide to Natural Food Restaurants*. The chapter listed natural food restaurants in the southern California area.

☐ **Establish your company name and image** more firmly in the minds of booksellers and media. Book shows are one of the best ways to gain such exposure. At BookExpo America, I've met media contacts for *CBS This Morning, Good Morning America, New York Times Book Review, National Enquirer, C-SPAN, Time Magazine, USA Today, Tonight Show*, and many radio and TV shows.

☐ **Make valuable marketing contacts.** In many cases you will have an opportunity to meet with buyers for major chain stores, wholesalers, and corporations. At no other events can you find such a concentration of buyers. At the 1988 BEA, Coffee House Press found foreign reps for their books in Holland, France, and Germany.

☐ **Take time to learn**—to see how others display and merchandise their books, to network with other publishers to discover new ways to market your own books, and to meet booksellers face to face to learn what more you can do to fill their needs.

☐ **Sell subsidiary rights.** Not only can you sell rights to your books, but you can also pick up the rights to other people's books. Even smaller publishers can get into the act. I know of a good number of smaller publishers who have obtained English language rights to books by attending the Frankfurt show and other international shows. At the 1997 BEA, Career Press sold foreign rights to many of its books, making more than enough from rights sales to pay for the exhibit.

☐ **Do market research.** In just two to three days, you can get a detailed overview of the industry, discover what sorts of books other publishers are promoting, and learn what new lines your competitors are bringing out. You may even uncover an emerging trend that you can exploit before others follow suit.

☐ **Meet new and established authors** and come up with great ideas for new books. This book grew out of my experience at the 1985 ABA Convention in San Francisco. Almost every publisher I talked to at that convention had one question to ask me: "How do I get my books into the hands of the people who can use them most?" This book, I hope, provides a few answers to that question.

☐ **Bring your authors to the major book shows.** If possible, try to get them booked as one of the major speakers at the breakfast meetings with booksellers because these meetings (more than any other event at BEA) are the major showcases for authors. Since only a few authors and celebrities will be invited to speak at the meetings, try to get your authors a spot in the autographing booths (where you can give away 200 copies in half an hour). These booths are open to any author, no matter who the publisher is, although celebrities will still have the longer lines. You can also have your authors autograph in your booth.

Authors — You, too, should attend these major trade shows, Indeed, some 4,000 authors attend BookExpo America every year. If you would like to share the spotlight with fewer authors, ask your publisher to send you to the regional booksellers convention nearest you.

13:18 How to Exhibit Your Books

To mount a successful exhibit, you must plan ahead. Not only should you design your booth, but you should also decide which of your books you will display (and which will get the limelight), what promotions you will run, who will staff the booth, and how the booth will be shipped, set up, maintained, dismantled, and shipped home. Here are a few other pointers on how to exhibit your books:

☐ **Make appointments.** If there are certain people you want to be sure to meet during a convention, contact them in advance to arrange an appointment to see them during the show. Don't expect that you will be able to just drop by their booth and meet them. Chances are that they will be out on the floor just like you. So be sure to make appointments ahead of time with any major buyers or key contacts that you want to meet. Then confirm those appointments the first day of the convention by dropping your card off at their booth with a short message confirming the time and place of your meeting.

☐ **Be accessible.** In his *Book Marketing Handbook*, Nat Bodian summed up the best way to work a show: 1. Make the booth accessible. 2. Make your books accessible. 3. Make yourself accessible.

☐ **Arrange your booth** so people can get in and out easily. Have your books, catalogs, and other sales literature readily available so that people can reach them without having to run an obstacle course.

☐ **Hire a professional to design your booth** or, at least, make it look like it was designed by a professional. It should be attractive, open, and inviting. It should project an image compatible with the one you want for your company.

☐ **Keep an extra chair or two empty for visitors.** Booksellers appreciate a ready and inviting place to rest. As Thomas Perrin of Perrin & Treggett Booksellers once noted, "If your sales reps are occupying the only chairs in your booth, I won't stop. If I do stop to rest my feet, the chances are good that you will get an order form me."

☐ **Arrange your books so they are easy to find**—either by subject, title, or author. Display new titles up front where they will get the most attention. Again, as Thomas Perrin pointed out, "In order to sell me books, the publisher needs to make them visible."

☐ **Give away samples of your books**—either advance review copies or at least sample chapters. This is one of the best ways to get people talking about your major titles months before their publication dates.

☐ **Staff your booth with friendly, knowledgeable salespeople.** The people in your booth must know your line of books well enough to talk intelligently about any title. They must also know your company's terms and discounts, upcoming promotions, and other policies. And they must be ready to help your customers. As John Randall of the Salt of the Earth bookstore once noted, "What makes a good booth is one where the people who staff the booth pay attention to your needs."

☐ **Make sure you have enough people to staff the booth.** Staffing a booth can be tiring, especially after four days, so be sure each person in your booth has enough time off to rest between work periods. Also, make sure each person has some time to scout the convention.

☐ **Train the people who will staff your booth.** They should be ready to answer any questions that might come up. If they cannot answer a question, they should write it down and be sure to get an answer or follow up with a letter after the convention. They should be alert and willing to help any passersby. They should not smoke in the booth. They should not be sitting down. They should not be reading or eating in the booth.

☐ **Have your staff make notes** of those books which attract the most attention from browsers and buyers. These notes might come in handy in planning future exhibits or sales promotions following the convention. Have them also make notes of any questions, comments, inquiries, or other conversations which might come in handy for future promotions.

☐ **Co-op exhibit.** If you cannot afford to rent a booth on your own, then join cooperative exhibit. Several of the publishers associations, including SPAN, PMA, Publishers Association of the South, and Rocky Mountain Book Publishers, offer cost-effective group exhibits at the major shows. Combined Book Exhibit (http://www.combinedbook.com) and Association Book Exhibit (http://www.bookexhibit.com) also offer group exhibits at many conferences, association meetings, regional library meetings, and smaller book fairs which you might not otherwise be able to attend.

☐ **Total all costs.** When considering your costs for exhibiting at a show, remember that the booth rental represents as little as 25% of your total cost. Other costs include travel expenses, housing and food, staff salaries, booth design and construction, promotional materials, shipping, labor setup, and miscellaneous booth charges. Note that it is often more cost-effective to exhibit at the regional trade shows.

Again, remember that the most important function of any exhibit is to sell your books. Keep that purpose in focus, and all the minor details will fall into place, making your job easier and more enjoyable.

13:19 How to Attract People to Your Exhibit Booth

When you have spent so much money on designing and staffing a booth, you don't want to leave it empty. While most of the attendees will pass by your booth sometime during the convention, many of them will probably pass by without much more than a glance—unless you provide them with some incentive to pause.

Display good books.

Of course, the best way you can ensure that they will stop to look is to have something worth looking at. If you publish good books (and people know it), people will stop by.

Advertise show specials.

Give a larger discount, offer free freight, or announce some other special for any order placed at the show. Announce your special offers ahead of time. Again, as bookseller Thomas Perrin points out, "The really smart publishers sent me catalogs, order forms, and announcements of their convention specials a month or two before the show."

- Prior to several BEA Conventions, Chilton Book Company placed an ad in *American Bookseller* offering a 10% discount to any bookseller who placed an order at the show and brought the coupon in the ad. Anyone who placed an order was also entered into a drawing to win the order they placed during the show.

- At another BEA, Krause Publications offered a 50% discount on selected titles, plus free freight on domestic orders over $300.00. Many other publishers also offered similar terms.

- At the 1997 BEA, Voyageur Press offered a 50% discount on backlist and 46% on frontlist for any orders of ten or more books. They also offered free freight if the bookseller prepaid.

- At the same convention, Creative Homeowners Press offered a thirteenth book free for every twelve books ordered. Plus free freight.

- Abbeville offered booksellers a choice between 120-day delayed billing on backlist titles or 50% discount.

Hold a drawing.

To encourage more people to leave their business cards, hold a drawing each day for a free prize. Place a basket at the front of your booth so people can enter the drawing. It's a perfect way to get the names and addresses of attendees so you can send them more promotional material.

- Perhaps the most attractive prizes given away in these drawings are free trips. To promote its series of travel guides, Viking Penguin held a drawing for a free one-week trip for two to Italy. To highlight its *Escape in Style*, Inner Traditions offered a week at a private villa in Jamaica. Several publishers offered free trips to the next year's trade show.

- Many publishers also hold drawings for free books. At the 1988 BEA, Woodbridge held a drawing for $1,000 worth of its books. Mustang Books and Indiana University Press gave away $500 worth of their books, while Moving Books and Steve Davis Publishing gave away $100 worth of books.

- To promote *Prove It All Night: The Bruce Springsteen Trivia Book*, Mustang Press gave away an autographed copy of Bruce Springsteen's *Born in the USA* album.

- Caedmon held drawings for three compact disc players. Indiana University Press raffled a VCR. The Better Baby Press gave away tuition for the "How to Multiply Your Baby's Intelligence" course. Bowker drew for a Hitachi CD-ROM drive. Four or five publishers gave away bottles of wine (a popular giveaway among booksellers).

- In a pre-BEA mailing, U.S. Games Systems asked ABA members to "staple your business card to the enclosed playing card and redeem in person during the ABA. ... You will receive in exchange one free deck of playing cards." In addition, their business cards could be entered into a drawing for $500.00.

- Little, Brown and Company held a drawing for an alligator purse as part of their promotion of the novel, *The Lady with the Alligator Purse*.

- To showcase *The Clairvoyant*, a novel about a man able to predict the future, Zoland Books held drawings for free one-hour sessions with a psychic so booksellers could learn which books were to be hot during the coming fall season.

Give away something attractive.

Many publishers give away advance reading copies of their books, posters, bookmarks, buttons, book bags, and other attractive gifts.

- Cliff Notes gave away free stuffed penguins to promote their new advertising slogan: "Our product line is dressed to sell."

- Advocacy Press gave away roses to women booksellers who came by their booth at BEA. The roses were in keeping with the floral cover design of their book, *Choices*, aimed at helping young girls make choices.

- At the ALA Convention, Festival Publications gave away 12,000 signs with humorous messages such as, "Ever meet a librarian who wasn't all booked up?" Each sign, of course, also carried a short sales message and ordering information for Festival's publications.

Give away a tie-in to your books

Find a small gift or something special that ties into one of your lead titles. Then give it away to booksellers who come by your booth. Or you could limit the gift only to those who place an order.

- To draw attention to Sara Shannon's *Diet for the Atomic Age*, Avery Publishing Group gave away personal radiation detectors.

- To promote their Best Places to Stay series, Harvard Common Press sent ABA members a guide to the best places to stay in Washington, DC just before the BEA in that city.

- Walker and Company gave away posters of an illustration by Greg Shed for Donald Hall's *The Milkman's Boy*.

Provide a service to the attendees.

If you can provide some service to the attendees, something they could really use, they'll flock to your booth.

- At the Triad Publishing booth, Deborah Caplan, author of *Back Trouble*, gave advice on how to make your back feel better.

- Staff members of the Lotus Light booth provided foot and back massages to anyone in need. Healthy Alternatives also gave free neck and shoulder massages. Ashley Books provided an electric foot massager. Professional Publications offered attendees free Dr. Scholls Air Pillow insoles. With so much walking and standing at conventions, anything that helps backs will be very attractive.

- At BookExpo America, Ransom Hill Press offered to read tea leaves for any booksellers passing by their booth.

- At the Christian Booksellers Association convention, Here's Life Publications invited booksellers to a free breakfast. 300 booksellers showed up! While the breakfast was served, some of Here's Life's authors stood up to say a few words about their books. What a great way to introduce your authors to booksellers!

- At the CBA, Wolgemuth & Hyatt invited booksellers to pose for a photograph with baseball pitcher, Orel Hershiser, who was promoting his autobiography, *Out of the Blue*. The next day, those booksellers could pick up the photograph. Accompanying the photo was a press kit individualized for their local city. As a result, not only did Wolgemuth and Hyatt encourage booksellers to stop by their booth twice, but they also provided booksellers with a superb opportunity to get local publicity for their stores while at the same time promoting Hershiser's book.

Leave promotional literature where it can be seen.

Besides offering promotional literature and catalogs at your booth, you might look for other ways to distribute your literature. If the convention has set aside a place where you can offer free literature, use it.

- At most BEAs, there are often tables in the convention hall where publishers can place free literature and announcements of any special promotions. I saw many booksellers sifting through the material to select items of interest to them. Such free material, especially if it has your booth number on it, might help to draw more people to your booth. Similarly, every show has a press office where media can sift through stacks and stacks of news releases. Be sure to drop off your news releases or press kits to the press office on the first day of the convention. I always check these news releases on the first day.

- To attract more people to their booths, publishers have placed napkins imprinted with their sales message and booth number on the counters of the coffee areas in the hall. Note: Some trade show organizers offer exclusive marketing opportunities such as this one, but they do charge for the exclusivity.

- One enterprising small publisher placed fortune cookies near the press room coffee pot. Each fortune asked a question and listed the publisher's booth number as the place to go to get the answer. Cable News Network and several other reporters followed up on the story.

Hold a special promotion.

At the 1985 Canadian Booksellers Association convention, McClelland & Stewart offered a free Macintosh computer to the bookseller who came closest to guessing what the total sales would be for the major M&S titles through December 1985. As part of the contest, they also asked the booksellers to estimate how many of each title they expected to sell. This contest not only helped to draw booksellers' attention to M&S's major titles, but it also gave M&S a breakdown of the sales expectations of the booksellers who came by their booth.

At BookExpo America, Learning Works put up a display of 300 paper dolls, all of which were topped by the photographic heads of real booksellers. Not only did the display attract all the booksellers featured in the display, but it also was an implied endorsement by those booksellers of the books published by Learning Works.

Get attention.

A recent Trade Show Bureau study demonstrated that the most effective way to get people to remember your product and company is to offer a product demonstration (a cookbook author offering sample food, an exercise author demonstrating stretches). Magicians were the second best attention-getters. Then came ad specialties and contests.

> **Authors** — Wear your book. T-shirts are effective attention-getters on a trade show floor because they allow you to showcase your book cover.

13:20 Get Listed in Trade References

To aid booksellers in finding you and your books, get listed in the major trade reference books. The references used most often by booksellers include *Books in Print*, *Publisher's Weekly* spring and fall announcement issues, *ABA Book Buyer's Handbook*, and *NACS Book Buyer's Manual*.

In a 1982 membership survey, 97% of the respondents said that the most valuable service provided by the American Booksellers Association was the *ABA Book Buyer's Handbook*. Hence, it is reasonable to conclude that the handbook is a vital source for them when they are ordering books. A listing in this handbook will bring you many S.T.O.P. orders.

Other directories you might want your company listed in include *Alternative Press Publishers of Children's Books*, *Black Resource Guide*, *Directory of Poetry Publishers*, *Directory of Women's Media*, *The Gardener's Book of Sources*, *International Directory of Little Magazines & Small Press*, and *Literary MarketPlace*.

If you don't sit down and talk to at least ten publishers each day
of the BEA convention, you have wasted your time at the show.
You've lost a golden opportunity to boost your business
in ways you can't begin to calculate.
You never know when that million-dollar idea will come your way
in some innocent side remark from a publishing buddy or a new friend.
— John Kremer, webmaster, BookMarket.com

The Distributor's Secret Sales Formula

by Clint Greenleaf and Meg La Borde of Greenleaf Book Group

Though the book industry is notorious for its complex supply chain full of middlemen, strong distributors are often the driving force behind self-publishers' sales. Because distributors make money on micro margins, volume is their number one priority. And they achieve this volume with a secret sales formula made up of four factors: cover design, placement, timing, and media. Here are some tips to increase your sales volume:

Cover Design

Because the book cover helps to sell the book, always solicit feedback from your distributor on your cover design before going to press. They can offer retail marketing and sales insight not available from other sources. And that can make the difference between lots of bookstores sales and no sales.

Placement

Front of store placement on new release tables, end cap placement within sections, and all other prominent placements in chain stores are paid for by publishers.

Your distributor can negotiate this co-op placement with national buyers, but unfortunately, they cannot simply offer a buyer money in exchange for national store placement. The sales rep has to convince the buyers that the book is worthy of placement in their prime retail spaces before negotiating payment, length of promotion, and buy size. Co-op placements often produce fantastic ROI, so you should arm your distributor with a healthy co-op budget and a stellar marketing plan for the buyers.

Timing

Get finished books to your distributor four to six months in advance of publication, so they have plenty of time to negotiate placement and make initial buys.

Media

Distributors need *impressive* media updates to move inventory before, during, and after publication. Big publicity makes all the difference in pre-publication negotiations. After the initial buy solicitation, distributors must have a reason to approach buyers for more sales. In order for distributors to sell the supply, publishers have to create the demand. That means lots and lots of publicity, the bigger the better.

Distributors can make or break the retail success of a book, so choose one you trust, communicate regularly, and nurture the relationship.

Here are a few other tips for authors and publishers to make the best use of their relationship with their distributor:

☐ **Leverage your publicity with the supply chain.** Update your distributor! If there is no supply to meet the demand your publicity is creating, you're wasting money and losing sales. Your distributor can target stores in the geographic markets your media coverage is reaching and use your publicity as leverage with national buyers to get more books in stores.

☐ **Make time for proper timing.** Things move fast in a publicity campaign, but it's nothing short of tragic when sales—big sales—are lost because of a silly detail like timing. If you think reviews will have a big impact on your book sales, make sure your publicist has galleys in hand at least four months prior to publication. If your publicist is booking radio or television interviews, give your distributor three to four weeks notice so they have time to work books through the supply chain. If you land a national TV interview, talk to your distributor immediately to troubleshoot any inventory issues and to give them the opportunity to use the hit to negotiate front-of-store placement with the chains.

☐ **Define three sales points to use in all media interviews.** Note: The hook that lands the interview is not necessarily the hook that sells the book. Be a good guest, but don't be shy about using free airtime to sell your book. Know your readers and appeal to their needs in your interviews. For example, if you landed the interview by positioning yourself as an expert on a newsworthy topic, don't assume people will go to a bookstore to buy your opinion. Instead, offer specific, usable content in the interview and clearly communicate (1) who needs the book and (2) what they will gain from reading it.

☐ **Say your title at least three times in every interview.** There will be times when this is impossible, and there will be times when this is tacky, but if you make it a rule and stick to it, you will sell more books. Erase the words "my book" from your vocabulary, and always use the full title to refer to your work. This is one easy way to sell books in an interview without sounding like an infomercial.

Greenleaf Book Group is the nation's leading consulting firm and book distributor for small independent publishers and self-publishers. For production, distribution, and marketing information, contact **Greenleaf Book Group**, 4425 Mopac South #600, Longhorn Building, 3rd Floor, Austin, TX 78735; 512-891-6100; 800-932-5400; Fax: 512-891-6150. Web: http://www. GreenleafBookGroup.com.

Chapter 14

Working with Bookstores

We can't afford to lose touch with the people
who are handselling our books.
To have a bookseller fall in love with your book
is the best thing in the world.
— Ina Stern, marketing director, Algonquin Books

Once you have a method of getting your books into the bookstores (via distribution), you must still work to see that your books move out of the bookstores. Besides promoting your books to the general public via advertising and publicity, you can also work with the bookstores to see that your books are properly displayed and merchandised. This chapter, then, will describe different ways to work with bookstores to increase the exposure and sale of your books.

14:01 Why Sell Through Bookstores?

Why would you want to sell your books through bookstores? First and foremost, because that's where most people go to buy books. Here, then, are a few reasons why you should work with bookstores to sell your books:

☐ **Bookstores sell lots of books.** According to a Gallup survey conducted in 1996, 52% of all books are purchased in bookstores, while 9% are bought in discount warehouses and price clubs, 7% from book clubs, and 5% direct from the publisher. Since bookstores are the primary source of books for most people, you would be wise to serve them well.

☐ **Bookstores are popular.** According to 1996 survey conducted by America's Research Group, Americans visit bookstores more frequently than any other type of store except for the large mass merchandisers such as Wal-Mart, Costco, and Target. 35 to 38% of Americans visit a bookstore at least once a month.

☐ **Booksellers handsell books.** According to a survey conducted by Cahners Publishing in 1997, children's booksellers report that more than 50% of their sales are made by hand. There are cases of booksellers who individually have handsold hundreds, even thousands of books.

For instance, Christy Pascoe of A Clean Well-Lighted Place for Books in San Francisco, handsold more than 1,500 copies of Sarah Smith's mystery, *The Vanished Child.* Similarly, when Warren Cassell, owner of Just Books, praised Robert Waller's *Bridges of Madison County* "as one of the finest first novels we have ever read," he ended up selling more than a thousand copies. And, finally, Roberta Rubin, owner of The Book Stall in Winnetka, Illinois, was one of the booksellers responsible for creating the buzz that made David Guterson's debut novel, *Snow Falling on Cedars*, a bestseller. Her store handsold more than 600 copies.

☐ **Bookstores sell books as gifts.** According to a 1996 Gallup survey, 23% of all books bought are intended as gifts. People are more likely to go to a bookstore rather than other outlets to buy books as gifts (*1996 Consumer Research Study on Book Purchasing*).

There are, of course, disadvantages to selling books through bookstores, including that fact that bookstores are accustomed to buying books on a returnable basis—which can lead to heavy returns. During the past few years, bookstore returns have caused many small and midsize publishers to suffer major financial crises. Returns have gone from an average of 15 to 25% fifteen years ago to as much as 35% in recent years. Hence, if you are going to sell to bookstores, be prepared for returns—and budget accordingly.

Also, another reason you might not want to sell books through bookstores is that they have little commitment to your books. The average shelf life of a book, according to Calvin Trillin, is "somewhere between milk and yogurt." In real life, that means your book gets about 90 days on bookstore shelves to prove itself. If it doesn't sell in that time, your book gets returned and forgotten. For this reason, you must do whatever you can to help get your books off those shelves. The rest of this chapter outlines some of the strategies you can use to sell your books into the bookstores and also make sure that your books sell once they are on the shelves.

14:02 Setting Priorities

To get the most out of your sales calls to bookstores, make your priorities clear. Decide what you want to accomplish with each visit (which books and authors you want to feature). Also decide which of your accounts you should visit first. Here are some guidelines to help you set priorities:

☐ **Remember the 80/20 rule.** 80% of your business will come from 20% of your accounts, so be sure to place your greatest emphasis on keeping in touch with these major accounts. At Bantam, they have a core group of experienced salesmen who handle only four or five accounts each. Since 25 major accounts make up almost 60% of their business, they give them extra special service and support.

☐ **Visit each major account at least twice a year**, preferably more often. At the very minimum, you or your reps should call on your key accounts to show them your spring and fall lists. Your key accounts would probably include several major wholesalers, the biggest chains, and 25 to 100 major independent bookstores.

☐ **Mail or phone key accounts.** If you are a smaller company without your own sales force or distributor, then you should certainly contact these key accounts by mail or by phone at least four times a year, or whenever you are bringing out a major new book.

☐ **Sell regionally.** If many of your titles are regional in content, place more emphasis on stores in your area. You could even visit the stores once a month or once every two months, thus providing them with far better service than they will ever get even from major publishers. New England Press does this with bookstores within the New England region.

☐ **Attend the regional bookseller trade shows.** The regional bookseller association trade shows in the fall have become important for book sales. Many independent bookstores are looking to these trade shows to find books they can sell during the coming holiday season.

14:03 Getting the Most from Your Sales Calls

In making direct sales calls to independent bookstores, smaller publishers have several advantages over major publishers. First, they can offer titles to the independent bookseller that most of the big chain and discount stores do not carry. Second, they can give more personal service to each store they visit. Third, they haven't worn out their welcome. Here are a few suggestions for making your direct sales calls to the independents more effective.

☐ **Locate booksellers to call on.** Here are some basic ways:

1. Check the yellow pages of each city you visit. You can also check the yellow pages directories on the Internet.
2. Go to the local library. Ask them if any new bookstores have started up. While there, also leave them one of your catalogs.
3. Use the following web resources: ABA Bookstore Directory (http://www.bookweb.org) and Christian Booksellers Association directory (http://www.cba-intl.org/st_city/index.htm).

4. Consult the *American Book Trade Directory.*

5. For direct marketing, American List Counsel offers a list of bookstore executives. For more information, contact **American List Counsel**, 4300 US Highway 1, CN-5219, Princeton, NJ 08543; 609-580-2800; 800-ALC-LIST; Fax:609-580-2988. Email: alcmgmt@. amlist.com. Web: http://www.amlist.com.

6. For new age bookstores, contact **Evolutionary Products**, 1667 N Maagnolia Avenue, Tucson, AZ 85712-4103; 520-323-1190; 800-777-4751. Web: http://www.evolutionaryproducts.com.

7. Some regional bookseller associations publish directories of their members. See http://www.bookmarket.com/pubassn.html for a directory of their web sites. Also check out http://www.bookmarket. com/bookstores.html for a list of web sites featuring bookstore lists.

8. Purchase the Top 700 Bookstores Data Files from Open Horizons. This list features more than 780 bookstores, with name, book buyer, address, telephone, fax, email, web site, and more. The cost is only $40.00. Web: http://www.bookmarket.com.

☐ **Call to set up an appointment** before you visit. Don't expect booksellers to drop everything to talk to you without an appointment.

☐ **Expect to make full sales calls** to two or three bookstores each day (four maximum when visiting a larger city). Prentice-Hall expects its sales representatives to visit about 80 bookstores four times a year.

☐ **Become friends.** When you visit booksellers, approach them as friends and coworkers. You can work with them to offer the best books to the reading public. Let them know you are there to help them.

☐ **Start your visit with some chitchat about books.** Ask them how their business is going? Who are their customers? Have they noticed any new trends? But keep it short. You don't want to waste their time.

☐ **Prepare a sales book which features your new titles** and key backlist titles. Start with your lead titles. The sales book should include a cover of the book, catalog copy (with one or two points highlighted), bulleted marketing points, any prepublication reviews or testimonies, and the major benefits of each book.

☐ **Prepare effective sales literature** that you can leave with the stores when you visit them. Always leave something behind. Give them your catalog, flyers, or brochures describing your new titles; a price list with your terms and policies; and any other literature that will aid them in making a decision on which books to buy. For all your new titles, have extra cover samples printed up so you can show the booksellers what the books will look like on their shelves. For major titles, carry the actual books with you if you have them.

☐ **Travel with a carload of books**, if possible, so you can stock the store immediately. Since they often have to wait three to six weeks to get books from major publishers, booksellers will appreciate the immediate response. Plus it will save them shipping costs and will save you the time you would otherwise have to spend in packing and shipping books.

☐ **Give samples of your major new titles** to your regular accounts. Not only will they appreciate this special service, but they are far more likely to order more copies of the books if they have read them.

☐ **Work with them to prepare an adequate order for your titles.** Don't push them to stock too many (if you can't afford heavy returns), but do let them know which titles you will be promoting most heavily so they can stock up on those titles.

☐ **Make frontlist sales.** Sales calls are your most effective way to promote new frontlist titles (bookstores do 40 to 45% of their business with front-list titles). Rodale Press likes to get advance orders of 15,000 to 20,000 copies for their main titles.

☐ **Offer special terms** for larger frontlist orders.

☐ **Make appointments.** Before you leave, set up your next appointment with them. Tell them when you will return and write it down on your calendar in front of them. Confirm that the day and time will suit them.

☐ **Check stock.** When you come back for a return visit, check their remaining stock of your titles and prepare a proposed reorder that takes into account which of your titles sold best in *their* store.

When you or your sales rep visit a store, be sure you are prepared to talk about your books. Reps who have read the books they represent and who can communicate their enthusiasm for a title will have an easier time selling to booksellers. You should also know enough about the booksellers you visit to know which of your titles will go best in their stores.

When the Viking rep made a sales call at Just Books, he didn't talk about print runs. Instead, he talked about the books he'd read and then recommended which ones he thought would go well at Just Books. As a result, the owner read two of the books and, in turn, recommended them to his customers—who bought over 200 of each title.

14:04 Make an Offer They Can't Refuse

Whenever you approach bookstores (whether in person, via telephone, via email, or by mail), offer them something special which will encourage them to place an order or increase their order for your titles. In granting special terms, you should be aware of your obligations under federal law. Here are a few offers that have worked successfully for other publishers:

Grant bookstores larger discounts on nonreturnable orders.

Because higher nonreturnable discounts will allow bookstores to make more profit on the sale of each book and because they cannot return the books, they are more likely to promote your books in their store. Hence, not only will the bookstores tend to sell more copies of such titles, but you will also save time and money by not having to process returns. Thus, the larger discounts will often pay for themselves.

- Open Horizons offers a 50% discount for orders of twelve or more books on a nonreturnable basis.

- On selected backlist children's titles, Macmillan offered a 55% discount plus free freight for orders placed on a nonreturnable basis.

- Sasquatch Books has an aggressive nonreturnable plan that has helped them to keep their returns average down.

Of course, most of the major publishers oppose nonreturnable terms because initial orders for new titles would plummet. When Ed Morrow, Jr., owner of the Northshire Bookstore, brought up the desire of booksellers to get more favorable discounts if they order nonreturnable, all three publishers on a panel at the New England Booksellers Association Trade Show—Larry Kirshbaum, CEO of Warner Books; Jack Romanos, president of Simon & Schuster; and Alberto Vitale, CEO of Random House—rejected that option. As one of them said, "Nonreturnability has never worked." For smaller publishers, however, the opposite is true. For most publishers and most bookstores, nonreturnable terms would make more sense.

According to Leonard Shatzkin, author of *The Mathematics of Bookselling*, "Returns are more costly to the bookseller than they are to the publisher. A return rate of 20%, for example, costs the bookseller the equivalent of ten percent profit on the store's total sales."

Offer free freight.

You can offer to pay shipping and handling fees on all orders of ten or more books (or some other limit you set). Free freight is one of the most requested items on the wish lists of bookstores. According to Ed Morrow, Jr., paying freight "will really help to overcome bookseller hesitancy to stock books from a small press."

- Many book publishers offer free freight on BookExpo America orders, holiday orders, or during other special promotions.

- In response to the growing trend among wholesalers to offer free freight, some publishers are now offering free freight on all orders over a certain dollar amount. As of January, 1998, Simon & Schuster has offered free freight on all orders. To compensate for the free freight, S&S revised their discount schedule to offer a 46% discount for a minimum order of $75.00 placed via electronic data interface compared to a flat 47% discount under their old schedule.

- On orders for ten or more books from accounts which are paid up, Globe Pequot pays all freight charges that exceed 3% of the net invoice.
- Some publishers offer free freight if stores pay invoices within 30 days.

Offer a freight pass-through plan.

With a freight pass-through plan, you price books so that the discount is taken after the freight has been subtracted. For instance, if your suggested retail price for a book is $9.95, you would invoice your discounts on the freight pass-through price of $9.45 (allowing an average of 50¢ in shipping costs per book). Note that few publishers are offering this option now. In fact, the following companies may no longer be offering this option.

- In the past, Addison-Wesley suggested that booksellers set the retail prices on freight pass-through books as follows: "Add 4% to the invoiced list price and round to the nearest nickel. List price of $25.00 or more, add $1.00 to list price."
- Houghton Mifflin determined freight pass-through prices by adding the following amounts to the invoiced list price: For books retailing for $34.00 or more, add $1.00; $10.00 to $33.95, add 50¢; $5.00 to $9.95, add 25¢; under $5.00, add 15¢. For a book they invoiced at $9.50 retail, they would suggest the bookseller set the retail selling price at $9.75.

Participate in the Single Title Order Plan.

The Single Title Order Plan (STOP) allows booksellers to send you a check for 40% of the list price (or whatever discount you've announced for STOP) plus shipping. When you offer STOP, be sure to let booksellers know that you do. Since most booksellers check STOP policies of publishers by looking in the *ABA Book Buyers Handbook*, be sure you are listed in this directory. Contact the American Booksellers Association at 800-637-0037 for more information on how to get listed.

The STOP offer may result in a trickle of single title orders in the beginning, but once stores have become accustomed to ordering from you (and have found your service to be fast and reliable), they are more likely to place larger orders with you when you approach them with titles that suit their customer profile.

Dover Publications offers their own Cash Order Plan (COP) for U.S. booksellers who want to place orders of $50 net or less. On these orders, Dover offers free freight and a 40% discount, regardless of quantity. In order to qualify, the bookseller must send in the order using Dover's COP order form, enclose full payment, include the ISBNs for the books they want and their account number, and write "Rush COP" on the envelope.

Offer white sales.

Run special sales on some of your slower moving titles to encourage bookstores to stock up on those titles.

- Houghton Mifflin has run white sales offering discounts of up to 85% on selected titles (all in mint condition). They require a minimum order of 25 assorted books on a nonreturnable basis.

- If you were going back to press on some backlist titles (and will be raising the prices of the books), you could offer a "Buy before the price increase!" promotion.

Offer a special anniversary discount.

If you are celebrating a company anniversary, a book anniversary, or an author's birthday, you could extend special discounts on certain titles or offer other incentives for ordering. To celebrate their first five years in business, Free Spirit offered booksellers a $5.00 certificate good toward their next purchase of $50.00 or more. Orders of $100.00 or more received a $10.00 certificate. They limited this offer to one certificate per customer.

Offer delayed billing.

You could offer delayed billing for holiday promotions or prepublication orders for major titles. Rather than invoice the bookstore at net 30 (which means they must pay in 30 days), you offer them delayed billing, either net 60 or net 90 days. In general, you will be better off if you offer delayed billing rather than extra discounts to entice booksellers to order. Why? First, because it will cost you less. Second, most booksellers don't pay on time anyway so the cost of delayed billing is minimal.

- To encourage larger stocking orders on its new edition of *The New Doubleday Cookbook*, Doubleday offered delayed billing on any order of ten or more copies.

- For major fall titles, some publishers offer to delay billing until after the holidays. Booksellers, of course, love this practice since it not only eases their cash flow problems, but it also means that they have one less thing to worry about during their busiest selling season.

- Thomas Nelson has offered Christmas dating *or* free freight on any order of 100 or more books. On any order of 500 or more books, they offered both Christmas dating *and* free freight.

- New American Library offered a choice of either delayed billing or an extra 1% discount on any backlist order of 250 or more books.

- To encourage face out display of certain titles in bookstores, both Viking and Macmillan have offered extended billing.

Set up an agency plan.

If you have a backlist of ten or more books within a specific subject area and publish three to four new titles each season in that same area, you might want to develop an agency plan that ensures that each participating store carries a minimum quantity of each of your current and future titles.

With agency plans, a store usually is required to order a minimum of five or ten copies of each title, guarantee that they will maintain a stock of at least two to three copies of each title (and reorder when the stock runs low), and put in a standing order for five or more copies of each new title you release. In exchange for such guarantees, you would offer them a 5% or greater bonus discount over your normal schedule. Agency plans are often used by professional and technical publishers who usually sell to booksellers on a short discount (a discount of no more than 20%).

Set up special merchandising programs.

To encourage booksellers to stock and display a wide range of your book titles, set up special programs that offer them higher discounts, free freight, or other incentives.

- Houghton Mifflin set up an In-Store Merchandising Program that offered booksellers incentives for stocking and displaying specific categories of HM titles. The incentive package included delayed billing, co-op money, rebates, plus a merchandising kit with materials for preparing special displays. Houghton Mifflin also offered prizes to the booksellers who set up the most effective displays. Over 400 independent stores plus a number of smaller chains took part in the first year of this program.

- When Candlewick Press announced its first list, it offered booksellers an irresistible deal—50% discount, free freight, double co-op merchandising points, and a visit from a local professional storyteller. All the booksellers had to do to become a Candlewick Corner Dealer was to order three copies each of 25 different titles from that first list and display them all in one place. Candlewick also provided these stores with sample newspaper ads and bag stuffers to promote the program.

   Also, when Candlewick promoted its new list direct to consumers via magazine ads, they featured a toll-free 800 number. Anyone who called the number was directed to local bookstores who had signed up to be Candlewick Corner Dealers.

- Zondervan created a handbook and CD designed to provide booksellers with creative ways to merchandise books on endcaps and tables. Of course, their books were featured in the samples.

Grant them a 5% discount for cash payment with order.

You can afford to give a 5% discount to prepaid orders since you will save billing and collection costs on such accounts. Plus, of course, you will get the money several months earlier.

Offer higher discounts in general.

Many booksellers have been calling on publishers to offer a higher discount—at least 42% on all orders, regardless of quantity. As Amy Thomas, owner of Pendragon Books, once noted, "Discount is our god right now." If you cannot afford to offer higher discounts all the time, offer them as a special incentive for booksellers to place their first order with you. Rodale, for example, offers an opening order discount to new accounts.

In 1970, the standard bookstore discount was 40%. Now most larger publishers are offering 46 to 47% standard discounts. Why? Because that's the only way they can compete for the business the wholesalers have taken from them. HarperCollins offers a discount of 45%, with an additional 1% discount for those bookstores that order via electronic data interchange.

In a survey conducted by *Publishers Weekly*, children's booksellers rated on a six-point scale five factors that affected their buying decisions. Greater discounts rated 5.6, free freight rated 5.2, quicker delivery time rated 5.2, delayed billing rated 4.2, and sales calls rated 3.5.

Don't require references for new customers.

One reason that booksellers don't like to open new accounts is that they have to fill out those silly forms asking for three industry references. Get their bank references. That's smart. But don't ask for the trade references. Most bookstores have at least three good references, so checking those out won't tell you anything. So don't waste your time or theirs by asking for it.

Give one free copy with a minimum order.

Free copy promotions are most commonly used when a publisher wants to place a countertop display in stores. Publishers also use the free-copy offer to promote new titles at BookExpo America or for fall stocking offers. For example, to encourage larger advance buys, a publisher might offer one free book with every order for 10 or more of that title. Brilliance Audio promoted its Nova line with a two-for-one giveaway. The promotion had a tremendous response: Orders for Nova titles doubled.

Organize a remainder-in-place program.

To encourage booksellers to sell your backlist and slow-moving titles rather than return them to you, set up a remainder in place program. Houghton Mifflin organized a Houghton Mifflin Markdown Program whereby the publisher and bookseller shared the cost of reducing prices on certain titles. Each book that was sold at a reduced price had to be clipped. The clippings then had to be submitted on a worksheet to Houghton Mifflin so the bookseller could get credit for the greatly reduced price. Waldenbooks, which participated in this program, noticed that sales went up dramatically for some discounted titles and several sold out.

Offer special discounts to promote a frontlist title.

Bantam offered a $5.77 credit for each copy of *Gift and Mystery* by Pope John Paul II that a retailer sold during March. This credit allowed booksellers to sell the book for half the retail price of $19.95. You could use a similar limited-time plan to push a title onto a bestseller list.

Offer no-hassle returns.

If there is one thing that booksellers ask for again and again, it is a liberal returns policy. Booksellers like to know that if they have to return a book because it isn't selling, they won't have to go through all kinds of roadblocks to make the return. The easier you make it for them to return a book, the more likely it is that they will order the book from you in the first place. Any returns penalty will kill a sale. So if you offer a returns option, make it easy to use. If, one the other hand, you want to discourage returns, your best option is to offer a complete nonreturnable option. Booksellers can live with such an option if you offer generous discounts.

Berkeley offered a retail incentive plan, where retail accounts which kept returns under 25% during a year can earn an additional 1% discount if their net dollar sales increased 5% to 7.9% over the past two years, or an additional 2% discount if their net increase was between 8% and 11.49%, or as much as a 4% discount if their net increase was over 13.5%.

Promote backlist titles.

Keep your backlist titles alive in the minds of booksellers. One way you can do this is to offer special discounts or billing options to encourage booksellers to stock select backlist titles.

- Schocken Books offered a 43% discount on backlist orders of 25-49 books and 10 titles or a discount of 48% on backlist orders of 100 books and 25 titles, plus delayed billing of 90 days end of month. In addition, backlist quantities combined with frontlist quantities to maximize the frontlist discount.

- In a fall stock offer, Workman gave a 55% discount on a minimum order of five copies each of select backlist titles; one order per store. Watson-Guptill offered a 50% discount or delayed billing on a minimum backlist order of 50 books and 25 titles per ship-to locations.

- One year after a book's publication date, Prentice-Hall sends out extra covers of the book to key bookseller accounts. On the inside of the cover, they print the book's sales history—thus reminding booksellers how well they did with the book.

- Chronicle Books has an ongoing spinner-rack program in which many of their backlist titles can be displayed.

- Knopf launched a backlist cookbook holiday promotion that featured extra advertising, author appearances, a recipe brochure, and special co-op.

Extend credit.

Be one of the first publishers to extend credit to a new bookseller. Act as a credit reference for them, and they will love you for life. How do you find out about new stores? Call the American Booksellers Association or your regional booksellers association (you can find addresses and phone

numbers at *http://www.bookmarket.com/pubassn.html*). Associations know
which stores are starting up. Indeed, ABA runs a school for new booksellers
and would be glad to list you as a prime credit reference for new stores.

Offer consignment terms.

If all else fails to entice a prospective account to order your titles, offer
to let them have the books on consignment—that means, they pay for the
books only after they've sold them. When Renny Darling of Royal House
Publishing published her first cookbook, *The Joy of Eating*, the book sold
few copies until she went down personally to the Beverly Hills B. Dalton
store and left five books on consignment for 90 days. Two days later the
store ordered fifteen more copies; two days after that, another 30; a few
days after that, several cases of the book. Her husband, seeing those results,
took to the road and began peddling copies of the book in all the bookstores
up and down the state of California. The book sold a half a million copies in
ten years, and Royal House went on to publish seven more books. It all
started, though, with that first small consignment.

Offer no-risk copies of a new title.

To promote the sale of *Off in Zora*, Booksellers Publishing made a special BookExpo America offer. Booksellers could come by their booth during
the trade show and pick up three copies of the novel to take home. After
180 days, the stores would be billed for $6.47 per copy. If the stores had not
been able to handsell those copies within that time period, the copies were
theirs to keep free. The stores only had to pay for the books they had sold
during that six-month period. That offer, of course, placed a lot of trust in
booksellers to report their true sales.

14:05 The Importance of Service

Once you have gained an account, the best way to keep that account ordering your titles is to provide them with fast and friendly service. Make it
easy for them to work with you, and they will remain loyal to you. Make it
tough, and they will find someone else who can provide similar titles (even
if those titles are not as good as yours).

Anytime you tighten up your terms or slack off in your service, booksellers will hesitate to order from you. Here are a few things you can do to
ensure that you keep a reputation for great service:

Fill orders promptly.

If possible, ship books the same day you receive the order. If you can't
offer same-day shipment, at least aim to ship all orders out in three days or
less. Believe me, you'll beat almost every major publisher if you do. And
booksellers will love you.

Hastings Books deals with suppliers from many industries. According to their president, John Marmaduke, book publishers are the slowest at filling orders. As he points out, "Toyota can build a car faster than most publishers can figure out an order." Next time you get an order from a bookstore, surprise them. Ship the order promptly.

Be willing to ship orders to any accounts, no matter how small. In early 1997, Macmillan decided to cut off any bookstores which did not order $10,000 net worth of books each year. They asked those bookstores to order through wholesalers. In response, the board of the American Booksellers Association gave Macmillan the first ever Rip Van Winkle Award for Out of Touch Management. Don't be the second publisher to get such an award.

When billing, send legible invoices.

More than one bookseller has complained of the sloppy business habits of smaller publishers. A bookseller will always choose to work with a company which is well-organized and efficient over one that is not. And, as one bookseller has noted, the ones who are organized are the first to be paid.

Invoices (and packing lists) should include the following information: ISBN, title (unabbreviated), author, price (if the price has changed, note the price change), discount, invoice date, invoice number, purchase order number, freight charge, and retail total.

Provide alternative ways to transmit orders.

More booksellers are asking for alternative ways to order—by telephone, by fax, via email, or via EDI (electronic data interchange). Independent booksellers are especially looking for ways to serve their customers better. If you provide them with ways to place orders more quickly, they will be more likely to order from you.

Many booksellers use fax machines to place their orders. Why? Because they can order quicker (even quicker than by voice because they don't have to repeat numbers, etc.), do not have to worry about mistakes, and can have printed confirmation of their order. To encourage bookstores to order by fax, Ingram offers an extra discount point for faxed orders.

Pack your books carefully.

Do not use styrofoam peanuts which are messy to unpack. Booksellers prefer heavy folded paper or confetti (shredded invoices will do) or, better yet, shrinkwrapping. If you want to see what a model shipment looks like, check any shipment from Ingram. They have packing down to a science. Use a sturdy box. If shipping multiple boxes, number them (1 of 4, etc.). Make sure the customer's purchase order number is on the mailing label.

Listen to booksellers.

First, of course, talk to them. Learn what their concerns are. Find out what you can do to make their jobs easier. And when they request a special service or an exception to the way you are accustomed to doing business, fill their request if it is reasonable.

To get a better idea of the concerns booksellers have, work in a bookstore at least one week every year. Some of the larger publishers now encourage their sales and marketing people to work at least one or two days every year, especially around the holidays to help their larger accounts handle the rush. If possible, work some of that time in the back room and some of that time up front at the cash register. You'll learn a lot.

Jacqueline Susann, author of *The Valley of the Dolls*, was a master at getting to know booksellers. Not only would she greet booksellers by name when she met them at trade shows, but she also sent birthday cards to them, each with an affectionate handwritten note. As each new book was published, she sent them signed advance copies, each boxed and gift-wrapped with a personal message enclosed. Jackie was the first author to really get out there and help sell her books. And sell she did!

> **Authors:** Get to know your local booksellers as well as those in others cities as you travel. James Redfield, author of *The Celestine Prophecy*, attributes much of his success to the personal relationships he developed with booksellers as he dropped off books to sell. Similarly, fantasy author Raymond Feist credits a good portion of his success to the fact that he has spent several weeks visiting bookstores up and down the California coast.

Send thank you notes.

Get in the habit of thanking new and old accounts who have placed especially large reorders. They'll appreciate the thought. It's just another way to build good will. And it works.

Promote to stores in the boondocks.

Stores off the beaten path rarely get any real attention from the major publishers or, for that matter, from most sales reps. These stores are virgin territory. If you promote to them on a consistent basis and build a relationship with them, they will respond—especially if you have books that fit well into their cultural milieu.

Woodbridge sends these stores catalogs enclosed in large envelopes. On the outside of those envelopes, the following message is printed: "New Catalogs. New Titles. Please order from these materials. (No Sales Rep will call in your area this season.)" It is important to alert these stores that no sales rep will call. Even major publishers, who have their own reps, promote to small town stores primarily through catalogs and phone calls.

Work the phones.

According to Charlie Winton, former president of Publishers Group West, one of the reasons Charles Frazier's novel *Cold Mountain* was so successful was that PGW worked the phones, making sure that accounts had enough of the books in stock as sales took off.

Support your books by advertising and publicity.

If you want to offer the greatest service you can to booksellers, promote your books well. No bookseller would want to carry a book which does not have the support and commitment of its publisher. Create the demand, and the booksellers will have to buy your books. As bookseller Sally Jordan once noted, "Parades don't draw much anymore, but homemade fudge does." By that she meant that all the details about terms, discounts, displays, posters, etc. are negligible compared to what the publisher does to promote its books. That's what will make booksellers!

Don't compete with bookstores.

If you want booksellers to get behind your books, don't compete with them. For instance, Elaine Petrocelli, owner of Book Passage, displays spine out any books with advertisements offering deep discounts on direct sales. These books never get face out display in her store. Other booksellers are as reluctant to promote books that blatantly advertise for direct sales.

Some bookstores will also not carry books that are heavily promoted on the web, especially if those books are sold at a discount. To get past this objection, Lonely Planet makes sure that it is not advantageous for someone to order directly from them. If a customers wants to order their travel books via the Internet, Lonely Planet charges full price, plus sales tax and shipping and handling. In addition, Lonely Planet provides links to independent bookstores who have sites on the web.

14:06 Keep in Touch with Your Accounts

As part of your overall service to your accounts, you should have some means of maintaining contact with them between actual sales calls. You can use the phone, email, direct mail, catalogs, or newsletters to keep in touch with them. The following sections provide a few suggestions on how to use each of these means to keep in touch with your bookstore customers.

To put these options in perspective, you might want to keep in mind the results of a survey of children's booksellers conducted by Cahners Research. When children's-only booksellers were asked what was the most useful source of information when buying children's books, 68.2% cited sales reps, while 58% cited catalogs. On the other hand, general bookstores that sell children's books cited catalogs as their most useful source (65.4%), while 48.9% cited sales reps.

After sales reps and catalogs, both types of stores cited the following sources of purchasing information: book reviews, word of mouth, articles in trade journals, trade shows, and input from staff.

14:07 Reach Out and Touch Someone

One of the best ways to keep in touch with your bookstore customers is to call them regularly. While this may not be practical if you have a large customer list, you can still use phone calls to keep in touch with your major accounts and other key contacts.

☐ As I've mentioned before, installing a toll-free number will encourage your customers to call you with new orders, questions, inquiries, suggestions, and other matters of importance to your relationship with them. When they do call, take the time to listen to them.

☐ Use outgoing calls not only to speed collection of past due accounts, but also to clarify any problems you might have encountered in fulfilling the order. For example, if the address is illegible or the purchase order number is missing, don't ship the order until you've called the bookseller and confirmed the order.

☐ Outbound sales calls preceded by a mailing of your catalog or other sales literature can increase your orders by as much as 60% (in the experience of at least one publisher).

☐ Use outbound phone calls to encourage orders from bookstores which have not previously ordered from you. While Carmichael's Bookstore had placed some special orders with Dalkey Archive Press, the store had never placed a stocking order until Dalkey's new sales manager called the owner. During a ten-minute call, the sales manager went through the Dalkey list with the store owner, who ended up ordering seven frontlist titles and twelve backlist titles. With Carmichael's computer tracking system, once a book gets into the store, the book is automatically reordered whenever a copy sells.

☐ When you have special publicity coming up in a region, call the bookstores in that area to alert them. Also alert bookstores whenever significant national publicity, such as an appearance on *Oprah!*, could affect the demand for your book.

☐ Use the phone to communicate with your sales reps. A few days before Abigail Van Buren mentioned Rhoda Levin's book for spouses of cardiac patients, *Heartmates*, in her column, she called the author and told her to "tell those Prentice Hall sales reps to get the book into the stores." Because Prentice Hall had established a digitized telephone message center, the author was able to leave a message for all sales reps with just one call. Since each sales rep checked into the message center every day, the word got out right away. That same day, the reps placed 1,000 orders for her book.

☐ Most bookstores now use fax machines to send out orders and receive information from publishers. Use broadcast faxes when you have to get out news to a lot of bookstores in a very short time. One distributor used "fax attacks" to alert its 300 core bookstore customers of developments with some of its bestselling titles. The distributor reported that their stepped up fax efforts helped to move more than 70,000 copies of *The World's Best Kept Beauty Secrets* by Diane Irons and 30,000 copies of *The Quickening* by Art Bell.

☐ For more pointers on using telephones in marketing your books, see sections 10:10 and 10:11 on advertising (Chapter 10 in this book).

14:08 Sell by Direct Mail to Bookstores

Direct mail can be an effective way to reach the person responsible for buying new titles at bookstores. Surveys show that chain store buyers rely on brochures and flyers as a major means for finding out about new titles. Review the first part of Chapter 10 for general pointers on using direct mail. Here, though, are a few tips for using direct mail in book trade promotions.

☐ **Mail to the book buyer.** Unless specifically requested to do so (or you have the names of subject-specific buyers), don't send your catalogs or other sales literature to more than one person at each store.

☐ **The best mailing list of bookstores** is the Top 700 Independent Bookstores list from Open Horizons. The cost is only $40.00. Order online at http://www.bookmarket.com.

☐ **Mail regularly.** Establish a certain schedule, two to four times a year (or more frequently for your best customers), so that booksellers begin to anticipate your mailings.

☐ **Establish a recognizable format** so that booksellers can easily recognize your promotions. This, again, will help to establish your company in the minds of the booksellers. The most effective format, according to reports from smaller publishers, is a postcard featuring a book cover on one side and a sales message on the other side.

☐ **Use statement stuffers.** When you send out invoices and statements, always include some announcement regarding one or more of your titles. Use these statement stuffers to offer special sales or promotions.

☐ **Try new formats.** When promoting to booksellers and wholesalers, try different formats to get their attention. Since most stores are inundated with catalogs, brochures, and media kits, try greeting cards, calendars, pop-ups, or other unusual formats. Try a Valentine card when promoting a book in February. A Mother's Day card during May. A flag on the 4th of July. Such items would stand out from the clutter on their desk.

☐ **Launch a letter-writing campaign** to your 100 best customers to encourage them to list your lead title or titles on their bestseller forms (for any lists they report to). Such a campaign has worked before.

Authors — You can also make effective use of direct mail to promote your books to booksellers. As a member bookstore of ABA, I've received numerous promotions from authors.

For example, to promote his novel, *Rush to Nowhere*, Howard Lewis Russell sent the following postcard to booksellers:

Dear Bookseller,

Enough about *The Mysteries of Pittsburgh*. Here's a mystery of New York: how do I make sure my book keeps selling? There's nothing sadder than a book that starts to sell well but doesn't catch on *because stores don't reorder*.

My book, **Rush to Nowhere**, has been in stores for two or three weeks now and, by all accounts, it's selling well. So: please reorder my book. I'd hate for the three years I spent working on it to become a **Rush to Nowhere**. Thanks for your support.

HOWARD LEWIS RUSSELL   124 East 91 Street NYC 10128

P.S.: It's available from Ingram, Baker & Taylor, and my publisher, Donald I. Fine.

[Notice how he personalized the postcard with his address.]

☐ Here are a few of the things that Thomas Gladysz of The Booksmith looks for in a personal letter from an author or publisher as he is tearing through his mail:

1. His name and store name must be spelled correctly.
2. Some handwritten ink must appear somewhere in the letter.
3. He always reads a handwritten post-it note or cover letter.
4. The book in question has to be relevant to his store.
5. The letter has to be different enough or personal enough to withstand his toss-now? Test.

14:09 Sell Via Catalogs to Bookstores

Your catalog is probably your best sales tool, other than your books themselves. Hence, design your catalog so it sells your books effectively. Design and publish a new catalog with each new list (usually in the spring and fall). To help you in designing and promoting your catalog, here are a few suggestions that might work for your books:

☐ **Mail your catalog to your own house accounts** and other major prospects. To save money, mail flyers or brochures to other marginal prospects offering them the complete catalog upon request.

☐ **Don't be stuck on one format for your catalog.** You can design your catalog for easy filing, or feature only frontlist titles, or make it so it stands out in the crowd—whatever works for your titles *and* the image you want to project for your company.

Stoller Publications' catalog for its line of calendars is a calendar itself with sample full-color pages from each of its major calendar titles. Not only is the catalog appropriate for its contents, but it also stands out from the crowd. Many booksellers undoubtedly put the beautiful calendar on the wall above their order desk, where it would be readily available when they got around to ordering.

Both Random House and Ballantine have put their frontlist catalogs on CDs to make it easier for computer-literate booksellers to find the books they need. With these CDs, booksellers are able to select titles and transfer them directly to their own computerized databases for order entry.

☐ **Organize your catalog so every title is easy to find.** Provide a table of contents and a cross-referenced index by author, title, and subject.

☐ **Include all appropriate bibliographic information** so it will be readily accessible to anyone wanting the information. Include the title, subtitle, author, price, publication date, ISBN, number of pages, trim size, type of binding(s), and the type and number of illustrations, indexes, appendices, and other information. Also describe the audience for the book, something about the book's contents and benefits, and any promotional information that will encourage booksellers to stock the book.

☐ **Make it easy to find the order form**, easy to detach from the catalog and mail, and easy to use to place an order. Include extra order forms so that the catalog doesn't become obsolete after the first order is placed.

☐ **Describe the shipping information**—how you ship the books, what the charges will be, and what your usual turnaround time is. Of course, if your turnaround time is unimpressive, don't mention it until you have taken steps to improve it.

☐ **Include a clear, concise statement of terms** and discounts, returns policy, and other information a bookseller might need before placing an order with your company. If you offer co-op advertising money or other merchandising programs, promote these programs in your catalog so the booksellers know that you support your books with advertising.

☐ **List the addresses of your sales representatives** or any distributors and major wholesalers who handle your book. Not only will this list make it easier for bookstores to consolidate their order for your books with other orders, but it will also encourage the wholesalers to stock more copies of your books. Be sure to send the wholesalers copies of your catalog so they are aware that orders will be coming their way.

☐ **Provide a return envelope** (whether prepaid or simply self-addressed is up to you) to make it easier for them to order.

☐ **Promote the use of your order phone number** so bookstores can easily find the information if they need to order quickly.

☐ **If you publish a catalog for direct sales to readers, don't send that catalog to booksellers.** Prepare a separate one for them, one that addresses their needs and concerns. Don't offer better discounts in your consumer catalog than you give to booksellers. Don't laugh. Some publishers have. Better yet, design your consumer catalog so it encourages bookstore sales. For instance, the order form of Picture Book Studio's consumer catalog featured the following words: "Look for Picture Book Studio Books at Fine Bookstores Everywhere"—a line that many publishers have used. But Picture Book Studio went one step further. They added the phrase: "and at These Special Dealers," and listed the names, addresses, and phone numbers of 250 bookstores! These stores had agreed to stock 28 titles (for a total order of 84 books) and display Picture Book Studio books in a section by themselves.

☐ **Print extra catalogs for bookstores**, which they can imprint with their store name and address and then send out to their best customers or give away in the bookstore. Ask bookstores first if they'd like this option.

14:10 Promote Via Newsletters

One of the best formats you can use to communicate regularly with your major accounts is a newsletter. Newsletters can be more personal, informal, and newsy than catalogs. Plus, since newsletters do not require extensive graphics or design, the cost of producing one (both in terms of time and money) will usually be less than the cost of producing a catalog or direct mail package. Indeed, with an email newsletter, the cost is almost zero.

Use your newsletter to let your key accounts know about new titles, upcoming promotions, updates on previous promotions, subsidiary rights sales, recent publicity, reprints or new editions, changing terms, and any other information that may be of use to them in selling your books. At the same time, be sure to keep the tone of the newsletter low-key and personal.

To encourage readership of your newsletter, add informative features on how to set up a display, how to run a book fair, or other how-to items which would make life easier for the bookseller.

You could include short camera-ready articles that booksellers could reprint in any newsletters or other mailings they make to their customers. This copy could feature a special theme or subject (travel, cooking, or back to school) and excerpt material from one of your books. In this way you would be helping booksellers to find good material for their newsletters while promoting your books at the same time. When you offer such material, make it clear to the booksellers that they have your permission to reprint the material in their promotions.

- Henry Holt lists six purposes for their bimonthly *Hooters* newsletter, which is sent to the book trade:

  1. To bring into closer perspective marketing, publicity, and sales objectives for new titles on each seasonal list.
  2. To stimulate consumer sales by coordinating in advance promotional plans with booksellers.
  3. To offer sales incentive programs.
  4. To bring retailers in close touch with the direction, development, and performance of Henry Holt and Company's publishing programs, order fulfillment, and customer service.
  5. To gauge sales performance factors through booksellers' input and response.
  6. To keep the trade current on special promotions and events that impact sales.

- Scribners publishes a quarterly newsletter featuring new titles from their line of mystery books. The newsletter also describes successes with previous titles. This newsletter is mailed to their house list of bookstores, agents who might buy subsidiary rights, individual readers who have requested to receive the letter, and to Baker & Taylor's 18,000 library and bookstore accounts.

- Pocket Books published a similar newsletter directed at science fiction and fantasy readers. At the World Science Fiction Convention, they offered a free subscription to anyone requesting one. Since the people who attend such conventions are among the most active and influential readers in that genre, Pocket Books was able to create significant word-of-mouth advertising. Pocket Books also offered this newsletter for bookstores to give away directly to their best customers.

- To promote their children's books, Dell sent the *Carousel* newsletter to 8,000 booksellers, librarians, educators, and media.

- To educate bookstores on how to merchandise audiotapes more effectively, Audio Renaissance Tapes published *New Audio Age*. This newsletter featured retail marketing ideas, industry stats, marketing tips, and a letters section where retailers could share ideas and concerns.

- Bantam started up a two-page newsletter, *The Bantam Independent*, for independent booksellers. In it, they listed upcoming advertising and publicity, co-op information, available promo materials, their recent award-winning books, and event marketing opportunities. Bantam also published the *Rooster Crows* newsletter sent to children's booksellers. In addition, Bantam asked its sales reps to identify bookstores that published newsletters so they could send materials to support those newsletters.

- Random House published a *Backlist Bulletin* that featured ideas for bookstore promotions, including display ideas, reviews of backlist titles, and upcoming promotional events. They also offered bookstores a special backlist catalog by category, a CD with all backlist titles, and backlist point-of-purchase displays.

- Random House sent out their *Kids' News* newsletter to children's booksellers and media as a follow-up to their seasonal catalogs.

- During the two-year book tour for Douglas Wood's *Old Turtle*, Pfeiffer-Hamilton sent out a regular *Turtle Talk* newsletter to inform booksellers about the latest publicity and solicit additional orders for the book. Since they had no sales reps, they used the mails as their rep. It worked. Over that two-year period, *Old Turtle* became a *New York Times* bestseller.

- Rough Guides publishes a tri-annual *RoughNews* newsletter featuring eight pages of travel articles about destinations covered in their Rough Guides travel books.

Authors — You can write and mail your newsletter not only to your fans but also to booksellers and jobbers. Julie Garwood, author of *The Lion's Lady*, offered to send a copy of her newsletter to anyone who wrote to her. Many romance novelists use newsletter to remain connected to their many fans.

14:11 Advertise in Trade Magazines

Another major way of keeping in one-way communication with your accounts (and other prospective customers) is to advertise your books in the major trade journals such as *Publishers Weekly, Library Journal, Foreword,* and some of the wholesaler and chain store publications. If you do not have a large ad budget yet want to promote your books to the trade, your first priority should be to promote your new lists in the spring and fall announcements issues of these magazines. Here is information on some of your major book trade advertising opportunities:

☐ **Publishers Weekly**, 245 West 17th Street, New York, NY 10011; 212-463-6758; Fax: 212-463-6631. Web: http://www.publishersweekly.com. One of the most cost-effective ways to advertise in *PW* is to take advantage of the co-op ads offered by PMA, SPAN, or your distributor.

☐ **ForeWord Magazine**, 129½ E. Front Street, Traverse City, MI 49684; 231-933-3699; Fax: 231-933-3899. Web: http://www.forewordmagazine.com. They offer special rates for smaller publishers.

☐ **Independent Bookstore**, Marion Street Press, P.O. Box 2249, Oak Park, IL 60303; 708-445-8330; 866-443-7987; Fax: 708-445-8348. Email: edavis@marionstreetpress.com. Web: http://www.marionstreetpress.com. A quarter-page ad in this quarterly newsletter only costs $200.

☐ **Publishers Lunch**, Cader Books. Email: sales@publishersmarketplace.com. Wet: http://www.publishersmarketplace.com. This daily email newsletter to the publishing industry is read by 35,000 readers.

☐ **Shelf Awareness**, Jenn Risko, Publisher; John Mutter, Editor-in-Chief, P.O. Box 43310, Upper Montclair, NJ 07043-0310; 973-953-0304. Email: Jenn@shelf-awareness.com. Web: http://www.shelf-awareness.com. This daily email newsletter for the book trade offers a great Author Buzz section for authors to advertise their books.

☐ **Bookselling This Week**, Rosemary Hawkins, Executive Editor, American Booksellers Association, 200 White Plains Road, Tarrytown, NY 10591; 800-637-0037. Email: rosemary@bookweb.org. Web: http://www.bookweb.org. Weekly email newsletter sent to association members.

Here, now, are a few ways you can make your advertisements more effective in reaching booksellers and convincing them to buy your books:

☐ **Feature booksellers in your ads.** In a full-page *Publishers Weekly* ad for Alice Hoffman's novel, *Turtle Moon*, Putnam featured the following headline: "From Moorestown, New Jersey, to Beaverton, Oregon, booksellers are falling in love with..." and a photo of the book jacket. The rest of the ad featured laudatory quotes from independent bookstores as well as buyers from Waldenbooks, Barnes & Noble, and wholesalers.

Warner produced a similar ad for Robert James Waller's novel, *The Bridges of Madison County*. Here's what Beth Robbins of Tecolote Bookstores had to say about this book: "The most profoundly moving book I have ever read in my life! Pulitzer Prize material!" *Bridges* went on to become a bestseller and stayed on the lists for over 200 weeks.

☐ **Recommend stores in your ads**. When advertising in consumer magazines, you might want to add a line such as the following: "Available at
your favorite local bookstore or direct from the publisher." If you are
creating a regional ad, convince several local booksellers to stock your
books in quantity in return for a free mention in your advertisement.

☐ **Include a coupon in your ad**. Coupons are a superb way to track advertising results. To use coupons effectively, you should arrange for certain
booksellers to accept your coupons and then feature them in your ad by
writing: "Redeem this coupon at the following cooperating bookstores."
When Harlequin advertised its line of romance novels in *People* magazine, they featured a coupon for a free quartz clock with purchase of a
novel (as evidenced by a cash register receipt from a retail store).

☐ **Provide ad slicks to bookstores.** When promoting specific titles to
bookstores, enclose camera-ready ad slicks that the bookstores can insert
into newspapers with their address. To encourage them to use these ad
slicks, provide co-op advertising money (see section 14:13 for details).

☐ **Thank bookstores.** In a full page ad in *Publishers Weekly* for Douglas
Kennedy's novel, *The Big Picture*, Hyperion thanked booksellers for
making the book a *New York Times* bestseller.

☐ **Offer free copies.** When Little, Brown advertised Anita Shreve's *The
Weight of Water*, they included a line at the bottom offering additional
advance copies for booksellers to share with their staff. To get copies,
booksellers simply had to call an 800 number.

In a full-page ad, Murdoch Books offered "Real Help for Parents" via
their *Projects for Parents* series. The ad offered booksellers free copies
if they had a story hour. In a Post-It note, the ad asked, "Do you have a
children's story hour? Call us at 800-262-5665 for free resource copies!"

In a classified ad, Travelers' Tales offered free reading copies of *Travelers' Tales: A Dog's World* to the first 100 bookstores to respond positively to the question: "Do you love dogs, travel, and reading?"

☐ **Advertise special promotions.** To promote *The Original Sin* by Marius
Gabriel, Bantam placed an ad in *American Bookseller*. Besides offering
advance reading copies to the first 500 booksellers to respond to the ad
by calling their 800 number, Bantam also promoted a contest to win a
seven-day trip to Barcelona, Spain, including a festive private dinner
with the author. To enter the drawing for this trip, booksellers had to
read the book, answer a simple question, and mail in the entry form.

☐ **Advertise your backlist.** Two or three times a year, Workman Publishing places a third-page ad in *Publishers Weekly* featuring titles which
have gone back to press. The ads include title, price, binding, authors,
copies in print, and the new printing. Since many of their books have
sold millions of copies, it makes for an impressive advertisement.

Similarly in *Publishers Weekly*, Conari Press advertised its top sellers, including *Random Acts of Kindness* (480,000 copies in print), *Coming Apart* (200,000 in print), *The Woman's Book of Courage* (180,000), and *More Random Acts of Kindness* (170,000). This was an effective way to advertise their backlist and company name.

☐ **Advertise regularly.** At one point Warner Books published a one-page newsletter, *The Latest Buzz*, in *Publishers Weekly*. In this ad, they highlighted their top books, book tours, rights sales, publicity successes, award winners, and most interesting authors. It offered some of the most interesting reading in the magazine.

14:12 Co-op Advertising

Perhaps the best promotional support program you can offer a bookseller is co-op advertising. Under co-op arrangements, a publisher rebates a portion of the bookseller's total purchase of eligible titles to be used by the bookseller to advertise the publisher's titles in local media. A typical rebate percentage would be about 8% of the net dollar amount of the bookseller's order. Manufacturers of all types now set aside more than $10 billion a year in co-op advertising funds (of which about 70% is actually used).

☐ **Offer the same terms to everyone.** If you offer co-op advertising to one bookseller, you have to offer the same terms to other booksellers. Not only is this the fair thing to do, it is an FTC regulation. So set your terms, and then stick to them.

☐ **Bookstores love co-op.** Both the chains and independent booksellers are open to co-op advertising. Few booksellers will refuse such help.

☐ **Offer co-op advertising only for your titles which have wide distribution.** Be selective. Titles of wide general appeal are best for national co-op programs; titles of regional appeal are best for regional co-op.

☐ **Beware of overstocking.** One drawback to co-op ads is that some booksellers may stock up heavily on your co-op titles in order to get a larger co-op advertising allowance and then end up returning most of the books. In such cases, there is no way for you to get any of the co-op money back, unless you subtract it from future co-op offers. To limit your risk, set an upper credit limit for such co-op ads.

☐ **Offer co-op for total purchases.** Rather than tie co-op to a specific title, you can award co-op moneys based on the bookseller's total buy for the previous year and allow booksellers to choose which titles they advertise. Booksellers, of course, like this option because it gives them the opportunity to push titles they are enthusiastic about and which they find most suitable for their market. Most booksellers find it a pain to be restricted to one or two titles.

Dial/Dutton makes available to bookstores 10% of their net order on a seasonal basis; they also offer 20% of the net sales on books sold during an autograph session. Houghton Mifflin makes available 10% of the store's previous year's buy. Macmillan offers 8% of the store's net buy from the previous season. Oxmoor House gives 10% of retail on co-op ads with a supporting order for all trade titles.

HarperCollins offers bookstores two options: Either 4% on the prior year's net on direct *or* indirect purchases or 2.5% of the prior year's net billings on both direct *and* indirect purchases.

Penguin Putnam offers either 4% of the prior year's net billing on titles purchased from the publisher *or* from distributors (not combined) or 3% of the prior year's combined direct *and* indirect net billing. They offer slightly less co-op percentages for mass market and trade paperbacks.

☐ **Set restrictions.** If you offer co-op based on total purchases, set some restrictions. Penguin, for example, limited spending on any one title to 25% of accrued co-op moneys. In another case, Putnam required that no more than 40% of co-op funds could be spent during the first six months of the year; the other 60% had to be spent during the second half.

☐ **Provide ad copy.** Give booksellers appropriate copy for co-op ads, preferably camera-ready ad slicks which can be inserted with the bookstore's logo and address (or prerecorded tapes for radio commercials). When Ballantine and St. Martin Press do national radio ads, they provide the tapes to retailers, who can then add their names at the end of the spot.

☐ **Allow alternatives.** Let booksellers use the co-op money for alternative advertising promotions as well as the usual newspaper and radio ads. For instance, if they want to feature your titles in their direct mail literature, newsletters, or catalogs, work with them to arrange an ad that satisfies both of you. In one instance, Putnam approved an unusual Earth Day promotion where one retailer produced green and tan reuseable canvas grocery bags with the latest book by Heloise imprinted on the side.

☐ **You can use co-op money to get floor placement.** For example, when Bantam Doubleday Dell published *The Pill Book*, they provided co-op funds to drug stores to ensure placement in or near the pharmacy department, using special floor displays, end caps, or shelf extenders.

☐ **Keep your co-op policy simple.** Booksellers often complain about the paperwork involved in co-op ad programs. If you make yours simple to use, they will be more likely to work with you to promote your titles.

☐ **Offer credit.** The best way to deal with co-op fund requests is to credit the bookstore's account after they provide you with a copy of the appropriate supporting invoice and a copy of the applicable ads.

☐ **As an alternative to co-op ad funds**, you could offer to list the stores in your major consumer advertisements if they purchase a minimum quantity of the advertised titles. For instance, for an ad in *Parents* magazine, Macmillan promoted six of its books for children and listed twenty member bookstores of the Association of Booksellers for Children.

Basil Blackwell placed a four-page spread in the *New York Review of Books* in which they displayed 50 titles and featured the names and addresses of 74 bookstores. The booksellers qualified for the free listing by ordering 40% of the chosen titles, with no minimum quantity. Also, by listing 74 bookstores, the publisher qualified for the lower retail ad rate.

☐ **Offer kickbacks for author events.** Instead of offering co-op moneys, offer the stores as much as 20% kickback on any book order for a specific event (to be used to promote that event).

☐ **Give newsletter allowances.** For bookstores that publish a newsletter, offer them a payment ($25 to $50) for any review or feature for one of your titles or authors. Random House offers bookstores a $750 per year newsletter allowance; Little, Brown offers $1,000 per year. In both cases, credit is given when the newsletter highlights one of their titles.

☐ **Offer books in trade for bookstore promotions.** Since the books cost you about 10¢ on the dollar, you get inexpensive advertising and bookseller goodwill.

14:13 Support Your Independent Bookseller

Do whatever you can to help bookstores sell more books (whether your own titles or books in general). Provide them with display materials, promotional literature, or other services that make their job easier, more productive, and more profitable.

☐ **Provide bookstores with camera-ready copy for their newsletters.** Since their regular customers enjoy the informative sales format of newsletters, many bookstores have found newsletters to be their most effective advertising media. Any help you can give them to make their newsletters better will certainly be appreciated. For instance, you could provide them with photos or sample reviews to use in their store newsletters. Or perhaps a quiz that features information about yourbook.

☐ **Provide support materials.** Among other things, you could provide support material for bookstores who want to host open houses or book fairs for librarians and school teachers. Let bookstores know that you are willing to supply them with giveaway items that would interest teachers and librarians—items such as bookmarks, bookplates, stickers, display materials, and other giveaways.

☐ **Prepare audio or video excerpts.** Prepare excerpts of some of your books and send them to booksellers who host local radio or TV book programs. You could also send such excerpts to other radio/TV book reviewers. Videos can also work as in-store ads. For instance, Gulf Publishing promoted its book, *Know your Rights*, via in-store videos featuring author interviews interspersed with ads for the book.

☐ **Provide imprinted material.** Personalize your promotional material by providing bookstores with flyers and brochures imprinted with their name and address (or flyers which can be imprinted by the store). Such promotional literature will be most effective if it is targeted at a specific audience (such as school teachers, craft people, corporate accounts, or travelers). Gulf Publishing provides brochures and fliers with a blank space for an address for those bookstores who want to mail to their own customers or who would use the pieces for statement stuffers, bounceback offers, or counter pieces to solicit special orders.

☐ **Provide support for school book fairs.** Houghton Mifflin, for example, underwrote a special issue of *Instructor* magazine which focused on helping schools to establish educational partnerships with local businesses and community groups. Their suggestions included establishing an after-school read-aloud program, donating a library of special titles to a retirement home, and giving free book coupons to students who help to tutor fellow students to read. If you would like to support school reading programs, you could provide stores with cents-off coupons redeemable for those of your titles which would appeal to young readers.

☐ **Provide support for reading groups.** Many of these reading groups are sponsored by bookstores who have found that these groups sell books. As Carla Cohen of Politics & Prose noted, "When one group reads a book, we can sell 50 copies!"

To support reading groups, Vintage included an audio author interview in each reading group guide. Doubleday provided reading groups with a 20-minute video of Margaret Atwood reading excerpts from her novel *Alias Grace*. Harvest Books offered themed brochures with author interviews, news, and views for reading group titles. If you want to provide material inexpensively, make it available online. Then let booksellers know that reading groups can go online for support material.

Dell developed Consumer Reading Group Kits, bookstore displays, TV spots, window streamers, door decals, co-op ad slicks, bookmarks, bag stuffers, sign-up pads, buttons, and more to support Danielle Steel Reading Groups. The consumer kits included membership cards, color-coded checklist bookmarks, self-adhesive stamps and stamp book to track each purchase of a Steel novel, plus a reading group newsletter.

☐ **Support other bookstore outreach programs.** Besides providing material for school book fairs and reading groups, check for any other audiences which bookstores might want to tap—such as corporate accounts, senior citizens, fundraising organizations, churches—and offer to provide the stores with material appropriate for that audience.

John Wiley launched a marketing program to help local bookstores sell more business books. In one instance, Wiley helped a store in Colorado send out a direct mailing to businesses in Wyoming and Colorado. They provided the store with a mailing list and produced the direct mail piece while the store used its co-op money to pay for the postage.

Zondervan started up a Retail Continuity Program to support the direct marketing programs of Christian booksellers. As part of that program, they sent participating stores a free video training kit that described the six secrets of direct marketing. In addition, Zondervan placed national ads to tell pastors to sign up for special books at the local bookstores.

Harlequin began a retail-based loyalty program called Pages & Privileges, which rewarded frequent romance buyers with gifts, travel discounts, and other benefits in return for proof-of-purchase coupons and cash register receipts. Such a frequent-buyer program, of course, can only work with publishers of series that attract multiple buys.

☐ **Keep them up-to-date on your successes.** Keep bookstores informed on your books, even your backlist titles. For example, one year (or some other suitable time period) after publication of important titles, you could send extra covers of the book printed on the inside with the book's sales history and any other important information.

When Chip Fleischer of Steerforth Press heard a great merchandising tip from Rob Mitchell of the Harvard Book Store, he passed that tip on to every bookseller who stopped by his booth at BEA. What was the tip? Simple: Sales took off when one of Mitchell's coworkers had shelved Robert Clarke's biography of James Beard next to Beard's cookbooks rather than in the biography section.

☐ **Offer bookstores a lamp.** Booksellers can use the lamp to highlight your book. Studies of bookstore browsers have shown that they tend to gravitate to those parts of the bookstore which are lit best. In other words, a light sells books. While you cannot make this offer to all bookstores, you sure can test it out with one or two of your local booksellers.

☐ **Encourage bookstores to sample your books.** The more booksellers know about your books, the more likely they are to recommend your books to their customers. The most effective way to introduce them to your books is to send them advance reading copies of special books. While such advance copies might not carry that much weight with some booksellers, when they *ask* for a galley copy from you, be sure to send it. If you want to ruin your reputation with booksellers, just ignore their requests for advance reading copies. To facilitate getting your reading copies out, participate in BookSense's white box mailings (for details, check out the BookSense.com web site).

Newmarket Press offered to send booksellers, librarians, and teachers a review copy of *Lynda Madaras Talks to Teens about AIDS* if they sent their request on their letterhead plus included $1.00 for shipping (a small charge to make sure the requesters were seriously interested).

M. Evans offered booksellers a chance to see galley copies of their new book, *The I-Like-My-Beer Diet*. With the galley copies, they offered a free case of beer to any bookseller willing to try out the diet.

Knopf credited the rise of Dean Koontz's *Intensity* to the bestseller list to the word of mouth generated by the multiple copies of reader's editions that they had sent out to bookstores.

Ballantine created a First Look program to bring attention to books that could benefit from handselling. Several weeks before the books reach the stores, Ballantine sends finished books to the homes of booksellers.

Zondervan created the Premiere Readers Fiction Club for bookstore managers, fiction buyers, and other retail staff (aka *frontliners*). These people were sent new fiction releases, previews of upcoming titles, and a bimonthly newsletter about the growing Christian fiction market.

☐ **If you have a potential bestseller, send advance copies not only to booksellers but also to their best customers.** That's what William Morrow did with *Morning's Gate* by Ann Roberts. When they sent out 5,000 galley copies to booksellers, they also enclosed a letter asking them to return a postcard giving the name and address of a favorite customer who would also be sent a copy of the book. 600 booksellers responded to this offer. Not only did this program excite the readers who received free books, but it also pleased the booksellers who were able to do something nice for some of their best customers.

To promote the romance novel *A Night in Eden* by Carolyn Nichols, Random House sent hundreds of galleys to booksellers along with a letter, comment form, and postcard. They also sent 10,000 copies of the first three chapters to romance readers. Later they sent those same readers an announcement when the book actually arrived in the stores.

☐ **Conduct market research.** In researching the market for their *Country Inns of New England*, Globe Pequot visited inns to find out who stayed at the inns. They discovered that the largest number of visitors to New England inns were coming from California. Armed with this data, they approached Waldenbooks and convinced them to test the guidebooks in their California stores. When the books sold out, Waldenbooks bought more. Now the California stores are steady customers for the book.

Zondervan sponsored a Cahners Research survey where it was shown that 88% of the people who shop at general bookstores are Christians. The survey also showed that 42% of all general bookstore shoppers have purchased a Bible or religious title during the past year.

Ask bookstores for feedback on your titles. While many publishers now turn to chain store buyers for feedback on their titles, covers, and marketing plans, you can and should do the same with major independents.

☐ **Sponsor in-store contests.** Bookstores like contests that draw browsers and opportunity seekers into their stores, but they don't want to get in the middle. That means: Don't expect them to track contests, pick winners, or send results to the publisher. Keep contests simple and have all responses sent back to you.

To encourage bookstore personnel to read David Sandison's *Once Upon a Christmas*, Barron's held a contest to name the rock stars hidden in the book's artwork. The contest was only open to bookstore personnel. The winner received $1,000 worth of stereo equipment.

Times Books sponsored a "Win a Great Meal" contest to publicize *Mariani's Coast-to-Coast Dining Guide*. Winners, chosen in a random drawing, were given dinners for two at selected restaurants featured in the book. Several winners were chosen in each of fifty major cities. Free dinners for two were also given to the bookstores where the winners had picked up their entry blanks for the contest (these free dinners were incentives for the bookseller to promote the contest).

Golden Aura Publishing offered to give five free copies of *The Basketball Player's Bible* to bookstores for use as contest giveaways (for the best essays on the importance of fundamentals in basketball). But their other requirements were pretty strict. Bookstores had to agree to put two copies of the title in a window display, send a letter suggesting a news story to the local sports editor, and provide copies of the winning essays as well as photographs of the winners.

☐ **Offer consumer rebates.** Macmillan Computer Publishing offered a $10.00 consumer rebate on all titles published by its divisions, including Sams Publishing, sams.net, and Que. Bookstores were encouraged to call their sales rep at a toll-free number for more details on the program.

☐ **Advertise in a holiday bookstore catalog.** Ingram and Baker & Taylor as well as several bookseller associations produce retail holiday catalogs that bookstores give away free to customers and also insert into newspapers or magazines. If you are publishing a title that you think will sell well during the holiday season, such an ad would spur consumer interest as well as spark sales to bookstores (since they have to stock books in the catalog). Note that the closing dates for ads in these catalogs are usually late June, so plan ahead.

Over 800 stores and 55 publishers participated in the 1985 ABA *Time* magazine insert which promoted buying books for gifts. 90% of those bookstores participating in the insert were satisfied with the results. The 1986 insert, which cost publishers almost $7,000 to participate (with a photo and short description of one book), ran not only in *Time* but also in the *New York Times* and *New Yorker* magazine.

In 1986, five regional bookseller associations sponsored holiday catalogs. The New England Booksellers Association's catalog was sent to

2,000,000 people through inserts in twenty major Sunday papers. Publishers were charged $2,000 for a listing in the catalog. The combined catalog of the Mountains and Plains Booksellers Association and the Intermountain Booksellers Association was inserted in seven Sunday papers with a combined circulation of 1,200,000. Listings cost $950.

Instead of being inserted in newspapers, the 1986 holiday catalog for the Upper Midwest Booksellers Association was mailed to 300,000 customers on the combined mailing lists of member stores, plus 65,000 copies were inserted in the December issue of *Minnesota Monthly* magazine. Publishers paid $850 per book for a listing.

☐ **Do something special.** Show your key accounts that you appreciate their business. When William Morrow published Paul Prudhomme's *Louisiana Kitchen*, they invited key wholesalers and booksellers to New York to sample a dinner cooked by Prudhomme.

To promote John Lanchester's first novel, *The Debt to Pleasure*, Henry Holt pulled out all the stops. In each city that the author appeared as part of his book tour, they invited the top independent booksellers out to dinner at the fanciest restaurant in town. Invitations were sent out in a fancy wooden box. The dinner and invitation, according to the buyer for Black Oak Books in Berkeley, California, "told me Holt really planned to do something with this book."

☐ **Get customers into the stores.** Above all, when thinking about supporting bookstores, be sure to focus on getting customers into their stores. The best salespeople for your books, ultimately, are the bookstore's customers. After the third or fourth person walks into a bookstore asking for a book, the booksellers will order that book. Guaranteed.

☐ **Work with the bookstore to sell premiums.** You can make bookstores your partner in selling your book as a premium to local companies, doctor's offices, accounting offices, churches, schools, and so on. I'll discuss this option in greater detail in Chapter 19.

14:14 Point of Purchase Displays

As many as 50% of all bookstore customers have no specific purchase in mind when they first enter a store. Because such a large percentage of readers come to browse and window shop, you should do everything you can to encourage impulse sales of your books.

Many booksellers will tell you not to send them displays, posters, bookmarks, and the like because these things will go into their trash can. Besides, they'll tell you, consumers rarely notice. Yet most of the major publishers continue to send them, and they wouldn't do that if these things didn't work (well, okay, some of them would). Furthermore, you only have to walk the aisles of BookExpo America for a little while to see how much booksellers go after such free items. Their bags are full of posters, book-marks, buttons, and other gimmicks (and only a few catalogs).

In a 1996 survey of children's bookstores, booksellers reported using 50.5% of the promotional materials sent to them. Still, 64.4% of those book-sellers reported that the availability of such promotional material had no impact on whether or not they bought the books.

There are any number of point-of-purchase (POP) sales aids which you can provide bookstores to help them sell your books. Of these, here are the most popular promotional items as reported by children's booksellers: 44.1% used posters, 31.9% bookmarks, 5.4% floor displays, 5% pins and buttons, 5% postcards, 4.5% mobiles, 4.1% balloons, and 3.2% counter displays. The following pages describe these promotional materials as well as many others used by general bookstores.

Bookmarks

Supply bookstores with attractive bookmarks featuring your lead titles. Since many readers collect bookmarks, such giveaways help to attract buyers into stores while also bringing attention to your books. Booksellers give away more bookmarks than any other in-store promotional item.

What should you put on a bookmark? How about the cover of the book? Or a photo of the author? Both of these have been used successfully by authors of romance novels (especially covers which feature real hunks). You could also feature an excerpt from your book. For example, the bookmark could feature ten ways to cook potatoes, five things every man should know about women, or ten tax tips that can save you money on this year's taxes.

* To promote Leo Buscaglia's *Bus 9 to Paradise*, Morrow distributed approximately 100 bus-shaped bookmarks to each bookstore.

* AMACOM featured "the top five reasons why you need more than one copy of *Your Intelligent Heart*"on bookmarks.

* To promote *Memory Can Be Murder*, a mystery by Elizabeth Daniels Squire, Berkley created a bookmark that read, "Of all the things I've lost, I miss my mind the most!"

* The Insiders' Guides provided booksellers with up to seventy-five book-marks for each of its *Insiders' Guides*.

> **Authors** — Many romance novelists produce bookmarks which they send to members of their fan clubs or to people who write to them. For instance, Linda Randall offered to send an auto-graphed bookmark to any reader who wrote in care of her home post office box. Any book, whether fiction or nonfiction could benefit from this special attention to potential fans. With laser printed bookmarks, it wouldn't cost much to test it out.

Book Covers as Billboards

The covers of your books should be designed to sell books. Think of your book covers as billboards which must attract the attention of the casual bookstore browser—and then make the sale. If you're not sure if your book cover does the job, contact John Kremer about his Book Cover Critique service. See http://www.bookmarket.com/consulting.html.

Posters

If your cover is well designed, blow it up and provide a copy for bookstores to use in their window displays. You could provide free posters with any order of ten or more books. Posters can be especially helpful in promoting children's books and science fiction books or, for that matter, any other books which are valued for their cover designs or interior illustrations. On the blowups of your book covers, you could print the tag line, "Available Here" across the top or bottom of the poster. Or you could print favorable reviews or testimonials.

As noted on the previous page, bookstores like to receive posters more than any other promotional items. Besides using posters in window or in-store displays, booksellers give them to their teacher customers to use in classrooms or post them in the back room where their buyers, shelvers, and sales people see them every day.

- To promote religious books in general, Abingdon Press sent out a poster that read, "Books about religion are also about love, sex, politics ... history, death and LIFE!" Many bookstores featured this poster at the entrance to their religion section because it was, as one bookseller noted, "a great way to reassure people that it's okay to browse" in that section.

- Arbor House, Delacorte, Harper & Row, and Random House, among others, all provide big blowups of book covers if a bookstore is sponsoring an autograph party. Bantam also supplies such blowups for bookstores to use in creating window displays.

- Natalie Windsor, author of *1,000,001 Things That Make You Crabby*, polled dozens of booksellers at BookExpo America to find out what made them crazy. Then Corkscrew Press, her publisher, took the results and produced a poster which they sent to any bookstore which ordered 10 or more copies of the book. Besides attracting the attention of booksellers, the poster also was featured in *Publishers Weekly* and *American Bookseller*. What was the top bookseller complaint? Running out of copies of *1,000,001 Things* (okay, the publisher padded the ballots).

- White Pine Press provided bookstores with a letterpress poster featuring their A World of Voices theme. The finely crafted poster was appropriate for bookstores attempting to create an air of sophistication.

- To promote the 10th anniversary of the Arthur series of children's books, Atlantic Monthly gave away "Happy Birthday, Arthur" posters.

Shelf-Talkers

Shelf-talkers are promotional cards, tags, or labels which help to draw attention to books on the shelf. According to research conducted by Zondervan, booksellers said that "the number one thing they want in a shelf-talker is flexibility," so it could be placed conveniently on the shelf.

- Crown used tent cards to promote a number of its cookbooks as lifestyle books. They found that when cookbooks are promoted in this way, they sell far faster than they would if shelved along with other cookbooks.

- To promote *The New Doubleday Cookbook*, Doubleday provided a shelf talker with a pad of tear-off recipe cards which had a cookbook comparison chart on the back side. Guess whose cookbook came out on top?

- Avon provides booksellers with folding cards which announce that a book is by a local author.

- For a new edition of *Streams in the Desert*, Zondervan published a booklet containing a week's worth of devotions from the book. They then created a merchandising kit to allow booksellers to display the free booklets on a poster, an end cap, a shelf-talker, or a counter top display.

- Rand McNally made a fold-out shelf-talker available to promote their *Fold-Out Rainforest* books.

- To draw attention to Jim Jinkins's *Doug* books, Disney Press created a shelf-talker where Doug is seen high-fiving his dog (who is on a spring and high-fives him back). This moving shelf-talker attracted attention. In addition, Disney sent booksellers a "Do You Dig Doug?" button to wear in the store and at the checkout counter.

- Besides shelf-talkers, Scholastic provided counter displays, endcap signs, ad slicks, and reading circle kits for *Dear America: A Picture of Freedom* by Patricia McKissack.

Bag Stuffers

Some bookstores are open to stuffing bookmarks or other items into each order that goes out their doors. Why? Because they know that these bag stuffers sell books.

- Orca Book Publishers encouraged stores to stuff bags with recipe samplers from Nadja Piatka's *Outrageously Delicious* cookbook.

- For *The New Doubleday Cookbook*, Doubleday provided recipe cards in loose packs so booksellers could place the cards into the bags of any book buyer who purchased a related title.

Book Bags

You can help bookstores save money by providing them with shopping bags advertising your books (and, if practical, imprinted with the store name). One advantage of imprinted bags is that they expose your advertising not only to the book buyer but also to the general public.

Note: If you produce bags to give away at BookExpo America, you might want to print more bags to give to stores (or sell to them at a low price) to promote a book, a series, or your company as a whole. Avon provided imprinted shopping bags to promote Gail Godwin's *The Finishing School*. Dell did the same for Richard Adams's *Maia*.

Postcards

While the favorite bookstore giveaways are bookmarks and posters, booksellers also like the more practical giveaway, the postcard. Such cards, if featuring a beautiful scene from a travel guide or a colorful illustration from an art book or children's book, can be effective in promoting titles since not only does the bookseller and customer see your subtle advertisement, but so does the recipient of the postcard.

- The Insiders' Guides provided postcards featuring scenes from *The Insiders' Guide to Cape Cod*, *The Insiders' Guide to Golf in the Carolinas*, and other books in the series.

- HarperCollins provided both posters and postcards for several of its children's titles, including *Detective Donut and the Wild Goose Chase* by Bruce Whatley and *Chasing Redbird* by Sharon Creech.

Door Hangers

To promote *Merry Christmas, Amelia Bedelia* by Peggy Parish, Greenwillow Books gave away door hangers that announced, "Do not disturb—I'm reading." A great promotion to give to children. Not only did it attract them to the book being advertised, but it also reinforced that reading books is a special activity.

Buttons

Send bookstores buttons advertising your titles. Such buttons are always one of the most popular giveaways at ABA conventions. The bookstores can give these buttons to their employees to wear while working, or they can give the buttons away to customers. Children's booksellers love to use buttons during author appearances, in-store parties, and school visits, but buttons also work for adult titles. NAL, for example, used buttons to help promote the mass-market edition of *Smart Women, Foolish Choices*.

T-Shirts

Provide imprinted T-shirts for each employee of your major bookstore accounts. Encourage them to wear the shirts on (and off) the job. In a recent survey of children's booksellers, many reported that T-shirts for staffers are a great way to publicize a book.

- Whenever you provide imprinted items to bookstores, be sure that the imprint has some connection to the book you are promoting. To promote its book *Boomerang*, Workman handed out T-shirts that read "I Am the Thrower" on the front and "I Am the Catcher" on the back.

- 4,000 stores participated in The American Girls Collection's "Proud to Be an American Girl" T-shirt promotion, where stores sold T-shirts for $6.95 to customers who purchased an American Girls book. As one bookseller noted, "These were good quality shirts, and we got a terrific response to them. In fact, we sold out in very little time."

To locate provides of imprinted items, check out the supplies listed at http://www.bookmarket.com/imprint.html.

Coupon Pads

Along with free posters for display in bookstores, you could provide a coupon pad that would allow consumers to order a free copy of the poster with the purchase of your books. Such offers would be especially suited to books which are valued for their cover designs or interior illustrations.

Window Streamers and Banners

Since most bookstores have only a limited amount of space to devote to window streamers, don't use them for any but your major books which you will be advertising and promoting extensively.

- NAL sent stores window streamers to help promote *Smart Women, Foolish Choices* as well as Robin Cook's *Mindbend*.

- To celebrate the 50th anniversary of *Goodnight Moon*, HarperCollins sent booksellers festive banners to use inside their stores.

- To promote *The 20th Century Art Book*, Phaidon Press provided stores with full-color banners printed on cloth.

Mobile Displays

Mobile displays and hanging signs can be used by bookstores to hang over a table of related books or to hang from the ceiling over a subject section in the store. These mobiles have several advantages. First, they attract attention. Second, they take up no selling space. Third, they're festive and add a lively air to bookstores.

- Tyndale House not only supplied shelf talkers and full-color posters to promote their *Campus Life* series; they also provided a full-color mobile.

- For their *You & Your Pet* backlist promotion, Random House created a bright mobile featuring a tabby cat, a Dalmatian, a Palomino horse, and a neon yellow and blue tropical fish. The header said, "You & Your Pet," so it was perfect for hanging over the pet book section.

  In previous years, Random had produced other mobiles and hanging signs featuring Audubon, Fodor's travel books, *Your Baby & Child*, the *Vintage Crime Gun*, and the Dictionary sign. Random's experience has been that many bookstores use these hanging shelf talkers.

- To draw attention to its 1992 $10,000 college scholarship sweepstakes, Merriam-Webster provided an inflatable Merriam-Webster character to hang over their dictionaries and the pad of entry forms. More than 2,500 bookstores participated in the sweepstakes.

- To celebrate Clifford's 25th birthday and to promote *Clifford's Birthday Party* by Norman Bridwell, Scholastic provided a two-color mobile, posters, and red and white birthday balloons.

Floor Displays

Any time you can get booksellers to give you exclusive space for your books, the better chance you have of attracting the attention of browsers and impulse buyers. Floor dumps or risers are an effective way to convince booksellers to give you that space. Note, however, that booksellers are not likely to give up such space except for titles expected to be bestsellers. Indeed, because such displays may look tacky or cluttered, many bookstores won't use floor displays. You might want to check with your local booksellers before you commit money to producing such displays for your books.

- To promote John G. Jones novel, *The Supernatural*, Tudor provided retailers with a full-color, motorized, traffic-stopping display. The motor turned the header card to reveal three different posters.

- Delacorte designed a pagoda-type floor display to promote Robert Duncan's novel, *China Dawn*. The bottom consisted of a corrugated cardboard base imprinted to look like wicker. The base could hold ten copies of the book. The display was topped off with a large red umbrella imprinted in bright gold lettering with the novel's title.

- When Harper designed the Harper Growing Tree floor display to feature a dozen of its titles, their California sales rep, Nancy Kellogg, was able to place the display in almost all of her accounts. As she pointed out, "Booksellers will make room for something of value."

- Hyperion shipped more than 3,000 floor displays to promote *McDuff Moves In* and *McDuff Comes Home*. Each display held ten books as well as ten plush McDuff dogs. The display headline, "Take Me Home," worked to get people's attention. By the time publication date rolled around, Hyperion had already sold out of the 50,000 first printing.

- Workman designed a hardworking display, the Workman Clock Tower, that made it possible for retailers to display such disparate titles as the *Brain Quest* series and *The Muppets Make Puppets*.

- To encourage sales in outlets other than bookstores, Random House created a large rotating metal display headlined, *Reading House from Random House*. This store-within-a-store with modular components provided stores with lots of flexibility in displaying Random's titles.

- Harlequin offers retail accounts pocket displays, rotating booktiques, and two-tower Romance Centers for displaying their large line of romance novels. Indeed, they pride themselves on their ability to provide a display for every shape and size to fit a bookstore's sales areas.

- If you can combine copies of previous titles from the same author in the display with his or her newest bestseller, you'll have a good chance of increasing sales of those backlist titles.

- To test a display, you can order samples from many display providers. For a list of providers, see http://www.bookmarket.com/14.html#displays.

Counter Displays

Booksellers prefer counter displays over floor displays because they offer more options for in-store placement. For publishers, counter displays have one great advantage over almost any other display: They can be placed right next to the checkout counter to encourage last minute impulse sales. Such displays work best for inexpensive humor and novelty books.

- Klutz Books was able to get prominent display of its instruction books on how to juggle and how to use hacky sacks by providing stores with ready-to-use counter packs of ten books each. Klutz also provides stores with spinner racks that can hold up to thirty titles in multiple copies.

- Philomel's counter display for Eric Carle's children's book, *Have You Seen My Cat?*, included a riser and a mobile to draw attention to it.

- As part of its *Bear Necessities* program, Candlewick provided bookstores with a permanent acrylic display that featured Candlewick's bear logo and a header saying, "Staff Picks." Booksellers were offered a wide range of titles at generous terms.

- In another promotion for their series of Lucy Cousins books, Candlewick offered retailers a pair of bookends featuring the author's Maisy character if they bought a minimum of fifty copies of at least twelve titles.

- To promote its travel guides, Moon offers bookstores a counter display that holds free copies of their newsletter, *Travel Matters*.

Window Displays

By encouraging booksellers to display your books more creatively, you will help them increase their sales at the same time you increase the sales of your titles. For your main titles, you can provide special display materials to any bookseller ordering ten or more copies. Encourage them to use these materials to create a window display.

- Addison-Wesley supplied booksellers with a watering can and other gardening paraphernalia to promote the sale of their book, *Gardening*.

- Wilshire Books provided booksellers with copies of the sheet music from Tommy Boyce's most famous songs ("Last Train to Clarksville," "Come a Little Bit Closer," "I Wanna Be Free," and "Valerie") to accompany displays of his book *How to Write a Hit Song and Sell It*.

- To draw attention to his book about two famous dogs, *Bummer and Lazarus*, Malcolm Barker of Londonborn Publications had a designer prepare a display for his exhibit at BEA. Because these two dogs were said to be so close that their "tails wagged as one," the display showed two dogs with their tails wagging in unison. After the convention, Malcolm offered the display to a local bookseller who put it in his window. Not only did the display help the bookseller sell ten copies of the book every week, but it also drew people into the store. The bookseller loved the display so much that he refused to give it up.

• Friendly Press offered touring window display materials for two of its titles. They provided an expensive antique kimono to use in designing window displays for *Once Upon a Time: Visions of Old Japan* and blowups of filmstrips to promote *The Most Beautiful Place in the World*. Friendly Press coordinated the tour. Each bookstore was expected to ship the display materials on to the next bookstore on the list after their week or two was up.

Window Display Contests

To encourage booksellers to use the materials you provide or to develop their own displays for your books, offer a prize for the bookseller who puts together the best display.

• To promote *The Mollen Method* exercise book, Rodale Press offered a free four-day Caribbean cruise to the bookseller who put together the best display for the book. Rodale supplied a fitness display kit including a gym bag, T-shirt, ankle weights, sweatband, jump rope, and poster to be used in putting the display together.

• For a display contest for *Nuts!*, their bestseller about Southwest Airlines, Bard Press offered five lucky bookstores two round-trip tickets to any Southwest destination. In addition, every entry received a $25 discount coupon off any Southwest round-trip full fare ticket. Winning entries could be window displays, floor displays, or front-of-store displays.

• Paris seems to be the most popular destination for display contest winners. Pantheon Books offered a two week vacation in Paris for the bookseller who came up with the best display for its *Hachette Guide to France*. Whole Earth Provision of Austin, Texas, won by setting up a temporary outdoor cafe offering French food and music.

• Another popular destination is Hawaii. Summit Publishing Group offered a free trip for two for the bookseller who designed the best display for Jim Miller's *Best Boss/Worst Boss*.

• Trips are not the only prizes you can offer. Some publishers have offered cash prizes, free books, even handmade quilts. Papier-Mâché Press offered thirteen prizes, including cash awards and a handmade quilt, to those stores who created the best in-store displays for their two titles, *When I Am an Old Woman, I Shall Wear Purple* and *If I Had My Life to Live Over, I Would Pick More Daisies*.

- At the suggestion of their sales reps, Little, Brown offered bookstores a window display allowance over and above their normal co-op allowance.

Other Displays

- As part of its promotion for the 40th anniversary of Dr. Seuss's *The Cat in the Hat*, Random House sent bookstores a six-and-a-half foot cutout of the Cat, which held coupons redeemable for a birthday party kit (with proof of purchase of a Dr. Seuss book).

- To promote its titles about ballet, Putnam produced a party kit, a child-sized tutu for display, yards of pink tulle, and a cardboard cutout of a life-sized young ballerina. They received so much feedback for the promotion that they repeated it the next year, sending out 600 packages.

- To increase their chances of getting face-out display in the chain stores, some publishers have begun suggesting thematic arrangements of books (including their own) that would fit on the endcaps of the shelves, one of the most visible selling spaces in these stores. To propose such displays, contact the merchandising department at chain headquarters.

- Little, Brown offers co-op advertising dollars to bookstores in trade for front-of-store placement. They have found that this is one of the best uses for co-op dollars because it gets them the best placement in stores.

- Zondervan formed a partnership with Family Christian Stores to set aside a dedicated space in the New Arrivals section for upcoming titles published by Zondervan. A reservation pad attached to the signs above the area allowed customers to order advance copies of new titles.

Boutiques

Some publishers offer special discounts, free freight, custom displays, or other incentives for bookstores to set aside separate display areas for their book lines. If you publish a recognizable and desirable line of books, this strategy could work for your books as well.

As part of its 50th anniversary celebration, Penguin offered booksellers a 47% discount on any order of ten or more books if they would establish a permanent boutique consisting of a wall section or floor fixture given over solely to Penguin titles. They also offered a 50% discount on all orders of ten or more books to any bookseller joining their 2500 Club, which required the bookseller to commit to stocking all 2,500 Penguin titles and to buying at least three copies of each new Penguin title.

In-Store Video Ads

If you have a recognizable or livewire author who comes over well on video, you could produce a DVD that could be used to promote the author's book in retail stores. Fleming H. Revell provided bookstores with videotapes of Zig Ziglar in action to promote his book, *Top Performance*. Note that only stores with a DVD player will be able to use such a promotion.

Special Handouts

For indie publishers, the best point-of-purchase display you could provide bookstores would be excerpts from your books—a printed item that would draw the attention of browsers, something they would pick up and read, something they could take home with them. Or, if you can't afford to print that many handouts (about 50 to 100 per store), prepare an excerpt or promotion that would draw the attention of booksellers.

• To promote Gloria Steinem's *Revolution from Within*, Little, Brown reprinted Bibliotherapy, a chapter that described the books Steinem found helpful in writing her book and in living her life. They sent 50,000 copies of this pamphlet to 1,000 of their major bookstore accounts who, in turn, passed them out to their customers.

• How about printing a recommended reading list for an area that you specialize in—and feature not only your books but also those of other publishers (books that don't compete with yours)? You can use the one of the lists you've created for Amazon.com's Listmania or for a Squidoo.com lense.

• To promote *Earth Right*, Prima mailed a flyer listing 10 ways a bookseller could help to save the earth. These tips included using paper rather than plastic shopping bags, recycling shipping boxes, and offering a small discount to customers with a proof of mass transit ridership.

• To promote their book on *Marketing Without a Marketing Budget*, Bob Adams produced a four-page flyer called *Marketing Without a Marketing Budget (for Booksellers)*. Besides listing 15 ways for booksellers to promote books inexpensively, the flyer also featured eight frontlist and backlist books from Bob Adams.

• To encourage bookstores to stock more business books, Dearborn Trade published a short brochure titled, *Business Books Mean More Business*. Among the tips they offered were the following (of course, they also made a pitch for their business books).

1) Tap into local professional associations. You may even be able to work out an arrangement to sell books at local meetings.

2) Set up a customer sign-up book, or offer a weekly drawing with a bowl next to the checkout counter to collect business cards.

3) Sell books directly to companies in your area. While each firm has different needs and buying structures, a simple mailing could net multiple-copy orders.

4) Get to know local authors. Often they speak to the audiences that you're beginning to serve.

• For *Dr. Nancy Snyderman's Guide to Good Health (For Women Over Forty)*, Harvest Books provided bookstores with a point-of-purchase brochure, *Health Tips for Women over Forty*.

> **Authors** — Don't wait for your local booksellers to come and find you. Go out and introduce yourself. Offer to assist them in selling your book as well as books from other authors. Autograph the copies of your books that are in the store already. In addition, you could offer to do a special event in their store: a reading, a signing, a demonstration, or whatever. You could also get a free lunch by offering to participate in a Take an Author to Lunch promotion sponsored by the store. Look, especially, for ways to help them bring more customers in.

14:15 How to Book Author Signings and Readings

One thing bookstores seem to agree on is that author events sell books. While author readings are effective for poetry and fiction, workshops and seminars seem to work best for nonfiction books. For an author to be considered for bookstore appearances, Leona Weiss, owner of A Clean Well-Lighted Place for Books, has said that "The author must be a powerful draw or have a strong local presence."

For smaller publishers, the best option is a passive author tour. That happens when a publisher schedules signings or readings when the author will be in a specific city for other business (so the publisher doesn't have to pay the air fare or lodging expenses). Otherwise, full-fledged author tours can cost $1,000 or more a day.

Don't expect a big turnout for any author event unless you work with the bookseller to publicize and promote the event. And don't judge an author appearance just on the number of books sold. Such events can have many intangible benefits for a publisher, from increased recognition for the author to better relations with booksellers. Here are a few notes on how to set up and carry out successful author appearances at bookstores:

☐ **Start locally.** It's more convenient and less expensive to work with local bookstores first to develop the author event that will work best for your book and the capabilities of your author.

☐ **Find the best stores.** To locate those stores which do the best job of promoting author events, check out the event calendars of the Friday or Sunday issues of the local newspapers. Those bookstores which regularly promote author events are featured in almost every issue.

☐ **Work with the chains.** For the bookstore chains, you can schedule appearances through the local events coordinator or through the district manager. When Papier Mache Press worked with the chains to book author tours, they coordinated with the specific subject buyer when working with Waldenbooks and with local and district managers when working with B. Dalton and Barnes & Noble.

☐ **Give stores eight weeks lead time.** To do a good job with publicity and in-store promotion, most stores need a two to three month lead time.

☐ **Contact by telephone.** Make initial contacts by telephone. Then follow up with written confirmation. Be ready to make your sales pitch right away. Make it short and make it strong.

☐ **Try to arrange for signings later in the month.** Raleigh Pinsky, author of *101 Ways to Promote Yourself*, found that signings in the last two weeks of the month tend to draw better. Why? Because bookstores put out their event calendars at the beginning of the month, and you have more chance for people to see your event and plan to attend.

☐ **Get publicity.** Work with event coordinators to generate publicity for your appearance. The stores should have media contacts that they work with regularly. John F. Blair won't schedule an author event unless they can also book a TV or radio appearance. As they noted, "We tend to have pretty successful autographing sessions because of this."

☐ **Make sure the store orders books.** They should have enough copies to fill orders during the author's appearance. Try to get them to order 20 to 40 copies and display them near the cash register for the week before. This exposure alone can be worth the time and expense of the event.

☐ **Coach your authors.** Work with your authors to prepare an event that will draw in bookstore browsers and get them excited about buying the book. Prepare the author to give a talk as well as read from the book.

☐ **Bring a prop.** Work with your authors to prepare something they can bring along to draw attention to themselves. At least bring a poster of the book's cover. Lisa Ferguson, author of *Raising Kids with Just a Little Cash*, not only brought a One-Pan, No-Bowl Banana Cake (recipe from her book), but also gave away stick frisbees (which the book describes how to make). Both were popular with her audiences.

☐ **Talk to the booksellers.** When authors appear at a bookstore, encourage them to get to know the people working there. Have them ask the booksellers to place their book on the staff recommendations shelf. That's what Jeannette Belliveau, author of *An Amateur's Guide to the Planet*, does wherever she speaks.

> **Authors** — If you'd be willing to do bookstore events for your book, let your publisher know. Also, don't be afraid to contact local bookstores to arrange such readings. Just be sure to coordinate such contacts with your publisher.

14:16 Author Events: Make Them Interesting!

Don't settle for signings only. Except for major celebrities, they rarely pay off. Instead, make your author appearances into events. Read from your book. Do a demonstration. Make a party of it. Mary Alice Gorman, owner of Mystery Lovers Bookshop, actually sells tickets to author events at her store. The tickets, she explains, sets a value to the event and allows her to use many author appearances to tie into community events via fundraising. Below are a few of the ways to make your author events more interesting.

Author Readings

- Black Oak Books sponsors four to ten in-store events each month. While some of these events include autograph sessions, photography exhibits, and charitable benefits, their most popular events are author readings. They feature fiction authors such as Ursula LeGuin, Elmore Leonard, and E. L. Doctorow, as well as nonfiction authors in psychology, philosophy of science, and mathematics. From 35 to as many as 500 people attend these readings.

- Milkweed Editions has set up seven partner stores with active reading programs. Twice each year, they send authors on tour to seven cities where these stores are located.

- Patti Gross, author of the *Adventures in the Roo World* series, goes to a Barnes & Noble store in her area at least once a month to read from her book and to teach children about safety.

Authors: You, too, can set up your own readings. John Thorndike, author of *Another Way Home*, set up a four-month auto tour across the country, making appearances in fifty-three stores along the way. As he traveled, he visited many other stores and arranged radio and newspaper interviews. He knew that since he wasn't John Grisham or John Updike, he'd have to do his own promotion if his book was going to have a chance to sell.

Author Signings

While author signings pay off biggest with celebrities, sometimes that is all the commitment you can get from a bookseller. If that is the case, take the opportunity to make inroads with the bookstore. You have to start somewhere and, if they won't allow you to do a reading or demonstration, then do the signing. Here are a few success stories:

- When Villard published *Two Guys, Four Corners* by Don Imus and his brother Fred, Imus gave the book a big plug on his national radio show.

During his two-week, nine-store author tour, he signed at least 750 copies per store. At one store, he signed more than 3,200 copies, of which at least 800 were phone orders.

- Richard Evans, self-publisher of *The Christmas Box*, signed more than a thousand copies at each store he appeared at during the holiday season.

- When Ann Martin, author of the *Baby-Sitters Club* series, appears at a bookstore, about 500 girls show up at each signing.

- When humorist Jeff Foxworthy went on tour to promote *No Shirt. No Shoes. No Problem.*, he signed 600 books per location. It took him about four hours to sign that many books.

- When The Andover Bookstore hosted a signing of Jay Leno's *Leading with My Chin*, they sold more than 800 copies of the book.

- When General Colin Powell went out on tour for *My American Journey*, he autographed more than 53,000 copies.

Author Workshops and Demonstrations

Besides author signings and readings, you could also arrange special demonstrations linked to your books. Demonstrations might include a cooking class for a cookbook or gardening tips for a gardening book. Similar demonstrations could be arranged for craft books, how-to books, and even travel guides (with tips for travelers about how to pack).

- For a cookbook featuring Virginia seafood recipes, GB Publishing arranged for a chef to give cooking demonstrations at local bookstores. As part of the demonstration, they also gave away seafood samples.

- Helen Rathbone of Powell's Books for Cooks has said that in-store demonstrations are one of the best ways that they have found to promote a book. As she points out, not only do such demonstrations give people a chance to sample recipes from the book, but they also make the bookstore staff more familiar with the book.

- The Children's Bookstore in Chicago has sponsored such diverse in-store events as book talks for parent groups, small pet show-and-tells, dance workshops, writing contests, child development workshops for parents, bilingual story hours as well as performances by storytellers, musicians, clowns, puppeteers, theatre groups, magicians, and dancers. Do you have any books or authors that would be suitable for such performances?

- When Elisha Cooper, author and illustrator of *A Year in New York*, autographed copies of his book at a SoHo gift store, he sketched the customers as well. As a result, the store sold over 1,000 copies of his book.

- Harlequin worked with Chapters to create a Passport to Romance event. As customers entered stores, they received a passport that, as they moved through the aisles, were stamped by famous romantic look-alikes such as Antony and Cleopatra. Once the passport was filled, the customers received a free book signed by the authors. Customers also received a coupon good towards purchase of additional Harlequin romances.

- Bard Press worked with Southwest Airlines to host parties for *Nuts!* at bookstores in the forty-eight cities where Southwest flies. Southwest volunteers gave away peanuts, tattoos, T-shirts, and other prizes. Each person who bought a copy of *Nuts!* received a $25 coupon good toward any Southwest flight. Two round-trip tickets on Southwest were also raffled off at the end of each party.

- When Laura Rosetree, author of *I Can Read Your Face*, returned to Greetings and Readings bookstore to sign books, she offered to read people's noses as she signed books. During her first visit, when she only signed books, the store sold seven copies of her book. During her second visit, when she offered free Nosographs, the store sold forty-two books.

Authors — If you have an idea for an in-store demonstration, let your publisher know what you can do and when and where you would be available. If you work up a demonstration, make it lively, visual, and educational.

Party Kits

When you can't afford to send your authors out on tour, send party or event kits instead. The items you include in the kit depend on the books you are promoting. For these kits, listen to an experienced bookseller: "Don't include activities that are too complicated, time-consuming, or call for additional materials we have to purchase." Make sure the events aren't messy. Below are a few of the party kits that have been sent out by publishers.

- When Thomas Pynchon, noted for his reclusivity, wouldn't tour for his *Mason & Dixon* novel, Holt provided support to any bookstore that wanted to host a Pynchon event. The Booksmith in San Francisco hosted an open mike night with attendees dressed as various characters from Pynchon novels. The KBG literary bar in Manhattan hosted a Pynchon imitation contest. Shaman Drum Bookshop in Ann Arbor held a party and raffle for a first edition cover of the book.

- Pfeifer-Hamilton sent out birthday party kits to celebrate the fifth year of *Old Turtle* by Doug Wood. The kits included party ideas, invitations, an *Old Turtle* audio tape, stickers, coloring sheets, and more.

- In promoting *The Berenstain Bear Scouts and the Sinister Smoke Ring* by Stan and Jan Berenstain, Scholastic worked with the American Lung Association to create a Berenstain Bear Scouts Smoke Ring Kit to educate children about the dangers of smoking.

- For their *Kids' Paper Airplane Book*, Workman sent out Flight School Event Kits, which included T-shirts, coloring pages, balloons, and more.

- For Winnie-the-Pooh's 70th birthday, Dutton published *The Complete Tales of Winnie-the-Pooh*. They created birthday party kits featuring tattoos, stickers, balloons, posters, hats, Pooh door signs, and reproducible activities. This kit, according to Penguin, was "the most successful promotional item we've produced in recent seasons."

- To promote its *Star Trek* books, Pocket Books worked with Paul Tunney of Brookline Booksmith to produce a *Star Trek* party kit. Tumey wrote a report on *How to Host a Star Trek Party in 8 Easy Steps*, which included recipes for Cardassian popcorn and Klingon warnog as well as tips on planning a party, lining up media interest, and working with local *Star Trek* fan groups. The party kit also included bookmarks, posters, trivia contests, signs, and activity suggestions.

- Scholastic created 100,000 copies of its party kits for the *Goosebumps* series. Most publishers create anywhere from 300 to 3,000 kits. If you've never used a party kit, you can test one by making a prototype and allowing a local bookstore to use it.

- Here are a few other items publishers have included in party kits: name tags, banners, CDs, DVDs, craft materials, coupons, display ideas, contest ideas, games, and costumes.

Costumes

If a book has a strong lead character, send a costume of the character to the stores for them to use in creating special events.

- To celebrate *The World of Beatrix Potter* (and their backlist of Beatrix Potter titles), Viking Penguin and Frederick Warne provided stores with a kit containing posters, streamers, bookmarks, balloons, buttons, and more. Plus, they made available costumes of many of the characters.

- Scholastic has 36 costumes of Clifford the Big Red Dog, which they keep circulating among bookstores. Clifford, the costume, makes about 800 bookstore appearances each year. While the publisher pays to ship the costume, the store is generally responsible for cleaning the costume and returning it to the publisher or sending it on to another store.

- With the success of a Lilly cutout (from *Lilly's Purple Plastic Purse* by Kevin Henke), bookseller's demands for visits from Lilly herself caused Greenwillow to create three mouse costumes which were immediately booked up for a year in advance once word got out to booksellers.

Group Events

Besides organizing individual author tours and events, you can also sponsor group author events, from autograph sessions to readings to demonstrations to special weeks.

- Colorado Governor Roy Romer proclaimed Colorado Authors' Week. 150 authors participated in the week's events, including a reception at the Governor's Mansion.

- The Chesapeake Regional Association of Booksellers sponsored Chesapeake Regional Authors Week. Member stores presented book signings, readings, children's events, and more.

> **Authors** — If you hear about any such upcoming weeks, especially local ones, let your publisher know about them as soon as possible so they can sponsor your participation *and* ensure that your books are stocked in all stores in the region.

14:17 Author Event Resources

To locate those bookstores which regularly sponsor author readings and signings, contact the following sources:

☐ **Poets & Writers Readings and Workshops**—Literary and poetry publishers should look into these programs in California, New York, and the Midwest. Under these programs, *P&W* matches any fees paid to authors who do readings or workshops. They fund about 350 events each year. For details on this program, contact **Poets & Writers**, 72 Spring Street, New York, NY 10012-4019; 212-226-3586; Fax: 212-226-3963.

☐ **Authors on Campus**—The National Association of College Stores publishes the *Directory of College Stores Interested in Hosting Authors for Campus Appearances and Book Signings*, which lists 70 stores which have agreed to set up a promotional display and publicize any author event at least ten days beforehand. In addition, these stores agreed to order at least 25 copies of the author's titles. For a copy of the directory, contact the **NACS**, 500 E. Lorain Street, Oberlin, OH 44074-1294; 216-775-7777; Fax: 216-775-1920. Web: http://www.nacs.org.

☐ **Top 700 Independent Bookstores**—Open Horizons maintains a database of the top 780 independent bookstores. Most of these stores regularly sponsor author signings and readings. For more information, check out the BookMarket.com web site: http://www.bookmarket.com.

14:18 Author Events in Other Venues

If you can't book your author into a bookstore, you don't have to give up. There are plenty of other places that will host a book signing or author workshop. Here are just a few other possibilities:

☐ **Grocery stores**—First and foremost, grocery stores get more foot traffic than bookstores. From anecdotal evidence, most grocery stores that host author appearances favor local authors. During the three weeks after Gregg Olsen, author of *Starvation Heights*, appeared at their store, Mostly Books sold 40 copies of his book. In contrast, Al's Grocery and Meats, which had never carried books before, sold more than 400 copies when it hosted a signing by Olsen.

☐ **Lingerie shops**—Andrew Wilson signed his *Handbook of Lingerie* at the Chelsea of London lingerie shop in Denver, Colorado—a most appropriate fit.

☐ **Art galleries**—Johnnie Walker Black Label sponsored Jennifer Egan, author of *The Invisible Circus*, as she did readings in alternative art galleries, cafes, and bookstores in six major cities.

☐ **Restaurants**—Since the main character of her mystery novel was the daughter of a restaurateur, Jane Rubino, author of *Death of a DJ*, hosted a mystery dinner and reading at a restaurant. Ann Chandonnet, author of *The Alaska Heritage Seafood Cookbook*, signed her books at the Nordstrom Cafe in Anchorage, Alaska.

☐ **Jewelry stores**—Warren Buffett, owner of Berkshire Hathaway as well as the Borsheim's jewelry store, hosted a book signing for Katharine Graham, author of *Personal History*, at Borsheim's.

☐ **Donut shops**—There's an owner of a donut shop in Grand Rapids, Michigan, that loves to host author workshops. She's found that more people come into her donut shop for these events and, as a result, she sells more donuts. The authors, in turn, have found that people who come to their events also buy books.

☐ **Other locations**—Department stores, health food stores, new age centers, travel stops, resorts, bars, cruise ships, garden centers, pet shops, sports stores, theaters, hotels, car dealerships, home stores, and other retail shops (see the next chapter for more ideas!).

> *Just thought I'd share my good news.*
> *I managed to market my newest book, The Thyroid Diet,*
> *for maximum publication release impact.*
> *It spent the month before publication in the Amazon top 100,*
> *and publication week in the top ten, with 2 days at #5,*
> *generating 3 printings in the first week of publication,*
> *and landing me a space on the NY Times Bestseller list!*
> *This just shows the power of author marketing,*
> *as the HarperCollins marketing, radio tour, etc. haven't even started yet!!*
> — Mary Shomon, author

Reaching Independent Bookstores: Exposure Pays

by Ed Avis, publisher of Independent Bookstore newsletter

Independent booksellers can be your best friends! Having your book sold by Barnes & Noble and Borders is nice for sales, but the independents still represent a major market for books, And independent bookstore are often more open to books from small publishers. How do you reach the independents? Here are some strategies we've used at Marion Street Press.

Work with the ABA

The American Booksellers Association, the trade group that all the important independent bookstores belong to, has a number of programs that you can tap to reach their members.

Advance Access: This is a great way to tell stores about your books. Send an email to Peter Reynolds at ABA (peter@booksense.com) set up in this format:

Wrong Word Dictionary by Dave Dowling, (Marion Street Press, Inc., ISBN 0972993770, $14.95, softcover, September 2005, Reference). A handy reference to commonly confused words. Illustrated with 25 cartoons. 50 sample copies available. mailto:edavis@marionstreetpress.com.

Peter assembles all the emails he gets, and a couple of times each month he sends all the offers to ABA members. If they're interested in your book, they send an email directly to you. You send them a sample copy, along with a cover letter and other marketing info. If they like it, hopefully they order copies. The Advance Access program costs $100.

Book Sense: A potential side effect of participating in Advance Access is that your book may get nominated for Book Sense. Book Sense is a monthly list of books that ABA members recommend to other members. ABA prints the list in a handsome flyer each month, and sends hundreds of thousands of these to members so they can distribute them to customers.

We've had the good fortune of four Book Sense picks over the past few years, and each time our sales took a great bump.

Direct Mail

Bookstores get tons of direct mail from publishers. If you want your book to rise about this crowd—and stay out the trash—you need to be innovative.

At Marion Street Press we started a newsletter, *Independent Bookstore*, that we send to bookstores instead of regular direct mail. The newsletter contains how-to articles for booksellers, so they read it. In fact, we frequently get comments from booksellers telling us how much they enjoy it! We never got that when we sent regular direct mail.

We don't use the editorial side of *Independent Bookstore* to promote our books. All the articles are non-biased, helpful articles. We promote our books by running ads for them. When booksellers read the newsletter, they also see our ads. And if they pass the newsletter among staff, more potential buyers see it. We also publish other small publishers' ads in *Independent Bookstore* (see below if you'd like more information).

Another direct mail idea is to work with other publishers in your genre to create one flyer or info packet. For example, you could create a flyer promoting three different travel titles from three publishers. The flyer would be more interesting to the bookseller because it contained a diverse collection of books, and you'd cut your costs by two thirds.

If you opt to send postcards, make them special. Have your author write a quick personal note to the bookseller inviting him or her to order the book. Or use the entire space to feature one amazing blurb. Or send three postcards, each with a different feature of the book mentioned.

The Direct Approach

Sometimes the best way to get your book on bookstores shelves is direct action. This works best for local stores, and there are basically two ways to do this effectively.

First, carry your books to the stores (choose a slow time) and speak to the owner about them. Most stores pay special attention to books from local authors and publishers, and often have shelves devoted to those books.

Second, offer to do a signing or some other event based on your book. These events—such as a workshop or reading—bring customers into the store, so owners are usually happy to accommodate you. Once your book is on the shelf because of a signing or event, the store owner will often keep it in stock, especially if you keep in touch.

These three methods won't necessarily get you a bookstore bestseller, but they will greatly increase your chances that you'll someday see your baby in a bookstore window display.

Ed Avis is the publisher at Marion Street Press, an independent publisher of books about journalism and writing. Marion Street Press also publishes *Independent Bookstore* newsletter. For advertising information, email him at edavis@marionstreetpress.com or call 866-443-7987.

Chapter 15

Selling through Other Retail Outlets

Everyone's doing it, or so it seems—selling children's books.
Walk into a T.J. Maxx, Bed Bath and Beyond, the gas station, the grocery
store, the pet store, even the car wash, and there they are.
— Judith Rosen, *Publishers Weekly*

According to publisher David Godine, only 32% of the population of the United States has ever been in a bookstore, much less bought a book there. Whether their figures are accurate or not, there is certainly a large proportion of people who do not visit bookstores regularly. Hence, if you want to reach these people, you have to get your books into the places where these people will see them.

In Los Alamos, New Mexico, there are two full-service bookstores—and twenty-eight other stores in the town that sell books. Similarly, of the 200 stores at the huge South Coast Plaza in Costa Mesa, California, only two are bookstores, but at least another twenty-five stores sell books. Nationwide, there are about ten times as many non-bookstore retail outlets as there are bookstores—over 200,000 such outlets. These retail outlets currently account for several billion dollars worth of book sales every year. That's a market worth pursuing.

In 1995, for the first time ever, the majority of books were sold through non-bookstore outlets. While book clubs and mail order accounted for 23% of all books sold, other retail outlets accounted for 30%. Bookstores accounted for only 47% of all books sold. (*1996 Consumer Research Study on Book Purchasing*). In 1996, bookstores' share of book sales dropped another 4% to only 43% (ABA study conducted by NPD Group). This sales trend has continued and gotten stronger in the past ten years.

For children's books, other retail outlets account for even greater sales. In 1995, according to a study sponsored by the American Booksellers Association, 39% of children's books were bought through mass market outlets (grocery stores, drug stores, price clubs, and discount stores) and another 20.9% were bought through specialty retail outlets (toy stores, variety stores, etc.). Only 17% of all children's books were bought via bookstores. Book clubs and mail order accounted for the remaining 22.5%.

One children's book publisher, Klutz Press, sells 45% of its books to bookstores while gift stores, toy stores, and other retail outlets account for the other 55% of sales. As their publicity director Sheila Wolfson once noted, "We're in park bookstores, car washes, pet stores, theatrical supplies, magic shops, luggage stores, and in the fall we'll be in nail salons." That's in addition to the toy stores, variety stores, and other mass market outlets that account for so many of their sales.

15:01   The Advantages of Other Retail Outlets

The major advantage of distributing your books in non-bookstore retail outlets is that you can get your books before people who would not otherwise enter a bookstore. That means, if the previous estimates are true, that you could triple the number of people you reach by getting your books into other retail outlets. Here are a few other advantages of distributing your books through these outlets:

☐ Your books do not have to compete with as many other books. Bookstores carry anywhere from 500 to 125,000 titles in stock. How many of your books could possibly stand out in such a crowd? On the other hand, most specialty retail outlets carry only a few other books (as few as three or four to as many as 500), thus giving your books a better chance of attracting the attention of casual browsers.

☐ You can target your audience much more sharply by distributing through specialized retail outlets. For example, you are far more likely to sell books about fishing or hunting in a sports shop than in a bookstore.

☐ Your books are more likely to be displayed prominently in specialty retail outlets. In some stores, your books will be given space right next to the cash register.

☐ Your books can be sold just about anywhere. New England Press, for example, sells its Vermont titles in cider mills, wood-products stores, pottery shops, T-shirt shops, country stores, drug stores, lodges, and even the ferries which cross Lake Champlain.

☐ These markets are easier to break into. For instance, because there are no wholesalers in the gift industry and because the gift trade thrives on novelty, retailers are more accessible to anyone with a fresh idea.

☐ Some specialty retail outlets have greater in-store traffic than most bookstores. This is especially true of tourist spots, stationery stores, drug stores, and supermarkets. Foghorn Press, publisher of outdoor books, now does 50% of its business with outdoor specialty stores such as REI and Eastern Mountain Sports (as compared to 30% just a few years ago).

☐ In these alternative markets, smaller publishers stand on more equal footing with major book publishers. Indeed, I've seen smaller publishers stand toe to toe and even beat out bigger publishers in some of these markets. For instance, in computer gaming books, Prima was #1, besting all the major publishers. So Random House bought them!

15:02 Alternative Retail Outlets: Some Examples

Because books provide information, instruction, and entertainment applicable to just about every field of life, they can be sold in almost any type of retail outlet. Here are a few examples of how other publishers have approached selling their books through alternative retail outlets.

Supermarkets

There are some 150,000 grocery stores in the United States of which 50,000 are supermarkets. Supermarkets currently account for about 8% of all books sold each year. While most of their sales are mass-market paperbacks, a number of publishers have been successful in selling hardcovers through supermarkets.

• Before the rise of the chain bookstores, HP Books sold almost all their books through supermarkets. To make it easy for the supermarkets to offer their books, HP designed spinner floor racks which could display a range of their cooking, crafts, and gardening titles. HP also pioneered the use of cross-merchandising in selling books to other retail outlets. For example, they supplied wire racks that would allow their pasta cookbooks to be displayed right next to the boxes of noodles and spaghetti. Finally, HP Books also offered supermarkets highly competitive terms including far better discounts than they were accustomed to getting from other suppliers.

• A grocery store in Gregg Olsen's hometown of Olalla, Washington, sold more than 1,200 copies of his book, *Starvation Heights*.

Home Improvement Centers

According to *National Home Center News*, 30% of all how-to books on home repair and interior decorating are sold through home improvement centers. Because how-to books teach customers how to do their own home improvement work, these centers encourage the sale of such books. About 21,000 retail outlets (hardware stores, decorating shops, and home centers) service this market. Besides home repair books, these outlets often carry books on cooking, exercise, gardening, entertaining, decorating, crafts, and architecture.

Ortho Information Services published an entire series of gardening and cooking books, all with first print runs of 50,000 copies. Using the 250 sales representatives of its parent company, Chevron Chemical, Ortho made over half its sales through garden centers and hardware stores.

Gourmet Shops

Besides the independent gourmet shops, many gift shops and cookware departments in major department stores also feature cookbooks. Regional and specialty cookbooks are big hits in these retail outlets. Most publishers reach these stores using gourmet sales representatives.

- Barron's has more than 40 representatives selling their cookbooks to gourmet and gift shops.

- 101 Productions set up their own distributorship network to sell their cookbooks to gourmet and gift shops.

- Wellton sold 150,000 copies of its *Cooking in the Nude* series each year. 85% of their business came via the gift and gourmet trade. It took them five years to develop a solid repping network for these stores. Displays and packaging also helped their books to stand out from the crowd.

- For Ten Speed Press, more cookbook sales take place outside book-stores. Gourmet and cookware stores, which feature books such as their *100 Top Pasta Sauces* next to pasta bowls, now constitute a large part of their business.

Food Stands

Food stands are a seasonal alternative to gourmet shops. If you can offer them an extra sale, a book that fits in with the food they are selling, many stands will be happy to sell your book, especially if you are a local author or publisher. The only disadvantage is that there are no distribution net-works for food stands, so you have to make each sale one stand at a time.

- Garden Way sold *The Apple Cookbook* and *Simply Strawberries* in or-chards and at roadside fruit and vegetable stands.

- A Good Thing Publishing sold *The Florida Citrus Cookbook* at citrus stands across the state.

- Globe Pequot sold its *The Bluefish Cookbook* through fish stands and stores up and down the Atlantic Coast.

Toy Stores

In 1995, 24.2 million books were sold through the 8,000 toy stores in the country. If you want to sell to the top chains in this market, you will need to produce full-color story or learning/activity books which can retail for less than $8.00 (most titles sell for prices ranging from $1.00 to $5.00). You'll have a better chance of placing your books with toy stores if you offer them sets or series of books.

Record Stores

Wilshire Books sold more copies of *How to Write a Hit Song and Sell It* in record stores than they did in bookstores. Here was another case where matching the book to its audience allowed a publisher to open new markets.

Auto Supply Stores

With 40,000 outlets, this is a large and virtually untapped market. Currently, some of them do carry books on auto repairs, tune-ups, and other do-it-yourself subjects. But don't overlook other possible topics for sale to this market. Other male-oriented topics, such as sports, home repair, and electronics might sell well. And how about a novel? *The Body in the Volvo*, a mystery novel by K.K. Beck, was carried by her local Volvo dealer.

Pet Shops

Pet care and training books have always sold well in pet shops, vetinarian centers, and aquariums.

* Green Turtle Publications sold over 55,000 copies of the *Marine Aquarium Handbook*. Most of those sales were made through pet stores.

* T.F.H. Publications, probably the world's largest publisher of pet and animal books, started out selling small pamphlets through pet shops. While most of their sales are still through pet shops, seven of their books are now on the ABA Basic Book List (a list of recommended titles which every bookstore should stock).

* Within a year after Jerry Pallotta self-published *The Ocean Alphabet Book*, the gift shop at Boston's New England Aquarium had sold more than 4,000 copies.

Drugstores

There are some 45,000 drugstores and pharmacies in the U.S., of which about half are chain stores. Drugstores currently account for about 3% of all consumer book purchases. While most of their book sales are mass-market paperbacks, some also carry hardcovers and trade paperbacks as well. To reach the drugstore market, you would probably go through the same magazine/paperback jobbers who service supermarkets. Afcom Publishing's *The Complete Guide to Home Remedies* has sold well in drugstores.

Beauty Salons

Among the hottest outlets for books lately has been beauty salons. Jack Canfield and Mark Victor Hansen, the authors of the *Chicken Soup for the Soul* series, promoted their first book by sending reading copies to hair salons and chiropracters. Their thought was that people would read a few of the stories in the book while waiting, get engrossed, and then go out and buy their own copy. It worked!

- New Leaf, a wholesaler of new age books, has found that hair salons and health food stores are great outlets for the books it carries.

- When F. Lynn Harris self-published his first novel, *Invisible Life*, he had two main outlets for his book: black-owned bookstores and beauty salons. He sold 5,000 copies before signing with Anchor to do a paperback edition. *Essence* magazine named his book one of the year's ten best.

Shoe Stores

New England Press sold its autobiography of running great Clarence De-Mar in the Bill Rodgers chain of athletic shoe stores. It was their only title to sell in those stores, but because it tied in so well with the main line of those stores, the book sold well.

Camera Shops

Through a network of sales representativess who sell to camera shops across the country, Amherst Media has sold over 45,000 copies of *Basic 35mm Photo Guide for Beginning Photographers*. To encourage sales in non-bookstore outlets, they provide free counter-top displays with the purchase of twelve or more copies. Besides its own titles. Amherst also distributes about 30 other books on photography.

Gift Shops

Of the 150,000 gift stores in the United States, most are mom and pop independents. To do well in this market, you need to organize a network of forty to one hundred sales reps in ten to twelve regions. But to support such a network and to make it worth their while to represent you, you need to publish at least three to ten new titles twice a year. If you only have one title, try to hook up with another publisher who already has distribution to the gift store market.

Blue Mountain Press has sold more than ten million copies of Susan Polis Schutz's poetry books as well as three hundred million greeting cards. One of their hardcover books, *To My Daughter with Love*, sold out its first printing of 70,000 copies in just one month. Since, however, most copies of the book were sold in gift and card shops rather than bookstores, the book never showed up on any bestseller list.

Movie Theaters

If you publish a book that ties in with a movie coming out, check with local theaters or movie chains to see if they'd like to sell copies to patrons coming to see the movie when it appears.

- Doubleday sold 100 copies of *Like Water for Chocolate* at the Angelika Film Center in New York City while the movie of the same name was presented there. The film center put up a sign at the box office and sold books to people standing in line, people coming out of the theater, and people passing by. Doubleday went on to sell many more copies at theaters across the country.

• The Angelika Film Center sold more than 200 copies of *How to Make Love to a Negro Without Getting Tired* by Dany Leferriere, who also co-wrote the screenplay.

15:03   Alternative Retail Outlets: A Checklist

Use the checklist below to aid you in locating other possible outlets for your books. For example, if you publish cookbooks, you could sell to appliance stores, beauty shops, campgrounds, candy shops, Christmas stores, coffee houses, cookware stores, doctor's offices, fish markets, fitness centers, food stands, garden supply stores, gift stores, grocery stores, gourmet shops, health food stores, hospital gift shops, houseware shops, marinas, supermarkets, and tourist shops. Of course, out of this list you would have to select those shops which are most appropriate for your particular cookbook titles. A regional cookbook could be sold in gift shops, campgrounds, and tourist shops while a natural foods cookbook would be most appropriate for health food stores and fitness centers. Here, then, is a checklist of alternative retail outlets for your books:

☐ **airport shops** — fiction, business, self-help, biographies, travel

☐ **art supply stores** — graphics, art, architecture

☐ **appliance stores** — house & home, how-to, cookbooks

☐ **automobile dealerships** — automobiles, how-to, travel, recreation

☐ **barber shops** — sports, recreation, novelty, humor

☐ **beauty shops** — beauty care, fashion, diet, exercise, relationships

☐ **camera shops** — photography, art, travel, coffee-table books

☐ **campgrounds** — recreation, sports, travel, novelty, regional books

☐ **candy shops** — cookbooks, diet, relationships

☐ **car washes** — automobiles, how-to, travel, recreation, novelty

☐ **chain stores** — general, mass-market, novelty, celebrity bios

☐ **children's stores** — juveniles, games, humor, child care

☐ **Christmas shops** — holiday, decorating, cookbooks, crafts

☐ **churches** — religious, family life, inspirational

☐ **clothing stores** — fashion, beauty care, diet, exercise

☐ **coffee shops** — cookbooks, poetry, literary fiction, general

☐ **college stores** — textbooks, general, literature, novelty, music, art

☐ **comic book retailers** — humor, entertainment, music, graphic novels

- ☐ **computer stores** — computers, business, technology
- ☐ **cookware stores** — cookbooks, diets, health
- ☐ **craft stores** — crafts, how-to, hobbies, cookbooks
- ☐ **discount stores** — general, remainders, mass-market, biographies
- ☐ **doctor's offices** — health, diet, cookbooks, recreation
- ☐ **dress shops** — fashion, beauty care, sewing, diet, exercise
- ☐ **drug stores** — general, mass-market, novelty, beauty care
- ☐ **fabric shops** — sewing, crafts, fashion, beauty care
- ☐ **fish markets** — seafood cookbooks, recreation, sports
- ☐ **fitness centers** — health, diet, recreation, cookbooks
- ☐ **florists** — gardening, how-to, crafts, entertaining, romance
- ☐ **food stands** — cookbooks, gardening, how-to, regional books
- ☐ **garden supply stores** — gardening, crafts, cookbooks
- ☐ **gas stations** — travel, atlases, humor, novelty, regional books
- ☐ **gift stores** — coffee-table books, humor, novelty, hobbies
- ☐ **golf clubs** — sports, recreation
- ☐ **gourmet shops** — food, cookbooks, diet, crafts
- ☐ **grocery stores** — food, cookbooks, diet, crafts
- ☐ **gun shops** — sports, recreation
- ☐ **hardware stores** — crafts, how-to, sports, recreation
- ☐ **health food stores** — cookbooks, diet, health, alternative lifestyles
- ☐ **hobby shops** — crafts, hobbies, how-to, games, novelty
- ☐ **home improvement centers** — house & home, how-to, crafts, design
- ☐ **hotel gift shops** — travel, novelty, coffee-table books, regional
- ☐ **hospital gift shops** — cookbooks, diets, humor, health
- ☐ **houseware shops** — cookbooks, crafts, how-to
- ☐ **law offices** — business, law, politics, social issues
- ☐ **luggage stores** — travel, regional, coffee-table books, lifestyle
- ☐ **magic shops** — humor, science, novelty
- ☐ **marinas** — seafood cookbooks, recreation, sports
- ☐ **maternity shops** — juveniles, child care, education, diet, exercise
- ☐ **military PX's** — general, military, adventure, recreation
- ☐ **movie theaters** — celebrity biographies, movies, entertainment
- ☐ **museum shops** — coffee table books, art, literature, juveniles, crafts
- ☐ **music stores** — music, celebrity biographies, entertainment
- ☐ **newsstands** — local titles, general, novelty, mass-market, genre novels
- ☐ **novelty shops** — humor, games, novelty, recreation
- ☐ **office supply stores** — business, humor, novelty, computers

- ☐ **pet shops** — pet care, animals, recreation, gardening, hobbies
- ☐ **print shops** — graphics, art, novelty, business, writing
- ☐ **prison commissaries** — general, literature, self-help
- ☐ **record shops** — music, celebrity biographies, novelty
- ☐ **religious stores** — religion, family life, general, inspirational
- ☐ **school supply stores** — education, juveniles, crafts, how-to
- ☐ **shoe stores** — fashion, beauty care, running, exercise
- ☐ **specialty shops** — novelty, regional, entertainment
- ☐ **sports shops** — sports, recreation, games, humor, novelty
- ☐ **stationery stores** — novelty, humor, calendars, business, careers
- ☐ **supermarkets** — cookbooks, mass-market, juveniles
- ☐ **tourist shops** — travel, regional titles, novelty, humor
- ☐ **toy stores** — juveniles, child care, novelty, games, sports
- ☐ **travel agencies** — travel books, regional titles, recreation
- ☐ **video stores** — movies, entertainment, games, novelty, biographies
- ☐ **warehouse clubs** — novels, children's, remainders, entertainment

15:04 Tips on Marketing to Other Retail Outlets

To work with other retail outlets, you must first learn what their standard operating procedures and expectations are. Few other stores operate in the same way as bookstores. For example, grocery stores operate on a 20% discount for many food items (they make up for the low discount with much higher volume), though they've come to expect and appreciate higher discounts for non-food items. Gift stores, on the other hand, buy almost all products at a 50% discount (they have a lower volume, higher risk business where fads and heavy promotions play an important role).

These differences in operating procedures and expectations are governed by several factors: the type of product the store normally sells, the average price of items sold, the sales volume, the type of customer, the distribution network for that industry, and tradition. If you are not aware of these differences, learn them. Ask local retailers how their industry works, who they buy from, what kind of discount they get, what their expectations are, and any other questions that will help you to sell books to similar stores.

To refresh yourself on how to sell to specialty retailers, re-read Chapter 5 on How to Open New Markets. To supplement that chapter, here are a few other tips on how to market your books to other retail outlets:

☐ **Find out how they learn about new products.** According to a survey of toy stores conducted by *Toy & Hobby World*, here are the ways that chain and independent stores learn about new products:

Source of Information	Chain Stores	Independent Stores
trade publications	64%	73%
sales representatives	51%	42%
conventions	37%	34%
toy & hobby markets	40%	30%
consumer media	18%	20%
exhibits / trade shows	18%	16%
competitors	17%	12%

☐ **Many retail outlets are accustomed to buying direct from manufacturer's sales representatives** (perhaps even more so than in the book industry where many bookstores have now become accustomed to buying through major wholesalers). To locate commission sales reps for these other outlets, go to the trade shows for that industry, read their trade magazines, ask your local retailer who their favorite reps are, and visit showrooms of reps in the nearest major city.

In the gift industry, reps are accustomed to commissions of 12% to 20%. Many reps won't even take on a new item unless they get at least a 15% commission. So your pricing formula must be able to support the larger commissions and higher discounts of the gift industry if you hope to sell to that market. When you are ready to sign up commission sales reps to represent your line, be sure you get a signed agreement that outlines their responsibilities, territories, and markets.

To facilitate their sales to specialty outlets, Globe Pequot Press has four sets of sales representatives for 1) the book trade, 2) library sales, 3) the gift and stationery trade, and 4) the gourmet trade. The Mountaineers has separate sales groups for both the book trade and outdoor trade. Chronicle Books has twenty-five reps calling on the book trade; they have four times that number calling on other retail markets. Andrews and McMeel has set up nineteen rep groups to cover the gift trade for their books.

☐ **Attend the trade shows for that industry,** especially when you are first starting out. Trade shows are the best place to get an overall view of the industry as well as an education in the detailed policies and procedures of that industry. Later, if your sales in those retail outlets are good, you might consider exhibiting at the trade shows.

To give you an idea of the variety of trade shows that are held every year, a few that might be appropriate for books are listed below:

Map & Travel Products Trade Show in September
World Sports Expo, in mid-October
School & Home Office Products Association Show, in December
Consumer Electronics Show, in early January and early June
American International Toy Fair in February
National Variety Merchandise Show, in mid-February
International Cat Show, in early March
National Sewing Show, in early March

National Hunting, Fishing, and Camping Show, in mid-March
Natural Foods Expo West, in mid-March
Educational Dealers and Suppliers Trade Show, in April
National Stationery Show, in mid-May
International New Age Trade Show in late June

WRC Publishing and Garden Way Publishing both exhibited special cookbooks at the San Francisco Gourmet Products Show. Among their titles, WRC displayed *Chocolate Truffles* and *Knowing Beans About Coffee*, while Garden Way displayed *Simply Strawberries*.

☐ **Read the trade magazines**. In the gift industry, this means reading *Gift and Decorative Accessories* and *Giftware News*. In the toy industry, trade magazines include *Toy and Hobby World* and *Playthings*. These magazines not only give you a good idea of what is currently happening in the industry, but they also provide many key contacts (such as sales reps, wholesalers, and retail stores). Also get to know the editors because they are the ones who will feature your book to the new industry.

☐ **Learn where to go for distribution.** You will discover that there are some book distributors or publishers who can already provide you with distribution into these other markets. In some industries, though, you will be better off working within their distribution system. This is especially true in the drugstore and toy markets, where major wholesalers dominate local and regional markets. Again, you can learn who these major wholesalers are by asking your local stores, going to trade shows, and reading the trade magazines. Also, if you've set up a rep network, they will undoubtedly take care of these contacts for you.

Besides working with sales reps or distributors, you could also work with another company which already has great distribution into a special market. For example, Kartes Video signed an agreement to have Hanes distribute their videos to 90,000 supermarkets, drugstores, convenience stores, and other outlets where Hanes sells L'Eggs panty hose. Hanes reps not only installed the video display racks, but they also checked the racks regularly, restocked them, and removed tapes that were not selling.

Jack Canfield and Mark Victor Hansen, authors of the *Chicken Soup for the Soul* series, worked with a beauty supply company in order to get their books into hair salons.

You can, of course, also set up your own distribution. That's what Rand McNally does for its atlases. That's also why Sourcebooks set up a distribution network to gift stores.

☐ **Set your discount schedule and terms to suit the industry.** In the gift industry, this means giving 50% discounts for packaged deals (such as a prepack display of ten or more books). In most cases you need not offer a returns policy. Let your sales reps and local retailers help you to set a reasonable discount schedule and statement of terms. As a caution, always verify advice you get from one source by checking with others.

☐ **Design packaged programs** that make it easy for retailers to order, stock, and display your titles. Since many retailers may not be set up to display books, offer a display with your books. The easier you make it for them, the more likely they will be to buy. To facilitate the sales of *US* magazine, Wenner Media designed display racks that featured its magazine along with music CDs. This allowed them to capitalize on cross-promotional opportunities in many specialized outlets.

☐ **When you send out display packages, include reordering instructions with the display.** You might put these instructions in front of or inside of the last copy in the display. Since the stores will not be accustomed to reordering from your company, you have to provide some procedure such as this to make it easy for the retailer to place a reorder.

☐ **Convince retailers that they can make an easy profit**, that your title or titles will sell well. Perhaps the best way to accomplish this is to demonstrate how well other stores have done. If you can tell them how often your books turn at retail (how often other stores have to reorder) or can demonstrate the profit potential of your books (how many dollars in sales they can expect to make per square foot per year), then you increase your chances of making the sale.

☐ **Show them how well your titles fit into their product mix**, how your titles can help them to sell other products. One way to convince them is to show how your books can serve as easy reference guides for their customers. For example, Aris Books placed *The Grilling Book* in hardware stores and *The California Seafood Book* in fish markets because both books were superb guides to using the products of those markets.

Autumngold focused on selling *The Ultimate Cigar Book* via tobacco shops and specialty liquor stores. As a result, they sold out the first edition within three months and had to go back for four more printings.

☐ **Show stores how they can cross-merchandise your books with their product line.** Barron's offers dumps to supermarkets so their seafood cookbooks can be placed near the fresh fish and their salad cookbooks near the fruits and vegetables. They have also packaged dessert cookbooks with baking trays so the books could be sold in cookware departments of stores. Similarly, 101 Productions has recommended to stores that they package a few tools with their book about kitchen tools.

Kathleen Fish decided to create her own products to cross-merchandise with her *Monterey's Cooking Secrets*. She worked with a restaurant chef to create bottled oils and vinegars as well as some three-way spreads. Not only did this give stores something to cross-merchandise with her book, but it also gave her gift/gourmet reps additional product to sell.

The Rotation Diet was highly promoted and cross-merchandised with many recommended food products in supermarket chains across the country. As a result, it sold well over a million copies.

☐ **Publish special editions for some markets.** For example, pop-up and other special effects books sell better in toy stores than do books with no play value. To make their booklet *Key to North American Waterfowl* more usable by hunters and bird watchers (who could easily drop the book in a lake or swamp), Schroeder Prints printed the booklet on special waterproof paper which actually floats. Because of its unique design, the book has sold well in sporting goods stores where it is often displayed submerged in a pail of water.

☐ **Don't overlook a store just because it doesn't sell books when you approach it.** Perhaps no one has ever shown them how they can make money selling books. Diana Brown convinced a jewelry store chain to showcase her novel, *The Emerald Necklace*, during May because emeralds are the birthstone of that month. All she had to do was give them a reason to stock her book.

Jon Gindick, author of *Harmonica Americana*, was able to convince Urban Outfitters to carry his book.

The Los Angeles representative for Prentice Hall approached a store that sold smoke, goo, and gum for use in special effects. That's all they sold. Their market was solely people from the movie industry. So why would they be interested in selling books? Well, the rep convinced them to sell science books for adults and kids. And the books sold. Indeed, they sold so well that now the store sells smoke, goo, gum, and books.

☐ **Make a commitment.** Don't think that opening special markets is something you can do on a lark. It must be seen as a long-term commitment, because that is what it takes to be successful.

Bonus Books sells many books to K-Mart, Osco Drugs, and Toys R Us. How do they do it? Generally, they start by calling the chain to find out the name of the buyer. Then they send a review copy of the book. Then they start the round of follow-up calls. Sometimes it takes as many as 20 calls to the same person before they get an order. The key here, of course, as in most sales is to be persistent. It's the only thing that works. And it works every time.

Here's Jim Donovan's story of how he sold his *Handbook to a Happier Life* to the Successories stores: "I contacted the Successories office and was given a name to submit the book to. After several phone calls, I was informed that I had the wrong person. I then resubmitted to the right buyer and followed up—for almost a year. I called, never reaching the actual person (voice mail, you know), faxed, and promised myself I would continue knocking on their door until I was successful. Every time I received a good review or some other bit of news, I faxed it to them. Finally, after a year, I was given an intent to order. Weeks passed, still no order. Another fax of a great review in *Home Business Journal* got their attention, and I received an order to drop ship to 47 stores." What he did you can do as well, as long as you are persistent.

Authors — You can help your publisher open up new retail outlets by doing some of the preliminary research for them. If you think your book would do well in sporting goods stores, visit some local stores and ask the manager a few questions. See Chapter 5 for a list of appropriate questions. Then follow up on the information yourself or pass it on to your publisher.

15:05 Some Key Contacts for Other Retail Markets

Here is a sampling of key distributors, publications, and organizations that can help you research and sell to specialty retail outlets. This list is nowhere near complete.

Gift Retailers

☐ **Gift & Decorative Accessories**, 360 Park Avenue South, New York, NY 10010; 646-746-6400; Fax: 646-746-7431. Email: qhalford@reed-business.com. Web: http://www.giftsanddec.com. This monthly is the major gift trade magazine.

☐ **Giftbeat**, 317 Harrington Avenue, Closter, NJ 07624; 800-358-7177; Fax: 201-768-3894. Email: editors@giftbeat.com. Web: http://www.gift-beat.com. Another trade magazine for the gift industry.

☐ **Giftware News**, 20 West Kinzie, 12th Floor, Chicago, IL 60610;312-849-2220; Fax: 312-849-2174. Web: http://www.giftwarenews.com. The third major trade magazine for the gift industry.

Computer Retailers

☐ **Cromland**, 1995 Highland Avenue #200, Bethlehem, PA 18020; 610-997-3000; 800-944-5554; Fax: 610-997-8880. Email: info@cromland.com. Web: http://www.cromland.com. This company wholesales computer and technology books.

☐ **The Innovative Alliance**, 1205 Osage Street, Denver, CO 80204; 303-825-1535; 800-870-8374; Fax: 303-825-1535. Email: info@tiabooks.com. Web: http://www.tiabooks.com. Bargain computer books.

Gourmet and Food Retailers

☐ **Pig Out Publications**, 6005 Martway #107, Mission, KS 66202; 913-789-9594; Fax: 913-789-9592. Email: kadler@pigoutpublications.com. Web: http://www.pigoutpublications.com. This company wholesales barbecue and grilling cookbooks.

☐ **Nutri-Books**, Royal Publications, 790 W. Tennessee, Denver, CO 80223; 303-778-8383; Fax: 503-744-9383. Email: nutribooks@royal-publications.com. Web: http://www.nutribooks.com. This wholesaler distributes books and other supplies to 6,000 natural food stores.

☐ **Whole Foods Markets**, 550 Bowie Street, Austin, TX 78703-4677; 512-477-4455; Fax: 512-482-7000. Web: http://www.wholefoods.com. Operater of 175 natural foods stores, they offer a large collection of books on cooking, health, gardening, child care, nutrition, and so on.

Hobby Retailers

☐ **Diamond Comic Distributors**, 1966 Greenspring Drive #300, Timonium, MD 21093; 410-560-7100; 800-452-6642; Fax: 410-560-7589. Web: http://www.diamondcomics.com. This comics distributor also features books on movies, pop culture, music, comics, etc.

☐ **Quilters' Resource, Inc.**, 2211 N. Elston, P.O. Box 148850, Chicago, IL 60614; 773-278-5695; 800-676-6543; Fax: 773-278-1348. Email: info@quiltersresource.com. Web: http://www.quiltersresource.com. This company wholesales 4,000 books and magazines to independent quilting, sewing, and needle art stores.

☐ **Specialty Book Marketing**, 443 Park Avenue South #800, New York, NY 10016; 212-685-5560; Fax: 212-685-5836. Email: billbooky@aol.com. Web: http://www.specialtybooks.com. This company provides sales representation for books into the hobby trade. Specialties: military history, aviation, and children's books.

Home and Garden Retailers

☐ **Earthworkers Emporium**, Denver Merchandise Mart #2333, 451 East 58th Avenue, Denver, CO 80216; 303-292-4141; Fax: 303-292-4126. Email: eeearthworkers@aol.com. This company has sales reps who sell books and other products to garden stores in Colorado, Wyoming, New Mexico, and Utah.

☐ **Home Channel News**, Lebhar-Friedman, 425 Park Avenue, 5th Floor, New York, NY 10022; 212-756-5228; Fax: 212-756-5295. Web: http://www.homechannelnews.com. This trade magazine serves the home improvement center market.

☐ **Smith & Hawken**, New Product Review Committee, 4 Hamilton Landing #100, Novato, CA 94949. New product hotline: 800-566-4383, ext. 7923. Web: http://www.smith-hawken.com. This company features several hundred books in its many stores.

Pet Retailers

☐ **Pet Age Magazine**, H.H. Backer Associates, 200 S. Michigan Avenue #840, Chicago, IL 60604; 312-663-4040; Fax: 312-663-5676. Email: petage@hhbacker.com. Web: http://www.petage.com. This monthly trade magazine goes to 25,000 pet retailers.

☐ **Pet Food Express**, 2131 Williams Street, San Leandro, CA 94577; 510-346-7773; Fax: 510-346-7788. Email: mark&michael@petfoodexpress. com. Web: http://www.petfoodexpress.com. This chain of 24 pet stores features books on animal and pet care.

☐ **Pet Industry Distributors Association**, 2105 Laurel Bush Road #200, Bel Air, MD 21015; 443-640-1060; Fax: 443-640-1031. Email: pida@ ksgroup.org. Web: http://www.pida.org. Their web site lists many pet product distributors.

Sports and Recreation Retailers

☐ **Alpenbooks**, 4602 Chennault Beach Road #B1, Mukilteo, WA 98275; 425-290-8587; 800-290-9898; Fax: 425-290-9461. Email: cserve@alpenbooks.com. Web: http://www.alpenbooks.com. This wholesaler features 4,000 outdoor books to outdoor, recreation, and bicycle shops.

☐ **Common Ground Distributors**, P.O. Box 25249, Asheville NC 28813-1249; 828-274-5575; 800-654-0626; Fax: 828-274-1029. Email: tips@ comground.com. Web: http://www.comground.com. This company wholesales gardening, home style, cooking, outdoors, natural history, and children's books to nature centers, museums, and other specialty retailers.

☐ **Eastern Mountain Sports**, 1 Vose Farm Road, Peterborough, NH 03458-2128; 603-924-9571; 888-463-6367; Fax: 603-924-4320. Web: http://www.ems.com. This company operates 80 outdoor recreation stores which feature about 500 titles on recreation.

☐ **Discovery Channel Stores**, 1608 4th Street, Berkeley, CA 94710; 510-528-9924, ext. 4313 (for how to submit products). Web: http://www.Discoverystore.com. Operates more than a hundred retail stores that feature 500 books on animals, nature, astronomy, birding, and children's nonfiction, especially science and how-to.

☐ **Sporting Goods Business**, VNU Media, 770 Broadway, 6th Floor, New York, NY 10003; 646-654-4997. Email: rcarr@sportinggoodsbusiness. com. Web: http://www.sportinggoodsbusiness.com. This monthly sports trade magazine has a circulation of 27,000.

☐ **Sports Market Place Directory**, Grey House Publishing, 185 Millerton Road, Millerton, NY 12546; 518-789-8700; Fax: 518-789-0554. Email: books@greyhouse.com. Web: http://www.sportsmarketplace.com. Features 13,000 sports organizations, teams, media, associations, and more.

Toy Retailers

☐ **Toy Industry Association**, 1115 Broadway #400, New York, NY 10010; 212-675-1141; Fax: 212-633-1429. Email: toyfairs@toy-tia.org.

Web: http://www.toy-tia.org. Contact them for information about the Toy Fair (held every February in New York) as well as regional toy shows.

☐ **Playthings**, 360 Park Avenue South, New York, NY 10010; 646-746-6400; Fax: 646-746-7433. Web: http://www.playthings.com. The major toy trade magazine.

☐ **Toys 'R' Us**, One Geoffrey Way, Wayne, NJ 07470-2030; 973-617-3500. Web: http://www2.toysrus.com. This company is the largest toy chain with more than 1,500 stores.

Miscellaneous Retailers

☐ **Museum Store Association**, 4100 E. Mississippi Avenue #800, Denver, CO 80246-3055; 303-504-9223; Fax: 303-504-9585. Web: http://www.museumdistrict.com. This association sponsors an annual trade show in May and publishes a quarterly magazine, the *Museum Store*.

☐ **Shopko Stores**, 700 Pilgrim Way, Green Bay, WI 54304; 920-497-2211; 800-791-7333. Web: http://www.shopko.com. This chain of 140 discount variety stores features books and other items. Also owns Pamida stores.

15:06 Discount Stores and Warehouse Clubs

Discount and department stores currently account for about 10% of all book sales. Meanwhile, the hundreds of warehouse clubs have had a growing impact on book sales, especially the higher priced coffee-table and reference books which can be discounted more deeply than lower priced books. Sales through warehouse clubs now total over $100 million yearly. While it is a limited market (few warehouse clubs stock more than 200 titles), they buy big (from 10,000 to 50,000 copies).

Here are a few major buyers and wholesalers of books to the mass merchandisers and warehouse clubs:

☐ **Advanced Marketing Services**, 5880 Oberlin Drive #400, San Diego, CA 92121-9653; 858-457-2500; 800-695-3580; Fax: 858-452-2237. Web: http://www.advmkt.com. This wholesaler services many mass merchandisers and warehouse buying clubs. They also have a division that serves office products warehouses.

☐ **Best Buy**, P.O. Box 9312, Minneapolis, MN 55440-9312; 612-291-1000. Web: http://www.bestbuy.com. 500 electronics stores. Best Buy hosts author signings in its stores. For instance, Olympic gymnist Kerri Strug appeared at several Best Buy stores in the Kansas City area to sign her biography, *Landing on My Feet*.

☐ **Anderson Merchandisers**, 421 East 34th Street, P.O. Box 32270, Amarillo, TX 79120-2270; 806-376-6251; Fax: 806-374-0010. Web: http://www.amerch.com. This company supplies books for Wal-Mart.

☐ **Costco Wholesale**, 999 Lake Drive, Issaquah, WA 98025; 425-313-8100; Fax: 425-313-8343. Web: http://www.costco.com. This company has 300+ warehouse stores that feature about 200 book titles.

☐ **Levy Home Entertainment**, 4201 Raymond Drive, Hillside, IL 60162-1786; 708-547-4400; Fax: 708-547-4503. Web: http://www.levybooks. com. This wholesaler services discount stores and warehouse clubs, including Wal-Mart, Best Buy, Toys 'R' Us, Meijer, and others.

☐ **Sam's Wholesale Club**, 608 S.W. 8th Street, Bentonville, AR 72716; 888-746-7726. Web: http://www.samsclub.com. This division of Wal-Mart, which has 600 warehouse stores, usually buys books through one of the following distributors: Advanced Marketing Services, Anderson Merchandisers, Ingram, or Levy Home Entertainment

☐ **Target Stores**, 33 South 6th Street, Minneapolis MN 55402; 612-304-6073; 800-440-0680; Fax: 612-304-3711. Vendor hotline: 612-696-7500. Web: http:// www.targetstores.com. This chain of 1,400 stores features juvenile, promotional, and new titles.

15:07 The Military Market

As Nat Kornfield, the advertising director of *Army Times*, once noted, "The military is the only market in the country that has no recession, no unemployment, and no pay cuts." While that may no longer be true, the market is still big. It consists of 2,200,000 active-duty personnel plus their dependents, 1,200,000 civilian employees, and 1,500,000 retirees. With a combined total income of over $160 billion, it is a significant market. To help you reach that market, here are a few resources:

☐ **Army and Air Force Exchange Service**, Yolanda Thursby, Book and Magazine Buyer, AAFES Headquarters, 3911 S. Walton Walker Boulevard, Dallas, TX 75236-1598; 214-312-2011, ext. 6659; Fax: 214-312-3000. Web: http://www.aafes.com. Check out the *Selling to AAFES* report at http://www/aafes.com/pa/selling/selling-to-aafes.htm.

☐ **Coast Guard Exchange System**, U.S. Coast Guard HQ, 870 Greenbrier Circle, Greenbrier Tower II #502, Chesapeake, VA 23320-2681; 757-420-2480; Fax: 757-420-0286. Web: http://www.cg-exchange.com.

☐ **U.S. Marine Corps Exchange**, USMC Building, 3044 Catlin Avenue, Quantico, VA 22135-5099; 703-640-3821; Fax: 703-640-7291. Web: http://www.usmc-mccs.org.

☐ **Navy Exchange Service Command**, NEXCOM, 3280 Virginia Beach Boulevard, Virginia Beach, VA 23452-5724; 757-631-3852; 800-628-3924; Fax: 757-631-3659. Web: http://www.navy-nex.com. Vendor info: http://www.navy-nex.com/command/contractor_vendor/cv-vendor.html. They buy books for all Navy Exchanges.

- **M.J. Daniel Company**, 1000 Belt Line Road #200, Carrollton, TX 75006-6282; 972-245-3600; Fax: 972-245-3896. Email: info@mjdco.com. Web: http://www.mjdco.com. This sales rep group sells to military exchanges around the world.
- **Byrrd Enterprises**, 1302 LaFayette Drive, Alexandria, VA 22308; 703-765-5626; 800-628-0901; Fax: 703-768-4086. Email: byrrd-books@aol.com. Web: http://www.byrrdbooks.com. Vendor info: http://www.byrrdbooks.com/distribution.html. Military books only. No fiction or bios.

Is Your Book a Good Fit for the Gift Market?

by Paul Weber, formerly with Sourcebooks

Due to the current state of the publishing industry, more and more publishers are looking to their special sales departments as a means to increase sales. Many have found that the gift trade is a lucrative market for books. Since, however, there are major differences between the book trade and the gift trade, you should consider these differences in deciding whether your book is a good fit for the gift market.

Gift Trade vs. Book Trade

The general public does not search out local gift shops when looking for a book. Whereas publicity plays a major part in driving sales in bookstores, it may not have any effect on sales in gift shops. If your book requires publicity to sell, gift shops are not for you.

Gift shops feel that a great deal of their patrons are regular customers. Therefore, they try to keep their inventory fresh. At times, this means not replenishing a title even though it sold well. Hence, don't expect that sales will lead to more sales.

Seasonal holidays are key selling periods. Books that fit greeting card buying seasons are great (such as, Valentine's, Mother's Day, Graduation, Father's Day, Halloween, Christmas, etc.). Certain other categories that sell well throughout the year are golf, aging, cats, humor, and inspiration.

80% of the sale of a book in a gift store is due to the title and cover. I can't stress the importance of that enough. At Sourcebooks, we've turned down many submissions not because the content was poor, but because the title and cover didn't work together to communicate who should buy the book or to whom the book should be given.

These are only the most basic guidelines when considering whether a book is a good fit for the gift market. Obviously there are many contributing factors to the success of a book in this market.

Reaching the Gift Market

How do we reach the gift market? The same way any other company would have to do. Here are just a few of the ways we use that you could also use if you were to try reaching the gift market on your own.

☐ **Rep Groups** — We have independent sales representatives thoughout North America who promote and sell our book selection to the gift trade, including card and gift shops, department stores, and other specialty stores.

☐ **In-House Sales** — Our in-house sales department represents a large portion of our overall gift division business and has experienced tremendous increases every year. They are responsible for implementing our Light Bulb Club, which is made up of our most frequent buyers. These members received promotional mailings, free freight, and other incentives rewarding their loyalty. Our in-house sales staff is also responsible for calling the mail order catalog trade, music store trade, and other large specialty markets.

☐ **Direct Mail**—We design and mail various offers to a variety of markets. We've done mailings to more than 9,000 accounts for every major holiday (Valentine's, Mother's Day, Father's Day, Christmas), 500 new age stores and retreat centers, 200 museum stores, 400 Unity Church stores, and educational supply stores.

☐ **Trade Shows**—Besides being represented at every major gift show through our rep groups, we also participate with our in-house staff at many other trade shows, including the National Stationery Show.

☐ **Publicity**—We have an in-house gift division publicist who nurtures relationships with the major gift trade publications as well as responds to media with information on current trends and our gift division introductions.

If you can give your son or daughter only one gift, let it be enthusiasm.

— Bruce Barton, advertising executive

Marketing Your Self-Published Book

by Sam Henrie, founder of Wheatmark

You've already taken one of the most important steps in successfully marketing your self-published book—you are reading *1001 Ways to Market Your Books*. Here are some additional tips specifically for you, the self-published author, to keep in mind:

DON'T focus on bookstores first. Brick-and-mortar bookstores are the obvious place to start selling, right? Wrong! On top of the problems that all publishers bemoan, including heavy discounts, substantial returns, lack of pricing flexibility, and stiff on-shelf competition, your self-published book has a couple of additional disadvantages in this market. Without a distributor it is difficult to get bookstores to carry a self-published book, and with only one or two titles it can be difficult to get a good distributor. Bookstores, especially the large chains, frequently have a bias against self-published books, making it an uphill battle to get book signings, good shelf placement, and reasonable inventory levels. Luckily, less than half of all books are sold in brick-and-mortar bookstores, so there are plenty of opportunities in markets that are friendlier to self-published books. Develop a track record of sales before trying to tackle the more difficult brick-and-mortar bookstore market.

DO focus on online bookstores and online marketing. Each year online bookstores grab a larger share of the total book market. Online bookstores are perfect for the self-published book because they offer a level playing field. Your book gets equal shelf placement with the titles from major publishers. Many publishing houses are slow to take advantage of the cornucopia of marketing opportunities available on the Internet, creating an opportunity for the self-published author who does her homework.

DO focus on nontraditional and special sales. Nontraditional sales markets include specialty stores, discount stores, libraries, supermarkets, retailers, book clubs, specialty catalogs, websites that sell books, promotional product companies, display marketers, corporations and associations that give away books as premiums, and schools that use books as textbooks. Many of these markets require direct sales, at which self-published authors have a distinct advantage—the person making the sales pitch is the person who wrote the book. These markets also offer greater pricing flexibility, better profit margins, and often fewer returns.

Think backlist, not frontlist. Ask the typical book marketing and publicity expert how to market and promote your book, and they'll usually describe the process used to sell frontlist titles in bookstores. Most bookstore sales happen during the first six months after a title's release. Thus, it's critical to schedule highly synchronized PR, advertising, and distribution campaigns right after publication. Conversely, sales on online bookstores tend to take several months to get going. It takes time to accumulate online reviews, reciprocal links, high search engine rankings, and Internet buzz. The same is true with selling into nontraditionalmarkets, which typically have long sales cycles. So, you may be better off using the marketing and publicity strategies traditionally recommended for backlist titles. Keep this in mind as you plan.

Manage your own marketing and publicity. No one can represent your book like you can. Contract marketing and PR services can be a great help, but you are hiring them for their contacts and for their understanding of how to get these contacts to pay attention to a product. You are still the keeper of the message and the spokesperson for your book. No one will ever understand you, your book, your message, and your audience the way you do.

Saturate your local market. We all know the cliché: it takes seven impressions to make a marketing message stick. Good luck making that happen on a national level! Local news programs, radio shows, libraries, schools, independent bookstores, and museums, however, love booking local authors. You can easily find seven or more inexpensive ways to get your message out to your local market.

Choose self-publishing services carefully. If you are going to use one of the many firms that help authors self-publish and distribute books, study your options carefully before making a decision. Print-on-demand publishers, subsidy presses, custom publishers, and self-publishing services vary widely in their offerings. Make sure you compare their distribution discounts, author discounts, royalty calculation methods and percentages, retail pricing systems, returns policies, rights policies, upfront costs, editorial and design capabilities, imprint policies, and marketing programs before making a decision. You don't want to find out after your book is published that you can't make a bulk sale because your self-publishing service doesn't allow for returns and/or only sells at short discounts.

Create a website and an online media room. A promotional website is an essential component of your marketing arsenal. Similarly, an online media room is an essential component of your publicity arsenal. Whether you create these yourself or hire someone else to do it, you'll need both to succeed.

Sam Henrie is founder and president of Wheatmark, a self-publishing service focused on helping authors maximize their book sales. A frequent speaker on special market sales and self-publishing, Sam's expertise includes new directions in production, distribution, publicity, and marketing. Sam is president of the Arizona Book Publishing Association (2005–2007) and an active member of PMA. For more information about their services, contact **Wheatmark**, 610 E. Delano Street #104, Tucson, AZ 85705-5210; 520-798-0888; 888-934-0888; Fax: 520-798-3394. Email: submissions@wheatmark.com. Web: http://www.wheatmark.com.

Chapter 16

Selling to Schools and Libraries

Textbooks are still the first source of reference. But in a society that is having to pay more attention to the rest of the world, people are now looking for answers beyond the scope of an average textbook.
— Andrew Dunning, director of school and library sales,
Barron's Educational Series

In 1996, U.S. sales of school textbooks and supplements amounted to more than $5.4 billion while retail trade sales amounted to $5.6 billion. Sales of books in the elhi supplemental publishing market grew to $1.53 billion in 2002 (Association of Educational Publishers). Add in the sales to libraries, and the school and library markets actually constitute a larger market than bookstores. Hence, if you are looking for new markets for your books, look into selling to these two major book markets.

16:01 School Textbooks: How to Get Adopted

Textbooks make up the major portion of book sales to schools and colleges. The best way to get your books adopted for classroom use is to get samples of your books into the hands of the instructors or school boards who make the adoption decisions. And the best way to reach these decision makers is through direct mail. According to a survey conducted by CMG Information Services, 90% of teachers purchase educational products through direct mail. The same survey found that 60% of teachers buy five or more educational products each year and that the best response month for mailings to teachers is August, followed by September, April, and March.

To obtain lists of schools and teachers, contact the following mailing list suppliers: American Student List Company, Consolidated Mailing Service, Mailings Clearing House, Market Data Retrieval, Quality Education Data, Willowood Lists, or Wilson Marketing Group. You can find their contact information at http://www.bookmarket.com/lists.html.

Another source of school lists, one highly recommended by at least one small publisher, is the state departments of education. Most have staff who specialize in sending out lists to people who request them. Costs are usually minimal. Use Google or another search engine to locate DOE addresses.

Note that you might also be able to trade, rent, or purchase lists from other publishers. For example, Prufrock Press has offered for rent a list of 19,634 K-12 teachers who have bought books about creative and critical thinking via mail order.

If the number of instructors in a particular discipline is small, you could send them review copies of your books right away. In most cases, however, you will want to pre-qualify recipients to make sure that they are responsible for making the adoption decision. Hence, when you send them your direct mail package describing your new textbook, enclose a reply card that allows them to request a complimentary examination copy (also known as a teacher's desk copy). On the card, ask them to answer these questions:

1. Instructor's name

2. Department and school where course is taught

3. Address of school (where book should be shipped)

4. Title of course

5. Current and/or previous textbooks used in the course

6. Age and grade level of students taking the course

7. Estimated number of students in the course

8. Date course will begin

9. Office phone number and office hours

10. Author and title of book they'd like to review

Not only will requesting this information weed out casual inquirers, but it will also provide you with some valuable marketing data for future promotions. When you send the review copy, enclose a review slip which asks the instructors to give you feedback on why they did or did not select your title for adoption. This feedback will be helpful in producing future textbooks and marketing promotions.

Besides using direct mail to contact decision makers, you can also use sales visits or telemarketing. For textbook adoptions, most major publishers use in-house sales reps who visit teachers, school boards, and state departments of education directly. Most successful smaller publishers, who cannot afford in-house sales reps, make use of many other channels to market their books to schools and colleges: direct mail, catalogs, advertising, card decks, distributors, publicity, exhibits, conferences, and telemarketing.

Textbook sales, of course, are not the only way you can sell to schools. Other options will be discussed later in this chapter.

16:02 How to Deal with Requests for Comp Copies

To sell college textbooks, you should offer complimentary copies to faculty members so they can review the textbook before assigning it for a course. Unfortunately, many college professors have gotten into the habit of requesting review copies for any book that might remotely interest them—even if they have no intention whatsoever of assigning the book for a class. Indeed, some college professors sell these complimentary copies to used-book wholesalers who, in turn, resell them to college bookstores which, in turn, resell them to students. It is estimated that the resale of these comp copies cost publishers $80 million dollars per year in lost sales. How can you cut these losses? Here are a few suggestions:

☐ **Don't give away comp copies at all**. One publisher of a scientific reference textbook reports that they "would go bankrupt if we gave away books to potential buyers. Professors who write asking for a free desk copy are sent a polite note with advertising material."

Another small publisher has sold over 2,000 *examination* copies of textbooks to teachers who otherwise would have asked for a free copy. Whenever he publishes a new book, he sends teachers a sales leaflet with the following offer:

Send for your professional sample now. The price is $12.50, but for a limited time you'll receive 20% off and free shipping—total $10.00. Please enclose payment—no invoicing. Sorry, no free copies. Of course, if you don't like the book, we'll gladly send a refund. But if you like it enough to assign it to your students, you'll receive a double refund of $20 upon any order of 15 copies or more.

☐ **Invoice for examination copies**. Many small publishers are now invoicing professors for examination copies. As in the example above, they might offer a 20% professional discount, but they require that if the professor is not going to adopt the book, then he or she must pay the invoice within 30 or 60 days. If the professor does not return the book or pay the invoice, he or she is put on a "book grabber" list.

☐ **Require a license agreement**. Send the license agreement with the review copy or, better yet, require that a teacher sign the agreement before they receive a comp copy. The license agreement should specify restrictions on its use (i.e., for examination purposes only, not for resale).

☐ **Use a special book design for examination copies** that indicates the book is free (under the assumption that students will refuse to pay for something marked free). Scott Foresman and St. Martins both use such examination copy designs.

☐ **Charge a processing fee**. Globe Pequot Press charges a $3.00 processing fee with every request for an examination copy.

☐ **Pay for book returns**. To make it easy for the professor to return a comp copy, accompany the book with a prepaid return envelope.

16:03   Factors Affecting Textbook Adoptions

When instructors review books for possible adoption, the most important factor influencing their decision is the quality of the text. The book must provide a reliable and comprehensive treatment of the subject. Here, though, are a few other factors that could influence their decision:

☐ **The timeliness of the information**—The book must be current; it must reflect the trends of the time. As a result, you should consider updating a textbook at least every three or four years.

☐ **Author's reputation**—The author's reputation is not that important for elementary textbooks or, sometimes, for introductory college-level texts, but it can be crucial for upper-level textbooks. In such cases, the author should be a recognized expert in the field.

☐ **Suited to the teacher's style**—The book must suit the teaching style of the instructor who will be using it in the classroom. If the instructor is uncomfortable with the format, style, or content of the text, she will not use it unless there are no comparable texts on the market.

☐ **Special features**—If the textbook includes quizzes, exercises, review questions, or other material that makes the teacher's job easier, it is more likely to be selected.

☐ **Teacher's guide**—A good teacher's guide is essential for any textbook adoptions. Besides providing lesson plans or ideas, it might also include student handouts, bibliographies, tests, and so on. If you provide accompanying transparencies, graphics, multimedia supplements, and other teacher's aids, so much the better. According to Ray Short, senior editor at Alan & Bacon, "Teaching aids are increasingly important to textbook sales, as they are often a deciding factor when colleges choose one text over another."

To facilitate the use of *The World Almanac for Kids* in schools, the publisher offered fifteen softcover copies, one hardcover copy, twenty-four pages of blackline masters, a teacher's guide, and two hundred bookmarks—all for only $99.00 (half the retail price of the fifteen copies).

☐ **Binding**—Because they tend to take more abuse and thus last longer, hardcover bindings are preferred over paperback bindings. This can be a crucial factor in school districts which provide textbooks for their students. It is not so important at the college level where the students have to buy their own texts. When the book is a supplement to the main textbook, its binding is not nearly as important. Indeed, many supplemental books are perfectbound rather than casebound.

☐ **Price**—Price is more important to school districts which must pay for the texts than it is for colleges where the students must pay the price. At the college level, the text quality is given primary consideration.

☐ **Graphic design**—The design of a book is becoming more of a factor in the decision. The design especially comes into play when two textbooks are equally matched on all other points, but one is more graphically appealing than the other. Hence, college publishers now use lots of graphics in introductory textbooks.

16:04 The El-Hi Textbook Adoption Market

Getting a textbook adopted in the el-hi market is a complicated, often years-long process, not something for the beginner or faint of heart. Few small companies can compete with the established publishing companies for a national market, but they can compete for specific state markets.

A state market can be worth many millions. For example, when Georgia school districts chose their K-8 reading textbooks in 1997, six of the top ten districts bought more than $11 million worth. Of the four publishing groups competing for the business, Houghton Mifflin sold $3.7 million worth of textbooks to these six districts alone.

Several years ago, Carolina Academic Press entered into competition for 7th and 8th grade science textbooks for the North Carolina adoption cycle. While they didn't have the money to give things away like the major publishers, they did have books that exactly followed the state science curriculum and they were able to spend more time teaching the teachers how to use their books. As a result, they captured 63% of the market and the cash flow allowed the company to survive and expand.

The el-hi textbook adoption market is complicated by the varying standards and requirements set by state departments of education. Some states restrict teacher options to only those books approved by the state; others allow more flexible purchasing. At present, twenty-one states (primarily southeastern and western states, including California, Texas, and Florida) have state adoption boards that must approve all K-12 textbooks sold to school districts. Individual districts in these states can only select from those texts approved by the state. Most states with approval plans review potential textbooks every four to eight years.

For more information on adoption procedures, write to the individual state departments of education. Or check out the adoption schedule prepared by the AAP School Division (Association of American Publishers).

One other disadvantage of competing in the textbook market is that it takes a lot of time and money to create a textbook that meets the changing requirements of various state agencies. For example, Macmillan/McGraw-Hill began market research in April, 1994 for social studies textbooks that would be shipped to Texas grade school students in the fall of 1997.

16:05 Other Sales in the El-Hi Market

Breaking into the el-hi textbook market could be difficult against the dominance of the already established textbook publishers, but there are other ways to sell books to schools. Here are a few examples of how smaller publishers are selling books in the school market:

☐ **Publish workbooks, practice guides, and other supplemental texts** which do not have to be approved by state agencies and which may be purchased from supplemental funds. 50% of elementary schools now use children's books as part of their reading curriculum in conjunction with a basic reading series. Another 20% use trade books as the sole component of their reading curriculum. For the entire K-12 market, sales of ancillary materials are well over $2 billion.

More than one smaller company has built up its value by selling to this market. The Tribune Company paid $100 million for The Wright Group, which sold $34 million in supplementary materials in 1993.

☐ **Go private.** When selling ancillary materials, also market to private school teachers since they tend to avoid many public school textbooks which are often designed for political rather than pedagogical reasons.

☐ **Follow the money.** Many ancillary products are bought with funds for Title 1, multicultural education, and other special programs. If you can show how your books help to meet the objectives of these programs, the schools can then use the special funds to order your books.

☐ **Go regional.** Instead of trying to compete with the major textbook publishers for national adoptions, publish regional books that might be adopted by your state or states in your region. For instance, why not publish a language arts book based on stories from regional authors? Or publish a state history book. Or a social studies program featuring regional problems, organizations, companies, and governments.

Tomato Enterprises has had great success selling pioneer history books to school districts in California that teach state history in the fourth grade. One of their books is on the state's framework (recommended list). Another sells well as a supplement.

☐ **Sell your books through school supply stores** where teachers go to buy teaching aids and other supplies to enrich their lessons. To learn more about this market, read **Educational Dealer**, P.O. Box 1080, Geneva, NY 14456: 315-789-0458; 800-344-0559; Fax: 315-789-4263. Web: http://www.eddealermagazine.com.

☐ **Attend the major trade show for this industry.** Here is the address and convention date for the School Products Expo: **National School Supply and Equipment Association**, 8300 Colesville Road #250, Silver Springs, MD 20910-3243; 301-495-0240; 800-395-5550; Fax: 301-495-3330. Web: http://www.nssea.org. The show is held in March.

Another association serving the school market is the **School, Home, & Office Products Association**, 3131 Elbee Road, Dayton, OH 45439-1900; 937-297-2250; 800-854-7467; Fax: 937-297-2254. Email: info@shopa.org. Web: http://www.shopa.org. Their trade show for the school, home, and office products market is held in September.

Not only does Music in Action sell its books to public school music teachers via direct mail, but it also works through a network of 75 educational music dealers, many of who it found through trade shows.

☐ **Market directly to teachers.** Many grade school teachers spend their own money to buy supplementary materials for their classrooms. Besides direct mail packages, you can also approach teachers through card decks such as those published by Learning Magazine or Prentice Hall Direct.

☐ **Organize book fairs.** Or sell to existing book fairs. Book clubs and fairs account for 20% of the market for K-8 educational materials. The largest company in this field is **Scholastic Book Fairs**, 1080 Greenwood Boulevard, Lake Mary, FL 32746; 407-829-7300. Web: http://www.scholastic.com/bookfairs. In 1994, this company hosted 60,000 book fairs.

Gryphon House sells preschools sample copies of their books which the schools can display at their book fairs. The schools take orders for additional copies which they, in turn, buy from Gryphon at a 20% discount.

☐ **Form a book club.** Again, Gryphon House mails a tabloid listing about 100 of its titles to over 10,000 preschool centers. The teachers at these schools, in turn, consolidate orders received from parents and send them on to Gryphon for fulfillment. Gryphon processes the combined order and ships the books to the schools where the books are distributed to the students. Under this program, the schools get to choose free books for their libraries, the number of books dependent on the amount of orders which were placed by the parents.

☐ **Sell to other book clubs.** If you don't form your own book club, work to get your books carried by the other book clubs that specialize in serving elementary schools. Here is the major one: **Scholastic Book Services**, 557 Broadway, New York, NY 10012; 212-343-6100; Fax: 212-389-3063. Web: http://www.scholastic.com.

☐ **Work through distributor catalogs.** A number of companies distribute books to schools and teachers through direct mail catalogs. To locate some of these companies, check with your local school teachers. They will be able to show you the catalogs they receive. Then write to those catalogs about your books.

Hertzberg New Method, 617 E. Vandalia Road, Jacksonville, IL 62650-3544; 217-243-5451; 800-637-6581; Fax: 800-551-1169. Web: http:// www.perma-bound.com. This company offers a number of book catalogs aimed at elementary schools.

Paperbacks for Educators, 426 W. Front Street, Washington, MO 63090-2103; 636-239-1999; 800-227-2591; Fax: 636-239-4515. Email: paperbacks@usmo.com. Web: http://www.any-book-in-print.com. This catalog features books on careers, children's books, education, child development, family life, psychology, and counseling.

Social Studies School Service, 10200 Jefferson Boulevard, P.O. Box 802, Culver City, CA 90232; 310-839-2436; 800-421-4246; Fax: 310-839-2249. Email: access@socialstudies.com. Web: http://www.social-studies.com. This company publishes thirty-five catalogs for K-12 teachers of social science, health, and language arts.

☐ **Offer your books to school fundraisers**. Student clubs, bands, sports teams, and even the PTA might be willing to sell some of your titles in order to raise funds for their programs. For example, sports teams could sell your fishing guides or other sports books to help raise money for special team trips. Look into any student function that might tie into one or more of your titles. Then send information on your fundraising programs to the faculty advisors at those schools which you feel would be most open. Before committing a lot of time or money into such a program, however, first test it with some local schools.

☐ **Sell site licenses**. George Moberg of The Writing Consultant offered site licenses to schools. His offer reads as follows:

For a small fee, your school or district can now create (in your duplicating room or at a local printshop) as many legal copies of the student text Writing on Computers *as needed for your classes. This is moneysaving even for as few as 30 copies (for your lab or one class). At list price they would cost $435, whereas your Share-Text / Site-Licence, plus original copy, would come to only $117.00—a nifty savings of about $300 to $400, depending on duplicating costs.*

Because this program increased his company's cash flow, he offered similar programs for school districts and even states.

☐ **Sell to adult education programs**. Because teachers of adult education programs usually have more flexibility in choosing which textbooks they use for their courses, you might be able to establish your new textbooks first through these programs. Sales to these programs could be enough to support the development and marketing of your textbooks until you are able to work your way through all the ins and outs of the school adoption processes in various states. For example, Dobry Enterpress sells their instructional drapery textbooks to home economics programs, extension services, and continuing education programs.

☐ **Promote to the home schooling movement**. With 500,000 children being schooled at home, there are many active organizations across the country promoting home schooling as an alternative to public and private schools. Many of the people involved in this movement are actively looking for alternative textbooks as well. There are a number of web sites, magazines, and catalogs that service this market. Google them.

☐ **Develop web sites aimed at educators**. Random House, for example, developed the Teachers@Random site (http://www.teachersatrandom. com) to support the classroom use of its books and educational materials. As part of that effort, they provide many ancillary materials on their site.

☐ **Sell your books to school libraries**. While school libraries may buy only one copy of each title, there are so many school libraries (over 120,000 public, private and parochial school libraries) that even one copy per library could make your books bestsellers. School libraries buy more than $400 million worth of books every year. Here are a few wholesalers that sell to school libraries:

Book Wholesalers, Inc., 1847 Mercer Road, Lexington, KY 40511; 859-231-9789; 800-888-4478; Fax: 859-225-6700. Web: http://www.bwi-books.com. This company distributes children's books to public libraries.

Sundance Publishers, One Beeman Road, P.O. Box 740, Northborough, MA 01632-0740; 508-571-6500; Fax: 508-571-6510. Email: info@sun-dancepub.com. Web: http://www.sundancepub.com. Using forty-five sales reps, Sundance distributes paperbacks and other supplementary materials to the school market.

☐ **Get your books reviewed** and/or recommended by *School Library Journal, Booklist, Horn Book, Instructor, Learning, Teaching K-8*, and other publications aimed at teachers and librarians.

☐ **Have your author tour schools and libraries**. Author appearances at schools and libraries have always been a part of the marketing programs of many major publishers of children's books. Why not make it a part of yours? Even if you don't have the time or money to arrange author appearances at schools and libraries yourself, support your authors when they are able to arrange such appearances. Note that many publishers offer a 40% discount to schools that sponsor such visits.

To book school visits, start with local schools and then branch out to other schools in your state or region. If you don't know who to contact, start by asking any teachers you know. They should be able to tell you who to contact for the local school district. From there you can ask for referrals to other schools.

If you need additional help setting up school appearances, check out **School Bookings**, Five Star Productions, P O Box 6698, Chandler AZ 85246-6698; 480-940-8182; 866-471-0777; Fax: 480-940-8787. Email: info@schoolbookings.com. Web: http://www.schoolbookings.com.

Authors: School visits can be a good source of additional income for authors of children's books. In a 1996 survey of twenty authors conducted by Raab Associates, the authors reported making an average of 23 visits per year, with honorariums ranging from $500 to $2,000 (average: $1,200). In addition, of course, you get the chance to interact with some of your greatest fans.

16:06 Other Sales to the College Market

In 1996, college instructional materials accounted for $1.9 billion in sales, with the ten largest publishers accounting for more than 95% of the sales (Cowles/Simba Information). The largest college publisher, Simon & Schuster, accounted for $516 million in sales, or about 27% of the market. That doesn't leave much room for the little guy.

However, besides the textbook market, the 15 million college students also represent a $20 billion market for non-school related items, from cars and clothing to records and movies to magazines and books. According to one study, the average college student spends $121 a month on consumer and entertainment items. They spend over half a billion dollars a year on books from college stores and bookstores.

The major way to reach the college textbook market is to get your books into the hands of the instructors who make the adoption selection. Here on the following pages are a few other things you can do to sell more of your books (both textbooks and regular trade books) in the college market.

☐ **Direct mail to faculty members** is still the best way to reach this market. Whether you want to sell textbooks, supplemental readings, or reference books to colleges, instructors are still the people who make the major adoption decisions.

One publisher offered professors a choice between an attractive pen and an abacus as incentives if they would read several chapters of an innovative computer textbook, provide their comments in writing, and return a survey card by a particular date. The promotion worked like a dream. It prodded the professors to open the book, read the chapters, and consider a new way of presenting introductory computer curricula. Additionally, thousands of cards were returned and the publisher's salespeople, armed with each professor's favorable comments or concerns, were able to gauge their prospect's degree of interest and answer objections faster.

☐ **Be alert to adoption cycles.** For college textbooks, 80% of adoption decisions are made in the spring (February through April) for fall courses. The other 20% are made in the fall for spring courses.

☐ **Enclose a library routing slip** in your direct mail packages to college instructors. Such a slip makes it easier for them to recommend your titles to their libraries. In 1996, college libraries bought $427 million worth of books. If you want to sell to the 3,000 college and university libraries, you need to bring your books to the attention of librarians. Faculty members can help you to do that if you make it easy for them.

☐ **Adapt your trade titles as supplemental readings** for college courses. Just as with elhi textbooks, you may find it easier to compete against the major publishers by going after these supplemental sales.

☐ **Don't compete for lower division core courses.** These courses, such as Principles of Economics or Introductory Psychology, have huge enrollments but are already served by major publishers. Instead, aim to serve the upper level courses. When approaching professors, encourage them to look at your book as a new approach for a course they are already teaching or as a basic text for a new course they might like to teach.

☐ **College travelers (sale representatives) can help to bring your books to the attention of faculty members.** While fewer publishers are currently using travelers, you might test using reps in certain regions (or try doing your own repping in your local area).

Here's one agency that serves Canada: **Savant Books**, Penelope Grows, Etobicoke, ON Canada; 416-231-6119; Fax: 416-231-5114. Email: savantbooks@primus.ca.

☐ **Sell to college wholesalers.** While college wholesalers often focus on used textbooks, they also sell new books.

One such company is **Tichenor College Textbook Company**, 5005 N. State Road 37 Business, Bloomington, IN 47404-1626; 812-332-3307; 800-367-4002; Fax: 812-331-7690. Web: http://www.tctcbook.com.

☐ **Exhibit your books at academic conferences** to bring your books to the attention of specific faculty. For example, you could exhibit your city planning texts at the American Society of Public Administration, the Urban Affairs Association, or the Population Association of America.

To promote its books on management, health, education, psychology, and public administration as textbooks, Jossey-Bass exhibits at professional academic conferences such as the Academy of Management, American Association of Higher Education, and American Psychological Association. Combined with direct mail and online marketing, Jossey-Bass now makes about a third of their sales from textbook adoptions.

☐ **Use an exhibit service to reach these conferences.** Association Book Exhibit exhibits books at a hundred conferences each year.

Association Book Exhibit, 8727A Cooper Road, Alexandria, VA 22309; 703-619-5030; Fax: 703-619-5035. Email: info@bookexhibit.com. Web: http://www.bookexhibit.com.

☐ **Get reviews in the appropriate scholarly journals**, especially those which are most applicable to your specific titles. If the reviews bring good results, then test an advertisement in subsequent issues to capitalize on that interest. Of course, you should also try for reviews in the book review media appropriate for college level books—*Choice, Library Journal*, and *Reference Quarterly*, among others.

☐ **Advertise in *The College Store Journal*** to bring your books to the attention of college store buyers. These bookstores carry not only textbooks and supplemental readings, but also general trade titles that they feel will interest college students. For more information on advertising in the *Journal* and exhibiting at Camex (Campus Market Expo) in April, write to the **National Association of College Stores**, 500 E. Lorain Street, Oberlin, OH 44074; 440-775-7777; 800-622-7498; Fax: 440-775-4769. Web: http://www.nacs.org. At one point they published a *Directory of College Stores Interested in Hosting Authors*. NASCORP, a division, is also a book wholesaler to college stores.

☐ **Mail directly to college bookstores** to promote specific titles or to feature your entire list in a catalog. Besides getting lists from NACS, you can also locate the addresses of Follett and Barnes & Noble college stores as noted below. You can also rent lists from Cahners Lists.

When one publisher found that bookstores would order fifty copies of a book, then a month later send twenty back, and then several months later order another fifty copies, they instituted a 15% restocking fee to help cut down on returns and paperwork. As a result, more bookstores began to keep books in stock and sell them rather than return them.

☐ **Sell to the college chain stores**. Follett College Stores operates several hundred stores on college campuses. Besides textbooks, they also buy trade books, t-shirts, coffee mugs, and other paraphernalia.

Follett College Stores, Follett Higher Education Group, 1818 Swift Drive, Oak Brook, IL 60523-1576. Web: http://fheg.follett.com. They list all their bookstores on their web site (searchable by state).

Barnes & Noble also operates many college stores. For a list of B&N college stores, contact their vendor relations at 212-539-2300.

☐ **Work with college store alliances.** John Wiley & Sons, Addison Wesley Longman, and International Thomson Publishing worked with Collegiate Stores Corporation (now Connect2One) to create a campaign to increase the sales of new textbooks. The promotion was supported with point-of-purchase displays, posters, ads, shelf-talkers, a web site, an online contest, coupons, and an instant-win sweepstakes.

The primary buying alliance for college stores is **Connect2One**, 5412 Courseview Drive #150, Mason, OH 45040-2364; 513-754-0111; Fax: 513-754-0110. Web: http://www.connect2one.com. It services more than 500 college stores.

☐ **Promote directly to students for bookstore sales.** Merriam-Webster used a college scholarship sweepstakes to promote its latest *Collegiate* dictionary to college students.

☐ **Mail your catalog direct to students.** According to a recent survey, 55% of all college undergraduates have bought by mail or telephone during the past year. Of those who did, 45% bought books.

☐ **Advertise in media aimed at students.** Or, better yet, get publicity in these media. Here are a few magazines published for college students: *The Black Collegian, Campus Life, College Outlook,* and *Panache. Newsweek* and a few other magazines publish special college editions.

Be sure to promote to the college newspapers. To promote *Making College Count,* Patrick O'Brien wrote a weekly column that was syndicated nationally to 400 college newspapers.

☐ **Promote on campus.** Below are the names of a few companies that can help you promote on campus, from campus trial packs to take-one displays, from postering to mailings. Other services can be found at http://www.bookmarket.com/16.html.

Campus Dimensions, 1717 Arch Street, 33rd Floor, Philadelphia, PA 19103; 800-592-2121; Fax: 215-568-1701. Web: http://www.cdicccc.com. This company specializes in programs directed at high school and college students, including bulletin board postering, campus reps, college tours, and sampling programs.

The College Kit, The Gigunda Group, 540 N. Commercial Street, Manchester, NH 03101; 603-314-5000; Fax: 602-314-5001. Email: info@gigundagroup.com. Web: http://www.collegekit.com. They conduct college sampling programs.

360 Youth, 151 West 26th Street, New York, NY 10001; 212-244-4307; Fax: 212-244-4311. Email: marketing@360youth.com. Web: http://www.360youth.com. This company's promotions range from trial packs and sampling to a Term Planner advertising publication and Campus Source billboards.

16:07 The Importance of Sales to Libraries

Since libraries buy over $1.6 billion worth of books every year, they represent a major market you should not ignore. Library sales are especially crucial for the more than 2,000 children's titles published every year, the majority of which are still bought by schools and libraries. Libraries offer several other advantages to book publishers:

• You can sell books to libraries at little or no discount for single copy orders but, if you want libraries to order direct, offer a higher discount for quantity orders (match the discounts offered by wholesalers).

- You don't have to offer a return privilege to libraries. They seldom return a book.

- Libraries offer great exposure for your books. Americans make some 3.6 billion visits to libraries every year. 57% of American adults visited a library at least once during the past year (*U.S. News*/CNN poll). 80% of them go to borrow books.

- The greatest advantage of library sales, though, is that they often result in further sales. If your book is the kind that readers would want to refer to again and again, those readers who first discover your book in a library will often order the book direct from you rather than continue to check the book out of their local library. At Open Horizons, we receive many orders from people who first see our books in libraries.

  One study of technical book buyers discovered that 2% to 3% of all such buyers bought the book because they had first seen the book in a library. When telephone operators at John Wiley & Sons asked where callers had heard about a title, 15% said they had seen the book in a library.

  Tikka Books has found that some public libraries order a dozen or more copies of its *Easy Halloween Costumes for Children* because "their patrons admit while checking the book out that they have no intention of returning it ever and would rather pay the $10 penalty or whatever to keep it forever."

16:08 The Diversity of the Library Market

The library market is not a homogeneous whole. Instead, it is made up of many smaller markets, each with its own special audience and interests. Of the $1.6 billion in library sales made in 1996, 40% of those sales were made to public libraries, 25% to el-hi school libraries, 25% to college libraries, and 10% to special libraries.

There are more than 150,000 libraries in the United States, including 9,000 public library systems, 3,275 college libraries, 100,000 el-hi libraries, 1,000 governmental libraries, 2,000 business libraries, 2,000 medical libraries, 1,000 law libraries, and more than 1,000 formal church libraries (and an estimated 50,000 smaller church libraries). Plus almost every organization in the country has its own small collection of books.

☐ Most of the above figures are taken from the mailing list catalog of DM2, the major supplier of library mailing lists. For more information, contact **DM2**, 2000 Clearwater Drive, Oak Brook, IL 60523; 800-321-4958; Fax: 630-288-8390. Web: http://www.dm2lists.com.

When Publishers Marketing Association surveyed the recipients of its library mailings (addressed to the acquisition librarian), it found that 92% of the recipients were directly responsible for placing orders. 37% also passed on the material to others for review.

☐ Another source of library lists is the list department of the **American Library Association**, 50 E. Huron Street, Chicago, IL 60611; 312-944-6780; 800-545-2433; Fax: 312-440-9374. Web: http://www.ala.org.

☐ One publisher reports that many state libraries maintain lists of all the libraries in that state. For example, the state library in Tallahassee offers publishers free access to its list of Florida libraries.

☐ For a list of 6,000 Canadian libraries, write to **Micromedia**, 20 Victoria Street, Toronto M5C 2N8, Ontario, Canada; 416-362-5211; 800-387-2689; Fax: 416-362-6161. Email: info@micromedia.ca. Web: http://www.micromedia.ca.

☐ For 12,000 special libraries, write to the **Special Libraries Association**, 331 S. Patrick Street, Alexandria, VA 22314-3501; 703-647-4900; Fax: 703-647-4901. Email: sla@sla.org. Web: http://www.sla.org.

☐ For a list of the top 2,300 public libraries for only $40.00, see the Book Market.com website at http://www.bookmarket.com/databases.html.

16:09 Why Libraries Buy from Library Jobbers

According to several studies, anywhere from 65% to 75% of all library orders are placed through wholesalers. Indeed, recent studies indicate that the percentage is even higher. According to a Cahners Research study of children's librarians conducted in 1991, 81.7% of all children's books are purchased through wholesalers, while 15.2% are bought direct from publishers (3.1% are obtained through donations). In a late 1992 survey of librarians, Publishers Marketing Association found that 95% of public librarians order from wholesalers while 36% of them also order direct from publishers.

Regardless of the actual percentage, wholesalers play an important role in getting your books to libraries. Of these wholesalers, Baker & Taylor is far and away the most significant for library sales. As many as 50% of all library sales for smaller publishers will come through Baker and Taylor. Other major library wholesalers include Brodart, Blackwell North America, Coutts Library Services, Emery-Pratt, Midwest Library Service, Yankee Book Peddler, as well as a good number of specialized wholesalers such as J. A. Majors (medical books), Bilingual Publications Company (Spanish books), and Small Press Distribution (literary and poetry books).

For an updated inexpensive list of the top book wholesalers, library jobbers, and book distributors, see the *Book Distribution MiniGuide* from John Kremer at http://www.bookmarket.com.

Why do libraries prefer buying from these wholesalers rather than direct from publishers? Here are just a few reasons:

☐ Library jobbers provide many more services, such as cataloging cards, book processing, and special bindings.

☐ Jobbers offer a greater selection than any one publisher can hope to offer. In essence, they offer the library one-stop shopping.

☐ There is less paperwork and check writing involved in placing a large order from one source as compared to placing many smaller orders from a number of sources.

☐ There is also less work in processing the books when they are received as one shipment.

☐ Jobbers usually offer equal or higher discounts than those offered by publishers, especially on larger orders (which the library can place when it consolidates orders for books from many different publishers).

☐ Jobbers, in general, offer faster and more reliable service than publishers. We as publishers should not be proud of this fact, but a fact it is.

☐ Jobbers tend to publish more frequent catalogs and other announce-ments of new titles. Many publish monthly announcements, thus enabling the librarian to keep up to date on all new titles.

☐ Many jobbers offer continuation, standing order, or on-approval plans for specific subjects. Because most publishers do not publish enough books in any one subject area, they can't possibly compete with jobbers in offering a comprehensive standing order plan for specific subjects.

16:10 How to Appeal to Libraries

To make it easy for librarians to order your books, provide them with the information they need to make informed decisions. Do not clutter your sales literature with hype. Instead, provide them with the following information in a clear and simple presentation:

☐ **ISBN and LCCN numbers**—State the ISBN and Library of Congress Cataloging numbers for every title listed. If you are publishing both a hardcover and paperback edition, be clear on which ISBN belongs to which edition. Each format requires a separate ISBN number. If possible, also include the Dewey classification numbers to facilitate distribution to subject specialists within the library.

☐ **Publication dates**—List the publication dates for your new and forthcoming titles so librarians can be sure when the books will be available; then be sure to meet those publication dates. List the month and year of publications for your backlist titles as well; librarians like to know how current the information is in any book they order. Providing the copyright date and ISBN numbers also help librarians to avoid ordering books or editions they already have.

☐ **CIP data**—If you participate in the Library of Congress's Cataloging in Publication program, be sure to indicate this. The CIP program provides ready-to-use cataloging information which any library may use. Librarians are more likely to order a book if they know that catalog card information will be readily available.

☐ **Prices**—Indicate the prices for each and every edition of your books. Librarians must have prices if they are to prepare book orders within their allotted budget. Librarians rarely choose on the basis of price alone, but if your book is less expensive than an equivalent book on the same subject, most librarians would order yours. The key word is "equivalent." If one book has gotten better reviews, even if it is more expensive, librarians will almost always order it. Quality of content and format is far more important to them than the price.

☐ **Edition statement**—When one of your titles has been published in a new edition (or as part of a continuing series), make that fact clear. Many libraries which have been satisfied with previous editions of a book will order new editions of the book to keep their collections as current as possible.

☐ **Contents**—Give the librarians some idea of what your books contain. Either reprint the table of contents, print a short representative excerpt, or write a good descriptive statement.

☐ **Reviews**—Quote favorable reviews from library journals or from endorsements by people who are well-known in the book's field. These outside testimonials carry far more weight than anything you can write about the book. Reviews are by far the most important criteria used by librarians in making their buying decisions. When quoting reviews, indicate the month and year of the review as well as the journal's name, so the librarian can go back to read the review or cite it when ordering.

☐ **Supplementary material**—State the number of pages, number of illustrations (photographs, drawings, tables, forms, graphs, etc.), and whatever additional information the book provides—especially whether it has appendices, a glossary, bibliography, index, and so on. The fact that your book has an index or a bibliography is important to librarians. It makes it easier for them to provide support to people who want to research a subject in greater depth.

☐ **Author credentials**—If the author is an expert in the field or has other credentials that make him or her particularly suited to writing the book, be sure to state these facts.

☐ **Physical qualities**—Indicate whether your books are available in both casebound and paperback versions and, if so, at what prices. Also indicate any editions with special library bindings or acid-free paper which make for a more durable, longer-lasting book.

☐ **Availability**—If your book is available through library wholesalers or distributors, list the specific names of the most prominent ones.

☐ **Index your catalogs**—If you mail catalogs to libraries, index the catalog listings by author, title, *and* subject. Give librarians as many ways as possible to locate the titles that interest them.

☐ **Enclose posters or bookmarks**—If you enclose a bookmark, poster, or mobile featuring your book, more librarians will order it—just so they can use your book in a special display. In the Cahners Survey, 93.8% of the libraries reported using posters, 83.6% used bookmarks, 49.2% used mobiles, and 40.6% used other displays supplied by the publisher.

In short, provide libraries with any information that 1) demonstrates the benefits of your books for readers, 2) makes it easier for the librarian to place an order, 3) indicates that your books will stand up to heavy library use, and 4) shows that your books are readily available.

16:11 Some Tips on Selling to Libraries

Libraries are really quite easy to sell to if you publish books that fill a need, whether it be entertainment, information, inspiration, or instruction. Once you've produced a book of quality, all you have to do is to let the librarians know about the book.

Perhaps I make it sound too simple but it is easier to get the attention of librarians than it is to reach booksellers or consumers. The main point to remember is that librarians are information specialists. They are continually and actively seeking new titles which can help them better serve their patrons. Hence, you don't have to overcome as much sales resistance as you would with consumers or booksellers who have many other activities demanding their attention. On the next few pages I've listed a few of the many ways you can attract the attention of librarians to your books:

Work to get reviews.

Work to get good reviews of your books in library review media such as *Publishers Weekly*, *Library Journal*, *Booklist*, *Kirkus Reviews*, *Choice* (for books of interest to graduate and undergraduate libraries), *Horn Book* and *School Library Journal* (for children's books), and *Foreword* magazine (for small press titles), as well as in the general review media which librarians rely upon (such as the *New York Times Book Review*).

Since they don't have time to read every book that is published, librarians rely on reviews from respected media to help them make informed buying decisions. A review in *Library Journal*, for instance, can sometimes result in orders for 1,000 books or more.

What are your chances of getting a review in these journals? *Library Journal* reviews 4,000 books per year and *School Library Journal* 5,000. Yet these two journals receive 600 books a week—that's over 30,000 new books every year. As a result, your chances of getting a review in one or both of these journals is somewhere between 1 in 6 and 1 in 8.

A Cahners Research survey had librarians rate the various criteria that influence their decision to purchase a book. Below are listed the results of that survey (on a scale of 1 to 6, with 1 not important and 6 extremely important). Note how important reviews are.

5.6 reviews in journals
5.5 starred reviews in journals
5.0 requests of patrons
3.9 reading copies
3.5 quote advertisements in journals
3.5 publishers' catalogs
3.4 internal review publications
3.2 wholesalers' catalogs
2.7 visits from sales representatives
2.5 direct mail offers
2.5 author appearances
1.9 telemarketing

Get other notices in library journals.

These journals provide other possibilities for being featured, including roundup articles, resource listings, interviews, and feature stories. For example, in each issue *School Library Journal* publishes a listing of new award recipients. Hence, if your authors or books receive any awards, send information to the library and other book trade journals.

* One issue of *School Library Journal* listed the following awards: Detroit Public Library's Author Day Award, Dorothy Canfield Fisher Award (voted by Vermont children in grades 4-8), Paul A. Witty Award, Iowa Children's Choice Award, Judy Lopez Memorial Award (for preteen books), National Jewish Book Awards, Young Reader's Choice Award (Schaumburg Public Library), and others.

* Both *School Library Journal* and *Library Journal* feature free or inexpensive posters, pamphlets, calendars, bibliographies, and other library resources in their monthly Checklist departments. *Pueblo Stories and Storytellers*, a children's paperback costing $9.95, was featured in the Checklist department of *School Library Journal*.

* One author regularly writes informative, educational letters to the editor of library journals offering free fact sheets on topics in her subject area. Each year she succeeds in placing two to three letters which each result in a hundred to five hundred requests for the fact sheets. She always sends her catalog with the free fact sheets.

Advertise in these journals.

If you have a choice, advertise in *Library Journal*, *School Library Journal*, and *Booklist*. Librarians like to know they are dealing with reputable and reliable suppliers. Advertisements in these journals help to reinforce your company image and also indicate to librarians that you are seriously pursuing their market. In a survey conducted by ABC-CLIO, they found that the key factor in getting librarians to open your promotional material and place an order was whether or not they recognized your company name.

Send your catalogs and other seasonal announcements to libraries.

Arrange your catalogs by subject area, then by author. Clearly indicate any new or forthcoming titles with the month and year of publication. Use simple, clear layouts with wide margins (for making notes). Show the covers of the books. If room allows, also include a table of contents or sample page. Provide an easy-to-use order form arranged by subject.

Provide incentives for ordering direct.

If you want libraries to order direct from you, provide some incentive for them to do so. Offer sale prices on certain titles, or prepayment discounts, or free postage. Be sure to set a time limit on these sales to encourage the libraries to order right away and to prevent orders from trickling in for years (which could cause all sorts of problems in your fulfillment department). At the same time, since many libraries have rather elaborate purchasing procedures, allow ample time for ordering; hence, set a deadline that is at least 60 to 90 days from the date you will be mailing the promotion.

Direct mail does work.

In a survey of librarians in England, the most cited source of information used in making acquisition decisions was direct mail from publishers.

- Twin Peaks Press has continued to sell their book, *All about Sewing Machines*, to libraries via direct mail and still gets lots of reorders even though the book was originally published in 1970.

- In a 1988 issue of *Library Hotline*, one librarian shared the following "time-and-money saving idea" with his fellow librarians. At his library they have their mail clerk automatically throw out all mail with a bulk rate or nonprofit mail insignia—without even opening it. As he put it, most of it is of little interest to the library anyway. Since this rather dubious idea was shared with about 2,000 other librarians, you might want to reconsider using bulk rate for your mailings to libraries.

Offer standing order plans.

For annuals, series, or subject areas where you publish many books (such as poetry books or children's books), offer a standing order plan where the library signs up to receive one copy of every new book you publish. Such standing order plans can be effective with large city and county systems. If you can get them to order one copy for the main library, chances are that if they like what they see, they'll order more copies for the other libraries in the system.

Gale Research offers the Gale Advantage Plan which allows libraries to earn a 7% discount on all standing orders plus free shipping and handling. They also receive a one-year money-back guarantee on all books shipped on standing order: "If for any reason a book does not meet your expectations, it may be returned within 12 months for a full credit or refund—no questions asked." Finally, all books still in print are covered by Gale's free book insurance policy. Under this policy, Gale will "replace any publication that is lost, damaged, or stolen—free of charge."

Refer readers to their local library.

Librarians are especially sensitive to the requests of people who use their library and will often order a book simply because one or two people request the title. Melvin Powers of Wilshire Books often sends readers of his advertisements to their local library to check out his books before they buy them. Not only does this allow readers to preview the books, but it also increases the demand at local libraries which, in turn, order extra copies if the demand persists. He claims to have sold thousands of copies in this way.

Offer prepublication savings.

In addition to their standing order plan, Gale also offers a PrePub Club where librarians can save 15% on titles they pre-select from a quarterly list. Librarians can earn a 25% discount if they choose to receive every new title in a specific category (general reference, business, literary/biography, environmental, or all new titles). Under either of these two discounts, librarians have up to six months to return the books for a full refund if they decide the books are not for them. Librarians receive a 50% discount if they choose to receive every new title in a specific category—and they buy nonreturnable.

Work with the major library wholesalers.

Send wholesalers information on forthcoming titles in plenty of time for them to order before they receive purchase orders from libraries. Remember that 75% of your library sales will come through these jobbers so make it easy for them to work with you.

Baker & Taylor runs an ad in many issues of *School Library Journal* that lists all titles reviewed in that issue with a blank space to allow librarians to enter how many copies they want to order. All books reviewed in that issue are advertised as being available through Baker & Taylor.

Provide libraries with display materials.

Almost every library has one or two display areas which they change every month or two. If you provide them with posters, extra book jackets, or other display material, they are more likely to order your book *and* feature it in one of their displays. Indeed, try including an extra copy of the book jacket with any direct orders from libraries. Remember: 95% of librarians report using posters while 83.6% report using bookmarks.

Provide libraries with cataloging cards.

If your primary market is libraries, offer library cards with your books. This makes it easier for librarians to catalog and shelve your book. You can order cards from the Library of Congress. Just send them your LCCN (Library of Congress Cataloging Number) and 65¢ for each set of 8 cards you want. They only sell main entry cards in sets of eight. Before ordering from them, write for complete details. Write to: **Cataloging Distribution Service**, Library of Congress, Washington, DC 20541; 202-707-6100. Of course, once you have a complete sample, you can print your own cards locally.

Exhibit your books at the major library association meetings.

Exhibit at any of the major meetings: the American Library Association convention in midsummer, their midwinter meeting, and the conventions of the Special Library Association, the Association of College and Research Libraries, and the many regional associations.

If you cannot afford to exhibit on your own, join one of the cooperative exhibits, such as those provided by Conference Book Service, Publishers Book Exhibit, SPAN, and Publishers Marketing Association.

- **Combined Book Exhibit**, 277 White Street, Buchanan, NY 10511; 914-739-7500; 800-462-7687; Fax: 914-739-7575. Email: info@combined- book.com. Web: http://www.combinedbook.com. This company provides co-op exhibits at many library association meetings.

- **The Reference Shelf**, 88 N. Main Street, Concord, NH 03301; 603-229-0662; Fax: 603-226-9443. Email: trs@basch.com. Web: http://www. Basch.com/ref_home.asp. This company displays directories and other reference works at many library conferences.

Speak at libraries.

At one time Baker & Taylor published a state-by-state directory of 140 public libraries that hosted author readings. That directory was obviously a short list. Many more libraries host talks. Ask your local library how to set up a talk there—and to recommend other libraries where you can talk.

> **Authors** — If your publisher is not able to put much attention on arranging appearances for you at libraries, you can arrange your own. Arrange to read during one of their children's book hours, speak to the Friends of the Library group, or answer questions on what it is like to write a book.

Besides speaking at libraries, you can also exhibit illustrations from your books. Grace Housholder, author of *The Funny Things Kids Say Will Brighten Any Day*, has found that having exhibits of the original watercolors from the book is a good way to promote the book to libraries. She has also provided libraries with matted, illustrated pages from the book to use for month-long displays.

The American Library Association and Association of American Publishers is offering a new Authors @ Your Library online matchmaking service for librarians seeking authors and for authors/publicists looking for library speaking opportunities. For authors or publicists, log on to the web site at http://www.authorsatyourlibrary.org to tell libraries how to contact you about speaking events.

Join cooperative mailings to libraries.

Publishers Marketing Association, other associations, and some specialty publishers offer co-op mailing programs to libraries. PMA, for instance, does mailings quarterly to public libraries, biannually to K-12 libraries, and three times a year to college libraries. Many publishers have reported good results using these inexpensive promotions.

Arrange distribution in special subject catalogs

Several publishers issue specialty catalogs that they mail to libraries. Among such catalogs are those published by North Carolina Biological Supply, Social Studies School Service, Tools of the Trade, and Gryphon House. Some of these are cooperative ventures; others are catalogs issued by publishers who also distribute other publishers' books.

Get listed in the standard reference works.

Get listed in the directories and bibliographies used by librarians to place orders, such as *Books in Print, Small Press Record of Books in Print,* and *Publishers Trade List Annual.*

Few librarians will track down a publisher who is not listed in these standard reference works if there is another publisher who is listed and who can supply a similar title. Moreover, such listings can lead to direct sales since librarians use these books to locate books of special interest. For example, Davis Publications found that most of the library sales for Carolyn Hall's *Soft Sculpture* were attributable to the fact that it was the only book listed in the title volume of *Books in Print* under "soft sculpture."

Publish a newsletter for librarians.

Another way to promote to libraries is to publish a newsletter targeted directly to them. While you might not be able to hire someone full time to provide such a newsletter, you could work with your local librarian to publish a quarterly or semiannual newsletter that features reviews of your books from a librarian's perspective.

Random House publishes *Random Revelations,* a newsletter targeted to librarians that is written by a former librarian. Nolo Press sends libraries a free subscription to *Nolo News,* their quarterly newsletter.

Sponsor a column in *Library Journal*.

If you have a number of books that would appeal to libraries, you might want to sponsor a full-page column or department in *Library Journal*. Baker & Taylor sponsored Literacy Clearinghouse, which features new books to encourage people to read. Gale Research sponsored Ready Reference, which featured submissions from librarians on techniques and rules of thumb that work for them. Gale paid libraries $50 for each tip used in the column.

Sponsor a library.

Besides supporting several library associations, Nolo Press has also supported libraries in the following ways: 1) They sponsor an annual library contest with three libraries winning $1,000, $500, or $200. 2) For every dollar Nolo's customers give to their favorite library in the form of Nolo gift certificates, Nolo doubles the amount. Under this program, Nolo gave out gift certificates worth over $10,000 in 1994. Their matching cost, of course, was $5,000. But their actual cost is much less since all certificates will be spent on Nolo books. 3) At various library conventions, Nolo gives out coupons which allow libraries to replace one stolen Nolo book for free. Because of the nature of their books and the demand, Nolo's books often get stolen.

Hire sales representatives.

Generally speaking, hiring your own sales representatives would not be cost-effective unless you publish many new titles each year for the library market. Doubleday has a special sales force which represents their line of science fiction hardcovers (and other titles) to libraries and institutions, which sign up for a year's worth of books at a special discount.

Sign up with a library distributor.

For many smaller publishers, signing up with one or more distributors has provided a significant jump in sales. Below are four distributors of small press titles to libraries.

- **Quality Books**, Vendor Relations Department, 1003 W. Pines Road, Oregon, IL 61061-9680; 815-732-4450; 800-323-4241; Fax: 815-732-4499. Web: http://www.quality-books.com. Using sales reps, Quality, the top small press distributor to libraries, distributes books and videos to libraries around the country using sales reps.

- **Superior Books**, 141 Dishman Lane, P.O. Box 1371, Bowling Green, KY 42102-1371; 270-781-9946; 800-532-5232; Fax: 270-781-9963. Using 22 sales reps, this company distributes 15,000 titles to libraries nationally. They prefer lines of books versus single title publishers.

- **Unique Books**, Product Development, 5010 Kemper Avenue, St. Louis, MO 63139; 314-776-6695; 800-533-5446. Email: uniquebks@aol.com. Web: http://www.uniquebooksinc.com. Unique distributes 12,000 books and videos from 1,600 publishers to libraries.

- **Librarian's Book Link**, P.O. Box 1199, State College, PA 16804-1199; 866-618-2665; Fax: 866-718-2665. Email: service@librariansbooklink. com. Web: http://www.librariansbooklink.com. This company has sales reps who make calls on high school, public, and academic libraries.

While library wholesalers rarely not go out of their way to promote your titles (but, instead, passively process the orders they receive from libraries), Quality Books actively distribute nonfiction adult books to libraries throughout the country. They exhibit at the major library conventions, have field sales reps which cover the entire U.S., offer standing order plans, telemarket, mail catalogs, and do whatever else they can to sell small press titles. And they have been successful: They have sold more than a million small press books. Besides that, they are easy to work with and pay on time. What more can you ask for?

Publishing houses now expect authors to play
an up-close-and-personal role in promoting their books.
And that means getting on the road to make appearances
at bookstores, libraries, writers conferences, schools
and other venues to read from, talk about and sign copies.
— Carole Goldberg, *Harvard Courant* Books Editor

The Ideal Product —
What We Are Looking For

by the staff of Quality Books

The following list, courtesy of the Quality Books web site, lists some of the basic criteria they use when selecting titles for the library market. This list should give you an idea of what sells best into public libraries.

☐ Adult nonfiction, selected children's titles, video/DVD/CD/CD-ROM titles (we do not stock poetry titles or novels).

☐ Timely subject matter.

☐ Recent copyright date (a must for most of our large customers). Ideally, we like to hear about a new title 90 days before the publication date.

☐ Well organized.

☐ Includes an index and table of contents.

☐ Title: Should be the same everywhere it appears on the product and packaging.

☐ Readily available information.

☐ No fill-in-the-blanks workbooks.

☐ Product title has not been exposed to the library market.

☐ Publisher's/producer's primary market is outside of the library market.

☐ Subject coverage fills a gap. Title is clearly differentiated from others in the field.

☐ The cover and title effectively and clearly convey the product's purpose at a glance. It is important that all product covers receive the same attention. Covers may be black & white or four-color.

☐ Binding or packaging is durable and cannot be easily damaged.

☐ Product is freestanding—not including or necessitating accompanying material, i.e., booklet with video.

☐ Video/DVD producer must be able to grant public performance rights for the U.S. and Canada.

Chapter 17

How to Sell Subsidiary Rights

The smart way for a new publishing venture to hit the ground running is to choose books geared to the sub-rights market.
— Paul Nathan, former Rights Columnist, *Publishers Weekly*

The sale of subsidiary rights is now a major source of income for trade book publishers. If you were to look at the accounting records of any major book publisher, you would discover that they lose money publishing books —that their income from rights sales exceeds their profits every year. What this means, in essence, is that major publishers are in the business of selling rights. They publish books, in effect, to establish the value of the rights. For this reason, many publishers have established a department of three or more people whose sole responsibility is to arrange sales of subsidiary rights.

Given the potential for income, you too should seriously consider establishing your own subsidiary rights department or, at the very least, you should assign someone to spend a portion of each day pursuing sales of subsidiary rights. The Lyons Press, a midsize New York City publisher, has set up such a department which now brings in more than $200,000 a year from rights sales. If you publish five or more titles of general interest every year, you might well discover that an organized, full-time pursuit of subsidiary rights sales will more than pay for itself.

17:01 Seven Benefits of Subsidiary Rights Sales

While subsidiary rights sales are a great source of income for any publisher, there are many other reasons why you should pursue the sale of subsidiary rights. Here are seven of them:

☐ **Rights income will help to pay for the printing and promotion of your books.** Such sales are useful in paying for an increased advertising budget which can, in turn, mean increased sales in the retail stores.

☐ **You can make money on a book even before you publish it.** For example, on one book Grove/Atlantic sold paperback rights to Vintage for $300,000, book club rights to Book-of-the-Month Club and Quality Paperback Book Club, and foreign rights in three languages—all before publication date. As a result, the publisher was able to commit $100,000 to the initial promotional budget, a far larger sum than it would otherwise have been able to do for that book.

☐ **Prepublication rights sales increase the visibility of your titles** and lead to larger advance orders from bookstores, more prominent displays, and greater sales. Warner Books had to increase the first printing of *The Notebook* by Nicholas Sparks to 250,000 copies after booksellers responded to the enthusiasm of rights buyers from New Line Cinema (film rights), *Good Housekeeping* (first serial rights), an auction for mass-market reprint rights, and sales of translation rights to a dozen countries.

☐ **Rights sales increase the credibility of any book.** A rights sale says that at least one person or organization has sanctioned the book as something worth being excited about. Hence, whenever you make a rights sale, be sure to let your distributor or sales reps know about the sale. As one distributor noted, "Outside validation is a vital selling tool!"

☐ **Rights sales beget other rights sales.** For instance, a first serial sale to a major magazine can spark interest in the book from the major mass-market reprinters or from independent movie producers.

☐ **The exposure given a book by a first serial can increase bookstore sales.** The serialization of Erich Segal's *Love Story* in *Ladies Home Journal* caused such a positive reaction that many readers bought the book. The excerpt put the book on the road to bestseller status.

☐ **The sale of movie or TV rights can create a second wave of book sales** when the movie plays in the theaters or the TV show is aired. This second wave of sales can sometimes be greater than the first wave.

Few publishers have ever reported losing any bookstore sales as the result of subsidiary rights sales. Indeed, in most cases, rights sales actually spur bookstore sales.

> **Authors** — Subsidiary rights income can be substantial and continue for years. Originally published in the 1960's, John Knowle's novel, *A Separate Peace*, has consistently earned royalties of $100,000 or more every year. Recently, Macmillan renewed the mass-market paperback rights for another 10 years by asking Bantam to pay an advance of $1 million.

17:02 Tips on Selling Subsidiary Rights

To make subsidiary rights sales, you must be well-organized, persistent, and attentive to details. When I published *Mail Order Selling Made Easier*, I actively promoted rights sales. As a result, I sold U.K. rights to McGraw-Hill, book club rights to The Executive Program and Fortune Book Club, serial rights to *Income Plus*, and reprint rights for a new trade paperback and casebound edition to John Wiley & Sons (who, in turn, published the update as *The Complete Direct Marketing Sourcebook*). Total income from rights sales amounted to more than $18,000 before royalties. And Wiley sold book club rights for their edition to Fortune Book Club again!

On the following pages are a few steps you can follow to increase your effectiveness in selling subsidiary rights:

☐ **Develop a contact list** for subsidiary rights. Include potential buyers of serial rights, audio/video rights, reprints, book clubs, and so on. Break down the list by category—those interested in fiction, those interested in biography, those interested in science, or whatever other categories you publish so you can match your new titles to each potential buyer.

☐ **Keep these key contacts informed of any forthcoming books.** Send news releases to them the moment you have signed an author for a new book and have set a proposed publication date. Send them your catalogs, noting those titles which would most interest their audience. Finally, once you have a manuscript in hand, send a letter to each of your contacts offering them a preview galley or photocopy of the manuscript.

☐ **Send out review copies** (either copies of the manuscript or galley copies) as soon as you receive requests. The quicker you send them out, the less chance the editor or buyer will have to lose interest in your book. In most cases, these review copies must be in the hands of major rights buyers at least six months before publication date so they have plenty of time to make a decision and schedule their use of the rights they buy.

☐ **Include the following information when you send out review copies.** You can add reviews, testimonials, and so forth if you have them.

1. A cover letter outlining why the book should interest their audience.
2. A biography of the author.
3. A fact sheet highlighting the contents of the book and your promotional plans for it.
4. If you have prepared a mockup of the book's cover, send that also.
5. Finally, be sure to note the publication date.

☐ **Don't be afraid to approach more than one rights buyer at a time.** It's standard operating procedure at major publishing houses. As a courtesy, though, let the buyers know that others are also being approached. The advantages of such multiple submissions are:

1. You can approach more potential buyers in a shorter period of time.

2. If more than one buyer expresses an interest in your book, they might bid against each other thus raising the final price for the rights.

☐ **Call or write key contacts.** Some rights buyers prefer to be telephoned first so they can screen a title. Others prefer to have some promotional literature or a review copy in hand before you call. Here are general guidelines on how to decide whether to call first and mail later or mail first and call later: If you are unsure whether or not rights buyers would be interested in a particular title, call them and ask. On the other hand, if you are sure that the book will interest them (because the book is highly targeted to their audience), then send the book or promotional literature first and follow up with a call.

☐ **Follow up.** Always be sure to do some sort of follow-up on every contact you make. Don't assume that just because they have not contacted you that they are not interested. There could be any number of reasons why they have not contacted you yet.

☐ **Don't hurry.** When you do get an offer or expression of interest from a buyer, don't sell that subsidiary right until you have heard from other potential rights buyers who've received a review copy. If the others haven't contacted you, call them and ask if they are interested in the book.

☐ **Hold an auction.** If more than one rights buyer expresses a strong interest in one of your books, you could hold a *rights auction*. To hold an auction, set a closing date for bids, lay down the basic rules for the auction, and set the minimum opening bid you will accept. You may offer the *floor* to any buyer who will guarantee payment of that minimum opening bid. In exchange, that buyer usually gets the right to sit out the bidding and to top the last bid by 10% or some other agreed upon percentage (that's called a *topping privilege*).

You can ask for written bids to be submitted by the closing date, or you can accept telephone bids on the closing date. In either case, once the auction date has arrived, you should review all the bids and then call the lower bidders to see if any of them want to top the highest bid. Continue this procedure until every bidder but one has dropped out. Then sell the rights to that highest bidder.

Note that with a telephone auction, you should go through the list of bidders in the same order during each round of bidding.

If someone has a topping privilege, call them back at the end to see if they'd like to top the final bid by the agreed upon percentage. If they'd like to, then they gain the rights. If not, the highest regular bidder gains the rights for their bid price.

When Conari Press announced a rights auction for Daphne Kingma's *Coming Apart: Why Relationships End and How to Live Through the Ending of Yours*, nine mass-market publishers responded. Conari set the lowest acceptable advance at $50,000. The bidding by telephone went on for ten rounds over two days. Ballantine eventually bought the rights for an $85,000 advance.

☐ **Prepare for the unexpected.** While the best policy is to pursue rights sales in an organized way, there have been a number of cases where rights buyers discovered the book rather than the publisher discovering the rights buyer. Sometimes this has occurred even several years after the original date of publication. So don't give up. If you have published a worthwhile book and it is selling well, the subsidiary rights buyers will come to you sooner or later if you don't find them first.

A little luck and persistence resulted in Naiad Press selling the movie rights to Jane Rule's novel, *Desert of the Heart*. The publisher gave a copy of the novel to a friend who, in turn, happened to meet independent producer Donna Deitch at a party one evening. Donna became interested in the book and went on to buy movie rights.

☐ **Try again.** If your book is rejected once, it doesn't mean you can't later offer the book to the same rights buyers again. If your book goes on to gain great reviews, large sales or some other sort of notoriety, you would certainly be justified in resubmitting the book for consideration. Quality Paperback Book Club, for instance, often buys backlist titles once they have established some sort of track record. They have even succumbed to other convincing arguments.

After QPBC first rejected the *Greystone Bakery Cookbook* by Helen Glassman and Susan Postal, Shambhala Publications sent the club editor a chocolate cake (made from a recipe in the book). Not only did QPBC rethink its decision and buy the book club rights, but so did the Cooking and Crafts division of Book-of-the-Month Club.

As a hardcover, Geneen Roth's *When Food Is Love* did not make it onto any bestseller lists, but when the paperback edition was discovered by Oprah Winfrey (who gave a copy to every member of her studio audience), the book made both the *New York Times* and *Publishers Weekly* bestseller lists. A year and a half after its first publication, *When Food Is Love* was bought at auction by the Literary Guild as a featured alternate.

☐ **Get attention.** If you want to attract the attention of other rights buyers, send notice of rights sales to the rights columnist at *Publishers Weekly*. That's how Conari Press first attracted the attention of mass-market publishers. When Literary Guild made *Coming Apart* one of their selections, Conari immediately sent a note to *PW*. Soon after the *PW* notice, Ballantine inquired whether the mass-market rights were available. As a result, Conari ran the auction described earlier. Note that reviews and other notices in *Publishers Weekly* also draw the attention of rights buyers.

☐ **Advertise.** Advertisements in *Publishers Weekly* have also been effective in drawing the attention of rights buyers. Among the many readers of *Publishers Weekly* are rights buyers for book clubs, magazines, movies, TV, and foreign rights. The only other print media that would draw as much attention might be the *New York Times Book Review*.

When Publishers Marketing Association placed twenty-one pages of advertisements for its member publishers in *Publishers Weekly*, within two days PMA received a call from Touchstone Pictures which wanted to discuss movie rights for one of the books. *Single White Homesteader*, which was featured on a page with six other history titles, also drew the attention of a video rights buyer. A few days later, a mass market publisher called to find out if paperback rights were available for Evelyn Kaye's *EcoVacations* published by Blue Penguin.

☐ **Build on publicity.** Another way to attract the attention of rights buyers is to build on any other publicity that ties into the book. Again, Conari's auction worked even better than expected because the author appeared on the *Oprah Winfrey Show* just days before the auction.

Similarly, just before the Naval Institute Press was to hold an auction for the mass-market paperback rights to *Flight of the Intruder* by Stephen Coonts, one of their people noticed the galley copy of *Flight* on President Reagan's desk (in a photo that appeared in *Fortune* magazine). The Press rounded up five copies of the magazine and air expressed them to the five publishers bidding for the rights. By the time the auction was over, Pocket Books bought the mass-market rights for $341,000.

☐ **Feature rights availability on your web site.** Many foreign publishers now track down books and authors via the Internet. On your book pages, always feature a list of what rights are still available and which have already been sold. Via our BookMarket.com web site, we've sold foreign rights to China and Korea for several titles.

☐ **Get an agent.** If you don't want to sell the rights yourself, work through an agent. Below is one literary agency that specializes in making subsidiary rights sales for independent publishers. For a list of other agents, see John Kremer's *Literary, Subsidiary, and Foreign Rights Agents* report which sells for $30.00 and lists more than 1,400 agents.

Writers House, Inc., Michele Rubin, Subsidiary Rights Manager, 21 West 26th Street, New York, NY 10010; 212-685-2400; Fax: 212-685-1781. Email: mgrubin@writershouse.com. Web: http://www.writers-house.com. They handle subsidiary rights sales for a number of smaller publishers. One publisher, who discovered Writers House through a previous edition of this book, worked with them to sell movie rights for six figures as well as reprint rights for another six figures for a dramatic book about Alzheimer's disease.

Other literary agents may also handle subsidiary rights sales for smaller publishers. If you'd like one of these agents to represent your company, send them your catalog. You should not have to pay agents to represent you; they work for a percentage of the sale (plus expenses). Generally, their percentages would be 10 to 20%.

When Libra Publishers needed help selling rights, they turned to Mary Jane Ross. She sold book club rights to *Hidden Bedroom Partners* to three different book clubs, mass-market reprint rights to Pocket Books, and first serial rights to *Glamour*.

Authors — If you have retained most subsidiary rights, you can sell them yourself or work with your literary agent to sell them. Even if you have assigned these rights to your publisher, you can and should help if you have some key contacts.

17:03 The Subsidiary Rights Contract

While many subsidiary rights buyers have a contract which they require you to sign when they buy rights from you, you may also want to develop your own contract. Here are the major points which need to be covered in any subsidiary rights agreement:

☐ **Title and author of book**—Be sure that the title, edition, and name of author are spelled out correctly in the agreement.

☐ **Rights being granted**—State exactly what rights are being granted. Be as specific and as clear as possible. Make sure that both parties clearly understand which rights are involved. Note whether the rights are exclusive or nonexclusive.

☐ **Territory covered**—State whether the rights are for North America only, or the English language only, or whatever territorial restrictions might apply.

☐ **Duration of rights**—State the term of the assignment of rights. For example, most mass-market paperback rights are sold for a term of five to seven years. Other rights might be sold for the life of the copyright. Others, such as serial rights, are only sold for one-time use.

☐ **Use of the book material**—If there are any questions about how the rights may be used, spell them out clearly. Can the rights buyer change or edit the material? Are there any restrictions on how they may advertise or promote their version of the book?

☐ **Amount to be paid**—The amount to be paid should be clearly spelled out, including any advances and royalties. Due dates for payments and methods of accounting also need to be delineated in detail.

☐ **Other limitations**—For certain rights you might want to include some other limitations. For example, in selling mass-market rights, you will undoubtedly want to require a limitation stating that no such edition can be published until at least one year after the publication date of your hardcover edition. That will give your hardcover edition a decent chance to sell out before the mass-market edition is published.

> **Authors** — Make sure your contract with your publisher specifies which rights you own and which rights you assign to your publisher—or what percentage of any rights sales you and your publisher share. Generally speaking, unless you are a well-known or well-connected author, it is to your advantage to let your publisher handle these rights sales.

According to *Entertainment Industry Contracts*, the split of subsidiary rights between author/publisher is generally as follows:

50/50	Mass-market paperback rights (author/publisher)
50/50	Book club rights
75/25	First serial rights
50/50	Second serial rights
90/10	Movie or TV rights
80/20	Foreign rights
50/50	Licensing or merchandising rights
50/50	Audio, video, or filmstrip rights

The above percentages should only be taken as guidelines. All such percentages are negotiable. As a publisher, always get as large a percentage as you can negotiate so you can afford to promote the book. As an author, always negotiate for the largest percentage you can get or retain as many subsidiary rights as you can for yourself, especially if you are in a position to exploit the rights yourself.

> **Authors** — Hold out for a 90/10 split on licensing or merchandising rights or, better yet, retain those rights for yourself. Most publishers really don't know how to exploit these rights effectively but they can add up to significant income for you.

17:04 First Serial Rights

First serial rights are the rights sold to magazines and newspapers to excerpt part (or sometimes all) of a book before its date of publication. While most first serial rights are sold for anywhere from $400 to $5,000, they have gone for as high as $200,000. *Woman's Day* paid that much for exclusive rights to excerpt Rose Kennedy's autobiography, *Times to Remember*.

Aside from the income such sales can generate, the other main benefit of first serial rights is the exposure they provide for new titles. This exposure can sometimes make or break a book. For example, Lee Iacocca's autobiography was launched through a prepublication excerpt and interview in *Newsweek*. This cover story was all the publicity Iacocca did for his book, and yet it was enough to create the word of mouth which made his book one of the first mass-market hardcover bestsellers. *Newsweek* has since provided similar (though less effective) sendoffs for Geraldine Ferraro's biography and David Stockman's *The Triumph of Politics*.

Since first serial rights can be so important to launching any major title, here are a few guidelines on how to handle such sales:

☐ **To place first serial rights, contact the book editors** (or whoever is responsible for buying serial rights) at magazines which you believe would be interested in the subject of your book. Send them a copy of the manuscript at least six months in advance of the book's publication date.

For a highly illustrated book (such as a travel guide or photography book), it is better to send a copy of the finished book or *F&Gs* (folded and gathered galley copies), if at all possible, or quality photographs with the manuscript if no finished book is available. Be sure to indicate those pages or passages in the manuscript that would be most appropriate for each serial rights buyer. Also enclose a cover letter highlighting why the book would be ideal for their magazine or newspaper. Finally, also provide some details on your marketing plan for the book.

☐ **First serial rights can be sold on a non-exclusive basis.** That means that you can sell excerpts from different parts of the book to as many buyers as are interested.

For example, Holt, Reinhart & Winston made ten first serial sales for Louise Erdrich's novel *Love Medicine*. They sold chapters from the book to *Ms.*, *Atlantic*, *Mother Jones*, *Kenyon Review*, *North American Review*, *North Dakota Quarterly*, *New England Review*, and *Chicago*.

Stanton & Lee, a regional publisher out of Wisconsin, sold thirty-four separate serial rights to their book *Haunted Heartland*, a collection of 150 stories of the occult by Beth Scott and Michael Norman. Because these stories take place in 108 different locations in the Midwest, Stanton & Lee found it easy to sell first serial rights to thirty-four Midwestern newspapers including the major ones. Because of the attendant publicity, the first printing of the book sold out the day after publication.

Hyperion sold first serial rights for *The Rise and Fall of Gay Culture* by Daniel Harris to *Antioch Review, Baffler, Bay Area Reporter, Harper's, Harvard Gay and Lesbian Review, Salmagundi,* and *Word*.

Three magazines bought first serial rights to *How to Make Love All the Time* by Barbara De Angelis. *Cosmopolitan* paid $1,000 for first North American rights only. *Family Circle* paid $4,000 for world rights to its excerpt. And *McCall's* paid $1,500 for a four-page quiz.

☐ **You can sell exclusive first serial rights to various categories of publications.** For example, Marcia Chellis's agent sold exclusive newspaper syndication rights for her book, *Living with the Kennedys*, to the New York Times Syndicate for $30,000 and exclusive tabloid rights to the *National Enquirer* for $75,000, for a total first serial sale of $105,000.

Doubleday sold first serial rights for *His Holiness* by Carl Bernstein and Marco Politi to *Reader's Digest* for a preemptive bid of $100,000. They then sold a five-part series to the *New York Post*. In addition, they sold syndication rights to the Los Angeles Times Syndicate. Finally, they sold foreign rights to the book, where serial rights were sold once more to *Paris Match, London Sunday Times*, and *Expresso*.

☐ **First serial sales can be made to newspapers, magazines (both consumer and business), tabloids, and syndicates.** Plus, within each category you can make sales to any number of publications. For example, if you have a health book, besides selling first serial rights to *Prevention* or *Today's Health*, you might also be able to sell rights to sports magazines such as *Running*, women's magazines such as *Self* or *New Woman*, alternative magazines such as *Mother Earth News*, and business magazines such as *Inc.*—all depending on how appropriate the contents of the book are to the different audiences. Don't overlook potential sales just because a magazine has never used such material in the past. Editorial trends are always changing. Keep up with them—or even ahead of them.

☐ **When negotiating book contracts with your authors, ask for a 50/50 split on the income from serial rights sales.** While some authors (or their agents) insist on an 90/10 or 80/20 split, you should try to convince them to go for a more equitable split—one which would make it worth your while to pursue such sales. The income generated from such rights sales should at least pay for your costs in obtaining the sales, and that usually requires at least a 50/50 split, especially for second serial rights.

Authors — If you decide not to handle your own serial rights sales (by yourself or through your agent), give your publisher an adequate share of the rights sales so they can afford to pursue such sales. Remember: The more such rights sales your publisher can afford to make, the better off both of you will be—not only because you will both get more income but also because of the attendant publicity (which will mean greater sales for the book itself). If, on the other hand, your agent wants to sell those rights, work with her to make those sales.

☐ **Get some of the major bidders interested in the book.** These include *Cosmopolitan, Redbook, National Enquirer, Ladies' Home Journal*, and *Self*. This will help you get the most money for those rights.

☐ **Try Sunday supplements to the local newspapers** in the author's home state (or your own home state). Your author should be able to help you make contacts.

17:05 How to Determine a Fair Price

With first serial rights going for as much as $200,000 and for as low as $400, you should carefully consider what price to ask for such rights. You don't want to price your book out of the market, but at the same time you do want to get a fair price for the book—the highest possible fair price. Here are a few guidelines to use in determining a fair price:

☐ **What is the circulation of the periodical?** The higher the circulation, the more the periodical can generally afford to pay. Hence, while *Playboy* can afford to pay $3,500 or more for first serial rights to a story, *Fantasy and Science Fiction* could hardly afford to pay more than its going rate per word which would result in a far smaller payment.

☐ **What does the periodical normally pay for such rights?** And what is the maximum amount it has been willing to pay in the past? Here are a few examples of higher prices paid by major buyers of first serial rights:

Redbook—$44,000 for *Breaking Point* the story of John Hinkley written by his parents and $30,000 for an excerpt from Carol Botwin's *Men Who Can't Be Faithful*.

Good Housekeeping—In the upper five figures for Eddie Fisher's autobiography *Eddie: My Life, My Loves* and for *The Pritikin Diet*.

Ladies' Home Journal—$120,000 for Betty Ford's autobiography *The Times of My Life*, $100,000 for Sophia Loren's autobiography *Sophia*, and $87,500 for Gail Sheehy's novel *Pathfinders*.

Woman's Day—$200,000 for Rose Kennedy's autobiography *Times to Remember*.

Family Circle—$100,000 for Lauren Bacall's autobiography *By Myself*, $75,000 for Richard Simmon's *Never Say Diet Cookbook*, and $35,000 for Nancy Sinatra's *Frank Sinatra, My Father*.

National Enquirer—$37,000 for the *I Love Lucy Book* by Bard Andrews, $27,000 for *The Duke: The Life and Times of John Wayne* by Donald Shepard and Robert Slatzer, and $70,000 for a four-parter from Shirley Temple Black's autobiography, *Child Star*.

☐ **How much do they want to excerpt?** The more they want to excerpt, the more they should pay. *Family Circle* paid $125,000 for five installments of Marjorie Craig's *10 Minutes a Day Shape-up Program*.

☐ **Does the publication want exclusive rights to the entire book or to just a part?** You would, of course, charge more for exclusive rights to the entire book since you would be giving up the possibility of any other serial rights income. *Good Housekeeping* paid $90,000 for the exclusive right to use a 2,000-word excerpt from Bill Cosby's book on *Fatherhood*. That's $45.00 per word, far higher than normal for such rights.

☐ **If they do want exclusive use of all or a part of the book, how long do they want such exclusivity?** The longer they want such exclusivity, the more they should pay.

☐ **How badly do they want the book excerpt?** Again, the more they want the excerpt, the more you can charge for it. Probably the only way, though, that you will ever be able to tell how much they want it is if some other competitor also bids for the rights. Of course, the more competition there is for the rights, the higher the price will go.

☐ **First serial rights are worth more than second serial rights** because of their *scoop value*. The buyer of first serial rights is paying for the opportunity to give the world its first look at a new book.

☐ **Syndication rights should sell for more** than first serial rights to one publication. Remember that most syndicators are going to make back whatever they pay for the rights by reselling the rights to syndicate members. For example, the Los Angeles Times Syndicate paid almost a $100,000 for the syndication rights to Anthony Summer's biography of Marilyn Monroe, *Goddess*. Within 48 hours they had recouped their investment by reselling the abridgment to seventeen newspapers.

☐ **Your book excerpt is easier to edit.** When pricing the first serial rights to your books, remember these two points: 1) Most first serial rights go for a little less than it would cost the magazine to commission an article from a freelance writer. 2) A book excerpt is easier to edit than an original article (which saves the periodical both time and money in editorial costs). So don't hesitate to ask for a fair price for such rights.

17:06 Second Serial Rights

Second serial rights are those serial rights which are sold after a book's publication date. Since the printing of excerpts from a book after its publication does not have the scoop value of excerpts prior to publication, second serial rights are usually sold for a lot less than first serial rights. Standard payment for second serial rights can range from $50 to $2,000, depending primarily on the circulation of the publication and the number of first and second serial rights which have previously been sold. Nonetheless, payments for second serial rights can sometimes rival those made for first serial rights.

National Enquirer paid $20,000 to reprint portions of Robert Lenzner's biography of John Paul Getty, *The Great Getty*. For second serial rights, *Redbook* paid $25,000 for Judith Krantz's novel, *Till We Meet Again*.

Why would magazines buy second serial rights? Besides the fact that such rights are cheaper, the magazine gets the benefit of the book's promotion. Plus, the editor can work from a finished, completely edited and proof-read book, thus making her job easier. Finally, before buying such rights, the editor has a chance to gauge readers' response and, hence, can better decide if the book would be appropriate for the magazine's readership.

When you approach periodicals about second serial rights, let them know of any previous serial rights sales. Not only is this common courtesy, but it also demonstrates to the prospective buyers that the book has material that lends itself to being excerpted. *Reader's Digest* bought second serial rights to Stephen Covey's *The 7 Habits of Highly Effective Families* after sections of the book had already appeared in *Family Circle* and *Working Mother*.

Note that you could theoretically continue to sell second serial rights for the life of the book's copyright. While this is rarely done, second serial rights have been sold several years after a book's publication.

Open Horizons sold second serial rights for *Turntable Illusions* to *Games* magazine several months after the book was published. While we had sent a prepublication review copy to the book review editor, the main editor had never seen the book. He bought the rights only after finding the book in a Manhattan bookstore. *Games* paid $500 for a three-page excerpt.

17:07 Freebies, Adaptations, and P.I. Deals

Rather than sell second serial rights, you could give away excerpts of your book in order to increase the book's exposure to its major audience. These freebies benefit the periodical by providing it with solid editorial material, and they benefit your book by increasing its visibility at no cost to you. These freebie deals can be arranged in at least four different ways:

☐ **Offer free excerpts of the book to any magazine or newsletter that expresses an interest** (or reaches your target audience). Stipulate that they may reprint the excerpt free as long as they provide a resource box at the end of the article. That *resource box* should include the title and author of the book, the name and address of your company, and the price of the book, plus any other ordering instructions.

Open Horizons has offered excerpts of its books to the newsletters of publishers associations. These associations rarely have a budget for such articles, yet their members would clearly be interested in the information in our books and would be likely to order our books if they had a chance to sample the contents. We look on these freebies as samplers which we are able to get into the hands of prime prospects at no cost to us. Similarly, we've offered excerpts to Internet web sites and email newsletters.

☐ **Offer freebies in trade for advertising space.** Since the ad space you get will often have gone unsold anyway, the article doesn't cost the magazine anything. At the same time, you are able to get a free ad which will reinforce the article's impact and increase direct sales of your book. Since the ad is yours to do as you please, you can have the orders come direct to you. A number of business opportunity and trade magazines regularly participate in such exchanges. So do many limited circulation magazines and newsletters.

☐ **If the magazine will not trade advertising space, you could offer them a per inquiry (P.I.) or per order (P.O.) deal.** Under such an arrangement, they not only run an excerpt of your book, but they also run an advertisement or bingo card which allows readers to order the book through them. The magazine then sends the orders to you for fulfillment (after taking their cut, which may be anywhere from 40 to 60% off, depending on the discount you've negotiated).

For its *Office Purchasing Guide*, Lowen Publishing permitted a chain of twenty regional purchasing management magazines to run a yearlong series of articles excerpted from the book in exchange for monthly P.I. ads for the book. This arrangement gave double exposure for the book to its prime market.

☐ **Rather than excerpt part of the book, you could adapt material from the book to create new articles.** These articles, in turn, could be sold in the same way as any other freelance article or could be given away under one of the above arrangements.

The one disadvantage of giving away freebies is that such arrangements make it harder to sell second serial rights for your other books. Magazines, which previously have gotten articles for nothing, are not likely to want to pay for excerpts of new books if they can still make other arrangements. Perhaps the best policy, then, is to offer freebies only to limited circulation magazines or newsletters who cannot afford to buy serial rights in the first place. All others pay cash.

Authors — Once any serial rights sales have been made, you can explore these freebie options. Before you do, however, coordinate your efforts with your publisher so you don't interfere with their ongoing publicity or rights sales. Ask them if they have any plans to sell second serial rights. Note: Most publishers do not have active programs for selling second serial rights.

17:08 Mass-Market Paperback Reprint Rights

Here's where the big money is. Paperback rights have gone for as high as $3.2 million (that's what Bantam paid for Judith Krantz's *Princess Daisy*). Even reprint rights for midlist titles will often sell for $25,000 to $100,000 or more. Hence, of all subsidiary rights, these reprint rights are probably the most important. So research this market carefully. Find out who the major players are, what categories of books they buy, and how much they are willing to pay for major titles. To give you a beginning, here are a few brief notes about some of the major mass-market publishers:

☐ **Avon**—A member of the Hearst Group, Avon has previously paid $1.9 million for Colleen McCullough's *The Thorn Birds*, $1.5 million for Collins and LaPierre's *The Fifth Horseman*, and $1.5 million for Woodward and Bernstein's *The Final Days*.

☐ **Ballantine**—Owned by Random House, this house publishes both general fiction and nonfiction. Its Del Ray line publishes some of the best science fiction and fantasy novels. Fawcett is also now owned by Random House. Ballantine has previously paid $1.9 million for Marilyn French's *The Bleeding Heart* and $1 million plus for Erich Segal's *Man, Woman and Child*.

☐ **Bantam**—Besides being a major publisher of hardcover bestsellers, Bantam is also known for its paperback bestsellers, including its two lines for young adults, Sweet Dreams and Sweet Valley High (which do not currently buy reprint rights). Besides paying $3.2 million for Krantz's *Princess Daisy*, Bantam has paid $1.8 million for E. L. Doctorow's *Ragtime*, $3.0 million for James Herriott's *The Lord God Made Them All* (along with the renewals for three previous titles), and $1.9 million for Cynthia Freeman's *No Time for Tears*. Note: Bantam and Dell, another paperback reprinter, are also divisions of Random House.

☐ **Berkley**—Part of the Penguin Putnam group which includes Jove, Ace, Viking, Dutton, Riverhead, and several other lines, Berkley publishes general fiction and nonfiction. Berkley paid $825,000 for Gerald Browne's *Stone 588*.

☐ **New American Library**—Also a part of the Penguin Putnam group, NAL has a hardcover line as well as the Signet line of paperback classics. NAL has paid $2.6 million for rights to Robin Cook's *Brain* and *Sphinx* and over $3 million for two new Cook novels. NAL has also paid $2.2 million for Mario Puzo's *Fools Die* and $1.5 million for Irma Rombauer's *The Joy of Cooking*. In an auction involving three other paperback publishers, NAL acquired *Pleasure in the Word: Erotic Writings by Latin American Women* from White Pine Press for $15,000.

☐ **Pocket Books**—Part of Simon & Schuster, Pocket Books publishes in most fields including a separate science fiction line, Tapestry romances, and Washington Square Press high-quality paperbacks. Pocket has paid over $2 million for John Irving's *Hotel New Hampshire* and $1.6 million for Judy Blume's *Smart Women* and a renewal of her *Wifey*. When Walter Mosley offered his Easy Rawlins mystery, *Gone Fishin'*, to Black Classic Press for hardcover rights, Black Classic, in turn, sold paperback rights to Pocket Books for a large six-figure advance.

☐ **Warner**—A division of Time Warner, Warner Books publishes contemporary fiction and general nonfiction. Warner has paid $1.2 million for Judith Rossner's *August*. They have also paid $2 million for Richard Nixon's *Memoirs* and $2 million for Woodward and Bernstein's *All the President's Men*.

☐ Other mass-market paperback lines include Baen Books, Harlequin, DAW, Eos, Leisure, Lynx, Tor, Mysterious Press, Pageant, Paperjacks, Penguin, Edge Science Fiction, Questar, Revell, One World, Scholastic, St. Martin's, Tudor, Pyr, and Zebra. Many of these lines specialize in various genre of fiction.

Once you've located those paperback houses you think would be most interested in your titles (you can find their editorial addresses listed in *Literary MarketPlace* available at your local library), send them a copy of your book for consideration.

Reprint rights can be sold at almost any time—at the time of signing the hardcover edition (a joint hard/soft deal), prior to hardcover publication, or any time after publication. But the best time to solicit potential buyers is before your book goes to press—the sooner, the better.

What are your chances of selling reprint rights to your titles? Very good if your book is fiction, since 80% of the 4,000 mass-market paperbacks produced each year are fiction titles. While many of those 3,200 fiction titles are original paperbacks, perhaps as many as a third are reprints of the 15,000 hardcover or trade paperback fiction titles published each year. That would mean that about one-twelfth of all fiction titles are sold for paperback reprinting each year. And most of those sales come from the major publishing houses.

For nonfiction titles, however, the prospects for mass-market reprint rights sales are not that good either. Each of the 140,000 hardcover and trade paperback nonfiction titles published each year in the U.S. must compete to be one of approximately 800 mass-market nonfiction titles produced in the U.S. each year. Since a number of those 800 titles are originals, the opportunities are even more limited.

Here are the odds for a number of categories (based on entries in the *Weekly Record* and *Paperbound Books in Print* databases for 1981 and 1982): For cookbooks and juveniles, about an 8% to 10% chance. For sports and recreation titles, about a 15% chance. For biographies, about a 4% chance. For all other titles, about a 1% to 2% chance. Chances for nonfiction titles have only decreased since that time.

If you make a sale, the basic terms of the contract would be about the same as for any other subsidiary right. Royalty rates range anywhere from 6% to 10% (and higher for a few brand name authors). The term for such rights is usually five to seven years. Most contracts also stipulate that the mass-market edition may not be published until a year after the publication of the hardcover edition. This delay allows the hardcover a decent life span.

17:09 Trade Paperback Reprint Rights

If you don't publish trade paperback editions, you can sell such reprint rights before you sell mass-market rights. In this way, a book can have three full lives—as a hardcover, as a trade paperback, and as a mass-market paperback. *The Joy of Cooking*, for example, has been a bestseller as a hardcover (over 12 million), a trade paperback (over 2.5 million), and as a mass-market paperback (over 7 million). Trade paperback reprint rights usually sell for a royalty between 6% and 10%. Other provisions of the contract are similar to mass-market rights and subsidiary rights in general.

- In 1996, Berkley paid six figures to Ability Workshop Press for trade paperback reprint rights to *The Gift of Dyslexia* by Ronald D. Davis.

- Jeremy Tarcher, a division of Penguin Putnam, bought six titles from Piñon Press, including *Your Fat Is Not Your Fault, A Cancer Battle Plan, Food Smart, Healthy Living in a Toxic World, Healthy Habits*, and *Reclaim Your Health*.

- Collier published a paperback edition of *Joshua*, a parable originally self-published by Fr. Joseph Girzone, a retired priest. The book had sold 45,000 hardcover copies in its self-published edition; it sold 100,000 more copies in Collier's trade paperback edition and spawned a series of popular novels.

17:10 Hardcover Reprint Rights

One of the major trends in publishing has been the selling of hardcover reprint rights of self-published books to major publishers. For example, Hampton Roads sold hardcover rights for Neale Donald Walsch's *Conversations with God, Book I* to Putnam for a seven-figure advance. As Bob Friedman, publisher of Hampton Roads noted, the reason they sold the reprint rights is because they knew that "Putnam could push this book into the mainstream very quickly and get it a lot of exposure."

Once Putnam had established the first book as a bestseller, Hampton Roads was able to publish the second book, *Conversations with God, Book II*, and make it a bestseller on its own (having learned what worked and what didn't from Putnam).

In the past few years, many self-published authors have made the bestseller lists once they were picked up by a major publisher. The list is long: James Redfield's *The Celestine Prophecy*, Marlo Morgan's *Mutant Message Down Under*, William Byham's *Zapp: The Lightning of Empowerment*, David Saltzman's *The Jester Has Lost His Jingle*, F. Lynn Harris's *If This World Were Mine*, and Richard Paul Evans's *The Christmas Box*. As *Publishers Weekly* rights columnist Paul Nathan once wrote, "Gone are the days when self-publishing was virtually synonymous with self-defeating."

As a small publisher, be on the lookout for rookie editors at the major publishers. These people are more likely to be interested in titles from self-publishers and small publishers. As Laurie Chittenden, at that time a new editor at Simon & Schuster, noted after buying the rights to *The Christmas Box*, "Self-published books are really a good route for an assistant editor to go. It's hard to get agents to send manuscripts." As it turned out, Evans's *The Christmas Box* became one of only a few books that made it onto the hardcover and softcover bestseller lists at the same time.

- After the success of Mary Pipher's *Reviving Ophelia*, Ballantine bought hardcover rights from Adams Media Group for Pipher's previous book, *Hunger Pains*. In 1997, Ballantine gave the book, which originally had limited distribution, star treatment as a lead title.

- With the help of an enthusiastic bookseller (Susan Wasson of Bookworks in Albuquerque, New Mexico), Calyx Books was able to interest a number of New York publishers in their trade paperback edition of Jean Hegland's environmental tale, *Into the Forest*. As a result of a spirited auction conducted by two agents, Calyx sold North American hard/soft reprint rights to Bantam Books for $700,000.

17:11 Selling to Book Clubs

In 1996, book clubs represented a billion dollar market for publishers. Book club sales, however, have since fallen as Internet booksellers took more and more of the market away from the book clubs. Besides the extra income that book club sales generate, there are a number of other advantages to such sales:

☐ If the book club joins your print run, you could save 10% or more on the production costs of your own copies.

☐ Book club sales rarely eat into normal trade sales or other sales by mail. They are, in effect, add-on sales you probably would not have gotten in any other way. Rodale, for instance, has never seen a negative impact from book club sales on their own direct mail promotions or retail sales.

☐ The promotional exposure provided by book club catalogs helps to support your promotional efforts and often leads to more bookstore sales.

☐ Book clubs get your book into the hands of more people. If your book has good word-of-mouth appeal, then you should sell even more books as a result of being selected by a club.

☐ Your authors will love it. Such sales increase their income and status.

☐ As with other rights sales, a book club sale provides an independent endorsement of the value of the book. In effect, the book club is saying that the book is worth selling. That's a message you can repeat to your distributor, sales representatives, wholesalers, booksellers, and any other people in your chain of distribution.

☐ Such sales also increase the prestige of the publisher.

Royalties for book club sales are usually around 10% of the club's list price (which itself is often 70 to 80% of the book's original list price). The royalty decreases to 5% if the book is used as a premium. The average advance against royalties offered by the major book clubs for a main selection is between $95,000 and $200,000 (to as high as $1,000,000). For featured alternates, the advance is generally around $25,000; and for other selections, advances can range from $4,000 to $10,000. For smaller clubs, the advance may be as small as $1,000, even for a main selection.

Book club deals come in three varieties: 1) They print their own copies, and pay the publisher a royalty (which the publisher, in turn, usually splits with the author). 2) They join the print run of the publisher, pay for the books they order, and pay a royalty as before. 3) They buy books from the publishers stock at a set price which includes printing costs and royalty. If they are doing their own print run, the smaller book clubs usually offer an advance of half the royalties expected to be earned based on the club's initial print run. Overall, book clubs try to get their costs under 25% of their proposed selling price.

The term for book club contracts runs from two to seven years, during which time the book club has the right to distribute the book to its members as they see fit. Generally, the major book club license contracts require exclusive book club rights. Most smaller book clubs do not require exclusivity. With nonexclusivity it is possible to sell a title to more than one club. For instance, St. Martin's Press sold book club rights for Roger Shattuck's *Forbidden Knowledge* to four clubs: Book-of-the-Month Club, Quality Paperback Book Club, History Book Club, and Reader's Subscription.

Submit books for consideration at least six months before your publication date (for alternate selections). If you want your book to be a main selection of one of the major book clubs, begin to approach them 1½ to 2½ years before your publication date. The sooner, the better. You can start by sending them information about the book and author. As soon as a manuscript and cover concept is ready, send that. When Storey Communications went from one year to three years in advance planning for its titles, its sub rights income jumped to a million dollars annually.

When submitting books to various book clubs for consideration, don't pass by a book club just because it has never offered a similar book in the past. If you believe that their members would be interested in one of your titles, send them a copy. Don't rule out any club; let them make the selections. For example, M. Evans sold Rodale's Prevention Book Club (which normally featured health and nutrition books) Julia Grice's *How to Find Romance After 40*. Although the book is clearly not a health book, it still had a natural appeal to the club's members, most of whom are over 40.

Chapters Publishing in Shelburne, Vermont, calls itself "the little house that has made a big business of selling to major book clubs." In late 1996, it auctioned off rights to Anne Fletcher's *Eating Thin for Life* to Book-of-the-Month Club for a $40,000 advance after it had already sold the book as a main selection to the Prevention Book Club. In three years, the company had placed seven main selections with either Rodale or BOMC.

Below is a list of various categories of book clubs. For a more complete list of book clubs, see *Literary MarketPlace* or http://www.bookmarket.com/bookclubs.html.

☐ **General-interest hardcover book clubs**—Book-of-the-Month Club and Literary Guild (and its sister club, Doubleday Book Club) are the two major ones.

☐ **General-interest paperback book clubs**—Quality Paperback Book Club is the major paperback book club. Interested in backlist as well as frontlist, hardcover as well as softcover, they are one of the prime book club buyers of small press titles.

☐ **Book condensations**—Reader's Digest Select Editions are the leaders in this field. While book condensations are not technically book club sales, we list them here because in most ways they are similar. *Reader's Digest* paid $40,000 to abridge *The Judgment* by Howard Goldfluss.

☐ **Professional book clubs**—BOMC has a number of professional book clubs for nurses, scientists, architects, and so forth.

☐ **Book clubs for teachers**—Early Learning Book Club and Instructor Book Club are two that serve teachers. Bright Ring Publishing sold rights to both of these clubs for its *Scribble Cookies and Other Independent Creative Art Experiences for Children*.

☐ **Children's book clubs**—Scholastic (with their Arrow, See-Saw, and Teen Age Book Clubs), and Book-of-the-Month Club are major companies in this field. There are two kinds of children's book clubs: those that sell direct to children and their parents and those that sell through schools. Scholastic runs their clubs through schools, while Book-of-the-Month Club sells direct.

☐ **Special interest book clubs**—There are many book clubs offering books for almost any interest, including writing (Writer's Digest Book Club), science fiction (Science Fiction Book Club), cooking (The Good Cook), military (Military Book Club), crafts (Crafter's Choice and WoodWorker's Book Club), and political (Conservative Book Club).

Open Horizons has sold the rights for *1001 Ways to Market Your Books* to Writer's Digest Book Club for the first, third, and fifth edition.

☐ **Religious book clubs**—There are book clubs for Catholics, Protestants, Evangelicals, and Jews, ranging from the Jewish Book Club to Guideposts Theological Book Service to the One Spirit new age book club.

☐ **Subscription book clubs**—Franklin Mint, for example, offers a fifty-volume series on Great American Fiction. The Easton Press offers a limited edition collection of the Masterpieces of Science Fiction.

☐ **Other language book clubs**—Circulo de Lectores, with 75,000 members, is the major Spanish-language book club in the United States. Book clubs in many languages are very big in Europe.

☐ **Alumni book clubs**—Several universities, including Notre Dame and Marquette, have book clubs that feature books by alumni and/or faculty of the university (or other books that might interest the alumni). Books are featured in and sold through the alumni magazine.

Authors — Check to see if your university has such a book club. If so, let your publisher know so they can send a review copy of your book to the university book club. Also, if you know of any special interest book clubs that you think would be appropriate for your book, tell your publisher. Especially alert them to any online book clubs you know about. You'll be able to find these online clubs easier than your publisher since they are working on so many titles at one time.

To give you a little better idea of how to approach book clubs, here are a few notes from the guidelines offered by Book-of-the-Month Club (which is now a member of the BookSpan group of book clubs):

☐ They are always on the lookout for books that will appeal to their members. They select about 1,500 titles from the 10,000 manuscripts they receive each year.

☐ "It is both a key part of our work and a personal pleasure for the editorial staff to discover worthy books from smaller publishing houses."

☐ Books offered to members must have "genuinely broad appeal within their subject area."

☐ Submit manuscripts to the editorial department of the appropriate club at **Book-of-the-Month Club**, Doubleday Entertainment, 15 East 26th Street, 4th Floor, New York, NY 10010; 212-651-7400; Fax: 212-651-7124. Web: http://www.bookspan.com.

☐ It is essential that you include a cover letter with the manuscript. This letter should list the publication date, estimated retail price, estimated number of pages, a brief description of the book and summary of its content, and the number and type of illustrations. Also include a brief bio of the author, especially noting any previous books.

☐ Expect to hear from them, if they are interested, in about two months. They do not encourage frequent follow-up calls.

☐ With the advent of their web site in 1997, the BookSpan clubs are keeping more of their selections in stock longer than before.

17:12 Motion Picture Rights

Except for mass-market reprint rights, sales of movie and TV screenplay
rights probably generate more excitement than any other sale. Why? Because they usually involve more money. Options can go for anywhere from
$500 to $100,000, with an average of about $10,000. Pickup rights go for
anywhere from $25,000 to $8 million plus (that's how much Warner Brothers paid for John Grisham's *The Runaway Juror*). The average pickup prices
for movie rights are between $75,000 and $300,000.

Options allow movie producers to gain exclusive rights to a book while
they arrange for financing of the movie, assemble the necessary talent
(screenwriters, directors, actors, and other necessary personnel), and explore
the feasibility of making a movie based on the book. The term of most options varies from ninety days to one year. Option payments are nonrefund-
able. That means that the author and publisher keep the money even if the
option is not exercised (i.e., the movie is not produced). If the option is exercised, the option payment is applied to the purchase price of the movie,
which is usually stated in the option contract.

Besides the pickup or purchase price, brand name authors can sometimes
negotiate for a percentage of the profits after the pickup price has been covered. In any movie or TV rights contract, there should be a provision allowing for the reversion of rights to the author if the movie or TV series is not
produced within so many years (for instance, five years).

While most books are optioned for movies as the result of sustained publicity efforts by the publishers and the work of TV/movie agents, happenstance can also play a role in which books are chosen for production. For
example, Calvin Floyd of Producers Enterprises optioned Judith Richards's
1978 novel *Summer Lightning* after his Swedish-born wife happened to pick
up a Swedish translation of the novel while they were visiting Stockholm.

Besides selling original screenplay rights, here are four other ways that
you could profit from movie rights to a book:

☐ **Novelizations and movie tie-ins**—Not only do producers buy screenplay rights to books, but publishers buy novelization rights to screen-
plays. Novelizations of *Rocky*, *Return of the Jedi*, *Raiders of the Lost
Ark*, and *E.T.* all became bestsellers as a result of tie-ins to the movies.

On the other side, previously published novels such as William Styron's
Sophie's Choice, Tom Wolfe's *The Right Stuff*, and Isak Dinesen's *Out of
Africa* have all become bestsellers for a second time after the release of a
movie by the same name. Because the one media helps to spur sales in
the other media and vice versa, both book publishers and movie producers benefit from the sales of such rights.

☐ **Sequel rights**—If the producer decides to do a second movie based on
the book, the purchase price is usually about half of the price for the

original movie. Of course, if the original movie is a blockbuster, sequel rights could sell for a lot more. J. K. Rowling became the first billionaire author as a result of the movies made from her *Harry Potter* books.

Chartoff Productions in association with Fresco Pictures paid $1 million plus a percentage of the profits for Orson Scott Card's novel, *Ender's Game*. A short time later, Fresco bought the rights for Card's entire oeuvre of twenty-six novels and dozens of short stories and plays.

☐ **Remakes**—Payments for remakes are usually less than the payment for the original version (unless the original version was made many years ago). The 1960's musical movie *Shangrila* was a remake of the 1930's movie *Lost Horizons*, which was based on James Hilton's novel.

☐ **Consultant fees**—One of the ways that authors can make additional money from movie rights is to also sign to write the screenplay or to act as a consultant. When Walt Disney Pictures optioned *Scam!*, a self-published book by Don Wright, they also offered him a consulting job for an additional $100,000 if the movie went into production.

You can sell movie rights to nonfiction books. Memoirs and biographies, of course, have been used as the basis of many movies. Here are a few movies based on the lives of real people: *Selena, The Elephant Man, Rob Roy, In Love and War, Papillon*, and *Out of Africa*. RDR Books, a small publisher, recently sold the rights to Hilda Hollingsworth's childhood wartime memoir *Places of Greater Safety* to a team of independent producers.

Movies have also been based on stories of actual events: *The Right Stuff, In Cold Blood, The People vs. Larry Flynt, Dead Man Walking, Blaze, The Accused*, and *Escape from Alcatraz*.

Authors — You can take an active role in selling movie and TV rights. For instance, Gerald Locklin, author of *The Case of the Missing Blue Volkswagen*, helped his publisher, Applezaba Press, to sell movie rights. As a teacher at California State University in Long Beach, he kept contact with his former students. One of those students was a Hollywood screenwriter with Mark Bark Productions. When one of the producers wanted a black comedy, the first book that the screenwriter thought of was the one written by his former teacher. As a result of that personal contact, a deal was made within one week.

A few movies have also been based on nonfiction books that are not themselves derived from real people or events. For instance, Dreamworks bought the rights to Terence Dickinson's *Extraterrestrials: A Field Guide to Earthlings* from Camden House.

One final note: Don't ever give up on selling movie rights. Even self-publishers have sold movie rights. For instance, Turk Pipkin sold rights to his self-published golf novel, *Fast Greens*, to Warner Brothers. And Elissa Wald sold movie rights to her *Meeting the Master* to producer Mack Brown.

17:13 Television Rights

Often TV rights are sold at the same time or in lieu of motion picture rights. In general, the option and pickup prices for prime time TV movies are lower than those for movies. While TV movie rights might sell for anywhere from $25,000 to $75,000, miniseries rights sell for about $20,000 to $40,000 per two-hour segment. Besides rights to adapt a book to a TV movie or miniseries, there are several other TV rights which can be sold:

☐ **Specials**—Rights can be sold to produce a one-time special based on a book. Motown bought rights to produce a show about weight loss and fitness based on Harvey and Marilyn Diamond's *Fit for Life*.

☐ **Installments**—Scripps-Howard Productions and ABC-TV paid John Saul $1.7 million for rights to broadcast his novel series, *The Blackstone Chronicles*, in installments.

☐ **Series**—The ABC TV series *Spenser: For Hire* was based on Robert B. Parker's series of novels about a detective named Spenser. Rights for a television series go for $1,000 plus per episode for a half-hour show and about $1,500 or more per episode for a full hour show.

Klutz Press signed with JP Kids to produce a new TV comedy series called *Klutz-TV*. The series, based on Klutz's fifty-five titles, would blend animation, live action, puppets, and digital graphics to teach science and problem solving.

New Horizons Press, which publishes twelve titles a year, sold TV rights to four of its books in one year. Three books were sold as movies of the week. One other, *Chased* by Billy Chase and Lenny Grimaldi, was sold as a possible TV series. The book featured an undercover cop who risked death from gangs as well as fellow cops while fighting drugs.

Judith Orloff, a psychiatrist who tells readers how to develop their psychic gifts in her book, *Second Sight*, worked with her agent Michael Katz and a dramatic rights agent from William Morris to sell Atlas Entertainment an option for a possible TV series.

Francine Pascal's Sweet Valley High series, published by Bantam since 1983, was made into a syndicated TV series and became a full-fledged hit with teen audiences.

The Ramona Quimby young adult novels by Beverly Cleary were produced as a TV series for PBS. To tie into this series, Yearling reissued the novels with new covers. In addition, Morrow Junior Books published a book about the production of the series, *Beverly Cleary's Ramona: Behind the Scenes of a Television Show* by Elaine Scott.

☐ **Miniseries**—Bestselling author Tom Clancy sold rights to ABC-TV for a network miniseries, *Tom Clancy's NetForce*. He then turned around and sold Berkley rights to the resulting books for several million dollars.

☐ **TV anthology series**—NBC optioned five books for a possible anthology series called *NBC Bestsellers*. The five books were *Erotic Silence of the American Housewife* by Dalma Heyn, *Women Who Love Too Much* by Robin Norwood, *Women and Doctors* by John Smith, *Jennifer Fever* by Barbara Gordon, and *Stepmothers: Keeping It Together with Your Husband and His Kids* by Merry Bloch Jones and JoAnne Schiller.

☐ **TV movies**—Pelican Publishing sold an option for TV movie rights to Columbia Pictures Television and ABC for Jean Hill's book on the Kennedy assassination, *JFK: The Last Dissenting Witness*. The pickup price was $125,000 plus percentages. One of the higher prices for a two-hour TV movie was the $400,000 TriStar paid to Nora Roberts for her novel, *Montana Sky*. RDR Books worked with a literary agent to sell an option on Marianne Rogoff's *Sylvie's Life*, which told the story of Rogoff's daughter who was born with severe brain damage.

☐ **TV episodes**—Book rights can also be sold as the basis for one episode in a dramatic or informative series. The American Master Series on PBS bought rights to Neil Baldwin's biography, *Man Ray: American Artist*.

☐ **Reruns**—Reruns pay about 20% of the fee for the original show.

☐ **Cable TV**—Rodale Press has produced special shows on gardening and other how-to subjects for distribution to cable TV stations. Since cable is made up of a variety of submarkets, no standards have been set for payment, terms, or other conditions of sale.

☐ **Cable networks**—HBO, other movie channels, and specialized cable networks are all potential buyers of TV rights to books. For instance, HBO produced a documentary based on *My Book for Kids with Cansur*, written by eight-year-old Jason Gaes when he was a cancer patient. A number of bestsellers have come out of original HBO programming. Rich Hall's bestselling trade paperbacks, *Sniglets* and *More Sniglets*, came out of HBO's *Not Necessarily the News*. Xerox sold 50,000 copies of an activity book tied into HBO's *Brain Games* series created by Jim Henson of Muppet fame.

With the proliferation of cable channels, there are many opportunities to sell TV rights to books on all subjects, from history to gardening, from cookbooks to music. And this market is only growing bigger as cable channels produce their own shows.

☐ **Videotapes**—Probably the fastest growing area of TV rights sales is the area of video rights (rights to reproduce books as videotapes or DVDs for direct sale or rental to consumers). MGM/UA Home Video paid a

$50,000 advance against a 20% royalty for video rights to Stuart Berger's *Dr. Berger's Immune Power Diet*. While that is a higher advance and royalty than most books will get, the field is wide open.

DVDs and videotapes have had a secondary effect on the sale of movie tie-in books and novelizations. Since DVDs and videos usually do not go on sale until after the original run of the movie, they can create a secondary burst of sales for tie-in books. Scholastic didn't even publish its novelization of *The Karate Kid* until after the film, yet the book sold so well that they published a sequel. Similarly, just before the release of the video two years after the movie's premiere, Tor published a novelization by Richard Mueller of *Ghostbusters*.

When selling movie and TV rights, don't overlook nonfiction books. Certainly biographies, histories, and current events stories such as *All the President's Men* are all adaptable to the screen. Plus feature films and TV movies have been made of such prosaic titles as *How to Succeed in Business Without Really Trying*, *Everything You Always Wanted to Know about Sex*, and *Sex and the Single Girl*. Plus, of course, some of the biggest selling videotapes have been nonfiction titles such as *Jane Fonda's Workout*.

17:14 Tips on Selling Movie/TV Rights

Most rights sales to movie and TV producers are made through literary agents who specialize in this field. You can search on the Internet for such agents or buy the $30.00 *Literary, Subsidiary, and Foreign Rights Agents* report from Open Horizons. Order at http://www.bookmarket.com.

If you'd like to handle your own rights sales for movies and television, you have several options on how to proceed:

☐ **Hope for an act of God or lucky happenstance** (with a little push from you). That's how Naiad Press sold the movie rights of Jane Rule's novel, *Desert of the Heart*, to Donna Deitch, an independent producer. The publisher gave a copy of the book to a friend who, in turn, happened to meet Deitch at a party. The rest, as they say, is history.

☐ **Work through scouts.** These people work for producers or production companies scouting for literary properties that might be suitable for making into movies. My favorite scout is Ron Martino, available via email at mmg7@aol.com.

☐ **Sell rights direct to the studios**, producers, or other decision-makers. To locate independent producers and other influential people in the entertainment industry, check out the following directory at your local library or buy it from: **Hollywood Creative Directory**, 5055 Wilshire Boulevard, Los Angeles, CA 90036-4396; 325-525-2369; 800-815-0503; Fax: 323-525-2398. Web: http://www.hcdonline.com.

☐ **List your books with an online web site** such as StoryBay.com. More than 500 producers and publishers are users of this service.

☐ **Build your network.** The motion picture industry is a people business: the more connected you are, the more successful you will be. Hence, build up your network of contacts. Or, perhaps better yet, hire someone who already has developed a good set of contacts.

> **Authors:** When writing your book, be aware of movie rights. As novelist Niven Busch, "The writer who doesn't angle his books for film sales is an idiot.... What you have to do is select a subject ... a subject which will appeal to a large audience and hence merit, and probably get, exposure in films, television, and whatever electronic devices for communication the future may provide."

17:15 Audio Rights

During the past ten years audio publishing has outpaced book publishing in growth. It is now estimated that more than 20 million U.S. households have bought books on audio. Aaudio rights can bring in significant royalties. Warner Audio paid a $37,000 advance for exclusive audio rights to *The IBM Way* by Buck Rogers (which it recouped by sublicensing audio rights to several companies selling to non-retail markets). Nightingale-Conant paid an advance in the high five figures for George Burn's two bestsellers, *How to Live to Be 100 or More* and *Dr. Burns' Prescription for Happiness*.

☐ **Multiple sales**—Audio or recording rights can be sold separately for audiotapes, records, CDs, MP3s, etc. The standard royalty is around 5% to 10%. The term of such recording rights is usually two years with automatic renewals until one or the other party serves notice.

☐ **Unabridged/abridged**—You can sell audiotape rights more than once—for unabridged rights and for abridged rights. In 1986, *The Collected Stories of John Cheever* were available in three different audiotape packages: as an eight-cassette unabridged package from G. K. Hall ($49.95 retail), as a two-cassette package from Listen for Pleasure ($13.95), and as a one-cassette Audiobook from Random House ($7.95).

☐ **Dramatization rights**—Audio rights can also be sold separately for excerpt rights versus dramatization rights. Audio dramatization usually involves multiple actors (or voices), music, and sound effects.

☐ **Direct marketing rights**—Audio rights can also be divided between direct marketing rights (for tapes to be sold only by mail order or telemarketing) and retail rights (tapes to be sold only through retail outlets). Jenn Crowell's *Necessary Madness* was sold to Books on Tape for rental and direct mail rights as well as to Brilliance for abridged and un-abridged readings.

Nightingale Conant is the major producer of self-help 6-tape audio sets which they direct market effectively. To sell rights, contact **Nightingale Conant**, 7300 N. Lehigh Avenue, Niles, IL 60714; 847-647-0306; 800-572-2770; Fax: 847-647-9243. Web: http://www.nightingale.com.

☐ **Audio book club rights**—There are a number of audio book clubs, but most now work mainly as online services. The largest membership based audio club is **Audio Book Club**, 2 Ridgedale Avenue #300, Cedar Knolls, NJ 07927; 973-539-9528; Fax: 973-539-1273. Web: http://www.audiobookclub.com.

☐ **Subscription services**—Audio rights can be sold to subscription services such as Soundview Executive Summaries and Audio-Tech Business Book Summaries, which feature audio summaries of business books.

☐ **Broadcast rights**—The right to broadcast a recording of a book via radio can be licensed separately. There are a number of radio programs on both public and commercial networks which feature readings or dramatizations of books. Among other books, Jeffrey Archer's *Kane and Abel* and a number of James Herriott's books have been broadcast on radio.

There are about two hundred major producers of audiobooks. To locate these producers to sell rights, get a copy of the *Resource Directory* of the **Audio Publishers Association**, 8405 Greensboro Drive #800, McLean, VA 22102; 703-556-7171; Fax: 703-506-3266. Email: info@audiopub.org. Web: http://www.audiopub.org.

17:16 Electronic Rights

As time goes on, electronic rights are going to become more and more important. While they don't generally bring a lot of money at this point for each individual sale, they can be broken up in so many ways that they can still generate a good income.

Because these rights can be important for promoting your books as well as generating additional income, it is important that the publisher control the rights. In your contract with your authors, be sure to include a *future technology clause* that will allow you to exploit technologies yet to be developed. With all the changes in hardware and software, the opportunities will be endless. Below are just a few of the ways you can break up electronic rights and make sales:

☐ **Computer CD-ROMs**—The sales of books on CD-ROMs have never lived up to expectations but, nonetheless, they can be a source of rights income. Random House, for instance, licensed its dictionary and thesaurus to be used in the computer spell check program of *Reference Desk*. Rights can be sold for the book as a whole or for excerpt rights of part of the book. IVI Publishing, which had licensed the CD-ROM rights to *Mayo Clinic Family Health Book*, sold more than three million copies of the CD-ROM version. The book, published by Morrow, sold for $42.50 while the CD-ROM from IVI sold for $39.95.

☐ **DVDs**—DVDs are the new hot format and could result in many retail sales for books that can be visually adapted to the medium. The cost to create DVDs is still too high for most publishers to get involved in creating DVDs themselves. It makes sense to license rights to a company that produces many DVDs and has the talent to do it well.

☐ **Computer software**—Open Horizons sells the *Celebrate Today Special Events* data files on CDs where we provide the files in five formats: Microsoft Access, Microsoft Excel, tab-delimited ASCII, comma-delimited ASCII, and dBase. People who buy the data files can then transfer the file formats they are most comfortable using to their computers' hard disks. By providing only data files, we don't have to get involved in supporting software. We are now in the process of setting up automatic downloads of any file format for all our databases, including the *Top 700 Independent Bookstores* and the *Catalog Sales Directory*. This would allow our customers to have almost instant access to our data.

Chef Paul Prudhomme's *Magic Seasoning Blends Cookbook* has been made available as freeware on disk. *Freeware* is software that is offered freely to anyone who wants to download it or copy it from a disk.

☐ **Online subscription databases**—Almost all reference books are now published in computer-friendly formats—CDs or online subscription databases—as well as in book format. It won't be long before the print editions will no longer be published. In the meantime, if you have published a book that might be a good supplement to an existing online subscription service, contact them about licensing the rights to your book. That could make a lot more sense that trying to establish an online market for your book alone.

☐ **Web site rights**—You can sell rights to all or part of your books for use by other web sites. Since commercial web sites need to have interesting content in order to attract visitors, the door is open for book publishers to provide that content. Don't sell such rights short. Be sure to get a fair price for your content. Also be sure to set a time limit on the use of your content, especially since the value could go much higher in the coming years. The University of Illinois Press sold rights to Golfweb for *Babe*, its biography of Babe Didrikson Zaharias. The rights covered an excerpt from the book, an author profile, a press release, and copies of reviews.

Macmillan Publishing licensed rights to many of its computer titles to Developer.com, which offers users free access to individual chapters and complete text from a thousand of Macmillan's titles.

☐ **Interactive novels**—Spinnaker, a publisher of interactive crime detective novels for home computers, paid a five-figure advance against royalties for the right to adapt an Ellery Queen novel.

☐ **Electronic games**—Software rights can be sold for computer games. For example, Roger Zelazny's *Nine Princes of Amber* was licensed to Telarium Corporation for its role-playing game. In addition to selling video rights to Twentieth Century Fox, Scholastic Productions sold CD rights for the *Goosebumps* series to DreamWorks and electronic game rights to Tiger Electronics. Mindscape bought game rights to John Saul's terror series, *The Blackstone Chronicles*.

Electronic rights can sell for major money. When Rabbit Ears Productions developed a line of audiobooks based on classic tales (such as *The Ugly Duckling* and *Goldilocks*) narrated by veteran actors (such as Danny Glover and Jodie Foster), they sold more than $12 million in rights, including more than a half a million for book rights to eighteen titles by Simon & Schuster. Showtime bought domestic TV rights for $150,000 per episode; Phillips Interactive Media paid $50,000 per story for CD-I rights; Microsoft paid more than $1 million for CD-ROM rights to eight titles.

17:17 Other Subsidiary Rights

There are many other subsidiary rights that you can sell, everything from dramatic rights to merchandising rights to other print rights. Indeed, you can sell rights from books for almost any product or service that uses words or illustrations—tee-shirts, clothing, stuffed animals, food, toys, home furniture, and so on. Just use your imagination. To help your imagination, though, here are a few of the other subsidiary rights that are regularly sold.

Dramatic rights

Books are sometimes made into stage plays before or even after they have been made into movies. These dramatic rights may be for amateur or professional productions, on Broadway or off, for serious drama or musical comedies. Prices can range from $1,000 on up.

- Sam Gallu, a playwright, paid a $2,000 advance for rights to adapt Curtis Bill Pepper's *An Artist and the Pope* for the Broadway stage. If the play was actually produced, he would pay more.

- Patrick Dennis's *Auntie Mame* began life as a book but has since gone on to be a play, a motion picture, a Broadway musical, and a movie musical. Then, it was licensed once again for a movie.

- Broadway plays have been produced from *A Bell for Adano*, *The King and I*, *Les Misérables*, *Mister Roberts*, *My Sister Eileen*, *Phantom of the Opera*, *South Pacific*, and *Teahouse of the August Moon*. All were later made into movies (for which separate movie rights were sold).

- John Gray's one-man show based on his bestselling book, *Men Are from Mars, Women Are from Venus*, packed Broadway's biggest theater.

- A musical stage play based on Robert Fulghum's *All I Really Need to Know I Learned in Kindergarten*, was held over at the Tiffany Theatre because of popular demand. Through monologues, music, and intimate scenes, the play brought Fulghum's stories to life.

Ballet or Opera

Although such rights are rarely sold, choreographer John Butler prepared a ballet based on stories by Southern authors. The ballet, commissioned by the public TV station in Jackson, Mississippi, aired in 1987.

Filmstrips, microfiche, microfilm, transparencies

These rights rarely bring in much money. Such rights are used primarily in preparing educational support material for schools, government programs, and business training programs.

Limited editions

It is possible to sell rights to another publisher to produce limited editions of your books. For example, both Phantasia Press and Underwood-Miller publish autographed, numbered and slipcased editions of books by well-known science fiction authors (such as a $50.00 autographed edition of Roger Zelazny's *Trumps of Doom* or a $40.00 autographed edition of C. J. Cherryh's *Cuckoo's Egg*). These higher priced editions rarely compete with standard hardcover or paperback editions since they are issued in limited runs of 250 to 1,000 copies and are sold primarily to collectors.

Library editions

Some publishers like Gregg Press specialize in publishing library editions of books whose hardcover editions have gone out of print. These editions are sold only to libraries.

Large print editions

As baby boomers have grown older, large print editions have sold more copies—and brought higher prices for rights (usually between $5,000 and $15,000). There are fewer than ten companies that specialize in printing large print editions, so it's not hard to find them. Just visit your local bookstore or library and browse the large print section.

- Thorndike paid $36,000 in an auction against G.K. Hall for large print rights to Anne Tyler's novel, *Breathing Lessons*.

- Thorndike paid $9,500 for large print rights for Barbara Delinsky's first book, *For My Daughters*. G.K. Hall paid $10,500 for Delinsky's second book, *Together Alone*.

- Large print rights for Toni Morrison's bestselling novel, *Beloved*, went for $7,500.

Syndication

You can sell syndication rights (a version of serial rights) for any book that would interest a mass audience. Most syndication rights are bought for articles to be syndicated through newspapers.

- The New York Times Syndication company syndicated the *Legal Question & Answer Book* published by Reader's Digest in a weekly column.

- Entertainment News Service syndicated questions and answers from John Kremer's *Tinseltowns, U.S.A.* in 70 newspapers across the country.

Permissions

If another author or publisher wants to use a short section, chapter, or several chapters from one of your books in one of their books, they must request permission from you to reprint. You will then have to decide how much to charge for such permission. Permission rates range from token charges for shorter quotes to charges comparable to second serial rights for anthology selections.

Direct marketing rights

You can sell rights to direct market your book to specific markets or to a general market. For instance, *Encyclopaedia Britannica* bought the direct marketing rights for Glenn Doman's *How to Teach Your Baby to Read* and its accompanying kit. They sold 120,000 copies via direct mail and space ads in magazines such as *Parents, American Baby*, and *Redbook*.

Board games

Board games drawn from books are especially popular among children's books. For example, Beatrix Potter, author of *Peter Rabbit*, also designed a board game, the *Peter Rabbit Race Game*. That game has gone through three editions since it was first published in 1917. More recently, TSR brought out a board game of Tom Clancy's *The Hunt for Red October*.

Card games

Sapiens Press sold game rights to U.S. Games Systems for three *Enjoyable English* card games, *Challenges*, *Winning Words*, and *Fool 'Em*. New age publishers have sold rights to U.S. Games for a series of Tarot card decks featuring the characters or symbols from their titles. These new versions of Tarot have been very popular.

Role-playing games

Victory Games bought rights to produce a role-playing game based on the *James Bond* books. A number of other books, especially in fantasy and science fiction, have also been licensed for role-playing games. Sean Curran and Hans Rueffert of Zehrapushu Inc. bought rights from Clive Barker to create a collectible card game based on his bestselling novel, *Imajica*.

Posters

While many posters are produced from book covers for promotional reasons, posters can also sell on their own. Conari Press licensed the rights to produce a poster from its book, *True Love*, to Ten Speed Press. Conari sold 250,000 copies of the book, while Ten Speed Press sold 100,000 copies of the poster.

Merchandising rights

Also known as *licensing rights*, these rights can cover any commercial reproduction of words, illustrations, or characters from a book, movie, game, or whatever. Almost any product can be—and has been—licensed, from T-shirts to coffee mugs, from greeting cards to rubber stamps, from dolls to toys, from carpets to salad dressing. Licensed merchandise is a $100 billion annual market.

- Wendy's Restaurants licensed the rights to *The Rotation Diet* by Martin Katahn for its Rotation Diet salad and dressing. A number of fast-food restaurants licensed the *Atkins Diet* name for a special line of dinners.

- Jack Canfield and Mark Victor Hansen sold excerpts from their *Chicken Soup for the Soul* books to be used in two mini-books published by Andrews McMeel: *A Little Sip of Chicken Soup* and *Another Sip of Chicken Soup*. Andrews McMeel also licensed the rights to create mugs and bookmarks based on the series.

- Viking Penguin licensed its *Little Chef* series of books to Riegal Textiles for a book/apron combination package.

- Both Mudpuppy Press and Learning Curve Toys license characters from children's books for their puzzles.

- Acropolis Books licensed rights to *Your Colors At Home* by Lauren Smith and Rose Bennett Gilbert to the following companies:

    Ceramic Fashions—vases
    Ex-Cell Home Fashions—shower curtains, bath ensembles
    Linde Company—decorative pillows, chair pads
    National Ceramics—lamps

  Acropolis also actively looked for *Your Color At Home* licensees in the following product areas: at-home wear, blankets, broadloom carpet, ceramic tiles, china, closet accessories, drapes, floral arrangements, plumbing fixtures, soap, wallpaper, and window treatments.

- In 1997, Yankee Publishing licensed its *Old Farmer's Almanac* name for a new line of seventy-five food items, from tomato sauce to snack foods, from baked goods to breakfast food. The *Almanac*'s name has also been licensed to garden supplies and Old Farmer's Almanac General Stores.

- At the height of *Gnomes*-mania in the late 70s, Abrams sold more than $10 million in licensed products for the book, *Gnomes*, created by Dutch artist Rien Poortvliet and writer Wil Huygen. While its subsidiary,

Abrams Art Papers, produced *Gnomes* calendars, stationery, note cards, gift tags, wrapping paper, posters, and jigsaw puzzles, Abrams licensed merchandising rights to other companies for clothing, jewelry, plates, music boxes, figurines, dolls, games, tie tacks, key chains, bookmarks, soaps, figurines, wristwatches, wall clocks, infantware, and many other items. Department stores opened *Gnomes* boutiques and window displays to sell the collection.

- Marcus Pfister is the author/illustrator of nearly two dozen children's books featuring such characters as Penguin Pete, Dazzle the Dinosaur, and Hopper. While North-South, his publisher, produces some products based on his characters (such as buttons and finger puppets), the characters have also been licensed to appear on the following products:

  Antioch—bookmarks, bookplates, journals
  Galison/Mudpuppy Press—puzzles, note cards, magnet sets
  Glitterwrap—giftwrap, tote bags
  Marcel Schurman—greeting cards
  Springs—fabrics
  There's Kids Line—infant bedding, lamps, etc.

- Paddington Bear, the hero of a dozen novels, two collections of short stories, and dozens of pop-up and picture books, has been licensed all over the world. The Copyrights Group sold licenses to twenty-four companies in Japan, thirty-seven in the U.S., and dozens more in South Africa, Southeast Asia, Australia, and Europe. Here are a few of the companies which have licensed Paddington Bear in the U.S.:

  American Greetings—Christmas ornaments
  American Traditional Stencil—blue laser stencils, brass stencils
  The Bradford Exchange—collectable plates
  Classico San Francisco—paper postcards, gift enclosure cards
  CTI Industries—mylar balloons, boxed gift mugs
  Eden Toys—plush, musical toys, mobiles, clip-ons, puppets, etc.
  Evenflo—nursers, pacifiers, bibs, teethers, and baby care accessories
  Hand & Hammer Silversmiths—sterling silver jewelry and ornaments
  Harper Collins—board books, novelty books, flap books, etc.
  Hope Industries—watches
  Infantino—dimensional fabric wall hangings and mirrors
  Inscribe—computerized stationery and greeting cards
  Jerry Leigh—women's and junior's apparel
  Kidstamps—rubber stamps
  Kurt Adler—holiday ornaments, stockings, lights, etc.
  Noel Joanna Inc.—infant bedding and fabric accessories
  Princess Fabrics—fabrics
  Random House—picture story books
  Royal Doulton—figurines
  Sangamon Company—greeting cards, note cards

Thomas Nelson—baby books, brag books, growth chart, gift bags
Westland Giftware—musical waterglobes and figurines

- Of course, you can also turn around and license characters from other companies to feature in your books. For example, Freedom Publishing licensed the Chicago Bulls mascot, Benny the Bull, for two children's books, *Benny Gets a Bully-Ache* and *Benny's Coloring Book from A to Z*, as well as a Benny Bookmark.

17:18 Slicing and Dicing Rights

One of the most important things to remember when buying and selling subsidiary rights is that every right can be cut into as many pieces as you want. If you want to maximize your subsidiary rights income and at the same time retain greater control over your intellectual property, learn how to slice and dice rights. Below are a few of the ways that you can do that.

☐ **First and second** — When selling magazine reprint rights, you can sell first serial rights and second serial rights. First rights are those sold for publication before the book's publication date. Second rights are those sold after the book has been published. You could use a similar breakdown for selling some other rights as well.

☐ **Duration** — Any right can be sold with a time limit attached. For example, mass-market reprint rights are often sold for a set time limit, from three to seven years. Foreign rights are also often limited to a certain number of years. If you have any concerns about the rights buyer, one of the best ways to retain control is to set a time limit for those rights.

☐ **Timing** — In addition to setting a limit, you can also require that the buyer exercise the right within a certain time period. If they fail to exercise it during that time, rights revert back to you. When I sold Chinese rights to *1001 Ways* the first time, the publisher failed to publish an edition in the time required so the rights reverted back to me. As a result, I am able to sell the Chinese rights to this new edition without any conflict with an old edition still being out there.

You could also set a time limit on when they can begin to exercise the right. For instance, to give your hardcover edition time to sell, you can require that a mass-market publisher wait one year from the signing of the contract before publishing their edition.

☐ **Grant an option** — Movie rights are often sold with an option first. The option allows a buyer to pay a smaller amount while trying to put a deal together. If he can't put the deal together, then the rights revert back to the seller without a high cost to the buyer.

☐ **Format** — Rights are naturally broken down by format: book, audio, video, electronic, performance, etc. I've already outlined most of these format possibilities in the previous points. In any rights contract, be sure to specify exactly what rights you are granting. All other rights should be retained by you.

☐ **Sub-formats** — You can also sell rights by sub-formats. For example, sell book rights to reprint in hardcover, trade paperback, mass-market paperback, limited edition, miniature format, etc. Each of these rights can be sold separately.

☐ **Medium** — When selling some rights, you can also restrict the rights to specific media. For example, break down audio rights to records, audio-tapes, CDs, and mp3 in addition to any new audio formats to be created. The best way to do this is to specify the actual media that the right includes and exclude all others unless the buyer also wants to buy the rights to reproduce audio for those media. You can do the same with video, books, etc.

☐ **Pieces** — You can sell rights to pieces of the book, not just for serial rights but also for reprinting as premium editions, purse books, miniature books, pocket guides, etc. Don't think you have to sell the entire book. Sell whatever portion a buyer wants to buy. Retain rights to the rest to sell to another buyer (even a competitor to the first buyer).

☐ **Abridgements** — Audio rights are often broken down to abridged or unabridged rights, but you can do the same for book rights, video, electronic, or other formats. By distinguishing between abridged and unabridged, you can sell the same format or medium rights more than once. For example, the first *Chicken Soup for the Soul* book also was reprinted in an abridged version as *A Cup of Chicken Soup for the Soul*.

☐ **Dramatic rights** — With audio especially, you can distinguish between dramatic and non-dramatic readings of the book. But you could possibly do the same with video and performance rights.

☐ **Exclusivity** — With any right, you can sell an exclusive or a nonexclusive right. Whenever possible, sell nonexclusively. If someone wants an exclusive, they should pay more for that right. While some rights require exclusivity (e.g., translation or movie rights), others can readily be sold on a nonexclusive basis (e.g., serial or book club rights).

☐ **Audience** — You can limit the exercise of a right to a specific audience. For example, you could sell first serial rights to an excerpt to a travel magazine and sell the same excerpt again to a food magazine—if you have limited the serial right to a specific audience.

☐ **Markets** — You can grant one publisher the right to publish a book for the religious market and sell the book rights for the general bookstore market to another publisher. Or you can sell book rights to a publisher but retain rights to publish and sell another edition to premium and corporate buyers.

☐ **Means of reaching a market** — In selling rights, you could distinguish between the means a publisher uses to reach a market. For example, you could sell the rights to publish the book for the bookstore market but retain rights to sell via mail order, telephone sales, the Internet, etc. If you retain such rights explicitly in a contract, you are free to exercise those rights later yourself—or sell them to someone else. This could be critical if someone wants to build an infomercial around your book.

☐ **Territory** — You can restrict any right by the territory where it is used, for example, North America, France, Spain, South America, etc. While this restriction is most used in selling foreign rights, it is possible for you to set regional restrictions within a country as well. I don't know when that would be practical or reasonable, but don't rule it out.

> **Authors:** It is important to remember when selling first serial rights that you sell first North American serial rights rather than world rights. Most magazines are now trying to grab all rights or *simply* world rights, but you should restrict the rights to first North American serial rights. If they want other rights, they should specify each right separately and how much they are willing to pay for each one. Don't sell yourself short. Negotiate for each right they want to exploit.

☐ **Language** — All subsidiary rights can be sold separately for every language on earth (if someone is interested in buying them). Generally, when you sell translation rights to your book, the foreign publisher also specifies the right to many of the subsidiary rights within that language. The most important subsidiary translation rights are serial, book club, audio, and electronic rights. Note: You would not sell movie rights in another language because then you'd be undermining your ability to sell movie rights in English.

☐ **Editorial restrictions** — When selling any right, you can always specify your right to approve any editorial changes. This could be important if you are concerned about the integrity of the content, especially when selling condensation rights, reprint rights, or translation rights. Such restrictions can also be important when licensing merchandising rights so that your brand image or title is not used inappropriately on t-shirts, calendars, posters, coffee mugs, etc.

> **Authors:** If your content or style is important to you, ask your agent to negotiate some sort of editorial approval clause in your contracts. While most sane publishers would refuse an author's right to change editorial (the headaches an author could cause could be tramatic, frustrating, and incapacitating), you have to decide what is important to you—and fight for it.

☐ **Advertising restrictions** — If it is important how your brand is presented, you should also set advertising and promotional restrictions so that the buyer doesn't advertise your brand inappropriately.

☐ **Other restrictions** — When selling rights, read any contract offered you as carefully as possible. Similarly, when offering a buyer a contract to license any rights, be sure to include every point that is important to you. If you have any other concerns, be sure to specify them in a contract. All rights are fully negotiable. Set any restrictions you need to set to be comforatable in selling a right.

The world can be yours, or at least one billion dollars of it (as is the case with J. K. Rowlings), if you know and understand how intellectual property rights work. Don't be stupid. If you don't know what you are signing, don't sign it. Keep asking questions until you are satisfied you understand exactly what rights you are granting and how you will be paid, how much, what kind of accountability is in place, etc. You can't be shy when it comes to your intellectual property rights. Stand up for your rights!

Authors: CDS Books, a division of Perseus, offers an attractive alternative for authors, one that I think you should seriously consider. While they offer no advance, they offer high royalties, contractually guaranteed promotion dollars, limited license of rights (you retain most rights), and monthly payments (based on actual sales as recorded by Bookscan). They have published at least one bestseller, Dan Burstein's *Secrets of the Code*. They are now expanding their outreach to authors and I wouldn't be surprised to see more publishers adopting this author-as-partner model.

For most authors, this model is definitely better than the big advance, no support, horrid contract, and no more payments model that is currently the vogue among larger publishers, especially now that they have cut advances so much. When negotiating with your potential publisher, be sure to bring up this model as an alternative to whatever they are offering. It pays to partner if you are willing to take some of the risk.

Chapter 18

Selling Your Books Overseas

What can you really get out of a foreign rights deal?
First of all, found money. You already have the product.
Now you will license that product to another company so that they
may pay you a fee to become the publisher of your title in that country.
— Jan Nathan, Executive Director, Publishers Marketing Association

In 1995, according to Euromonitor, global retail book sales totaled $80.1 billion. The top ten book markets sold $65 billion as follows: United States, $25.5 billion; Japan, $10.5 billion; Germany, $10 billion; United Kingdom, $3.6 billion; France, $3.4 billion; Spain, $3 billion; South Korea, $2.8 billion; Brazil, $2.5 billion; Italy, $2.2 billion; and China, $1.8 billion. Other top markets were Canada with $1.3 billion and Mexico with $1 billion.

For a smaller publisher with a limited list of titles, the best way to sell books overseas is to sell translation rights rather than the books themselves. Translation rights require no shipping, warehousing, distribution, or customs clearance. Even then, translation sales are not likely to make you rich. Not only do translation rights usually sell for less than a $5,000 advance, but payment can also be reduced by agent fees, taxes, exchange rates, shared translation costs, and the author's share of the sale (usually 50 to 80%).

Besides translations rights, there are a number of other ways to arrange distribution of your books overseas.

18:01 Two Kinds of Foreign Rights

You have two basic options when you sell foreign rights: You can sell reprint rights (such as British Commonwealth rights) or translation rights (e.g., French language rights). In each case you can divvy up these rights into certain territories. For example, you can sell English language rights to the entire British Commonwealth or to Great Britain only (thus allowing you to sell separate rights to Australia, India, South Africa, and other countries).

Reprint rights allow a foreign publisher to reprint the English language edition of the book and market it in certain territories. The most common English language reprint rights are for British Commonwealth rights (exclusive of Canada), Canadian rights, ANZAC rights (Australia and New Zealand), Indian rights, and South African rights.

- Crown sold British rights to Payne Harrison's technothriller, *Storming Intrepid*, for $105,000.

- The Atlantic Monthly Press sold British rights for Rian Malan's *My Traitor's Heart* to The Bodley Head for $38,000.

- Collins Harvill paid almost $480,000 for the British rights to two novels by Martin Cruz Smith. Italian rights sold for $125,000 and Japanese rights for $100,000.

- Alti Publishing's *At Century's End*, edited by Nathan Gardels, sold English-language reprint rights in the U.K., Singapore, Hong Kong, the Philippines, Malaysia, Indonesia, Sri Lanka, and South Africa. In addition, translation rights were sold for Spanish, Chinese, Japanese, Korean, Italian, Bulgarian, and Turkish.

Translation rights permit a publisher to translate the book into another language and then sell that book in any country speaking that language. Because of the cost of making good translations, translation rights are rarely divvied up into smaller territories, except for Spanish rights, which are often divied up between continental Europe and Latin America. For instance, translation rights for *His Holiness*, a book about Pope John Paul II written by Carl Bernstein and Marco Politi, was sold to Planeta in Spain and Norma for Latin America.

- Japan is a growing market for American books. As an example of some of the higher sales, Japanese publishers have paid $40,000 for Payne Harrison's *Storming Intrepid*, $30,000 for *Raymond Chandler's Philip Marlowe*, and $80,000 for Daniel Burstein's *Yen! Japan's New Financial Empire and Its Threat to America*.

- Other strong markets for U.S. books include France, Germany, Spain, Italy, the Scandinavian countries, and Holland. Because these markets are often smaller, translation rights can go for less than English language reprint rights. For instance, Permanent Press sold U.K. rights to Philip Metcalfe's *1933* (an account of Hitler's rise to power) for $25,000, while Dutch rights went for $6,600 and Swedish rights for $6,000.

- Philip Margolin's novel, *Gone, But Not Forgotten*, earned over $250,000 in advances from rights sales to the United Kingdom, Germany, Holland, Sweden, Italy, and Japan.

- *The Day After Tomorrow* by Allan Folsom earned advances on foreign rights of more than $1,500,000 with sales to the United Kingdom and France, $750,000; Japan, $300,000; Korea, $200,000; Spain, $100,000; Holland, $75,000; Sweden, $65,000; Germany, $50,000; Finland, $20,000; Norway, $13,000; Denmark, $10,000, and China, $2,000.

- During the first year, David Guterson's *Snow Falling on Cedars* sold 21,000 copies in Italy, 160,000 copies in France, 8,000 copies in Sweden, 400,000 copies in England, as well as many thousands of copies in Germany, Denmark, Finland, Japan, Norway, Iceland, Brazil, Portugal, Greece, Israel, Taiwan, Poland, Romania, and Spain (in two editions, one in Spanish, the other in Catalan).

18:02 Advantages of Selling Foreign Rights

When you sell foreign rights, you give away most of your control over how your books are to be packaged and marketed in those countries. Nonetheless, if you are careful in your selection of which publishers you sell rights to, the advantages to selling foreign rights far outweigh the disadvantages. Here are a few of the advantages:

☐ You don't have to deal with the vagaries of selling your books in a foreign country. Foreign publishers are much better prepared to deal with the laws, customs, and changing tastes of their own countries.

☐ With the sale of foreign rights, you don't have to arrange customs clearances, shipping, distribution, and fulfillment.

☐ Translating American books offers a clear advantage to foreign publishers. According to Herbert Lottman, International Correspondent for *Publishers Weekly*, "Printing an American name on the jacket (sometimes a British one) is a guarantee of success" in Italy. The average print runs of translations is double that of Italian originals.

☐ You receive payment for the rights up front. Most advances for rights go for about $1,000 to $5,000, with a royalty of 8 to 10%.

☐ You can draw on the experience of these publishers to sell to a number of related countries. For example, by selling British Commonwealth rights to a British publisher, you not only get distribution in Great Britain, but also in Australia, New Zealand, India, South Africa, and other members of the British Commonwealth. In most cases the British publisher will also handle distribution of English language books to other European countries, Africa, and Asia.

☐ Sales of a translated edition can also spur sales of the English language edition, especially among libraries and scholars.

☐ Foreign rights have little if any downside impact on domestic sales.

☐ Translation sales can be a significant source of income for smaller publishers. 70% of Impact Publisher's titles have been published in international translations covering eighteen languages. For larger publishers, foreign rights can help a publisher to earn out the advance they've paid to the author, sometimes even before the book is published.

☐ John Oakes, publisher of Four Walls Eight Windows, attributed their success with subsidiary rights as one of the factors that led to their long-term success. With the help of Writer's House, Four Walls sold translation rights for *Fermat's Last Theorem* to fifteen countries.

☐ Authors like having their work translated into other languages, so another plus to such rights sales is author loyalty.

☐ One note of caution: If the potential foreign market for your book is only a few thousand copies, you might be better off exporting your title rather than selling translation rights.

18:03 How to Sell Foreign Rights

Out of almost 52,000 titles published by West German publishers in 1984, slightly over 4,000 (or about 8%) were translations from English. Similarly, out of over 32,000 titles published by Spanish publishers in 1982, almost 4,000 (or about 12%) were translations from English; by 1996, however, one book in four were translations. At the same time, in Italy translations accounted for one book in three with English accounting for 54.3% of the translations.

In general, if we allow for duplication, anywhere from 9,000 to 14,000 English language titles are bought for translation each year. Since up to half of these titles were originally published in Great Britain, the annual market for translation rights of American books was probably about 7,000 titles—or about 5% of all titles produced in the U.S. each year.

What all this means is that each new book has about one chance in twenty of selling some translation rights. Since a good number of the books produced in the United States have a limited foreign market, your chances of selling translation rights to your books increases even more. Indeed, your chances of selling foreign rights are probably greater than your chances of selling mass-market reprint rights or any dramatic rights.

The most important thing you can do to sell foreign rights is to get reviews and distribution in the U.S. or to make a big impact on the Internet. If the book sells well here and has a potential market overseas, you'll be contacted. Below are a few of the choices you have in selling foreign rights:

☐ **Contact foreign publishers on your own**. If you want to sell direct to foreign publishers, start by compiling a list of such publishers who specialize in the same subject areas as you do. Mail them your catalog

(Attn: Rights Manager), with a list of what rights are available and a letter in English introducing your company and pointing out which of your new titles might be of most interest to them. Be sure to include your fax number or email address, since those are the most likely ways they will respond if they want to see a specific title.

☐ **Hire a U.S. literary agent** who specializes in foreign rights sales. For a list of such agents, see my special report, *Literary, Subsidiary, and Foreign Rights Agents.* Writers House helped Wildcat Canyon Press sell rights to *Girlfriends* in five languages and Hampton House sell rights to *Conversations with God: Book 2* in eleven languages.

Here is another literary agent who specializes in foreign rights: **Linda Michaels, Ltd.**, Linda Michaels, President, 130 West 56th Street, 2nd Floor, New York, NY 10019; 212-247-0700; Fax: 212-247-0301. She sold rights for Richard Carlson's *Don't Sweat the Small Stuff* to the U.K., Australia, Germany, Czech Republic, Sweden, Taiwan, Thailand, Israel, Lithuania, Brazil/Portugal, Estonia, Korea, Hungary, Turkey, France, and French Canada.

☐ **Hire foreign agents** who handle English language rights sales in their own country. Here, for example, are two rights agencies in Japan: The Japan Uni Agency and The English Agency. For the addresses of 325 such agents, again see my special report, *Literary, Subsidiary, and Foreign Rights Agents.* You can order it at BookMarket.com for only $30.

Work with foreign agents in the same way you'd work with U.S. literary agents. Keep them up to date on what you are publishing. Send them copies of your major titles, supporting material, and any major reviews. The main advantage of using agents when you are first starting out is that they know the market better than you could possibly get to know it without devoting full time to the project. Agents are well worth the 10% to 20% fee that they charge.

Danny Baror of Baror International worked with overseas subagents to sell rights to Joseph Finder's *The Zero Hour* in twenty-one countries. Total rights income for these foreign rights was over $750,000.

Isobel Dixon of Blake Friedmann in England sold rights to New Zealand author Cherry Simmond's self-published memoir *Nobody in Particular* to Bantam. The book also inspired a radio series on Radio New Zealand.

☐ **Work with scouts** (U.S. agents of foreign publishers). These scouts are also listed in *Literary, Subsidiary, and Foreign Rights Agents.* Send them your catalog regularly. While they will not represent your books, they might buy rights for the foreign publishers they represent.

☐ **Attend major international book fairs.** While it is possible to find an agent or to sell rights direct to publishers via phone calls and letters, the most practical way to make the necessary contacts is to attend the major international book fairs.

BookExpo America has become a major foreign rights fair. It's a great place to make initial contacts. I know one publisher who spent most of his time at one BEA meeting with Japanese, Chinese, and other foreign publishers. His rights sales to them more than paid for his exhibit at the trade show—even without making one sale to a bookstore.

The major international trade event is the Frankfurt Book Fair, held the beginning of October in Frankfurt, Germany. 320,000 people representing about 9,000 firms from around the world attend this fair every year. For more details, contact **Frankfurter Buchmesse**, Ausstellungs und Messe GmbH, Frankfurt Book Fair, Reineckstrasse 3, 60313 Frankfurt am Main, Germany; (49) 69-2102-0; Fax: (49) 69-2102-227. Email: info@book-fair.com. Web: http://www.frankfurt-book-fair.com.

At one Frankfurt fair, HarperCollins sold more than $300,000 in foreign rights to Ralph Helfer's biography of *Modoc*, a circus elephant.

Other international book fairs of importance to general trade publishers are the Bologna Children's Book Fair in early April in Italy and the London Book Fair in March. Fairs are also held annually or biennially in Jerusalem, Barcelona, Quebec, Mexico City, Cairo, Belgrade, Guadalajara, Warsaw, Moscow, New Delhi, and other cities. Some of their addresses are listed on the 1001 Ways update site at http://www.bookmarket.com/18.html. More are listed at the Frankfurt Book Show web site.

Whether you have a display or participate in a cooperative exhibit, you should attend one of these book fairs if you are serious about pursuing overseas sales. Attending such fairs, especially the Frankfurt fair, will enable you to make invaluable contacts, learn firsthand how foreign rights are sold, and perhaps even buy some translation rights from others (to expand your own list of titles here in the U.S.).

Before you attend an international book show, send letters and your catalog to those publishers or agents you'd like to meet. Use *International Literary MarketPlace* or the Internet to locate their names and addresses. Make appointments beforehand. Because the Frankfurt fair is spread over six buildings and thousands of exhibits, it is impossible to meet with anyone unless you already have an appointment prior to the fair.

☐ **Join a co-op exhibit.** If you cannot afford to display your books on your own, you can join one of the cooperative exhibits put on by Publishers Marketing Association, International Titles, Columbine Communications, Overseas Book Service, Rights & Distribution, or International Publishers Alliance (addresses at http://www.bookmarket. com/18.html). They offer an inexpensive way to expose your books to foreign publishers. The cost of a co-op display, travel, food, lodging, and other expenses can run anywhere from $1,500 to $8,000, depending on where you stay and how extravagant you are. The cost is much less if you simply exhibit.

Some wholesalers, such as Baker & Taylor, have mounted group exhibits at international book fairs. Finally, the U.S. Department of Commerce sponsors some co-op exhibits at book fairs around the world. For more information about their exhibits, email William Lofquist, publishing analyst, at william_lofquist@ita.doc.gov or call 202-482-0379.

When Dennis Lewis exhibited his self-published book *The Tao of Natural Breathing for Health, Well-Being and Inner Growth* at the PMA exhibit at Frankfurt, a foreign rights rep saw his book and offered his services. Within months he and subagents found buyers in Germany, Russia, Bulgaria, Poland, Holland, Portugal, France, Spain, and Croatia.

Robin Sharma used a co-op exhibit at Frankfurt to sell translation rights to *MegaLiving* to publishers in India, Malaysia, Singapore, Indonesia, Dubai, and Italy.

☐ **Participate in PMA's Foreign Rights Virtual Book Fair.** As an alternative to exhibiting live at the trade shows, you could exhibit all year long via the Internet for only a small amount per title per month. Titles are grouped by genre, with a short description and the rights available. If you are looking to buy rights, you can get a free listing; you only pay if you are looking to sell rights. For more information, see the PMA web site at http://www.pma-online.org/pmafair.

☐ **Enclose a fact sheet.** When you send out information to prospective rights buyers, include a fact sheet (or *rights sheet*) which describes the book, its author, its audience, and what rights are available. This fact sheet should provide all the information a rights buyer would want to know in a clear and concise format. Be sure to include your address, phone and fax numbers, email address, and web site.

☐ **Be persistent.** If the first publishers you approach are not interested in your books, ask them what publishers in their country they think would be most interested in your line. These references can be the most valuable leads you receive.

☐ **Don't overlook the third world countries.** While they might not have that much money to spend, they can be a continuing source of sales for your future titles. The third world is still a wide open market. Another fast-growing market includes the countries in eastern Europe and the countries of the former Soviet Union.

☐ **Look for publishers you'd like to work with.** Try to establish long-term working relationships with them. When selling rights, don't settle for the first offer or the highest advance; look for the publisher who can best market your book. Check out the publisher. What other titles do they offer? How are their sales? What is their reputation in their market?

☐ **Get noticed.** Reviews in the appropriate trade magazines go a long way to helping you sell foreign rights just as they do for other subsidiary rights. Edin Books, for example, made its first foreign rights sale for *Interview with an Angel* after it was advertised on the cover of *Publishers Weekly* as part of the Small Press Week cover sponsored by PMA.

Also make contact with foreign trade publications like *The Bookseller* and *London Review of Books* as well as foreign bookseller and publishing associations such as the Booksellers Association in Great Britain (web site at: http://www.booksellers.org.uk) and The Independent Publishers Guild (http://www.ipg.uk.com).

☐ **Remember the bandwagon effect.** Once you make one foreign rights sale, publishers from other countries are more likely to jump on the bandwagon as well. One rights sale often leads to another which leads to another until you've signed up five or six countries.

☐ **Get a clear contract.** Before signing a contract, make sure the copyright is credited to your author and permission credited to your company. Also ensure that your author has a chance to look at any translation before publication. In addition, insist that you receive at least annual reports on sales, royalties earned, and payments due. While most contracts run for ten years or the life of the copyright, there should be a clause which states that the rights revert back to you if they don't sell more than 250 copies a year (or whatever number you feel should be a minimum). Be sure to specify the territories and/or languages covered by the contract. Finally, make sure payments are expressed and made in U.S. dollars; otherwise you could be very surprised by variable exchange rates. For a sample foreign rights contract, see my special report, *Literary, Subsidiary, and Foreign Rights Agents*.

☐ **Clear up the taxes.** You should learn the relevant tax laws in the various countries to ensure that you get the most income from rights sales. Apply for tax exemptions wherever applicable to avoid paying double taxation, here and abroad.

18:04 Other Ways to Sell Overseas

While selling translation rights may be the quickest and easiest way to get your books distributed abroad, it is not always the most financially rewarding. Moreover, you do lose control over the presentation and marketing of your books. If you decide you'd rather market the books yourself, there are a number of arrangements you can make: direct sales, co-publishing, export sales agents, agency arrangements, bookselling distributors, U.S. exporting distributors, and subsidiaries. Here are a few resources that may help you explore the various options for selling your book overseas:

☐ *Basic Guide to Exporting.* This 173-page book is available free from any local office of the International Trade Administration of the Department of Commerce. Or you can buy it for $20.00 from the U.S. Government Printing Office at http://www.access.gpo.gov.

☐ **Export-Import Bank of the United States**, 811 Vermont Avenue, Washington, DC 20571-0001; 202-565-3946; 800-565-3946; Fax: 202-

565-3946. Web: *http://www.exim.gov*. This bank is chartered to facilitate export of U.S. goods through loans, guarantees, and insurance programs.

☐ **Foreign Book Distributors, Wholesalers, & Sales Reps** — This report features more than 345 companies that provide foreign distribution or sales representation. This report also includes a sample foreign distribution contract. Just $30.00 from *BookMarket.com*.

18:05 Selling Direct to Overseas Customers

Exports account for about 8% of all U.S. book sales. Foreign markets, thus, represent a significant market for English language books. For direct sales, the bestselling American titles are in the fields of business, science, technology, and reference.

☐ The major markets for direct sales of American books are Great Britain, continental Europe, Japan, and Australia. Smaller markets for STM (scientific, technical, medical) titles exist in almost every country.

☐ Almost any mailing list broker can provide you with mailing lists that might work for you in approaching consumers directly overseas. But note that direct marketing via airmail can be expensive.

☐ Another source of targeted mailing lists of international book buyers are the foreign subscribers of U.S. magazines. The *Harvard Business Review*, for example, has more than 30,000 foreign subscribers.

☐ Foreign members of professional associations would also be prime prospects for books in their areas of interest.

☐ Besides direct mail promotions, you could test advertisements in leading overseas journals. For periodicals that might reach the same audience as your books, check *Ulrich's International Periodicals Directory* (available in most libraries).

☐ The main advantage of direct sales is that you are in total control. The main disadvantages are the expenses of mailing promotions overseas and the problems with collecting payments with changing foreign currency rates. One way to avoid the second problem is to request payment in U.S. dollars (with a check drawn on a U.S. bank). Better yet, have them pay via credit card.

☐ To cut your costs for mailing promotional literature and packages overseas, use the U.S. Postal Service's International Surface Air Lift (ISAL). To use this service, you must have enough volume to be able to ship in bulk. Plus, you need to be near an ISAL airport (most large cities). Write to the **U.S. Postal Service**, Customer Service Department, Room 5520, 475 L'Enfant Plaza WSW, Washington, DC 20260-6342; 202-268-2000. Or contact the customer service representative at your local post office.

☐ To cut the costs of international direct sales to consumers, try to do most of your foreign promotions via email and the Internet.

18:06 Co-Publishing

When two publishers agree to share the costs of acquiring, producing, and marketing a book, this arrangement is known as *co-publishing*. Such arrangements are usually made between two English-language publishers since the main benefit of co-publishing is the savings in typesetting and production costs. Co-publishing is also the standard for producing full-color art and children's books where all the publishers join in the color print run and then print the black text separately for each language. Co-publishing offers a number of advantages:

☐ The two publishers can share the costs of production. Sometimes one publisher simply joins the print run of the other publisher so each gains from the reduced costs of a larger print run. In other cases, the originating publisher provides camera-ready copy to the other publisher, thereby eliminating duplicate typesetting and preparation costs.

☐ They can share marketing costs as well, especially when exhibiting the book at international book fairs and when selling translation rights.

☐ Promotional efforts by one publisher will often spill over into the other publisher's marketing area. For example, advertisements or reviews in *Publishers Weekly* or the *New York Times Book Review* will benefit other English-language publishers of the same book since many international buyers read these publications.

18:07 Export Sales Agencies

Export sales agencies are U.S. organizations which act as distributors of books by American publishers in overseas book markets. They function in much the same way as an American distributor.

☐ They represent the titles of a number of different publishers (anywhere from ten to one hundred publishers).

☐ Their sales representatives call on the book trade (booksellers, schools, and libraries) in each country they serve.

☐ They handle all distribution and collections.

☐ They handle most of the promotion of the titles they carry in the markets they serve.

If you are a smaller publisher who wants to avoid all the hassles of marketing to the book trade overseas and would rather not have to worry about the details of distribution, fulfillment, and collection, an export sales agency will serve you well. On the other hand, if the overseas market is a significant source of sales for your books and you'd like to market your books more aggressively, you would probably be better off seeking other arrangements. Since an exports sales agency may be serving as many as a hundred different publishers, you can't expect your books to get the royal treatment.

Export sales agencies expect a discount and commission structure similar to many U.S. distributors (40% to 45% discount with a 15% commission). They pay quickly with checks drawn on U.S. banks. Most export sales agencies do not warehouse books, but rather place orders as they receive orders through their sales visits and other promotions in the countries they serve.

Here are two of the major export sales agencies in the U.S.:

☐ **Baker & Taylor International**, 800-775-1800. Email: btinfo@btol.com. Web: http://international.btol.com. They represent books to all countries. They also publish a new quarterly magazine, *Baker & Taylor's Book Watch*, designed to help international booksellers select U.S. titles. B&T stocks all titles featured in this magazine.

☐ **Book Network International**, 3 Front Street #331, P.O. Box 338, Rollinsford NH 03869; 603-749-9171; Fax: 603-749-6155. Email: bizbks@aol.com. This company distributes business books overseas.

18:08 Agency Arrangements

An agency is a foreign company (either another book publisher or a sales representative) which stocks books, fulfill orders, and handles billing and collection for other publishers. Some agencies will also handle marketing, including sending out review copies, mailing promotions, advertising in journals, exhibiting at conferences and book fairs, and visiting stores and jobbers. In many ways, they act in the same way as a distributor in the United States. The services they offer are determined at the time you sign a contract with them. Their services can be either exclusive or non-exclusive.

The main advantage of agencies is that they stock books in the countries they represent. Hence, you can refer orders from overseas customers direct to a distributor in their own country. This saves them time and money as well as saving you the hassle of handling such orders. Plus the agencies know the markets and media in the countries they represent and can therefore often do a better job than you could in promoting your books in these countries. The disadvantages of such agencies are:

☐ They can be expensive, especially considering the cost of shipping books to them on consignment. You might want to start off with small quantities to see how they perform before committing more inventory to them.

☐ Agencies may be not be able to offer the kind of marketing service you'd like because they are representing too many other companies.

☐ Since they take books on consignment, they may tie up stock that you could be selling.

☐ They may not cover all areas of their market territory as well as you or another agent might do.

The actual terms for such arrangements vary depending on the services provided and the territories covered. As a general rule, agencies expect a discount between 45% and 55%. They handle all costs of shipping, insurance, warehousing, trade discounts, fulfillment, and promotion.

The best place to make agency arrangements is at an international book fair such as Frankfurt or London. If that is not possible, then locate another publisher who works through an agency and see if their agency would be willing to take your line on as well. Of course, be sure to ask the other publisher if they are happy with the agency before making an initial contact.

• Berrett-Koehler uses a combination of companies to sell its books overseas. Linda Michaels handles translation sales, while a network of agencies handles direct sales outside the United States (McGraw-Hill Ryerson in Canada, John Wiley in southeast Asia, WoodsLane in Australia and New Zealand, McGraw-Hill Europe in the U.K. and Europe, Knowledge Resources in South Africa, and Livraria Canuto in Brazil.

• In late 1997, Zondervan entered into new distribution agreements with Family Reading Publications for Australia and Omega Distributors for New Zealand. Previously Zondervan had been distributed in these countries by its parent company, HarperCollins, but when HarperCollins restructured and decided to discontinue distribution of all religious titles, Zondervan had to make other arrangements. Zondervans Bibles are still distributed by the Bible Societies in Australia and New Zealand.

• In 1997, Abrams signed with Thames & Hudson to have them distribute its titles throughout the world, except for the U.S., Canada, and France.

You can find the addresses, phone numbers, email, and web sites for most of these companies in *Foreign Book Distributors, Wholesalers, & Sales Reps* report, which sells for $30.00 (avalable at BookMarket.com).

18:09 Bookselling Distributors

Distribute your titles overseas by using library jobbers, booksellers who act as distributors, and academic booksellers (such as Blackwell's). Most such distribution arrangements, like those with library jobbers in the U.S., are nonexclusive.

Such distributors will usually stock your books, take orders, bill, and distribute for a 20% to 30% discount. If these distributors also do major advertising and promotion, the discount goes up to 40% or 50%.

18:10 U.S. Exporting Distributors

A number of U.S. library jobbers and wholesalers also offer export services to other countries. Among these are Baker & Taylor (which exports to all areas of the world including the Soviet Union and the People's Republic of China) and Ballen Booksellers International. You might want to check with these companies to see if they would like to participate in any joint promotions of your titles.

18:11 Establish Your Own Subsidiary

One final way to distribute your books in other countries is to establish your own subsidiary in that country. The subsidiary would not only distribute your books but also acquire and publish original editions in that country. Such arrangements are not for small companies. To justify the costs of establishing a subsidiary, you would probably need a million dollar a year market potential in the area served by the subsidiary.

While a number of U.S. publishers have Canadian subsidiaries, only a few have established subsidiaries elsewhere. The prime other market area for U.S. subsidiaries is Great Britain. Here are a few U.S. publishers who have established foreign subsidiaries.

- John Wiley has established subsidiaries in Canada, Great Britain, Singapore, and Latin America.

- HarperCollins has offices in Great Britain, the Netherlands, Australia, Mexico, and Brazil.

- McGraw-Hill has subsidiaries in Australia, Brazil, Canada, Colombia, France, Great Britain, India, Japan, Mexico, New Zealand, Panama, Portugal, Singapore, South Africa, Spain, and West Germany.

- Rodale's international operations contributed $25 million to its bottom line in 1997.

- To take advantage of the growing strength of the European Economic Community, five religious publishers banded together to form Alban Books in the United Kingdom to distribute their books throughout Europe. The five publishers were Abingdon Press, Augsburg-Fortress Publishers, Crossroad/Herder, Eerdmans, and Orbis Books.

18:12 Selling Books to Mainland China

China has become a major market for English language books. The market is wide open to small publishers as well as large publishers, especially publishers of scientific, medical, and technical books. Here are a few pointers on how to get your books distributed in China:

☐ Several book import agencies are currently active in seeking out new titles from American and Canadian publishers. Since they are more likely to respond to publishers whose names they recognize, make sure you send them your catalog and new title information on a regular basis.

☐ When import agencies receive your catalog, they thoroughly review it, select those titles which would most interest Chinese readers, clip out the information, publish a collection of these clippings grouped by subject, and send the resulting catalog to bookstores, libraries, and universities around the country. A network of foreign-language bookstores receive the orders from these institutions, send them on to the import agencies who then order the books from the appropriate publisher.

☐ The largest of these import agencies is the China National Publications Import and Export Corporation. They buy books from every subject category. Send your catalogs and other correspondence to **China National Publications Import and Export Corporation**, P.O. Box 88, Beijing 100020, People's Republic of China; 86-10-6508-2324; Fax: 86-10-6508-2320. Email: info-center@cnpeak.com. Web: http://www.cnpeak.com/eng.

☐ They have a subsidiary in the U.S. for handling the shipping of books to China. Their address is **Beijing Book Company**, 701 E. Linden Avenue, Linden, NJ 07036-2495; 908-862-0909; Fax: 908-862-4201.

☐ Shanghai Book Traders is an importer and distributor (through its chain of Shanghai Foreign Language Bookstores). Send your discount schedule, payment requirements, and freight arrangements along with your catalogs for review. If they feel your titles are appropriate for their audience, they will ask you to send sufficient catalogs and other promotional material on a regular basis so they can, in turn, distribute them to their prospective book buyers. **Shanghai Book Traders**, 390 Fuzhou Road, Shanghai 200001, People's Republic of China; 86-21-63-223-200; Fax: 86-21-63-516-864. Email: crisbtb@online.sh.cn or chsbtb@online.sh.cn.

☐ *The China List*, a database of 5,900 institutional buyers of scientific, technical, medical, engineering, and professional books in China, is available from James Chan, a consultant on selling books to Asia. For more details about his services, contact **Asia Marketing & Management**, James Chan, 2014 Naudain Street, Philadelphia, PA 19146-1317; 215-735-7670; Fax: 215-735-9661. Email: jameschan@comcast.net. Web: http://www.asiamarketingmanagement.com.

☐ You can also, of course, sell translation rights to Chinese publishers. They have been very active in acquiring rights to books in English. Your best bet is to work through a literary agency such as Cassidy and Associates that works with Chinese publishers. For a list of such agents, see John Kremer's *Literary, Foreign, and Subsidiary Rights Agents* report, available at http://www.bookmarket.com.

Chapter 19

Special Sales: Special Opportunities

If I had to rely on bookstore sales to stay in business, I would close up shop. Fortunately, bookstores now account for less than 5% of my business. Where I might sell 2,000 copies of a title through bookstores in a year, I can sell 50,000 copies to one phone company.
— Robert Mastin, publisher, Aegis Publishing Group

Special sales are those sales made outside the normal book trade and other retail channels. Some standard special sales outlets include corporate sales, premium uses, catalog items, fund-raisers, and remainders. Nonetheless, you need not be limited to these outlets. Because books both inform and entertain, they can fulfill almost any need and appeal to almost any audience. Hence, in reality, the range or extent of your special sales are limited only by your imagination.

The great incentive for pursuing special sales is the real possibility of making high volume sales in a single stroke. It is not unusual for a key contact to result in sales of thousands of copies of a book. The other great advantage of special sales for smaller publishers is that the major publishers do not—and cannot—have a stranglehold on the distribution and sales network since, in fact, there is no such network. For that reason, it is possible for a small unknown publisher to compete for the biggest sales in this area.

19:01 How to Make Special Sales

Since special sales are—as their name implies—special, there are no standardized channels for making such book sales. Nonetheless, there are certain marketing steps you can take. Here are a few of them:

☐ **Work directly with people, not titles**. When you contact a company to make a sale to their sales division or personnel division, get the name of the sales manager, brand manager, or personnel manager. Then call him or her direct. If he or she seems interested, send a sample book and appropriate sales information. As with most key contacts, follow up with a phone call within a few weeks after sending out the book.

☐ **Reach the decision makers.** According to an Incentive Federation Survey, 79% of senior management are involved in the decision to implement incentive programs and select appropriate awards. Other departments involved in such decisions include sales (65%), marketing (58%), and human resources (32%). What do these numbers mean to you? Simple: Go to the top if you want to get a decision fast.

☐ **Keep in touch**. Cultivate a lasting relationship with these people. Even if they do not buy your first book, or second, or whatever, continue to approach them. Sooner or later, if you have done your research and your books do meet their needs, they will place an order with you.

☐ **Be prepared to wait.** In the case of most special sales (especially catalog and premium sales), be prepared to wait as long as six months or more before any final decision is made. Even then, it may be another three to six months before you receive the order. Most catalogs, for instance, work with at least a nine-month lead time.

☐ **Make a clear and direct connection between your book and their needs**. When approaching these special contacts, don't assume they'll make the connection. Point out the benefits of your book to their target audience (whether it be consumers, salespeople, or buyers). For example, when you know the catalog, tell them exactly on what page of their current issue your book should appear. When you can show them that kind of detailed knowledge about their needs, they are more likely to buy.

☐ **Prepare a merchandise data sheet** or other fact sheet which provides all the details about your book at a glance. For a sample Merchandise Data Sheet, see http://www.bookmarket.com/mds.pdf.

☐ **Offer them an exclusive.** If the deal has the potential of being big (25,000 or more unit sales), offer them exclusive use of the book within their market. Otherwise, it is not necessary to offer exclusives.

☐ **Give higher discounts.** Some special markets will insist on a discount as high as 60% or 75%. If you are not prepared to give discounts that high, then you should reconsider whether you want to invest the time and money to enter those markets. Note, however, that you should not offer high discounts unless they, in turn, are prepared to order large quantities. Arrange your discount schedule so that higher discounts are available only if they order sufficient quantities to make it worth your while. If they want they higher discount, they buy the larger quantity.

To give you an idea of what kind of discount to offer, here are the discount schedules of two publishers.

The following discount schedule was offered by Rayod House for the trade paperback edition of *In Search of Excellence*, which sold for $8.95 retail. Note that Rayod House is not the publisher; hence, the publisher is probably offering even a deeper discount.

Copies	1-11	12-239	240-499	500-999	1000-4999	5000+
Price	$4.95	$4.50	$3.95	$3.25	$2.95	$2.50
Discount	45%	50%	56%	64%	67%	72%

Here is a representative discount schedule once offered by Time-Life Books for premium sales:

Copies	50-199	200-1999	2000-4999	5000+
Price	$9.72	$8.97	$8.22	$6.73
Discount	35%	40%	45%	55%

☐ **Most special markets will require some sort of assurance that you can fulfill their order**. This means that you must be able to prove to them that you either have the manufacturing capacity, stock on hand, or reputation to be able to handle whatever volume they require.

☐ **For some special markets, there are sales representatives or distributors who can do most of your selling for you**. For example, the premium and incentive field has premium rep groups, jobbers, wholesale distributors, and premium promotion houses who provide many businesses with prearranged premium programs.

☐ **Exhibit at appropriate conventions** such as the Premium/Incentive Show or the Licensing Show. If nothing else, you should attend such shows to learn more about the industry. Plus, of course, they provide great opportunities to make connections with sales reps, wholesalers, distributors, and buyers. A number of publishers, such as Penguin Putnam and Warner Books, have exhibited at the New York Premium Incentive Show. At the 1986 show, Viking exhibited *The Essential Wine Book*, *Lyn St. James' Car Owners Manual for Women*, and *Fitness after 50*—all superb candidates for incentive programs.

☐ **Advertise in appropriate magazines**. In the case of premium sales, you could advertise in *Potentials in Marketing, Incentive,* or *Promo*. Warner Books, Addison-Wesley, Hammond, Penguin, Random House, Time Life Books, and Rand McNally, among others, have advertised in these magazines. You could also advertise in sales and marketing magazines (if you are offering a book as a sales incentive) or in personnel or training magazines (if offering a book for health or training programs).

☐ **Use consultants**. Crisp Productions was successful approaching personnel and training consultants to sell their *Retirement Planning Book* and other titles. They had about 400 such consultants selling their titles. Each consultant worked on a non-exclusive basis and received discounts or commissions ranging from 40 to 50%. As a result of these sales, Crisp produced many private label versions of their books for companies.

The advantages of using such consultants are that 1) They already have established clients. 2) They know the needs of their clients. 3) Their clients will usually have confidence in their recommendations.

For the consultants, such sales offer two benefits: 1) They are able to provide an additional service to their clients. 2) They are paid a commission on the sale. One consultant working with Crisp Productions sold 800 copies of their *Retirement Planning Guide* to Monsanto.

☐ **Work with booksellers.** Some bookstores, such as Harry W. Schwartz in Milwaukee, Wisconsin, cultivate strong relationships with local businesses and corporations (they operate 1-800-CEO-READ). If you offer bookstores a much larger discount for quantity nonreturnable orders, you can encourage such sales. Times Business Books, for example, offers a 65% discount on orders of more than 500 nonreturnable copies. To encourage corporate sales through bookstores, Pitman Publishing launched a Frequent Flyer program which offered free customized flyers for bookstores to use as mail stuffers or in other direct marketing programs.

☐ **Publish a newsletter for special markets.** If you make lots of sales in special markets, you might want to publish a newsletter directed at these markets. Besides featuring your new titles which have the best possibilities of being a premium or catalog item, you could also publish examples of what other companies are doing with your books.

Bantam Doubleday Dell publishes a separate newsletter just for the premium markets. They mail this newsletter to 20,000 premium buyers at least twice a year.

HarperCollins publishes *Special Markets News* twice a year. They send it to many catalogs as well as all companies which have opened up a HarperCollins special markets account. To accompany the newsletter, they insert their special markets discount schedule and a Request for Review Copies form.

Authors: If you'd like to pursue special market sales, be sure to negotiate a decent discount from your publisher for quantity orders of your book. You will need to get a minimum 50% discount, but try to get 70 to 75% for large orders of 1,000 or more copies. Get these discounts written into your initial contract or get a separate contract stating the discounts you get when you place quantity orders for your books. Your publisher, if they are smart, will grant you good discounts.

19:02 Premium and Incentive Sales

American businesses spend $30 billion dollars on premiums and incentives. Of that amount more than 71% was spent on incentives (42% for dealer incentives and 29% for sales incentives). Another 18.5% was spent on consumer promotions. The remaining 10.5% was spent on gifts and travel incentives for non-sales employees. According to the 1997 Incentive Federation Survey, there's plenty of room for growth since 74% of survey respondents reported that they do not use incentives.

Of the $30 billion dollars in premium sales, about half a billion was spent on books. Books can be used in many different ways as either premiums or incentives. You should be aware of these different ways so you can adapt your promotional literature so it clearly addresses the needs of companies and other organizations who buy premiums.

Books have a number of advantages over other premiums. They have a high perceived value. The premium buyer does not have to worry about styles, colors, sizes, breakage during shipping, or service problems afterward. Plus, books are available to suit almost any need, for any audience, at any price range. Perhaps the major advantage of books is that they can be inexpensively imprinted with almost any message. Finally, books have staying power. People tend to keep and cherish books for a long time, even after they have read them. On the next ten pages are listed just a few of the ways that companies might use your books as premiums:

Dealer incentives

Dealer incentives reward retailers and other dealers for displaying a manufacturer's wares prominently and/or for selling a significant amount of those wares. While most dealer incentives are for larger gifts such as trips, appliances, and gift certificates, books can supplement other promotions.

- Coors Beer bought 100,000 copies of *The Colorado Scenic Calendar* from Westcliffe Publishers to give to their distributors who, in turn, gave them to their retail accounts. While these calendars were a small gift, they did help to keep Coors's name in front of their key accounts, both distributors and retailers.

- Kevin Krueger, director of department store sales for Regal Ware, has noted that "books are not the most exciting or visible premium, but we've found them to have a very high perceived value." As a bonus, books are "a relatively cheap and easy premium to offer."

- Time Life Books offered a display loaded with various 32-page booklets (excerpted from its series of do-it-yourself books) to manufacturing companies who could, in turn, offer the display to home centers, lumber yards, and other places that would sell their product to consumers. Included in each booklet, which sold for $1.00 each, were coupons from the manufacturer.

Sales incentives

To encourage salespeople to better their previous sales records, companies often give them prizes (the greater their sales, the larger the prize). Again, most sales incentives involve higher priced prizes such as trips or appliances. Nonetheless, books could be used to spur the salespeople along during the middle of a competition.

- For example, a travel guide book for Italy could be offered to any salespeople meeting a minimum sales goal. Not only would such a prize give a boost to their sales enthusiasm during the middle of a contest, but it could also be tied into a grand prize trip to Rome and, thus, as the salespeople read the guidebook, they would be inspired to work that much harder to win the trip.

- San Francisco-based incentive house CMI regularly uses Insight Pocket Guides as mid-program teasers in incentive travel programs. Other companies have used travel books for post-trip gifts, in-room extras, awards, and pre-trip promotions.

- To reinforce a conference's message, Carlson Marketing Group sends participants titles authored by the speakers.

Employee incentives

Employee incentives are given to employees who meet certain goals (other than sales goals). For example, they might have been responsible for increasing production, setting new safety records, or simply completing an important project on time.

- For example, *In Search of Excellence* or another business bestseller would make a great incentive for employees who come up with suggestions that save time or make the business environment a better place in which to work.

- Intracorp, a HMO, gave a copy of *Health Promotion and Medical Guide* to every one of its client's employees who chose it as their HMO. The book, culled from three other books published by Random House, was designed to give these employees the message that they don't have to go to the doctor; they can use the book instead. By providing this book, Intracorp hoped to decrease the number of medical claims filed by these employees and thereby cut their health care costs. In less than two years, Intracorp gave out 50,000 copies of the book. Since Random House probably sold the book for around $10.00 per copy, they netted close to half a million dollars in sales from this one customized book.

Business gifts

To show their appreciation to their major customers, businesses often give gifts during the holiday season. While in many cases, these gifts involve food for the body, there is no reason such gifts could not involve food for the mind. Why not encourage businesses to give holiday bestsellers instead of food? Or a beautiful four-color coffee-table book that major customers could enjoy for years to come.

The major reasons businesses give gift are to thank customers, to develop business, to recognize employees, and because customers or employees expect it. Here are a few other occasions for giving gifts: to commemorate an anniversary, to celebrate the closing of a deal, to congratulate, or to apologize. Companies can also give books to their employees for birthdays, weddings, illnesses, deaths, retirements, promotions, meeting deadlines, completing projects, or other major events. Where might your book fit into these gift-giving occasions?

Remember the power of gifts. As Neal Sofman of A Clean Well-Lighted Place for Books once noted, "When was the last time you ever received a tie that changed your life?"

- To show the dynamism of south Florida, the Swedish-American Chamber of Commerce sent copies of *Miami: City of Dreams* as Christmas gifts to ambassadors, government leaders, and other opinion leaders. SunTrust Bank of Miami gives a different book every year during the holidays to their most important customers.

- To show appreciation to its *Yellow Pages* advertisers, U.S. West bought 2,000 copies of *Talking with Your Customers* at a 60% discount from Dearborn. The person responsible discovered the book in a bookstore.

- The American Hospital Association gave several hundred copies of Dartnell's *A Professional Secretary's Survival Guide* to its secretaries in honor of Secretaries Day. In addition, the association brought in the book's editor, Doug Leland, to speak to the secretaries.

Company celebrations

Upjohn celebrated its 100th anniversary by having Benjamin Company prepare a history of its first 100 years, which it gave to its employees and customers. To celebrate its 100th anniversary, Pet Foods offered consumers a cookbook using recipes from Pet products. The book, *Celebration of Cooking in America*, sold for $8.95.

Opening celebrations

A Santa Barbara bank celebrated a new branch opening by giving away 5,000 copies of Judy Dugan's self-published book, *Santa Barbara Highlights and History*, to every customer that came in during the first week.

Publicity

Benjamin Company produced a *Consumer's Buying Guide* for a number of Better Business Bureaus who, in turn, sold them to utilities and banks to be used in their public relations programs. The Benjamin Company produced a similar book for banks on *How to Manage Your Money*.

Name recognition

To increase their name recognition among a target audience, companies often use books. Companies that want to appeal to college students, medical patients, doctors, and other specific audiences have found books to be a good way to introduce themselves.

- As part of its continuing promotion to the youth market, Coors bought the exclusive rights to Edward J. Rogers's *Getting Hired* to distribute free to students. The first year Coors distributed 165,000 copies on college campuses. The agent who put this deal together, Jeff Herman, notes that such a promotion need not be a one-time thing since every year there is an entirely new crop of graduating seniors.

- James Malinchak, self-publisher of *From College to the Real World*, has found that corporations will pay him from $3 to $5 per book for him to speak on behalf of the corporation at colleges and then give away copies of his book to students.

Private label gifts

Shepherd's Garden Seeds featured cookbook author Alice Water in its private label seed gift products. Their bestseller was Alice Water's Salad Garden Mix. In this case, no book was used, but the author's name was licensed for use.

Traffic builders

Books can also be used to help build traffic for a department store, bank, restaurant, or other retailer. With their high perceived value, books have great pulling power.

- Bamberger's department stores gave away 50,000 copies of Hammond's *A Taste of German Cooking* to promote store restaurants during Octoberfest celebrations.

- More than 3,000 Dairy Queen restaurants featured *The Busy World of Richard Scarry* in a summer-long promotion. Finger puppets featuring characters from the book were given away inside each children's meal bought at the restaurants. In addition, many stores also promoted frozen cakes with *Busy World* themes.

Attention-getters

To reinforce its image as an air cargo service, United Airlines shipped a book case, magnifying glass, and *Doubleday Dictionary* to 1,700 freight forwarders and commercial shippers. Later, they also sent copies of the *Hammond Almanac*, *Guinness Book of Records*, and *Hammond World Atlas*. Each book had a specially printed jacket outlining United's services. For example, the Guinness book carried the following legend: "Who holds the record for serving the commercial shipper? United Airlines Cargo."

Bonus premiums

Bonus premiums are items given to someone when they order or buy another product. Below are a few ways books have been used as bonuses:

- To encourage subscriptions, *Working Woman* gave new subscribers free copies of *Boss Lady*, the autobiography of advertising executive, Jo Foxworth. The response rate to their direct mail promotions increased by 25% as compared to other bonuses they had been using.

- Frigidaire increased sales of refrigerators by 44% when they offered a free book from Better Homes & Gardens Books with purchase.

- Reader's Digest Condensed Books gave away 750,000 copies of Judith King's *Greatest Gift Guide Ever* as a premium for joining the condensed book club.

- To differentiate its bread machine from others, Regal Ware gave consumers a copy of *The Best Bread Machine Cookbook Ever* with each purchase. The program was available at select retailers.

- To promote its Amaretto di Saronno liquor, Paddington hosted Summer Midnight Parties where it gave away copies of Sidney Sheldon's novel, *Memories of Midnight*, to any bar customers who ordered the drink.

- Pfeifer-Hamilton worked for more than a year and a half to make a deal with Manco Duct Tape to feature its *Duct Tape* book. The deal never happened, but a similar deal did get worked out with Wal-Mart, which packaged duct tape and the book together.

Self-liquidators

Many cereals and other food products offer items for sale at very low prices with a small payment plus proof of purchase. Self-liquidating offers allow the company making the offer to cover some or all of its costs in buying the books (or other premiums) and shipping them out.

- Life cereal offered a *Rand McNally Road Atlas* for $3.50 and two UPC symbols. Post Grape Nuts, to reinforce its natural image, offered a free copy of a *Rand McNally Nature Guide* for three box tops or one box top and $2.00. Gerber baby foods offered a Rand McNally *Travel with Baby* manual for 50¢ and 24 UPC symbols.

- Total cereal offered a *Reader's Digest Do-It-Yourself Manual* for $1.30 and two UPC symbols. Bran Chex offered three books (*The New Aerobics*; *Dr. Abravanel's Body Type Program for Health, Fitness and Nutrition*; and *Running for Health and Beauty*) for two proofs of purchase plus 50¢ postage and handling for each book ordered.

- To promote its Ziplock storage bags, Dow Chemical gave away 250,000 copies of a 22-page, four-color recipe collection excerpted from Dom DeLuise's book, *Eat This—It'll Make You Feel Better*. Since DeLuise was the TV spokesman for Ziplock bags, the promotion was a perfect tie-in. Simon & Schuster, publishers of the book, also benefited—not only for the money they earned from the excerpt, but also because the excerpt promoted the book for five months before its publication date!

- To encourage sales of Kellogg's Mueslix cereal, Random House provided copies of the $13.95 *Fodor's Touring Europe* as a self-liquidator for only $3.95 plus two proofs of purchase.

- Grosset & Dunlap sold over a million Nancy Drew and Hardy Boys books when they were offered as a self-liquidating premium on 20 million boxes of Post Raisin Bran cereal. Not only do such on-pack offers sell a lot of books, but they also provide incredible exposure to your books. Sales of the Nancy Drew and Hardy Boy titles in retail bookstores increased during this same promotional period.

- Meow Mix offered *The Meow Mix Guide to Cat Talk* as a self-liquidator to people who bought a bag of the cat food. The book was customized for Meow Mix by simply changing the title of Jean Craighead George's *How to Talk to Your Cat*.

- Random House made the largest single sale in company history to Kellogg. Besides giving away 500,000 copies of Dr. Seuss books to 2,000 schools, Kellogg also offered another 1.6 million copies of twelve different Dr. Seuss titles free to kids who returned box tops from these Kellogg cereals: Froot Loops, Rice Krispies, Cocoa Krispies, and Smacks.

- To encourage sales of Complete Bran Flakes, Kellogg offered a gardening book from Meredith in exchange for one UPC symbol. Four different titles were featured in the promotion, including books on perennials and low-cost landscaping. The program proved so enticing to consumers that Kellogg had to double its order.

- General Mills had to come back for three additional orders when it offered books from the First Time series featuring the Berenstain Bears in exchange for two UPC symbols from Kix cereals. Kix later offered three Golden Books with a proof of purchase and shipping. This program was featured on General Mills's web site (http://www.youruleschool.com).

- Procter & Gamble used Fodor's *Great American Vacations* as a self-liquidating offer with proofs of purchase for its Pepto-Bismol and Metamucil brands.

- Abrams sold copies of a biography, *Jackie Robinson: An Intimate Portrait*, to General Mills for use as a self-liquidating premium on special commemorative boxes of Wheaties cereal. To get the $29.95 book, fans had to send in a Wheaties boxtop and $9.95.

- Diane Pfeifer of Strawberry Patch sold 15,000 copies of her *Gone with the Grits* cookbook to Quaker Oats, the major supplier of grits to grocery stores. The self-liquidating offer for the cookbook was printed on 16.5 million packages of grits. What a free advertising opportunity!

In-packs

With in-packs, the premium is offered inside the package. When the customer buys the product, they get the premium.

* Alka-Seltzer has used excerpts from several books as in-packs to promote its "relief-giving" properties. During tax time, they gave away *Tax Relief*, an excerpt from *J.K. Lasser's Your Income Tax*. In another promotion, they gave away *Hot & Spicy Favorites* recipes excerpted from various Better Homes and Gardens cookbooks.

* To promote Charlie perfume to busy young women, Revlon included a purse-size date book from Simon & Schuster as an in-pack bonus to all fall and Christmas buyers.

* Frito-Lay inserted three mini-books written by R.L. Stine, collectively called the *Goosebumps Thrillogy*, into 32 million bags of Doritos, Ruffles, and other Frito-Lay chips. *Goosebumps* also formed partnerships with Taco Bell, Pepsi, and Hershey. Later, Parachute Press, developers of *Goosebumps*, formed a similar partnership with Pizza Hut.

* To encourage sales of their Swiss Army knife, the Forschner Group created a gift set that combined The Weekender Swiss Army knife with the *Mr. Boston Official Bartender's and Party Guide*.

On-packs

With on-packs, the premium is offered on the outside of the package. Most on-packs are short quizzes, puzzles, or other items that can be printed on the package (for instance, a follow-the-dots drawing on a box of cereal). These quizzes, of course, could be excerpted from books. Other on-packs are shrink-wrapped or put into a pouch on the outside of product packages.

* Kraft Foods offered an unusual on-pack premium for their frozen cocktail sausage rolls. They packaged the sausage rolls with one of thirty different romance novels from Mills & Boon, a British publisher of mass-market romance novels. With more than 30 titles to choose from, Kraft didn't have to worry about consumers ignoring the offer once they had collected one premium. As a result of this promotion, sales of the sausage rolls exceeded projections by 50%.

* To promote sales of Marlboro cigarettes as well as the image of the Marlboro Man, R.J. Reynolds distributed 1.5 million copies of the *Great Trails Road Atlas* as an on-pack premium on cartons of Marlboros.

Near-packs

Near-packs are premiums that are offered at the point of purchase but which are not in or attached to the product being promoted.

* Rand McNally designed a glove-compartment size atlas complete with coupons and best buy recommendations as a near-pack to promote Cambridge cigarettes from Philip Morris.

- Consumers who bought two jars of Smucker's ice-cream toppings were given a copy of *Richard Scarry's Best Back-to-School Activity Book Ever* at the in-store display. The 32-page book was compiled for Smucker by incorporating the back-to-school activities featured in Richard Scarry's other books. The cover also featured Smucker's logo and various characters eating ice cream. Random House printed hundreds of thousands of copies of this custom premium.

Coupons

In Zebra's *Spring Bouquet* romance novel, they included back-of-the-book coupons good for $10 off all flower orders from Superflora.

Educational promotions

Dorsey Laboratories in cooperation with Random House developed a children's book, *The Care Bears Help Chase Colds*, to promote the sale of their Triaminic cold care product. Not only did this promotion help them to sell two million units of Triaminic (each with a free book), but it also helped them to get better display space in stores.

New product introductions

When O.M. Scott introduced its new line of lawn care products, it decided to use a book that would appeal to the same audience as its products. So it offered a free copy of *How to Watch Pro Football on TV*, prepared by the Benjamin Company. During their promotion, they gave away almost 1.5 million copies of the book.

Product promotions

Meredith prepared a *Best You Can Bake Chocolate Desserts* cookbook for Nestlé. This 32-page booklet was given away to two million buyers of Nestlé Tollhouse Morsels. Western Publishing created an even fancier cookbook for Hershey's called *Hershey's Chocolate Treasures*.

Sweepstakes prizes

Any company offering a grand prize of a trip in a sweepstakes promotion could use a travel guide to the trip's destination as third or fourth prizes to be given away at the same time. Since sweepstakes tend to work better when there are more prizes to be awarded, such low-cost yet valuable prizes can add considerably to the perceived value of the sweepstakes. Would your titles work for frequent sweepstake offers? Keep a watch out for tie-ins.

Frequent buyer programs

One of your travel books, for instance, could be used as a premium in a frequent flyer program for one of the airlines—especially if it featured one of the airline's destinations. Books can also be used to encourage retail customers to spend more.

- Pier 1 Imports offered anyone buying $50 of Pier 1 merchandise (and who returned a special card sent to them in the mail) a free copy of *Better Homes & Gardens New Decorating Book.*

- To encourage people to renew their membership in a frequent stay club, a national hotel chain gave out 15,000 copies of *The Restaurant Companion: A Guide to Healthier Eating Out.* The publisher happened to call the chain just when they were searching for a giveaway.

Customer loyalty programs

To encourage repeat purchases, Nestlé offered consumers a $5 cash rebate for each purchase of $20 worth of selected products. At the same time, Nestlé also offered consumers $5 worth of books to be given to the public school of their choice. The schools were able to choose from a selection of 400 titles from Time-Life, Little, Brown, and Warner Books (which Nestlé had bought at a big discount).

Door openers

A company could offer one of your books as a free gift to prospects who will listen to their sales presentation. For instance, an insurance saleswoman could give away a tax guide to everyone who listens to her sales pitch.

- To encourage people to test drive their cars, Chrysler Motors gave away free copies of Little, Brown's *American Roads,* retitled as *Rediscover American Roads* so it would fit in better with Chrysler's advertising. Chrysler paid about $25 each for 25,000 copies of the book. Honda Acura dealers used a similar book, Fodor's *Great American Vacations* to bring in people for a test drive.

- Pharmaceutical companies have found that doctors love to get books. One pharmaceutical company used Simon & Schuster's *Hugh Johnson's Pocket Encyclopedia of Wine* as a door opener to doctor's offices.

- In the spring of 1997, AT&T offered a free copy of *Maxi-Marketing* by Stan Rapp and Thomas Collins to anyone who called to listen to their sales pitch for AT&T Solutions for Direct Marketers. Their full-page advertisements ran for many months in a dozen business magazines, thus offering incredible exposure for the book.

Customer relationships

As a means of establishing a continuing relationship, salesmen can give away a volume from a series each time they call on a client. Do you have a book that would fit such a need for a company you know?

Referral premiums

A company could give away a book each time one of their customers refers a friend to their products or services. The book should tie in somehow with their product or service and be something the customer would value.

Educational premiums

Drug manufacturers are now required to help educate users of their drugs, not only on how to use the drugs but also on how to change their lifestyles to improve their chances of improving under such drug use. For example, manufactures of cholesterol-lowering drugs often give away low-cholesterol cookbooks to help educate people on how to lower cholesterol. Not only does this make the company look good in the eyes of the consumer, but it also increases the chance that the company's drug will actually produce useful results.

19:03 Some Premium/Incentive Resources

Where will you find customers for your books? You don't have to look far for companies interested in premiums and incentives. They are all around you. To help get you started, here's a "short" list of some of Hammond's premium clients for its line of atlases:

Allied Chemical, American Express, Amoco Oil, AT&T, Audubon Society, Avis, Avon, Award Lines, Bank of the South, Barclays Visa, Bendix Corporation, BMW, Book-of-the-Month, Bristol-Myers, Burger King, Britches of Georgetown, Byron Broadcasting, Cadillac, Chemical Bank, Citibank, Coca-Cola, Contadina Foods, Crown Life Insurance, Diamond Shamrock, Doubleday, ESPN, Exxon, Farmers & Merchants Bank, Firestone, Fortune Magazine, Ford, GAF, Gallo Winery, General Motors, GEO Magazine, Glendale Federal S&L, Green Giant, Gulf, Honda, Indiana University Alumni Association, Playtex, J.C. Penney Life Insurance, Johnson & Johnson, J. P. Stevens, KLM, Kawasaki, Keystone Automobile Club, Leathersmith of London, Lever, Liberty National Life, Lumbermans Mutual Insurance, Mazda, Mercedes Benz, Merrill-Lynch, Mister Doughnut, Money Magazine, Mother's Trucking, Nabisco, New York Life, Paine Webber, Parents Magazine, Parke-Davis; Peugeot, Pfizer, Pitney Bowes Credit, Pontiac, Prudential, RCA, Reader's Digest, Royal Crown Cola, Shell Chemical, Sandoz, Seagrams, Stanley Tools, Sunshine Specialties, Texaco, Time Magazine, Travel Masters, Truckstops of America, TWA, Union Pacific, United Technologies, U.S. Air Force Academy, U.S. Golf Association, Volkswagen, Volvo, Warner Brothers, and Warner Lauren.

How do companies select premiums to use in their promotions? According to a study in *Business & Incentives*, here's how:

25.1%   while brainstorming with management
18.7%   from seeing ads in trade magazines
12.5%   during trade shows
10.7%   through manufacturers' representatives
 8.3%   because of the popularity of past awards
 8.0%   from incentive house suggestions
 7.2%   by reading new product announcements in trade journals

Since trade magazines and trade shows play such an important part in their selection process, if you are serious about the premium field, you should read at least one of the following magazines and attend one of the two major trade shows held every year.

Premium/Incentive Magazines

Besides reading the following magazines, you should also send them your publicity and possibly test an advertisement for your premium offers. Send full-color as well as black-and-white shots of your book covers for possible use in their new product departments.

☐ **Corporate Meetings & Incentives**, Barbara Scofidio, Editor, 132 Great Road #120, Stow MA 01775; 978-448-8211; Fax: 978-448-8212. Email: bscofidio@primediabusiness.com. Web: http://www.meetingsnet.com.

☐ **Incentive**, William Flanagan, Editor-in-Chief, VNU Business Publications, 770 Broadway, New York, NY 10003; 646-654-5000; Fax: 646-654-7633. Email: wflanagan@vnuuspubs.com. Web: http://www.incentive mag.com. If you are serious about selling to the premium market, be sure to have your company listed under books in their annual buyers guide.

☐ **Potentials**, William Flanagan, Editor-in-Chief, VNU Business Publications, 770 Broadway, New York, NY 10003; 646-654-5000; Fax: 646-654-7633. Web: http://www.potentialsmag.com.

☐ **Promo Magazine**, Kathleen Joyce, Editorial Director, 11 River Bend Drive South, P O Box 4242, Stamford, CT 06907-0242; 203-358-4226. Email: kjoyce@prismb2b.com. Web: http://www.promomagazine.com. This magazine covers all promotions including premiums. Surrey Books was one of five book publishers featured in *Promo's Sourcebook '97*, an annual directory of promotion suppliers and services.

☐ **Sales & Marketing Management**, Christine Galea, Executive Editor, VNU Business Publications, 770 Broadway, New York, NY 10003; 646-654-7606. Email: cgalea@salesandmarketing.com. Web: http://www. salesandmarketing.com/smm/index.jsp.

Premium/Incentive Trade Shows

The Motivation Show and Premium Incentive Show are the two major trade shows for premium sales. They are good places to prospect for customers, incentive reps, or other companies to work with.

☐ **The Motivation Show**, Hall-Erickson, 800-752-6312. Web: http://www. motivationshow.com. Held in Chicago in late September.

☐ **Premium Incentive Show**, VNU Expositions; 703-488-2743; 800-765-7615. Web: http://www.piexpo.com. Held in New York City in May.

☐ **Promotional Products Association International Trade Show**, Promotional Products Association International, 3125 Skyway Circle N., Irving

TX 75038-3526; 972-252-0404; 888-426-7724; Fax: 972-258-3007. Web: http://www.ppa.org. Two shows held in August and January.

Lists of Premium Buyers

☐ **Directory of Premium, Incentive & Travel Buyers**, Douglas Publications, 2807 N. Parham Road #200, Richmond, VA 23294; 804-762-9600; 800-794-6086; Fax: 840-217-8999. Web: http://www.salesmans guide.com. This directory features 21,000 premium buyers.

Premium Sales and Human Relations Associations

☐ **Incentive Marketing Association**, 1805 N. Mill Street #R, Naperville, IL 60563; 630-369-7780; Fax: 630-369-3773. Web: http://www.incentive marketing.org. Members of this association work on commission to represent products to potential premium and incentive users.

☐ **Society for Human Resource Management**, 1800 Duke Street, Alexandria, VA 22314; 703-548-3440; 800-283-SHRM; Fax: 703-836-0367. Web: http://www.shrm.org. For sales to training and human resources programs, as described in the next section.

☐ **Promotion Marketing Association**; Email: pma@pmalink.org. Web: http://www.pmalink.org.

Special Sales Company

☐ **Jenkins Group**, Andrew Parvel, Director of Special Market Sales, 400 W. Front Street #4A, Traverse City, MI 49684; 231-933-0445; Fax: 231-933-0919. Web: http://www.specialmarketbooksales.com. Sell books as premiums or as catalog items.

19:04 Other Corporate Sales

Besides premiums and sales incentives, corporations and other organizations can use books to aid their other departments. Here are just a few of the other approaches you can use to sell your books to corporations:

Training programs

Corporations and government units spent $58.6 billion in 1997 to train their employees. Of that amount, $13.6 billion was spent on outside training goods and services. The cost of such training has only gone up since then. Why shouldn't your books be used as resources in their training programs?

• Addison-Wesley has a separate sales force that calls only on businesses. One of their trade bestsellers, *Born to Win*, originated in a Bank of America training program. Since expanding that book to the trade market, they have sold almost two million copies plus sold the mass-market reprint rights for over $1 million.

- Roger Von Oech sold many copies of his self-published book, *A Whack on the Side of the Head*, to corporations who used them in training their creative staffs. IBM bought 2,000 copies, Hewlett Packard 700 copies, and Control Data 600 copies.

- Jossey-Bass Publishers sold 4,000 copies of *The Empowered Manager* to Sears and another 2,000 copies to AT&T to use in their manager development programs.

Health care programs

In order to promote the health and well-being of their employees (and to save money on insurance or HMOs), many corporations have established health care programs. To support these programs, companies often buy books to give to employees to help them understand how to take better care of themselves.

- Over the years, Addison-Wesley has sold three million copies of D.M. Vickery and J.F. Fries's *Take Care of Yourself*. 450,000 copies of the book were sold in 1985 alone, yet the book never showed up on the bestseller lists because more than 90% of those copies were sold to corporate health care programs.

- To promote employee health awareness, the Texas Medical Association and the University of Texas have offered copies of *The American Medical Association Family Medical Guide* to their employees. Some companies bought as many as 75,000 copies of the book at $7.25 each—that's a half a million dollar sale!

Retirement planning

Because of certain laws and union contracts, some corporations are now required to provide retirement planning as well as help for those they lay off or fire. Books are great resources for either program.

- Monsanto bought 800 copies of Crisp's *Retirement Planning Guide* to give to its employees to help them with their retirement plans.

- Cosmair bought 500 copies of *The 17 Laws of Successful Investing* at a 20% discount to use in a retirement planning program for its employees.

Public service

To better their reputations and serve the communities in which they operate, many companies get involved in public service or volunteer efforts. Books can become an integral part of those efforts.

- Coors Brewing Company spent more than $300,000 advertising Judith McNaught's romance novel, *Perfect*, as part of its $40 million, five-year campaign to end illiteracy. The advertising helped *Perfect* make the bestseller lists and, better yet, during the first few months more than 6,000 people returned postcards requesting more information on how to help with literacy programs.

- DC Comics produced a *Supergirl* comic promoting car safety for Honda who, in turn, gave the comic away free to driver's education classes around the country.

Sponsorships

As part of their ongoing public relations programs, some companies will sponsor worthy causes and book publishing projects related to those causes.

- Collins used corporate sponsors to help underwrite the costs of producing their *Day in the Life* series of books. Sponsors included Kodak, Canon, American Express, and Apple Computers, as well as many hotels and airlines, plus some nonprofit associations and governmental agencies. Every sponsor was given credit in the front of each book.

  One corporate sponsor, Petro Canada, offered a free copy of *A Day in the Life of Canada Road Atlas* to patrons of its gas stations just prior to the publication of the larger book, *A Day in the Life of Canada*. Not only did this provide income for Collins from the sale of the atlas, but it also provided some of the best prepublication promotion the book received.

- Weyerhaeuser donated $25,000 worth of paper to Melior Publications for the publication of *Washington: Images of a State's Heritage* to celebrate the state's centennial in 1989.

Bundling

- Apple Computer bundled Addison-Wesley's two books about PostScript along with every LaserWriter it sold. A number of other laser printers bundled the books with their machines as well.

- Wham-O bundled Para Publishing's *Frisbee Player's Handbook* with many of its frisbees.

Examples of their work

Companies will buy copies of books that showcase their work. If you use a printer, typesetter, cover designer, or similar service to produce your book, those services might be interested in buying copies of your book to showcase their work, especially if your book appeals to one of their market segments.

- McNaughton & Gunn, printers of several editions of Dan Poynter's *The Self-Publishing Manual*, gave a free copy of the book to each new publisher who requested a quotation from them.

- As a thank you gift to producers who had filmed in the Miami area as well as a promotional item to give potential producers a taste of Miami, the Miami Dade Office of Film, TV and Print sent out copies of Alan Maltz's self-published book, *Miami: City of Dreams*. The book did a far better job of showcasing Miami than any brochure could ever do.

Company connections

When Prentice Hall published Eddie Rickenbacker's autobiography, they offered to print a special edition for Eastern Airlines (Rickenbacker had been chairman of Eastern's board of directors). Eastern bought 15,000 copies of the special edition.

Editorial mentions

I've always encouraged authors and publishers to edit their books for promotional clout. If, for example, you were editing a gardening book, why not list specific seed and tool companies as resources in the appendix? Not only do such lists benefit the reader, but they also provide you with potential premium sales.

- That's what Warner Books did with the resource directory in the back of Howard Ruff's bestselling book, *How to Prosper During the Coming Bad Years*. They mailed a copy of the resource directory to each company on the list with a note suggesting that they might offer the book to their customers. As a result of this one simple promotion, they received many orders. In fact, one dehydrated food company ordered 1,000 copies every month for many years.

- When they published *The Best of Everything*, St. Martin's Press did a similar promotion. As a result, they sold a premium edition of the book to Sylvania, whose nineteen-inch color TV had been voted the best in the field.

Speaking opportunities

- MasterMedia runs a full-service speakers bureau to support the authors of its management titles. At one conference, they sold more than 2,600 copies of four books from T. Scott Gross's *Positively Outrageous Service* series.

- When the authors of *Looneyspoons* sold 20,000 copies of their cookbook to Avon Canada, they spoke at many local Avon meetings as a way of turning the Avon salespeople into ambassadors for their book.

Cross promotions

Look for ways to cross promote your book with someone else's product. For instance, add a coupon for birdseed with a book on bird care or bird watching if the birdseed company will, in turn, feature a coupon or other promotion for your book.

- To bring greater attention to their holiday book, *There's No Place Like Home for the Holidays*, Papier-Mâché Press joined with Continental Airlines to sponsor a free-trip sweepstakes. The sweepstakes entry form was bound into the book along with a coupon worth up to $200 on two Continental tickets.

Corporate libraries

Many corporations have business or technical libraries to support their administrative, sales, marketing, training, or research personnel. Some of your initial contacts with corporations could result in orders trickling in from these libraries even if you don't make a direct premium or corporate sale. You could even approach these libraries directly. There is an association of specialty librarians that services this market. You might rent their list of members to do specific promotions to them.

Brand publishing

One way to build upon the strengths of other companies and their brands is to publish books based on those brands—books such as *Classic Cooking with Coca Cola, Campbell's Creative Cooking with Soup, Pillsbury Complete Book of Baking, The Wall Street Journal Guide to Who's Who and What's What on Wall Street, The Purina Encyclopedia of Cat Care,* and *Volvo Guide to Halls of Fame.*

HarperCollins once formed an imprint, HarperHorizon, devoted to brand publishing. The imprint's first major program featured books published in cooperation with NASCAR. Titles ranged from expensive coffee-table books to inexpensive children's books. HarperHorizon has also signed agreements with other brands, including the NBA and QVC.

Authors — If you or your book have connections with any companies, clubs, or associations, be sure to let your publisher know so they can explore various sales possibilities. You might want to make some contacts yourself. Indeed, you might be a more effective salesperson than someone from your publisher. But before making any personal contacts, coordinate your activities with your publisher's marketing department.

19:05 Selling to Associations

Besides selling to corporations and small businesses, you can also sell to associations, clubs, and other organizations. Just as companies need premiums, employee gifts, and training guides, so do associations. Don't overlook them. They can lead to significant sales.

Fundraising Sales

Schools, churches, clubs, and other organizations often sell books as a means of raising money to support their activities. Schools, for example, sponsor book fairs to raise money for their libraries. Churches often have book sales tables where they sell books after church services. Other groups use books as premiums in their direct mail fundraising programs.

To reach groups which might use books as fund-raisers, advertise in appropriate media (such as a magazine for church leaders or a journal aimed at faculty advisors of school clubs). You can also use direct mail aimed at church leaders, faculty advisors, or association personnel. The standard discount schedule for such sales is 20 to 40% on sales of 25 or more books.

- Advocacy Press, the publishing arm of the Girls Club of Santa Barbara, sold over 100,000 copies of *Choices*, a career planning workbook for teenage girls, and *Challenges* (for boys). Both of these titles were used as fund-raisers for other girls clubs, YWCAs, YMCAs, and scout troops.

- Covenant House has found that a book freemium sent along with their direct mail fundraising promotions brings in more responses and higher average gifts. Other fund-raisers have also discovered the power of books when used as premiums.

- Horizon Publishers promotes its titles in various fundraising programs to scouting groups, high school bands, PTAs, and other nonprofit groups. Horizon supplies the brochures, order forms, processing system, and guidance to make fundraising campaigns run smoothly. They offer different brochures to satisfy various groups: *Make Learning Fun!* (15 books that appeal to families with grade school children), *Leisure Learning* (15 books for families with high school children), and *Books on Camping and Outdoor Crafts & Skills* (12 books). Their discounts range from 20% for 11 to 25 books through 56% for 3,001+ books.

- Pauline Bartel, author of the *Complete Gone with the Wind Trivia Book*, contacted her local public broadcasting station when she heard that they would be broadcasting *Gone with the Wind* during their annual membership drive. She convinced them that her book would be a perfect premium for new members. Not only did her book gets lots of exposure on TV during the membership drive, but she also sold many, many autographed copies of her book.

- The publishers of *The Soccer Mom Handbook* sell cases of their book to soccer clubs and tournaments which, in turn, sell the books to their members or attendees. Since tournaments draw from 1,000 to 5,000 kids and clubs may have as many as forty teams, most groups buy at least one case (100 books) to sell. For each case they sell, they make $500. The publishers recommend that when selling books as fund-raisers, look for groups that are accustomed to fundraising. That saves you time and increases your rate of success, since you only have to sell the groups on using your book instead of having to sell them on fundraising first and then sell them on your book.

- The American Indian Movement bought many copies of Steve Wall's *Wisdom Keepers* to use as gifts to special donors.

Educational Sales

When you approach associations, be sure to emphasize the educational value of your books as well as their sales value. Books are far more likely to tie in with the group's purposes and activities than are other standard fundraising items such as cookies, candy, or magazines. Indeed, some books might actually be used in their educational activities.

• King County Rape Relief sells many copies of *He Told Me Not to Tell* and *Top Secret* to PTAs, state agencies, schools, scouting organizations, doctor's offices, and counselors.

• New Society Publishers has sold their books on social change to Seneca Women's Peace Encampment, San Diego Peace Resource Center, New England Greenpeace, Resource Center for Nonviolence, Maine Nuclear Freeze Campaign, National Fellowship of Reconciliation, and Women's Division of the Methodist Board of Global Ministries. These associations have used the books for both educational and fundraising work.

• Wilshire Book Company has sold more than 1.1 million copies of *Guide to Rational Living* by Albert Ellis. Many of those sales were made direct to psychologists and self-help groups.

Membership Training

Besides educating people about the values and purposes of a group, books can also be used to train or inform members of that group. When they published the story of the CanSurmount cancer patient program, *I'm a Patient, Too*, Nick Lyons Books sold 5,000 copies of the book to the CanSurmount organization and even more copies to *Cope*, a new magazine for cancer patients.

Membership Acquisition

Encourage associations to use your books as premiums when someone joins the association. Dan Janal, self-publisher of *How to Publicize High-Tech Products and Services*, sold 1,000 copies to the Software Publishers Association, which gave them to new members.

Conferences

For many publishers of special-interest titles, one of the largest markets for their books are sales at association conferences and seminars. Be sure you have a presence at those conferences where your target audiences gather. Exhibit if possible, have your authors speak, advertise in conference programs, etc. There are many opportunities to expose your books to association members during conferences.

• Susan Setley made good sales by getting her book, *Taming the Dragons: Real Help for Real School Problems*, in conference bookstores at many educational conferences.

- Besides exhibiting their books at psychological association conventions, Professional Resource Press also exhibits books from other publishers.

- When Deer Creek Publishing exhibited Dale Smith's novel for young readers, *What the Parrot Told Alice*, at the annual convention of the American Federation of Aviculture, they sold 200 copies.

Catalog Sales

Besides buying books for training and fundraising, some associations also buy books to sell to members as part of a regular bookstore or catalog.

- Each of the sixty-nine offices of the Auto Club of Southern California operate small bookstores (display stands near the reception desk) where they sell books at a discount to their members. Over a 14-month period, they sold 1,600 copies of Bill Gordon's *Ultimate Hollywood Tour Book.*

- Sagamore Publishing overprints its catalogs for some of the State Park & Recreation Associations. In return for mailing out these catalogs to their members, the associations receive a 20% royalty on all sales. Sagamore receives the orders, processes them, mails out the books, and sends royalty payments quarterly to the participating associations.

- The Automobile Association of America offered its members *Birnbaum's Europe for Business Travelers* as a self-liquidating premium.

Co-Publishing Books

Rather than selling your own books to associations, you can work with them to co-publish books that would interest their members but would also interest others. Sourcebooks, the fast-growing trade publisher, got its start working with the Bank Marketing Association to produce new books of interest to its members. The association ordered 1,000 copies for their own members. That sale alone paid for the entire first printing.

Cause-Related Marketing

One of the best ways to work with associations is to donate money to them for every book sold—and then work with them to co-promote your book to their members, the media, and the general public. For cause-related marketing to work, your book has to be related to the cause advocated by the association. Research has shown that 66% of consumers will change brands to support a social cause important to them. Think about that when you publish your next book.

Here are just a few of the associations and charities willing to work with companies to promote causes: American Heart Association, American Lung Association, Camp Fire Boys & Girls, CARE, Global Releaf, Habitat for Humanity, Literacy Volunteers of America, March of Dimes, Mothers Against Drunk Driving, National Kidney Foundation, National Safety Council, North Shore Animal League, Paralyzed Veterans of America, Special Olympics, United Cerebral Palsy, and Vegetarian Awareness Network.

Some of these groups charge as much as $300,000 for a company to use their logo or name in a cause-related marketing program. Other associations, however, can be convinced to work with you for little upfront costs as long as you commit a minimum donation to their cause (based on sales of the related book).

- Health Communications donated 50¢ to the American Red Cross for every *A 3rd Serving of Chicken Soup for the Soul* book sold. They advertise this donation on the book cover as well as in their trade ads to bookstores. One million 16-page samplers, featuring a $1.00 off coupon for the book, were given free to blood donors at Red Cross donation centers nationwide. Participating bookstores, which would redeem the coupons, were provided posters to announce their participation.

- Troll Communications donated $10,000 from the sales of their *Pocket Dictionary of Signing* to the Helen Keller Foundation. The donation established the Troll Communications Scholarship Fund to fund rehabilitation programs for deaf-blind children.

- To promote *Merlin's Journey* by Jonathan Gunsen and Martin Coombe, HarperCollins offered a prize to the one person in the world who could first figure out the spell being cast by Merlin in the book. If after two years no one won, the prize would be donated to Save the Children Fund. For every book sold, the prize would increase by 32¢.

- To promote her new novel, *Come the Spring*, bestselling author Julie Garwood hosted special Toys for Tots events at bookstores in nine cities. During the weeks prior to each event, the bookstores displayed Toys for Tots collection receptacles where people could donate toys. Donations of toys were also accepted during her book signings.

- Foghorn Press, a publisher of outdoor recreation titles, won't publish a book without working with some worthwhile organization. In 1993, under their Books Building Community program, they donated more than $40,000 to participating organizations. Here are a few of the organizations they've worked with in the past (and the related titles):

  Trout Unlimited — *California Fishing*
  Greenbelt Alliance — *Great Outdoor Getaways to the Bay Area*
  The American Hiking Society — *Pacific Northwest Hiking*
  The American Lung Association — *California Golf*
  San Francisco SPCA — *Bay Area Dog Lover's Companion*

Other Ways to Work with Associations

Besides selling books to associations, you can also work with them to promote your books direct to their members, either by renting their lists, by advertising in their journals or newsletters, by getting publicity in their publications (reviews or articles by your author), by joining in with them for a mailing or other promotion, or by giving them books for their libraries (in the hope that members will see your books in the library and want to buy copies for themselves).

Resources

☐ **American Society of Association Executives**, 1575 I Street N.W., Washington, DC 20005-1168; 202-371-0940; 888-950-2723; Fax: 202-371-8315. Web: http://www.asaenet.org.

☐ **Encyclopedia of Associations**. This online database features detailed information on 135,000 organizations worldwide, including 22,000 national associations in the U.S.

☐ **National Trade and Professional Associations of the United States,** Columbia Books, Editorial Offices, 1825 Connecticut Avenue N.W. #625, Washington, DC 20009; 202-464-1662; Fax: 202-464-1775. Orders: 888-265-0600. Web: http://www.columbiabooks.com. Online at http://www.associationexecs.com. Also publishes *State and Regional Associations of the United States*.

☐ **Associations Yellow Book**, Leadership Directories, 104 Fifth Avenue, New York, NY 10011; 212-627-4140; Fax: 212-645-0931. Web: http://www.leadershipdirectories.com. Features 1,045 national trade and professional associations.

☐ **Oasis Events**, 1507 Western Avenue #507, Seattle, WA 98101; 206-624-0083; Fax: 206-624-0198. Web: http://www.oasisevents.com. This company provides event marketing, mobile marketing, media relations, cause marketing, mall tours, and teen marketing.

Also check out *Promo* magazine (http://www.promomagazine.com) for its regular listings of cause-related marketing services and associations actively seeking out cause relationships.

Authors — If you are a member of an association or if you know of an association that might be interested in offering your book as a premium, fundraising item, educational guide, or whatever, tell your publisher. As a member, you might be the best person to contact the association about selling your book. If you are not a member, let your publisher make the contacts.

19:06 Selling to Corporations: An Alternative

If you would like to make more sales to corporations, small businesses, professionals, associations, or other groups, partner with independent bookstores. Why? Because they are located in most major cities around the country, have a vested interest in selling more books, and have built relationships with many companies.

Unless your book is appropriate for use by only one or two corporations, you need help to reach all the markets you could reach. You can't begin to sell to every bank, every doctor's office, every association, etc. You need help. In my experience, that means you need the support of independent booksellers.

Several years ago, I spoke to some 200 independent booksellers at BookExpo America. My topic? How to work with local businesses and other groups to sell more books. These booksellers were actively looking for ways to make more sales outside the bookstore. If you approach them with a workable plan, they could easily become your partners in selling to small companies and groups.

Here are some possible steps to take to build a workable plan:

☐ Start by going to the largest independent bookstore in your area and ask to speak to their outside sales coordinator. Most of them will have someone with such a title or something closely related.

☐ Sit down with them and talk about your idea for making special bulk sales of your book to doctors' offices (or whatever your special market forcus is). Work with them to develop a plan to approach and sell to the doctors' offices in the area.

☐ Phone to set up an appointment at the one of your prime prospects.

☐ When you go to the doctor's office (we'll use that as the example here), both you and the bookseller should go together. Lay out your proposal to them: Why your book would be appropriate for their use. How it would be used. What it could do to increase their business or serve their patients. Ask them questions to find out what they need and what would get them to use a book as a premium, corporate gift, or educational tool. Even if they are not interested, ask for their help in learning how to speak to other doctors' offices that might be interested.

☐ If they are interested, sign the order. Chances are, though, that it will take more than one follow-up meeting, phone call, letter, or plea to convince them that your proposal will work for them.

☐ As you make each follow-up, record what you say or write. You want to develop the sales letters, phone call scripts, and in-person scripts that can be used again and again in approaching other doctors' offices.

☐ Deliver the books and track the results.

☐ If you make a sale and the doctor's office gets the results they want, ask them to provide you with a testimonial.

☐ Then use the scripts you've developed to solicit additional doctor's offices. Again, work with the bookseller to do this.

☐ Once you've established a program that makes it easy to sell to the doctor's offices (that is, one where 2 out of 5 offices you approach buy the program) and get a number of testimonials from offices describing how your program works wonders for them, then you want to export the program to other bookstores.

☐ Start by getting a testimonial from the bookseller you've been working with, a testimonial that gives the numbers: how m any books sold, how easy it was to make the sale, how big the market is, etc.

☐ Then write a great sales letter aimed at other booksellers that includes the bookseller's testimonial and some of your program details. Tell them that if they want to be involved, you can provide them with a great sales kit with all the scripts, promotional letters, order forms, and other items to make it easy for them to carry out your program.

☐ Send the sales letter to the appropriate person at each bookstore. Write to the attention of the outside sales coordinator or manager. You can use the Top 700 Bookstores list from Open Horizons or another list that you develop on your own.

☐ Call some of the bookstores to follow up and make the sale.

☐ When offering such a program to bookstores, be sure to give them a great discount (50% or more). They will handle all sales to the offices, plus all collections and other service. Your job is simply to develop the program and then franchise it around the country to an independent bookstore in each major city.

☐ Offer each store an exclusive for their city.

☐ Note that any bookstore that gets involved with your program and makes more sales will love you—and will feature your book on their shelves as well as in the program you've developed.

☐ In rolling out your franchised system of outside sales, you might want to start slowly by rolling out to a few more cities first to make sure the system works everywhere.

19:07 Selling to the Government

Just as corporations and associations can use books for premiums and other special purposes, so can various governmental units. For instance, Graphics Arts Center sells many of its regional pictorial books to state governments to be used as honoraria gifts for visiting dignitaries.

As a $225 billion dollar market for supplies and services, the federal government is a large potential market for your books. Contrary to popular belief, a large portion of federal business is done with small companies. If you are interested in selling to a specific government agency, start by asking to talk to their small business representative.

If you are interested in exploring options for selling to government, check out the following resources. By the way, the government buys products using the Standard Industrial Classification Code (SIC), which for books is 273. Also, the GSA Federal Supply Class (FSC) number for books is 7610. You will need both of the above numbers when completing various applications and forms used by the government.

☐ **Government Product News**, Penton Media, 1300 East 9th Street, Cleveland, OH 44114-1503; 216-696-7000; Fax: 216-931-9799. Web: http://www.govpro.com. This magazine is sent to government executives, administrators, engineers, and purchasing officials. The July, 1987, issue of the magazine featured *Facts about Aids* from Evergreen Publications.

☐ **Commerce Business Daily** (http://cbdnet.access.gpo.gov) — This web site provides access to the daily notice of what government agencies are buying. You can also subscribe via the Government Printing Office (http://www.access.gpo.gov) or to a daily email update via the Govcon Resource Center (http://www.govcon.com), which also provide lots of other information and links on selling to the government.

☐ **Central Contractor Registry** (http://www.ccr.gov) — Get listed in this central referral system of small businesses interested in selling to the government.

☐ **Minority Business Development Agency** (http://www.mbda.gov) — This agency was established to encourage the creation, growth and expansion of minority-owned businesses in the United States. It's web site is very slow, but check it out anyway if you qualify.

☐ **Small Business Administration** (http://www.sba.gov) — Check out this site for information on SBA loans as well as the address of your local office, which will be able to help you navigate the waters of selling to the government.

☐ **General Services Administration**. (Http://www.gsa.gov) — The GSA is the federal government's largest purchaser. Check out their site for information on marketing to them. You'll also find the addresses of the GSA Small Business Centers located around the country.

☐ **Panoptic Enterprises**, P.O. Box 11220, Burke, VA 22009-1220; 703-451-5953; 800-594-4766. Web: http://www.fedgovcontracts.com. They publish the *Federal Contracts Perspective* newsletter and *Getting Started in Federal Contracting*, a book aimed at companies providing construction or manufacturing services to the federal government.

☐ **Federal Marketplace** (http://www.fedmarket.com) — This web site provides lots of information as well as links to many sites that will help you sell your books to the federal government.

> **Authors** — As a published author, you are an expert in your field. If you feel qualified and inclined, you might explore the possibilities of doing consulting work for some local, state, or federal government agencies. The above resources should help you to orient yourself.

19:08 Selling to Mail Order Catalogs

While the major mail order catalogs drive a hard bargain—requiring as much as an 50 to 70% discount—they can move a lot of books. Not only that, but the exposure they give your books to their customers will often result in spillover sales through bookstores. Where else could you find outlets who are willing to pay you so they can advertise your books to as many as five million people?

- Irena Chalmers Cookbooks have sold more than 250,000 books through the *Lillian Vernon* catalog, which is mailed to over five million people. They have also sold many cookbooks through *Jessica's Biscuit*, a mail order cookbook catalog which is mailed to almost a million people. Indeed, they have found catalogs to be far more productive than book clubs.

- During the 1996 holiday season, Hyperion sold 30,000 copies of *Balance: A Guide to Life's Forgotten Pleasures* even though the book was only available through the *Eddie Bauer* catalog and retail stores.

There are some 6,000 companies in the U.S. that sell products through catalogs. Annual catalog sales were over $60 billion. More than 110 million people buy items from a catalog each year.

According to one Gallup Survey, 80% of the people who receive a catalog in the mail actually read some portion of the catalog, and 93% of the people who have bought something by mail or by phone within the past six months are avid catalog readers. According to one survey, more catalog shoppers (62%) bought books, videos, or music via catalogs than any other item. In contrast, 60% bought gifts, 54% bought women's apparel, 33% bought kitchen or household products, and 32% bought gardening items.

To sell to catalogs, first research those catalogs which target the same audience as your book. If possible, get a sample copy of their catalog and review it to see if they offer any other books. Then send a finished copy of your book to those catalogs which you think would do the best job of presenting and selling your book. In your letter, tell them what page your book would fit on in their current catalog. Be specific. Where on the page would it fit? Next to what product? Why there? If you can show the catalog merchandise director that you know the catalog, he or she is far more likely to buy from you, rather than from someone who shows no such knowledge.

At the same time, enclose a Merchandise Data Sheet (see an example in John Kremer's *Catalog Sales MiniGuide*, available at BookMarket.com). This data sheet should provide all the details about your book, from its shipping weight and size to its potential markets to a good discount schedule.

Be persistent. Ernie Zelinski, author of *The Joy of Not Knowing It All*, approached many catalogs, but it was the last two catalogs he approached that sold the most books. *Pacific Spirit* sold 700 copies and *Loompanics* sold 250 copies. If he hadn't been persistent or, in his words, "unreasonable," he'd never have gotten those sales.

One other note: Catalogs like books that can be paired with other products that they sell. One reason that *Edmund's Scientific* carries books on astronomy is to help them sell more of the high-ticket telescopes they carry.

Catalogs can be broken down into a number of different categories. Here are a some of the major categories, with a few examples for each. To locate additional catalogs, see the *Catalog Sales Data Files*, available at BookMarket.com or use some of the online resources described later.

☐ **General catalogs**—Lillian Vernon, Miles Kimball, Hanover Direct, Walter Drake, Harriet Carter, Signals, and others.

☐ **High-ticket catalogs**—Bloomingdales, Metropolitan Museum of Art, Circa, Ross-Simons.

☐ **Business catalogs**—Office Depot, Office Max, Tools of the Trade, G. Neil, Successories.

☐ **Children's catalogs**—PlayFair Toys, Hearthsong, Toys to Grow On, Invisible Ink, Smart Starts, Childs Work Childs Play.

☐ **Collectible catalogs**—All American Products, Lighthouse Depot, West-Tex Collectibles, Pieces of History, Esoterica.

☐ **Computer catalogs**—PC Zone, PC Mall, Mac Connection, Computer Gear, Global Computer Supplies, J&R Computer World.

☐ **Cooking catalogs**—Jessica's Biscuits, Kitchen Arts and Letters, Wine and Food Library, Spices Etc., Spice Merchant, Salsa Express, Chef's Catalog, San Francisco Herb Company, Just Pasta, Seafood Direct.

☐ **Crafts catalogs**—Herrschners, Suncoast Discount Arts, Dick Blick, Lark Books, The Basket Maker's, Maplewood Craft, Craft King, Creative Craft House, Stitcher's Sourcebook, Eastern Art Glass, Newark Dressmaking Supply, Kirchen Bros., Clotilde, Keepsake Quilting, Jax Photo Books, Woodworker's Store, Bud Plant's Incredible Catalog (art).

☐ **Games and novelties catalogs**—Game Room, Johnson-Smith, Bits & Pieces, Ann-dy's Magic Shop, Spy Headquarters, Magic Masters, Whole Mirth, Spilsbury Puzzle, Gambler's Emporium.

☐ **Garden catalogs**—Carnivorous Plants, Langenbach Garden Tools, Burpees, Smith & Hawken, Stark Brothers, Teas Nursery, Gardener's Supply, Backyard Gardening, Capability's Books.

☐ **Health catalogs**—Indiana Botanic Gardens, Healthy Back Store, Robert Anderson Publishing, The Vitamin Shoppe, Aroma Therapeutix, Allergy & Asthma Catalog, Allergy Resources, Healthy Living, Priorities.

☐ **Home catalogs**—Country Store, Simply Southwest, Cumberland General Store, Yield House, Renovator's Supply, Alsto's Handy Helpers, Tapestry, Improvements, Reverie, Williams-Sonoma.

☐ **Music catalogs**—Lark in the Morning, The Music Stand, Dance Mart, Rhino Records, Elderly Instruments, Opera Box, Mix Bookshelf.

☐ **Pet catalogs**—Valley Vet Supply, Cats, Cats & More Cats, Creative Pet Supply, Pet Warehouse, Care-A-Lot Pet Supply Warehouse.

☐ **Religious catalogs**—Christian Book Distributors, Best to You, Believers Book Distributor, Abbey Press.

☐ **Science and technology catalogs**—Edmund's Scientific, Brainstorms, Sharper Image, The Brain Store, Storm Tech, Hello Direct.

☐ **Self-help and new age catalogs**—Courage to Change, Goddess Connection, Real Goods, DharmaCrafts, Inner Dimension, Kama Sutra.

☐ **Sports catalogs**—Harbour Bay Golf Classics, Bart's Watersports, Adelson Sports, Golf Day, Mueller Sporting Goods, Austad's, Performance Bicycle, Bike Nashbar, Sports Fan Memorabilia, Overton's.

☐ **Travel catalogs**—Magellan's, Pentrex, J.C. Whitney, Mach 1, Historic Aviation, Family Travel Guides, TravelSmith.

☐ **Alternative catalogs**—Northern Sun, Loompanics, Armageddon Books, Eden Press Privacy Catalog.

☐ **General book catalogs**—A Common Reader, Bas Bleu.

19:09 Resources for Selling to Catalog Houses

To help you sell to mail order catalog houses, here are a few magazines, directories, and web sites which cover the catalog industry. Plus, I've listed several major catalog houses that feature books as well as other products.

Magazines

☐ **Multichannel Marketer**, 11 River Bend, P.O. Box 4949, Stamford, CT 06907-0949; 203-358-9900; 800-775-3777; Fax: 203-358-5821. Web: http://www.prismb2b.com. This monthly is the main trade magazine covering the catalog industry. This company also publishes *Direct* magazine (Fax: 212-206-3618; http://www.directmag.com).

☐ **DM News**, Mill Hollow Corp., 100 Avenue of the Americas, New York, NY 10013; 212-925-7300; Fax: 212-925-8754. Email: editor@dmnews. com. Web: http://www.dmnews.com. This weekly tabloid newspaper is the prime source of direct marketing news.

☐ **Direct Marketing**, Hoke Communications, 224 Seventh Street, Garden City, NY 11530-5771; 516-746-6700; Fax: 516-294-8141. Email: http:// www.directmarketingmag.com. The only paid subscription magazine in the field and one of the first.

☐ **Catalog Success**, North American Publishing, 1500 Spring Garden Street #1200, Philadelphia, PA 19130-4094; 215-238-5224; Fax: 215-238-5270. Web: http://www.catalogsuccess.com.

☐ **Target Marketing**, NAPCO, 1500 Spring Garden Street #1200, Philadelphia, PA 19130-4094; 215-238-5300; Fax: 215-238-5270. Email: editor.tm@napco.com. Web: http://www.targetonline.com.

Directories

☐ **The Directory of Mail Order Catalogs**, Grey House Publishing, 185 Millerton Road, P.O. Box 860, Millerton, NY 12546; 518-789-8700; 800-562-2139; Fax: 518-789-0556. Email: books@greyhouse.com. Web: http://www.greyhouse.com. Lists many catalogs but does not indicate which ones carry books. This company also publishes a *Directory of Business to Business Catalogs*, which lists many business catalogs. Both directories are now available only online for a subscription.

☐ **Catalog Sales Directory**, Open Horizons, P.O. Box 205, Fairfield, IA 52556-0205; 641-472-6130; Fax: 641-472-1560. Email: info@bookmar-ket.com. Web: http://www.bookmarket.com/catalog.html. $30.00. Features more than 1,300 catalogs known to carry books, with info on buyer's names, addresses, phones, faxes, email address, and URL.

☐ **National Directory of Catalogs**, Oxbridge Communications, 186 Fifth Avenue, New York, NY 10010; 212-741-0231; 800-955-0231; Fax: 212-633-2938. Email: info@oxbridge.com. Web: http://www.mediafinder. com. $995.00. Lists 11,000 catalogs classified by subject.

Web Resources

☐ **Buyers Index**, Wired Markets, 1045 Via Mil Cumbres, Solana Beach, CA 92075; 858-793-0085; Fax: 858-793-3680. Web: http://www.buyers index.com. Features 20,000 web shopping sites and mail order catalogs with over 300 million product offerings for your home or business.

☐ **CatalogLink** (http://cataloglink.com) — A good site for researching mail order catalogs.

☐ **Shop at Home Catalog**, Belcaro Group, 7100 E. Belleview Avenue #305, Greenwood Village, CO 80111; 303-843-0302; 800-315-1995;

Fax: 303-843-0377. Web: http://www.shopathome.com. A catalog and web site that features catalogs from 400 companies.

☐ **The Catalog Shop** (http://www.catalogs.com). A catalog search site for consumers.

☐ **Free Shop** (http://www.freeshop.com). Another catalog search site.

Other Catalog Resources

☐ **Catalog Solutions**, 19 Ketchum Street, Westport, CT 06880; 203-454-1919; 800-240-6766; Fax: 203-226-7333. Email: info@asseenonpc.com. Web: http://www.asseenonpc.com. This company helps other companies to sell products to mail order catalogs. Their specialty is products featured in TV infomercials.

☐ **Telebrands Corp.**, A. J. Khubani, President, 7 Telebrands Plaza, Fairfield, NJ 07004; 973-277-8777; 800-777-4034. Web: http://www.tele brands.com. This company has handled catalog and direct to retail distribution for some major TV infomercial products.

☐ **ACCM**, Prism Business Media, 11 River Bend South, Stamford, CT 06907; 203-358-9900; 800-559-0620; Fax: 203-358-5816. Web: http://www.catalogconference.com. The annual conference on catalogs which is held in early May or early June, generally in Chicago.

Major Catalogs

To help you get started in making a list of key contacts, here are the addresses of a few major mail order catalogs that carry books. For the addresses of other catalogs, see the directories listed above.

☐ **Hanover Direct**, 1500 Harbor Boulevard, Weehawken, NJ 07087-6788; 201-863-7300; Fax: 201-272-3280. Web: http://www.hanoverdirect.com. This company publishes catalogs that carry gifts (and sometimes books): Domestications, The Company Store, and Silhouettes.

☐ **Harriet Carter Gifts**, Catalog Manager, 425 Stump Road, Montgomery-ville, PA 18936-9631; 215-361-5100; Fax: 215-361-5344. Web: http://www.harrietcarter.com. They feature many books in their catalogs— books on sports, cars, railroads, trivia, humor, word origins, crafts, and cooking. This catalog circulates to 30 million people every year. A product review board makes decisions on what products they carry.

☐ **Publisher's Clearing House**, 382 Channel Drive, Port Washington, NY 11050-0002; 516-883-5432, ext. 4723; Fax: 516-767-3650. Web: http://www.pch.com. Along with American Family Publishers, this company is a major magazine subscription agency. Both are now offering books as well as magazines in their sweepstakes mailings. But note that both have cut back drastically because of sweepstakes controversies.

For instance, American Family Publishers offered *Jane Fonda's New Workout & Weight-Loss Program*, *Betty Crocker's Christmas Cookbook*, Velveteen Rabbit Set, Little Treasury sets, and *Freebies for Cat Lovers*.

Publisher's Clearinghouse once offered an all-books catalog. Among the books they offered were *The Homeowner's Journal* by Vic Spadoccini and *Common Sense: The Complete Money Management Workbook* by Judy Lawrence. They also featured practical books on cooking, crafts, consumer reference, self-improvement, personal finance, and children's books (both fiction and nonfiction). When they selected a book, they bought from 2,000 to 10,000 copies at a time.

☐ **Taylor Gifts Catalog**, New Item Committee, 600 Cedar Hollow Road, Paoli, PA 19301; 610-725-1122, ext. 205. Email: newproducts@taylor-gifts.com. Web: http://www.taylorgifts.com. This catalog features low-priced gifts including some books.

Their web site currently features *Natural Cures They Don't Want You to Know About, 515 Scrapbooking Ideas, Club the Bugs and Scare the Critters, 100 Best One-Dish Meals, Over 50 Jokes, Real Simple Solutions, Why Do Cats Do That?, Irish Pride, Italian Pride, German Pride, 1000 Places to See Before You Die, 1001 All Natural Secrets to a Pest-Free Prpoerty, The Right Words for Any Occasion, Speed Cleaning, Getting a Good Nights Sleep, Super- market Diet, Travel Mate Sudoku Puzzle Book*, and *Mayo Clinic* self-help books.

☐ **Miles Kimball**, 250 City Center, Oshkosh, WI 54906-6047; 920-231-3800; 800-255-4590; Fax: 920-231-4804. Web: http://www.mileskimball. com. This general interest catalog features low-priced gifts, books, clothing, and other items. It is mailed six times a year to 3.5 million people. Their web site currently features *The Home Owners Journal, The Big Book of American Trivia, 500 Uses for Baking Soda, The Ultimate Christmas Fake Book, This Is the Ultimate Fake Book with Over 1200 Songs*, and a *Crossword Puzzle Dictionary*.

☐ **Signals Catalog**, 5581 Hudson Industrial Parkway, P O Box 2599, Hudson OH 44236-0099; 800-669-5252. Web: http://www.signals.com. Their web site currently features the following books: *Walking the Bible, What a Year It Was, A Bookshelf of Our Own, What Would Jackie Do?, Horse Fever, No, David!, Great American Houses and Gardens Pop-Up Book, Knuffle Bunny Book*, and many other titles. The guidelines *Signals* used to send out to inquiring companies provides good pointers on how to sell to catalogs in general. Here are a few:

- *Please do not send samples unless requested. Initially a catalog sheet or detailed letter describing your product is sufficient.*

- *Photographs are always helpful as is retail and wholesale pricing info and sales history data.*

- *If there is any special significance or story behind the product or its design, let us know that also.*

- *If you are sending several different designs, let us know which are your bestsellers.*

- *Signals is always interested in doing custom products and catalog exclusives.*

- *We expect to receive your lowest possible price. This can be accomplished through the use of volume discounts, negotiable minimum purchases, and/or advertising allowances (5 to 10% usually).*

Note: Many catalogs ask for an advertising allowance, which usually takes the form of an additional discount off the price of the product to the catalog. Essentially, the ad allowance is the price you pay for space in the catalog. Look on this cost as if you were buying a display ad in a magazine.

Authors — Watch for catalogs that could be appropriate for your books. If you discover any, send them to your publisher so the special sales department can make bulk sales to the catalog. To receive catalogs in the subject areas that interest you, get your name on related lists. For instance, if you want to receive photography catalogs, subscribe to a photography magazine, or buy a camera or supplies by mail, or join an amateur photography club—anything to get your name on some lists.

19:10 Sales through Other Direct Marketers

Besides catalogs, there are a number of other ways to market your books through mail order book sellers. For example, there are many smaller enterprises which sell books by mail. To reach these dealers, you can advertise in *BookDealers World, Entrepreneur, Spare Time,* or other magazines where people read the classifieds to find moneymaking opportunities. Wilshire Books and George Sterne's Profit Ideas are two publishers who have been using such mail order dealers for many years—and selling books as a result.

You can offer these independent dealers 50 to 70% discount depending on the quantity they order. These discounts are justified since all sales should be prepaid with no returns allowed (these are the standard terms). As an option, you can offer to dropship books for these dealers at a 50% discount plus postage and handling. Under these arrangements, they send you a check for the appropriate amount plus a label already made out to their customer. Then all you have to do is stuff the book into a shipping bag, attach the label and appropriate postage, and mail.

Lowen Publishing sold thousands of copies of *The Secretary's Friend* through dropship agreements with independent publishers and marketers. They also sold many copies through office supply catalogs.

Many book publishers have started their own catalogs to resell books from other publishers as well. That's how the *Firefighter's Catalog* first started. To locate these publishers, just contact other publishers who sell books that complement yours. If they don't have such a catalog, ask them if they know someone who does.

Para Publishing, publishers of *The Self-Publishing Manual*, sold several thousand copies of *1001 Ways to Market Your Books* over the years. In turn, we sold several thousand copies of their book. It was a win-win situation for both of us—as well as for our customers!

19:11 Home Party Sales

How many of you have attended a Tupperware party? The Tupperware Company built up an incredible market almost solely on the basis of home party sales. Why not apply the same technique to advertise and distribute your books? Lions Head Press has found that home party sales can be effective for selling religious books. They use individuals to demonstrate their entire line of books at in-home parties. Sales, thus far, have been good enough to continue the program.

19:12 Display Marketers

Display marketers are companies that buy books in large quantities (30,000 to 100,000 copies) at large discounts (about 80% of retail price) to sell in schools and corporate settings through independent sales reps who set up displays in those settings. What kind of book works best for them? Cookbooks, gift books, coffee-table books, children's books, sports, how-to, and other titles that have an impulse appeal to a mass audience. Novels don't work for them, but books like *Chicken Soup for the Soul* and *Men Are from Mars* have. They prefer hardcover editions that they can sell at a 50% discount. They generally test books in smaller quantities before rolling them out nationally. Every year, they are presented thousands of titles, test about a thousand, and sell several hundred in major quantities.

☐ **Books Are Fun**, New Publisher Department, 1680 Highway 1, P.O. Box 2468, Fairfield, IA 52556; 641-472-8301; 800-966-8301; Fax: 641-469-3915. Web: http://www.booksarefun.com. This company is now owned by Reader's Digest, which bought it from the owner for $300 million.

☐ **Imagine-Nation Books**, Tim McCormick, Senior Buyer, P.O. Box 27672, Tempe, AZ 85285-7672; 480-838-4309; Fax: 480-820-1011. Email: TMcCormick@ImagineNation.us. Web: http://www.imagination-books.info. Another display marketer founded by the former owner of Books Are Fun.

☐ **Readon Publications**, Henry Delmar, President, 8241 Keele Street, #9-10, Concord, Ontario L4K 1Z5, Canada; 905-761-9666; Fax: 905-761-1377. Email: henry@readon.com. Web: http://www.readon.com. Jennifer Handy, Buyer; Email: jennifer@readon.com. The Canadian version of Books Are Fun.

Authors — If you see a sales representative for one of these book display marketers, talk to them. They are encouraged to bring new titles to the corporate offices. You could end up making a sale for your book in a huge quantity.

19:13 Bartering for Books and Other Services

You can also use your books as exchange items for other services. I know of a number of poets who have bartered their poetry books for goods or services from family and friends.

When I published the third edition of my *Directory of Book Printers*, I exchanged several hundred copies of the second edition for books from other publishers. They, in turn, distributed the extra copies to their customers or friends. In this way I made sure that the outdated books were distributed rather than trashed.

Jeff Justice, author of *The Pregnant Husband Handbook* and a professional speaker, regularly barters for speaking engagements. In one case, he spoke at a printing association meeting in return for thousands of laminated humor cards. In another case, he spoke at the Atlanta Gift Mart in return for several advertisements. And, finally, he bartered half his wife's maternity fees in return for entertaining at a big party for the regional ob/gyns. At the same party, he sold many copies of his book.

Authors — You, too, can barter your books or speaking for other products and services. Since books have such a high perceived value, it is easy to trade them for many other items. But don't trade unless you really want the other item.

19:14 Sell Advertisements in Your Books

To increase the income from your books, you can sell ads for related products in the back of your books. Though some people would question whether such advertising corrupts the editorial integrity of books, ads have not interfered with the quality of most magazines which carry advertising nor with the many directories (such as *Literary MarketPlace* and the *Thomas Register*) which also carry advertising.

Indeed, I see ads as being a service to readers, especially for users of directories. Giving advertisers the opportunity to tell their story their way is, in my mind, an integral part of any really useful directory.

Why couldn't other books carry advertising as well? Recently, I saw an ad for a new quarterly fantasy magazine in a trade paperback fantasy novel. Such advertising might be the only feasible way for a quality magazine to reach the target audience for its editorial content. Why not give readers an opportunity to learn about related products or services?

You could accept just about any advertising which targets the same market as your books. For example, romance novels could carry ads for soaps, beauty aids, and diet plans while westerns could carry ads for chewing tobacco or Marlboro cigarettes. Such ads could, of course, get too commercial, but they could also help to hold the line on rising prices for mass-market paperbacks and hardcovers. Perhaps there could be some selection criteria which would limit ads to certain clearly defined commercial products that you feel would be compatible with the book's content and style and which would actually be a service to the reader.

The following idea, which was used to promote a newsletter, might be adapted for promoting books as well. In the 1980s, Milton Zelman launched *Chocolate News*. As a subscription premium, Zelman used a coupon book consisting of $25.00 worth of discount offers for chocolate bars, cookbooks, baking supplies, and so on. Because this *Chocolate Bonus Book* had a high perceived value, it worked wonders as a premium. Now, here's the great part of the promotion: It didn't cost Zelman a cent. Why? Because he charged each company offering a coupon a fee to be included in the book. Each year, he published a new edition of the book so he could continue to use it as a renewal premium indefinitely.

To add greater value to their atlases and to keep the prices down, Rand McNally includes pages of coupons for free information, lower entrance fees for parks and museums, discount room charges, two-for-one meals, etc. Each year, of course, the offers change. And Rand McNally makes money on the coupon ads as well as from atlas sales.

19:15 Selling Sponsorships

For a book on wealth preservation, one self-publisher charged contributors to write the book for him. He brought in fifty-four contributors at a price of $20,000 each. Do the numbers—more than a million dollars! In return for his $20,000 and answering questions for the book, each contributor received copies of the book with his name on the front as one of the co-authors. In addition, his photograph and biography was featured on the back cover. Finally, all contributors were featured in the back of the book. The contributors were willing to pay so much because they wanted the exposure before so many potential customers for their services. Given how much financial planners, especially estate planners, charge, the fee was a small amount for such valuable exposure.

When preparing this fifth edition of *1001 Ways*, I decided to solicit sponsors as well. I had two basic motivations in doing so: 1) I could use the upfront payments to pay for the printing of this edition, and 2) I wanted to add some outside perspective to this book. In soliciting sponsors, I contacted 120 individuals and companies that I thought did a good job serving the needs of book publishers and authors. I asked them to participate in an experiment. Fifteen of them chose to respond. Each paid from $400 to $1,000 to participate by writing a contribution to this book. I believe those contributions added to the book.

I hope you agree since I've done the same thing for this edition (but I charged more for the sponsorships). The income from the sponsorships allowed me to print 10,000 copies of this book for literally nothing. The neat thing, again, is that I got some great editorial content for free as well. That means you the reader also got some great editorial content as a bonus.

19:16 Remainder Sales: The Final Frontier

At some point in the life of a book, no matter how committed you are to keeping your books in print, you must consider whether or not to sell any leftover stock to remainder dealers. Sometimes you will have to remainder a book simply because it is outdated or because the author wants to do another edition, but the major reason most books are remaindered is that the book is no longer selling enough copies to justify the costs of warehousing.

Remaindering is actually just another way to keep a book alive rather than, as many publishers think, a way to bury a book. John Fielder of Westcliffe Publishers, which produced many fancy photo books, actually welcomed remaindering. It is, he said, a way to reach an entirely new market. When you cut the price of a book by half or more, you make your book affordable to a whole new group of book buyers.

Indeed, a number of publishers are now actually publishing books for the remainder market. They don't really expect the books to sell that well in a bookstore at a high price, but they do expect them to sell quite well when they are marked down to the remaindered retail price.

True remainders are not damaged or returned copies which have been sitting on some bookseller's shelves for months; rather, true remainders are actual publishers' overstocks which have never been distributed. Most books are bought by remainder dealers at or below the publisher's actual productions costs (between 5% and 15% of the list price, or at a cost about ¼ that of the retail price the remainder will carry when sold in stores). There are two basic ways to sell your books for remaindering:

☐ You can offer a packaged deal to one or more remainder dealers. Send them copies of the titles you want to remainder, along with inventory information for each title. Once the dealers have had a chance to review the books, you can negotiate a price with them either over the phone or by mail. This is a quick and easy method to remainder a few titles.

☐ You can offer a larger list of titles on a **bid-list** basis. Send the list to all remainder dealers who might be interested in bidding on the books. The list should include the following information about each book: title, name of author, other biographical details about the author that might encourage them to stock the book, the copyright date, original retail price, and remaining inventory.

Offer review copies of any title they could interested in reviewing more closely. In your cover letter, indicate a closing date for receiving bids, the terms of payment you expect, and information about how (and where) the books are stored. Under this, the remainder dealer who offers the highest price for each book gets all the inventory for that book.

The Chicago International Remainder and Overstock Book Exposition is a good show to sell remainders at since it's all business. One publisher reported selling "a ton of books" at one show. The show is held in October or November in Chicago. For more information, contact **CIROBE**, 1501 East 57th Street, Chicago, IL 60637; 773-404-8357; Fax: 773-955-2967. Email: info@cirobe.com. Web: http://www.cirobe.com.

Also, you can approach the major remainder dealers at the BookExpo America convention. Since most of the people staffing their booths will be there to take orders from booksellers, ask to see the person responsible for buying remainders. Make an appointment to show him or her your books. It is possible to make a deal right at the show.

Authors — At some point, your publisher will remainder your books. Make sure your contract specifies that you have first right to bid on any remainders. You should be able to buy these remainders at production cost. While your publisher may no longer think it can sell your books, you know better. As long as your heart is in your books, you can sell them forever and ever, wherever you speak, wherever you travel, wherever you have friends. When St. Martin's decided to let her memoir, *Love and Rutabaga*, go out of print, Claire Shu Accomando bought up a large quantity of the book, which she sold wherever she spoke. She even paid her agent a percentage of every sale she made.

For the addresses of major remainder dealers, see the BookMarket.com website at http://www.bookmarket.com/19.html#remain. Note that the major chains and some independent bookstores also have buyers who specialize in purchasing remainders.

19:17 Books as Donations

If you would rather not sell your overstocked books at a loss, you can donate them to a charity and take a deduction on your income taxes. Below are two services that will accept your excess inventory and channel these donations to worthy causes (schools, colleges, literacy groups, prisons, etc.) or sell them to fund scholarships and other grants. For other such services, see the bottom of the following page: http://www.bookmarket.com/19.html.

☐ **Books for Asia Program**, The Asia Foundation, 465 California Street, 9th Floor, San Francisco, CA 94104; 415-982-4640; Fax: 415-392-8863. Email: info@asiafound.org. Web: http://www.asiafoundation.org. Books are sent to schools and libraries in developing countries in Asia.

☐ **National Association for Exchange of Industrial Resources**, 560 McClure Street, Galesburg, IL 61401; 800-562-0955; Fax: 309-343-0862. Web: http://www.naeir.org. Books are donated to schools and non-profit organizations.

Before submitting any books to these programs, call or write first to verify that they would like to receive the titles you wish to donate. Also, check to see how many copies they can use and whether they will provide you with forms to allow you to write off the donations on your taxes. Note that some of these programs are quite formal, while others are informal.

Besides donating to these general programs, you can also donate books to specific causes. For example, in the past publishers have donated books to schools, libraries, churches, prisons, charities, public television stations, 4-H clubs, scouting groups, garden clubs, and other nonprofit groups. Publishers can deduct 100% of the production costs of any books donated (200% if the company is incorporated), plus 100% of the freight and 100% of administrative fees.

- In 1996, religious publisher Zondervan donated a box of thirty books to each of eighty-four black churches that had been burned since 1990. The donation, designed to rebuild the church libraries, had a retail value of more than $30,000.

- Wade Cook, author of *Business Buy the Bible*, donated copies of his book to every prison in America. As he noted when making the donation, "This donation is a way to do something positive for those most in need of hope and inspiration."

Authors — You, too, may qualify for tax deductions by donating your books to worthy causes. Check with your accountant to find out what deductions you can take.

Beyond talent lie all the usual words:
discipline, love, luck—but, most of all, endurance.
— James Baldwin, author

In three words I can sum up everything I've learned about life.
It goes on.
— Robert Frost, poet

Conducting a PR Campaign
Online and Offline
by Imal Wagner of Phoenix Rising PR

The Power of Publicity

You can be the greatest in the world at what you do, but if no one knows about you, you will never achieve the wealth and fame you deserve.

While searching the internet for articles published about *Cracking the Millionaire Code* (a book I worked on), I found a small story about Alex Tew and his website (*http://www.MillionDollarHomePage.com*). I contacted Alex and we began working together within days. My first placement was an exclusive magazine interview with *Vanity Fair*. The photographer who flew to London to photograph Alex had just finished a shoot with Madonna.

I created a series of exclusives in print, radio, newspaper, and TV coverage including ABC news radio, *The Jim Bohannon Radio Show*, *The Wall Street Journal*, *The Neil Cavuto* Fox TV show, and several high-tech California TV shows. Articles were printed around the world with TV networks providing additional coverage. Alex was offered a six-figure book deal, but turned it down so he could tell his story online as an e-book. His site became the first pixel site to sell $1 million in ads, all in just a few months!

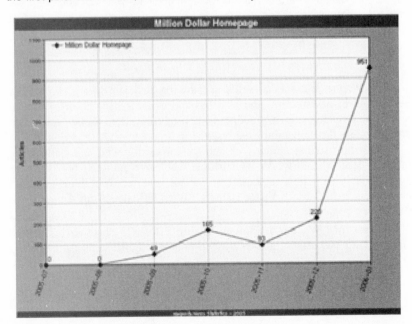

I am now working on a wonderful website developed by Seth Godin called *Squidoo.com*. At this site, anyone can build a *lense*, which is a web page featuring one person's expert view of a particular topic. Lenses are made from building blocks featuring Amazon.com books, news feeds, blogs, Google maps, CafePress items, eBay, Flickr images, and hundreds of online merchants. Be sure to create your own lense so you can piggyback on the publicity this site will be getting over the new months.

Seth is the bestselling author of eight books, including *Unleashing the Ideavirus*. As my newest client, he has already been interviewed by CNN.com and the *New York Times*. Already several hundred thousand people visit the *Squidoo* website every month.

Cross-Promotions

If you are publishing a book, you know that publishing is not just creating a book. It is also creating a product. When companies create products, the main goal is to sell those products. If the products don't sell, the business doesn't exist.

Now, doesn't it sound like the perfect opportunity to figure out a way to work with other businesses who are selling other products, in order to increase both of your sales? This kind of arrangement between companies is often called cross-promotion and it is a fantastic way to sell more books. Don't overlook this very important component of your book marketing plan.

There are countless ways to set up cross promotions. Here are just a few of them: Gift with purchase incentives, educational tools, and charitable support promotions. Partner with companies in such a way that you both win. That's the perfect promotion and the perfect way to create relationships that last and last.

Imal Wagner has special skills in knowing how and where to promote her clients in newsrooms. She also has the extraordinary ability to forge long-lasting relationships with editors and producers. Her unique capabilities and relentless determination have resulted in an impressive newsroom list of *NY Times* best-selling authors, up-and-coming performers, and trailblazing business leaders. She works with people who have authored books in the areas of self-help, how-to, business, finance and family/children's issues. Her clients include Mark Victor Hansen, Robert G. Allen, Tom Antion, Seth Godin, and John Kremer.

Contact Imal Wagner at **Phoenix Rising PR**, 9627 Shadow Oak Drive, Gaithersburg MD 20886; 301-840-5999. Email: authors@comcast.net. Web: http://www.imalwagner.com.

Chapter 20

Authors: How to Capitalize on Your Books

My advice is not to create something totally different from what you are now selling until you have pursued every means of marketing your existing information. The best strategy is to repackage your bestselling, proven products and market them to a brand new audience. . . .

Don't be shy about selling your repackaged information for a higher price. People want your information but may not have the time or desire to read a book. They will gladly pay more to get the same information presented in a convenient form. That's why you see the exact same information sold as a $10 book, a $25 cassette series, a $40 noncredit course, a $75 videotape, a $100 newsletter, a $150 per hour consultation, a $250 seminar, etc.

— Mark Nolan, *The Mark Nolan Letter*

No other publication establishes the credentials of an author the way the publication of a book does. Until you've written a book and had it published, you will always be an incomplete writer in the eyes of many people. Why is this? I don't know. Perhaps it's because books are more substantial, more impressive. Maybe it's because the book stands or falls on your work alone. Or maybe it's because a book takes a major commitment to finish. Whatever the reason, you should be ready to capitalize on the increased recognition that a published book gives your work.

This chapter lists some of the ways that you can use your newfound recognition to expand the audience for your creative endeavors—and make more money in the process. While some of these opportunities will come your way unasked, don't wait for them to happen. Instead, envision what you really want, and then create it on your own.

Note: Many of these ways of capitalizing on your book will also be useful in helping you to promote your book to a wider audience.

20:01 Sell Your Writing Skills

Once you have demonstrated that you can write a book that merits publishing, you will find that many new opportunities begin to open up for you in the writing field. Here are just a few of them:

☐ You'll finally be able to convince a literary agent to take on your work. Few agents will represent authors who only produce short pieces simply because there's not enough money in selling articles and short stories. The agents have to be able to justify the time and money they spend on representing their clients. Representing one book is more cost-effective for them than trying to sell dozens of articles to generate the same amount of income.

☐ Magazine editors will take you more seriously since you have demonstrated that you can produce major works. Also, by getting your book published, you've passed a screening test far more rigorous than any magazine writer. Your book is one out of 55,000 new titles, while a magazine article is only one out of half a million or more features.

☐ With the publication of your book, you become an instant expert. People will seek you out for advice. Editors will pay more attention to your article proposals, especially those having to do with your area of expertise (as indicated by your book). You might even find yourself teaching Ph.D. candidates even though you have nothing more than a B.A. or high school diploma.

☐ You'll also find more doors open to you in the business world and other areas where your knowledge and/or writing skills are needed. Indeed, you could well be offered job opportunities that are more in line with what you really want to do with your life.

☐ A published book will increase your chances of obtaining grants to continue developing your skills as a poet or fiction writer. Foundations and other organizations are more willing to support authors who have demonstrated that they can produce a significant work.

20:02 One Book, Two Ways

Once you have established your reputation as an expert on one subject, why not write another book on the same subject? Not only is it easier to write another book on the same subject, but you will also be able to use many of the same contacts to promote, market, and distribute your new book. Just as a publisher benefits from specializing in specific areas, so can a writer.

Here are a few examples of how other writers have drawn upon their previous books to create new books:

- Sheldon Gerstenfeld, a veterinarian, wrote one book on *Taking Care of Your Cat*. Then, using much of the same information and advice, he wrote another book on *Taking Care of Your Dog*. Both books used the same cover design, format, and style (thus saving the publisher time and money in designing and producing the books). Later, Gerstenfeld wrote still another book, *The Bird Care Book*, which incorporated much of the same information and made use of the same book design.

- Archie Satterfield and Eddie Bauer put together three related books for Addison-Wesley, all using the same format and design. The first book, *The Eddie Bauer Guide to Cross-Country Skiing*, was followed by two other books aimed at a more general audience, *The Eddie Bauer Guide to Family Camping* and *The Eddie Bauer Guide to Backpacking*.

- When Durk Pearson and Sandy Shaw wrote their book on *Life Extension*, they filled it with many complicated and technical articles, which made the book difficult for the average reader to follow. Nonetheless, the book sold more than a million copies. To make the information more accessible to the average person, they wrote a second book, *The Life Extension Companion*, which used less technical language to make the same points as the first book. Later they wrote a third book, *The Life Extension Weight Loss Program*, to reach an even greater audience.

- Recently, I took parts of five chapters from this book, rewrote them, and incorporated them into a new book, *High Impact Marketing on a Low Impact Budget*, which I co-authored with Dan McComas. Prima Publishing released the book in the fall of 1997.

- It's possible to write one book aimed, for instance, at doctors and another one aimed at patients. Both books could contain much of the same information; only the angle of approach would be different.

  For instance, in my previous editions of the Directory of Book Printers I included several sections giving publishers pointers on how to select a book printer and work with that printer to produce a high quality yet inexpensive book. At one point I considered taking that same information and adapting it for a report aimed at printers who wanted to develop more short-run business. The report, How to Sell Your Short-Run Production Services to Book Publishers, would have shown book printers how to adapt their advertising and actual capabilities to serve the short-run needs of book publishers.

20:03 Self-Publishing Successes

For those of you who are thinking of self-publishing your own book, here are a few examples of other writers who have done so successfully— and then sold their book to a major publisher in order to gain even wider distribution.

- After having triple bypass surgery at the age of 32, Joseph Piscatella was forced to change his eating habits. As a result, he and his wife developed 400 recipes for foods low in salt, sugar, and fat. In the spring of 1983, he self-published 5,000 copies of *Don't Eat Your Heart Out.* Within a month the entire edition had sold out. Later that fall Workman Publishing published the book, printing 30,000 copies in their first edition. Since that time, they've sold well over 940,000 copies of the book at the rate of about 6,000 copies per month.

- When Jim Everroad lost his job as a high school athletic coach, he decided to become a sportswriter. The first job he tackled was to write an article describing the exercises he had developed to tighten his pot belly. After selling the article to a newspaper, he expanded it into a full book (6,000 words plus several dozen photographs) and printed a first edition of 3,000 copies. That edition sold so quickly that he ordered another edition of 50,000 copies, which he sold primarily in his own home region of Indiana. Later the book was discovered by Price/Stern/Sloan who published a national edition of the book, which became a bestseller. The book has since sold over 2,000,000 copies.

- Richard Paul Evans self-published a little holiday story, *The Christmas Box*, and sold thousands of copies in the Salt Lake City area. When the major publishers became interested in the book, dozens participated in a two-day auction. Simon & Schuster came out the winner. They only had to pay Evans a $4.2 million advance (which included the rights to a prequel as well). He retained the rights to his softcover edition. The next year, both editions ended up on the bestseller lists.

- Spencer Johnson and Kenneth Blanchard originally self-published *The One Minute Manager* because they wanted to sell their book at a $15.00 cover price (a price few major publishers would have dared set for such a slim book). After they had sold more than 20,000 copies of the book in a very short time, seventeen publishers bid for the rights to republish the book. Since then, the book has sold millions of copies and been on the bestseller lists for both hardcovers and trade paperbacks. Plus, it spawned an entire line of other *One Minute* books.

- Turk Pipkin sold many copies of his self-published novel, *Fast Greens*, via reviews in golf magazines and word of mouth. A literary agent then contacted him and sold the movie rights for the book to Warner Bros. and reprint rights to Dial.

- Wess Roberts paid for and promoted four printings of his book, *Leadership Secrets of Attila the Hun.* After getting a strong endorsement for the book from H. Ross Perot, Roberts decided to approach New York publishers once again. As a result, Warner Books featured the book as their lead title for March, 1989, and the book went on to become a bestseller. Foreign rights were sold to publishers in England, Holland, Spain, Germany, Norway, Sweden, Mexico, and Brazil. Total advances ran into six figures. Plus Literary Guild bought book club rights, Nightingale-Conant bought audio rights, and *Success* magazine bought first serial rights.

- After twenty years in show business, Mike Martineau self-published *The Strokers*, a novel about the rise to stardom of a British rock musician. He started out by distributing the novel only to bookstores in the Virgin Islands. Tourists there bought out the first and second printings of the novel. Hallmark Press, a Miami publisher, then took over the publication of the book. Meanwhile, Martineau sold movie rights to Joseph E. Levine Presents for a $25,000 option against a final pickup price of $250,000. He also received $35,000 for writing the movie screenplay.

- Vicky Lansky sold 300,000 copies of her self-published parenting title, *Feed Me, I'm Yours*, and then sold the rights to Bantam, which went on to sell millions of that title and millions more of other books that Vicky wrote. That first book helped to establish Meadowbrook Press, now operated by her ex-husband, and The Book Peddler, Vicky's publishing firm where she republishes books when the big publishers let her books go out of print. Lately, Vicky is publishing many new titles, both those written by herself as well as those written by other authors.

- JoAnna Lund self-published the *Healthy Exchanges Cookbook* after going from 300 lbs. and a size 28 to 170 lbs. and a size 14 using the low-fat recipes collected in the book. After selling 150,000 copies, she sold reprint rights to Putnam for a six-figure advance. Several books later, JoAnna is now the cookbook queen of QVC, having sold more books via the home shopping network than any other author.

- With the help of his parents, 18-year-old Christopher Paolini self-published 10,000 copies of *Eragon*, the first book of his fantasy Inheritance trilogy in February 2002. Dressed in a medieval costume, he spent a year hawking the book at various festivals, schools, and bookstores, often selling 100 or more copies. A few months after the book appeared, the stepson of bestselling writer Carl Hiassen bought a copy while vacationing in Montana and told Hiassen that the book was "better than Harry Potter!" Hiassen took the book to his editor at Knopf. With the help of agent Simon Lipskar of Writer's House, Paolini sold rights to the entire trilogy to Knopf Books for Young Readers in a major deal worth half a million dollars. The books in the series have all gone on to become major bestsellers.

- While Tom Clancy did not self-publish his first book, *The Hunt for Red October*, it was published by a small publisher, Naval Institute Press. Since then, he's had many bestsellers. In the summer of 1997, Putnam paid $50 million for world English-language rights to two new titles plus another $25 million for a four-year book/multimedia deal with his Red Storm Entertainment. In addition, Berkeley paid around $22 million for twenty-four paperbacks tied into his ABC miniseries, *Tom Clancy's Net-Force*. According to *Forbes* magazine, Clancy was among the top thirty highest paid entertainers in 1996. At one point, he was in the bidding for becoming the owner of the Minnesota Vikings NFL football team.

- For a much longer list of books that were originally self-published and went on to become bestsellers, see the Self-Publishing Hall of Fame at http://www.selfpublishinghalloffame.com. Or buy my special ebook, *John Kremer's Self-Publishing Hall of Fame*, for only $20.00.

20:04 Syndicating Your Expertise

Having a book published establishes your credentials both as a writer and as an expert. You can use both these credentials to syndicate your knowledge via radio stations and newspapers or to obtain a position as a commentator on a radio or TV show. Below are a few examples of what other authors have done.

Syndicated newspaper columns

- Mary Ellen Pinkham, author of a number of books on helpful hints, wrote a syndicated column that was carried by over 125 newspapers with a combined circulation of well over ten million readers.

- Tom Peters, co-author of *In Search of Excellence*, wrote a weekly syndicated newspaper column on business management for the Tribune Company. At one point, he also wrote a regular magazine column.

- John Javna, publisher of *50 Simple Ways to Save the Earth*, wrote a syndicated column that featured practical ecological tips.

- Gene and Adele Malott, self-publishers of *Get Up and Go: A Guide for the Mature Traveler*, wrote the Mature Traveler column, which was syndicated by the New York Times Syndicate.

- Jacqueline Mitchard, author of *The Deep End of the Ocean*, wrote a column on family issues for her local paper. When her novel made the bestseller lists, Mitchard sold the column for syndication by Tribune Media Services.

For more information on syndicating a column, see John Kremer's special report on *Syndicating a Column*.

Television shows

- Besides the newspaper column, Tom Peters also appeared weekly on the cable TV show, *Business Times*.

- After publishing her books on helpful hints, Mary Ellen Pinkham joined *Good Morning America* for two years as a commentator on helpful hints.

- Kurma Dasa, author of *Great Vegetarian Dishes*, used the book as the basis for twenty-six half-hour cooking shows. ITV Productions produced the shows which were broadcast on eighty-five PBS stations.

- Lucille Treganowan, author of *Lucille's Car Care*, appeared as herself on an episode of Tim Allen's *Home Improvement*.

- The Romance Classics cable TV channel hired romance novelists Barbara Bradford, Mary Higgins Clark, Olivia Goldsmith, and Nora Roberts to act as hostesses.

- Robyn Spizman hosts a weekly gift segment for her local NBC affiliate and also serves as the gift expert for *The Today Show* on NBC.

- Deepak Chopra, Wayne Dyer, and other authors have done one-hour specials for PBS that have not only resulted in lots of book sales but are also used by local PBS affiliates during their fund-raising weeks.

- Other authors who have had nationally syndicated TV shows include Dr. Phil McGraw, Suzy Orman, Rachel Ray, and Chef Harry Schwartz.

- Many TV hosts, in turn, have created bestselling books. For example, almost all of the chefs featured on the Food Channel have written at least one bestselling cookbook. In most cases, their shows predated their cookbooks and were the reasons their books were published.

Radio shows

- Tony Hyman, author of the *Handbook of American Cigar Boxes*, hosted a weekly radio show that was syndicated to more than 100 stations.

- Beverly Nye, self-publisher of *A Family Raised on Sunshine*, syndicated her own series of shows on homemaking tips to radio stations across the country. Not only did the radio stations pay her royalties for airing the show, but she was able to use the show to plug her own books.

- Arthur Frommer hosted a weekly *On Travel* radio show for the United Stations Talk Radio network.

- Many authors are now creating and hosting their own radio shows via the Internet.

Magazine columnist

- Herschell Gordon Lewis, author of *Direct Mail Copy That Sells*, writes a monthly column for *Direct* magazine. At the end of each column, the magazine prints a short biography which plugs his books and copywriting services.

- Steven Covey, author of *The Seven Habits of Highly Effective People*, wrote a regular column on leadership for *Incentive* magazine.

- Donna Erickson, author of *Prime Time Together ... with Kids*, was a contributing editor of *Parent's Magazine* and author of its monthly "Do It Together" section. In addition, she wrote a weekly column for King Features and hosted *Donna's Day*, an award-winning PBS series. In addition, she appeared regularly on major national TV shows such as *The Today Show* and *Oprah*.

- Diane Harris, author of *It Takes Money, Honey*, is a contributing editor and Money Matters columnist for *Parenting* magazine.

- Chris Epting, author of *James Dean Died Here: The Location of America's Pop Culture Landmarks*, is the travel editor for the new *Chicken Soup for the Soul* magazine where he specializes in telling it-happened-here stories. As the author of another book on baseball landmarks, he also podcasts for Major League Baseball's radio web site.

- *O*, the Oprah magazine, features the following authors as columnists and contributing editors: Sharon Salzberg, Julie Morgenstern, Suze Orman, Dr. Phil McGraw, Martha Beck, and Dr. David Katz.

- *Redbook* featured authors John Gray, Karen Karbo, and Laura Berman Fortgang as contributing editors and columnists.

Newsletter columnist

- For two years I wrote a regular column about book marketing for a publishing association newsletter. Although I received no compensation for this column, I did receive a short plug for my books, which helped to sell many copies.

20:05 Publish a Newsletter

Once you've established your expertise, you might consider publishing a newsletter, especially if your expertise is in a rapidly changing field. Newsletters can command high prices and, because they are shorter than books, can be easier to produce. The major drawback to newsletters is that they do require a long-haul commitment to meeting deadlines (whether weekly, monthly, bimonthly, or quarterly). Because of the high startup costs of getting subscribers, it's not worth publishing a newsletter if you don't intend to continue publishing it for at least two years. Of course, with email and the Internet, many of those cost factors have changed.

- Howard Ruff's *Financial Success Report* at one time had 115,000 subscribers paying $109.00 per year (that works out to more than $12 million per year in subscription income).

- For several years Robert Ringer, author of *Winning Through Intimidation* and *Looking Out for #1*, published a newsletter, *The Tortoise Report*, which was an expression of his personal philosophy. Two hundred thousand subscribers paid $59.00 per year for the monthly newsletter.

- Dr. Andrew Weil, author of *Spontaneous Healing*, works with Thorne Communications to publish a monthly newsletter for consumers called *Dr. Andrew Weil's Self Healing*. With more than 145,000 subscribers at $19.95 per year, the newsletter generates $3 million each year. Plus the company rents out its subscriber list for additional income.

- Jerry Baker, America's Master Gardener, hosts a syndicated radio show as well as edits a monthly newsletter with a circulation of 155,000.

- I started up the *Book Marketing Update* newsletter as a way of keeping authors and publishers up-to-date on industry changes in between editions of this book. Several years ago I sold the publishing rights to this twice-monthly newsletter to Bradley Communications, but I still write a column for every issue. To subscribe, just call 641-472-6130.

- Deepak Chopra, author of a dozen *New York Times* bestsellers, worked with his publisher, Crown Publishers, to produce a monthly newsletter, *Deepak Chopra's Infinite Possibilities for Body, Mind & Soul*. Besides extending the information contained in his books, the newsletter was also used to promote his books, speaking engagements, and the Chopra Center for Well Being.

If you decide to publish a newsletter, join the **Newsletter & Electronic Publishers Association**, 1501 Wilson Boulevard #509, Arlington, VA 22209; 703-527-2333; 800-356-9302; Fax: 703-841-0629. Email: nepa@ newsletters.org. Web: http://www.newsletters.org.

20:06 Speak Out Your Knowledge

As a book author, you will often be asked to speak before groups. At some point you need decide if you will charge for your speaking services or continue to offer them gratis. To be honest, the lecture circuit could provide you with more income than your writing. Mary Cunningham, author of *Powerplay*, commands $10,000 per speaking engagement. In 1994, Anthony Robbins got $65,000 for a one-hour speech; Alvin Toffler, $45,000; Faith Popcorn, $30,000; Ken Dychtwald, $25,000; William Buckley, $20,000; Jane Bryant Quinn, $12,500; Dennis Waitley, $10,000; and Dr. Joyce Brothers, $7,500. Those prices have only increased in the intervening years.

After Harvey Mackay's first book, he had enough speaking offers to make $3 million per year if he had wanted to devote full-time to speaking. Faith Popcorn, at $30,000 per talk, spoke at forty events a year for a speaking income over a million dollars. Jim Fixx, author of *The Complete Book of Running*, made $500,000 from book sales and another $500,000 from the speaking engagements he was able to book after becoming famous. If you are serious about a career as a speaker, explore the following resources:

☐ **National Speakers Association**, 1500 S. Priest Drive, Tempe, AZ 85281; 602-968-2552; Fax: 602-968-0911. Web: http://www.nsaspeaker. org. This association, which publishes the *Professional Speakers* magazine, is the best resource for authors who want to make money speaking. Their semiannual conferences are incredible resources for networking.

☐ **Toastmasters International**, P.O. Box 9052, Mission Viejo, CA 92690; 949-858-8255; Fax: 949-858-1207. Web: http://www.toastmasters.org.

Contact them to get the address for a local group where you can build your speaking skills before a supportive group.

☐ **Sharing Ideas**, 18825 Hicrest Road, P.O. Box 398, Glendora, CA 91740; 626-335-8069; Fax: 626-335-6127. Web: http://www.walters-intl.com. They also operate Walters International Speakers Bureau.

After checking out the web sites listed above, also look over the following web sites. Then follow their links to even more resources.

☐ **Speakers On-line**, 130 Lubrano Drive #110, Annapolis, MD 21401; 410-897-1970; Fax: 410-897-1971. Web: http://www.speakers.com. A great place to be listed if you want to establish yourself as a speaker.

☐ **Speakers Platform Bureau**, 475 Hampshire Street #4, San Francisco, CA 94110; 415-861-1700; 877-717-5327. Email: speaker@speaking. com. Web: http://www.speaking.com. Showcases the best speakers, trainers, and consultants. Must be a member of the bureau to be listed.

☐ **Experts.com**, 2800 W. March Lane #340, Stockton, CA 95219; 209-477-5100; 866-239-7378; Fax: 209-477-7611. Email: info@experts.com. Web: http://www.experts.com. Be listed here if you want to establish yourself as an expert. Search here for experts.

☐ **Book Organizations of Colorado**. Web: http://www.coloradobook.org. They list more than 100 local authors who can speak at libraries, classrooms, or bookstores. The listing is free. They also sponsor a chat group to discuss writing, getting an agent, etc.

According to a survey of corporations and associations conducted by Walters Speakers Bureau, here are the most popular ways that these organizations go about selecting speakers:

80.2%	word-of-mouth and references
56.1%	seeing speakers at other conventions
45.6%	through speakers bureaus and agents
29.1%	speakers brochures and marketing material
24.1%	universities
23.6%	current celebrity personalities
14.3%	speakers directories and advertising
6.3%	convention bureaus

According to an earlier survey conducted by Walters, here are the ten most popular topics requested by speakers bureaus and meeting planners: motivation, change, sales, team building, future trends, humor, leadership, customer service, celebrities, and entertainers. On the following pages I list a number of ways you can earn money as a speaker.

Begin speaking

Start speaking wherever you can book a talk, even for free. The possibilities for speaking are almost endless. Not only can you speak at local club meetings, but you can also speak at sales meetings, seminars, conventions, association meetings, company training programs, cruise ships, and any-where else that people go to find useful information. Almost every company and association has need of speakers at least once a year (for their annual conference or meeting) and many require speakers more often than that (for monthly sales meetings, training programs, and other educational seminars).

Once you've had experience, you'll start to develop a repertoire of talks that will get people talking about you. As noted in the Walters survey above, word-of-mouth is the most important factor in building your career as a speaker. Alvin Donovan, author of *Make More Money Now*, almost canceled a small speaking engagement because he wasn't being paid much. Fortunately for him, he did it anyway. The top executive from Excel was in attendance, like what he heard, and hired Donovan to do a national seminar tour for their sales reps (at $30 a head, with 2,000 to 5,000 at each stop).

When you speak before a group, try this bookselling technique: Put your book into the hands of the audience. Raleigh Pinskey, author of *101 Ways to Promote Yourself*, suggests placing a copy of your book directly in front of each member of the audience. When Dan Poynter tried this, book sales shot up from 10% of the audience to 50%. While he speaks, he draws attention to something in the books so listeners have a reason to handle the books.

Lecture agents

Engage a lecture agent to represent you. Like other agents, they work on a commission (usually anywhere from 15% to 30%).

Speakers bureaus

Register with speakers bureaus who work on a nonexclusive basis. Speakers bureaus assist organizations looking for speakers to address their meetings and conventions. When they book a speaking engagement for you, the speakers bureau will charge a percentage of your speaking fee (generally somewhere between 10% and 30%).

Libraries

Speak at libraries. Some libraries have funds to pay well-known authors to come and speak to the community. In other cases, the Friends of the Library will invite authors to speak to the group. Finally, some state associations publish directories of authors who are available to speak at libraries. For example, the Southern Connecticut Library Council publishes an annual directory of state authors willing to speak at libraries. For an application (if you live in the state), contact the **Southern Connecticut Library Council**, 2405 Whitney Avenue #3, Hamden, CT 065180-3235; 203-248-6370. You might find a similar directory for your state, either in print or online.

Bookstores

Some authors charge for giving workshops or lectures at bookstores, es-pecially new age stores. Here, for example, are the fees charged by some authors (as reported by *New Age Retailer*):

Marc Allen	$500 for an afternoon workshop
Brother Bob	$100 to $125 for a lecture
	$150 minimum for workshops (60% of fees)
Lee Ann Dzelzkalns	$150 per hour for lectures
	65% of collected fees for workshops
Marie-Clair Wilson	$500 for workshops up to four hours
	$200 for one-hour lectures, plus expenses
J. Donald Walters	$200 for one to two-hour lectures

Seminars

Organize your own seminars. Once you've had some experience as a speaker, you might consider setting up seminars, such as the "Implementing In Search of Excellence" seminars (informally known as skunkcamps) put on by Tom Peters. The skunkcamps are only one of five services offered by the Tom Peters Group; the other four are consulting, research, publishing, and audio/video products.

Peter Lowe International sponsors success seminars around the country. In 1997, more than 200,000 people paid from $49 to $225 to hear authors such as Zig Ziglar and Dan Kennedy speak about success.

When Charles Givens first started offering his money strategy seminars, he spent $15,000 on advertising and had seventeen takers. Next, he decided to publicize his talks via TV talk shows. During his first interview, he announced that he would be lecturing the next day on investing, buying real estate, reducing taxes, and getting rich. Five hundred people showed up the next day. Since that time, Givens has built a fortune worth more than $200 million through his seminars, TV infomercials, and books. He now owns a recording studio, radio stations, financial services, a travel agency, and a half dozen real estate holding and management companies.

In the spring of 2006, I offered a seminar on marketing novels several days before BookExpo America. I charged $300 for a four-hour seminar. With less than six weeks promotion, I drew 50 participants. A nice income, for sure.

Workshops

Offer workshops. The main distinction between a workshop and seminar is that a workshop is more hands on, with more give and take, more examples, more exercises. For instance, Holly Ebel, the author of *Christmas in the Air*, offered a Christmas workshop every fall.

I regularly offer Book Marketing Blast-Off Seminars in various parts of the country. These three-day hands-on workshops cover everything from making a marketing plan to setting up distribution, opening new markets, getting publicity, selling rights, working with bookstores to sell more books, and Internet marketing. I make more from my Book Marketing Blast-Off seminars than I do from any other speaking engagements. All sign-ups and promotions are done via my email newsletter and web site. The cost of putting on the seminars now only includes hotel room rental, my sleeping room, and my air fare. At $495.00 per attendee, the net income is often $10,000 or more.

Conventions

Organize your own conventions. In the late 1970s Howard Ruff organized a number of Ruff Times National Conventions featuring well-known political and business figures giving advice on how to survive in the coming hard times. In 1979, the cost for the three-day convention was $95.00. Many conventions, of course, charge much more than that.

Cruise ships

Some authors get free trips and extra income by speaking on board cruise ships. For example, Parachute Properties, the packager of the *Goosebumps* series, hosted a Sail with the Stars cruise. Families cruised with R.L. Stine, author of the *Goosebumps* books. Not only did he sign books, but he also hosted photograph sessions, mystery solving adventures, story writing, and make-up sessions.

Churches

Many bestselling authors of the past few years have built their reputation and book sales by speaking at Unity churches around the country. James Redfield, John Gray, Barbara De Angelis, Neale Donald Walsch, Deepak Chopra, Jack Canfield, Mark Victor Hansen, and many others have sold many books while speaking at Unity churches and other religious organizations. Similarly, many Christian authors have built up their audiences by speaking at Protestant and Catholic churches around the country.

How do you set up such talks? For Unity churches, you can contact the program director at each church. To locate addresses for these churches, some authors have used the phone book directories available on the web. Or, you can use computer phone book programs. Note that there are 600 Unity churches worldwide.

Learning centers

Another great source of speaking engagements in most big cities are the learning centers where authors are regularly invited to offer ongoing classes or special one-time workshops. These centers generally promote their classes by mailing out thousands, sometimes millions, of catalogs. Most of these centers pay speakers a portion of the income generated by the classes. In addition, some also allow speakers to sell related books at the end of a class session (if they don't allow back of the room sales, see if they will include your book as a required class material). Below is a list of some of these learning centers along with the cities where they are located.

- **Colorado Free University** — Denver, CO; Colorado Springs, CO.
- **Discover U** — Seattle, WA.

- **Knowledge Shop** — Orlando, FL.
- **Learning Annex** — San Francisco, CA; Los Angeles, CA; San Diego, CA; Chicago, IL; Vancouver, BC; Toronto, ON; New York, NY. These centers pay 20% of the gate, but allow you to sell product in the back of the room.

Check out other centers such as the Palm Beach Center for Living, C.G. Jung Educational Center, Science of Mind centers, and Unity Churches around the country. You can locate many of these by doing a Google search.

For a *Learning Centers* database featuring 125 such centers for only $15.00, order from BookMarket.com.

Overseas

Speak overseas. Not only can you write off a vacation overseas, but you can actually be paid a decent speaking fee. Alvin Donovan and Meg Northcroft presented more than 500 of their Make More Money Now programs overseas. They suggest that if you want to start speaking in Europe, contact Management Center Europe, a subsidiary of the American Management Association located in Brussels, Belgium (call AMA at 800-262-6969 for current contact information). Once you've done a program for MCE, many other European groups will be interested in having you speak for them. Note: MCE specializes in business talks.

Become a spokesperson

If you think you'd make a good spokesperson for a product related to your book, you should begin to contact the companies that produce that product. Contact their brand manager, marketing manager, or advertising agency to see if they're looking for a spokesperson. To become a spokesperson, you should be personable, videogenic, and willing to travel.

Tom Ninkovich of Reunion Research was paid $80 per hour by Dow Brands to act as a spokesperson for their Handiwrap food wrap. Golan Harris, their advertising agency, hired him for the job. Besides acting as a spokesperson for Dow, Tom also sold time capsules, cookbooks, T-shirts, and ad specialties from other companies to planners of family reunions, genealogy fairs, and military reunions. In addition, he taught seminars on how to plan reunions.

Sherri Athay, author of *Present Perfect: Unforgettable Gifts for Every Occasion*, made $35,000 for six hours of work as a corporate spokesperson for a major national gift certificate distributor. The typical daily rate, though, is more like $3,000 (less when you are just beginning).

Chris Epting, author of *James Dean Died Here: The Location of America's Pop Culture Landmarks*, has been the official spokesperson for Hampton Inns' Hidden Landmarks program for more than three years. The chain approached him after one of their marketing people saw his book in a store.

As part of the arrangement, Hampton regularly sends Epting on media tours where he goes to landmarks and does press interviews, promotes Hampton Inns, and encourages people to visit the Hidden Landmarks web site (http://www.hamptonlandmarks.com). Within the first fifteen days of building this active web site, Hampton Inns generated almost $42,000 in additional hotel bookings (every page features a link to find an Inn near the landmark).

Other authors who have acted as spokespeople include Jack Canfield and Mark Victor Hansen for Campbell Soup, Dr. Ruth Westheimer for the Wallcoverings Association of America (who was quoted in one ad as saying, "Don't be afraid to do it in the kitchen."), Deborah Madison for The Artichoke Board, and Lucille Treganowan for Jiffy Lube.

If you'd like to become a spokesperson, check out the following services which specialize in hooking up celebrities with companies looking for spokespeople and endorsers. These services have worked with authors as well as actors, sports stars, and other celebrities. Send them a photo, your bio, and something about your book along with a cover letter outlining the tie-in possibilities for you and your book.

☐ **Celebrity Endorsement Network**, Noreen Jenney, President, 23679 Calabasas Road #728, Calabasas, CA 91302; 818-225-7090; Fax: 818-225-5343. Web: http://www.celebrityendorsements.com. This company has worked with Revlon, Denny's, and Anhauser-Busch.

☐ **FoodSpeak**, Melanie Young, M. Young Communications, 7 West 18th Street, 3rd Floor, New York, NY 10011; 212-620-7027; Fax: 212-645-3654. Email: melanieyoung@myoungcom.com. Web: http://www.myoungcom.com/foodspeak.htm. This company provides training, counseling, and placement for culinary spokespeople.

☐ **Spokespersons Plus Network**, Deborah Dunham, President, 3600 Cerillos Road #719-A, Santa Fe, NM 87507; 505-471-2760. Email: deb@spokespersons.com. Web: http://www.spokespersons.com. Books spokespeople for media events and other needs.

20:07 Making Money as a Teacher

One thing I've learned in all the years I've taught classes is that the teacher always learns more than the student. This, perhaps, is the strongest argument that can be made for teaching at least a few classes a year. You will always come away from classes with renewed enthusiasm for your subject, renewed interest and, if my experience is any indication, a mind bursting with ideas for new books. So get out there and enjoy.

While speaking before large groups might pay better, teaching classes can often be more fulfilling. Teaching is an especially good way to gain experience talking before groups, and it is possible to arrange classes so you are well compensated for your time. Below are a number of possibilities.

Continuing education classes

Teach continuing education classes for adults. Most high schools and colleges offer evening and weekend courses for adults who are not able to attend classes during the day. These continuing education courses are usually noncredit courses, so even if you don't have a teaching certificate, you can still teach these classes. Indeed, as an author, you are probably more experienced and qualified than many other people teaching such courses.

Since most schools charge students a fee (anywhere from $20 to $50) for a three to ten hour course, the teacher usually gets paid a portion of the course fees collected (anywhere from 30% to 60%). Hence, if 30 students were to take one of your courses, you could well make $500 or more for a five hour course. Plus, you can assign your book as the textbook for the course and gross another $300 or more. Since you will undoubtedly be teaching a course related to your book, it is certainly reasonable to draw upon your book as the course text.

Another benefit of teaching continuing education classes is that your course and book will be publicized before many potential customers. For instance, when a large university system offers your course in its continuing education program, it sends out catalogs announcing its courses to an entire metropolitan community. Many of the seminars that Gordon Burgett teaches every year are offered through colleges and continuing education programs.

College campuses

You could teach courses or speak on college campuses. Many colleges bring in authors to speak at classes, teach complete courses, speak at extracurricular events, or speak at student-sponsored events. In addition, some corporations will pay authors to speak on college campuses.

☐ Brian Krueger, author of *College Grad Job Hunter*, was asked by a corporation to do a tour of twenty-one campuses in the Midwest. They didn't blink when he asked for $1,500 per campus plus expenses.

☐ James Malinchak, author of *From College to the Real World*, works with Admire Entertainment, a collegiate booking agency, to set up talks at colleges around the country. His fee? $2,500 per engagement. In addition, he sells corporations quantities of his book which he then gives out on behalf of the corporations to students who attend his talks. James now teaches a course on getting paid to speak on college campuses. For more information on his programs, call 888-793-1196 or see http://www.collegespeakingsuccess.com. Tell him I sent you.

Schools

Some children's book authors have, according to *U.S. News & World Report,* "made a career of author visits" to schools. For instance, months after self-publishing *Buck Wilder's Small Fry Fishing Guide*, Tim Smith had established a second career as a motivational speaker to school groups.

Most schools have budgets to support authors who come speak to classes (as authors in residence), while others make use of PTA funds. In at least some cases, the school librarian books the authors. One librarian scouts out the best authors by sizing them up during the American Library Association annual conferences. Note: most children's book publishers have someone who is responsible for helping authors to book appearances in schools.

Fees for speaking at schools range from $100 for a new author to $2,000 for established authors, with an average fee of $1,200. Not only can you make money speaking, but you can sell books. In some instances, authors have sold 1,000 to 1,500 books during a three-day school visit. Publishers often offer schools a 40% discounts on books bought for resale to students.

In a survey of twenty authors conducted by Raab Associates, the authors reported making an average of twenty-three school visits per year. Some made as few as four visits, while others made as many as a hundred. In an average visit, the author appeared before three classes.

Here are a few tips on how to do a school appearance: Think like the children. Use visuals. Bring things related to your book that the children can touch. Move around during your presentation. Involve the quiet students as well as the talkative ones. Share personal stories, especially childhood memories. When appearing at schools, be open to giving a talk to teachers during lunch or to parents in the evening.

Note: **Smart Writers** (http://www.smartwriters.com) features children's book writers and illustrators who are available for school visits, book signings, and other public appearances.

Local stores

Teach classes at local stores. For instance, if you write cooking, craft, or how-to books, you could arrange to teach classes at local gourmet shops, other retail stores, community centers, or shopping centers. Jack Mandel, author of the *Arts, Fine Crafts, and Collectibles Directory*, regularly teaches business workshops at Bloomingdale's and Macy's department stores. Not only do they pay him to put on the workshop, but they also pay for the books used in the workshop.

Correspondence courses

You could teach correspondence courses like the ones offered by the Writer's Digest School and the Children's Literature Institute. This possibility is a much greater and more practical opportunity now that the Internet makes distance learning easy.

Your own school

You could open your own school. For example, if you write cookbooks, why not open a cooking school. Not only could the school bring in additional money, but it could also give you a place to develop new recipes, test new cookbook ideas, and experiment with cooking techniques.

20:08 Making Money as a Consultant

If you are not comfortable speaking before large groups, you can still put your expertise to work as a consultant. No matter what your subject area, somewhere at sometime someone is going to need your expertise—and be willing to pay well for your services. Here are two resources

☐ **Consulting Magazine**, 3 Park Avenue, 30th Floor, New York, NY 10016; 212-563-6054; Fax: 212-563-6138. Email: editors@consulting-mag.com. Web: *http://www.consultingmag.com*.

☐ **Consultants News**, Kennedy Information, 1 Phoenix Mill Lane, 3rd Floor, Peterborough, NH 03458; 603-924-0900; 800-531-0007; Fax: 603-924-4460. Web: *http://consultants_news.consultingcentral.com*. For management consultants.

Here are a few ways other writers and publishers have put their expertise to work as consultants:

Become a consultant.

• Sheilah Kaufman, author of eleven cookbooks including *Sheilah's Fearless Fussless Cooking*, does consulting for gourmet, gift, and houseware companies. She also travels around the country teaching cooking classes.

• Besides producing about 50 seminars every year on construction estimating and project management, the R. S. Means Company also publishes software and offers consulting services (where they send experts to work with construction companies on site).

• Sheila Lukins, author of *The Silver Palate* cookbook, was asked by United Airlines to redo its economy-class menus. With her input, passengers enjoyed Red and Yellow Bell Pepper Penne Pasta and Shaker Cranberry Basket. In introducing the new menus, United also heavily promoted Lukins's cookbooks, including her *USA Cookbook*. Too bad, the airlines don't offer such great meals anymore.

Offer consulting services via the mail.

Herschell Gordon Lewis, author of a number of books on direct marketing, has his own business called Communicomp, which offers direct mail copywriting for a wide variety of companies and organizations including the U.N. Children's Fund, Grolier Enterprises, Heritage House, and American Bankers Insurance Company. All his business is conducted through the mail and by phone.

Offer consulting services via the phone.

As the author of a number of books on book marketing as well as the editor and publisher of the *Book Marketing Update* newsletter, I offer consulting advice via the phone to anyone having questions about book publishing and marketing. When I first started consulting, my fee was only $25 per hour. Now it's $500 per hour—and I'm worth every dollar of it.

While I do little promotion for this service and don't actively solicit consulting work (except for the web page at http://www.johnkremer.com), I still end up consulting about 5 to 10 hours per month for a significant income from consulting. To set up an appointment with John, call Open Horizons at 641-472-6130.

I charge people $500 per hour for consulting. I'm worth it. But, you know, many times the people who pay me that kind of money don't follow my advice. Such stupid people. Why pay me that much and then not listen to my advice? I only give the best advice in the world on book marketing. If you're going to pay me, pay attention to me.

Someone on my last Book Marketing Blast-Off Seminar suggested that I start charging people $1,000 per hour for consulting. And then, only if they actually do what I say, I can refund them $500 per hour. That made sense to me. I think I might just start doing that. The refund will only be given if I judged that they followed my advice. Watch for an announcement if I do it.

Franchise your consulting services.

Carole Jackson, author of the multi-million copy bestseller, *Color Me Beautiful*, franchised Color Me Beautiful consultants all over the country. When Acropolis Books came out with a new book, *Always in Style with Color Me Beautiful* by Doris Pooser, their 30-city publicity campaign was fully supported by Color Me Beautiful consultants in each of those cities.

Establish an institute.

John Naisbitt, author of the bestselling book *Megatrends*, organized an institute to study trends. The institute offered consulting services, a newsletter, and seminars, plus a number of annual reports.

One of Tom Peter's five businesses, as noted previously, is a research institute. This institute provides research data and other information to support the other businesses in his group.

Establish a center.

To help promote his exposé of the genetically modified crops industry, *Seeds of Deception*, Jeffrey Smith founded the Institute for Responsible Technology in 2003. The Institute has since taken on a life of its own as it works to stall the introduction of additional genetically engineered crops into the American food chain. The Institute publishes a free monthly ezine called *Spilling the Beans*.

Jed Diamond, author of *Inside Out: Becoming My Own Man*, and Carlin Diamond, author of *Love It, Don't Label It*, have organized the Center for Prospering Relationships to promote the principles and practices they believe in. Both books were published by their own press, Fifth Wave Press.

Lee and Marlene Canter, who started off by self-publishing their first book *Assertive Discipline: A Take Charge Approach for Today's Educator*, have since trained more than a million educators in their Assertive Discipline program. Their company, Canter & Associates, not only publish books and teacher planning aids, but also trains teachers in ongoing programs. It is the largest teacher education organization in the country.

Deepak Chopra, bestselling author of many books on Ayurveda and Eastern thought, created the Chopra Center Spa at La Costa Resort in Carlsbad, California. That center is now open year around to provide rest, healing, wellness, and renewal to many people. He also offers many workshops on body, mind, and spirit at the center.

Form an association

Chase Revel formed the American Entrepreneur's Association to promote his line of business startup manuals. Through the association's *Entrepreneur* magazine, books, reports, and other services, it actually provides much support for business newcomers.

20:09 Become a Legal Expert Witness

A number of authors have found a lucrative sideline income from appearing as expert witnesses for various legal questions. As a legal expert, you may be called upon to investigate cases, testify at trials, give depositions, counsel attorneys, or provide other advice either by mail or over the phone. The standard fee for such work is $100 or more an hour. If you have to go out of town to do on-site investigations or testify at a trial, the standard fee is anywhere from $500 to $1,500 per day, plus expenses.

How do you become an expert witness? First, of course, you need to be an expert. While writing a book on a particular subject will authenticate your expertise, you should also have a lot of experience in that subject because you will have to stand up to cross examinations in court. Being an expert witness can be hard work since you must do your homework for each case, so if you are not enthusiastic about studying or learning more about your subject, you should not get into this field.

If you do decide to become a legal expert, visit your local law library (at the county courthouse or local law school) and check out the directories of legal experts. Review these directories to see if your area or areas of expertise are listed. If so, write to those directories and request an application to be listed. You'll also find many expert witness directories online by Googling *expert witness directory*.

Dan Poynter, author of *The Parachuting Manual* and *Parachuting, The Skydiver's Handbook*, does expert witness work. Besides being the author of eight books on the subject, Dan also spent seven years as a skydiving instructor and is still an active member of several parachuting associations.

Dan has written a book on how to be an expert witness, *The Expert Witness Handbook*. For details, contact **Para Publishing**, P.O. Box 8206, Santa Barbara, CA 93118; 805-968-7277; Fax: 805-968-1379. Web: http://www.para publishing.com.

Dick Murdock, a former railroad engineer and author of several books about the old days of railroading in northern California, also does legal expert work for railroads. As a side benefit to his legal expert work, Dick sold 1,000 copies of one of his railroading books to a law firm which specialized in railroad cases (and for whom Dick had often done consulting).

Over the years I've been called upon to do expert witness work for several publishing cases. One involved a sales agent who began publishing competitively against the original self-publisher. Another involved two co-authors, one of whom felt that the other was stealing all their consulting and speaking engagements. I've never had to go to court, but I have responded to depositions in writing. My responses have resulted in my clients winning their cases.

20:10 Open a Bookstore

While a number of authors have opened bookstores to sell only their books, others have open bookstores that reflect their thought and life.

- Melody Beattie, author of *Co-Dependent No More*, opened her own bookstore, A Different Dimension, in Malibu, California. She hand-picked the titles in the store, which reflected "almost the story of my life," from addiction to healing, from holy books to enlightenment.

- Al Fahden, author of *Innovation on Demand*, opened the Readundant Bookstore in downtown Minneapolis, Minnesota, to showcase his management consultancy business focused on creativity. In his bookstore, his book was shelved under business, sports, philosophy, religion, music, math, even fiction ("There's some lies in the book," he explained). The store's in-house bestseller list featured his book in all ten spots.

- Wade Cook, author of *The Wall Street Money Machine* and other business bestsellers, operated Get Ahead Bookstores in Seattle and Tacoma, Washington, as a subsidiary of his Wade Cook Financial Corporation. His corporation also offered seminars, workshops, home study courses, audio and video tapes, software, and other services (including a travel agency, incorporation office, and Wealth Information Network). He certainly did not get bored.

- Larry McMurtry, author of *Lonesome Dove* and other bestselling novels, opened a used bookstore in his home town of Archer City, Texas. The Booked Up bookstore now features more than 300,000 used books in four buildings. A national legend and tourist attraction, it's the largest business in Archer City.

20:11 Fringe Benefits

One of the fringe benefits of being a writer is that you are often sent free products to review. I know of a number of cookbook writers, for instance, who have received dozens of blenders or microwaves to test while they were preparing cookbooks featuring those machines.

When writing his book on word processing, Dan Poynter received a free Xerox word processor to review. Similarly, when Peter McWilliams was producing all his books on computers and word processing, he would receive a new machine to review almost every month. He had machines sitting in his hallways, kitchen, even his bathroom.

While preparing my books on publishing, I've received a good number of complimentary review copies of books on publishing and marketing. I still do. I feature them all in the Bibliography for this book. That book list is located at http://www.bookmarket.com/1001bib.html.

When you are preparing a new book, don't overlook the possibility of receiving complimentary review copies of materials that you require in your research. It never hurts to ask for such review copies. Remember, if you feature anything in your book, you will be giving it publicity that no amount of advertising could possibly buy.

These fringe benefits may not amount to much, but they do help you to cut down your upfront costs in producing a book. So don't be shy about making an honest request for review material needed for your book.

Here's a short tale of another added benefit of authorship. Richard Pinsker made a U-turn while driving to a seminar in Chicago, Illinois. When he was pulled over by police, the lady cop asked to see his license. When Pinsker produced his California license, the cop ask for another ID, one with a photo. Well, Pinsker had no other ID, but he did have copies of his book, *Hiring Winners*. So he produced one of those instead, complete with a photo of him on the jacket. On seeing the photo, the cop asked, "Is that really you?" Pinsker admitted it was. Well, the cop grinned, "Hey, I can't give a published author a ticket."

On a lecture trip, I realized I'd forgotten my driver's license. Nowadays, you need one to get on the airplane, but back then it wasn't an absolute requirement. So, when the lady at the airport counter asked for my ID, I pulled out a copy of my book. Well, in this case, it didn't work. But it was certainly worth the try.

20:12 A Few Unusual Spinoffs

Don't limit your vision. Anything can be related to your book if you take the time to make the connections that are most important to you (as an author, as a reader, or as a publisher). Take time to consider why you wrote or published your book. Then look to see if there are any other products, services, or ways of marketing that will help you to bring your message, idea, cause, entertainment, or whatever to the attention of more people. Finally, decide whether you want to spend your time marketing this new product or service, licensing it to another company, and/or writing a new book.

- Jim Everroad, author of the two million copy bestseller, *How to Flatten Your Stomach*, endorsed the Belly Burner, an exercise device. Commercials for this product appeared on TV all over the country. A copy of his book was enclosed as a bonus with every order for the Belly Burner.

- Chef Paul Prudhomme, author of *Louisiana Kitchen*, published a catalog featuring cast-iron skillets and other cookware necessary for preparing Cajun foods, plus his own brand of herbs and seasonings, Cajun Magic Seasonings, and several Cajun delicacies (Tasso Ham and Andouille sausage, both of which are prepared in his manufacturing plant in Melville, Louisiana). He distributed these catalogs through his three Louisiana Kitchen restaurants in New Orleans, New York, and San Francisco, as well as to people who had written in asking for more information. He has advertised the catalog in *The New Yorker* and *Cook's Magazine* as well as on the Owen Spann syndicated radio show, via postcard decks, and now via the Internet (http://www.chefpaul.com). Since then, he's been featured in a TV commercial for a Crest toothpaste and still does many motivational speeches every year.

- Gourmet cook Kathleen Fish, self-publisher of *San Francisco's Cooking Secrets* and other cookbooks, worked with restaurateur Suzette Cognetti to design and package original dips and spreads. With an initial budget of $40,000, they developed bottled oils and vinegars as well as a series of three-way spreads called Trios under her Bon Vivant label. While some outlets ordered both the books and spreads, others ordered only the spreads. The interest in the food line became so strong that Bon Vivant went mass market. Then responding to requests from retailers, the company developed boxed sets featuring cookbooks, aprons, and food items.

- Marjorie Ainsborough Decker, the Christian Mother Goose, has written books Christianizing basic fairy tales. Among her books are *Humpty Dumpty's Together Tales*, *Nothing-Impossible-Possum Stories*, and *Grandpa Mole and Cousin Mole's Journeys*. In partnership with Ebenezer Toys, her press produced and marketed plush animals based on characters in her books. She also formulated three skin care products to ensure that "our precious children can have happy-soft skin." The three Christian Mother Goose Skin Care products included a lotion, a body soap, and an oil.

- Drawing on her reputation as a romance novelist, Barbara Cartland has gone on to endorse lines of bedsheets, greeting cards, perfume, and vitamins. She also recorded an album of love songs. A few nice hobbies to pass the time between novels!

20:13 Become an Industry Unto Yourself

Some bestselling authors have now become industries all by themselves. For instance, Debbie Macomber, author of many romance novels, supports a staff of three (an assistant, publicist, and production manager) who are responsible for producing everything from motivational tapes to promotional aprons based on her novels. Here are a few more prominent examples.

Money Is from Mars

John Gray, author of *Men Are From Mars, Women Are From Venus*, has developed a line of products and services to go with the book.

- Even before the book became a ten-million-copy bestseller, Gray was conducting seminars on relationships and communication. Afterwards, of course, he could charge more and pack in even larger crowds.

- He starred in his own one-man show on Broadway. Previously he had played to a sold-out crowd at Carnegie Hall.

- He starred in an infomercial that sold a taped course developed around his book.

- A new magazine, *Mars & Venus*, edited by Gray, premiered right before Valentine's Day in 1998. It bombed. It just wasn't a very good read compared to competing magazines.

Getting Goosebumps

R.L. Stine, bestselling author of the *Fear Street* and *Goosebump* children's horror series, developed a number of offshoots of these series. Here are a few of them:

- His licensing company, Parachute Enterprises, joined with Disney's Hollywood Pictures to produce feature films based on the books.

- ABC developed a TV series called *Ghosts of Fear Street*.

- Walt Disney Records produced a series of *Goosebumps* audio books.

- MGM Studios created a Goosebumps HorrorLand attraction. Walt Disney World theme park attractions were also in the works.

- Parachute Entertainment and the Disney Cruise Line put together a special family cruise designed around the *Goosebumps* theme.

Seven Habits of Success

Stephen Covey, author of *The 7 Habits of Highly Effective People*, formed the Covey Leadership Centers to spread his message via seminars, audiotapes, books, and training workshops. In 1996, the Center had revenues of $100 million and in 1997, Covey merged the Center with Franklin Quest, a time-management company. Here are just a few of the current offerings of the new $450 million Franklin Covey Company:

- They operated 120 Franklin Covey stores nationwide, plus stores in Canada, Hong Kong, and Mexico. These stores sell self-improvement books, audiotapes, videotapes, software, planners, and cards.

- More than 3,000 schools and many communities have signed up for *7 Habits* programs.

- They publish a bimonthly magazine called *Priorities: The Journal of Personal Success.*

Deepak Inc.

Deepak Chopra, bestselling author of *The Seven Spiritual Laws of Success*, diversified into so many new fields that *Newsweek* ran a multi-page feature on him in October, 1997. His enterprises at the time brought in more than $15 million per year. Among other things, Deepak was involved in the following:

- He was the editor-in-chief of *Deepak Chopra's Infinite Possibilities* newsletter discussing human potential, health, and spiritual progress.

- The first Chopra Center for Well Being opened in August 1996 in La Jolla, California. He hoped to open additional health centers worldwide.

- He signed a two-album deal with Tommy Boy Records, one featuring poetry with music and the other featuring Chopra's lyrics with pop music and South Asian music.

- He wrote movie scripts, including *The Lords of Light*, which has been described as *Independence Day* meets *Siddhartha*.

- He authored more than a dozen books which sold well over ten million copies worldwide. His book, *Ageless Body, Timeless Mind*, sold more than 130,000 copies in just one day.

- He wrote a novel, *The Return of Merlin*, which went on to become a bestseller.

- He translated other authors, including the Persian poet Rumi.

- He formed the Global Network for Spiritual Success, which was created to support individuals committed to expanding their knowledge of human potential. The network linked more than 5,000 members in a hundred study groups in fifty countries.

- He offered three five- to seven-day seminars worldwide. In March, 1998, he offered a *Seduction of Spirit* seminar in Goa, India.

- His Infinite Possibilities Seminars group scheduled lectures around the world, where he charged up to $25,000 per talk.

- Nightingale-Conant produced bestselling audiotape sets featuring his talks on health and success. In addition, Deepak's Quantum Publications produced tapes on weight loss, insomnia, and chronic fatigue as well as video tapes on *Waking the Power Within* and *The Healing Mind*.

- PBS featured several top-rated television shows based on his talks. A TV series was in the works.

- He developed a line of Ayurvedic herbal supplements, such as OptiCalm and OptiEnergy, as well as seasonings and massage oils.

- He was working to set up a spiritual cable TV channel.

- He taught meditation and primordial sound techniques—and taught others how to do so.

How did he do it all? Where did he find the energy? As Deepak noted in his book on *The Seven Spiritual Laws of Success*, "When your actions are motivated by love, your energy multiplies and accumulates—and the surplus energy you gather and enjoy can be channeled to create anything that you want, including unlimited wealth."

20:14 Do It Once, and Sell It Forever

When John Shuttleworth started *The Mother Earth News* magazine, his guiding principle was this: Do it once, and sell it forever. And that's just what he did. Not only did he write and edit the bimonthly magazine, but he also wrote a syndicated newspaper column three times a week, hosted a spot radio program five times a week, wrote several books, conducted dozens of seminars, and ran a mail order business.

How did he do all this? By doing something once and then selling it over and over again. He'd write a magazine article and then whittle it down to three or four key paragraphs for the newspaper column. He'd then take the newspaper column, make a few minor changes in it, and use it as the script for his radio spots. One of the books he wrote was essentially a collection of his newspaper columns. And all the material was used as background for his seminars.

There's no reason you can't do the same with your books. Just follow John Shuttleworth's golden rule: **Do it once, and sell it forever.**

Someone once asked me how much I made for my first
Guerilla Marketing *book. The answer I gave was $10 million.*
The book itself only paid me about $35,000 in royalties,
but the speaking engagements, spinoff books, newsletters, columns,
bootcamps, consulting, and wide open doors resulted
in the remaining $9,965.000.
— Jay Conrad Levinson, author, *Guerilla Marketing*

Making Your Marketing Click
Three Ways to Help You Lock
1001 Marketing Ideas into Place

by Tami DePalma and Kim Dushinski of Marketability

It's wonderful to have so many amazing marketing action steps at your fingertips. Your next step involves finding the ways that are best for your book and putting them into a guess-free plan that is ready to easily implement. Where do you start?

If you can count to three, you can make your marketing click. Just keep the following three things in mind and you will find that marketing your book is not only easy; it becomes fun, even inspiring. And you will enjoy much stronger results for your book.

Target Market

While it may be alluring to think that everyone wants your book, it is simply not true. The single best thing you can do to set your marketing on track is to define your target market. Knowing who wants to buy your book is as important (perhaps even more important) to effective marketing as writing a good book in the first place.

Simply stated, your target market is the group of people who are most likely to buy your book enthusiastically, without even giving it a second thought. The people for whom buying your book is a no brainer. They do *not* need to be informed, educated, coerced, convinced, or converted. They want your book. Now.

What do these people who want to buy your book have in common? They may be the same gender, work in the same industry, live in the same geographical area, or have a common interest. Once you figure out all of the characteristics these people have in common, you have found your target market. And you can reach them effectively.

This makes your marketing much easier. Less expensive. Less frustrating. More rewarding.

Your Goals

People write and publish books for many reasons. What are yours? State and prioritize your goals and you find yet another key to lock-down success for your book.

Among at least 1,001 opportunities for books, how do you distinguish the ones right for your book? Compare each opportunity to your goals. If an opportunity does not take you closer to your goals, turn it down. Do not do something just because it is expected or because everybody else is doing it. (Some advice never goes out of style!)

Budget

Anyone who writes or publishes a book puts into it their heart and spirit. When something like a book is so intimate, it can be difficult to talk about money. But whether or not you choose to identify and set aside a specific budget, you will spend both time and money on your book. No budget is wrong, as long as it works with your pocketbook, your daily calendar and your expectations.

The blunt bottom line about budgeting is that how much money you are *able* to invest will tell you how much time you will *have* to invest. How much of each you *do* invest will control how many books you sell.

Budgeting allows you to balance what you will do with what you hire done. Invest in services or tools that accomplish the things you are unable to do. And make sure that your investment in time and money realistically lines up with your goals.

Kim Dushinski and Tami DePalma are the partners of MarketAbility, a Denver-based book marketing consulting firm. MarketAbility connects authors and publishers to the right marketing information and services for their books. To receive a free customized list of recommended marketing solutions for your book visit **http://www.HowToMarketMyBook.com**.

Contact **MarketAbility**, 8031 Wadsworth Boulevard #B4-188, Arvada, CO 80003; 303-279-4349. Email: twist@marketability.com. Web: http:// www.marketability.com.

Chapter 21

What to Do Next

---

*That's where the magic and the power is — in doing that which
you know you need to do. No matter what the obstacles.
No matter what your trepidation. No matter how impossible it might seem.
Nothing happens unless you do it. No media or market can respond
to you until you ask for a response. No sales, no TV interviews,
no major reviews, nothing — until you ask. Ask today.*

— John Kremer, editor, *Book Marketing Update*

This book, as I noted in the introduction, was designed to be a potpourri of ideas, examples, tips, and suggestions to encourage you to explore new ways to market your books. I hope the book has achieved this purpose for you. To be honest, I'd be surprised if you didn't come away from this book with at least a dozen new promotional possibilities for your books.

As a caution, however, I'd like to repeat what I said in the introduction. Don't get so excited about all the possibilities for marketing your books that you try to do everything at once. It won't work. Instead, focus your attention on those markets and promotional methods that offer the best possible return for your time and money. Then work hard.

Remember the old 80/20 rule. Put your attention on your prime markets first because those markets are the ones that are going to produce the vast majority of your sales and profits.

21:01 The Open Horizons Book Marketing Library

To supplement the information in this book, I've developed a line of books, kits, mini-guides, and databases to help any author or publisher sell more books. The following pages feature a few of them.

To order any of the following items, go to the *BookMarket.com* web site. Most of the items can be downloaded right away. Some, however, will require you to wait until the U.S. Postal Service delivers your mail.

☐ **Do-It-Yourself Book Publicity Kit** — Do you have trouble writing effective news releases or coming up with innovative ideas for promoting your books? This special report provides you with scores of examples of successful PR releases, author bios, background releases, fact sheets, Q&As, and other press kit materials. In addition, it provides you with samples and procedures for booking TV and radio interviews, dealing with media, and tracking your results. It also includes details on all major media directories and update services. Newly expanded and updated as a PDF download. Available in late summer 2006. $30.00 download.

☐ **Celebrate Today** — This book features 3,000 reasons to throw a party, take the day off, or promote a product by tying it into a special day, week, month or event. Celebrate Today! features 3,400 special days (e.g., Homemade Bread Day and Woman's Equality Day), weeks (Therapeutic Recreation Week and Cleaner Air Week), months (Good Nutrition Month and Children's Books Month), and other events (such as the anniversary of the Social Security Act or the first U.S. bank).

Whether you are publicizing a book or other product, planning a meeting, or designing a retail display, this book will provide you with the inspiration and facts to make your promotions livelier and more interesting. Published in January, 1995. 224-page softcover. $9.95.

Now also available as an up-to-date **Celebrate Today Special Events** database of 18,500 events. $30.00 download.

☐ **The Joy of Publishing** by Nat Bodian — In the bestselling tradition of *The Joy of Cooking* and *The Joy of Sex*, this book offers a wealth of entertaining anecdotes about world-renowned literary figures. It takes you on a never-to-be-forgotten, behind-the-scenes tour of the world of book publishing. A fact-filled treasury for anyone who loves books!

Look behind the scenes at the world's largest and most unusual bookstore. Read about the advertisement that started the mass-market paperback revolution in America. Learn from the mail order advertiser who sold over 500 million books. Discover Ernest Hemingway's Rule for Life. Find out about the origins of the dime novel, detective mystery, *Who's Who*, and *Grimm's Fairy Tales*. Published in June, 1996. 240-page hardcover. $19.95.

☐ **John Kremer's Self-Publishing Hall of Fame** by John Kremer — This book features the stories of hundreds of self-publishers who have gone on to great success. It also features tips from many of the hall of famers on how to do what they did. I publish this book as a print-on-demand book because I'm continually adding new heroes to it. Published in May, 2006. 205-page softcover. $20.00.

Also available as an ebook download for $20.00.

21:02 John Kremer's Book Marketing Mini-Guides

For many years now, I've been selling a series of inexpensive short reports. I've now taken these reports and put them together as longer reports with more detail than ever before. I call these expanded reports mini-guides. These mini-guides are published as PDF files and are continually being updated by me.

Note that some of the following reports will be available after June 2006. Since I'm still updating most of them, I can't give you the page count yet. Here are a few of the mini-guides now available. More will be added soon. Stop by BookMarket.com to discover new additions every month.

☐ **Book Marketing 101: How to Create a National Bestseller** — How to out-sell the *New York Times* bestsellers without breaking the bank. This is an inside guide on how other authors and self-publishers have created national bestsellers with persistence, elbow grease, and some investment of time or money. Also includes John Kremer's insight on how to create a bestseller. Ebook download, $30.00.

☐ **Book Marketing 102: Editorial as the First Step in Marketing** — An incredible book about creating effective editorial that will sell a book, when you should publish a book and when you should not, how to get the best testimonials, creating selling book titles, and more. 78 pages, ebook download, $20.00.

☐ **Book Marketing 103: Designing Your Books as Sales Aids** — You can sell a book by its cover. Learn how to design both the inside and outside of your books for most effective sales. No other investment can increase the sales of your books more than effective designs. In addition, learn how to price your books for greatest sales and ask for the order. 60 pages, ebook download, $20.00.

☐ **Book Marketing 104: 192 Marketing Ideas I've Learned from Other People** — In this mini-guide, I describe 192 marketing ideas I've learned by reading bestselling books and magazines, attending seminars, and watching TV. Learn the seven successful strategies of every bestseller, the ten secrets of publishing success, guerilla marketing for writers, the meaning of success, a bestseller's take on selling books, Mohammad's guide to gaining paradise, how to be a good talk radio guest, how Terry McMillan became a bestselling author on her own, and how Elmore Leonard became HOT! Ebook download, $20.00.

☐ **Book Marketing 105: Choosing a Book Distribution System** — This vital report includes criteria for deciding how you will distribute your books. Also includes complete information on 30 distributors, 4 library distributors, 89 book publishers who also distribute for other publishers, 3 sales representatives to the chains, 27 bookstore wholesalers, 34 library wholesalers, and 23 Spanish-language wholesalers. Plus a sample book distribution contract. Ebook download, $20.00.

☐ **Book Marketing 106: Working with Bookstores to Sell More Books** — A detailed strategy on how to work with bookstores to sell more books, both inside and outside the store. This mini-guide features so many incredible tips. It will help you to become a bookstore star! Ebook download, $30.00.

☐ **Book Marketing 107: Everything You Ever Wanted to Know about Internet Marketing with a Little Help from My Friends** — Features hundreds of Internet marketing secrets, both from John Kremer and from his friends. This mini-guide features advance information not available in this book. Ebook download, $30.00.

☐ **Book Marketing 108: How to Sell More Books via Publicity** — Includes 29 ways to break into the media, the promotional power of radio, the value of persistence, the essence of marketing, hiring and working with publicists, 40 ways that book reviews can help you sell more books, 50 creative book marketing ideas, and much more. Ebook download, $30.00.

☐ **Book Marketing 109: How to Make Money with Your Mailing List** — Most of us go to mailing list brokers only when we need to rent a list for a direct marketing campaign. That, I believe, is a mistake. While going to a good list broker to find the right list for a direct marketing campaign is vital to the success of any mailing, list brokers offer so many other possibilities. Learn how to make money with your list. Plus who to contact for the best results. Ebook download, $30.00.

☐ **Book Marketing 110: How to Sell More Books Via Amazon.com** — This is an advanced version of the few pages on selling via Amazon.com contained in this book. This 100-page ebook has all the secrets for making a big, big splash at Amazon.com.

☐ **Marketing Your Novel 101: How to Market Your Novel** — This mini-guide features the top 400 editors who buy first novels, the top 350 literary agents who represent first novelists, success stories from first-time novelists, a sample author book contract, and key marketing strategies for novelists. Ebook download, $30.00.

☐ **Foreign Book Distributors, Wholesalers, & Sales Reps** — This mini-guide features more than 345 companies that provide foreign distribution or sales representation. This report also includes a sample foreign distri-bution contract. Ebook download, $30.00.

☐ **Literary, Subsidiary, & Foreign Rights Agents** — This mini-guide includes more than 1,425 literary agents, including 325+ agents that sell foreign rights, 400 that have sold a first novel, and another 50 or so that handle subsidiary rights sales. This mini-guide also includes a sample foreign rights book contract. Ebook download, $30.00.

☐ **How to Sell More Books via Google and Yahoo** — An excerpt from *1001 Ways* sold as an Amazon Short. Ebook download, $10.00.

21:03 Book Marketing Update Newsletter

Book Marketing Update is the twice-monthly 12-page print newsletter for any author or publisher who wants to sell more books. It is chock-full of information, resources, tips, and real-life examples to help you market your books more effectively. For more than twenty years, John Kremer has edited this newsletter. The newsletter is now published by Bradley Communications, but John still writes a regular column revealing new book marketing ideas, tips, and techniques.

Below are a few of the testimonials John received during the years that he edited the newsletter.

☐ *We have been trying to get our books into* Cabela's, *a major sporting catalog, for the past two years with no response. Our first issue of your newsletter gave* Cabela's *contact info. We tried it one more time and* Cabela's *took on our sports book for inclusion in the catalog. Your newsletter paid for itself on the very first issue and is worth thousands of dollars. A very good investment for any publisher.* — James Russell, publisher, James Russell Publishing

☐ *As each issue comes, I think, "There's no way you can top this"—and your next one does.* — Alex Combs, publisher, Alpenglow Press

☐ *As a small, vigilantly independent publisher, we are always on the look-out for new customers, new reviewers and their publications, new publicity avenues, and so on.* Book Marketing Update *has saved us countless hours in such prospecting and research.* — Christopher Carey, former sales and marketing, Lyons & Burford

☐ *I am forever in your debt. The leads you've provided in* Book Marketing Update *have resulted in thousands of dollars in sales for Surrey Books over the past year.* — Margaret Liddiard, former director of marketing, Surrey Books

☐ *Please send your publication to my home address. When it comes to the office, it tends to vanish for days, later to mysteriously turn up in my "in" box! Talk about a hot publication!* — Jeff Stevenson, sales department, Franklin Watts Inc.

To order this newsletter, go to http://www.bookmarket.com. Get a $1.00 trial subscrption by visiting http://www.freepublicity.com/transcript/?10005.

21:04 Top 800 Independent Bookstores

Working with subscribers to the *Book Marketing Update* newsletter, hundreds of other book publishers, and participants in several Internet discussion lists, I have compiled a database of the best bookstores in the country. These are the stores that support small presses and new authors, the ones that work well with their communities, the ones that sponsor author signings and talks. This is just one of a number of databases that I've created to help authors and publishers sell more books.

Here are the databases I currently have for sale:

☐ **Top 800 Independent Bookstores** — This listed started out as 500, then 600, then 700, and now 800 top bookstores. It includes names of the buyers and event coordinators, address, phone, fax, email, website, and other information about each bookstore. Data file download, $40.00.

☐ **Public Libraries Data Files** — Features the top 2,300 general public libraries, with library name and address only. No phones, faxes, or emails. Can be addressed to any department. Data file download, $40.00.

☐ **Catalog Sales Directory** — Would you like to sell thousands of books with only one contact? This data file features 1,350 catalogs that are known to carry books, audiotapes, videos, software, gifts, and other items. Includes contact names, addresses, phone numbers, websites, subject interests, and other vital details to help you sell more books to catalogs. As of January 2006, one-third of this database has been verified; the rest is being worked on. Data file download, $30.00

"John, thanks for providing us with your specialty retailer and catalog databases. We have sold more than 3,000 copies of one of our books to customers from these two lists ... none of whom had ever ordered from us before. Well worth the money we paid for the two lists!" — Steve Deger, sales and marketing manager, Fairview Press

Note that our *Specialty Retailer Data Files* will soon be available at our new user-generated website: http://www.hotstuffcoolplaces.com.

☐ **Learning Centers** — This database features the contact information for the Learning Annex, Baywinds, Colorado Free University, Discover U, Open University, Learning Tree University, Fun Ed, Knowledge Shop, and 130 other places where you or your authors can speak and teach for a fee. A great resource for authors and speakers who want to earn money teaching while they also sell more books. Data file download, $15.00.

☐ **Celebrate Today Special Events Data Files** — This expanded version of the *Celebrate Today* book features more than 18,500 annual events in a variety of database formats for easy sorting, targeting, and display. Always updated for the current year. Data file download, $30.00.

21:05 Book Marketing Consulting

Since I like to practice what I preach, I have been expanding the services I offer to other publishers and writers. For more than twenty years now, I've been doing consulting in the design, development, and promotion of books. Now my consulting services are available to anyone within reach of a telephone.

I offer telephone consulting for anyone with questions regarding the marketing of their books. I've worked with self-publishers, book publishers of all sizes, authors who have books published by the top ten book publishers and, perhaps most important of all, those authors who are in the process of writing a book. I help them develop marketing plans, prioritize their sales efforts, select distribution options, publicize their books, develop a brand, and position their books for maximum success.

Among other services, I provided the strategy that took Deepak Chopra from a vanity press author to being on the *New York Times* bestseller list many times. Jack Canfield and Mark Victor Hansen, authors of *Chicken Soup for the Soul*, credit *1001 Ways to Market Your Books* as the guiding light for their rise to bestseller status. As a consultant, my clients have included a self-published author who has sold more than two million books, a new age publisher with sixty titles, and a general publisher who eventually sold out to a New York publisher for many millions of dollars.

John's consulting clients have gotten stories in *Wall Street Journal, New York Times, Newsweek, Playboy, Scientific American, Chicago Tribune, Los Angeles Reader*, as well as been featured on *Oprah, Today Show, Fresh Air, All Things Considered*, and many other local and national shows.

Call 641-472-6130 or email JohnKremer@BookMarket.com to schedule an appointment. The charges for this service are $500.00 per hour, billed by the portion of an hour you use. Use as many minutes as you need to have your questions answered. Note: Most appointments last from thirty minutes to an hour. Long-term consulting, however, is also available.

☐ *You have an uncanny ability to find out the needs of countless number of authors you have advised and counseled so that individually we feel you've tuned into us. Yet your ideas have a universal appeal. One of my areas of interest is in creativity. You certainly have a most unusual creative spirit. You come up with ideas so spontaneously and offer them so easily and warmly it's like you've been thinking of the subject forever. And as I mentioned to you, I know how much you enjoy giving to others. Your laughter and good humor punctuate what you give.* — Marv

☐ *After studying all the self-publishing books and putting together a busi-ness plan and marketing plan, I still had questions which could only be addressed by the voice of experience, such as how to time the whole process. Sometimes there is nothing like talking one-on-one with an ex- perienced individual. John offered several ideas for marketing which were specific to my book. I'm certain these will more than pay for the consultation. For a new publisher like myself it was just what I needed to put all the pieces together. As for the more experienced publisher, I'll bet he could give you a few ideas to spark your promotional efforts.* — Brian Scott, Systematic Publications

☐ *For the past few years I've been asking John Kremer's advice on handling the complexities of the book publishing business. Here are two examples where his advice and experience has proven invaluable.*

When sales of the hardback edition of one of my books stalled (even after receiving wonderful reviews), John suggested that I work with the publisher to repackage and revise the material in the form of a paperback. He explained exactly how I should pitch the idea and exactly what to say to the publisher. His strategy resulted not only in a second chance for the book but an additional advance! The revised edition quickly ate through both advances and I eventually received several royalty checks before the paperback finally went out of print.

Then, more recently, when I found myself without an agent, I called John to ask him the best way to get an agent. He told me to call everyone who I knew who might know a good agent, especially people whom I had interviewed (for articles and such) who had bestselling books. I did as he suggested, separating my possible sources into A, B, and C depending on the likelihood that they'd have a good contact. By the time I had called everyone on the A list, the name of one agent had come up twice. I sent him an email describing myself and my work (with which he was familiar) and now I'm being represented by one of the top agents in the country. Thanks John!!! — Geoff James, author of *Success Secrets from Silicon Valley* and *The Tao of Programming*

John Kremer's Book Cover Critique Service

I've watched key book wholesalers, chain store buyers, and producers of major TV shows pick up a book and make an instant decision on the book *without* opening the book. How important is your book cover? Without a good one, your book won't sell.

If you'd like feedback on your cover from a book marketing expert, then call me at 641-472-6130 or email me at JohnKremer@bookmarket.com. I'll help you to pass that First-Look Test. All for only $100.00. Each critique includes a 10-minute feedback session via telephone. In this session I will critique your front cover, spine, back cover, and title, or whatever portion you have ready for me to critique at the time.

☐ *That $100.00 was the best investment I've made on this book.* — Sandra Lewis, publisher, *My Health Record*

☐ *The cover you helped me design, and some of the verbiage, is selling the book. It's already attracting international attention, besides local and regional sales. What a great way to start!* — Pat Yanello, publisher, Personality Reality

John Kremer's Book Title Critique Service

Before you spend time and money designing a book cover, be sure you have the title you want—one that is brandable, memorable, and effective in selling books. If you are still at an early stage in writing or designing your book, you might want to make sure you have a title that is really the best one for your book. I can help you develop a bestselling title and subtitle for your book. Again, the fee is $100 for such a critique. Each critique includes a 10-minute feedback session via telephone.

If you'd like feedback on your title from a book marketing expert, then call me at 641-472-6130 or email me at JohnKremer@bookmarket.com.

John Kremer's News Release Critique Service

I see dozens of news releases every day. Few make the grade. Most are uninteresting, unnewsworthy, and product-oriented. What does it take to sell books with a good news release? In a 10-minute phone call, I can give you feedback on your news release to help you make it one that sells books. All for only $100.00. Need help? Call me at 641-472-6130. Or email your news release to JohnKremer@BookMarket.com, and I'll get back to you right away. Each critique includes a 10-minute feedback session via telephone.

☐ *I want to thank you again for your generous help with our press release problem. The responses we've gotten for our latest release are much better than what I'm used to. A large percentage of that is (obviously) due to your suggestions.* — Thomas Shelby, Hohm Press

21:06 Book Marketing Blast-Off Seminars

I am available to speak to groups of publishers and writers. In the past few years I've spoken to dozens of groups around the country. If you know of a group that would like me to speak on publishing, marketing, or publicizing books, have them give me a call at 641-472-6130. Or check out my speaker web site at http://www.JohnKremer.org.

I've spoken at book publishing and marketing seminars in New York, Los Angeles, San Francisco, San Diego, Chicago, Orlando, Miami, Denver, Boulder, Tucson, Phoenix, Portland, Seattle, San Antonio, Houston, Austin, Toronto, Kansas City, Saint Louis, London, Atlanta, Milwaukee, Minneapolis, Las Vegas, Washington DC, and many other cities around the country. My speeches have ranged from half-hour talks on book marketing to two-hour sessions on getting national publicity to three-day seminars on how to open new markets for your books. Here are just a few of the hot topics I have presented:

☐ Seven Secrets of Success in Marketing

☐ How to Open New Markets

☐ 25 Ways to Make the National News

☐ How to Create a National Bestseller without Breaking the Bank

☐ How to Sell to Special Markets: Catalogs, Premium Sales, Etc.

☐ 50 Creative Book Marketing Ideas

☐ The A to Z Guide to Building Brands and Selling Rights

My talks are loaded with practical step-by-step directions, real-life examples, and plenty of humor. Why not book me today?

Here are a few testimonials from people who have attended my talks:

☐ *John Kremer was the keynote speaker. He not only gave us many, many tips about marketing, but also through his appealing personality and presentation skills showed us ways for wowing audiences and selling books.* — Jane Trittipo, author/publisher, *The Marvelous Microwave: Good Food in Practically No Time*

☐ *John Kremer spoke for two hours, and it seemed like he was just warming up when we had to stop for lunch. He hung around for the entire day, answering questions cheerfully and generally contributing to an overall good feel. His support, enthusiasm, and generosity infected everyone. I guarantee that any small publisher's group will get more than their money's worth if they bring John Kremer in to speak.* — Jon Sievert, author/publisher, *Concert Photography: How to Shoot and Sell Music-Business Photographs*

☐ *John Kremer spoke to us on March 7th about book marketing. He spoke until almost 9:45 p.m.. A few people grabbed their cell phones to tell whoever was on the other end that they'd be coming home late, but no one left early. I couldn't and wouldn't try to summarize everything John said. He mixed some of the practical tips from his book with a perspective that gives an overarching meaning to all the things we do every day to sell our books. These activities are parts of life and living, much more a state of mind than a state of desperation. His presentation was enormously and uniquely valuable. Those who missed this event should be kicking themselves right now.* — Bob Goodman, San Diego Publishers Alliance

☐ *Caught your schtick last night at Borders. I was reluctant about missing my Studebaker Drivers Club meeting in favor of your presentation. I made a good choice. Your passion is pervasive and you inspired me. Don't get all teared up. I figure you are probably tired of people telling you how encouraging you are but I want to take the risk you won't be bored by my comment. Thanx.* — Michael McKinney Black

Book Marketing Blast-Off Seminars

In addition to talks for other groups, I also sponsor a three-day seminar on a regular basis. My Book Marketing Blast-Off Seminars are three-day, information-packed seminars. In those three days, I teach the inside secrets of how other authors and book publishers are selling more books every day. In this seminar, I cover distribution, opening new markets, publicity in all media, subsidiary rights sales, special sales, working with bookstores to sell more books, Internet marketing, and creating a marketing plan.

Here are a few things people have written about my Book Marketing Blast-Off Seminars:

☐ *We are just a bit excited about being nominated for Book of the Year! You know it all started when Denise and Cari took your workshop. Since then we won the Ben Franklin Award for Children's Picture Books. We spent 10 weeks plus on the BookSense bestseller list and for two weeks at Christmas we were #4 putting us ahead of two of the four Harry Potter Books. We have spent 12 weeks on the NY Times bestseller list and have gone as high as #2. We have won the International Reading Association Young Readers Award for fiction. What we are most proud of is that we have raised over $50,000 for wishes for kids and for protecting special places with the Nature Conservancy since the book was released. Thank you setting us off in the right direction.* — Carl R. Sams II, author/publisher, *Stranger in the Woods*

☐ *Georgia and I thank you from our hearts for presenting such a great seminar. You gave us wonderful ideas for which we are doing our best to carry through! ... We try to make contacts every day and see the light to start our new book!* — Cyndi Duncan, co-publisher, C&G Publishing

☐ *Enclosed is some show-and-tell to demonstrate the learning that I internalized from your seminar last winter! First, you will see some significant changes to the Energize resource catalog. Initial response to the catalog from our traditional audience has been very positive. I certainly feel that we are gaining momentum and thank you for your advice.* — Susan J. Ellis, president, Energize, Inc.

☐ *Thanks again for a super fantastic class this past weekend! I've taken over 100 classes and seminars and yours was by far the best in all categories: valuable content, organized delivery of content, interesting, value for the money.* — Jill Ferguson, publisher, Truth Endeavors

☐ *I highly recommend John Kremer's Book Market Blast-Off Seminar. Within two weeks of attending, taking pages of notes and firmly deciding to actively market my book, I was called out of the blue and interviewed by an editor of Money Magazine. Take note, that I had only made a List of 100 Things To Do and done four of them when I received this call. John's seminar made the difference. John knows what he is talking about and will save you tons of money and lots of missteps. Plus he's funny, kind and wise. Go, just go! It will be the best marketing money you spend during the first five years of your publishing career.* — Suzan Hilton, author of *The Feng Shui of Abundance*

Other bestselling graduates of John Kremer's Book Marketing Blast-Off Seminar include Robert Allen, author of *Multiple Streams of Income*; Richard Nelson Bolles, author of *What Color Is Your Parachute?*; Greg Godek, author of *1001 Ways to Be Romantic*; Dan Gookin, author of *PC for Dummies*; Teri Lonier, author of *Working Solo*; Robyn Freedman Spizman, The Gift Guru; and Fred Gleeck, the Product Guru.

To find out when a Book Marketing Blast-Off Seminar is coming to your area, check out http://www.JohnKremer.net.

Book Marketing for Novelists Seminar

I used to think that my general book marketing advice was enough to help most novelists sell their books. While I still believe that is true, I have found that many novelists are not at all prepared to do what is necessary to make their books into bestsellers. They can't figure out how to apply my general advice to their specific needs. Well, that's something I can do—and have done. So I created a half-day seminar on how to market novels. The first such seminar was held in Washington, D.C., in mid-May 2006.

If you want to know when I'm doing more such seminars, watch for updates at http://www.novelbestsellers.com.

☐ *Just a quick note to tell you how fortunate I feel that I was able to attend your seminar this past weekend. I found you to be such a warm and generous person not to mention vastly knowledgeable and patient. ... On a practical level, I feel I have been grounded in terms of what I need to do every step of the way for my book. It has helped put my fear and anxiety in check and has left me energized and motivated. Thank you. —* Cara Johnson, author of *Mama Do-Right and the Black Cat Bone*

21:07 Book Marketing MBAs

Beginning in June, 2006, I am offering four new year-long courses as part of John Kremer's Book Marketing Masters Institute where you can earn a master's degree in book acceleration (an MBA). *Book acceleration* is my new term for book marketing actions that accelerate your book into the upper atmosphere of big sales and wide-spread author recognition. My new Book Marketing Masters Institute will offer four MBA courses:

☐ **Marketing Novels** and Creating Fiction Bestsellers

☐ **Branding, Subsidiary Rights, and Special Sales:** The Gold Mine in Your Book

☐ **Marketing Books Via the Internet:** How to Create MegaSales for Your Book Using Viral Marketing, Google, Amazon Bestseller Campaigns, Blogs, Podcasts, Videos, and Much, Much More

☐ **Book Publicity and Promotion:** How to Get Top Media to Pay Attention to and Promote Your Books and Authors

You will be able to sign up for one or more of these year-long courses. Each course includes the following tools to help you sell more books, make more money, and create the business you want.

☐ **A daily email tip** (featuring key resources, incredible ideas, up-to-the-minute sales leads, answers to questions, and other guidance). These daily emails will give you continual access to John Kremer's book marketing experience and knowledge. Each course will feature its own tips. A $495 value. You can subscribe separately to these tips if you like.

☐ **Daily one-hour classes** via the web and telephone where you and others in the program can ask me questions (this will include audio and video options). I will be available for one hour each morning, Monday through Friday, to answer questions, give feedback, and help you build your marketing plan. These classes give you unprecedented access to the top book marketing expert in the world! That's more than 250 hours of access in just one year. At $500 per hour, that's a $125,000 value.

☐ **Email Q&A** whenever you need it. Again, unprecedented access to me. A $1,200 value. Again, you can subscribe separately to this service if you like.

☐ **John Kremer's Rolodex** of key contacts (more than 8,500 key bookstores, wholesalers, specialty chains, catalogs, magazine editors, newspaper editors, radio producers, TV producers, syndicated columnists, and rights sales contacts). $3,000 value.

☐ **Free attendance at any seminars** that I host during the coming year, including my Book Marketing Blast-Off Seminars and Book Marketing for Novelists Seminars. $495.00 value.

All this for only $1,200 per course. If you sign up for one for the first three MBA courses, you'll get the Book Publicity and Promotion MBA course for free! If you sign up for two courses, you pay only $2,000. If you sign up for all three, you pay only $2,800—and you still get the fourth MBA on Book Publicity and Promotion for free! To sign up, call 641-472-6130 or email JohnKremer@bookmarket.com.

The cost of one of these courses is far less than most of the artificial programs out there to help you sell books. This is the real deal. You can have day by day feedback on how well you are doing, incredible key contacts and ideas any one of which could pay back the course fee many times over.

This is the one new program that I'm offering that I'm really excited to do. I really expect to help dozens of authors to bestseller status in the coming two years. That's my goal.

21:08 John Kremer's Rant

Below is a rant I wrote recently on my Book Marketing Bestsellers blog. I thought it would be useful to include it here.

Well, I'm tired of authors, print-on-demand published authors, and self-publishers who continually spend money trying to get other people to do what they should be doing.

I am sick and tired of that. I hate the griping that no one wants to listen to you. I hate the whining when another service provider takes you by the nose and wrings out all your money without providing much. I hate the statement so many make that "I'm giving up because no one cares."

Everyone cares. Dang it. Everyone cares.

Except you. If you fall into one of the three whining patterns I've out-lined above, I know exactly what is going on. You don't care. Because if you really had any true passion for your book, nothing would stop you. You wouldn't wait for someone else to champion your book. You would do it. You would climb the highest mountain if need be, so people would know about your book. Or you would parachute into Windsor Palace. Or you would stand in front of a speeding truck. You would die for your book.

If none of this makes sense to you, you are not an author. You are a dil-ettante.

My apologies if this rant offends you, but some days I really get tired of authors who expect other people to do the work they should be doing.

I know the above is some tough talk, but it really frustrates me when people have written a good book but won't take the time to do the promo-tion necessary to get people to read their book. What a shame.

Yes, there is a time when you can hire someone else to do some of the work, or pay someone to help you make your plans, or employ a service for a specific need. But you should still be intimately involved in whatever someone else is doing. Learn from them. Help them. Incorporate their serv-ice into the other steps you are taking to marketing your book.

12:09 What I've Learned in 24 Years of Book Marketing

During the past year I've been giving a talk on the top ten things I've learned in the past 20+ years of marketing books and helping others sell more books. Here is the short notes for that talk:

☐ **90% of marketing efforts are wasted.** This is not a bad thing. This in-sight tells you that you have to keep knocking on doors, making calls, and sending out letters until your target audience answers.

☐ **Book marketing is all about creating relationships.** The only reason to hire a publicist is to hire them for their relationships. Ask, "Who do you know?" It's all about creating friends. You have to take the first step to create a relationship. *The Wall Street Journal* will not approach you.

If you want to sell to a catalog, get the catalog. Say to them, "Here on page 49 is where my product would fit." Watch Oprah if you want to be on Oprah. If you want to be in a magazine, read the magazine first. Fo-cus on the key media important to you.

You need to create relationships with the media contacts. If a news re-lease comes from two different people, they'll pay attention to the re-lease from the person they know. Your job is to make friends. The beauty is, one relationship lasts a long time.

☐ **You can't do everything.** Prioritize what you do best. Focus on the four or five actions that give you the best return on your time and money.

☐ **Packaging is important.** As an author, this offends me, but the reality is that if a book isn't packaged well, it won't sell. An instant judgment on your book is based on the cover, the packaging. Packaging not only includes the cover, but also the title, the contents, and the interior design.

☐ **Build a brand with your books.** For example, consider the *Dummies* brand or the *Chicken Soup of the Soul*. You should create a brand for two reasons: 1. There is greater value in branded product. 2. A brand by its very nature is more memorable. That makes word of mouth easier and more effective.

☐ **We are in the business of creating and selling rights.** Licensing rights can make the difference between a profitable publishing operation and a losing operation.

For example, you can go to audio publishers and offer them the rights to your books. The *Chicken Soup of the Soul* people have given 45 licenses. They probably made more money on rights than from the sale of their books. New York publishers lose money publishing books. They make their money (profits) selling rights to their books.

Do not give away electronic rights. Web sites, CDs, and e-books are all considered to be electronic media. Be sure sites that use your material on the web ask for your permission. Grant them the rights in writing.

For premiums, don't hesitate to sell part of your book, a chapter or something less. For example five to ten recipes from a cookbook could be licensed by a food manufacturer who would feature the recipe with its product. They don't need to buy rights to the entire book. That leaves you room to license other recipes to another manufacturer.

☐ **Remember that small presses can create bestsellers.** In fact, they've created more than 400 bestsellers in the past 20 years. If you'd like to see a list of the bestsellers from small presses, go to the BookMarket.com web site at http://www.bookmarket.com/bests.html.

☐ **New standards are coming for submitting info to booksellers.** You need ONIX compliant data. Get familiar with it. ONIX is a standard format that publishers can use to distribute electronic information about their books to wholesale, e-tail, and retail booksellers, other publishers, and anyone else involved in the sale of books.

The Internet has grown as a popular place to buy books. Online, however, there is no physical book to pick up and peruse. What has replaced it is a web page devoted to the book that can be designed to carry all the rich information of the jacket cover, audio and video files pertaining to the book, and all the bibliographic details. The richer the data, the better the chances are for selling the book.

ONIX specifies over 200 data elements, each of which has a standard definition, so that everyone can be sure they're referring to the same thing. Some of these data elements, such as ISBN, author name, and title, are required; others, such as book reviews and cover image, remain optional. While most of these data elements consist of text, some are multimedia files, such as images and audio files. It is these optional fields—excerpts, reviews, cover images, author photos, etc.—that lead to more online sales.

In time, it is hoped that all companies along the distribution line, from publishers, distributors, wholesalers, online booksellers, and retailers use the same data. For more information on the implementation of this new stantard, see http://www.bisg.org/onix/index.html.

☐ **What was your strength can become your weakness.** For example, New York publishers depend on the chains and have almost lost touch with the independents. Macintosh could have been the standard in computing, but Apple kept everything exclusive and thus killed any chance of dominating the market.

☐ **Make no little plans**, because they have no power to move the hearts of men and women. So many books are published that don't come to their potential because the publisher didn't have the confidence. Let your vision shine through. Don't let the media sell you short.

Well, we've come to the end of my contributions to this book. I hope you enjoyed it and found it useful. Please send me your success stories. I love to hear how other publishers market their books—and, in most cases, I share this information with the readers of my newsletter. Meanwhile, enjoy yourself. And sell those books!

John Kremer

Make no little plans. They have no magic to stir men's blood
and probably themselves will not be realized. Make big plans;
aim high in hope and work, remembering that a noble,
logical diagram once recorded will never die, but long after
we are gone will be a living thing, asserting itself with ever-growing
insistency. Remember that our sons and grandsons are going
to do things that would stagger us. Let your watchword be order
and your beacon beauty. Think big.

— Daniel Burnham, Chicago architect

Advice for Authors

by Seth Godin, author of *All Marketers Are Liars*

The following is an excerpt from Seth Godin's Blog (http://sethgodin. typepad.com). Seth is the author of many great books on marketing, including *All Marketers are Liars, Free Prize Inside, Purple Cow, The Big Red Fez, Permission Marketing*, and *Unleashing the Idea Virus*. In this excerpt from his blog, he gives advice to authors.

Always beware free advice. It is worth what it costs!

That said, I get a fair number of notes from well respected, intelligent people who are embarking on their first non-fiction book project. They tend to ask very similar questions, so I thought I'd go ahead and put down my five big ideas in one place to make it easier for everyone.

I guarantee you that you won't agree with all of them, but, as they say, your mileage my vary.

1. Please understand that book publishing is an organized hobby, not a business. The return on equity and return on time for authors and for publishers is horrendous. If you're doing it for the money, you're going to be disappointed.

On the other hand, a book gives you leverage to spread an idea and a brand far and wide. There's a worldview that's quite common that says that people who write books know what they are talking about and that a book confers some sort of authority.

2. The timeframe for the launch of books has gone from silly to unrealistic. When the world moved more slowly, waiting more than a year for a book to come out was not great, but tolerable. Today, even though all other media has accelerated rapidly, books still take a year or more. You need to consider what the shelf life of your idea is.

3. There is no such thing as effective book promotion by a book publisher. This isn't true, of course. *Harry Potter* gets promoted. So did *Freakonomics*. But out of the 75,000 titles published last year in the US alone, I figure 100 were effectively promoted by the publishers. This leaves a pretty big gap.

This gap is either unfilled, in which case the book fails, or it is filled by the author. Here's the thing: publishing a book is really nothing but a socially acceptable opportunity to promote yourself and your ideas far and wide and often.

If you don't promote it, no one will. If you don't have a better strategy than, "Let's get on Oprah," you should stop now. If you don't have an asset already—a permission base of thousands or tens of thousands of people, a popular blog, thousands of employees, a personal relationship with Willard Scott... then it's too late to start building that asset once you start working on a book.

By the way, blurbs don't sell books. Not really. You can get all the blurbs in the world for your book and it won't help if you haven't done everything else (quick aside: the guy who invented the word "blurb" also wrote the poem *Purple Cow*).

4. Books cost money and require the user to read them for the idea to spread. Obvious, sure, but real problems. Real problems because the cost of a book introduces friction to your idea. It makes the idea spread much much more slowly than an online meme because in order for it to spread, someone has to buy it. Add to that the growing (and sad) fact that people hate to read. Too often, people have told me, with pride, that they read three chapters of my book. Just three.

5. Publishing is like venture capital, not like printing. Printing your own book is very very easy and not particularly expensive. You can hire professional copyeditors and designers and end up with a book that looks just like one from Random House. That's easy stuff.

What Random House and others do is invest. They invest cash in an advance. They invest time in creating the book itself and selling it in and they invest more cash in printing books. Like all VCs, they want a big return.

If you need the advance to live on, then publishers serve an essential function. If, on the other hand, you're like most non-fiction authors and spreading the idea is worth more than the advance, you may not.

So, what's my best advice?

Build an asset. Large numbers of influential people who read your blog or read your emails or watch your TV show or love your restaurant or or or...

Then, put your idea into a format where it will spread fast. That could be an ebook (a free one) or a pamphlet (a cheap one—*The Joy of Jello* sold millions and millions of copies at a dollar or less).

Then, if your idea catches on, you can sell the souvenir edition. The book. The thing people keep on their shelf or lend out or get from the library. Books are wonderful (I own too many!) but they're not necessarily the best vessel for spreading your idea.

And the punchline, of course, is that if you do all these things, you won't need a publisher. And that's exactly when a publisher will want you! That's the sort of author publishers do the best with.

Seth Godin's latest venture is *Squidoo.com*. Check it out!

Bibliography

The following books are the major resources used in writing this book. For a more complete bibliography of books and other publishing resources, see the BookMarket.com website at http://www.bookmarket.com/1001bib.html.

Blanco, Jodee, *The Complete Guide to Book Publicity*, 2nd Edition (New York: Allworth Press, 2004)

Bodian, Nat, *Book Marketing Handbook*, Volumes One and Two (New York: R.R. Bowker, 1980)

Bodian, Nat, *How to Choose a Winning Title* (Phoenix, AZ: Oryx, 1989)

Bodian, Nat, *The Joy of Publishing* (Fairfield, IA: Open Horizons, 1996)

Cardoza, Avery, *The Complete Guide to Successful Publishing* (New York, NY: Cardoza Publishing, 1995)

Hill, Brian and Dee Power, *The Making of a Bestseller: Success Stories from Authors and the Editors, Agents and Booksellers Behind Them* (Chicago: Dearborn Trade, 2005)

Huenefeld, John, *The Huenefeld Guide to Book Publishing, Fifth Edition* (Lexington, MA: Mills-Sanderson, 1992)

Jud, Brian, *Beyond the Bookstore: How to Sell More Books Profitably to Non Bookstore Markets* (New York: Reed Press, 2003)

Kremer, John, *The Complete Direct Marketing Sourcebook* (New York, NY: John Wiley & Sons, 1992)

Lant, Jeffrey, *How to Make a Whole Lot More Than $1,000,000 Writing, Publishing, and Selling How-To Information* (Cambridge, MA: JLA Associates, 1989)

Levinson, Jay Conrad; Rick Frishman; and Michael Larson, *Guerilla Marketing for Writers* (Cincinnati OH: Writer's Digest Books, 2000)

Mettee, Stephen Blake, editor, *The Portable Writers' Conference* (Fresno, CA: Quill Driver Books, 1997)

Poynter, Dan, *The Self-Publishing Manual*, various editions (Santa Barbara, CA: Para Publishing, 2005)

Rose, M. J., and Angela Adair-Hoy, *How to Publish and Promote Online* (New York: St. Martins, 2001)

Ross, Marilyn and Tom, *The Complete Guide to Self-Publishing, 4th Edition* (Cincinnati, OH: Writer's Digest Books, 2002)

Ross, Marilyn and Tom, *Jump Start Your Book Sales* (Cincinnati, OH: Writer's Digest Books, 1999)

Warren, Lissa Warren, *The Savvy Author's Guide to Book Publicity* (New York: Carroll & Graf, 2004)

Woll, Tom, *Publishing for Profit* (Tucson, AZ: Fisher Books, 1998)

Woll, Thomas, *Selling Subsidiary Rights: An Insider's Guide* (Tucson, AZ: Fisher Books, 1999)

John Kremer's Websites

The following are some of the websites I currently operate or will soon operate. Add http://www to each listing for the full URL website address.

BookMarket.com — My main book marketing website, with key resource listings, halls of fame, and top 101 sites.

Book-Marketing-Bestsellers.com — An information website based on my PromotingYourBooks blog, organized by subject. Lots of free information and articles. Also known as PromotingYourBooks.com.

AllBooksFree.com — A website featuring free ebook novels, short stories, and poetry collections.

BestsellerGhostwriter.com — A website featuring my new service providing complete book proposals for non-fiction books.

BiologyOfBusiness.com — A website featuring my on-going entries for a new book called *The Biology of Business*.

BookAcceleration.com — The website for my new Book Marketing MBA program.

CelebrateToday.com — A website of special events, holidays, and historical anniversaries.

FreeBooksForAll.com — A website featuring free ebook non-fiction books: business, self-help, relationships, travel, cookbooks, etc.

HotSpotsCoolPlaces.com — A travel trivia and information website.

HotStuffCoolPlaces.com — A user-generated website featuring their favorite specialty retailers, with full contact information, tagging, and reviews.

JohnKremer.com — John Kremer's consulting web page.

JohnKremer.org — John Kremer's speaking web page.

JohnKremer.net — John Kremer's Book Marketing Blast-Off Seminar page.

JohnKremerSentMe.com — A website featuring various ebooks, seminars, and other information programs I recommend to help authors and publishers sell more books via the Internet.

NovelBestsellers.com — A website featuring John Kremer's book marketing seminars and programs for novelists.

PromotingYourBooks.com — See Book-Marketing-Bestsellers.com above.

Self-Publishing-Bestsellers.com — Features the *Self-Publishing Hall of Fame* page on my main BookMarket.com website. A tool for getting my main website featured higher on Google for *self-publishing*.

SelfPublishingHallOfFame.com — A website featuring famous and successful self-publishers, the Self-Publishers Hall of Fame.

WayBackWords.com — A website featuring backwords, reduplicatives, portmanteaus, other word play, and lots of quotations.

Indexes

The 5th Edition of this book was the first book in history to have four indexes: a general index, an index of authors, an index of book titles, and an index of publishers. In the 5th edition, the general index was included with the book. The other three indexes for that edition were located on the Book-Market.com website.

For this 6th edition, since I didn't have room for the general index (because Chapter 12 on Internet marketing more than doubled in size), I have placed all four record-setting indexes on the BookMarket.com website. Here are their locations:

☐ **General Index** — http://www.bookmarket.com/6index.htm

☐ **Author Index** — http://www.bookmarket.com/6iauthors.htm

☐ **Book Title Index** — http://www.bookmarket.com/6ititles.htm

☐ **Publisher Index** — http://www.bookmarket.com/6ipublisher.htm

Please Note: Besides the indexes on the website, you can find most of the details you want to locate simply by reviewing the comprehensive Table of Contents at the front of this book.

About the Author

John Kremer is the owner of Open Horizons as well as editor-in-chief of the *Book Marketing Update* newsletter. He is the author of *1001 Ways to Market Your Books, The Complete Direct Marketing Sourcebook, High-Impact Marketing on a Low-Impact Budget, Do-It-Yourself Book Publicity Kit, Celebrate Today*, and many other titles.

As a consultant, his clients include a self-published author who has sold over a million books, a new age publisher with 60 titles, and a $100,000,000 publisher with a rapidly growing list of 1,000 titles.

John is 57 years old. His wife Gail, a storyteller, is author of *Little Fox and the Golden Hawk*. They live in a small town in Iowa, where they take care of two dogs named Lisa and Elsie as well as a cat named Gray.

To contact John, email him at JohnKremer@BookMarket.com.

I just spent some time listening to John Kremer speak last night. Wow! If you want to learn every angle to marketing, listen to John, look for his books, and sign up for his consulting. Anyone who devotes himself so faithfully to his craft is worth listening to... even just for 15 minutes. He tells you the best things to do and the worst things to do in the most succinct, common-sense manner. Awesome!

— Valerie Atkinson Brown, author, International Thomson Publishing